The Early Church
at Work and Worship

The Early Church at Work and Worship

Volume 3
Worship, Eucharist, Music, and Gregory of Nyssa

EVERETT FERGUSON

CASCADE Books • Eugene, Oregon

THE EARLY CHURCH AT WORK AND WORSHIP
Volume 3: Worship, Eucharist, Music, and Gregory of Nyssa

Copyright © 2017 Everett Ferguson. All rights reserved. Except for brief quotations in critical publications or reviews, no part of this book may be reproduced in any manner without prior written permission from the publisher. Write: Permissions, Wipf and Stock Publishers, 199 W. 8th Ave., Suite 3, Eugene, OR 97401.

Cascade Books
An Imprint of Wipf and Stock Publishers
199 W. 8th Ave., Suite 3
Eugene, OR 97401

www.wipfandstock.com

PAPERBACK ISBN: 978-1-6089-9366-6
HARDCOVER ISBN: 978-1-4982-8590-2
EBOOK ISBN: 978-1-5326-3411-6

Cataloging-in-Publication data:

Names: Ferguson, Everett, 1933–, author.

Title: The early church at work and worship , vol. 3, worship, eucharist, music, and Gregory of Nyssa / Everett Ferguson.

Description: Eugene, OR: Cascade Books, 2017 | Includes bibliographical references and indexes.

Identifiers: ISBN: 978-1-6089-9366-6 (paperback) | ISBN: 978-1-4982-8590-2 (hardback) | ISBN: 978-1-5326-3411-6 (ebook).

Subjects: LCSC: Christian literature. Early—History and criticism | Fathers of the church | Theology—History—Early church, ca. 30–600 | Church music—To 500—History and criticism | Lord's Supper—History—Early church, ca. 30–600 | Gregory, of Nyssa, Saint, approximately 335–approximately 394 | Athanasius, Saint, Patriarch of Alexandria, –373.

Classification: BR67 F47 2017 v. 3 (print) | BR67 (ebook).

Manufactured in the U.S.A.   09/15/17

To
Carl Holladay
Teachers rejoice when their students excel

Contents

Acknowledgments | ix
Abbreviations | xii
Preface | xiii

1 Spiritual Sacrifice in Early Christianity and Its Environment | 1
2 Praising God with "One Mouth" / "One Voice" | 45
3 The Liturgical Function of the *Sursum Corda* | 62
4 The Lord's Supper in Church History: The Early Church through the Medieval Period | 67
5 A Response to Robin Darling Young on The Eucharist as Sacrifice according to Clement of Alexandria | 97
6 Psalm-Singing at the Eucharist: A Liturgical Controversy in the Fourth Century | 107
7 The Art of Praise: Philo and Philodemus on Music | 127
8 Toward a Patristic Theology of Music | 164
9 The Active and Contemplative Lives: The Patristic Interpretation of Some Musical Terms | 185
10 Athanasius' *Epistola ad Marcellinum in Interpretationem Psalmorum*, Part I | 197
11 Athanasius, *Epistola Ad Marcellinum in Interpretationem Psalmorum*, Part II | 214
12 Words from the Ψαλ- Root in Gregory of Nyssa | 241
13 Progress in Perfection: Gregory of Nyssa's *Vita Moysis* | 253

14 God's Infinity and Man's Mutability: Perpetual Progress according to Gregory of Nyssa | 262

15 Some Aspects of Gregory of Nyssa's Moral Theology in the Homilies on Ecclesiastes | 282

16 Some Aspects of Gregory of Nyssa's Interpretation of Scripture Exemplified in his *Homilies on Ecclesiastes* | 298

17 Images of the Incarnation in Gregory of Nyssa's *Vita Moysis* | 304

Bibliography | 325
Subject Index | 339
Ancient Sources Index | 359

Acknowledgments

THE AUTHOR AND PUBLISHER are grateful to the original publications and publishers for permission to reprint articles. All used by permission.

1. "Spiritual Sacrifice in Early Christianity and Its Environment" first appeared in *Aufstieg und Niedergang der römischen Welt* II: *Principat* 23.2, edited by Hildegard Temporini and Wolfgang Haase, 1151–89. Berlin: deGruyter, 1980.

2. "Praising God with 'One Mouth'/'One Voice'" first appeared in *Renewing Tradition: Studies in Texts and Contexts in Honor of James W. Thompson*, edited by Mark Hamilton, et al., 3–23. Princeton Theological Monograph Series 65. Eugene, OR: Pickwick Publications, 2007.

3. "The Liturgical Function of the *Sursum Corda*" first appeared in *Studia Patristica* 13 (1975) 360–63.

4. "The Lord's Supper in Church History: The Early Church through the Medieval Period" first appeared in *The Lord's Supper: Believers' Church Perspectives*, edited by Dale R. Stoffer, 21–45. Scottdale, PA: Herald, 1997.

5. "A Response to Robin Darling Young on the Eucharist as Sacrifice according to Clement of Alexandria" first appeared in *Rediscovering the Eucharist: Ecumenical Conversations*, edited by Roch Kereszty, 104–15. New York: Paulist, 2003.

6. "Psalm-Singing at the Eucharist: A Liturgical Controversy in the Fourth Century" first appeared in *Austin Seminary Bulletin* 98 (1983) 52–77.

7. "The Art of Praise: Philo and Philodemus on Music" first appeared in *Early Christianity and Classical Culture: Comparative Studies in Honor of Abraham J. Malherbe*, edited by John T. Fitzgerald et al., 391–426. Novum Testamentum Supplements 110. Leiden: Brill, 2003.

8. "Toward a Patristic Theology of Music" first appeared in *Studia Patristica* 24 (1993) 266–83.

9. "The Active and Contemplative Lives: The Patristic Interpretation of Some Musical Terms" first appeared in *Studia Patristica* 16.2 (1985) 15–23.

10. "Athanasius' *Epistola ad Marcellinum in Interpretationem Psalmorum*, Part I" first appeared in *Studia Patristica* 16.2 (1985) 295–308.

11. "Athanasius' *Epistola ad Marcellinum in Interpretationem Psalmorum*, Part II" first appeared in *Ekklesiastikos Pharos* 16 (1978) 378–403.

12. "Words from the Ψαλ- Root in Gregory of Nyssa" first appeared in *Studien zu Gregor von Nyssa und der christlichen Spätantike*, edited by Hubertus R. Drobner and Christoph Klock, 57–68. Vigiliae Christianae Supplements 12. Leiden: Brill, 1990.

13. "Progress in Perfection: Gregory of Nyssa's *Vita Moysis*" first appeared in *Studia Patristica* 14 (1976) 307–14.

14. "God's Infinity and Man's Mutability: Perpetual Progress according to Gregory of Nyssa" first appeared in *Greek Orthodox Theological Review* 18 (1973) 59–78.

15. "Some Aspects of Gregory of Nyssa's Moral Theology in the Homilies on Ecclesiastes" first appeared in *Gregory of Nyssa: Homilies on Ecclesiastes*, edited by Stuart George Hall, 319–36. Berlin: de Gruyter, 1993.

16. "Some Aspects of Gregory of Nyssa's Interpretation of Scripture Exemplified in His *Homilies on Ecclesiastes*" first appeared in *Studia Patristica* 27 (1993) 29–33.

17. "Images of the Virgin Birth in Gregory of Nyssa's *Vita Moysis*" first appeared in *Jesus Christ in St. Gregory of Nyssa's Theology: Minutes of the*

Acknowledgments

Ninth International Conference on St Gregory of Nyssa, Athens 7–12 September 2000, edited by Elias D. Moutsoulas, 285–305. Athens: Eptalophos, 2005.

Abbreviations

ANRW	*Aufstieg und Niedergang der römischen Welt*
Aug	*Augustiniana*
EB	Études bibliques
FC	Fathers of the Church
GNO	*Gregorii Nysseni Opera*
HTR	*Harvard Theological Review*
JEH	*Journal of Ecclesiastical History*
JTS	*Journal of Theological Studies*
NHC	Nag Hammadi Codices
NovTSup	Novum Testamentum Supplements
NPNF	Nicene and Post-Nicene Fathers
n.s.	new series
PG	*Patrologia graeca*. Edited by J. Migne
PL	*Patrologia latina*. Edited by J. Migne
StPatr	Studia Patristica
TS	*Theological Studies*
VigChr	*Vigiliae Christianae*

Preface

VOLUME 3 BRINGS TOGETHER articles on aspects of worship and on one of the great spiritual masters of the ancient church, Gregory of Nyssa.

The concept of spiritual sacrifice was the great revolution in the religious language and understanding in the ancient world. Although it had analogs in pagan philosophy and Judaism, Christianity made the greatest use of the concept and carried it through most comprehensively.

The focal point of spiritual sacrifice in the church was the Eucharist, the central activity of the Christian assembly.

The theology and practice of music have drawn my attention, in part because they are so little studied and thus much misunderstanding abounds.

Gregory of Nyssa is important for the study of the terminology and spiritual interpretation of music, especially as represented in the Psalms. He also made significant contributions to the understanding of the spiritual life. Gregory followed Origen as an important theorist of the non-literal interpretation of Scripture, which ties him with the contents of volume 2 as well.

As this collection opened in volume 1 with a theological contribution to the imagery of ecclesiology, it closes with a contribution by Gregory of Nyssa to Christology in his imagery of the incarnation that encouraged the increasing veneration of the virgin Mary.

1

Spiritual Sacrifice in Early Christianity and Its Environment

GREEK AND ROMAN POETS AND PHILOSOPHERS

Ethical Requirements

ALREADY IN CLASSICAL TIMES the Greek playwrights protested against the conception of sacrifice characterized as *do ut des*. An important principle of the later philosophical criticism of sacrifice in popular religion was stated by Euripides, "For God, if indeed he truly is God, has need of nothing."[1]

The early philosophers stressed the need for purity of soul and life to accompany the outward offering of sacrifices. Socrates was remembered as saying that the gods could not delight more in great offerings than in small, for in that case the gifts of the wicked would often find more favor than the gifts of the good; rather the gods rejoiced more in the gifts of the most pious.[2] Plato learned the lesson well and taught that to sacrifice and commune with the gods by prayers, offerings, and devotions was profit-

---

1. *Hercules furens* 1345: δεῖται γὰρ ὁ θεός, εἴπερ ἔστ' ὀρθῶς θεός οὐδενός.

2. Xenophon, *Memorabilia* 1.3,3: οὔτε γὰρ τοῖς θεοῖς ἔφη καλῶς ἔχειν, εἰ ταῖς μεγάλαις θυσίαις μᾶλλον ἢ ταῖς μικραῖς ἔχαιρον. πολλάκις γὰρ ἂν αὐτοῖς τὰ παρὰ τῶν πονηρῶν μᾶλλον ἢ τὰ παρὰ τῶν χρηστῶν εἶναι κεχαρισμένα . . . ἀλλ' ἐνόμιζε τοὺς θεοὺς ταῖς παρὰ τῶν εὐσεβεστάτων τιμαῖς μάλιστα χαίρειν. Cf. Xenophon, *Anabasis* 5.7.32: πρὸς Διὸς πῶς ἢ θεοῖς θύσομεν ἡδέως ποιοῦντες ἔργα ἀσεβῆ;

able for the good man, but that it was not right for the wicked man with an unclean soul to receive gifts from the gods.³ His followers picked up the thought: the wicked offer gifts and sacrifices in vain, for the gods are not seduced by gifts; the gods have regard for the holiness and justice of the soul rather than the gifts and sacrifices.⁴

The Roman Stoics continued the emphasis. Seneca, for example, defined a *beneficium* by the intention of the giver and applied this to sacrifice:

> The honor which is paid to the gods lies, not in the victims for sacrifice, though they be fat and glitter with gold, but in the upright and holy desire of the worshippers. Good men, therefore, are pleasing to the gods with an offering of grain, but the bad do not escape impiety although they dye the altars with streams of blood.⁵

The first-century satirist Persius, who was influenced by Stoic thought, expressed a similar sentiment:

> Tell me this, you priests, what avails gold inside the sanctuary? . . . Rather let us offer to the gods . . . a heart rightly attuned towards God and man; a mind pure in its inner depths, and a soul steeped in nobleness and honor. Give me these to offer in the temples, and a handful of grits shall win my prayer for me!⁶

---

3. *Leges* 4, 716D–E: ὡς τῷ μὲν ἀγαθῷ θύειν καὶ προσομιλεῖν ἀεὶ τοῖς θεοῖς εὐχαῖς καὶ ἀναθήμασι καὶ ξυμπάσῃ θεραπείᾳ θεῶν κάλλιστόν καὶ ἄριστον καὶ ἀνυσιμώτατον πρὸς τὸν εὐδαίμονα βίον καὶ δὴ καὶ διαφερόντως πρέπον, τῷ δὲ κακῷ τούτων τἀναντία πέφυκεν. ἀκάθαρτος γὰρ τὴν ψυχὴν ὅ γε κακός, καθαρὸς δὲ ὁ ἐναντίος. παρὰ δὲ μιαροῦ δῶρα οὔτ' ἄνδρ' ἀγαθὸν οὔτε θεὸν ἔστι ποτὲ τό γε ὀρθὸν δέχεσθαι.

4. Ps. Plato, *Alcibiades* II, 149E: οὐ γὰρ, οἶμαι, τοιοῦτόν ἐστι τὸ τῶν θεῶν, ὥστε ὑπὸ δώρων παράγεσθαι . . . καὶ γὰρ ἂν δεινὸν εἴη, εἰ πρὸς τὰ δῶρα καὶ τὰς θυσίας ἀποβλέπουσιν ἡμῶν οἱ θεοί, ἀλλὰ μὴ πρὸς τὴν ψυχήν, ἄν τις ὅσιος καὶ δίκαιος ὢν τυγχάνῃ. Cf. Plutarch, *Isis and Osiris* 11 (*Moralia* 355B): καὶ δρῶσα μὲν ἀεὶ καὶ διαφυλάττουσα τῶν ἱερῶν τὰ νενομισμένα, τοῦ δ' ἀληθῆ δόξαν ἔχειν περὶ θεῶν μηδὲν οἰομένη μᾶλλον αὐτοῖς μήτε θύσειν μήτε ποιήσειν κεχαρισμένον, οὐδὲν ἂν ἔλαττον ἀποφεύγοιτο κακὸν ἀθεότητος δεισιδαιμονίαν.

5. *De beneficiis* 1.6.3: *Non est beneficium ipsum, quad numeratur aut traditur, sicut ne in victimis quidem, licet opimae sint auroque praefulgeant, deorum est honor sed recta ac pia voluntate venerantium. Itaque bone etiam farre ac stitilla religiose sunt; mali rursus non effugiunt impietatem, quamvis aras sanguine multo cruentaverint.* Cf. the passage cited by Lactantius, *Div. inst.* 6.25. Seneca, *Ep.* 95.47, 49; Cicero, *Nat. Deo.* 271.

6. Persius, *Sat.* 11.69–75: *dicite pontifices: in sancto quid facit aurum? . . . quin damus id superis . . . compositum ius fasque animo sanctosque recessus mentis et incoctum generoso pectus honesto. haec cedo ut admoveam templis, et farre litabo.*

Epictetus said that it was fitting to sacrifice according to ancestral custom but to do so purely.[7]

This viewpoint was adopted by the rhetoricians and through them became not just a philosophical commonplace but also a part of the educated person's outlook. Isocrates had already counselled:

> In the worship of the gods, follow the example of your ancestors, but consider that the noblest sacrifice and greatest service is to show yourself the best and most righteous person, for such persons have greater hope of enjoying a blessing from the gods than those who slaughter many victims.[8]

The rhetorical topic was expressed, "It is not customary for the gods to rejoice in the cost of what is sacrificed but in the piety of those sacrificing."[9]

Rational Worship

Theophrastus, Aristotle's successor, also advocated that the deity has more regard for the pure motives of the one sacrificing than for the size of the sacrifice, but he initiated another line of thought in his repudiation of animal sacrifice.[10] According to his theory, the original form of sacrifice was the fruits of the earth, and animal sacrifice began in a time of famine.[11] He claimed that the gods should be honored with the fruits of the field, since these were the most valuable benefits they had granted us.[12] The rejection of animal sacrifice and replacing it with God's most valuable gifts to man, when combined with the Stoic doctrine that man's rational nature is his highest possession and what he shares with the gods, led to the conception of "rational sacrifice."

---

7. *Enchiridion* 31.5: σπένδειν δὲ καὶ θύειν καὶ ἀπάρχεσθαι κατὰ τὰ πάτρια ἑκάστοτε προσήκει καθαρῶς. Cf. Diogenes Laertius, VII.119 (Zeno).

8. *Or.* 11 (To Nicocles).20: Τὰ μὲν πρὸς τοὺς θεοὺς ποίει μὲν ὡς οἱ πρόγονοι κατέδειξαν, ἡγοῦ δὲ θῦμα τοῦτο κάλλιστον εἶναι καὶ θεραπείαν μεγίστην, ἂν ὡς βέλτιστον καὶ δικαιότατον σαυτὸν παρέχῃς· μᾶλλον γὰρ ἐλπὶς τοὺς τοιούτους ἢ τοὺς ἱερεῖα πολλὰ καταβάλλοντας πράξειν τι παρὰ τῶν θεῶν ἀγαθόν.

9. Anaximenes, *Ars Rhet.* 2, ed. Spengel and Hammer in *Rhetores Graeci* 1, 20: οὐκ εἰκὸς τοὺς θεοὺς χαίρειν ταῖς δαπάναις τῶν θυομένων, ἀλλὰ ταῖς εὐσεβείαις τῶν θυόντων.

10. Bernays, *Theophrasts Schrift über Frömmigkeit*. For the philosophical criticism of material sacrifice, see Norden, *Agnostos Theos*, 37ff.

11. Cf. Clement of Alexandria, *Strom.* 7.6.32.

12. Porphyry, *De Abstinentia* 2.32.

Shortly before the beginning of the Christian era there was a revival of Pythagoreanism which reinforced the vegetarianism of Theophrastus. It was recalled of Pythagoras that he abstained from meat and would not stain altars with blood. He offered to the gods honeycake, frankincense, and hymns of praise as more welcomed by the gods.[13] Apollonius of Tyana adopted Pythagoras' manner of life and offered sacrifices "of a bloodless and pure kind."[14] He wrote, "The gods do not need sacrifices. What then can one do to win their favor? In my opinion one can acquire wisdom and do good so far as he can to such men as are worthy."[15] He advised others to avoid offering to God any victim at all. "We should make use in relation to him solely of the higher speech, I mean of that which issues not by the lips; and from the noblest of beings we must ask for blessings by the noblest faculty we possess, and that faculty is intelligence, which needs no organ."[16]

The philosophical principles that God does not need man's gifts and is best worshipped by that highest part of man's nature which is most akin to God are given warm religious expression in the "Corpus Hermeticum." The author prayed, "Accept my rational sacrifices, pure from soul and heart always stretched up to thee . . . whose name nothing but silence can express."[17] The collection contains in hymn the request, "Thy reason sings through me thy praises. Take back through me the All into thy Reason—my rational sacrifice" and "Receive from all their rational sacrifice."[18] There is the further sentiment, "There is one way alone to worship God:

---

13. Philostratus, *Vita Apol.* 1.1: μὴ γὰρ αἱμάττειν τοὺς βωμούς, ἀλλὰ ἡ μελιττοῦτα καὶ ὁ λιβανωτὸς καὶ τὸ ἐφυμνῆσαι, φοιτᾶν ταῦτα τοῖς θεοῖς παρὰ τοῦ ἀνδρὸς τούτου, γιγνώσκειν τε, ὡς ἀσπάζοιντο τὰ τοιαῦτα οἱ θεοὶ μᾶλλον ἢ τὰς ἑκατόμβας καὶ τὴν μάχαιραν ἐπὶ τοῦ κανοῦ.

14. Ibid. 4.11: πολλὰ δὲ τῶν ἀναίμων τε καὶ καθαρῶν καθαγίσας.

15. Apollonius, *Ep.* 26: Θεοὶ θυσιῶν οὐ δέονται. τί οὖν ἄν τις πράττων χαρίζοιτο αὐτοῖς; φρόνησιν, ὡς ἐμοὶ δοκεῖ, κτώμενος, ἀνθρώπων τε τοὺς ἀξίους εἰς δύναμιν εὖ ποιῶν.

16. *De sacrif.*, quoted by Eusebius, *Praep. Evang.* 4.13 (*Dem. Evang.* 3.3.11): μόνῳ δὲ χρῷτο πρὸς αὐτὸν αἰεὶ τῷ κρείττονι λόγῳ, λέγω δὲ τῷ μὴ διὰ στόματος ἰόντι, καὶ παρὰ τοῦ καλλίστου τῶν ὄντων διὰ τοῦ καλλίστου τῶν ἐν ἡμῖν αἰτοίη τἀγαθά. νοῦς δέ ἐστιν οὗτος, ὀργάνου μὴ δεόμενος.

17. *Corp. Herr.* 1 [Poimandres].31: δέξαι λογικὰς θυσίας ἁγνὰς ἀπὸ ψυχῆς καὶ καρδίας πρὸς σὲ ἀνατεταμένης, ἀνεκλάλητε, ἄρρητε, σιωπῇ φωνούμενε. Cf. also 22. See the Hermetic tractate, "Discourse on Eighth and Ninth," in NHC VI.57.19: "Receive from us these spiritual sacrifices, which we send to thee with all our heart and our soul and all our strength."

18. *Corp. Herm.* 13.18,19: ὁ σὸς Λόγος δι' ἐμοῦ ὑμνεῖ σέ. δι' ἐμοῦ δέξαι τὸ πᾶν λόγῳ, λογικὴν θυσίαν . . . δέξαι ἀπὸ πάντων λογικὴν θυσίαν. Dodd, *The Bible and the Greeks*, 196–98.

not to be evil."[19] Belonging to the same literature is "Asclepius," which rejects the suggestion of adding incense to prayers as a profanation: "He stands in need of nothing, because he is all things and all are in him. But let us worship, pouring forth our thanks. For this is the best incense in God's sight, when thanks are given to him by men."[20]

Platonic, Aristotelian, Stoic, and Neo-Pythagorean streams flowed into the Neo-Platonic conception of spiritual sacrifice.[21] Porphyry developed Theophrastus into a comprehensive theory of sacrifice: each level of divine being is to be worshipped in a manner appropriate to his nature. (1) The highest God must be offered nothing by fire nor any of the things of sense, not even words. Silence and pure thoughts concerning him are the proper worship; the lifting up of the soul to God, when we are made like him, is the holy sacrifice and hymn to him.[22] (2) The intellectual gods, who are the highest of God's offspring, are honored by hymns of speech.[23] (3) The heavenly gods, planets and stars, are honored by offerings of honey, fruit, etc. but not animals. (4) The demons receive the usual sacrifices.[24] He summed up his thought in these words, "The best firstfruit offering to the gods is a pure mind and soul free from passion; also congenial to them is to offer the other firstfruits in moderation."[25] Or again, "For God, being the father of all, is in need of nothing; but it is well with us when we adore him by means of justice, chastity and other virtues, and so make our life itself a prayer to him by imitating him and seeking knowledge of him."[26]

---

19. Ibid. 12.23: θρησκεία δὲ τοῦ θεοῦ μία ἐστί, μὴ εἶναι κακόν.

20. Ascl. 41.2: *Nihil enim deest ei, qui ipse est omnia aut in eo sunt omnia. Sed nos agentes gratias adoremus. Haec sunt enim summae incensiones dei, gratiae cum aguntur a mortalibus.* This is quoted with approval in Lactantius, *Div. Inst.* 6.25. Apuleius, *Deo Soc.* 13.

21. See in general Young, "The Idea of Sacrifice."

22. *De abstinentia* 2.34: θεῷ μὲν τῷ ἐπὶ πᾶσιν, ὥς τις ἀνὴρ σοφὸς ἔφη, μηδὲν τῶν αἰσθητῶν μήτε θυμιῶντες μήτ' ἐπονομάζοντες. οὐδὲν γάρ ἐστιν ἔνυλον, ὃ μὴ τῷ αὔλῳ εὐθύς ἐστιν ἀκάθαρτον. διὸ οὐδὲ λόγος τούτῳ ὁ κατὰ φωνὴν οἰκεῖος, οὐδ' ὁ ἔνδον, ὅταν πάθει ψυχῆς ᾖ μεμολυσμένος, διὰ δὲ σιγῆς καθαρᾶς καὶ τῶν περὶ αὐτοῦ καθαρῶν ἐννοιῶν θρησκεύομεν αὐτόν. δεῖ ἄρα συναφθέντας καὶ ὁμοιωθέντας αὐτῷ τὴν αὐτῶν ἀναγωγὴν θυσίαν ἱερὰν προσάγειν τῷ θεῷ, τὴν αὐτὴν δὲ καὶ ὕμνον οὖσαν καὶ ἡμῶν σωτηρίαν. ἐν ἀπαθείᾳ ἄρα τῆς ψυχῆς, τοῦ δὲ θεοῦ θεωρίᾳ ἡ θυσία αὕτη τελεῖται.

23. Ibid. τοῖς δὲ αὐτοῦ ἐκγόνοις, νοητοῖς δὲ θεοῖς ἤδη καὶ τὴν ἐκ τοῦ λόγου ὑμνῳδίαν προσθετέον.

24. Cf. Iamblichus, *De myst.* 5.14 for material sacrifice to the material gods and immaterial sacrifice to the immaterial gods.

25. *De abstinentia* 2.61: θεοῖς δὲ ἀρίστη μὲν ἀπαρχὴ νοῦς καθαρὸς καὶ ψυχὴ ἀπαθής, οἰκεῖον δὲ καὶ τὸ μετρίων μὲν ἀπάρχεσθαι τῶν ἄλλων.

26. Porphyry, *Phil. ex or.*, quoted by Augustine, *Civ. Dei* 19.23: *Nam Deus quidem,*

Neo-Platonism attempted to unite a philosophical spiritual conception of worship with the traditional religion. The defence against Christianity echoes in Sallustius: "The divine nature is free from needs; the honors are performed for our good." Yet man is a composite being. Animal sacrifices represent the unreasonable life in us, and prayers the intellectual element. "Since everything we have comes from the gods . . . we offer first-fruits of our possessions in the form of votive offerings, of our bodies in the form of hair, of our life in the form of sacrifices." The accomodation to popular religion is evident: "Prayers divorced from sacrifices are only words, prayers with sacrifices are animated words, the word giving power to the life and the life animation to the word."[27] There has been a return to the earlier philosophical position, combining sacrifice with a pure life, only there is now a more sophisticated justification for offering animals: animal life provides an intermediary between human life and divine life.[28]

With reference to Porphyry's classification, Jews and Christians came to share the premises of a rational worship and a living sacrifice, repudiating animal sacrifice (4) on one hand but on the other largely ignoring the suggestion of silent prayer and song (1). The emphasis on attitudes of mind and purity of life continued, with priority given to verbal praise (2) and an acceptance in a limited way of the offering of the fruits of the earth (3) in the extension of sacrificial language to the elements of the eucharist. Man could commune directly with the divine; where an intermediary was necessary, for Christianity this was the sacrifice of Christ.

---

utpote omnium Pater, nullius indiget; sed nobis est bene, cum eum per iustitiam et castitatem aliasque virtutes adoramus, ipsam vitam precem ad ipsum facientes per imitationem et inquisitionem de ipso.

27. *Concerning the Gods and the Universe* 15;16: αὐτὸ μὲν γὰρ τὸ θεῖον ἀνενδεές αἱ δὲ τιμαὶ τῆς ἡμετέρας ὠφελείας ἕνεκα γίνονται . . . πρῶτον μὲν ἐπειδὴ πάντα παρὰ θεῶν ἔχομεν δίκαιον δὲ τοῖς διδοῦσι τῶν διδομένων ἀπάρχεσθαι, χρημάτων μὲν δι' ἀνιθημάτων, σωμάτων δὲ διὰ κόμης, ζωῆς δὲ διὰ θυσιῶν ἀπαρχόμεθα. ἔπειτα αἱ μὲν χωρὶς θυσιῶν εὐχαὶ λόγοι μόνον εἰσὶν αἱ δὲ μετὰ θυσιῶν ἔμψυχοι λόγοι, τοῦ μὲν λόγου τὴν ζωὴν δυναμοῦντος τῆς δὲ ζωῆς τὸν λόγον ψυχούσης.

28. Ibid., 16: ζωῆς οὖν μεσότητα ζωὴν ἐχρῆν εἶναι, καὶ διὰ τοῦτο ζῷα θύουσιν ἄνθρωποι.

JUDAISM

Jewish Bible

Hebrew poets and philosophers taught the priority of purity of heart. They did not, it seems, reject the sacrificial cultus per se but emphasized ethical relationships.[29] The passages most often cited by later Jewish and Christian authors may be grouped as follows:

(1) God's rejection of sacrifice unless obedience accompanies it—Prov 15:28 (cf. 21:27); Isa 1:10–17; Jer 6:20; 7:21–23; Mal 1:10–14; Ps 49:7–15 [50:8–15];[30]

(2) Obedience, or some quality, is better than sacrifice—1 Sam 15:22; Hos 6:6; Amos 5:20–25; Prov 21:3; Pss 39:7–9 [40:6–8]; 68:31, 32 [69:30, 21];

(3) Praise and obedience are the sacrifice—Pss 50:18, 19 [51:16, 17]; 140:2 [141:2].

Apocryphal, Pseudepigraphal, and Sectarian Literature

The necessity of combining obedience with sacrifice continued to be voiced in the Jewish wisdom tradition. Jesus ben Sira has a long passage on sacrifice (Sir 34:18—35:11). "The Most High is not pleased with the offerings of the ungodly; and he is not propitiated for sins by a multitude of sacrifices."[31] Proper conduct toward others must accompany ritual acts (34:18–26). The righteous man will offer the sacrifices prescribed (35:1, 4), but kindness and almsgiving are sacrifices, and avoiding wickedness is an atonement (35:2, 3). "Sacrifice by a righteous man is acceptable."[32]

---

29. Gaster, "Sacrifices and Offerings, OT," 157.

30. The Psalms are cited by LXX number with Hebrew number in brackets. The "sacrifice of praise" in 49:14, 23 may be an actual sacrifice offered in praise; cf. Lev 7:12 for this as one kind of offering. The same may be true for Ps 106 [107]:22; 26 [27]:6; and 115:8 [116:17]. On the other hand, "sacrifice" is clearly figurative in Ps 50:19, and so may be in the other Psalms references. Cf. Jonah 2:10. For the Old Testament passages used in the anti-sacrificial polemic of Christians and the theme that God does not need sacrifice, see Prigent and Kraft, *Épître de Barnabé*, 82–83, and references cited.

31. Sir 34:19: οὐκ εὐδοκεῖ ὁ ὕψιστος ἐν προσφοραῖς ἀσεβῶν οὐδὲ ἐν πλήθει θυσιῶν ἐξιλάσκεται ἁμαρτίας.

32. Ibid., 35.1–6: Ὁ συντηρῶν νόμον πλεονάζει προσφοράς, θυσιάζων σωτηρίου ὁ προσέχων ἐντολαῖς. ἀνταποδιδοὺς χάριν προσφέρων σεμίδαλιν, καὶ ὁ ποιῶν ἐλεημοσύνην

Purity of soul and moral conduct were evaluated more highly than sacrifice, especially in Diaspora Judaism. The highest form of glory is "to honor God, and this is done not with gifts and sacrifices but with purity of soul and holy conviction."[33] Judith says that every sacrifice is a small thing to God, but "he who fears the Lord shall be great forever."[34] The "Book of the Secrets of Enoch" or *2 Enoch* in one rescension implies a rejection of all material sacrifice, but in the more complete version makes purity of heart superior to sacrifice: "When the Lord demands bread, or candles, or flesh, or any other sacrifice, then that is nothing; but God demands pure hearts, and with all that only tests the heart of man."[35]

Several other religious acts were presented as sacrifices. *Jubilees* speaks of God's commands ascending "as a sweet savor acceptable before him" (2:22). The *Testament of Levi* gives as the ministry of the archangels who are nearest to the throne of God, "offering to the Lord a sweet smelling savor, a reasonable and bloodless offering."[36] The Prayer of Azariah 15–17, in the absence of sacrifice, offers the "contrite heart and humble spirit" as an acceptable sacrifice "as though it were with burnt offerings."[37] Tobit presents mercy (almsgiving) as "a good offering before the Most High" which "delivers from death and purifies from sin."[38] Fourth Maccabees

---

θυσιάζων αἰνέσεως. εὐδοκία κυρίου ἀποστῆναι ἀπὸ πονηρίας, καὶ ἐξιλασμὸς ἀποστῆναι ἀπὸ ἀδικίας . . . προσφορὰ δικαίου λιπαίνει θυσιαστήριον, καὶ ἡ εὐωδία αὐτῆς ἔναντι ὑψίστου. θυσία ἀνδρὸς δικαίου δεκτή, καὶ τὸ μνημόσυνον αὐτῆς οὐκ ἐπιλησθήσεται. Snaith, "Ben Sira's Supposed Love of Liturgy."

33. *Ep. Aristeas* 234: Τί μέγιστόν ἐστι δόξης; Ὁ δὲ εἶπε. Τὸ τιμᾶν τὸν θεόν. τοῦτο δ᾽ ἐστὶν οὐ δώροις οὐδὲ θυσίαις, ἀλλὰ ψυχῆς καθαρότητι καὶ διαλήψεως ὁσίας. Cf. 170, 172; also Josephus' paraphrase of 1 Sam 15:22 in *Ant.* 6.147–50.

34. Judith 16:16: ὅτι μικρόν πᾶσα θυσία εἰς ὀσμὴν εὐωδίας, καὶ ἐλάχιστον πᾶν στέαρ εἰς ὁλοκαύτωμά σοι. ὁ δὲ φοβούμενος τὸν κύριον μέγας διὰ παντός.

35. *Book of the Secrets of Enoch* 45:3 (Charles, *Apocrypha and Pseudepigrapha*, 2:458); 59:2 and 66:2 speak of actual sacrifice.

36. *Test. Levi* 3.5.6: Ἐν τῷ μετ᾽ αὐτῶν εἰσιν ἀρχάγγελοι οἱ λειτουργοῦντες καὶ ἐξιλαοκόμενοι πρὸς Κύριον ἐπὶ πάσαις ταῖς ἀγνοίαις τῶν δικαίων, προσφέροντες τῷ Κυρίῳ ὀσμὴν εὐωδίας λογικὴν καὶ ἀναίμακτον θυσίαν. Le Déaut, "Le titre de Summus Sacerdos," 228 notes the similarity to the canon of the Roman mass.

37. Dan 3:38–40, LXX: καὶ οὐκ ἔστιν ἐν τῷ καιρῷ . . . οὐδὲ ὁλοκαύτωσις οὐδὲ θυσία οὐδὲ προσφορὰ οὐδὲ θυμίαμα . . . ἀλλ᾽ ἐν ψυχῇ συντετριμμένῃ καὶ πνεύματι τεταπεινωμένῳ προσδεχθείημεν ὡς ἐν ὁλοκαυτώμασι κριῶν καὶ ταύρων . . . οὕτω γενέσθω ἡμῶν ἡ θυσία ἐνώπιόν σου σήμερον.

38. Tobit 4:10, 11: διότι ἐλεημοσύνη ἐκ θανάτου ῥύεται . . . δῶρον γὰρ ἀγαθόν ἐστιν ἐλεημοσύνη πᾶσι τοῖς ποιοῦσιν αὐτὴν ἐνώπιον τοῦ ὑψίστου. 12.9: ἐλεημοσύνη γὰρ ἐκ θανάτου ῥύεται, καὶ αὐτὴ ἀποκαθαριεῖ πᾶσαν ἁμαρτίαν οἱ ποιοῦντες ἐλεημοσύνας καὶ δικαιοσύνας πλησθήσονται ζωῆς. Cf. 12.12.

interprets the death of the Jewish martyrs as an atonement for the sins of the nation.[39]

Philo reported that the Essenes showed themselves "devoted servants of God, not by offering animal sacrifices but by resolving to sanctify their minds."[40] Josephus, however, reported that they sent votive offerings to the temple but performed their own sacrifices by themselves.[41] If Philo's and Josephus' "Essenes" are to be identified with the Qumran sect, then it seems clear that they did not reject sacrifice in principle but only the then current cultus in Jerusalem. The rejection of the Jerusalem priesthood, however, did put an emphasis on the prophetic teaching about the heart.[42]

> "They shall expiate guilty rebellion and sinful infidelity and procure loving kindness upon the earth without the flesh of burnt offering and the fat of sacrifice, but the offering of the lips in accordance with the law shall be as an agreeable odor of righteousness, and perfection of way shall be as the voluntary gift of a delectable oblation." (1QS 9:4, 5)

Is this an eschatological hope or a present reality in the life of the community?

Philo[43]

In Philo the currents of Greek philosophy and Hebrew prophetism flowed together in such a way that although he stayed within the river bed of Judaism his thought cut a channel for the later Christian apologists. This Jewish philosopher often put "sacrifices and prayers" together, showing

---

39. 4 Macc 6:29; 17:22.

40. *Quod omnis probus liber sit* 75: ἐπειδὴ κἀν τοῖς μάλιστα θεραπευταὶ θεοῦ γεγόνασιν, οὐ ζῷα καταθύοντες, ἀλλ' ἱεροπρεπεῖς τὰς ἑαυτῶν διανοίας κατασκευάζειν ἀξιοῦντες.

41. *Ant.* 18.19 (LCL IX, p. 16): εἰς δὲ τό ἱερὸν ἀναθήματα στέλλοντες θυσίας ἐπιτελοῦσιν διαφορότητι ἁγνειῶν, ἃς νομίζοιεν, καὶ δι' αὐτὸ εἰργόμενοι τοῦ κοινοῦ τεμενίσματος ἐφ' αὑτῶν τὰς θυσίας ἐπιτελοῦσιν. See Feldman's note ad loc. for the text. See also Wallace, "The Essenes and Temple Sacrifice," 335–38; and Beckwith, "Qumran Calendar and the Sacrifices of the Essenes."

42. Baumgarten, "Sacrifice and Worship."

43. Wolfson, *Philo*, II.241-52; I. Heinemann, *Philons griechische und jüdische Bildung*, 66, 472. Nikiprowetzky, "La spiritualisation des sacrifices."

that they formed a natural pair in his thinking.⁴⁴ Sacrifice is a medium of prayer and thanksgiving.⁴⁵

Philo defended the literal sacrifices at the temple as the outward form of the sacrifice of the soul.⁴⁶ The latter was expressed in intellectual and moral allegories of the ritual prescriptions in the Pentateuch.

Although Philo accepted the literal sacrifices, his principal thrust was to give moral allegories of the ritual prescriptions in the Pentateuch. The temple of God is the rational soul whose priest is the true man (*De somniis* 1.215). The light of the lamps in the tabernacle is a sacrifice of thanksgiving (*Spec. leg.* 1.297). "The true altar of God is the thankful soul of the wise man."⁴⁷ The sacrifice on the altar consists "not in the victims but in the offerer's intention and zeal."⁴⁸ or in the "pure and unstained life of a holy person."⁴⁹ God is not interested in the number of the victims but in the true purity of a rational spirit in the one who makes the sacrifice.⁵⁰ God cannot be bribed; he rejects the sacrifices of the guilty and accepts the guiltless even if he sacrifices nothing. He delights in an altar surrounded by a choir of virtues although there is no fire on it.⁵¹ The whole burnt offering is a symbol of a perfect and wholly sound frame of mind.⁵² "The mind

---

44. *Vit. Mos.* 2.147; 2.174; *Ebr.* 66; 79; *Decal.* 158; *Spec. leg.* 1.97; 1.113; 1.193; 1.229; 2.17; *Plant.* 162; *Somniis* 1.215; 2.72; 2.299. The "sacrifice of praise" was treated as a particular kind of sacrifice, not praise as itself a sacrifice—*Spec. leg.* 1.224.

45. *Spec. leg.* 1.195: τὰς διὰ θυσιῶν εὐχαριστίας ὁμοῦ καὶ λιτάς.

46. *De mig. Abrahami* 89–93.

47. *Spec. leg.* 1.287: πρὸς ἀλήθειαν τοῦ θεοῦ θυσιαστήμιόν ἐστιν ἡ εὐχάριστος τοῦ σοφοῦ ψυχή.

48. Ibid. 1.290: ὅτι οὐ τὰ ἱερεῖα θυσίαν ἀλλὰ τὴν διάοιαν καὶ προθυμίαν ὑπολαμβάνει τοῦ καταθύοντος εἶναι.

49. *Quaes. et sol. in Ex.* 2.98. In this and the preceding passage Philo's interpretation is based on his understanding of the literal meaning of altar as a place for keeping or preserving sacrifice (see *Vit. Mos.* 2.106).

50. *Spec. leg.* 1.277: παρὰ θεῷ μὴ τὸ πλῆθος τῶν καταθυομένων εἶναι τίμιον, ἀλλὰ τὸ καθαρώτατον τοῦ θύοντος πνεῦμα λογικόν. Cf. *Somniis* 2.73,74: τίς ἡ σεμίδαλις, ἐκκεκαθαρμένης ταῖς παιδείας ὑποθήκαις γνώμης σύμβολον . . . πλήρη τὴν ὅλην ψυχὴν εἰλικρινεστάτων καὶ καθαρωτάτων δογμάτων γενομένην αὐτὴν ὡς ἱερεῖον τὸ κάλλιστον ἀνάγειν προστέτακται.

51. *Plant.* 1.107,108: ἀδέκαστόν ἐστιν, ὦ οὗτοι, τὸ θεοῦ δικαστήριον, ὡς τοὺς μὲν γνώμῃ κεχρημένους ὑπαιτίῳ, κἂν καθ' ἅπασαν ἡμέραν ἑκατὸν βόας ἀνάγωσιν, ἀποστρέφεσθαι, τοὺς δ' ἀνυπαιτίους, κἂν μηδὲν θύωσι τὸ παράπαν, ἀποδέχεσθαι. βωμοῖς γὰρ ἀπύροις, περὶ οὓς ἀρεταὶ χορεύουσι. Cf. *Vit. Mos.* 2.279 for God not accepting the sacrifice of the impious.

52. *Spec. leg.* 1.253: ἑκάτερον σπεύδειν πρὸς ὁλόκληρον καὶ παντελῆ διάθεσιν, ἧς ἡ ὁλόκαυτος θυσία σύμβολον.

which is without blemish and has been purified with perfect virtue is the purest sacrifice and is completely pleasing to God."[53] Genuine offerings are those of "a soul bringing simple truth as its only sacrifice."[54]

Philo rose to the heights of pure spirituality, in language which indicates that Greek philosophy had attained ideas only documented now from later sources. After a discussion of the need to bring sacrifice with a pure body and mind, he says:

> Although the worshippers bring nothing else, in offering themselves they bring the best sacrifice—the full and most truly perfect sacrifice of noble living—as they honor their Benefactor and Savior, God, with hymns and thanksgivings, sometimes with the organs of speech, sometimes without tongue or lips when within the soul alone their minds recite or cry out.[55]

Philo felt that we cannot adequately present gratitude to God by buildings, oblations, and sacrifices. It must be expressed by hymns and praise, not such as the audible voice sings but what the purified mind expresses.[56] Solely silent sacrifice did not find much favor in Jewish and Christian sources; the inner sacrifice was expected to be accompanied by outward expressions, although of a rational kind.

Rabbinic Literature

After the destruction of the temple in AD 70 the rabbis continued to comment on the ritual prescriptions of the law, teaching that the amount of the offering was inconsequential and that the sacrifices were performed

---

53. Ibid. 1.201: νοῦς . . . ὅς ἄμωνος ὤν καὶ καθαρθεὶς καθάρσεσι ταῖς ἀρετῆς τελείας αὐτός ἐστιν ἡ εὐαγεστάτη θυσία καὶ ὅλη δι' ὅλων εὐάρεστος θεῷ. Cf. *Vita Mos.* 2.108: εἰ δ' ὅσιος καὶ δίκαιος, μένει βέβαιος ἡ θυσία, κἂν τὰ κρέα δαπανηθῇ, μᾶλλον δὲ καὶ εἰ τὸ παράπαν μηδὲν προσάγοιτο ἱερεῖον. ἡ γὰρ ἀληθὴς ἱερουργία τίς ἂν εἴη πλὴν ψυχῆς θεοφιλοῦς εὐσέβεια;

54. *Quod. det. pot.* 21: γνήσιοι δ' εἰσὶν αἱ ψυχῆς ψιλὴν καὶ μόνον θυσίαν φερούσης ἀλήθειαν. Cf. *Quaes. et sol. in Ex.* 1.11.

55. *Spec. leg.* 1.272: κἂν μέντοι μηδὲν ἕτερον κομίζωσιν, αὐτοὺς φέροντες πλήρωμα καλοκἀγαθίας τελειότατον τὴν ἀρίστην ἀνάγουσι θυσίαν, ὕμνοις καὶ εὐχαριστίαις τὸν εὐεργέτην καὶ σωτῆρα θεὸν γεραίροντες, τῇ μὲν διὰ τῶν φωνητηρίων ὀργάνων, τῇ δὲ ἄνευ γλώττης καὶ στόματος, μόνῃ ψυχῇ τὰς νοητὰς ποιούμενοι διεξόδους καὶ ἐκβοήσεις.

56. *Plant.* 2.126: θεῷ δὲ οὐκ ἔνεστι γνησίως εὐχαριστῆσαι . . . ἀλλὰ δι' ἐπαίνων καὶ ὕμνων, οὐχ οὕς ἡ γεγωνὸς ᾄσεται φωνή, ἀλλὰ οὕς ὁ ἀειδὴς καὶ καθαρώτατος νοῦς ἐπηχήσει καὶ ἀναμέλψει.

because they were commanded.[57] They also gave attention to religious duties which availed the same as sacrifice or could be claimed to be superior to sacrifice.[58] The special concern was atoning sacrifice.

1. *Reading and Study of the Law.* A possible explanation for the extensive attention given to the laws of sacrifice in rabbinic literature is the principle, "If you study the laws about sacrifice, that is to me as if you had offered them."[59] Reading the chapters about sacrifices would bring forgiveness.[60] God was said to account one day engaged in learning better than the thousand burnt offerings of Solomon (*b. Shabbath* 30 a end). It was affirmed that "the study of Torah is more beloved of God than burnt offerings" (*Fathers according to Rabbi Nathan* 4).

2. *Repentance.* The rabbis frequently reiterated that nothing expiates without repentance.[61] Yom Kippur atoned only for those who repented.[62] A man who repented was accounted as though he had sacrificed.[63]

3. *Prayer.* When sacrifices, temple, and altar were laid waste, nothing was left but prayer (*Midrash Psalms* on 5.4). For those unlearned in the law, God promised to forgive if they would weep and pray.[64] The poor man who could bring nothing else could come to God with words of prayer.[65]

Thus it was an easy step to say that prayer (Hosea 14:2) replaced animal sacrifice. Malachi 1:11 was interpreted as prayer, not literal sacrifices and incense.[66] The daily prayers were instituted to replace the daily

---

57. *Siphre Num.* 143, quoted by Montefiore and Loewe, *Rabbinic Anthology*, 151 no. 410.

58. Brown, *Temple and Sacrifice in Rabbinic Judaism*, 26–30. Cf. Mark 12:33.

59. *Pesikta of Rab Kahana* 60b, Montefiore and Loewe, *Rabbinic Anthology*, 25 no. 57. Cf. *b. Men.* 110a.

60. *b. Meg.* 31b [= *b. Ta'anith* 27b]; cf. *Sifre Deut.* 30b on Deut 32:2. The study of the Torah and acts of charity bring forgiveness of sins—*b. Berakoth* 5a,b. Cf. *Tanhuma* B., *Aharè Mot* 16–17 (35a) in Montefiore and Loewe, *Rabbinic Anthology*, 119, no. 313.

61. *Tos. Yoma* 5.9; Montefiore and Loewe, *Rabbinic Anthology*, 323, no. 843. See Brown, *Temple and Sacrifice in Rabbinic Judaism*, 11–13.

62. *b. Shebuoth* 13a [= *Kerioth* 7a]; cf. *m. Yoma* 8:8.

63. *Lev. R.* on *Zaw* 7.2.

64. *Ex. R.* 38.4, Montefiore and Loewe, *Rabbinic Anthology*, 343, no. 897.

65. *Tanhuma* B., *Zaw* 8, 9a, Montefiore and Loewe, *Rabbinic Anthology*, 346, no. 909. See G. F. Moore, *Judaism*, 2:218, for *'abodah*, which was used of the sacrificial cultus, applied to prayer, and for other references on this section.

66. *Tanhuma, Aharè Mot* 14 (34b–35a).

sacrifices.⁶⁷ It was further claimed that "prayer is greater than all the sacrifices" (Isa 1:11, 13).⁶⁸

4. *Works of Charity.* Johanan ben Zakkai was quoted as saying, "We have an atonement equal to the temple, the doing of loving deeds," quoting Hos 6.6 (*Aboth R. Nathan* 4, 11 a). Rabbi Eleazar said, "Greater is he who performs charity than he who offers all the sacrifices," quoting Prov 21:3 (*b. Sukkah* 49b). Sins not expiated with sacrifice and offering were expiated with Torah and charitable deeds (*b. Rosh Hashanah* 18a). "When the temple stood, a man used to bring his shekel and so make atonement. Now that the temple no longer stands, if they give for charity, well and good" (*b. Baba Bathra* 9a). Food given to the poor was accounted as if it were given to God.⁶⁹ Hospitality was particularly singled out as a charitable deed having sacrificial value (*b. Berakoth* 10b).

5. *Fasting.* "When the temple was standing, if a man sinned he used to bring a sacrifice and, though all that was offered of it was its fat and blood, atonement was made for him. Now I have kept a fast and my fat and blood have diminished. May it be thy will to account my fat and blood which have been diminished as if I had offered them before thee on the altar" (*b. Berakoth* 17a).⁷⁰

6. *Suffering.* The Tannaite scholar Rabbi Nehemiah said, "Even as the sacrifices brought acceptance, so sufferings bring acceptance . . . And not only so, but sufferings are more acceptable than sacrifices, because sacrifices affect a man's money, but sufferings affect his body."⁷¹ Sufferings are greater than offerings, because they atone for all sins (*Midrash Psalms* on 118.18). "The death of the righteous makes atonement" (*b. Moed Katan* 28a).

7. *Heart.* Various attitudes of the heart were also compared to sacrifice. "He who has a humble mind is regarded as if he had offered all the sacrifices of the law."⁷² Justice and righteousness are better than the sacrifices.⁷³

67. *b. Berakoth* 26a,b; cf. 15a; *Num. R.* 13 on Num 7:12.

68. *Tanhuma* 1, 31b; Montefiore and Loewe, *Rabbinic Anthology*, 357, no. 951. Cf. *b. Berakoth* 32b for prayer more efficacious than good deeds and offerings.

69. Montefiore and Loewe, *Rabbinic Anthology*, 414.

70. Cf. *b. Berakoth* 32b for fasting as better than charity, because the latter has to do with money but fasting with the body.

71. *Mekilta, Bahodesh, Yitro* 10, Montefiore and Loewe, *Rabbinic Anthology*, 545, no. 1531.

72. *b. Sotah* 5b [= *b. Sanhedrin* 43b].

73. *Deut. R.* 5.1–3; cf. *j. Berakoth* 1.1.

NEW TESTAMENT[74]

The Sacrifice of Christ

Jesus, as a good Jew, attended the festivals at the temple (Luke 2:41–49; Mark 14:12ff. and parallels), and his disciples continued to go to the temple (Acts 2:46; 3:1; 21:20ff.). Nevertheless, the temple ritual lost its significance for those disciples when they came to the understanding that Jesus' body was the temple (John 2:19–22; Eph 2:18–22) and that his death was an atoning sacrifice (Mark 10:45; Matt 26:28). The blood of Jesus now effected forgiveness (Eph 1:7). Since sacrifice was the universal language of worship in the ancient world, it was natural that the significance of Jesus' death should be interpreted in those terms.

The "Epistle to the Hebrews" most fully developed the sacrificial imagery in reference to Jesus' death.[75] What corresponded to the temple ceremony for Christians was the redemptive work of Christ (Heb 9:11–14). Christ is the high priest, superior in every way to the priests under the law (Heb 7:15–28), and serves in the true tabernacle, the heavenly sanctuary (Heb 8:1, 2; 9:11, 12). He is not only priest, but also victim, offering himself as the perfect sacrifice (Heb 8:3; 9:12–14, 25–28; 10:1–14). Christ thus prepared the way (Heb 6:20) so that his people could follow him boldly, with free access into the presence of God (Heb 9:9, 14; 10:19–22). Christians, forming the temple or house of God (Heb 3:6; 10:21; cf. 1 Cor 3:16; 2 Cor 6:16), worship God in Spirit (Heb 9:14; 10:23–25; cf. John 4:24).

The death of Christ continued to be interpreted by Christians as a sacrifice, replacing the sacrificial system of the Jewish law and temple.[76] This provided the essential background for the Christian spiritualization of sacrifice. Since atoning sacrifice was effected by Christ, Christian sacrifices were seen largely as thank offerings or else as enabling one to share in the sacrifice of Christ.

---

74. Young, "Temple Cult and Law in Early Christianity"; Young, "New Wine in Old Wineskins"; Wenschkewitz, *Die Spiritualisierung der Kultusbegriffe*.

75. Stott, "The Conception of 'Offering' in the Epistle to the Hebrews."

76. E.g., *Ep. Barnabé* 2.4–10; 7.3; Justin, *Dial.* 111.3; Origen, *Comm. Joh.* 1.35, 37, 39, 40. For the anti-sacrificial texts from the Old Testament used by the early Christians see Prigent, *L'Epître de Barnabé I—XVI et ses sources*; cf. 127–42 for this attitude in late Judaism. Eusebius, *Dem. Evang.* 1.10.

The Sacrifice of Christians

New Testament writers presented Christians as a priestly people. By reason of their incorporation into Christ, the High Priest, they shared in his priestly office.[77] The church, as the new Israel of God (Gal 6:16; Phil 3:3), occupied the priestly status of Israel.[78] The priestly work of Christians was to offer spiritual sacrifices.[79] The language of sacrifice employed in the New Testament about the offerings of the individual Christian to God served as one point of departure for later interpretations of the nature of Christian sacrifice.

1. *Praise and Thanksgiving.* The Epistle to the Hebrews 13:15 provided a sacrificial interpretation of the Christian life.[80] The passage abounds in Old Testament language.[81] The confession of God's name and praise to him, offered through the high priest Christ, were the Christians' sacrifice. The context refers to the sufferings of Jesus and sanctification by his blood (Heb 13:11, 12). There may, therefore, be a eucharistic reference in Hebrews 13:10,[82] but the primary reference would be to participating in the benefits of the death of Jesus, and the altar is probably the same as the one in the heavenly sanctuary in 9:1–14, 24; 10:19. Hebrews 13:15 would make explicit that the sacrifice was the verbal thanksgiving.

2. *Benevolence.* The Epistle to the Hebrews 13:16 continues by identifying good works and sharing with those in need as acceptable Christian sacrifices.[83] The verb translated "pleasing" or acceptable occurs as an adverb in Hebrews 12:28 for the Christians' worship or service to God. The word appears not to have been common in sacrificial contexts outside the

---

77. Rev 1:6: ἐποίησεν ἡμᾶς βασιλείαν, ἱερεῖς τῷ θεῷ.

78. 1 Pet 2:9: ὑμεῖς δὲ γένος ἐκλεκτόν, βασίλειον ἱεράτευμα, ἔθνος ἅγιον. Cf. Exod 19:5, 6. Best, "Spiritual Sacrifice."

79. 1 Pet 2:5: καὶ αὐτοὶ ὡς λίθοι ζῶντες οἰκοδομεῖσθε οἶκος πνευματικὸς εἰς ἱεράτευμα ἅγιον, ἀνενέγκαι πνευματικὰς θυσίας εὐπροσδέκτους θεῷ διὰ Ἰησοῦ Χριστοῦ. Cf. Rev 1:6; 5:8. Best, "I Peter 2:4–10."

80. Δι' αὐτοῦ οὖν ἀναφέρωμεν θυσίαν αἰνέσεως διὰ παντὸς τῷ θεῷ, τουτ' ἔστιν καρπὸν χειλέων ὁμολογούντων τῷ ὀνόματι αὐτοῦ.

81. "Sacrifice" and "praise" are combined in 2 Chr 29:31, and the exact phrase "sacrifice of praise" is common (see n. 30). Likewise, the "fruit of lips," instead of the fruits of the earth or of the flocks and herds, is found in Hos 14:2.

82. ἔχομεν θυσιαστήριον ἐξ οὗ φαγεῖν οὐκ ἔχουσιν ἐξουσίαν οἱ τῇ σκηνῇ λατρεύοντες. The commentaries discuss the different interpretations. For the context see Trudinger, "Sens de la Sécularité selon l'Evangile."

83. τῆς δὲ εὐποιΐας καὶ κοινωνίας μὴ ἐπιλανθάνεσθε. τοιαύταις γὰρ θυσίαις εὐαρεστεῖται ὁ θεός.

New Testament but pertained to one's total conduct before God. Sharing and doing good were such pleasing conduct and were here included by the writer in his spiritual reinterpretation of priestly activity.[84]

3. *Preaching.* Paul understood his apostolic ministry to the Gentiles in priestly terms. Sacrificial imagery dominates his account of preaching the gospel in Rom 15:15–21. Four words in vv. 15, 16[85] are drawn from sacrificial worship. "Minister" (*leitourgos*) is the noun of a word often used in the Greek Bible for the activity of priests.[86] "Priestly service" (*hierourgeō*) is regularly used for the sacrificial work of a priest. "Offering" (*prosphora*) is a common, general word for sacrificial offerings; by it Paul describes his Gentile converts as a sacrifice to God. "Acceptable" (*euprosdektos*) refers to a sacrifice (cf. 1 Pet 2:5) which is received by God. In this case, the Gentiles, previously considered unclean, are made acceptable as a sacrificial offering because they have been "sanctified" (*hagiazō*) by the Holy Spirit. Paul varied the imagery in Phil 2:17 from himself as the priest to himself as a drink offering poured on the sacrifice.[87] As Paul contemplated the possibility of his death because of his work of preaching the gospel, he could speak of pouring out his life as a drink offering. The faith of his converts was the "sacrifice and service" for which Paul was willing to give his life. Therefore, not only was teaching others a sacrificial act, but giving one's life in preaching the gospel was a sacrifice. The converts themselves and their faith, too, could be viewed as a sacrifice.

4. *Financial Support of Preaching.* Paul went further in writing to the Philippian Christians and identified their monetary contribution to support him in his work of preaching as a sacrifice. Philippians 4:18 overflows with sacrificial terms.[88] "Fragrant odor" (*osmēn euōdias*) is common in the Old Testament for a sacrifice pleasing to God.[89] "Acceptable and well pleasing" (*dektos* and *euarestos*) reflect a formula declaring that the sacrifice

---

84. Cf. Jesus' teaching in Matt 9:13, quoting Hos 6:6.

85. διὰ τὴν χάριν τὴν δοθεῖσάν μοι ἀπὸ τοῦ θεοῦ εἰς τὸ εἶναί με λειτουργὸν Χριστοῦ Ἰησοῦ εἰς τὰ ἔθνη, ἱερουργοῦντα τὸ εὐαγγέλιον τοῦ θεοῦ, ἵνα γένηται ἡ προσφορὰ τῶν ἐθνῶν εὐπρόσδεκτος, ἡγιασμένη ἐν πνεύματι ἁγίῳ.

86. Cf. Isa 61:6 for *leitourgos* applied to priests. Paul in 1 Cor 9:13, 14 compares the priests' *leitourgia* at the temple to preaching the gospel. See n. 101

87. Ἀλλὰ εἰ καὶ σπένδομαι ἐπὶ τῇ θυσίᾳ καὶ λειτουργίᾳ τῆς πίστεως ὑμῶν, χαίρω καὶ συγχαίρω πᾶσιν ὑμῖν.

88. πεπλήρωμαι δεξάμενος παρὰ Ἐπαφροδίτου τὰ παρ' ὑμῶν, ὀσμὴν εὐωδίας, θυσίαν δεκτήν, εὐάρεστον τῷ θεῷ. Cf. 2.25.

89. Note Ezek 20:40, 41 in a prophecy about God's people in the age to come.

is received and very satisfactory. Money given to support the gospel (the preaching of which was itself a sacrifice) was a gift to God.

5. *Life (Body or Self)*. Romans 12:1 catches up and unites all of these ideas and serves as the most comprehensive and challenging statement of the Christian conception of sacrifice. Once more notice may be taken of the piling up of sacrificial terminology.[90] "To present" (*paristēmi*) had among other uses "to present an offering to the deity." As well as presenting the converts to God (as in 15:16) Christians pesent their bodies, themselves, to God. "Holy and acceptable" (*hagios, euarestos*) mark the sacrifice as appropriate and set apart for divine use. The language, however, has an important contrast with traditional conceptions. The Christian's sacrifice is not the dead body of animals slain in the act of sacrifice; theirs is a "living" sacrifice, As Christians serve a "living God" (e.g., 1 Thess 1:9) instead of dead idols, so their sacrifice is living and not dead. It is the totality of life. As verse 2 proceeds to say, this means living all of one's life in obedience to God instead of in accord with the world's standards. Such a manner of life is a "rational service" (*logikē latreia*), a service to God that proceeds from man's spiritual nature, the highest part of his being. *Logike* is equivalent to *pneumatikē* in 1 Pet 2:5.[91] Life lived for God is the truly spiritual sacrifice. This verse is the high point of the sacrificial language of the New Testament and of all literature. The whole self belongs to God and is to be given to him. Throughout life one belongs to God, to worship and serve him.

OTHER CHRISTIAN LITERATURE TO EUSEBIUS

Apostolic Fathers

1. *Worship in General*. 1 *Clement*, on the analogy of the Old Testament and borrowing its terminology, suggests a sacrificial understanding of Christian worship and the Christian ministry. His only uses of *thusia* are in references to Old Testament sacrifice and in Old Testament quotations.[92] Other sacrificial and priestly words, however, are extended to Christian divine service. *Prospherō*, in addition to its occurrences in the same context with

---

90. Παρακαλῶ οὖν ὑμᾶς, ἀδελφοί, διὰ τῶν οἰκτιρμῶν τοῦ θεοῦ, παραστῆσαι τὰ σώματα ὑμῶν θυσίαν ζῶσαν ἁγίαν τῷ θεῷ εὐάρεστον, τὴν λογικὴν λατρείαν ὑμῶν.

91. Reitzenstein, *Die hellenistischen Mysterienreligionen*, 328–32.

92. 4:1–2—Cain and Abel; 10:7; 31:3—Isaac; 41:3—the daily sacrifices of the law: 18:16, 17; 35:12; and 52:3, 4—quoting Psalms 49 and 50 [50 and 51], favorites in the Christian argument for a spiritual interpretation of sacrifice.

thusia, appears in 36:1, "Jesus Christ, the high priest of our offerings,"[93] and three times in the crucial passage 40–44, associated with *leitourgia*. *Leitourgia* is a favorite word with Clement, reflecting his aquaintance with the Greek Old Testament.[94] The Old Testament language of offering and liturgy came naturally to Clement when speaking of Christian practices.[95] Chapter 40 is ambiguous: how much is referring specifically to the enactments of the law and how much to Christianity under the terminology of the law?[96] Clement's application to the disorders at Corinth is clear: "Let each one of us, brethren, be well pleasing to God in his own rank, having a good conscience and not transgressing the appointed rule of his service."[97] So each Christian has an appointed "liturgy." But Clement especially has in mind the presbyter-bishops. Their ministry was by apostolic appointment (44:2), was received with the approval of the whole church (44:3), and having been blamelessly performed should not be rejected (44:6). The service which they rendered was offering the gifts (44:4).[98] Since Clement is still following the language of his Old Testament analogy, it is not clear exactly what he includes in these gifts—prayers, the eucharist, or the total conduct of divine service. I am inclined to say the whole responsibility of the episcopate. Preaching is included in his understanding of *leitourgia* elsewhere: "The ministers of the grace of God [prophets] spoke through the Holy Spirit."[99] Clement included within the Christian worship or religion the contents of his whole letter, which touched on "the things befitting our worship [*thrēskeia*] and profitable for a virtuous life" (62:1).

2. *Preaching*. The *Didache* adds support to conclusions which can only be inferred from 1 *Clement*. Assuming the priestly connotation of *leitourgia* (which in view of the Jewish background of the *Didache* seems

---

93. Ἰησοῦν Χριστόν, τὸν ἀρχιερέα τῶν προσφορῶν ἡμῶν.

94. 9:2, 4—Old Testament worthies; 34.5 and 36.3—angels; 34.6 quoting Dan 7:10; 20:10—winds; 43:4—priesthood of Old Testament; 32:4 and 41:2—Levites who served the altar.

95. Noll, "The Search for a Christian Ministerial Priesthood in I Clement"; Jourjon, *Remarques sur le vocabulaire sacerdotal dans Ia Ia Clementis*, 107–10.

96. 40:2: τάς τε προσφορὰς καὶ λειτουργίας ἐπιτελεῖσθαι (ἡμᾶς). 40:3: ἵν' ὁσίως πάντα γινόμενα ἐν εὐδοκήσει εὐπρόσδεκτα εἴη τῷ θελήματι αὐτοῦ. 40:5: τῷ γὰρ ἀρχιερεῖ ἴδιαι λειτουργίαι δεδομέναι.

97. 41:1: Ἔκαστος ἡμῶν . . . μὴ παρεκβαίνων τὸν ὡριομένον τῆς λειτουργίας αὐτοῦ κανόνα.

98. ἁμαρτία γὰρ οὐ μικρὰ ἡμῖν ἔσται, ἐὰν τοὺς ἀμέμπτως καὶ ὁσίως προσενεγκόντας τὰ δῶρα τῆς ἐπισκοπῆς ἀποβάλωμεν.

99. 8.1: Οἱ λειτουργοὶ τῆς χάριτος τοῦ θεοῦ διὰ πνεύματος ἁγίου περὶ μετανοίας ἐλάλησαν.

probable), then the ministry of the word was a kind of sacrifice. "Appoint therefore for yourselves bishops and deacons..., for they also minister to you the ministry of the prophets and teachers."[100] The ministry of prophets and teachers was to "speak the word of the Lord" (4:1; 11).[101] The prophets, taking the place of the priests in Judaism, were to receive the firstfruits (13). The "Didache" further indicates that the ministry of prophets and teachers included the conduct of divine service, specifically pronouncing the eucharistic prayers (10:7).

3. *Eucharist.* The 'Didache' provides the first use in Christian literature of *thusia* in reference to the eucharist. "When you come together on the Lord's day of the Lord, break bread and give thanks, after confessing your transgressions, in order that your sacrifice may be pure."[102] The author points out that allowing a quarrel to go unreconciled will profane their sacrifice. He quotes Mal 1:11, 14 (the favorite Old Testament testimony to the eucharist in early Christian literature) as referring to the Christian sacrifice,[103] which however cannot be the "pure sacrifice" of that text if division exists in the community. The whole transaction of the Lord's Supper—the breaking of bread and the prayers of thanksgiving—are viewed as the sacrifice. Since the sacrifice is not identified with the material elements, this qualifies as rational or spiritual sacrifice, although the action of breaking bread as well as the words are included. In Jewish practice the gesture and the prayer went together in the thanksgiving with which a meal began.[104]

The *Didache* allows no compromise with paganism: the believer must abstain from food sacrificed to idols, "for it is the worship [*latreia*] of dead gods" (6:3).[105] Christians serve a living God and walk in the way

---

100. Didache 15.1: Χειροτονήσατε οὖν ἑαυτοῖς ἐπισκόπους καὶ διακόνους... ὑμῖν γὰρ λειτουργοῦσι καὶ αὐτοὶ τὴν λειτουργίαν τῶν προφητῶν καὶ διδασκάλων.

101. Assuming a Syrian provenance for the *Didache*(?), then it may be significant that Acts 13:2 uses *leitourgeō* of the prophets and teachers at Antioch.

102. *Didache* 14:1: Κατὰ κυριακὴν δὲ κυρίου συναχθέντες κλάσατε ἄρτον καὶ εὐχαριστήσατε, προεξομολογησάμενοι τὰ παραπτώματα ὑμῶν, ὅπως καθαρὰ ἡ θυσία ὑμῶν ᾖ. There is a voluminous literature on the eucharist as a sacrifice. See Watteville, *Le sacrifice dans les textes eucharistiques des premiers siècles*; Lampe, "The Eucharist in the Thought of the Early Church"; Rordorf, "Le sacrifice eucharistique"; Kilmartin, "*Sacrificium laudis.*"

103. Audet, *La Didachè*, 462–63, for Mal 1:11 in the *Didache*; for the Jewish background to the Christian use see Swetman, "Malachi 1,11: An Interpretation."

104. Cf. Mark 6:4 and parallels; Acts 27:35; as well as Mark 14:22.

105. In a similar way *2 Clement* declares, "We who are living do not sacrifice to dead gods and do not worship them" (6:3).

of life (1–4); hence the Christian (baptized in "living water"—7:1) in his sacrifice gives thanks for the life and immortality which are made known through Jesus, the Son of God (9:3; 10:2).

As the *Didache* has spoken of "coming together" to break bread, so Ignatius of Antioch gave great emphasis to the common assembly. In order to combat schism and heresy, Ignatius urged the necessity of unity and employed the sacrificial imagery of "one altar" to symbolize being together in the service of God. "All of you are to hasten to come together as to one temple of God, as to one altar, as to one Jesus Christ."[106] Either Christ himself, the assembly, or the activity in the assembly is metaphorically described as an altar, a place of sacrifice. The pure offering is possible only within the constituted meeting under the leadership of the appointed ministers.[107] This is in keeping with Ignatius' strong emphasis on union with the bishop, presbyters, and deacons in the face of heretical teachings.[108] The central point of the common assembly was the breaking of bread accompanied by prayer: "Unless a man be within the sanctuary he lacks the bread of God. For if the prayer of one or two has such power, how much more the prayer of the bishop and the whole church."[109] Thus Ignatius' language of "one altar" includes a eucharistic reference, if it is not confined to such:

> Be careful therefore to employ one eucharist [thanksgiving] (for there is one flesh of our Lord Jesus Christ and one cup for union with his blood, one altar, even as one bishop together with the presbytery and deacons my fellow servants) in order that whatever you do may be done according to God.[110]

---

106. *Magnesians* 7.2: πάντες ὡς εἰς ἕνα ναὸν συντρέχετε θεοῦ, ὡς ἐπὶ ἓν θυσιαστήριον, ἐπὶ ἕνα Ἰησοῦν Χριστόν.

107. *Trallians* 7.2: ὁ ἐντὸς θυσιαστηρίου ὢν καθαρός ἐστιν᾽. ὁ δὲ ἐκτὸς θυσιαστηρίου ὢν οὐ καθαρός ἐστιν. τοῦτ᾽ ἔστιν, ὁ χωρὶς ἐπισκόπου καὶ πρεσβυτερίου καὶ διακόνου πράσσων τι, οὗτος οὐ καθαρός ἐστιν τῇ συνειδήσει.

108. Cf. *Smyrnaeans* 9.1: "He who does anything without the knowledge of the bishop serves the Devil."

109. *Ephesians* 5.2: ἐὰν μή τις ᾖ ἐντὸς τοῦ θυσιαστηρίου, ὑστερεῖται τοῦ ἄρτου τοῦ θεοῦ. εἰ γὰρ ἑνὸς καὶ δευτέρου προσευχὴ τοσαύτην ἰσχὺν ἔχει, πόσῳ μᾶλλον ἥ τε τοῦ ἐπισκόπου καὶ πάσης ἐκκλησίας; Cf. Snyder, "The Text and Syntax of Ignatius ΠΡΟΣ ΕΦΕΣΙΟΥΣ 20:2c."

110. *Philadelphians* 4: Σπουδάσατε οὖν μιᾷ εὐχαριστίᾳ χρῆσθαι. μία γὰρ σὰρξ τοῦ κυρίου ἡμῶν Ἰησοῦ Χριστοῦ καὶ ἓν ποτήριον εἰς ἕνωσιν τοῦ αἵματος αὐτοῦ, ἓν θυσιαστήριον, ὡς εἷς ἐπίσκοπος ἅμα τῷ πρεσβυτερίῳ καὶ διακόνοις. Woodhall, "The Eucharistic Theology of Ignatius of Antioch."

"Altar" appears to be used metaphorically by Ignatius. His main emphasis was upon unity, expressed in a common assembly. The center of that assembly was the eucharist, so sacrificial connotations were given to the Christian meeting. If Ignatius was influenced by terminology reflected in the Apocalypse (from the same geographical area as the churches he addressed), where the prayers of the saints arise as incense from the altar (Rev 5:8; 8:3, 4), then Ignatius would have thought primarily of the prayers of thanksgiving accompanying the bread and cup.

4. *Martyrdom.* Ignatius provides two other uses of the words "altar" and "sacrifice" which show his spiritualizing of the concept of sacrifice. His association of martyrdom with an altar may also be paralleled from the Apocalypse (6:9). Ignatius urged the Roman Christians, "Grant me nothing more than to be poured out as a libation to God, while an altar is still ready, that forming yourself as a chorus in love you may sing to the Father in Christ Jesus."[111] His picture seems to be that of a chorus gathered around a pagan altar singing a hymn to the deity to whom the sacrifice was offered. Ignatius is himself the drink offering poured on the altar (cf. 2 Tim 4:6). He did not want to miss his opportunity for martyrdom. To give one's life because of his faith in Christ was a sacrifice:

> I am God's wheat, and I am ground by the teeth of wild beasts in order that I may be found pure bread of Christ. Rather entice the wild beasts that they may become my tomb . . . Beseech Christ on my behalf in order that through these instruments I may be found God's sacrifice.[112]

Ignatius' metaphor of the wheat and bread may give some support to a sacrificial interpretation of the eucharistic elements, but also may be natural to Ignatius' imaginative use of language. What is certain is that a martyr's death was a sacrifice to God.

Polycarp of Smyrna, one of Ignatius' correspondents, became a martyr because he refused to say, "Lord Caesar," and to sacrifice (*Mart. Polyc.* 8.2). In contrast to his repudiation of animal sacrifice and other elements of pagan worship (12.2), his own death was understood by Christians as

---

111. *Romans* 2.2: πλέον δέ μοι μὴ παράσχησθε τοῦ σπονδισθῆναι θεῷ, ὡς ἔτι θυσιαστήριον ἕτοιμόν ἐστιν, ἵνα ἐν ἀγάπῃ χορὸς γενόμενοι ᾄσητε τῷ πατρὶ ἐν Ἰησοῦ Χριστῷ. Corwin, *Saint Ignatius and Christianity in Antioch*, 172 and 250, on martyrdom in Ignatius as a sacrifice; for the idea of martyrdom as a sacrifice in early Christianity in general, see von Campenhausen, *Die Idee des Martyriums in der alten Kirche*, chapter 3.

112. Ibid., 4:2: . . . λιτανεύσατε τὸν Χριστὸν ὑπὲρ ἐμοῦ, ἵνα διὰ τῶν ὀργάνων τούτων θεοῦ θυσία εὑρεθῶ.

a sacrifice. He was led out "bound, as a noble ram out of a great flock, for an oblation, a whole burnt offering, prepared and acceptable to God."[113] Polycarp's prayer also employed sacrificial imagery in reference to his death: "Today may I be received among the martyrs before thee as a rich and acceptable sacrifice."[114] A person's giving his life in order to die for God might naturally be described in the same terms used for giving the life of an animal for God,[115] but Christian martyrdom gave the concept of sacrifice a new dimension which went beyond the human sacrifice of pagan antiquity.

5. *Benevolence.* Polycarp's own writing speaks of widows as an altar of God.[116] They were viewed as the place of sacrifice, because they received the church's gifts. It may be, further, that the association with altar was suggested because the widows were to be constantly at prayer (cf. 1 Tim 5:5), but more likely ceaseless prayer was simply part of the description of a total life of purity and virtue necessary for an altar which received the pure sacrifice (benevolence) of Christians.

The "Shepherd of Hermas" uses sacrificial language principally in reference to benevolent acts.[117] Fasting was to be observed, not as an ascetic discipline, but in order to give the price of the food "to a widow, orphan, or someone destitute," which would be a "sacrifice acceptable to God."[118] Fasting for benevolence was a sacrifice and a liturgy. The liturgy of bishops is explained by Hermas as including hospitality, sheltering "the destitute and widows," and conducting themselves with holiness.[119] Her-

---

113. *Mart. Polyc.* 14.1: ὥσπερ κριὸς ἐπίσημος ἐκ μεγάλου ποιμνίου εἰς προσφοράν, ὁλοκαύτωμα δεκτὸν τῷ θεῷ ἡτοιμασμένον. Cf. 15.2 for his burning body having the scent of incense.

114. Ibid., 14.2: τοῦ λαβεῖν μέρος ἐν ἀριθμῷ τῶν μαρτύρων ἐν τῷ ποτηρίῳ τοῦ Χριστοῦ... ἐν οἷς προσδεχθείην ἐνώπιόν σου σήμερον ἐν θυσίᾳ πίονι καὶ προσδεκτῇ.

115. Letter of Churches of Lyons and Vienne in Eusebius, *H.E.* 5.1.40, 51, and 56.

116. *Ep. Philip.* 4.3: τὰς χήρας σωφρονούσας περὶ τὴν τοῦ κυρίου πίστιν, ἐντυγχανούσας ἀδιαλείπτως περὶ πάντων... γινωσκούσας, ὅτι εἰσὶ θυσιαστήριον θεοῦ καὶ ὅτι πάντα μωμοσκοπεῖται.

117. An exception is *Mand.* 10.3.2 where prayer ascends to God's altar.

118. *Sim.* 5.3.7,8: καὶ ἐκ τῶν ἐδεσμάτων σου ὧν ἔμελλες τρώγειν συμψηφίσας τὴν ποσότητα τῆς δαπάνης ἐκείνης τῆς ἡμέρας ἧς ἔμελλες ποιεῖν, δώσεις αὐτὸ χήρᾳ ἢ ὀρφανῷ ἢ ὑστερουμένῳ... ἐὰν οὖν οὕτω τελέσῃς τὴν νηστείαν, ὥς σοι ἐνετειλάμην, ἔσται ἡ θυσία σου δεκτὴ παρὰ τῷ θεῷ, καὶ ἔγγραφος ἔσται ἡ νηστεία αὕτη, καὶ ἡ λειτουργία οὕτως ἐργαζομένη καλὴ καὶ ἱλαρά ἐστι καὶ εὐπρόσδεκτος τῷ κυρίῳ. Cf. 5.3.3 for the liturgy of fasting combined with keeping commands. *II Clement* 16.4 attributes atoning value to almsgiving as superior to fasting and prayer. Cf. Eusebius, *H.E.* 5.18.2 for a fraudulent use of alms as offerings.

119. *Sim.* 9.27.2,3: ἐπίσκοποι καὶ φιλόξενοι, οἵτινες ἡδέως εἰς τοὺς οἴκους ἑαυτῶν

mas (who was a prophet) describes his own life as a liturgy, but he places the emphasis on the need for purity of heart.[120]

6. *Purity of Heart and Life.* The *Odes of Solomon*, not included among the Apostolic Fathers but belonging to the same time period, give a pure spiritual expression to sacrifice:

> I am a priest of the Lord, and to him I do priestly service, and to him I offer the sacrifice of his thought. For his thought is not like the thought of the world, nor the thought of the flesh, nor like them that serve carnally. The sacrifice of the Lord is righteousness and purity of heart and lips. Present your reins before him blamelessly, and let not your heart do violence to another's heart nor you soul to another's soul.[121]

Thinking about God and giving expression to this in word and deed (see the remainder of the Ode) is the true priestly work.

Apologists

The Apostolic Fathers developed early Christian thought out of a predominantly Jewish background: prayer and alms as a sacrifice and death as atoning. The Apologists were especially aware of Greek philosophy where spiritual sacrifices were the non-material offering of the human mind. They emphasized that God does not need sacrifices (*Ep. ad Diog.* 3.4; cf. *Ep. Barn.* 2.4). The Valentinian Gnostic Ptolemy was very close not only to the time but also to the thought world of the second-century Apologists. His words, reflecting philosophical influence, may serve to introduce the concerns of his more orthodox contemporaries: "The Savior commanded us to offer oblations, but not those of irrational animals or incense, but of spiritual praises, gloryings, and thanksgiving, and of fellowship and doing good to our neighbors."[122]

πάντοτε ὑπεδέξαντο τοὺς δούλους τοῦ Θεοῦ . . . οἱ δὲ ἐπίσκοποι πάντοτε τοὺς ὑστερημένους καὶ τὰς χήρας τῇ διακονίᾳ ἑαυτῶν ἀδιαλείπτως ἐσκέπασαν . . . οὗτοι οὖν πάντες σκεπασθήσονται . . . ἐὰν ἐπιμείνωσιν ἕως τέλους λειτουργοῦντες τῷ κυρίῳ.

120. *Sim.* 7.6: cf. *Mand.* 5.1.2,3.

121. *Odes of Solomon* 20; Harris and Mingana, *The Odes and Psalms of Solomon*.

122. *Ad Floram* 3, from Epiphanius, *Haer.* 33.5.10: προσφορὰς προσφέρειν προσέταξεν ἡμῖν ὁ σωτήρ, ἀλλὰ οὐχὶ τὰς δι' ἀλόγων ζώων ἢ τούτων τῶν θυμιαμάτων ἀλλὰ διὰ πνευματικῶν αἴνων καὶ δοξῶν καὶ εὐχαριστίας καὶ διὰ τῆς εἰς τοὺς πλησίον κοινωνίας καὶ εὐποιίας.

1. *Knowledge of God*. Athenagoras closely followed philosophical thought in his statement of the Christian case.[123]

> First, as to our not sacrificing: the Maker and Father of all does not need blood, nor the odor of burnt offering, nor the fragrance of flowers and incense, since he is the perfect fragrance, needing nothing and selfsufficient.[124] The best sacrifice to him is for us to know who stretched out and vaulted the heavens and fixed the earth in its place … When, holding God to be this Maker of all things, who preserves them in being and superintends them all by knowledge and skill, we lift up holy hands to him, what need has he of a hecatomb? … And what have I to do with holocausts which God does not need? Indeed it befits us to offer a bloodless sacrifice and "the service of our reason."[125]

The best sacrifice is the knowledge of God, a bloodless sacrifice proceeding from the mind (Rom 12:1). Its outward expression was lifting up holy hands in prayer (1 Tim 2:8).

2. *Praise and Prayer*. The "Acts of Apollonius" contains two speeches of an apologetic character by the martyr. Although the surviving "Acta" are late, they contain an excellent brief statement of the position of the early Christian apologists with reference to sacrifice. Apollonius tells the proconsul: "1 and all Christians offer a pure and unbloody sacrifice to Almighty God who rules heaven, earth, and all breath, the sacrifice of prayers."[126]

---

123. Malherbe, "The Structure of Athenagoras, *Supplicatio pro Christianis*."

124. Aristides, *Apol.* 1.5 (Syriac) states a commonplace: "God requires neither sacrifice and libation nor anything that appears to sense, but all living creatures stand in need of him." Cf. 13.4.

125. *Legatio* 13: καὶ πρῶτόν γε περὶ τοῦ μὴ θύειν. ὁ τοῦδε τοῦ παντὸς δημιουργὸς καὶ πατὴρ οὐ δεῖται αἵματος οὐδὲ κνίσης οὐδὲ τῆς ἀπὸ τῶν ἀνθῶν καὶ θυμιαμάτων εὐωδίας, αὐτὸς ὢν ἡ τελεία εὐωδία, ἀνενδεὴς καὶ ἀπροσδεής. ἀλλὰ θυσία αὐτῷ μεγίστη, ἂν γινώσκωμεν τίς ἐξέτεινε καὶ συνεσφαίρωσεν τοὺς οὐρανοὺς καὶ τὴν γῆν κέντρου δίκην ἥδρασε … ὅταν οὖν ἔχοντες τὸν δημιουργὸν θεὸν συνέχοντα καὶ ἐποπτεύοντα ἐπιστήμῃ καὶ τέχνῃ καθ' ἣν ἄγει τὰ πάντα ἐπαίρωμεν ὁσίους χεῖρας αὐτῷ, ποίας ἔτι χρείαν ἑκατόμβης ἔχει; … τί δεῖ μοι ὁλοκαυτώσεων, ὧν μὴ δεῖται ὁ θεός; καὶ προσφέρειν, δέον ἀναίμακτον θυσίαν τὴν λογικὴν προσάγειν λατρείαν. Barnard, *Athenagoras*, 153–58, interprets the passage with reference to the eucharist.

126. *Acta Apol.* 8: θυσίαν ἀναίμακτον καὶ καθαρὰν ἀναπέμπω κἀγὼ καὶ πάντες Χριστιανοὶ τῷ παντοκράτορι θεῷ τῷ κυριεύοντι οὐρανοῦ καὶ γῆς καὶ πάσης πνοῆς, τὴν δι' εὐχῶν. Cf. Aristides, *Apol.* 16.1. See *Acta Apol.* 44 quoted below (n145).

Spiritual Sacrifice in Early Christianity and Its Environment

Justin Martyr had occasion to speak frequently against both pagan and Jewish sacrifice.[127] On the positive side, Justin set forth the Christian conception of sacrifice to pagans in the following way:

> What sober-minded man, then, will not acknowledge that we are not atheists, worshipping as we do the Maker of this universe, and declaring as we have been taught that he has no need of streams of blood and libations and incense. We praise him to the utmost of our power by the exercise of prayer and thanksgiving for all things wherewith we are supplied. We have been taught that the only honor that is worthy of him is not to consume by fire what he has brought into being for our sustenance but to use it for ourselves and those who need, and with gratitude to him to offer thanks by solemn hymns for our creation.[128]

Justin presents different kinds of prayers, emphasizing thanksgiving and detailing some of their content. He associates hymns with the prayers of praise (see below).

In setting forth Christianity with Jewish ideas in mind, Justin interpreted the prophecies as referring to "true and spiritual praises and thanksgivings."[129] He declared that Christ was the eternal Priest (*Dial.* 42.1; 118.2) and Christians the "true high priestly race of God," quoting Mal 1:11 (*Dial.* 116.3). Since God receives the sacrifices of Christians, they must be priests, for "God receives sacrifices from no one, except through his priests."[130] Justin knew that Trypho and like-minded Jews admitted

---

127. Against pagan sacrifice—*Apol.* I, 9.1; 24.2; 62; *Dial.* 46.7; against Jewish sacrifice—*Dial.* 19,6; 22.1; 43.1; 67.8; 92,5. Christ the perfect sacrifice—*Dial.* 40; 111; 13; 72. Old Testament quotations against sacrifice—*Dial.* 22; 28; 29; 73. Cf. *Ep. ad Diog.* 2.8 against pagan sacrifice and 3.2,5 against Jewish. Prigent, *Justin et l'ancien testament*, especially 273–79, 286–87.

128. Apol. I, 13: Ἄθεοι μὲν οὖν ὡς οὐκ ἐσμεν, τὸν δημιουργὸν τοῦδε τοῦ παντὸς σεβόμενοι, ἀνενδεῆ αἱμάτων καὶ σπονδῶν καὶ θυμιαμάτων, ὡς ἐδιδάχθημεν, λέγοντες, λόγῳ εὐχῆς καὶ εὐχαριστίας ἐφ' οἷς προσφερόμεθα πᾶσιν, ὅση δύναμις, αἰνοῦντες, μόνην ἀξίαν αὐτὸν τιμὴν ταύτην παραλαβόντες, τὸ τὰ ὑπ' ἐκείνου εἰς διατροφὴν γενόμενα οὐ πυρὶ δαπανᾶν, ἀλλ' ἑαυτοῖς καὶ τοῖς δεομένοις προσφέρειν, ἐκείνῳ δὲ εὐχαρίστους ὄντας διὰ λόγου πομπὰς καὶ ὕμνους πέμπειν ὑπέρ τε τοῦ γεγονέναι καὶ . . . τίς σωφρονῶν οὐχ ὁμολογήσει;

129. *Dial.* 118.2: μὴ δόξητε λέγειν Ἡσαΐαν ἢ τοὺς ἄλλους προφήτας θυσίας ἀφ' αἱμάτων ἢ σπονδῶν ἐπὶ τὸ θυσιαστήριον ἀναφέρεσθαι, ἀλλὰ ἀληθινοὺς καὶ πνευματικοὺς αἴνους καὶ εὐχαριστίας.

130. *Dial.* 116.3: ἀρχιερατικὸν τὸ ἀληθινὸν γένος ἐσμὲν τοῦ θεοῦ, ὡς καὶ αὐτὸς ὁ θεὸς μαρτυρεῖ, εἰπὼν ὅτι ἐν παντὶ τόπῳ ἐν τοῖς ἔθνεσι θυσίας εὐαρέστους αὐτῷ καὶ καθαρὰς προσφέροντες. οὐ δέχεται δὲ παρ' οὐδενὸς θυσίας ὁ θεός, εἰ μὴ διὰ τῶν ἱερέων αὐτοῦ. Quacquarelli, "L'epiteto sacerdote (ἱερεύς) ai cristiani in Giustino Martire (*Dial.* 116.3)."

that God had rejected the sacrifices at Jerusalem and claimed that God was now pleased with the prayers of Jews in the Dispersion, regarding them as sacrifices. Justin adds, "That prayers and thanksgivings by worthy persons are the only perfect and well-pleasing sacrifices to God I also affirm."[131] He claims, however, that Mal 1:10–14 is fulfilled in the prayers at the Christian eucharist and not in the Jewish prayers.

3. *Eucharist*. Justin often employs the pair "prayers and thanksgivings" and for Christians prayers of thanksgiving had their culmination at the bread and wine. Thus Justin follows his declaration that Christians are the true priestly people (*Dial*. 116.3 above) with the following words:

> Anticipating all the sacrifices which we [Christians] offer through this name [of Jesus] and which Jesus the Christ commanded to be done, that is in the thanksgiving of the bread and cup, which things are done by Christians in every place throughout the world, God bears witness that they are well pleasing to him but that he utterly rejects those which are done by you and your priests, saying [followed by the quotation again of Mal 1:10–12].[132]

It should be noted that Justin does not say here that the Christians' sacrifices are "the bread and cup of thanksgiving" but the "thanksgiving of the bread and cup." The sacrifice is the prayers offered for or in relation to the bread and cup. He declared (as cited above) that "prayers and thanksgivings" were the only acceptable sacrifices to God, and he continued "For such alone Christians have undertaken to offer, in the remembrance of both their solid and liquid food, by which the suffering which the Son of God endured for us is brought to mind."[133]

Justin's typological interpretation of the Old Testament sacrifices does lead him elsehere to speak of the "bread of thanksgiving and cup

---

131. *Dial*. 117.2: ὅτι μὲν οὖν καὶ εὐχαὶ καὶ εὐχαριστίαι, ὑπὸ τῶν ἀξίων γινόμεναι, τέλειαι μόναι καὶ εὐάρεστοί εἰσι τῷ θεῷ θυσίαι, καὶ αὐτός φημι.

132. *Dial*. 117.1: Πάσας οὖν διὰ τοῦ ὀνόματος τούτου θυσίας, ἃς παρέδωκεν Ἰησοῦς ὁ Χριστὸς γίνεσθαι, τοῦτ' ἔστιν ἐπὶ τῇ εὐχαριστίᾳ τοῦ ἄρτου καὶ τοῦ ποτηρίου, τὰς ἐν παντὶ τόπῳ τῆς γῆς γινομένας ὑπὸ τῶν Χριστιανῶν, προλαβὼν ὁ θεὸς μαρτυρεῖ εὐαρέστους ὑπάρχειν αὐτῷ. τὰς δὲ ὑφ' ὑμῶν καὶ δι' ἐκείνων ὑμῶν τῶν ἱερέων γινομένας ἀπαναίνεται, λέγων ... On the eucharist in Justin, see Barnard, *Justin Martyr*, 142–48.

133. *Dial*. 117.3,5: ταῦτα γὰρ μόνα καὶ Χριστιανοὶ παρέλαβον ποιεῖν, καὶ ἐπ' ἀναμνήσει δὲ τῆς τροφῆς αὐτῶν ξηρᾶς τε καὶ ὑγρᾶς, ἐν ᾗ καὶ τον πάθους, ὃ πέπονθε δι' αὐτοὺς ὁ υἱὸς τοῦ θεοῦ, μέμνηνται ... οὐδὲ ἐν γὰρ ὅλως ἐστί τι γένος ἀνθρώπων ... ἐν οἷς μὴ διὰ τοῦ ὀνόματος τοῦ σταυρωθέντος Ἰησοῦ εὐχαὶ καὶ εὐχαριστίαι τῷ πατρὶ καὶ ποιητῇ τῶν ὅλων γίνωνται.

Spiritual Sacrifice in Early Christianity and Its Environment

of thanksgiving" as themselves the sacrifices which fulfill Mal 1:10-12.[134] The elements of the bread and wine, therefore, could be called sacrifices,[135] but it would seem in a secondary sense through their association with the prayers of thanksgiving which accompanied them.[136] The prophecy of Malschi appears to have had a decisive influence in giving sacrificial associations to the Christian eucharist.[137]

Justin thus testifies to the extension of the word thanksgiving from the prayers to the food for which thanks was given (*Apol.* I, 66.1),[138] a usage which made eucharist a technical term in Christian language. Its frequency in early Christian literature points to what was originally central (thanksgiving) and the type of sacrifice intended (prayer or a thank offering). This extension to the elements accords with Justin employing the word commonly used for bringing a sacrificial offering (*prospherō*) to describe the act of bringing the bread and wine to the president of the assembly,[139] but it is not clear that the bringing of the gifts (by the people?) was understood as a sacrificial act. The important moment for Justin came when the president sent up "prayers and thanksgivings."[140]

4. *Hymns and Songs*.[141] The word *hymnos* meant praise and could be used of prose expressions of praise, but vocal sacrifice found expression also in songs of praise. The Christian *Sibylline Oracles* reflect the motifs of Athenagoras and Justin—the rejection of pagan sacrifice (*Or. Sibyl.* 8.487–

---

134. *Dial.* 41.1-3: καὶ ἡ τῆς σεμιδάλεως δὲ προσφορά . . . τύπος ἦν τον ἄρτου τῆς εὐχαριστίας, ὃν εἰς ἀνάμνησιν τοῦ πάθους . . . Ἰησοῦς Χριστὸς ὁ κύριος ἡμῶν παρέδωκε ποιεῖν . . . περὶ δὲ τῶν ἐν παντὶ τόπῳ ὑφ' ἡμῶν τῶν ἐθνῶν προσφερομένων αὐτῷ θυσιῶν, τοῦτ' ἔστι τοῦ ἄρτον τῆς εὐχαριστίας καὶ τοῦ ποτηρίου ὁμοίως τῆς εὐχαριστίας, προλέγει τότε, εἰπὼν καὶ τὸ ὄνομα αὐτοῦ δοξάζειν ἡμᾶς, ὑμᾶς δὲ βεβηλοῦν.

135. Casel, "Die Λογικὴ θυσία der antiken Mystik in christlichliturgischer Umdeutung," for the significance of the achievement of the Apologists in combining the idea of spiritual sacrifice with the eucharist.

136. Cf. *Acta Joh.* 109: "What praise, what offering, what thanksgiving shall we name as we break this bread?" In 110 the bread is called eucharist.

137. Harnack, *History of Dogma*, I, 210, suggests in addition the regard for prayer as a sacrifice, the command "Do this" which suggested a definite religious action, and the bringing of material offerings for the love feast.

138. *Apol.* I, 66.1: Καὶ ἡ τροφὴ αὕτη καλεῖται παρ' ἡμῖν εὐχαριστία.

139. *Apol.* I, 65.3: ἔπειτα προσφέρεται τῷ προεστῶτι τῶν ἀδελφῶν ἄρτος καὶ ποτήριον ὕδατος καὶ κράματος. So also 67.5.

140. *Apol.* I, 65.3: καὶ οὗτος λαβὼν αἶνον καὶ δόξαν τῷ πατρὶ τῶν ὅλων . . . ἀναπέμπει καὶ εὐχαριστίαν. Cf. 67.5: καὶ ὁ προεστὼς εὐχὰς ὁμοίως καὶ εὐχαριστίας, ὅση δύναμις αὐτῷ, ἀναπέμπει.

141. Quasten, *Musik und Gesang*, 69-77, discusses the general theme of λογικὴ θυσία and music.

92) and the knowledge of God which is expressed in praise (8.380–90). Instead of animal sacrifice, praise voiced in song is the proper worship:

> Put away the old ways and wash thyself with his blood;
> For he is not propitiated by your songs or by your prayers,
> Nor gives he heed to corruptible sacrifices, being incorruptible.
> But offering a holy hymn from understanding mouths
> Know who this is, and then shall you see your begetter.[142]
> ...
> But with holy understandings, rejoicing with merry heart,
> With abundant love and with generous hands,
> In gracious psalms and songs meet for God,
> To hymn you the immortal and faithful are we bidden,
> God the Creator of all, the Omniscient.[143]

5. *Virtuous Life.* The Apologists followed early Christian thought in including morality and good works in their conception of spiritual sacrifice. The section from the "Sibylline Oracles" quoted above has God identify benevolent deeds as sacrifice:

> Man is my image, possessed of right reason.
> For him set you a pure and bloodless table,
> Filling it with good things, and give to the hungry bread
> And to the thirsty drink, and to the naked body clothing,
> Of your own labors providing it with holy hands!
> Receive the afflicted, come to the aid of the weary,
> And present this living sacrifice to the living God.[144]

---

142. *Or. Sibyl.* 8.332–336:
τοὺς προτέρους δ' ἀπόθου καὶ λοῦσον ἀφ' αἵματος αὐτοῦ
οὐ γὰρ σαῖς οἴμαις ἱλάσκεται οὐδὲ λιταῖσιν,
οὐ θυσίαις προσέχει φθαρτοῖς ἄφθαρτος ὑπάρχων.
ἀλλ' ὕμνον στομάτων συνετῶν ἅγιον προφέρουσα
γνῶθι, τίς ἔσθ' οὗτος. καὶ τὸν γενετῆρα τότ' ὄψει.

143. *Or. Sibyl.* 8.496–500:
ἀλλ' ἁγναῖς πραπίδεσσι γεγηθότες εὔφρονι θυμῷ
ἀφνειαῖς τ' ἀγάπῃσι καὶ εὐδώροις παλάμῃσιν
μειλιχίοις ψαλμοῖσι θεοπρεπέεσσί τε μολπαῖς
ἄφθιτον ἐξυμνεῖν σε καὶ ἄψευστον κελόμεσθα,
παγγενετῆρα θεόν, πινυτόφρονα.

144. *Or. Sibyl.* 8.402–408:
εἰκών ἐστ' ἄνθρωπος ἐμὴ λόγον ὀρθὸν ἔχουσα.
τούτῳ θεὸς καθαρὰν καὶ ἀναίμακτον σὺ τράπεζαν
πληρώσας ἀγαθῶν καὶ δὸς πεινῶντι τὸν ἄρτον
καί διψῶντι ποτὸν καὶ εἵματα σώματι γυμνῷ
ἐκ μόχθων ἰδίων πορίσας ἁγναῖς παλάμῃσιν.
θλιβόμενον κτῆσαι καὶ τῷ κάμνοντι παράστα

Similarly the martyr Apollonius associated benevolence with prayer:

> I was hoping, proconsul, through my defence to give you a more pious reasoning and to enlighten the eyes of your soul, so that your heart, bearing fruit, might worship the God who is the creator of all things and thus daily by almsgiving and a philanthropic manner of life you might send up prayers to God alone as a bloodless and pure sacrifice.[145]

Justin set it in a more philosophical context:

> We have received the tradition that God does not need the material offerings of men, seeing that he is the provider of all things. We have been taught and are persuaded and believe that he accepts only those who imitate the good things which reside in him—temperance, righteousness, love of men, and whatever is proper to God.[146]

This thought, that virtue expressed in deeds is the best sacrifice, has a classic expression in the Latin apologist Minucius Felix:

> Do you think that we conceal what we worship, if we have not temples and altars? And yet what image of God shall I make, since, if you think rightly, man himself is the image of God? What temple shall I build to him, when this whole world fashioned by his work cannot receive him? And when I, a man, dwell far and wide, shall I shut up the might of so great majesty within one little building? Were it not better that he should be dedicated in our mind, consecrated in our inmost heart? Shall I offer victims and sacrifices to the Lord, such as he has produced for my use, that I should throw back to him his own gift? It is ungrateful since the best sacrifice is a good disposition, a pure mind, and a sincere judgment. Therefore, he who cultivates innocence supplicates God; he who cultivates justice makes offerings to God; he who abstains from fraudulent practices

καὶ ζῶσαν θυσίαν ταύτην τῷ ζῶντι πόριζε.

145. *Acta Apol.* 44: Ἐγὼ ἤλπιζον, ἀνθύπατε, τοὺς εὐσεβεῖς διαλογισμούς σοι παρεῖναι καὶ πεφωτίσθαι σοῦ τοὺς τῆς ψυχῆς ὀφθαλμοὺς διὰ τῆς ἀπολογίας μου, ὥστε τὴν καρδίαν σου καρποφοροῦσαν θεὸν τὸν ποιητὴν πάντων σέβειν τού τῳ τε καθ' ἡμέραν δι' ἐλεημοσυνῶν καὶ φιλανθρώπου τρόπου τὰς εὐχὰς ἀναπέμπειν μόνῳ θυσίαν ἀναίμακτον καὶ καθαρὰν τῷ θεῷ.

146. 1, 10.1: Ἀλλ' οὐ δέεσθαι τῆς παρὰ ἀνθρώπων ὑλικῆς προσφορᾶς προσειλήφαμεν τὸν θεόν, αὐτὸν παρέχοντα πάντα ὁρῶντες. ἐκείνους δὲ προσδέχεσθαι αὐτὸν μόνον δεδιδάγμεθα καὶ πεπείσμεθα καὶ πιστεύομεν, τοὺς τὰ προσόντα αὐτῷ ἀγαθὰ μιμουμένους, σωφροσύνην καὶ δικαιοσύνην καὶ φιλανθρωπίαν καὶ ὅσα οἰκεῖα θεῷ ἐστι, τῷ μηδενὶ ὀνόματι θετῷ καλουμένῳ.

propitiates God; he who snatches man from danger slaughters the most acceptable victim. These are our sacrifices, these are our rites of God's worship; thus, among us he who is most just is he who is most religious.[147]

Irenaeus

Irenaeus repeats many of the themes of the Apologists,[148] but his special concern was to turn the arguments which had been used against pagans in a new direction against the Gnostics. Christians do have oblations. "The church makes offerings to the omnipotent God through Jesus Christ."[149]

> The oblation of the church, therefore, which the Lord taught to be offered throughout the world is reckoned by God a pure sacrifice and is acceptable to him; not that he needs a sacrifice from us, but that he who offers is glorified in what he offers if his gift is accepted.[150]

God does not need the Christians' oblations, but they are for our benefit that, like the Jews, we may learn to serve God.[151] "Sacrifices do not sanctify a man, for God does not need sacrifice, but the conscience of him who

---

147. Octavius 32: *Putatis autem nos occultare quod colimus, si delubra et aras non habemus? Quod enim simulacrum deo fingam, cum, si recte existimes, sit dei homo ipse simulacrum? Templum quod ei extruam, cum totus hic mundus eius opere fabricatus eum capere non possit? Et cum homo latius maneam, intra unam aediculam vim tantae maiestatis includam? Nonne melius in nostra dedicandus est mente? in nostro intimo consecrandus est pectore? Hostias et victimas deo offeram, quas in usum mei protulit, ut reiciam ei suum munus? Ingratum est, cum sit litabilis hostia bonus animus et pura mens et sincera sententia. Igitur qui innocentiam colit, deo supplicat; qui iustitiam, deo libat; qui fraudibus abstinet, propitiat deum; qui hominem periculo subripit, optimam victimam caedit. Haec nostra sacrificia, haec dei sacra sunt: sic apud nos religiosior est ille qui iustior.*

148. God did not want sacrifices but commanded them to keep the Jews from idolatry—*Adv. haer.* 4.14.3; sacrificial system ceased with Christ—4.16.5; 4.17.5; 4.18.2; collection of Old Testament testimonia against sacrifice—4.17.1–5.

149. *Adv. haer.* 4.17.6: *Et in deo omnipotente per Jesum Christum offert Ecclesia.*

150. Ibid., 4.18.1: *Igitur Ecclesiae oblatio, quam Dominus docuit offerri in universo mundo, purum sacrificium reputatum est apud Deum et acceptum est ei, non quod indigeat a nobis sacrificium, sed quoniam is qui offert glorificatur ipse in eo quod offert, si acceptetur munus ejus.* Cf. 4.18.2 for sacrifice in the church as there was sacrifice among the Jews, only the kind has changed.

151. Ibid., 4.17.1: *et rursus quoniam non indiget Deus oblatione hominem, sed propter ipsum qui offerat hominem, manifeste Dominus docuit.* Cf. 4.18.6.

Spiritual Sacrifice in Early Christianity and Its Environment

offers, when it is pure, sanctifies the sacrifice."[152] The Christians' oblations are prayers, possessions, virtue, and the eucharist. The last item was particularly pertinent for Irenaeus' polemical purpose.

1. *Prayer.* Irenaeus quoted with approval Apocalypse 5:8.[153] He followed the Asian tradition of the heavenly altar: "He wants us to offer a gift at the altar, frequently and without intermission. The altar, then is in heaven, for there we direct our prayers and oblations."[154]

2. *Possessions.* The Jews gave tithes to God, but Christians as freedmen "set aside all their possessions for the Lord's purposes."[155] Irenaeus, following the Septuagint, understood Cain's sacrifice to have been rejected because he did not divide rightly, so he concluded that if one offers with all external correctness but does not share properly with his neighbor, his sacrifice is ineffective.[156]

3. *Virtue.* Sacrifice is profitable only if a man gives up evil (*Adv. haer.* 1.18.3). "It is necessary for us to make an oblation to God and in all things to be found grateful to God our Maker, with pure thoughts, faith without hypocrisy, firm hope, and fervent love."[157]

4. *Eucharist.* This which is offered sincerely in the church is "the firstfruits of his own created things. And the church alone offers this pure oblation to the Creator, offering to him the things from his creation with the giving of thanks."[158] The Jews do not offer this pure sacrifice because they

---

152. Ibid., 4.18.3: *quoniam non sacrificia sanctificant hominem, non enim indiget sacrificio Deus, sed conscientia ejus qui offert sanctificat sacrificium, pura existens.*

153. Ibid., 4.17.6.

154. Ibid., 4.18.6: *nos quoque offerre vult munus ad altare frequenter sine intermission. est ergo altare in caelis, illuc enim preces nostrae et oblationes diriguntur.*

155. Ibid., 4.18.2: *illi quidem decimas suorum habebant consecratas; qui autem perceperunt libertatem omnia quae sunt ipsorum ad dominicos decernunt usus, hilariter et libere dantes ea.* Cf. *Dem.* 96.

156. Ibid., 4.18.3: *quoniam non sacrificio placatur Deus. Si enim quis solummodo secundum quod videtur munde et recte et legitime offerre temptaverit, secundum autem suam animam non recte dividat eam quae est ad proximum communionem neque timorem habeat Dei, non per id quod recte foris oblatum est sacrificium seducit Deum.*

157. Ibid., 4.18.4: *Oportet enim nos oblationem Deo facere et in omnibus gratos inveniri Fabricatori Deo, in sententia pura et fide sine hypocrisi, in spe firma, in dilectione ferventi.* Cf. ibid.: *Quoniam igitur cum simplicitate Ecclesia offert, juste munus ejus purum sacrificium apud Deum deputatum est.*

158. Ibid., 4.18.4: *primitias earum quae sunt ejus creaturarum offerentes. Et hanc oblationem Ecclesia sola puram offert Fabricatori, offerens ei cum gratiarum actione ex creatura ejus.* Lawson, *Biblical Theology of Saint Irenaeus*, 267–71. Congar, *Jalons pour une theologie du laïcat*, 277–79, emphasizes that the whole Christian community offers the eucharistic sacrifice.

have on their hands the blood of the one through whom it is offered to God. Nor do the assemblies of the heretics offer this pure sacrifice, for they distinguish the Father from the Creator and so cannot offer to the Father the gifts of creation. "How can they be consistent with themselves, that the bread for which thanks is given is the body of their Lord and the cup his blood, if they do not call him the Son of the Creator of the world."[159] Since the Gnostics rejected that the Father of Christ was the Creator and looked on matter as evil, Irenaeus stressed the association of the material elements with the body of Christ (a fleshly and not a docetic Christ). Furthermore, for the same reason, he stressed that the material elements were the sacrifice: to offer the Father material bread and wine demonstrated that they were made by him and were gifts acceptable to him.

> [Jesus] gave directions to his disciples to offer to God the firstfruits of his created things—not as if he stood in need, but in order that they might be neither unfruitful nor ungrateful—and took bread (which is something created) and gave thanks, saying, "This is my body." And likewise the cup (which is part of creation) he confessed to be his blood, and he taught the new oblation of the new covenant. The church throughout the world, receiving this from the apostles, offers to God who gives us the means of subsistence the firstfruits of his gifts in the new covenant.[160]

The anti-Gnostic thrust accounts for Irenaeus' frequent reference to the Christian sacrifice as "firstfruits of God's creation" (4.18.1). "We offer him his own" (4.18.5). Moreover, this explains why he speaks of the eucharist as the bread (4.18.5) and speaks of it as the offering, although he knows that thanksgiving accompanies (4.18.4) and only by this blessing does it partake of a heavenly reality.[161]

---

159. Ibid.: *Quomodo autem constabit eis eum panem in quo gratiae actae sint corpus esse Domini sui, et calicem sanguinem ejus, si non ipsum Fabricatoris mundi Filium dicant.*

160. Ibid., 4.17.5: *Sed et suis discipulis dans consilium primitias Deo offerre ex suis creaturis, non quasi indigenti, sed ut ipsi neque infructuosi neque ingrati sint, eum qui ex creatura est panes accepit et gratias egit dicens: Hoc est meum corpus. Et calicem similiter, qui est ex ea creatura quae est secundum nos, suum sanguinem confessus est et novi Testamenti novam docuit oblationem; quam Ecclesia ab Apostolis accipiens in universo mundo offert Deo, ei qui alimenta nobis praestat, primitias suorum munerum in novo Testamento.*

161. Ibid., 4.18.5: Προσφέρομεν αὐτῷ τὰ ἴδια, ἐμμελῶς κοιωνίαν καὶ ἕνωσιν καταγγέλλοντες σαρκὸς καὶ πνεύματος. Ὡς γὰρ ὁ ἀπὸ τῆς γῆς ἄρτος προσλαβόμενος τὴν ἐπίκλησιν τοῦ θεοῦ οὐκέτι κοινὸς ἄρτος ἐστίν, ἀλλ' εὐχαριστία ἐκ δύο πραγμάτων

Alexandrians[162]

By the end of the second century the Christian interpretation of sacrifice was well established. It continued to be used against pagans,[163] Jews,[164] and Gnostics, but was free to be developed also in the interests of Christian spirituality. This is true in Clement of Alexandria and Origen, who repeat many traditional Christian concerns but were primarily concerned with developing the picture of the "true Gnostic"—orthodox in doctrine and practice but with an understanding of spiritual reality. The activity of the Gnostic is to have conversation with God through the great high priest and to serve God for the salvation of men through worship, teaching, and good works.[165]

1. *Self.* The ideal of the Alexandrians was the sacrifice of the self to God, "We glorify him who sacrificed himself for us, we also sacrificing ourselves."[166] "The one who brings a living sacrifice, his own body,to God is a priest."[167]

> Those who live their religion in a holy and priestly manner, not only those who are seated among the priests, but especially those who are led by a priestly spirit, whose portion is the Lord

συνεστηκυῖα, ἐπιγείου τε καὶ οὐρανίου.

162. Daly, "Sacrifice in Origen"; Lecuyer, "Sacerdote des fidèles et sacerdoce ministériel chez Origène"; Hermans, *Origène*.

163. Clement of Alexandria, *Strom.* 5.11.70.4; Origen, *C. Cels.* 6.70; Arnobius, *Adv. Nat.* is the strongest attack—see 6.1 and 3 and book 7, devoted to the refutation of different reasons advanced for animal sacrifice—but his thrust is wholly negative.

164. Clement of Alexandria, *Strom.* 5.11.74.5; *Paed.* 3.12.90; *Strom.* 7.6.32.7, "The sacrifices under the law are allegories of the religion which we practice," a principle exemplified in Origen's homilies on Exodus, Leviticus, and Numbers; Origen, *Sel. Ps.* 49.5, 6; Tertullian, *Adv. Jud.* 5; *Adv. Marc.* 2.22; Cyprian, *Test.* 1.16.

165. *Strom.* 7.3.13.2: αὕτη τοίνυν ἡ ἐνέργεια τοῦ τελειωθέντος γνωστικοῦ, προσομιλεῖν τῷ θεῷ διὰ τοῦ μεγάλου ἀρχιερέως, ἐξομοιούμενον εἰς δύναμιν τῷ κυρίῳ διὰ πάσης τῆς εἰς τὸν θεὸν θεραπείας, ἥτις εἰς τὴν τῶν ἀνθρώπων διατείνει σωτηρίαν κατὰ κηδεμονίαν τῆς εἰς ἡμᾶς εὐεργεσίας κατά τε αὐτὴν λειτουργίαν κατά τε τὴν διδασκαλίαν κατά τε τὴν δι' ἔργων εὐποιίαν. Cf. *Paed.* 1.12 and *Strom.* 7.12.

166. *Strom.* 7.3: οὐ θύομεν εἰκότως ἀνενδεεῖ τῷ θεῷ τῷ τὰ πάντα τοῖς πᾶσι παρεσχημένῳ, τὸν δ' ὑπὲρ ἡμῶν ἱερευθέντα δοξάζομεν σφᾶς αὐτοὺς ἱερεύοντες.

167. *Sel. Ps.* 65:13, 15: the passage is said to refer either to the sacrifices under the law before the coming of the Savior or to the spiritual sacrifices when one comes into the house of God, the church—namely, virtues and prayers. ἱερουργοῦντος τάχα γοῦν τοῦ προσάγοντος θυσίαν ζῶσαν τῷ θεῷ τὸ ἴδιον σῶμα (PG 12.1501 B–C). For the believer as a priest and the temple as within him, see "The Teaching of Silvanus," NHC VII.4.109,15–30. This work has been connected with Alexandria by Zandee, *"The Teachings of Silvanus" and Clement of Alexandria*.

and who have no inheritance on the earth, these are truly the priests and Levites of the Lord, who carry on their shoulders the law of God, for they accomplish in their works what is written in the law.[168]

2. *Martyrdom.* A special form of the sacrifice of self was martyrdom. Origen assimilated the shedding of the blood of martyrs to the sacrifice of Christ as also having atoning significance,[169] Martyrdom brings forgiveness of sins, and martyrs are priests who "offer themselves in sacrifice" and therefore appear beside the altar (in heaven).[170]

3. *Condition of Mind.* In accord with the Greek philosophical development, Clement understood the distinctive nature of man primarily in terms of his reason, so the sacrifice of the self pertained to the intellect, the abstinence from passion. "The sacrifice which is acceptable to God is unswerving separation from the body and its passions."[171] "A pure heart, a spotless soul, and spiritual perceptions which lead to deeds of piety and justice."[172] Origen developed the emphasis. After speaking of the rejection of animal sacrifice, he said, "The rational soul in us is an altar where the passions which have been put to death are sacrificed."[173] Origen explained the continual burnt offering of the Mosaic law in this way: "What other continual sacrifice can there be to the man of reason in the world of mind, but the Word growing to maturity, the Word who is symbolically called a lamb and who is offered as soon as the soul receives illumination."[174] The

---

168. *Hom. in Jesu Nave* 9.5: *Etenim quicumque sacerdotali religione et sanctitate vivunt, non solum hi qui sedere videntur in consessu sacerdotali, sed hi magis, qui sacerdotaliter agunt, quorum pars est Dominus nec ulla iis portio habetur in terris, ipsi sunt vere sacerdotes et Levitae Domini, qui in humeris suis legem Dei portant, agendo videlicet et implendo per opus ea quae scribuntur in lege.*

169. *Comm Joh.* 6.54.36: Καὶ ταύτῃ θυσίᾳ [τοῦ Ἰησοῦ τοῦ ἀμνοῦ] συγγενεῖς εἰσιν αἱ λοιπαί, ὧν σύμβολόν εἰσιν αἱ νομικαί. λοιπαὶ δὲ καὶ συγγενεῖς ταύτῃ τῇ θυσίᾳ θυσίαι αἱ ἐκχύσεις εἶναί μοι φαίνονται τοῦ τῶν γενναίων μαρτύρων αἵματος, οὐ μάτην ὁρωμένων ἑστάναι ὑπὸ τοῦ μαθητοῦ Ἰωάννου παρὰ τῷ οὐρανίῳ θυσιαστηρίῳ.

170. *Exh. Mart.* 30: ὥσπερ ὁ ἀρχιερεὺς θυσίαν ἑαυτὸν προσήνεγκεν Ἰησοῦς ὁ Χριστός, οὕτως οἱ ἱερεῖς, ὧν ἐστιν ἀρχιερεύς, θυσίαν ἑαυτοὺς προσφέρουσι. δι᾽ ἣν ὡς παρὰ οἰκείῳ τόπῳ ὁρῶνται τῷ θυσιαστηρίῳ. The whole chapter is pertinent. Cf. *Exh. Mart.* 39 and 50 for the presence of the martyrs at the heavenly altar.

171. *Strom.* 5.11.67.1: Θυσία δὲ ἡ τῷ θεῷ δεκτὴ σώματός τε καὶ τῶν τούτου παθῶν ἀμετανόητος χωρισμός.

172. *Acts of Phileas*, Bodmer Papyri, col. III (cf. Latin 2.1).

173. *Hom. Lam.* 2.7: ψυχῆς δὲ θυσιαστήριον τὸ ἐν ἡμῖν λογικόν, δι᾽ οὗπερ ἱερουργεῖται τὰ πάθη νεκρούμενα.

174. *Comm. Joh.* 6.52.33: ποία δὲ ἑτέρα θυσία δύναται ἐνδελεχισμοῦ εἶναι τῷ λογικῷ νοητὴ ἢ λόγος ἀκμάζων, λόγος ἀμνὸς συμβολικῶς καλούμενος ἅμα τῷ φωτίζεσθαι τὴν

inwardness of true sacrifice finds frequent expression: "The spiritual law demands of us for the tabernacle a gold which comes from within, a silver which comes from within ... You must not offer any sentiment or word if you have not first conceived that which is written in your heart."[175]

4. *Virtues.* The inner condition of the mind (the Biblical heart) must be virtuous. "Gentleness, philanthropy, magnanimous piety ... these virtues I say are 'the acceptable sacrifice' in God's sight."[176] "What gift has God made to man? The knowledge of himself. What offering does man present to God? His faith and love."[177] To offer perpetually is "to observe perpetually righteousness and abstain from sin" (*Hom. Num.* 23.3).

5. *Prayer.* Prayer is the activity most closely associated with the inner, rational and spiritual nature of man's service to God. The statements in Clement and Origen abound on this theme. Clement's major discussion of prayer occurs in the context of contrasting Christianity with pagan idols, temples, and sacrifices (*Strom.* 7.3-7). If the Deity by mature needs nothing but delights to be honored:

> It is not without reason that we honor God in prayer. We send up this best and most holy sacrifice with righteousness ... The altar, then, that is with us here, the terrestrial one, is the congregation of those who devote themselves to prayers ... Breathing together is properly said of the church, for the sacrifice of the church is the word rising like smoke from holy souls, when the whole mind together with the sacrifice is unveiled to God ... They do not believe us when we say that the righteous soul is the truly sacred altar and the incense rising from it holy prayer ... Therefore, we ought to offer God those sacrifices which he loves and not costly ones. And that compounded incense mentioned in the law is that which consists of many tongues and voices in prayer, or rather of different nations and natures prepared under the different covenants for the unity of the faith and gathered together in praises, with a pure mind and just and right conduct, and from holy works and righteous prayer.[178]

ψυχὴν καταπεμπόμενος.

175. *Hom. Ex.* 13.2 on Exod 35:5: *Spiritalis autem lex aurum requirit ad tabernaculum, quod intra nos est, argentum quod intra nos est ... Non enim potens aliquid de sensu tuo offerre Deo, vel de verbo tuo, nisi prius quae scripta sunt corde conceperis.*

176. *Strom.* 7.3.14.1: ἡμερότης δ', οἶμαι, καὶ φιλανθρωπία καὶ μεγαλοπρεπὴς θεοσέβεια ... ταύτας φημὶ τὰς ἀρετὰς θυσίαν δεκτὴν εἶναι παρὰ θεῷ. Cf. *Paed.* 3.12.90.

177. *Hom. Num.* 12.3 on Num. 21:18-20: *Quid dedit Deus homini? Agnitionem sui. Quid ergo offert Deo? Fidem suam et affectum.* Cf. 23.2.

178. *Strom.* 7.6.31.7: οὐκ ἀπεικότως ἡμεῖς δι' εὐχῆς τιμῶμεν τὸν θεόν, καὶ ταύτην τὴν

Prayer is the true sacrifice and priesthood.[179]

Origen pointed out that Celsus "does not perceive that our altars are the spirit of righteous men from which truly and inellectually there arises a sweet smelling incense, prayers from a pure conscience."[180] "He who does his duties, always praying, truly celebrates a feast, always sacrificing unbloody sacrifices by his prayers to God."[181] "To praise God and offer him the vows of prayer is to present immolations to him," but Origen reminded his hearers that they must pray not only with words and voice but also with the understanding.[182]

Prayers for the forgiveness of those undergoing the penance of the church are called a sacrifice.[183]

6. *Eucharist*. With the spiritualizing emphasis of the Alexandrians, the elements of the eucharist were not frequently associated with sacrifice. When Clement used the word oblation, there is an ambiguity whether the reference is to the elements, the eucharistic prayer, or the whole action?[184] Origen explained that Christians were not ungrateful because they did

---

θυσίαν ἀρίστην καὶ ἁγιωτάτην μετὰ δικαιοσύνης ἀναπέμπομεν. 7.6.31.8: ἔστι γοῦν τὸ παρ' ἡμῖν θυσιαστήριον ἐνταῦθα τὸ ἐπίγειον τὸ ἄθροισμα τῶν ταῖς εὐχαῖς ἀνακειμένων. 7.6.32.4: ἡ σύμπνοια δὲ ἐπὶ τῆς ἐκκλησίας λέγεται κυρίως. καὶ γὰρ ἐστιν ἡ θυσία τῆς ἐκκλησίας λόγος ἀπὸ τῶν ἁγίων ψυχῶν ἀναθυμιώμενος, ἐκκαλυπτομένης ἅμα τῇ θυσίᾳ καὶ τῆς διανοίας ἁπάσης τῷ θεῷ. 7.6.32.6: βωμὸν δὲ ἀληθῶς ἅγιον τὴν δικαίαν ψυχὴν καὶ τό ἀπ' αὐτῆς θυμίαμα τὴν ὁσίαν εὐχὴν λέγουσιν ἡμῖν ἀπιστήσουσιν. 7.6.34.2: Δεῖ τοίνυν θυσίας προσφέρειν τῷ θεῷ μὴ πολυτελεῖς, ἀλλὰ θεοφιλεῖς, καὶ τό θυμίαμα ἐκεῖνο τὸ σύνθετον τὸ ἐν τῷ νόμῳ τὸ ἐκ πολλῶν γλωσσῶν τε καὶ φωνῶν κατὰ τὴν εὐχὴν συγκείμενον, μᾶλλον δὲ τὸ ἐκ διαφόρων ἐθνῶν τε καὶ φύσεων τῇ κατὰ τὰς διαθήκας δόσει σκευαζόμενον εἰς τὴν ἑνότητα τῆς πίστεως καὶ κατὰ τοὺς αἴνους συναγόμενον, καθαρῷ μὲν τῷ νῷ, δικαίᾳ δὲ καὶ ὀρθῇ τῇ πολιτείᾳ ἐξ ὁσίων ἔργων εὐχῆς τε δικαίας.

179. Fragment 61 from *Sacra Par*. 300: Αὕτη ἐστίν ἱερατεία καὶ θυσία ἀληθινὴ ἡ εὐχή (Stahlin III, 227,28).

180. C. Cels. 8.17: οὐχ ὁρῶν ὅτι βωμοὶ μέν εἰσιν ἡμῖν τὸ ἑκάστου τῶν δικαίων ἡγεμονικόν, ἀφ' οὗ ἀναπέμπεται ἀληθῶς καὶ νοητῶς εὐώδη θυμιάματα προσευχαὶ ἀπὸ συνειδήσεως καθαρᾶς. Cf. 8.13; De or. 10.2; Dial. Heracl. 4 for prayers as offerings.

181. C. Cels. 8.21: καὶ ἑορτάζει γε κατὰ ἀλήθειαν ὁ τὰ δέοντα πράττων, ἀεὶ εὐχόμενος, διὰ παντὸς θύων τὰς ἀναιμάκτους ἐν ταῖς πρὸς τὸ θεῖον εὐχαίς θυσίας. Cf. Hom. Num. 23.3: the perpetual sacrifice is to pray without ceasing.

182. Hom. Num. 11.9: *Laudare ergo Deum, et vota orationis offerre, immolare est Deo . . . si non solum verbis et voce, sed et mente oremus et corde.*

183. De or. 28.9,10; cf. Hom. Num. 24.1.

184. Strom. 1.19.96.1: ἐπί τῶν ἄρτῳ καὶ ὕδατι κατὰ τὴν προσφορὰν μὴ κατὰ τὸν κανόνα τῆς ἐκκλησίας χρωμένων αἱρέσεων . . . εἰσι γὰρ οἵ καὶ ὕδωρ ψιλὸν εὐχαριστοῦσιν. If Strom. 6.14.113.3 alludes to activities in the assembly, the eucharist may be the oblation; on the other hand, the repetitions in the list may cause one to pair oblation with prayer.

not give sacrifices and thank-offerings to the pagan deities, but "the bread which we call 'eucharist' is for us a symbol of thanksgiving to God."[185]

7. *Songs.* Clement associated psalms and hymns with prayer as a sacrifice. The true Gnostic's "whole life is a holy festival. His sacrifices are prayers and praises, reading of the scriptures before meals, psalms and hymns in the evening before bed, and prayers again during the night."[186]

8. *Preaching.* The explanation of 1 Pet 2:9 based on Clement's "Hypotyposies" is that Christians form a priesthood "on account of the oblation which is made by prayers and the instructions by which are gained the souls which are offered to God."[187] As a preacher and teacher, Origen saw instruction as a priestly task. The priest is the teacher of the word (*Hom. Lev. 1.4*). Origen interprets the passages about priests in the Old Testament as often as he can in terms of imparting the word of God.[188]

9. *Benevolence.* Clement acknowledged that the Gnostic knew another kind of sacrifice, "the imparting both of doctrines and money to those in need."[189] Origen preached, "If one gives to the poor, if one performs any good work, he has offered to God a present according to the commandment."[190] The maxims known as the 'Sentences of the Sextus' belong in this environment: "Kindness to men on behalf of God is the only suitable sacrifice to God."[190a]

10. *Asceticism.* Origen laid much of the theoretical basis for monasticism's understanding of self-denial as a sacrifice. For instance, he affirmed that the perpetual sacrifice of the Old Testament was possible only "to one

---

185. *C. Cels.* 8.57: ἔστι δὲ καὶ σύμβολον ἡμῖν τῆς πρὸς θεὸν εὐχαριστίας ἄρτος εὐχαριστία καλούμενος.

186. *Strom.* 7.7.49.4: ἅπας δὲ ὁ βίος αὐτοῦ πανήγυρις ἁγία. αὐτίκα θυσίαι μὲν αὐτῷ εὐχαί τε καὶ αἶνοι καὶ . . . ψαλμοὶ δὲ καὶ ὕμνοι.

187. Stahlin III, 204,21–25. Cf. *Strom.* 7.7.

188. *Hom. Lev.* 5.8: *Caro quae ex sacrificiis sacerdotibus deputatur verbum Dei est quod in Ecclesia docent.* Cf. 8:11; *Hom. Luc.* 13 on Luke 8:16. Daniélou, *Origène*, 58–63, discusses Origen's view that the ministry of the word fulfills the Levitical priesthood.

189. *Strom.* 7.7.49.5: οὐ καὶ τὴν ἄλλην θυσίαν τὴν κατὰ τοὺς δεομένους ἐπίδοσιν καὶ δογμάτων καὶ χρημάτων γιγνώσκει;

190. *Hom. Num.* 11.9: *Si quis vel egentibus distribuat, vel faciat aliquid boni operis, pro mandato munus obtulit Deo.*

190a. *Sentences of Sextus* 47: θυσία θεῷ μόνη καὶ προσηνὴς ἡ ἀνθρώποις εὐεργεσία διὰ θεόν. Cf. also 217.

who has vowed perpetual chastity,"[191] for "one who lives in chastity vows his body to God."[192]

North Africans

1. *Self.* Tertullian in referring to the assembly of the church described its oblation as "offering to God our very body and our very spirit."[193] Cyprian, with his great emphasis on the unity of the church, saw peace and brotherly agreement as a greater sacrifice than anything offered in disagreement (*De dom. or.* 23). Lactantius spoke as a philosopher of religion when he concluded a discussion of daily life by saying:

> Whoever, therefore, has obeyed all these heavenly precepts is a worshipper of the true God, whose sacrifices are gentleness of spirit, an innocent life, and good actions . . . For God does not desire the sacrifice of a dumb animal, nor of death and blood, but of man and life.[194]

2. *Prayer.* Tertullian explained that Christians did not offer sacrifice to the emperor, but prayed for him. Christians offer to God alone "at his own requirement, that costly and noble sacrifice of prayer sent up from a chaste body, an innocent soul, a sanctified spirit."[195] After quoting Isaiah 1:11 and John 4:24, he affirmed, "We are the true worshippers and true priests who, praying in spirit, sacrifice in spirit prayer . . . This victim . . . we ought to escort with the pomp of good works, amid psalms and hymns to God's altar."[196] Tertullian interpreted Mal 1:10, 11 as referring to "simple

---

191. *Hom. Num.* 23.3: *Unde videtur mihi quod illius est solius offerre sacrificium indesinens, qui indesinenti et perpetuae se devoverit castitati.*

192. Ibid. 24.2: *Qui in castitate vivit, corpus suum vovit Deo.*

193. *De virg. vel.* 13: *debemus, cum tantam oblationem Deo offerimus ipsius corporis et ipsius spiritus nostri, cum illam ipsam naturam consecramus.* Fini, "'Sacrificium spiritale' in Tertulliano."

194. *Div. inst.* 6.24: *quisquis igitur his omnibus praeceptis caelestibus obtemperauerit, hic cultor est uerus dei, cuius sacrificia sunt mansuetudo animi et uita innocens et actus boni: quae omnia qui exhibet, totiens sacrificat, quotiens bonum aliquid ac pium fecerit. deus enim non desiderat uictimam neque muti animalis neque mortis ac sanguinis, sed hominis et uitae.* Cf. 6.1—innocence: *nihil enim sancta et singularis illa maiestas aliut ab homine desiderat quam solam innocentiam: quam si quis obtulerit deo, satis pie, satis religiose litabit.* Cf. 5.19.6.2—mind.

195. *Apol.* 30.5: *qui ei offero opimam et maiorem hostiam quam ipse mandavit, orationem de carne pudica, de anima innocenti, de spiritu sancto profectam.*

196. *De or.* 28: *Nos sumus veri adoratores, et veri sacerdotes, qui spiritu orantes*

Spiritual Sacrifice in Early Christianity and Its Environment

prayer from a pure conscience" (*Adv. Marc.* 4.1). Certain Old Testament sacrifices were types signifying that we are bound "to offer to God in the temple a gift, even prayer and thanksgiving in the church."[197]

3. *Eucharist*. The words "to offer" and "sacrifices" came naturally to Tertullian in reference to the eucharistic celebration (*Ad ux.* 2.8; *Exh. cast.* 7). The fullest development of the eucharist as a sacrifice in ante-Nicene writings comes from Cyprian, bishop of Carthage. He was the first to associate the eucharist specifically with priesthood (he regularly calls the bishop "priest") and to make the sacrifice of Christ the object of the eucharistic offering.[198] He spoke of the altar and sacrifices of a bishop.[199] "To offer" and "to give the eucharist" (to consecrate and to communicate) were the two parts of the ceremony.[200] The Lord's sacrifices were bread and wine.[201] Epistle 63 against the practice of celebrating with water and without wine shows most completely Cyprian's thought. He argued that the action of Jesus at the Last Supper must be imitated. Since the Lord used wine, "the blood of Christ is not offered if there be no wine in the cup, nor the Lord's sacrifice celebrated with a legitimate consecration unless our oblation and sacrifice respond to his passion."[202] "That priest truly discharges the office of Christ who imitates what Christ did; and he then offers a true and full sacrifice in the church to God the Father when he proceeds to offer it according to what he sees Christ himself to have offered."[203] "And because we

---

spiritu sacrificamus orationem Dei propriam . . . Hanc de toto corde devotam . . . cum pompa operum bonorum inter psalmos et hymnos deducere ad Dei altare debemus.

197. *Adv. Marc.* 4.9.9: *hominem quondam peccatorem verbo mox dei emaculatum offerre debere munus deo apud templum, orationem scilicet et actionem gratiarum apud ecclesiam per Christum Iesum, catholicum patris sacerdotem.* Cf. ibid., 4.22 that the true oblation is thanksgiving.

198. Wiles, "The Theological Legacy of St. Cyprian." Dugmore, "Sacrament and Sacrifice in the Early Fathers," notes how much of later Western theology of the eucharist can be paralleled in Cyprian.

199. *Ep.* 73.2; cf. 67.3 and *Ep. Firm. ad Cyp.* (*Ep.* 75.17).

200. *Ep.* 15.1 and 16.3 in reference to reconciling the lapsed.

201. *Ep.* 69.6. Note the reference to memorial eucharists for martyrs in *Ep.* 39.3, "We always offer sacrifices for them."

202. *Ep.* 63.9: *undo apparet sanguinem Christi non offerri, si desit uinum calici, nec sacrificium dominicum legitima sanctificatione celebrari, nisi oblatio et sacrificium nostrum responderit passioni.* Cf. 63.13 on offering wine mixed with water.

203. *Ep.* 63.14: *ille sacerdos uice Christi uere fungitur qui id quod Christus fecit imitatur et sacrificium uerum et plenum tunc offert in ecclesia Deo patri, si sic incipiat offerre secundum quod ipsum Christum uideat optulisse.*

make mention of his passion in all sacrifices (for the Lord's passion is the sacrifice which we offer), we ought to do nothing else than what he did."[204]

The bringing of the elements by the laity for use at the Lord's Supper was also a sacrifice.[205]

4. *Asceticism.* Tertullian accounted the self denials of fasting and celibacy as fragrant offerings acceptable to God.[206] A soul afflicted with fasts is a sacrifice (*De ieiunis* 16), especially as an accompaniment to prayer (*De ieiunis* 7).[207]

5. *Confession and Martyrdom.* To those sent to the mines and denied the opportunity of being present when "God's priests celebrated the divine sacrifices," Cyprian said that their contrite hearts and lives of faith were "a sacrifice equally precious and glorious."[208] Cyprian saw his priestly work of reconciling to the church those about to face martyrdom as preparing "offerings and victims for God."[209]

6. *Repentance for Sins.* Not many were so steadfast under persecution, so Cyprian was very much preoccupied with the problem of reconciliation to the church of those who had lapsed. He appears to call the penitential discipline which preceded reconciliation to the church a sacrifice.[210] And he considered "almsgiving and works of righteousness" as propitiatory for sins committed after baptism.[211]

7. *Benevolence.* Cyprian taught that prayers which are supported by good works quickly ascend to God. "When one has pity on the poor, he

---

204. *Ep.* 63.17: *Et quia passionis eius mentionem in sacrificiis omnibus facimus, passio est enim Domini sacrificium quod offerimnus, nihil aliud quam quod ille fecit facere debemus.* Cf. *De alea.* 4, 5, and 8.

205. *Op. et eleeom.* 15. Hamman, *Vie liturgique et vie sociale*, 229ff., discusses the liturgical offering.

206. *De res. care.* 8: *Nam et sacrifcia Deo grata, conflictationes dico animae, jejunia, et seras et aridas escas.*

207. Cf. *De cultu fem.* II.9. Harnack, *History of Dogma*, 11, 132–33.

208. *Ep.* 76.3: *quod illic nunc sacerdotibus Dei facultas non datur offerendi et celebrandi sacrificia diuina. celebrates immo adque offertis sacrificium Deo et pretiosum pariter et gloriosum et plurimum uobis . . .* (Ps 50:19). *hoc uos sacrificium Deo offertis, hoc sacrificium sine intermissione die ac nocte celebratis, hostiae facti Deo et uosmet ipsos sanctas adque immaculatas uictimas exhibentes.*

209. *Ep.* 57.3: *ut sacerdotes qui sacrificea Dei cotidie celebramus hostias Deo et uictinias praeparemus.*

210. *Lapsis* 16: *ante purgatam conscientiam sacrificio et manu sacerdotis.*

211. *Op. et eleeom.* 1 and 2.

lends to God; and he who gives to the least gives to God—he sacrifices spiritually to God an odor of a sweet smell."[212]

8. *Praise.* Tertullian in one place interpreted the pure sacrifice of Mal 1:10, 11 as "assigning glory, blessing, praise, and hymns."[213] Lactantius preferred the word praise when he spoke of Christian sacrifice. The "Divine Institutes," Book 6, sets out "to show by what rite or by what sacrifice God is to be fittingly worshipped" (6.1). Lactantius firmly grasped the principle that the nature of God dictates the kind of worship offered to him. Since God is unseen, sacrifice to him must be incorporeal. "His offering is innocency of soul; his sacrifice, praise and a hymn."[214] "We ought to sacrifice to God in word, inasmuch as God is the Word . . . Therefore the highest rite of worship to God is praise from the mouth of a just man directed to God."[215] For this to be accepted there is need of humility, fear, and devotion. Let God be consecrated in the heart, for a person is the temple of God.[216]

Other Third-Century Sources

In the apocryphal *Acts of Thomas* 76 the demon confesses to Thomas, "As you are refreshed by prayer, good works, and spiritual hymns, so am I refreshed by murders, adulteries, and sacrifices wrought with wine at the altars." Prayers (including the eucharist), hymns, and good works are a good summary of the spiritual sacrifices found in third-century sources.

1. *Prayers.* The *Didascalia Apostolorum* 9 instructs Christians to set aside tithes and firstfruits to Christ, the true high priest. "Instead of the sacrifices which then were, offer now prayers and petitions and thanksgivings."[217] The high priests are the bishops (who minister the word); priests and Levites are presbyters, deacons, widows and orphans.

---

212. *De dom. or.* 33: *Nam quando qui miseretur pauperi Deo faenerat et qui dat minimis Deo donat, spiritaliter Deo suauitatis odore sacrificat.*

213. *Adv. Marc.* 3.22: *et sacrificium mundum, gloriae scilicet relatio et benedictio et laus et hymni.* Cf. *Adv. Iud.* 5.5–7.

214. *Div. inst.* 6.25: *donum est integritas animi, sacrificium laus et hymnus.*

215. Ibid.: *uerbo enim sacrificari oportet deo, siquidem deus verbum est . . . summus igitur colendi dei ritus est ex ore iusti hominis ad deum directa laudatio.*

216. Ibid.: *et humilitate et timore et deuotione maxima opus est . . . secum denique habeat deum semper in corde suo consecratum, quoniam ipse est dei templum.*

217. *Quae tunc erant sacrificia, modo sunt orationes et praecationes et gratiarum actiones.* Connolly, *Didascalia Apostolorum*, 87, 89.

Offerings of produce are to be brought to the bishop who will distribute them justly.

2. *Eucharist*. Hippolytus' account of the eucharist uses sacrificial language freely: The church offers bread and wine, gives thanks for this priestly activity, and prays for the coming of the Holy Spirit on its Offering.[218] "Offering" appears repeatedly in Hippolytus' account of an agape also,[219] showing that the word meant to consecrate to a religious purpose and applied to the bringing of food and saying prayers at a love feast no less than the eucharist. Thus Hippolytus still moved in Irenaeus' thought world of a thank-offering, but his terminology prepared for the extended conceptions of Cyprian.

3. *Hymns*. The fragments of a commentary on the Psalms attributed to Hippolytus speak of David's hymns replacing the sacrifices instituted by Moses.[220]

4. *Good Works*: Chastity. Methodius presented chastity or celibacy in sacrificial terms. "To offer up oneself perfectly to the Lord" means the control and proper use of the mouth and eyes.[221] The "unbloody altar of God" is virgins and widows whose sacrifice is "the sweet savor of love" and "prayers."[222]

5. *Baptism*. Unique in the literature of this survey is the 'Ebionite' thought that baptism is parallel to the Old Testament sacrifices, because it has replaced them as the means of obtaining forgiveness of sins.[223]

---

218. *Apos. trad.* 4: *Illi uero offerant diacones oblationes, quique inponens manus in eam cum omni praesbyterio dicat gratias agens . . . offerimus tibi panem et calicem gratias tibi agentes quia nos dignos habuisti adstare coram te et tibi ministrare. Et petimus ut mittas spiritum tuum sanctum in oblationem sanctae ecclesiae.* Botte, *La tradition apostolique de Saint Hippolyte*, 10, 16.

219. *Apos. trad.* 26.1, 6, 29-30 (Dix, *Treatise on the Apostolic Tradition*, 45-52) = 23; 27, 25 (Botte, *La tradition apostolique de Saint Hippolyte*, 60-69).

220. PG 10, 712B.

221. *Symp.* 5.4: τὸ ἀναθεῖναι ἑαυτὸν τελείως Κυρίῳ. Cf. *De res.* III.3.

222. Ibid., 5.6 and 8: καὶ γὰρ θυσιαστήριον εἶναι παρεδόθη θεοῦ τὸ ἄθροισμα τῶν ἁγνῶν . . . τὴν εὐωδίαν τῆς ἀγάπης ἀναθυμιῶσαν Κυρίῳ . . . τὰς προσευχὰς ἀναπεμπάζουσα Κυρίῳ, δεκτὰς εἰς ὀσμὴν εὐωδίας.

223. Ps. Clement, *Recog.* 1.39: *et ne forte putarent cessantibus hostüs remissionern sibi non fieri peccatorum baptisma eis per aquam statuit, in quo ab omnibus peccatis invocato ejus nomine solverentur.*

Eusebius

1. *Self.* The historian and panegyrist of the Constantinian church summed up the philosophical and Christian understanding of spiritual sacrifice. Eusebius declared that Constantine, in contrast to traditional Roman practice, did not propitiate the deities with fire and smoke but "dedicated to the universal Sovereign a pleasant and acceptable sacrifice, even his own imperial soul and a mind truly fitted for the service of God." Having made this first and greatest sacrifice, he then offered the souls of the flock in his care whom he led to the pious worship of God.[224]

2. *Prayer and Eucharist.* Eusebius, as was the universal Christian language by his day, associated the eucharist with the spiritual worship of prayer. Thus he could speak, for example, of "offering the memorial of Christ's sacrifice."[225] Eusebius frequently contrasted Christian worship with the bloody sacrifices of paganism and ancient Israel.[226] Eusebius' panegyric on the building of the churches addressed to Paulinus, bishop of Tyre, spoke of Jesus as the high priest standing at the altar of the church to receive the "bloodless and immaterial sacrifices offered in prayer."[227] Although Eusebius' usual term for church buildings was "house of prayer," he could speak of the building as a temple[228] with consecrated oblations.[229]

3. *Other Uses.* The oration of Constantine "To the Assembly of the Saints" refers to the bloodless sacrifice of thanksgiving in memory of the martyrs.[230] Eusebius described the council of Nicaea as a "thankoffering"

---

224. *Laud. Const.* 2.5—3.1: τὴν δ' αὐτῷ τῷ βασιλεῖ τῶν ὅλων προσφιλῆ καὶ χαρίεσσαν θυσίαν, αὐτὴν δηλαδὴ τὴν αὐτοῦ βασιλικὴν ψυχὴν καὶ τὸν νοῦν τὸν θεοπρεπέστατον, ἀφιερῶν αὐτῷ. θυσία γὰρ αὕτη προσηνὴς αὐτῷ μόνη.

225. *Dem. Evang.* 1.10: οὐκοῦν καὶ θύομεν καὶ θυμιῶμεν. τοτὲ μὲν τὴν μνήμην τοῦ μεγάλου θύματος, κατὰ τὰ πρὸς αὐτοῦ παραδοθέντα μυστήρια ἐπιτελοῦντες, καὶ τὴν ὑπὲρ σωτηρίας ἡμῶν εὐχαριστίαν δι' εὐσεβῶν ὕμνων τε καὶ εὐχῶν τῷ θεῷ προσκομίζοντες.

226. *Laud. Const.* 16.9,10: Ἀναίμους δὲ καὶ λογικὰς θυσίας τὰς δι' εὐχῶν καὶ ἀπορρήτου θεολογίας τοῖς αὐτοῦ θιασώταις, τίς ἐπιτελεῖν παρέδωκεν ἄλλος, ἢ μόνος ὁ ἡμέτερος Σωτήρ; Διὸ ἐπὶ τῆς καθ' ὅλης ἀνθρώπων οἰκουμένης θυσιαστήρια συνέστη, ἐκκλησιῶν τε ἀφιερώματα, νοερῶν τε καὶ λογικῶν θυσιῶν ἱεροπρεπεῖς λειτουργίαι. Cf. *Praep. Evang.* 4.4; *Dem. Evang.* 1.10.

227. *H.E.* 10.4.68: τὰς δι' εὐχῶν ἀναίμους καὶ ἀύλους θυσίας. Cf. *Vita Const.* 4.45 and 1.48.

228. *H.E.* 10.2.1; 10.4.1; 4.69; *Vita Const.* 3.40.

229. *H.E.* 10.4.20 and 22.

230. *Or. ad sanctos* 12.

presented by Constantine to the Savior for the victories which he had obtained.[231]

CONCLUSION

Sacrificial language received a wide range of applications in Christian usage—the self, attitudes, virtues, praise, prayer, eucharist, song, preaching, benevolence, fasting, celibacy, martyrdom. What began in Christianity as a metaphorical and spiritual conception was by the age of Constantine ready to be taken literally again. The extension of sacrificial language had come to encompass the ministry as a special priesthood (Cyprian), the table as an altar, and buildings as temples (Eusebius). Sacrifice was increasingly materialized and traditional content was put into the words. Sacrifice became again not only praise and thanksgiving, but also propitiatory (Origen and Cyprian). A blending and transformation of conceptions—pagan, philosophical, Jewish, and Christian—created a new complex of ideas. We not only use words, but words use us.

---

231. *Vita Const.* 3.7; cf. 3.15.

2

Praising God with "One Mouth" / "One Voice"

THE GREEK PHRASES "ONE mouth" (ἐν στόμα) and "one voice" (μία φωνή) had multiple idiomatic uses, an important one of which had to do with music, especially vocal music. The principal study that sparked by interest in the phrase "one voice" was by Johannes Quasten, who found in the phrase support for the idea that early Christians favored monophonic singing. My wider examination of occurrences of the phrase shows the emphasis on unity and harmony, which Quasten also noted, but not an indication of monophony itself. Indeed there was a recognition by Christian authors of differences in human voices. The main idea in "one mouth" and "one voice" was the particpation by all of a given group in a unified expression.

"ONE MOUTH"

The Greek Bible represents some of the principal usages in Greek literature as a whole. Romans 15:6 provides my title and the starting point for this study.

> May the God of steadfastness and encouragement grant you to be of the same mind [τὸ αὐτὸ φρονεῖν] in accordance with Christ Jesus, so that together with one mouth [ἐν ἑνὶ στόματι] you may glorify the God and Father of our Lord Jesus Christ. (Rom 15:5–6)

This prayer is part of Paul's instructions on unity among Christians in Rome and how to co-exist with their differences in customs. He wanted them to live together in harmony, and this unity would find expression in praising God with one accord (ὁμοθυμαδόν) as if from one mouth.

Origen provides the earliest surviving commentary on the verse: "For 'one mouth' is uttered where one and the same understanding and speech proceeds through the mouths of diverse people." This seems to be a fair and accurate summary of the import of the phrase from a Christian scholar learned in secular and Biblical literature. To the uses of "one mouth" in that other literature we turn.

Second Chronicles 18:12 records what a messenger of kings Jehoshaphat and Ahab said to the prophet Micaiah: "Look, the prophets spoke with one mouth [ἐν στόματι ἑνὶ] good things concerning the king; let your words be as one of them." These court prophets delivered a common message, words with the same import.

Particularly important for our study, both for what it says and for its use later, is the introduction to "The Song of the Three Youths": "Then the three in the furnace as from one mouth [ὡς ἐξ ἑνὸς στόματος] hymned, glorified, and blessed God." The qualification "as" or "as if" was frequently used with the idiom to signal its non-literal use. The youths' words in their hymn of praise were the same so that it was as if they spoke with only one mouth.

The idiom "one mouth" had long been present in classical Greek. One usage was for a group voicing their viewpoint by acclamation. The playwright Aristophanes has a line, "All the council cried out with one mouth" (*Knights* 670). Plato emphasized common agreement by use of the phrase when he spoke of "the universal voice [literally 'one mouth'] of mankind" (*Republic* 2, 364a). He united the two phrases that are the subject of this study in making his point about unified agreement: "With one voice and from one mouth they must all agree that the laws are all good" (*Laws* 1, 634e).

Turning to Christian usage, we find that the earliest non-canonical Christian use of the phrase "one mouth" was with reference to prayer: "When we with harmony in conscience have gathered together in the same place, let us cry to God fervently as from one mouth" (*1 Clement* 34.7). The emphasis on harmony in the context adds to the sense of united prayer.

Irenaeus piles up the expressions of oneness in speaking of the church believing and teaching the same faith:

> The church, although scattered throughout the world, carefully preserves [this faith], as living in one house. She likewise believes these things, as having one soul and the same heart, and harmoniously preaches, teaches, and delivers them, as possessing one mouth. (*Against Heresies* 1.10.2)

The church everywhere (we allow Irenaeus some exaggeration) adhered to and taught the same message, as if speaking with one mouth.

The *Hortatory Address to the Greeks*, falsely ascribed to Justin Martyr and likely from the third century, speaks of the harmony of the prophets in revealing the things of God because of their inspiration by the divine Spirit: they gave divine instruction "as if with one mouth and one tongue" (8).

Gregory Thaumaturgus' *Paraphrase of Ecclesiastes* 12:11 says that "some people will pass on those wise lessons" they have received, "as if everyone from one mouth described in unison and in greater detail what was entrusted to them."

Returning to the motif of praising God, we find several fourth-century references. The *Apostolic Constitutions* in a chapter that refers to both praying and hymning unites heavenly and human beings in gorifying God: "As all the heavenly natures of the incorporeal powers glorify God harmoniously, so also all human beings on earth with one mouth and one attitude glorify the one true and only God" (7.56.1). The agreement in words of the mouth reflects the inner harmony of disposition. This work is now thought to reflect the hand of a Neo-Arian, specifically Eunomian, compiler, but the same thought is expressed by a champion of the Neo-Nicene cause, Basil the Great. In describing vigil by his congregation in Caesarea of Cappadocia, he says: "All in common as from one mouth and one heart, offer up to the Lord the psalm of confession, each making the words of repentance their own" (*Letter* 207.3). The description speaks of reciting the same words without indicating sameness of tone.

Basil's friend, Gregory of Nazianzus, juxtaposes the "one voice" of the tower of Babel (Genesis 11) and Christians with allusion to Rom 15:6: "We have become one lip, one voice [language] in contrast to those who built the former tower. They were in agreement for evil, but for us the things of harmony are for all the best in order that together we might with one mouth glorify Father, Son, and Holy Spirit" (*Oration* 23 ["On Peace"].3). Once more, the emphasis is on the "togetherness" of the group in its vocal praise rather than on the musical manner.

A later Latin contemporary, Paulinus of Nola, evoked The "Song of the Three" to describe Christian song: "So let the holy lyre of our combined voices resound as though three tongues were singing with one mouth" (*Songs* 21.275). This statement more nearly evokes the practice of monophony, but even so the context, where an instrument of discordant notes brought into harmony serves as an illustration of vocal harmony, stresses agreement and unity.

John Chrysostom did not preach on Rom 15:6 in his *Homilies on Romans*, but he did recall its phraseology. He describes monks rising and "having made one choir, with their conscience bright, all as if from one mouth sing hymns harmoniously to the God of all" (*Homilies on Matthew* 68[69].3). He continues in the next section to contrast the songs of monks with the music of the theater: "Here the grace of the Spirit sounds forth, employing instead of aulos, kithara, or syrinx, the mouths of the saints" (68[69].4). He combines the phrases "one mouth" and "one voice" in discussing 1 Cor 14:33, but "one voice" is used literally and only "one mouth" is used metaphorically. Rebuking his congregation for talking on other matters in church, he pleads for their silence so that the one leading an activity was the only person speaking.

> There ought to be always but one voice in the church, just as there is one body. The one reading speaks alone, and even the bishop sits and maintains silence. The chanter chants alone; although all give the response, the voice is borne as from one mouth. The one who preaches, preaches alone (*Homilies in 1 Corinthians* 36.9).

Chrysostom maintains his point about a single voice at a time by describing the congregational responses to the singing of the Psalms by the chanter as the many voices of the congregation so united as to come from one mouth.

The unifying theme in these varied uses of "one mouth" is that of different persons being in agreement, an agreement expressed principally of course in the spoken word. This agreement might take the form of acclamations, voicing a common opinion or judgment, teaching the same thing, prayer, or especially praising God in song.

"ONE VOICE"

"One voice" is a parallel phrase to "one mouth," but it is much more frequent and thus offers more variety in usage. Many of these uses are

Praising God with "One Mouth" / "One Voice"

the same as "one mouth," and the underlying idea again is agreement or harmony. The phrase sometimes has the literal sense in the forefront, yet some of the metaphorical uses lose a connection with vocal expression. Once more, I begin with texts from the Greek Bible.

Genesis 11:1 describes all the people of the earth at one time as having "one lip and one voice [φωνὴ μία]," meaning one language. In Exod 24:3 "all the people with one voice" gave their acceptance to the words of the Lord delivered to them by Moses. A musical use occurs in 2 Chr 5:13, where it is stated that "There was one voice [sound, i.e., harmony] in the trumpeting and singing and proclaiming with one voice of acknowledgement and praise to the Lord." The thought of the Greek translators here could hardly have been of monophonic or strictly unison sound, since trumpeters and singers were both involved, so the emphasis was upon the notes of the instruments and singers being in harmony. In 4 Macc 8:29, when the tyrant tried to persuade the seven brothers to eat defiling food, "they all with one voice together, as if from the same soul," refused. Thus was described their united response. These four texts exemplify the meanings for "one voice" of a common language, united expressions of acceptance (the words of God) or refusal (commands of a pagan ruler), and harmony of musical sounds.

The New Testament adds specific content to these usages. Paul is quoted in Acts 24:21 as referring to "this one statement [voice]" he made concerning the resurrection of the dead. Acclamations or shouting in unison is represented by Acts 19:34—the mob at Ephesus "became one voice, all crying out for about two hours, 'Great is Artemis of the Ephesians!'" This unison shouting involved all saying the same words together without any necessary implication of the same tone. There is a literal use of the phrase "one voice" in Rev 9:13, "I heard one [a single] voice from the four horns of the altar."

Classical usage of "one voice" is even more varied and more extensive. It was noted above that Plato uses "one voice" with "one mouth" (*Laws* 1, 634e). The same work witnesses to the classical usage of φωνή for language: "many slaves who speak the same language [voice]" (*Laws* 6, 777c). The literal meaning is found in the statement that "sound which passes through the mouth whether of all or of an individual is one yet infinite" (*Philebus* 17b). Plato gives an explicit statement to monody, but in the metaphorical language of the "harmony of the spheres." In speaking of the seven planets and the Siren, he has the phrase, "hymning a single tone [or note, i.e., sound]" with "the eight forming one harmony" (*Republic* 10, 617b).

Aristotle shows a literal use of "one voice."

> Why does a human being show great variety of voice, but other animals have only one, unless they are of different species? Or, has the human being only one voice, though many varieties of speech [or many languages]. (*Problems* 10.38, 895a)

Another literal use appears in an illustration from music. "The two [notes] played against one voice [or, sound] make the other note imperceptible" (*Problems* 19.16, 918b). A non-literal grammatical use of φωνή occurs in the phrase, "affirm a single predicate [meaning, significance]" (*Interpretation* 11, 20b).

Diodore of Sicily was fond of the phrase and often used it for unison acclamations. "They united in acclaiming him [Gelon of Syracuse] with one voice benefactor, savior, and king" (*Library* 11.26.6). Describing agreement on a course of action, he wrote, "with one voice they asked their commander to lead them" (ibid. 11.19.3). In keeping with the Greek custom of choosing their generals, the multitude cried out in an election "as if from one voice" (ibid., 16.10.3). (The qualification "as if" is frequent.) "When [Demetrius] had called together an assembly under arms . . . , the crowd shouted with a single [one] voice" (ibid. 19.81.2). There was always implicit or explicit that a large number were involved.

Dionysius of Halicarnassus employs the expressions, "The Romans cried out with one voice" (*Roman Antiquities* 4.67.2), and "one mind and voice" (ibid. 6.87.1). Dio Chrysostom expresses harmonious agreement with the phrase, "speaking the same language [voice]" (*Oration* 39.3).

Plutarch uses "one voice" with some frequency in his extensive works. Sometimes this is literal, "In the theater [at Delphi] one voice reaches all" (*The Obsolescence of Oracles* 8; *Moralia* 414c). Or again, "They give the name 'Seven-voiced' to the Stoa at Olympia, which reverberates many times from a single utterance [voice]" (*Talkativeness* 1; *Moralia* 502d). Or, "one voice" could be used for a phrase, "Then expressing this one word [voice]," followed by a short quotation (Pompey 72.2). Similarly, "So great influence had a flatterer's one word [voice]" (Demetrius 18.7).

A non-literal use by Plutarch is indicated by an incident where many were probably not shouting the same words but words that had the same meaning: The soldiers and horsemen were "crying out loudly with one voice," ordering the private citizens out of their way (*Galba* 26.3). The phrase often is used for acclamations, whether spontaneous or organized.

Praising God with "One Mouth" / "One Voice"

"One cry [voice] came from all, recognizing Galba as emperor" (ibid. 14.5). When Timoleon arrived at the theater, "the people would greet him and call him by name with one voice" (*Timoleon* 38.3). "The people of Utica assembled together, calling Cato with one voice their benefactor, savior, the only one free and only one unconquered" (*Cato the Younger* 71.1). As a general expression of unity and harmony Plutarch gives this description: "a lover of harmony among nations, community of cities, unanimity [one voice] of council and assembly [theater]" (*Aratus* 10.2).

Plutarch has one usage in a description of musical practice at Greek banquets that closely approximates Christian language: Some say "that first the guests would sing the god's song together [κοινῶς, 'in common'], all raising their hymn with one voice" (*Table-Talk* 1.1, *Moralia* 615b). Then each person who wanted to do so sang individually in turn to the accompaniment of a lyre. These solo performances thus were contrasted with the group or unison singing that was characterized as "with one voice."

A work of the first or second century ascribed to Apollodorus contains the riddle of the sphinx that uses the word "voice" with the meaning "name": "What has one voice [name] and yet becomes four-footed and two-footed and three-footed?" (*Library* 3.5.8). The answer is a human being, for a person begins by crawling on "all fours," learns to walk on two legs, and in old age requires the assistance of a walking-stick.

Lucian of Samosata describes a crowd in a theater displeased with an actor in this way: "They all cried out in a single [one] voice" (*On Dance* 76). In another place he speaks of a crowd shouting, "All cried out with one voice as if by pre-arrangement" (*Nigrinus* 14).

Athenaeus uses "one voice" to refer to the "same language" (*Learned Banquet* 1.6.87 and 2.1) or to making "one sound" (ibid.1.10.83). Chariton (second century?) employs the phrase to introduce a statement, "sending forth one voice" followed by a quotation (*Chaerea and Callirhoe* 8.1). The grammarian and rhetor Aelius Herodianus (second century) represents the literal meaning, "one sound among many languages," and the grammatical sense, "they seek two [grammatical] cases in one sound." Cassius Dio contains a literal use of "one voice" but qualified by "if indeed": "[M]ention the things which the whole people would have celebrated with one tongue, if indeed they could speak with one voice" (*Roman History* 44.36.2).

The Neoplatonist Plotinus describes complete unity with the phrase "It is as if one voice and one word" (*Enneads* 6.4.14). Toward the close of pagan Greek literature the rhetor Libanius has the phrase, "everywhere the same word [voice]" (*Letters* 1350.3).

Thus we find over the long span of classical Greek literature a variety of uses of "one voice," not always as a set idiom: the literal meaning of one sound, standing for a word or a statement, the same spoken language, agreement in attitudes or policies, most frequently in unison acclamations whether staged or spontaneous, and the heavenly bodies "singing" the same tone or a group singing the same words together.

Jewish authors picked up the Greek classical and biblical uses of the idiom "one voice." Philo quotes Gen 11:1 and then gives an allegorical interpretation of the "one lip" and "one voice" as the agreement in evil deeds (*Confusion of Tongues* 1.1; 5.15). He describes an occasion in Alexandria where the crowd called for the death penalty against Isidorus: "They all cried out together [ὁμοθυμαδὸν] with one voice" (*Flaccus* 17.144). In contrast to this shouting out a negative condemnation, there is a positive affirmation recorded by Josephus of the greeting the Jews gave to Alexander the Great: "All the Jews together greeted Alexander with one voice" (*Antiquities* 11.8.5, 332).

"The Book of the Similitudes," the latest component of *1 Enoch*, often speaks of praying and glorifying "with one voice." Thus, "[T]he holy ones who dwell in the heavens above will unite with one voice, and supplicate, and pray, and praise, and give thanks, and bless in the name of the Lord of Spirits (47.2).

> And all those in the heavens above received a command, and power and one voice and one light . . . [T]hey will all speak with one voice, and bless, and praise, and exalt, and glorify the name of the Lord of Spirits . . . [A]nd they will raise one voice, and will bless, and praise, and glorify, and exalt (him) . . . and they will all say with one voice: 'Blessed is he, and blessed be the name of the Lord of Spirits for ever and ever.' (61.6, 9, 11)

Although I have limited this study primarily to Greek literature without thorough examination of Latin and Hebrew texts, I note that the late rabbinic *Midrash Rabbah on Song of Solomon* gives as one interpretation of Song of Solomon 8:13, "When Israel go into their synagogues and recite the *shemaʿ* with devotion, with one voice and with one mind and thought." This kind of recitation is contrasted with reciting "inattentively, one before the other," and without fixing "their minds on the words" (8.13.2). An interpretation of 8:14 is, "When Israel recite the *shemaʿ* with one mouth, one voice, one chant" (8.14.1).

The Christan edition of the *Ascension of Isaiah* also has the motif of the angels in heaven praising God with one voice, stated three times. The angels on the right (who had the greater glory) and on the left of the throne in the fifth heaven "all sang praises with one voice" (7.15). In the sixth heaven all the angels were equal, and Isaiah joined in their praise: "And there they all named the primal Father and his Beloved, Christ, and the Holy Spirit, all with one voice" (8.18). In the seventh heaven there was one "whose glory surpassed that of all," and all the righteous from Adam forward and all the angels "worshipped him, and they all praised him with one voice, and I also was singing praises with them" (9.28). It is difficult to draw conclusions from these statements about the nature of the singing, but since a human joined with the angels ("my praise was like theirs," 8.18 and 9.28), the "one voice" would seem to refer to the content of the united praise and not to the tonal likeness of the sound.

This Jewish Christian theme of the righteous joining the angels in praising God with one voice occurs also in the *Apocalypse of Peter* 19. The righteous were in a place of bliss where angels were present, and "All who dwell there had an equal glory, and with one voice they praised God the Lord, rejoicing in that place."

This heavenly praise was a model for the earthly church. Ignatius of Antioch uses a comparison from instrumental music to express the unity desired in the congregation but then describes Christian practice as vocal music.

> For your justly famous presbytery, worthy of God, is attuned to the bishop, as strings to a kithara. On account of this by your unanimity and harmonious love, Jesus Christ is being sung. Now each of you together become a choir so that being harmoniously in unanimity and receiving the keynote from God in unity, you may sing with one voice through Jesus Christ to the Father. (*Ephesians* 4.1–2)

The emphasis in the passage is clearly on unity and harmony. The unison singing might have been monodic, but one thinks that what Ignatius had in mind was the whole congregation participating in a harmony that found expression in singing the same thing. Unison tonality would not seem to be required by "one voice" any more than by other words in the description; if it was practiced, that would have to be established by other information about vocal music practices of the time.

A papyrus of the *Acts of Paul* contains the statement, "The lion said with one voice" (Papyrus Hamburg 5, 4), followed by a long quotation, but this is conjectured to be a corruption for "a divine voice."

Besides speaking of "one mouth," Irenaeus offers two problematic references to "one voice." He describes Marcus the Gnostic as teaching that the restitution of the universe will occur when all things will return to one letter and make one and same sound [ἐκφώνησιν]. He proposes that the "Amen" that we say together is an image of this sound (*Against Heresies* 1.14.1).

Although using a different form of the word φωνή, Irenaeus's statement indicates that the unison congregational "Amen" at the conclusion of prayers could be expressed as spoken with "one voice." A textual problem attaches to a passage where the surviving Greek breaks off in the middle of a difficult Latin reading. I offer this translation, following a conjectural reading:

> All the Scripture given to us by God will be found by us to be harmonious, and the parables will agree with the things said plainly. The things said [in Scripture] clearly will explain the parables, and through the many varied expressions one harmonious melody will be sung by us while we praise God in hymns (*Against Heresies* 2.28.3).

I take it that something may have dropped out of the text in transmission that would clarify that Irenaeus was making a comparison between the varied voices of Scripture teaching a harmonious message and the varied voices of the congregation united in the praise of God.

A text of uncertain date, but probably later than Irenaeus, comes from one of those groups whom Irenaeus so strenuously opposed as Gnostic. The *Holy Book of the Great Invisible Spirit*, better known as *The Gospel of the Egyptians*, is preserved in Coptic in the Nag Hammadi codices. It contains a passage about singing similar to expressions in orthodox writers, except for its description of the objects of the praise:

> [T]he spiritual church increased in the four lights of the great, living Autogenes, the god of truth, praising, singing, (and) giving glory with one voice, with one accord, with a mouth that does not rest, to the Father, and the Mother, and the Son, and their whole pleroma. (NHC III, 2, 55, 5–11 = IV, 2, 66, 14–23)

Here praising, singing, and glorifying are combined as being done in accord or unanimity by the church with the one voice of the mouth. Despite

Praising God with "One Mouth" / "One Voice"

the uncertain date and certainly unorthodox character of the document, it well expresses the worship practices in song by the mainstream of the church.

Clement of Alexandria has a metaphorical use, "employing the only one voice of writing," that is, the one medium of writing instead of speaking (*Miscellanies* 1.1.14.4). Drawing on the language of sacrifice from the ancient world, Clement interpreted the altar as "the congregation of those devoted to prayer, as if having one common voice and one mind" (ibid. 7.6.31.8). The same imagery applies to song as to prayer.

> The union of many in one, a unity that out of many varied sounds receives a divine harmony, becomes one symphony [συμφωνία], following the one choir director and teacher, the Word, resting in the same truth and saying 'Abba, Father' [Rom 8:15]. (*Exhortation* 9.88)

Particularly important for our purposes is a passage that apparently quotes in part from Plutarch, *Moralia* 615b above:

> Among the ancient Greeks at their drinking parties and after-dinner cups they were accustomed to sing a song called the *skolion* in the manner of the Hebrew Psalms, for "all raise the paean in common with one voice." Sometimes they passed around in turn the toasts of the ode. (*Instructor* 2.4.44.3)

As in Plutarch, Clement uses "one voice" for the group singing together in contrast to the individual singing. For purposes of understanding Jewish and Christian musical practice, Clement gives the important testimony that the Hebrew Psalms were sung corporately.

Origen picked up the reference in Genesis 11:1 to one voice for one language. He also used the phrase for the unity of Scripture: "The prophecies are not divided but were spoken and written as by one Spirit truly working harmoniously and by one voice in one soul" (*Commentary on Matthew* 14.1 on Matt 18:19). Origen furthermore applied "one voice" to prayer and song.

> [Whether Greeks or Romans] each in his own language prays to God and praises him as one is able. And the Lord of every language hears those praying in every language as, if I may speak thus, one voice according to the meaning expressed in different languages. (*Against Celsus* 8.37)

Origen qualifies his statement, his philological training seeming to realize there was an accommodative sense in the phrase while he recognized it as a common usage.

Eusebius of Caesarea uses "one voice" in the sense of "identical utterance" for the message of two revelatory visions (*Church History* 6.11.2). "This one voice [=statement]" refers to a quotation from Psalm 29 (*Questions of the Gospel to Stephen*; PG 22.912); "with one word and one voice" introduces a quotation of Matt 28:19 (*Proof of the Gospel* 3.6; 132a). The most frequent metaphorical use in Eusebius, however, is to express agreement. Thus there is the combination "one mind and one voice" (*Preparation for the Gospel* 14.3; 719d). The agreement among the prophets was possible because "they all spoke with one voice by the divine Spirit" (*Proof of the Gospel* 5 int. 25; 208d). The two phrases of our study are combined in Eusebius's exaggerated rhetoric about Constantine: "All the nations . . . with one voice and one mouth confessed that Constantine by God's grace made the common good to shine upon human beings" (*Life of Constantine* 1.41.2). Eusebius often expresses the unity and harmony of Christian singing but without the use of the phrases in our study.

Athanasius uses the phrase "one voice" to describe a congregational acclamation, "O Christ, send help to [emperor] Constantius" (*Apology to Constantius* 10), and the congregational "Amen" at the conclusion of prayer—it is better to assemble in one place so as to speak "as with one and the same voice in perfect harmony" so that "such a great assembly of people might become one voice when they say the 'Amen' to God" (ibid. 16).

Basil the Great of Caesarea in Cappadocia represents the usages already established. The literal meaning of one sound occurs with reference to a mother sheep who recognizes her lamb, although all "have the same sound, color, and smell" (*Hexaemeron* 9.4.32). Basil picks up the meaning "one language" from Gen 11:1 (*Homily on Pentecost* 3; PG 52.811). "One voice" can stand for "one word" in the sense of a saying or statement, Basil's most common use of the phrase. Similar to this is the metaphorical use for the collective voice of people. For a group saying the same thing, he writes, "There is only one voice [or cry] in all, who recount their pitiable and sad condition" (*Letters* 243.2). One person can speak for others: "Your whole fatherland addresses these words to you through our one voice" (*Letters* 96.1). In a musical context for congregational singing Basil emphasizes its unifying quality:

> Who can consider as an enemy one with whom he has sung to God with one voice? Hence singing of the psalms in unity . . . harmoniously draws the people to a symphony of one choir. (*Commentary on Psalms* 1.2; PG 29.212)

"One voice" once more represents the communal singing, which here creates unity as well as expressing it.

The same pattern of usage recurs in Gregory Nazianzus. In a letter to Basil he could describe the latter's voice as "one [unique] among all things" (*Letters* 46.4). "One voice" stands for "a single expression" or phrase (*Oration* 43 ["Panegyric on Basil"].68), or to one statement from Isaiah (*Oration* 4 ["Against Julian"].15). We noted above on "one mouth" Nazianzen's allusion to Genesis 11; he uses the meaning of language also in reference to the Pentecost miracle: "Did they each hear in their own language so that, permit me to say so, one sound was spoken but many sounds were heard?" (*Oration* 41 ["On Pentecost"].15). (He preferred to punctuate Acts 2:6 so that the miracle was in the speaking of other languages rather than in the hearing.) There is an analogy from vocal music, with reference to Exodus 15, that fits what other Christian authors said: "Taking up one voice, harmonized by the one Spirit, let us sing that victory ode which Israel then sang over the Egyptians" (*Oration* 4 ["Against Julian"].12).

Gregory of Nyssa has a literal use of the phrase in reference to speech: [One] "cannot utter the names of three persons with one sound [voice] at the same time" (*Against Eunomius* 1.203 [16]; GNO 1,86,3; PG 45). His extensive use of "one voice" for the most part seems to be equivalent to "one word" or "one saying." Often the reference is to a text of Scripture, but other statements could be capsuled in the phrase. Among the notable applications of the usage is to the uniform message of Scripture: "You heard all [law, prophets, Gospels] calling out together with one voice 'love' and saying 'philanthropy'" (*Usury* 9; GNO 9, 204, 11). With allusion to Gen. 11:1 is the statement, "Whenever all the church in agreement with the good becomes one lip and one voice" (*Canticles hom.* 7 on Cant. 4:3; GNO 6, 228, 14). Gregory gives a similar metaphorical application:

> Just as there was "one lip and one voice" before the confusion of tongues, so also now all the nations and the whole world and all human beings become one hearing and one heart when the one Word resounds in them all. (*Inscriptions of the Psalms* 2.12.171)

Literal speaking is involved in a confession of faith: "One word [voice] was heard to all these things, Christ being confessed in the mouths of the saints" (*The Forty Martyrs* 1b [GNO 10.1, 149, 25; PG 46.764]).

The *Confessions of Cyprian* (of Antioch—apparently an invented person) mention the unison Amen as a response to songs:

> Thereupon we went into the church, and [one could there] see the choir, which was like a choir of heavenly men of God or a choir of angels taking up a song of praise to God. To every verse they added a Hebrew word [as] with one voice, so that one might believe that there were not [a number of] men but rather one rational being comprehending a unity, which gave off a wonderful sound. (17)

The huge corpus of John Chrysostom will serve to complete our survey of "one voice" in Greek patristic literature. He too frequently uses "one voice" for "one phrase" or "one saying." Thus in preaching on Acts 17:24 Chrysostom says that "one phrase [voice]" of Paul overthrew the ideas of philosophers (*Homilies on Acts* 38 (PG 60.270). "By one expression [voice]," Luke 23:43, Jesus introduced the thief on the cross into paradise (*On the Ascension*, hom. 4; PG 52.799). There are several references to the "one lip, one voice" of Gen 11:1. "One mouth" and "one voice" occur with reference to a secular acclamation: "In the theater as from one mouth they cry out all with one voice, they all in harmony call him protector and ruler of the city" (*On Vainglory and Education of the Young* 4).

With reference to verbal petition, Chrysostom speaks of the people of Antioch "calling upon God with one and the same voice with much earnestness" (*To the People of Antioch* 15.3). Prayer in the liturgical assembly is described in the following words:

> You are able to pray in private, but the prayer does not have such power as when done with all the members of the household, as when the whole body of the church together sends up petition with one voice, the priests being present and lifting up the prayers of the community. (*On the Obscurity of the Prophets*; PG 56.182)

This is a striking statement of the power of congregational prayer when prayed in unity. With that power in mind, Chrysostom exhorts, "Let us all join in prayer, and let us lift up one voice in their behalf" (*Homilies on Romans* 7 on Rom. 3:31).

A particularly interesting passage pertains to the singing of Psalms in church. Chrysostom has referred to young and old, rich and poor, women and men. His description of their equality in church includes this description of their participation (including women) in psalmody:

> Behold, when the Psalm is introduced it blends the different voices, provides one harmonious ode to be offered up, and joins the dead and the living.
>
> The blessed prophet (David) sings with us; he speaks and all answer with the responses.
>
> There is not here slave or free, rich and poor, ruler and private person. All have been welded together into one chorus out of all. Heaven and earth are combined. Neither does man have freedom of speech nor is woman silent and stands speechless; but all enjoy equal honor, and we offer up a common sacrifice, a common offering. This one does not have more than another, and that one more than this, but all in the same honor, one voice out of different tongues, offer to the Creator of the world. The difference is not in slave and free, not in rich and poor, not in female and male, but in attitude, in diligence, in readiness, in evil and in virtue. (*De studio praesentium* 5.1; PG 63.487)

Without using the exact phrase "one voice," as the preceding quotation does, Chrysostom elsewhere expresses the same thought: "Our tongues are the strings of our kithara, putting forth a different sound yet a godly harmony. For indeed women and men, old and young, have different voices but they do not differ in the word of hymnody for the Spirit blends the voice of each and effects one melody in all" (*On Psalms* 145 [English 146].2; PG 55.521.)

These passages demonstrates that the emphasis for Chrysostom was on agreement and unity in the words sung, not on identity of sound; the one melody was the work of the Spirit not of the unison voices of the congregation.

Although the burden of this paper has been on the Greek writers, the study may be rounded out by quoting two Latin authors contemporary with Chrysostom on the one voice of Christian music. Ambrose, bishop of Milan, borrowing in part from a passage in Basil quoted above, wrote:

> A psalm ... produces one song from various and sundry voices in the manner of a cithara ... The apostle admonishes women to be silent in church, yet they do well to join in a psalm; this is gratifying for all ages and fitting for both sexes ... With what great effort is silence maintained during the [scriptural] readings! If one person recites, the entire congregation makes noise; but when a psalm is read, it is itself the guarantor of silence because when all speak [in response] no one makes noise ... A psalm joins those with difference, unites those at odds and reconciles those who have been offended, for who will not concede

to him with whom one sings to God in one voice? (*Explanation of the Psalms* 1.9)

Singing together, by actively engaging the whole congregation, kept order in the assembly and had a unifying effect.

Niceta of Remesiana, in the Balkans where Latin and Greek met, wrote the first known treatise of hymn-singing:

> [After quoting "The Song of the Three Youths," Dan 3:51–52, he says,] You see that it was for our instruction that we are told that the three boys humbly and holily praised God with one voice. Therefore, let us sing all together, as with one voice, and let all of us modulate our voices in the same way. If one cannot sing in tune with the others, it is better to sing in a low voice rather than drown the others. In this way he will take his part in the service without interfering with the community singing . . .
>
> When we sing, all should sing; when we pray, all should pray. So when the lesson is read, all should remain silent, that all may equally hear. (*On the Utility of Hymn Singing* 13)

Niceta clearly envisions not everyone singing "on key," although that was desirable. His "one voice" is the joint participation by all.

Christian writers used the phrase "one voice" in a variety of ways: predominately to refer to a single saying or statement, "one word," to mean "one language" (in comments on or allusions to Gen 11:1), or for acclamations. In the context of worship the phrase was used for united prayer, the ratification "Amen," or for congregational psalmody (whether the whole song or more often the responses to the text sung by a cantor). The phrase emphasized corporate agreement.

CONCLUSIONS

It may seem obvious, but should be stated, that this study deals with vocal sounds. This is explicit in the phrase "one mouth," but it applies also to "one voice." Although the word φωνή could mean "sound" as well as "voice," in the phrase "one voice" it most often means vocal sound or in its idiomatic uses is derived from that meaning. Thus in musical contexts the phrases have to do almost exclusively with vocal music.

In keeping with the general metaphorical use of the phrases "one mouth" and "one voice," the emphasis in worship contexts also is on agreement and unity. The use of these phrases in reference to prayer parallel their use in reference to song. They should have the same meaning when used of prayer as they do of song. Hence, "one voice" did not mean "unison" in the modern sense of monophonic but "unison" in the sense of joint, unified participation by all. The singing may actually have been monophonic, but these phrases do not, as Quasten contended, establish this usage. The translation "unison" for "one voice" is not justified if by unison one means monophonic singing, but it is appropriate if by it one means congregational participation.

3

The Liturgical Function of the *Sursum Corda*

THE *Apostolic Tradition* of Hippolytus gives us the earliest text of the introductory dialogue preceding the eucharistic prayer.

> To him [the bishop] then let the deacons bring the oblation and he with all the presbyters laying his hand on the oblation shall say giving thanks: The Lord be with you. And the people shall say: And with thy spirit. [Bishop:] Lift up your hearts. [People:] We have them with the Lord. [Bishop:] Let us give thanks unto the Lord. [People:] It is meet and right.[1]

Josef Jungmann says concerning the middle phrase, "The precise origin of this preliminary *sursum corda* is not known."[2] Gregory Dix speaks more confidently of the words' meaning:

> They were confined strictly to use at the sacramental eucharist, unlike the other parts of the dialogue, and the reason is not far to seek. They are intended to remind the *ecclesia* that the real action of the eucharist takes place beyond time in "the age to come."[3]

---

1. *Apostolic Tradition* I.iv, according to Dix, *The Treatise on the Apostolic Tradition*, 6–7; Botte, *La tradition apostolique de Saint Hippolyte*, 10, 12. A different translation in Bradshaw et al., *The Apostolic Tradition*, 38.
2. *The Mass of the Roman Rite*, 369.
3. *The Shape of the Liturgy*, 127.

The Liturgical Function of the Sursum Corda

It is proposed here to suggest a specific context for the exhortation "Hearts above," or "Up with our hearts."[4]

The normal Christian posture for prayer (and this was by no means confined to Christians) in the worship assembly was standing, with the arms extended, and the palms and the eyes uplifted to heaven. We may cite only a few of the references from Hippolytus' near contemporaries.[5] A counterpart in the church order literature from the East, the *Didascalia Apostolorum*, mentions "When you stand up to pray."[6] Tertullian says, "To heaven Christians look up, with hands outstretched, because free from sin; with head uncovered, for we are not ashamed."[7] Origen declares, "There can be no doubt that the position of stretching out one's hands and lifting up the eyes is to be preferred."[8] Earlier Athenagoras in contrasting animal sacrifices with Christian prayer stated. "We lift up holy hands to God."[9]

The abundant literary references are illustrated by Christian art of the third and fourth centuries. Indeed the literary texts are few in comparison to the number of *orantes* to be found in catacomb paintings and

---

4. Compare the Ἄνω ἡμῶν τὰς καρδίας of the *Liturgy of St. Mark* (Brightman, 125) and the Ἄνω σχῶμεν τὸν νοῦν καὶ τὰς καρδίας of the Liturgy of St. James (Brightman, 50). In a non-liturgical context one may compare Hermas, *Vision* 3.10.9 and *Mandates* 10.1.6.

5. Among his predecessors see 1 Timothy 2:8; *1 Clement* 2 and 29; *Acts of Paul and Thecla* 34; Clement of Alexandria, *Strom.* VII. vii. 40. 1.

6. *Didas.* XII (Connolly, 119). This statement is about the people; chapter XI (Connolly, 117) has the bishop standing for the prayer.

7. *Apol.* 30. 4. Tertullian has a number of references: *De bapt.* 20, "When you ascend from that most holy washing of the new birth and for the first time spread out your hands with your brethren in mother church," a passage which reminds us that new converts went directly from baptism to their first communion (Justin, *Apol.* I, 65); *De or.* 14 and 17; *Idol.* 7. 1; *De spec.* 25 ("to raise your hands to God and then occupy them in applause of an actor") may have the order of the laity's participation in worship in its sequence of listening to prophetic appeals, singing Psalms, raising hands to God, saying "Amen" over the holy thing, and acclaiming "forever."

8. *De or.* 31. 2. The *Comm. Joh.* XXVIII. 4 on John 11:41 argues the necessity of lifting the eyes up to heaven in prayer, with special reference to the time of taking the bread and drinking the cup. Origen indicates that kneeling was appropriate for prayers of contrition, although not the normal posture. Tertullian in *De cor.* 3 and *De or.* 23 says that on Sundays and from Easter to Pentecost one stood in prayer in honor of the resurrection. The Pseudo-Justin, *Quaes. et resp. ad orth.* 115 assigns the same explanation to Irenaeus' (lost) treatise *De Pascha*. One may think of the distinction in Gregory Thaumaturgus, *Ep. can.* XI, between the penitents who are "kneelers" and depart with the catechumens and those who stand together with the faithful at communion.

9. *Leg. pro Chris.* 13. For the uplifted hands, cf. Hippolytus, *Comm. Dan.* II. 24.

on sarcophagi sculptures, not to mention other art objects.[10] This posture in prayer was the recognized symbol for piety and communion with God.

Specifically, Christians stood for the eucharistic prayer. So Justin Martyr informs us. After the Scripture readings and sermon,

> Then we all rise together and send up prayers. And, as we said before, when we cease from prayer, bread and wine with water are presented, and the president likewise sends up prayers and thanksgivings as he is able, and the people respond by saying the "Amen."[11]

We do not know the preceding posture, presumably sitting, but where would depend on the type of meeting place in which the liturgical celebration was held.

Moreover, the faithful appear to have taken the eucharist standing, at least according to some texts. Dionysius of Alexandria describes "one who had heard the thanksgiving and joined in repeating the "Amen"; who had stood at the table and had stretched forth his hands to receive the holy food."[12] Tertullian says of taking the eucharist, "You have stood at God's altar."[13]

There is a rather precise illustration of Hippolytus' words to be found in a painting from (a bit ironically) the Catacomb of Callistus.[14] It shows a large fish on a tripod table with one person extending his arms so as to place his hands on the fish in the act of blessing,[15] even as Hippolytus' bishop lays his hands on the elements at the consecration prayer. Another figure stands beside with arms raised in the *orans* gesture, exactly as we have seen the congregation standing for the eucharistic prayer.

All of this leads me to suggest the occasion which gave rise to the words "Lift up your hearts." They served as a rubric inviting the believers to lift their hands or, if seated, to rise and lift their hands for the eucharistic prayer. As they all in common rise, as Justin says, then the people lift up

---

10. For quality reproductions see André Grabar, *The Beginnings of Christian Art*, illus. 25, 26, 58, 96–98, 102, 104, 113–15, 119, 120, 135, 140, 146, and *Christian Iconography* (Princeton, 1968), illus. 188–94.

11. *Apol.* I, 67.

12. Eusebius, *H.E.* VII. ix.

13. *De or.* 19. 3. See also John Chrysostom, *II Cor. Hom.* XVIII. 3.

14. Reproduced in van der Meer and Mohrmann, *Atlas of the Early Christian World*, 43. Cf. Muñoz, *Il Codice Purpureo di Rossano*, Plate VI.

15. The Inscription of Abercius describes taking the eucharist as receiving the fish. Translation in Ferguson, *Early Christians Speak*, 3rd ed., 152.

The Liturgical Function of the Sursum Corda

their hands, look to heaven, and respond, "Our hearts are with the Lord." The congregation was hereby aroused for the high moment of its assembly. The people were invited to arise and thereby lift their hearts to God, this finding expression in the outward elevating of the arms for prayer. The people responded by their gesture and their words in the offering of themselves to God. The sacrifice of prayer and thanksgiving was thus accompanied by a symbolic sacrifice as the people presented themselves before God.[16]

There is perhaps some confirmation for this suggestion in the Ethiopic version of Hippolytus' instructions for an *agape*.

> The bishop standing in the midst of the faithful, before he gives thanks shall say: The Lord be with you all.
>
> And the people also shall say: With thy spirit.
>
> And the bishop shall say: Let us give thanks unto the Lord.
>
> And the people shall say: It is meet and right. Greatness and exaltation with glory are due unto Him.
>
> And he shall not say: Lift up your hearts, because that shall be said at the oblation.[17]

At the agape the people were reclining at table ready to eat the meal, and so they did not rise for the thanksgiving prayer. At the eucharistic assembly they did all rise together, so there the *sursum corda* was used.

Cyprian, too, may be taken as implying a connection between the standing posture and the spiritual significance of the call "Hearts upward."

> Moreover, when we stand for prayer, beloved brethren, we ought to be watchful and intent on our prayers with our whole heart. Let all carnal and worldly thoughts be far away, nor let the soul at that time think on anything except what is being prayed. For this reason, also the priest, as a preface before the prayer, prepares the minds of the brethren by saying, "Lift up your hearts," and when the people respond, "We have them with the Lord,"

---

16. Note also the close of Hippolytus' eucharistic prayer with its request that the people, filled with the Holy Spirit, might praise God (*Ap. Trad.* I. iv. 12, 13—Dix, *The Treatise of the Apostolic Tradition*, 9; Botte, *La tradition apostolique de Saint Hippolyte*, 16).

17. This passage (*Ap. Trad.* III. xxvi. 19–23, Dix, *The Treatise of the Apostolic Tradition*, 50–51) exists entire only in the Ethiopic version, but it is retained by Botte, section 25 in his numbering (*La tradition apostolique de Saint Hippolyte*, 64); Bradshaw, et al., *The Apostolic Tradition* (as section 29c), 156.

they are reminded that they ought to think of nothing other than the Lord himself.[18]

The suggestion of this paper should not be seen as reducing a beautiful piece of spiritual exhortation and confident response to the level of the commonplace. The providing of a concrete setting for the *sursum corda* is not a contradiction to a nobler understanding of its function. This would not be the first time nor the last that a physical response was given a spiritual meaning or that a religious attitude found expression in an outward action.[19]

---

18. *De Dom. or.* 31. Cf. *Acts of John* 43 "John stretched out his hands and with uplifted heart..."

19. After preparing this paper I found in Dölger, *Sol Salutis* (1920) pp. 228-44, a similar perspective. Perhaps the new collection of evidence and the independent formulation will yet make this contribution useful.

4

The Lord's Supper in Church History

The Early Church through the Medieval Period

INTRODUCTION

MANY ASPECTS OF THE Lord's Supper could be considered both liturgical and doctrinal. To limit the subject, I have chosen to consider the real presence, a topic where many of the confessional differences in the history of Christianity center. As a second limitation, I will largely confine myself to Western history, with apologies to my Orthodox and other Eastern Christian friends. As a further limitation, instead of attempting a complete survey,[1] I will make some soundings at strategic places in the history of eucharistic theology: the second century,

---

1. A fine older survey from a non-Roman Catholic perspective is Srawley, "Eucharist (to end of Middle Ages)." For more extensive surveys, see Briolioth, *Eucharistic Faith and Practice*; MacDonald, ed., *The Evangelical Doctrine of Holy Communion*; Clements et al., *Eucharistic Theology Then and Now*; Crockett, *Eucharist: Symbol of Transformation*; more popularly, Macy, *The Banquet's Wisdom*. For a Roman Catholic interpretation of the ancient period, see Battifol, *L'Eucharistie*. For a good collection of texts from the patristic period, see Daniel J. Sheerin, *The Eucharist*; for texts from the whole period topically arranged, Palmer, *Sacraments and Worship*, 38–215; for the ancient period and arranged by literary categories, Hamman, *The Mass*; a more extensive collection of texts in the original languages with Spanish translation is Solaro, *Textos eucaristicos primitivos*.

with attention to Justin Martyr and others on the topic; the fourth century, with special reference to Ambrose and Augustine; the ninth century, with its treatises by Radbertus and Ratramnus; the eleventh century, with the controversy involving Lanfranc and Berengar; and concluding in the thirteenth century, with special attention to the contributions of Thomas Aquinas.

I need to state my understanding of the apostolic and New Testament point of departure for thought about the Lord's Supper. If one has a different interpretation of the New Testament texts, then the course of development will look different. I think my understanding is consistent with the future unfolding of thought on the Lord's Supper, but I trust the sample excavations of certain chronological sites will be objective enough to hold up regardless of the starting point and interpretive framework.

I understand Jesus' words at the Last Supper in terms of the Old Testament description of the Passover, in keeping with the Passover atmosphere if not Passover context of the meal. The meal "is the passover of the Lord," according to the first reference to it in Exodus 12:11. The Passover meal commemorated the death of the firstborn of the Egyptians and the deliverance of the Israelites (Exod 12:14).[2] More than that, it was a reliving in the present of those events, a bringing of them into the present so that those participating could think of themselves as experiencing the exodus.[3] As the Mishnah put it, "In every generation a man must so regard himself as if he came forth himself out of Egypt" (Pesahim 10.5). I consider Jesus' words, "This is my body" (Mark 14:22), in the same way. The bread brings the body into the present. The presence is real, but not literal. The meaning of the event is made present once more. Similarly, the "remembrance" (*anamnēsis*) of 1 Corinthians 11:24–25, according to the Jewish background, was neither simply mental recollection nor the actual repetition of something but the celebration of a past event in order to live in its experience and to participate in its redemptive qualities. The historical deliverance is unrepeatable, but its effects are reaffirmed.

---

2. Exod 12:14 uses μνημόσυνον for "remembrance," the same word as Matt 26:13. Cf. ἀνάμνησις in 1 Cor 11:24–25.

3. McCormick, *The Lord's Supper*, 73–84; Léon-Dufour, *Sharing the Eucharistic Bread*, 102–16. On the theme of "remembering" in the Old Testament, Childs, *Memory and Tradition in Israel*; in the New Testament, Nils A. Dahl, "*Anamnēsis*: Mémoire et Commémoration dans le christianisme primitif," esp. 71–72 on this point; reprinted in English without complete annotation, "*Anamnēsis*: Memory and Commemoration in Early Christianity."

In biblical thought something, including food for nourishment, is sanctified to a given purpose "by God's word and by prayer" (1 Tim 4:5).[4] Similarly, the effects of commemoration are accomplished by reason of God's appointment of what is to be done (declared by the Word of God) and the human intention to do what is appointed (expressed by prayer). In the context of the Lord's Supper, this means that the bread and wine now have a different function from what they do as table food. Their purpose now is the memorial of Jesus' giving of himself for human forgiveness.

In this Jewish context of thought and practice, the first Christians broke bread and blessed the cup. In so doing, they relived their time when Jesus was personally present. They made Jesus' body and blood offered on the cross and its effects real in their assemblies. Other aspects were also present—fellowship, eschatological joy, a thank-offering to God, and so on. But for now we focus on the question of Jesus' "presence."

SECOND CENTURY

What happened to this Jewish understanding of memorial and sanctification by God's Word and by prayer in a Greco-Roman intellectual and social environment? How was this to be expressed in a different thought world? Greeks and Romans obviously had the concept of memorial and knew a distinction between the holy and the unholy, but other philosophical understandings were also at work.

This situation required Christians to make many adjustments and reinterpretations in their effort to communicate with their society. The interpretation of the Lord's Supper was included in those matters influenced by new ways of looking at things.[5] A major aspect was a shift from Jewish thought in terms of function and relationships, to Greek philosophical thought about ontology (or being, where Plato had directed his attention) and substance (where Aristotle had made important analyses).[6]

---

4. Atchley, *On the Epiclesis of the Eucharistic Liturgy*, surveys the history of an epiclesis or invocation in consecrating the eucharistic elements and the water of the baptismal font.

5. For the second century, see Swete, "Eucharistic Belief in the Second and Third Centuries"; Ferguson, *Early Christians Speak*, rev. ed., 93–127.

6. Crockett, *Eucharist: Symbol of Transformation*, 62, describes the shift as from Jewish and biblical models to naturalistic and philosophical models. He notes that there were biblical models for a language of transformation, but these were eschatological, having to do with resurrection and new creation.

Justin Martyr, who was born at the Roman colony near Samaria and died as a martyr at Rome ca. 165, knew well the Jewish context of Christianity but had his intellectual formation in Hellenistic philosophy.[7] He made the earliest surviving effort at communicating the words of the Last Supper in this philosophical environment.[8] In his *Dialogue with Trypho*, Justin recorded his debates with Jews who were quite hellenized. This work addressed Jewish concerns, even if Justin may have had his eye on Gentiles who wanted to know the differences between Jews and Christians.[9]

To Jews, Justin speaks of the eucharist (the common term in use from the second century until the Reformation) as a memorial. He describes the bread as a "memorial [ἀνάμνησις] of the incarnation" and the cup as a "memorial of his blood" (*Dial.* 70.4). In these things there is "remembered his passion" (*Dial.* 117.3). The word "memorial" suggests the intention or purpose behind the act. As we have said, a memorial for the Jews involved more than what the word itself said: it was to bring God's activity of the past into the present and to make it effective. How was this idea to be expressed to educated pagans?

Here we turn to Justin's *First Apology*, addressed to pagans. Justin includes two accounts of the eucharist. The first is in chapter 65 as part of a description of Christian initiation that included instruction and baptism and was followed by first communion. The second is in chapter 67 as part of the description of the continuing Christian life that included the regular Sunday assembly. This shows that the baptismal eucharist was not different from the weekly eucharist. Both observances had a congregational context in which the president and the people together were involved. Between the two accounts, there is an explanation of the meaning of the rite (chap. 66).[10]

Justin's "explanation" has been more confusing than helpful to modern readers. The difficulty that has plagued interpreters comes from his struggle to express a fullness of meaning that terminology carrying a Jewish content did not adequately convey to educated pagans. Justin says,

> We do not receive [the eucharist] as common bread and drink.
> In the same manner as Jesus Christ our Savior became flesh

---

7. Barnard, *Justin Martyr: His Life and Thought*; Osborne, *Justin Martyr*; Stylianopoulos, "Justin Martyr."

8. Jourjon, "Justin."

9. Nilson, "To Whom Is Justin's Dialogue with Trypho Addressed?"

10. Ratcliff, "The Eucharistic Institution Narrative of Justin Martyr's First Apology."

through the word of God and had flesh and blood for our salvation, so also the food for which thanks was given through the prayer of the word that is from him [or, through his word of prayer], from which our blood and flesh are nourished by metabolism, we have been taught to be the flesh and blood of that Jesus who became flesh. (*Apol.* 1.66.2)

The following points are important: (1) The bread and beverage were now no longer "ordinary" food and drink, for they now served another purpose. (2) This change was effected by the word of the Lord (he cites in the next section, 66.3, the institution narrative as the justification for the Christian practice) and by prayer, as in 1 Timothy 4:5. (3) The description of the prayer is so unclear as to be particularly puzzling,[11] but the nature of this prayer or formula of words is of more liturgical than doctrinal interest; for my purposes it is sufficient to note that Justin still reflects the Jewish and New Testament thought about what effects sanctification for a particular use. (4) The bread and wine are still real food, for they bring nourishment to our physical bodies by the regular process of digestion. (5) Nevertheless, the comparison with the incarnation opened up the line of thought along which doctrinal interpretation was to proceed.

Did Justin by his explanatory words intend to help his pagan readers understand the significance the bread and wine had for Christians and to emphasize the true humanity of Christ, or is he an early witness to a belief in the substantial conversion of the elements? By his comparison to the incarnation, is Justin describing the meaning that the consecrated ("eucharistized") elements had for Christians, that is, a change in their relationship or function so that the bread and drink now mean the real flesh and blood of Jesus that suffered for us? Or is he describing some real ontological change of the bread and drink into the flesh and blood of Jesus? Or is he suggesting in some sense an addition of the flesh and blood of Jesus to the material elements?[12] I do not know how literally to take Justin, but I am suspicious of efforts to read too much of later developments into his words. Nonetheless, his parallelism between the word of God giving flesh

---

11. Atchley, *On the Epiclesis*, section 3, understands Justin's phrase as "through the word [*logos*] of prayer" and as meaning a form of words, that is a prayer which he thought came from Christ; Curing, "*DIA EUCHES LOGOU*," translates, "a prayer of the form of words which is from Jesus," with reference to Justin, *Apol.* 1.13.1. Gelston, "*DI' EUCHES LOGOU* (Justin, Apology 1.66.2)," translates, "through the word of prayer from him," according to the example of Jesus' thanksgiving. See my discussion of other options in Ferguson, *Early Christians Speak*, 112–14.

12. Ferguson, *Early Christians Speak*, 113.

and blood to Jesus and the bread and wine becoming flesh and blood does show how the transition to a realistic interpretation could have occurred.

Irenaeus, bishop of Lyons in the late second century,[13] may serve as a supplement to Justin's words or possibly an interpretation of them. Irenaeus mainly makes incidental rather than deliberately descriptive remarks about the eucharist.[14] Most of his statements are in an anti-Gnostic context, stressing the real humanity of Christ.[15] He set up a three-track parallel between the Lord having flesh and blood, the material elements of bread and wine receiving the word of God,[16] and our human bodies having the hope of resurrection for a twofold purpose: to affirm the goodness of creation and the redemption of the body against the Gnostic denial of these doctrines, and to argue that the use of bread and wine is an indication that the Savior had a real human body.

> How can they [Gnostics] say that the flesh which is nourished from the body of the Lord and from his flesh comes to corruption and does not partake of life? Let them either change their views or avoid offering the bread and wine. But our view is in harmony with the eucharist, and the eucharist confirms our view. We offer to God his own things, proclaiming rightly the communion and unity of flesh and spirit. For as bread from the earth when it receives the invocation of God is no longer common bread but the eucharist, consisting of two things—one earthly and one heavenly—so also our bodies when they partake of the eucharist are no longer corruptible but have the hope of the resurrection to eternity. (*Adv. haer.* 4.18.5)

Irenaeus offers several parallels to Justin's language: "no longer common bread," yet this cup and bread furnish true physical nourishment,[17]

---

13. Lawson, *The Biblical Theology of St. Irenaeus*; Clark, "Irenaeus."

14. Hamman, "Irenaeus of Lyons"; Ferguson, *Early Christians Speak*, 114.

15. *Adv. haer.* 4.17.5; 4.18.4–5; 4.33.2; 5.2.2–3.

16. *Adv. haer.* 5.2.3, the cup and bread "receive the word of God and the Eucharist becomes the body of Christ." The parallel with 4.18.5, "receive the invocation of God," might indicate a reference to the prayer (so Atchley, *On the Epiclesis*, section 4); but "word of God" for Irenaeus normally means Christ, the Eternal Word, and if that is the meaning here, we have a possible explanation of what the heavenly reality in the quotation below is. Other possibilities besides the heavenly Logos for this heavenly reality would be the body and blood of the risen Christ, or the Holy Spirit, but these seem to me less likely.

17. Hence, there could be no change in the substance of the elements, or else his argument that our real physical bodies are raised would be compromised; everything depends on the physical elements being what they appear to be, nourishing food and

and the elements are sanctified by a prayer of thanksgiving (*Adv. haer.* 4.18.6). These similarities indicate that Irenaeus is acquainted with and developing Justin's thought. His statements, furthermore, make clear which option in the interpretation of Justin's ambiguous language he would take: the prayer to God adds a new dimension to the material elements; now they have a heavenly as well as an earthly reality. The partaking of this heavenly reality through the earthly brings eternal life. Nowhere does Irenaeus make a literal identification of the elements with the body and blood; his point is that Christ by acknowledging material elements in relation to his body and blood was affirming that they too were material realities. I would contend that for Irenaeus, there is not a conversion or change in the elements[18] but a new reality is added to them by reason of their consecration through calling upon God.

There were two other ways in which early Christian authors expressed the relationship between the bread and wine of the eucharist and the body and blood of Christ: in Greek by the word σύμβολον, as represented by Clement of Alexandria, and in Latin by the word *figura*, as represented by Tertullian.

Clement of Alexandria[19] makes such allusive reference to the eucharist in talking about other matters that his thought is difficult to interpret.[20] I want here only to note his use of the words "symbol" and "allegory" to describe the bread and wine of communion. "The holy Scripture named wine a mystical symbol of the holy blood" (*Paed.* 2.2.32). He interprets the eating the flesh and drinking the blood of Jesus in John 6:53–56 as spoken "through symbols" and "allegories" about the partaking of faith and the promises, of the Holy Spirit, and of the divine Word (*Paed.* 1.6.38, 43, 47).[21] Later he makes more explicit reference to the eucharist:

---

drink. Fragment 13 (Harvey, 2.482–83) affirms that the "divine communion" is the blood and body of Christ but not "true blood and flesh." This extract that Oecumenius attributes to Irenaeus appears to be based on the Letter of the Churches of Vienne and Lyons (Eusebius, *H.E.* 5.1.14–17).

18. He does report with scorn the quite literal changes in the elements effected as if through magic by the Gnostic Marcus, in *Adv. haer.* 1.13.2.

19. Osborn, *The Philosophy of Clement of Alexandria*; Wagner, "Clement of Alexandria."

20. Bigg, *The Christian Phitonists of Alexandria*, 103–7; Mehat, "Clement of Alexandria."

21. John 6 was a major source of both a realistic identification of the elements with the flesh and blood of Jesus (as witnessed by the frequent substitution of "flesh" for "body" in comments on the Eucharist) and of a symbolic interpretation of the benefits derived from participation.

> The blood of the Lord is twofold. There is his fleshly blood by which we are ransomed from corruption; and there is the spiritual blood by which we are anointed. And this is to drink the blood of Jesus, to partake of the Lord's immortality. The Spirit is the strength of the Word, as blood is of the flesh. By analogy, as the wine is mixed with water, so the Spirit is with man; the mixed wine and water nourishes to faith, and the Spirit leads to immortality. And the mixing of both the drink and the Word together is called eucharist, a praiseworthy and beautiful grace. Those partaking of it in faith are sanctified in body and soul. (*Paed.* 2.2.19–20)

Thus does Clement in his own highly symbolic style describe Irenaeus's earthly and heavenly realities.[22] By drinking of the eucharistic wine, a person partakes of the Lord's Spirit and so of his immortality.

Tertullian of Carthage, the formative influence on ecclesiastical Latin,[23] speaks more expressly than Clement about the Lord's Supper but again only in discussing other subjects.[24] His viewpoint seems to be the same as his predecessors we have considered. He alludes to the physical properties of the wine that Jesus consecrated as a memorial of his blood (*An.* 17.13), yet he expresses the concern felt when the wine or bread of the eucharist falls to the ground (*Cor.* 3). Realist language is joined to a spiritual benefit: "The flesh feeds on the body and blood of Christ," but the soul is nourished (*Res.* 8.3; *Pud.* 9.16).

In opposing Marcion, Tertullian had anti-Docetic concerns similar to those of Irenaeus, as shown in his use of the term *figura*.

> Taking bread and distributing it to his disciples, Jesus made it his own body by saying, "This is my body," that is a "figure of my body." On the other hand, there would not have been a figure unless there was a true body. (*Adv. Marc.* 4.40.3–6; cf. 5.8)

---

22. In Clement's collection of *Excerpts from Theodotus* 82, we read, "And the bread and oil are sanctified by the power of the Name, and they are not the same as they appeared to be when they were received, but they have been transformed by power into spiritual power. Thus, the water, also, both in exorcism and baptism, not only keeps off evil, but gives sanctification as well" (Casey, *The Excerpta ex Theodoto of Clement of Alexandria*, 88–91). This statement could have been subscribed to by Justin and Irenaeus; it contrasts with the kind of change expressed in the fourth century by Cyril, Gregory of Nyssa, and Ambrose.

23. Barnes, *Tertullian*; Sider, *Ancient Rhetoric and the Art of Tertullian*; Sider, "Tertullian."

24. Hitchcock, "Tertullian's Views on the Sacrament of the Lord's Supper"; V. Saxer, "Tertullian"; Ferguson, *Early Christians Speak*, 115.

Figura has a prophetic or typical meaning for Tertullian. The bread of the eucharist has the same significance as the words of the prophets: both proclaim or point to the body of the cross (*Adv. Marc.* 3. 1 9.3–4). A "figure" is not the same as something else; the symbolic or figurative meaning is confirmed by Tertullian's parallel use of image, allegory, and enigma. Nevertheless, there is a correspondence between a figure and what it reflects. "The bread . . . represents [Jesus'] own proper body" (*Adv. Marc.* 1.14.3). As the passage quoted from book 4 argues, "A phantom is incapable of a figure"; or to paraphrase, "Without a substance, there is no shadow."

Protestants have tended to make symbol mean "bare symbol" and figure mean "mere figure." Catholics and some others have stressed the connection in ancient thought (especially in Platonism) between symbol and reality; the symbol partakes of or participates in the nature of what is symbolized. Or from the perspective of Plato's theory of ideas, the reality manifests itself in material imitations. The usages of Clement and Tertullian lie somewhere between these interpretations. The philosophical language offered an approximation to the Jewish idea, so it presented a means of communication while at the same time carrying the potential of misunderstanding. The symbol or figure carries with it the reality of which it is a symbol; in this instance the symbol makes the body present and effective.

Certainly if one read the statements of Justin, Irenaeus, Clement, and Tertullian as a Platonist, attention was called to the heavenly reality behind the earthly manifestations. But the way was also opened for a more realistic understanding of the presence of the body and blood. That feature would have been preserved by the Jewish and early Christian emphasis on historical events. Some precision for their understanding is given if the Alexandrians and North Africans were trying to express in philosophical or legal-rhetorical language some grasp of the biblical-Jewish language of religious reality. The biblical-Jewish realism concerning the present benefits of historical events was combined with philosophical-Greek realism about ideas and their material manifestations. I think this best accounts for the dual language of symbolism and realism found in Christian thought about the Lord's Supper, often in the same writers.[25]

---

25. In a similar way Crockett, *Eucharist: Symbol of Transformation*, 80–81, says the distinction between a "realist" and "symbolic" understanding would have had no meaning in the early church, for whom the symbol is participating in the reality rather than just representing it. Because the symbol is the reality, yet distinguished from it, both kinds of language could be used interchangeably (87).

FOURTH CENTURY

Third-century thinkers sometimes expressed themselves in the language of figure or symbol that we have described; sometimes they employed the language of simple realism. At what point these statements are to be taken at face value is not clear. In the fourth century, however, we know that thought moved to a new level of explicitness, because of the use of the language of a conversion of the elements to express the real presence. The future of eucharistic theology belonged to this language of conversion.

The explicit language of conversion occurs first in Greek authors of the fourth century. Cyril, bishop of Jerusalem (ca. 349–78),[26] explained to the newly baptized the ceremonies they had experienced. He first speaks in general terms without detail:

> The bread and wine of the eucharist before the holy invocation of the worshipful Trinity was simple bread and wine, but when the invocation is done, the bread becomes the body of Christ and wine the blood of Christ. (*Catech. mys.* 1.7)

This statement does not reveal how realistic a content Cyril intends. But he later affirms that the elements in some sense really are the body and blood (*Catech. mys.* 4.1), the evidence of the senses to the contrary (*Catech. mys.* 4.6), and compares the wine becoming blood to the water becoming wine in Jesus' miracle at Cana (John 2:1–11; *Catech. mys.* 4.2). In further elaboration, he distinguishes between the elements and the gift but declares a real partaking of Christ:

> In the type (τύπος) of the bread there is given to you the body, and in the type of the wine there is given to you the blood, in order that you may become by partaking of the body and blood of Christ the same body and blood with him. For even so we become bearers of Christ since his body and blood are distributed in our members. (*Catech. mys.* 4.3)

Then he explains that in response to the invocation of God, the Holy Spirit effects a real change:

> We beseech the loving God to send forth the Holy Spirit upon what is offered in order that he may make the bread the body of Christ and the wine the blood of Christ. For whatever the Holy

---

26. Norris, "Cyril of Jerusalem."

Spirit touches he sanctifies and changes (μεταβάλλω). (*Catech. mys.* 5.7)[27]

The nature of the change is still not spelled out; Cyril only says that there is a reality present now that was not present before—the body and blood of Christ. It could be a functional change, but I suspect he means something more. At least, later thinkers, as we shall see, took the language of change more literally.

The language of change became more explicit with reference to the elements in Gregory, bishop of Nyssa (d. ca. 395).[28] Gregory might seem to be moving in the biblical frame of thought when he describes the working of the Spirit with material elements and describes how benediction consecrates something to the service of God. He illustrates the working of the Spirit through common water in baptism by the way an ordinary table of stone becomes an altar, common bread and wine become the body of Christ, oil becomes sacramental, and a man by ordination is set apart from the mass of men (*Bapt. Chr.*, in *Gregorii Nysseni Opera*, 9, 225).

Yet he means something more than biblical consecration, for he speaks of a transformation and gives examples of real change occurring, both in the Bible and in nature. Elsewhere he applies this idea of change in the elements expressly to the Lord's Supper. After noting that when Christ ate bread it was transformed (μεταποιέω) into his body and quoting 1 Timothy 4:5, Gregory affirms the effects on believers:

> He disseminates himself through that flesh whose substance comes from bread and wine in everyone who believes in the economy of grace, blending himself with the bodies of believers, as if by this union with what is immortal, man too may become a partaker in incorruption. He gives these things by the power of the benediction through which he transelements (μεταστοιχειόω) the natural quality of these visible things to that immortal thing. (*Or. catech.* 37)

Gregory was a pioneer here in expressing a thought that was to have an abundant future.[29]

Justin Martyr did not say that the bread and wine were "converted into" but that they "are" the body and blood. Irenaeus then spoke of a

27. The translations from Cyril and Gregory of Nyssa below are taken from Ferguson, *Early Christians Speak*, 108–9; briefly discussed on 116.

28. Balas, "Gregory of Nyssa."

29. John of Damascus in his presentation of the orthodox position on the Eucharist, in *Fide orth.* 4.13, borrows extensively from Gregory of Nyssa.

heavenly reality added to the material elements. Cyril and Gregory next spoke of a change in the elements, illustrating it but not explaining philosophically how it came about.[30]

This idea of a change in the elements was introduced from the East into the West by Ambrose, bishop of Milan (374–397).[31] He is the major representative of the realist strand of thought in the West, as Augustine, bishop of Hippo (395–430)[32] is of the symbolist strand of thought. Yet both have statements that sound like the other.[33] This fact indicates that thinkers at that time did not fit into the neat categories refined by later thought.

Ambrose affirms that John 6 means that we receive the Lord's "true flesh . . . and true blood"; lest this literalism be offensive, he also explains, "You receive the sacrament in a similitude, but truly obtain the grace and virtue [or power] of the nature." His addition, "You who receive his flesh partake of his divine essence in that food" (*De sacram.* 6.1.3, 4),[34] shows that the eucharistic food has a spiritual character. The sign and the reality are treated as identical so that the physical and the spiritual eating are united.[35]

The bread and wine become a sacrament by consecration, and that is effected by the working of the words of Christ. Ambrose declares that the

---

30. The same situation obtained in the arguments from the Eucharist in the fifth-century christological controversies. Both Cyril of Alexandria and Nestorius believed in a conversion of the elements without defining the manner of the change. But they drew opposite conclusions as to the relation of the divine and human in Christ. See Chadwick, "Eucharist and Christology in the Nestorian Controversy." Crockett, *Eucharist: Symbol of Transformation*, 61–62, notes the shift to the language of transformation in the liturgies of the fourth to sixth centuries. The Liturgy of St. John Chrysostom uses the language of "make" and "change" (μεταβάλλω) with reference to the elements, instead of the language of «consecration» or «epiphany» as in the earlier liturgies.

31. Swift, "Ambrose."

32. Miles, "Augustine." The literature on Augustine is enormous; for an introduction to him, see Battenhouse, ed., *A Companion to the Study of St. Augustine*.

33. For the interpretation of Ambrose and Augustine, I follow Dugmore, "Sacrament and Sacrifice in the Early Fathers"; see also Crockett, *Eucharist: Symbol of Transformation*, 88–98. The characterization of the two positions as realist and symbolic follows MacDonald, ed., *The Evangelical Doctrine of Holy Communion*; Ambrose and Augustine are discussed in chap. 2.

34. Doubts about the authorship of this work appear to "have been laid to rest" (Quasten and Di Berardino, *Patrology*, vol. 4, 172).

35. Theodoret, *Eccl. Hist.* 5.17, quotes Ambrose as speaking in terms of literal realism when he denies the sacrament to the emperor Theodosius for the massacre at Thessalonica. These words reflect Ambrose's thought, since Theodoret himself often speaks in symbolical terms.

priest uses the words of Christ himself at the Last Supper, which he quotes. Then he explains:

> Before consecration, it is bread, but when the words of Christ have been added, it is the body of Christ . . . And before the words of Christ, the cup is full of wine and water. When the words of Christ have operate*d, then is made the blood which redeems the people. (De sacram.* 4.5.23)[36]

Ambrose follows Cyril and Gregory in speaking of a change in the nature of the elements. But once more, there is an element of ambiguity for the modern reader. The flesh and blood of John 6:54 are the "merits and power of the Lord's death." "Now we, as often as we receive the sacramental elements, which by the mysterious efficacy of holy prayer are transfigured into the flesh and blood, 'do show the Lord's death'" (*De fide* 4.10.125). The significance of figure for Ambrose would seem to be still that of Tertullian, for he can speak of the manna in the wilderness and other experiences of Israel as a figure of the body of the Lord, and "the reality is better than the figure" (*Mys.* 8.49).[37]

At other times, Ambrose can speak of a metabolism that concerns the elements themselves, not simply their effects or power.[38] By a blessing "even nature itself is changed," as may be seen in Old Testament miracles of transformation. The words of the Savior are even more powerful, so as even "to make out of nothing what was not" as well as to change natures. A new reality is added to the elements. The body of Christ was not present before the consecration, but after the consecration it is, and that body is identical with the body born of Mary. But Ambrose then calls attention once more to the spiritual aspect. "Therefore it is not bodily food, but spiritual." This declaration follows from the teaching that "the body of Christ is the body of a divine Spirit, because Christ is a Spirit." The purpose of the bread and wine is to nourish and strengthen the church: "With these sacraments, therefore, Christ feeds his church."[39]

---

36. The passage begins at Ambrose, *Sacrum.* 4.4.13.

37. Similarly, the eucharistic sacrifice is called an 'image of truth," an image of future reality (Ambrose, *Enarrationes in Is.* 38.25).

38. The following sentences summarize some thoughts from *De mys.* 9.50–58, where the language is more precise than in *De sacram.*

39. Cf. *Enarrationes in Psalmos* 118, *Serm.* 18.26: "Christ is food to me; Christ is drink to me; the flesh of God is food to me, and the blood of God is drink to me . . . Christ is ministered to me daily."

Ambrose can be read as trying to elaborate the language of Irenaeus about two realities, earthly and heavenly, or as anticipating later language about a physical change in the elements. There are both components to his thought. He probably saw them as no different, for it is likely that by the language of physical change, he was making more vivid the presence of the spiritual blessings.

Later readers of Ambrose noted as distinctive in him the idea of a change in the elements effected by the repetition of the words of Christ at the Last Supper. They found in Augustine, on the other hand, an emphasis on the symbolic and spiritual aspects of the Lord's Supper. Nevertheless, there is once more a combination of language about a real presence and about a symbolism, so that both Roman Catholic and Protestant interpreters have claimed Augustine as supporting their views. Augustine, true to his Platonic philosophical heritage, put more emphasis on the spiritual reality than on the material sign, but true to his North African theological heritage, he took the material elements seriously.

Sometimes Augustine speaks in the ordinary realist language without explanation: "That bread you see on the altar, sanctified by the word of God, is the body of Christ. That cup, or rather what the cup contains, sanctified by the word of God, is the blood of Christ" (*Serm.* 227).[40] He anticipates the language of later Scholastic theologians, but I assume without their meaning: "The appearance is the same, but not the substance" (*Sermo Morin* 7). Augustine also connects the practice of adoring the Lord's Supper by bowing before it to the reality of Christ's flesh in it. He explains that Christ took flesh and "gave that very flesh to us to eat for our salvation; and no one eats that flesh unless he has first worshipped."[41] He continues, however, as an interpretation of John 6:54 and 63, by having Jesus say the following:

> Understand spiritually what I have said; you are not to eat this body that you see; nor to drink that blood that they who will crucify me will pour forth. I have commended to you a certain mystery; spiritually understood, it will give life. Although it must be visibly celebrated, yet it must be spiritually understood.

---

40. Cf. *Serm.* 234.2, "Not all bread, but only that which receives the blessing of Christ becomes the body of Christ"; *Sermo Denys* 6, "Add the word [prayer] and it becomes something very different"; *Trin.* 3.4.10 refers to consecration by "mystic prayer" and the Spirit of God working invisibly.

41. *In Psalm.* 98.8 (Engl. 99.8); cf. *In Psalm.* 33:1, 3, and 11 (Engl. 34), where Augustine speaks of Christ carrying his own body.

This latter statement agrees with Augustine's commentary on John 6, where he declares, "Believe, and you have eaten" (*In euang. Ioh.* 25.2). Or again, "This then is the eating of that meat and the drinking of that drink: to dwell in Christ and to have. Christ dwelling in him" (*In euang. Ioh.* 26.18).[42] These interpretations accord with and result from Augustine's understanding of a sacrament: "One thing is a sacrament [the sign]; another the virtue [power] of the sacrament" (*In euang. Ioh.* 26.11).[43] This definition he applies to John 6:50, "so that one may eat of it and not die":

> That which pertains to the virtue of the sacrament, not that which pertains to the visible sacrament: he that eats inwardly not outwardly; he that eats in the heart, not he that presses with his teeth. (*In euang. Ioh.* 26.12)

In another context, Augustine uses the word sacrament expressly of the Lord's Supper in comparison to baptism: "As, then, in a certain manner the sacrament of the body of Christ is the body of Christ, and the sacrament of the blood of Christ is the blood of Christ, so the sacrament of faith [baptism] is faith" (*Ep.* 98.9).[44] In addition to the words sign and sacrament, Augustine could also use the word *figure* with reference to the elements. He says that at the Last Supper, Jesus gave a *figuram* (*In Ps.* 3.1).

Augustine sometimes interpreted the symbolism of the bread and wine with reference to the unity of the church. Participation in the elements was a sign of incorporation into the mystical body of Christ, the church.[45] This understanding, also based on biblical language, was an extension of the symbolism of the body of Christ and was not itself a contradiction of a real presence.

I conclude that Dugmore's description of Augustine's doctrine is accurate: For Augustine, the sign is distinct from the reality, but the reality is

---

42. *Sermo Mai* 129 refers to eating Christ not just sacramentally but by abiding in him. Cf. *Doct. Chr.* 3.16.24, where John 6:53 is interpreted as a "figure" that we should have a share in the Lord's suffering.

43. Cf. *Serm.* 272, "These things, my brothers, are called sacraments because in them one thing is seen but another is understood. What is seen has a physical appearance, but what is understood has spiritual fruit."

44. Augustine's fullest definition of a sacrament occurs in reference to the salt given to catechumens: "The signs of divine things are, it is true, things visible, but the invisible things themselves are also honored in them, and that species which is then sanctified by the blessing is therefore not to he regarded merely in the way in which it is regarded in common use" (*Catech. rud.* 26.50).

45. *Serm.* 57.7 [7.7]; 272; *Sermo Denys* 3; *Sermo Morin* 7 ("sacrament of unity"); *In euang. Ioh.* 26.13.

conveyed by and through the sign. Augustine believed in a symbolism of the visible sign and the realism of the supernatural invisible gift.[46] There is one passage that comes the closest to bringing these two ideas together and seems to sum up his thought: "The body and blood of Christ will be life to each one, when that which is received visibly in the sacrament is in very truth spiritually eaten, spiritually drunk" (*Serm.* 131.1). The influence of Augustine maintained a dynamic alternative to the popular realism in medieval thought.

Ambrose and Augustine were major influences on the eucharistic theology in the West. That they themselves did not see symbolism and realism as opposed suggests to me that the realism was not what it became later. Indeed, each was interpreted in terms of the other. So, at times the emphasis was on Ambrose's metabolic realism; sometimes more emphasis was laid on Augustine's symbolic realism.

NINTH CENTURY

The succeeding centuries saw a growth of popular literalism about the real presence of the body and blood in the Lord's Supper. Authors sometimes made distinctions between the sign and the reality; often they did not. The next major period of writing on the subject of the Lord's Supper came in the ninth century in Carolingian Gaul. Many writers contributed to the discussion of the subject, including Rhabanus Maurus, Gottschalk, and John Scotus Erigena. The major alternatives of interpretation were voiced by Paschasius Radbertus and Ratramnus.[47] Quotations from Ambrose and Augustine recur in the writings of both men. The two "R's" assumed that the two "A's" agreed. However, Radbertus used Ambrose to interpret Augustine, and Ratramnus used Augustine to interpret Ambrose.

Radbertus was a monk at Corbie near Amiens (and its abbot from 844 to 853). His treatise, *On the Body and Blood of the Lord*, opened the discussion and indeed was the first treatise we have devoted to the eucharist.[48] It was written about 831 and then revised and sent to the Frankish King Charles II the Bald in 844. There followed a flurry of writing on the subject in the revived intellectual life of the Carolingian renaissance.

---

46. "Sacrament and Sacrifice," 24–37, esp. 33–34.

47. Brief but helpful summaries in Harnack, *History of Dogma*, vol. 5, 312–22; and Pelikan, *The Growth of Medieval Theology*, 74–80.

48. My quotations are taken from the selections translated by McCracken, *Early Medieval Theology*, 94–108.

Radbertus united the Augustinian with the Ambrosian-Greek view, borrowing the language of earlier writers but understanding the presence of Christ in the elements literally. Radbertus had two overruling points to make: (1) There is a real presence of the body and blood of Christ in the elements. (2) Body and blood in the eucharist are identical with the body and blood of the man who walked the earth and died on the cross.

For Radbertus, the appearance to the senses of the consecrated bread and wine is a symbol of Christ's body, but the essence of the consecrated elements is the true historical body itself.

> Because it is not right to devour Christ with the teeth, he willed in the mystery that this bread and wine be created truly his flesh and blood through consecration by the power of the Holy Spirit; . . . as from the Virgin through the Spirit true flesh is created without union of sex, so through the same, out of the substance of bread and wine, the same body and blood of Christ may be mystically consecrated. (*Corp.* 4.1)

Thus there is both a reality and a figure, because the appearances of bread and wine remained.

> He is speaking [John 6:53] about no other flesh than the true flesh and the true blood, that is, in a mystical sense. And because the sacrament is mystical, we cannot deny the figure, but if it is a figure, one must ask how it can be truth . . . That sacrament of faith is rightly called truth; truth, therefore, when the body and blood of Christ is created by the power of the Spirit in his word out of the substance of bread and wine; but a figure when, through the agency of the priest at the altar, outwardly performing another thing, in memory of his sacred Passion, the Lamb is daily sacrificed as he was once for all. (*Corp.* 4.1)

Radbertus used *figura* in the sense of "outward appearance" and *veritas* for "what faith teaches."

> It is rightly called both the truth and a figure, so that it is a figure or character of truth because it is outwardly sensed. Truth however, is anything rightly understood or believed inwardly concerning this mystery. (*Corp.* 4.2)

For Radbertus, it was important that Christ did not say, "This is a figure of my body," but, "This is my body." He made two fundamental affirmations: (1) At every eucharist there is a new creation of the body of Christ. (2) There is a complete identification of the sacramental body with the historical body. Through the agency of the priest in repeating Christ's words, the consecration by the Holy Spirit (*Corp.* 4.3) creates the sacrament of his flesh:

> No wonder that the Spirit which without seed created the man Christ in the womb of the Virgin, from the substance of bread and wine daily creates the flesh and blood of Christ by invisible power through the sanctification of his sacrament, though outwardly understood by neither sight nor taste. (*Corp.* 3.4)

Furthermore, there is more than an analogy between the creation of the body of Christ in the womb and the creation of the body on the altar. It is the same body that is created. Such is affirmed near the beginning of the treatise:

> These [bread and wine] must be believed to be fully, after the consecration, nothing but Christ's flesh and blood . . . And, to put it in more miraculous terms, nothing different, of course, from what was born of Mary, suffered on the cross, and rose again from the tomb. (*Corp.* 1.2)

The reader may have noticed how prominent the Holy Spirit is in Radbertus's exposition, a feature usually associated with Greek thought on the eucharist. It is important, also, to note the centrality of faith for Radbertus. The sacrament presupposes faith and is meant to arouse faith; hence, the physical appearance remains so that the body is hidden.

> He has left us this sacrament, a visible figure and character of flesh and blood, so that through them our soul and our flesh are richly nourished for grasping things invisible and spiritual by faith. (*Corp.* 4.2)

The believer alone receives the *virtus sacramenti*, the power of the sacrament. The unbeliever eats for condemnation, but the believer receives the body and blood for salvation.

> They all eat, without distinction, what they often receive as sacraments of the altar. They receive them, of course, but one man spiritually eats the flesh of Christ and drinks his blood; another man, however, does not, although he may seem to receive the wafer from the hand of the priest. (*Corp.* 6.2)

Radbertus stressed in his exposition the salvific purpose. "Therefore, the true flesh and blood of Christ, which anyone worthily eats and drinks, have eternal life abiding in them" (*Corp.* 1.5). "We do not spiritually take the flesh and blood for the sake of this life so that we may not die temporally, but for the sake of life eternal" (*Corp.* 5.2). This theme from John 6 may have contributed as much to the popularity among theologians of realist language about the body and blood as the literal reading of John 6 itself did.

We conclude this survey of Radbertus with a passage setting forth his synthesis of what a sacrament is.

> They are called sacraments either because they are secret in that in the visible act divinity inwardly accomplished something secretly through the corporeal appearance, or from the sanctifying consecration, because the Holy Spirit, remaining in the body of Christ, latently accomplishes for the salvation of the faithful all these mystical sacraments under the cover of things visible. (*Corp.* 3.1)

Many who disagreed with Radbertus might have subscribed to this statement. The difference was that Radbertus had a realistic understanding of the presence of Christ in the eucharist.

Ratramnus, another monk at Corbie, represents a different way of looking at what happens and what is involved in the sacrament of the altar.[49] Charles the Bald requested his views on the eucharist. Ratramnus responded with a treatise bearing the same title as Radbertus's, *On the Body and Blood of the Lord,* probably written shortly after 844.[50]

The king raised questions concerning the two points that were fundamental to Radbertus's exposition: (1) What is the nature of the presence of Christ in the elements?[51] (2) What is the relation of the eucharistic body to the historical body?[52] Ratramnus concludes,

> It has been most clearly shown that the bread which is called Christ's body, and the cup which is called Christ's blood, is a figure, because it is a mystery, and that there is no small difference

---

49. Fahey, *The Eucharistic Teaching of Ratramn of Corbie.*

50. I quote the English translation of McCracken, *Early Medieval Theology,* 118-47.

51. "Whether it contains some hidden element which becomes patent only to the eyes of faith, or whether without concealment of any mystery the appearance of the body is seen outwardly in what the mind's eyes see inwardly" (*Corp.* 5). If meant to reflect Radbertus's view, this is not a fair representation, but it may he an accurate statement of how the king interpreted him.

52. "Whether it is that body which was born of Mary, suffered, died, and was buried, and which, rising again and ascending into heaven, sits on the right hand of the Father" (*Corp.* 5).

between the body which exists through the mystery and that which suffered, was buried, and rose again. (*Corp.* 97)[53]

Ratramnus interpreted Ambrose as teaching not an actual but a sacramental presence of Christ. As human beings are body and soul, so the consecrated elements have an outward and inward aspect that nourish respectively the body and soul of the recipient.

> They are called Christ's blood and body, because they are received, not as what they outwardly seem, but as what inwardly, through the agency of the divine Spirit, they have been made ... Just as the substance of this visible bread and wine nourishes and stimulates the outer man, so the Word of God, who is living Bread, refreshes faithful souls that share in it. (*Corp.* 43)

The emphasis on the dual realities is a position that may he described as dynamic symbolism. There is, as for Augustine, a symbolism of the elements and a realism of the spiritual benefits. "In one respect they are what they outwardly signify, and in another they are what they effect inwardly and invisibly" (*Corp.* 47). The change is not in appearance or substance but in effective power.

> Christ's body and blood which are received in the mouth of the faithful in the church are figures according to their visible appearance; but according to their invisible substance, that is the power of the divine Word, they truly exist as Christ's body and blood. Therefore, with respect to visible creation, they feed the body; with reference to the power of a stronger substance, they feed and sanctify the souls of the faithful. (*Corp.* 49)

A superficial reading might not see a great difference in Ratramnus from some of Radbertus's statements, especially in the use of *figura*. However, Ratramnus normally made a different distinction between *figura* and *veritas* from the one Radbertus made. *Veritas*, or "truth," for Ratramnus is "representation of clear fact," or what is perceived by the senses; *figura* or figure usually refers to the "intent [or reality] under some sort of veil" that may be seen by the eye of faith.[54]

Drawing on Augustine's distinction between "sacraments" and "the things of which they are sacraments," Ratramnus offers an illustration. The giving of the name of the Lord's body and blood to the "sacraments of

---

53. Cf. *Corp.* 69 for the body of Christ that suffered as different from the "body which daily in the mystery of Christ's Passion is celebrated by the faithful."

54. *Corp.* 7–10; on "figure," cf. 91.

these two things" may be compared to the name Pascha for the annual celebration of the Lord's death and resurrection. Those things happened only once, yet the same name is used for the annual remembrance. In the same way, when the sacraments of the Lord's passion are celebrated, the name body and blood is employed. There is a resemblance, but not an identity.[55]

Within this framework of thought, the similarities with Radbertus are to be seen in their true light. The objective efficacy of the sacraments was due to the spiritual presence of the body and blood.[56] And this, no less than for Radbertus,[57] requires the exercise of faith: "They [the sacramental body and blood] are commonly called sacraments because under cover of corporeal objects the divine power secretly dispenses the salvation of those who receive it by faith" (*Corp.* 48).

The treatises by Radbertus and Ratramnus sharpened the issue by more fully presenting two different ways of looking at the sacrament: a change in the elements versus a change in their effects. Radbertus, however, offered no explanation of how the sacramental change in the elements could be understood (other than to state it was a mystery). Nevertheless, the future belonged to him. His viewpoint was dominant by the end of the tenth century.

ELEVENTH CENTURY

There was doctrinal disagreement over the Lord's Supper in the ninth century but not much evidence of real controversy. The eleventh century was different, for it saw genuine controversy—theological, conciliar, and political. The occasion was a letter in 1049 from Berengar, archdeacon and treasurer of the cathedral at Angers and later scholasticus (or master of the schools) at Tours, to Lanfranc, prior at Bec and later archbishop of Canterbury.[58] The ensuing controversy was the first in which dialectical

---

55. *Corp.* 37–38.

56. "This [change] was done figuratively, since under cover of the corporeal bread and of the corporeal wine, Christ's spiritual body and spiritual blood do exist" (*Corp.* 16). Cf. the reference to "the spiritual body" in the Lord's Supper (*Corp.* 62).

57. Ratramnus would say more so, for he sees the realist interpretation as removing the need for faith (*Corp.* 11).

58. A Protestant perspective by MacDonald, *Berengar and the Reform of Sacramental Doctrine*; Roman Catholic by Sheedy, T*he Eucharistic Controversy of the Eleventh Century;* balanced surveys by Southern, "Lanfranc of Bec and Berengar of Tours"; and J. Pelikan, T*he Growth of Medieval Theology*, 184–204; Macy, T*he Theologies of the Eucharist*, 1–72.

reasoning shaped by Aristotelian logic assumed a formative place. The outcome was the beginning of a philosophical explanation for the real physical presence that had been lacking from the presentations by Ambrose and Radbertus.[59] This explanation came to be formulated in terms of the Aristotelian distinction between substance (the essential underlying reality of what something truly is) and accidents (the thing's nonessential external appearances). This development was a response to dialectical arguments against the possibility of a real physical presence of Christ in the elements.

Roman Catholics charge Berengar with being an innovator because he placed dialectical reasoning at the foundation of his theology instead of starting with traditional theology. Protestants defend him by seeing him as part of a tradition that reached back through Ratramnus to Augustine. The main surviving source for Berengar's eucharistic teaching is *De sacra coena* (On the Holy Supper), written 1068–1070.

As first of all a grammarian, Berengar drew on grammar and logic to argue against the popular realism with regard to the Lord's Supper. We will give some samples of his reasoning that give the flavor of his use of both verbal and physical arguments.[60]

(1) Grammarians of the time said that a pronoun signified things in their substance only; nouns referred to substance and accidents. Hence, when Jesus said, "*This* is my body," he was referring to bread in its substance.

(2) No proposition can stand if the subject is denied, destroyed, or contradicted by the predicate. "This bread is the body of Christ" would be self-contradictory if it implied the substance of the subject of the sentence ceased to exist; the bread and wine must still exist or the proposition is false.[61]

---

59. "In the course of the Middle Ages, the Platonic dialectic between symbol and reality was obscured and the salvation-historical perspective gave way to a greater preoccupation with metaphysical questions" (Crockett, *Eucharist: Symbol of Transformation*, 87). The rediscovered philosophy of Aristotle provided a new way of looking at the problem and of explaining a change in the elements themselves.

60. Whalen, T*he Authentic Doctrine of the Eucharist*, 5–6, summarizes some of these.

61. These two arguments are explained by Southern, "Lanfranc of Bec and Berengar of Tours," 43–45.

The Lord's Supper in Church History

(3) "Qualities" or "accidents" of something cannot exist apart from their substance, and any change in substance would involve a change in its accidental qualities (the first use of this terminology so characteristic of later Scholasticism).

(4) A change into a real bodily presence is contrary to the senses.

(5) The resurrection body, since it is impassible and incorruptible, is incapable of being handled, broken into little pieces, and chewed.

(6) The doctrine of a real presence of the body and blood involved two bodies of Christ (one in heaven and one on earth).[62]

(7) A change into the body and blood is contrary to nature, for it requires either the breaking up or annihilation of what was originally there (denied by the senses) or the creation of a substance that had not existed before (contradicted by the teaching itself). The whole doctrine, therefore, was impossible and blasphemous.

Although Berengar often does not allow any form of real presence in his attacks on the current teaching, he does sometimes express himself in more positive ways. The only conversion that he allows, however, is of the spiritual significance of the elements, that is their value or efficacy. Moreover, he consistently maintained the distinction between realities that are spiritual and material, divine and earthly. A balanced statement of his positive teaching is found in the following quotation:

> The eucharistic sacrifice has two constituents, the sacrament, which is visible, and that to which the sacrament refers (the *res sacrarnenti*), which is invisible. The latter is the body of Christ. If it were before our eyes, it would be invisible, but being exalted into heaven and sitting at the right hand of the Father "until the time of the restoration of all things," . . . it cannot be summoned down from heaven, as the person of Christ consists of God and man.[63]

Although repeatedly condemned by councils, made to read a grossly materialistic oath in 1059, and finally made to submit to the doctrine of his opponents before Pope Gregory VII in 1079, Berengar was never excommunicated or officially declared a heretic. The defeat of Berengar limited

---

62. Macy, *The Theologies of the Eucharist*, 39.
63. Gibson, *Lanfranc of Bec*, 92.

the range of options in eucharistic thought but did not establish a single acceptable approach to the sacrament of the altar in Catholic thought.[64]

Apart from forcing his opponents to clarify their own views, Berengar made two contributions to the development of Catholic thought. His definition of a sacrament as a "visible form of invisible grace" became standard; and his use of Aristotelian categories of substance and accidents helped establish these concepts.[65]

Lanfranc was one of Berengar's principal opponents.[66] He championed with modifications the realistic interpretation of Radbertus. He recognized, however, that simply repeating the traditional realism was not sufficient to answer the objections, so he attempted to meet Berengar on his own grounds and provide a dialectical justification for the doctrine of Radbertus. In his work, *On the Body and Blood of the Lord*, he put forward in effect the theory of transubstantiation, that the substance of bread and wine changes while the accidents remain, but without using that terminology. He spoke instead of "to be changed in the essence."

> The material objects on the Lord's Table which God sanctifies through the priest are by the agency of God's power indefinably, wondrously, in a way beyond our understanding, converted to the body of Christ in their being (*converti in essentiam dominici corporis*). Their outward appearance and certain other qualities remain unchanged, so that those who receive them are not shocked by the naked flesh and blood, and so that believers may receive the greater rewards of faith . . .
>
> What we receive is the very body which was born of the virgin, and yet it is not. It *is*, in respects of its being and the characteristics and power of its true nature; it *is not*, if you look at the outward appearance of the bread and wine.[67]

This explanation of a change of the essence pointed toward the technical language of transubstantiation.

Berengar and Lanfranc themselves both preferred not to use the word substance (*substantia*), but the discussion they initiated was the first major controversy in the medieval Latin West to be dominated by this

---

64. Ibid., 89.
65. Macy, *The Theologies of the Eucharist*, 73ff.
66. Ibid., 40.
67. MacDonald, *Lanfranc*; Gibson, *Lanfranc of Bec*, 63–97, on the controversy with Berengar.

Aristotelian idea.[68] When Platonism was the ruling philosophy, theologians spoke of symbol and reality in explaining the real presence in the eucharist. With the (re)introduction of Aristotelian philosophy, substance and accidents became the way to account for the real presence. The concept of a change in substance made possible the affirmation of a real presence without there being a presence discernible by the senses.

The next century credited Lanfranc with the major part in the overthrow of Berengar's teaching. Yet Humbert, Cardinal-Bishop and papal adviser, appears to have had more to do in an official way with Berengar's condemnation. And Guitmund, a monk at Bec, had a more important role in the literary controversy.

Humbert, it seems, was responsible for drafting the oath of 1059 that many even of Berengar's opponents later found embarrassing. It stated the doctrine of the real presence in a way that was quite literal and even crude, some might say:

> The bread and wine which are laid on the altar are after consecration not only a sacrament but also the true body and blood of our Lord Jesus Christ, and they are physically taken up and broken in the hands of the priest and crushed by the teeth of the faithful, not only sacramentally but in truth.[69]

Berengar later repudiated his repeating this oath.

Guitmund's treatise *On the Reality of the Body and Blood of Christ in the Eucharist* shows him a more subtle thinker than Humbert. As a dialectical realist, he defined the change of the elements in clearer terms than his predecessors. He emphasized faith, but he also raised the doctrine of a metabolism of the elements to a more philosophical plane. He argued that Berengar's position robs human beings of salvation, for they must receive the substance of Christ in order to receive his immortal life. There is the total and complete presence of the body of Christ in the tiniest fragment of the consecrated bread. The eucharist represents a unique kind of change, known only by faith, the change of that which exists into something already in existence.[70] Guitmund did not introduce the wording *substantialiter mutari* ("to be changed in the substance") but he popularized it. This

---

68. Southern, "Lanfranc of Bec and Berengar of Tours," 34, 40.

69. Macy, *The Theologies of the Eucharist*, 36.

70. This represents a fourth kind of change in addition to the three stated by Berengar: a change from being to nonbeing, from nonbeing to being, and being into being.

modification of Lanfranc's formula became the accepted way of describing the sacramental change in the eucharist.

The oath required of Berengar in 1079 contained a variation on the wording of Guitmund:

> The bread and wine which are placed on the altar ... are changed substantially (*substantialiter converti*) into the true and proper vivifying body and blood of Jesus Christ our Lord, and after the consecration there are the true body of Christ which was born of the virgin ... and the true blood of Christ which flowed from his side, not however through sign and in the power of the sacrament, but in their real nature and true substance.[71]

The first uses of *transubstantiation* (*transsubstantiatio*) to express the change in the elements of bread and wine, but not their accidents, occurred about 1140 in a work of Rolando Bandinelli, the future Pope Alexander III, and about the same time in a work attributed to Stephen of Autun.[72]

THIRTEENTH CENTURY

Theologians of the twelfth century elaborated the doctrine of transubstantiation and related it to the rest of Catholic theology. In the thirteenth century, transubstantiation received official approval at the Fourth Lateran Council (1215) under Pope Innocent III, and full theological justification and philosophical explanation in the *Summa theologiae* of Thomas Aquinas.[73] Thus the doctrine of transubstantiation in the technical sense is a latecomer to Catholic theology. It functioned as an explanation of how the change in the elements occurred without affecting the sense perception of that change. The doctrine of the real presence is much older, going back at least to the fourth century, depending on how it is defined. Transubstantiation was a theory of how the real presence of body and blood was accomplished when the bread and wine continued to have the appearance

---

71. Macy, *Theologies of the Eucharist*, 37.

72. Pelikan, *The Growth of Medieval Theology*, 203; McCue, "The Doctrine of Transubstantiation from Berengar through Trent," esp. 387; dependent on Hans Jorissen, *Die Entfaltung der Transsubstantiationslehre*, McCue notes that Bandinelli favored a doctrine of succession rather than transubstantiation (394).

73. During this same period of time, the late-twelfth and early-thirteenth centuries, the words of consecration were fixed. See Pierre-Marie Gy, "Les paroles de la consécration."

of bread and wine. The doctrine, as we shall see more fully in Thomas Aquinas, made use of the Aristotelian distinction between substance and accidents. The substance, what something is in itself, becomes the body and blood of Christ, but the accidental qualities of what one sees, smells, tastes, and feels remain bread and wine.

The word *transubstantiation* occurs in the creed approved at the Fourth Lateran Council (the twelfth ecumenical council of the Western Church) in opposition to the Cathars, or Albigensians, who represented a revival or continuation of the ancient dualist heresy held by the Gnostics, the Manichaeans, and the Bogomils—a heresy that considered matter to be evil. Canon 1 of the council includes in its exposition of the faith the following statement:

> There is one Universal Church of the faithful, outside of which there is absolutely no salvation. In which there is the same priest and sacrifice, Jesus Christ, whose body and blood are truly contained in the sacrament of the altar under the forms of bread and wine; the bread being changed by divine power into the body, and the wine into the blood (*transsubstantiatis pane in corpus et vino in sanguinem potestate divina*), so that to realize the mystery of unity we may receive of Him what He has received of us.[74]

Theologians of the early thirteenth century did not understand this conciliar confession as containing a definitive statement on the mode of the real presence. They read it as a strong rejection of the anti-materialist heresy of the Cathars but not as deciding the manner of the eucharistic presence of the body of Christ.[75]

By the mid-thirteenth century, theologians began to give to the word *transubstantiation* a very exact meaning. Thomas Aquinas, Dominican friar and one of the great theological thinkers of all time, became the most influential defender and exponent of transubstantiation.[76] For him, transubstantiation provided the only way in which the real presence could be explained in such a way as to preserve the physical presence without gross materialism and to preserve the sign quality of the sacrament without a purely symbolic interpretation. This was one example of his theological

---

74. Schroeder, *Disciplinary Decrees of the General Councils*, 238–39.

75. Macy, *The Banquet's Wisdom*, 84, 104, following McCue, "The Doctrine of Transubstantiation," 385–412, esp. 389–403.

76. For a brief introduction, McInerny, "Aquinas, St. Thomas," but not discussing his views on the sacraments.

program of fusing Aristotelian philosophy with Catholic theology: to the eucharistic elements, he applied Aristotle's distinction between *substance* (what a thing is in itself as grasped by the mind) and *accidents* (the appearance of a thing as grasped by the senses). Actually, as his critics later pointed out, Aquinas departed from Aristotle in this instance by allowing the accidents to be separated from their substance.

Aquinas devoted questions 73 to 83 of part 3 of his *Summa theologiae* to the eucharist, and of these question 75 considers "The Change of Bread and Wine into the Body and Blood of Christ," in 8 articles. (1) "Is the body of Christ really and truly in this sacrament, or only in a figurative way or a sign?" He answers, "We could never know by our senses that the real body of Christ and his blood are in this sacrament, but only by our faith which is based on the authority of God."[77] (2) "Does the substance of the bread and wine remain in this sacrament after the consecration?" The position of those who say it does, he replies, "cannot be sustained." (3) The substance of bread and wine, however, is not annihilated or reduced to a more elementary kind of matter. (4) The bread can be turned into the body of Christ; "this conversion, however, is not like any natural change, but it is entirely beyond the powers of nature and is brought about purely by God's power." Such a change is unique and so has "a name proper to itself," "*transubstantiation*."

(5) Logically the accidents of bread and wine ought not to be present, but by God's power they remain when their substance is changed. (6) The substantial form (according to Aristotle's distinction of matter and form) of the bread does not remain after consecration. (7) The change is wrought instantaneously. (8) "The body of Christ comes from the bread." The conversion of the bread into Christ's body has certain resemblances both to creation and to natural change, but in some respects it differs from each of them. Aquinas, furthermore, affirmed that the whole Christ was present in each of the species (bread and wine) and in every part of each species (*Summa*, 3:Q. 76, art. 1–3), a doctrine that gave theological justification to communion in one kind.[78]

The importance of transubstantiation for Aquinas is that it guarantees the presence of Jesus Christ in the sacramental species on the altar. Transubstantiation is independent of place and all local movement, does not modify the quantity of the body of Christ, and is invisible. The great

---

77. I use the translation in *St. Thomas Aquinas Summa Theologiae*, vol. 58, 53–91.

78. Megivern, *Concomitance and Communion*, 237, points out that concomitance is an aspect of the doctrine of the real presence and a consequence of transubstantiation.

miracle of transubstantiation involves other miracles as well: the complete disappearance of the substance of bread and wine, the permanence of the accidents after the disappearance of their substance, the existence of a human body (in this case that of Christ) without any of its natural accidents, and (most extraordinary of all) the apparent "multilocation" of Christ (actually Christ is present in the elements because the accidents are present in him).[79] Throughout his treatment of the change of the elements, to overcome objections Aquinas constantly invoked the infinite power of God. God is able to effect what is contrary to sense and logic.

Aquinas's interpretation was disputed by theologians of the Franciscan order such as Alexander Hales and Bonaventura. One point of difference had to do with the connection between the body of Christ and the accidents of the elements. For Aquinas, the substance of the body of Christ after consecration remained attached to the accidents, whatever happened to the bread and wine; thus if a mouse ate them, the body of Christ was there, although Christ would be unaffected and the mouse would derive no benefit. For the Franciscans, on the other hand, the body of Christ was detachable from the consecrated elements so that only those capable of understanding (not a mouse) and believers (not Jews or pagans) could receive sacramentally.[80]

In the later thirteenth century, the Franciscan Duns Scotus (ca. 1265–1308) considered *consubstantiation* more plausible on philosophical grounds than transubstantiation. (Consubstantiation is the view that the substance of the body and blood of Christ is present along with the substance of the bread and wine in the eucharist.) Duns nevertheless adhered to transubstantiation on the authority of the church, and he appears to have begun the interpretation of the Fourth Lateran Council as a dogmatic affirmation of transubstantiation over against other alternatives.[81] These other alternative approaches continued to be taken by various theologians through the later Middle Ages. Transubstantiation remained one explanation among others but increasingly prevailed until the Council of Trent (1551) condemned those who rejected it.

---

79. Augier, "La transsubstantiation d'après S. Thomas d'Aquin."
80. Macy, *The Banquet's Wisdom*, 109–12.
81. McCue, "The Doctrine of Transubstantiation," 403–7.

SUMMARY

We have traced a long history of interpretation of the Lord's Supper, reflecting in turn the influence of Hebrew commemoration, Platonic ontology, and Aristotelian analysis of substance and accidents. This history has traveled from a Hebrew realism of meaning to a Greek realism of presence, or in other words, adding to a change in significance a change in the elements themselves. Within the context of Greek thought, the philosophical background moved from Plato's idealism of spiritual forms to Aristotle's explanation of material reality. These changes of intellectual climate culminated in the teaching of transubstantiation as an explanation of how the change in the reality of the sacrament of the Lord's Supper occurred.

Discussion continued among Roman Catholic theologians of the late Middle Ages concerning the correct and best way to define and explain the real presence in the Lord's Supper. Yet the stage was now set for the various options to be taken in the age of the Reformation.

The modern preference by some Roman Catholic thinkers for the term "transignification" promises a way to overcome the debates of the Reformation era. The term itself may fairly be interpreted in such a way as to agree with the early understanding of the Lord's Supper which was proposed at the beginning of this essay.

5

A Response to Robin Darling Young on The Eucharist as Sacrifice according to Clement of Alexandria

I APPLAUD THE CHOICE OF Clement of Alexandria as a representative of the eucharistic thought of the early Greek Christian writers. He is a thinker not given enough attention on this topic,[1] and he is one with whom I feel a kinship on many aspects of his attitudes. However, the choice immediately raises questions. There is no passage in Clement that has the Eucharist primarily in view; there are several allusions to it in passages discussing something else. And Clement's allusive style makes associations that a literal-minded person such as I has difficulty following.

Clement was a "man of the church," but I suspect that Professor Young has made him represent a more realistic sacramentalism than is the case. She is right to look for eucharistic associations where these may not be explicit, but may it be that instead of Clement providing the foundation for later Greek patristic thought, Professor Young has read later thought into Clement? I want to sketch a reading of Clement that supplements her treatment and offers an alternative interpretation. It seems to me that Clement assumed the Eucharist as part of Christian practice and used it

---

1. Representative of this neglect is Mazza, *Celebration of the Eucharist*, who does not mention Clement (the liturgical focus of the book does not exempt Tertullian and Cyprian from full treatment). Notable exceptions include Bigg, *The Christian Platonists of Alexandria*, 136–42; Tollinton, *Clement of Alexandria*, vol. 2, 137–39, 147–64; and especially Mehat, "Clement of Alexandria."

as a basis for the spiritual teaching that was his primary concern. Clement understands the Eucharist primarily in terms of receiving the Spirit of Christ through faith and acquiring the heavenly knowledge that leads to immortality.

Clement found Old Testament anticipations of the Eucharist. There is a liturgical allusion to the prayer of consecration in his interpretation of Gen 14:18: "[Melchizedek] gave bread and wine [to Abraham] as sanctified food for a type of the Eucharist."[2] He twice refers to Gen 49:11 ("Binding his foal to the vine and his donkey's colt to the choice vine, he washes his garments in wine and his robe in the blood of grapes"). The first reference gives this interpretation:

> He bound this simple and childlike people to the Logos, whom he allegorizes as a vine. For the vine produces wine, as the Logos does blood, and both are a drink for the welfare of human beings, the wine for the body and the blood for the spirit.[3]

The basis of the statement is obviously the association of wine with the blood of Jesus in the Eucharist, suggested by the parallelism in the biblical text of wine and the blood of the grape. It is characteristic of Clement that he sees a reference to both the physical and the spiritual. The other quotation is incidental to a larger treatment of John 6, to which we shall come shortly. It is to be noted that the most popular Old Testament text applied to the Eucharist in the second century, Mal 1:10–12 (the pure offering made by the Gentiles), is quoted by Clement only once and that without reference to the Eucharist.[4]

There are several incidental references to liturgical practices. Clement mentions standing with head looking up and hands upraised in prayer. This was the common posture of prayer in the ancient world and so not necessarily eucharistic,[5] but was a practice noted by Christian authors specifically in connection with the *sursum corda* preceding the Eucharist.[6] The eucharistic elements were bread (Clement uses the ordinary Greek word *artos*, as does the New Testament) and wine mixed with water.[7] A

---

2. *Stromateis* (*Str.*) 4.25.161. The passage is followed by a statement "The Savior initiates us into the mysteries"—4.25.162.3.

3. *Paidagogus* (*Paed.*) 1.5.153–4.

4. *Str.* 5.14.136.2. References to second-century usage in Ferguson, *Early Christians Speak*, 3rd ed., 117–18.

5. *Str.* 7.7.40.1.

6. Ferguson, "Liturgical Function," 360–63.

7. For wine mixed with water in ordinary as well as eucharistic usage, see Ferguson,

Eucharist with bread and water alone he identifies (in interpreting Prov 9:17) with heresies (Encratites and Marcionites) who do not follow the rule of the church.[8] Clement refers to the custom at the distribution of the Eucharist that the people are entrusted individually to examine their consciences when they take a portion.[9]

Clement refers in one passage to those who have been to church having heard a discourse about God and having hymned immortality.[10] He appears to give a fuller list of activities in the assembly of Christians in a passage where he characteristically says these things are to be done always.

> The soul that is always giving thanks (*eucharistousa*) in all things to God by righteous hearing and divine reading, by true inquiry, by holy offering, by blessed prayer, praising, hymning, blessing, and singing Psalms is never separated from God at any time.[11]

It is characteristic of Clement that he gives prominence to vocal musical activities, but that would be another paper.[12] If Clement was thinking of the worship assembly in this listing, the "offering" might be a reference to the Eucharist, but the pairing of items could as well link it with prayer. Liturgical activities would seem to be often in Clement's mind. And, granted that the heart of the liturgy is the Eucharist, we nonetheless must ask if everything that is liturgical is eucharistic. Professor Young appears to have assumed the Eucharist was in Clement's mind and then proceeded to interpret the texts accordingly.

"Wine as a Table Drink in the Ancient World."

8. *Str.* 1.19.96. The mixture of wine and water is also mentioned in *Paed.* 2.2.19.3, a passage discussed below, and later in the same passage the use of wine is defended against the Encratites.

9. *Str.* 1.1.5. There follows a quotation of 1 Cor 11:27–28.

10. *Paed.* 3.11.80.4.

11. *Str.* 6.14.113.3.

12. Ferguson, *A Cappella Music*, 19–23, 46.

Clement makes fairly frequent use of sacrificial language.[13] There is no doubt that his spiritualizing of sacrifice gives prominence to prayer.[14] One might think that sometimes the Eucharistic Prayer is in mind, but this would be an assumption to be tested in each case. Clement's little treatise on martyrdom uses the phrase "to drink the cup" for martyrdom.[15] The uniting theme is sacrifice, but the phrase is biblical (Matt 20:22).

If Clement gives sacrificial connotations to the Eucharist, we must still ask what kind of sacrifice. The Eucharist is of course associated with Jesus' sacrifice on the cross. Professor Young wants to connect the sacrificial theme in Clement with that atoning sacrifice. The prevailing association in the early church was of the Eucharist with a thank offering.[16] And that seems to be true for Clement as well.[17] Here we have continuity with Rabbi Stern's paper.

Clement makes two references to the institution narratives, both as part of a discussion of something else. In defense of drinking wine in moderation he cites Matt 26:27–29, and in this instance he explains the phrase "This is my blood" as "the blood of the vine, which is the Logos poured out for many for the forgiveness of sins."[18] In support of the need to speak well and to act well, Clement says, "The Savior taking bread, first spoke and gave thanks, and then breaking the bread, he presented it so that we might eat with reference to the Logos."[19]

---

13. Ferguson, "Spiritual Sacrifice," 1179–83. Like other Christians, Clement affirmed that Christ was the whole burnt-offering and offering without fire made for human beings and that the Logos prohibited all building of holy places and all sacrifices—*Str.* 5.1 1.70.4 and 5.11.74.5. An example of his spiritualizing of sacrifice is the reference to offering incense in a meal context: "If one should say that the Lord, the great High Priest, offers the incense of fragrance to God, we do not understand this as a sacrifice and fragrance of [literal] incense, but let us receive this as the Lord offering the acceptable sacrifice of love, the spiritual fragrance, on the altar—*Paed.* 2.8.67.

14. *Str.* 7.6.31.7; 7.6.31.8 (the altar is the congregation at prayer); 7.6.32.4 (prayer is incense); 7.6.32.6; 7.6.34.2 (prayer is incense); 7.7.49.4; Frg. 61 from *Sacr. Par.* 300 (Stählin III, 227, 28); *Hyp.* on 1 Pet 2:9 (Stählin III, 204, 21–25).

15. *Str.* 4.9.75.1. He refers to Jesus' calling his passion "a cup"—*Paed.*1.6.46.1.

16. Rordorf, "Le sacrifice eucharistique."

17. Note the association of thanksgiving with prayer in *Str.* 7.7.35.4, 6; 7.7.41.67 and with psalmody in *Paed.* 2.4.43.3. The offering of the "firstfruits of food and drink" with thanksgiving in *Str.* 7.7.3 6.4 reminds one of Irenaeus, *Adversus Haereses* 4.17.5.

18. *Paed.* 2.2.32.2. Cf. *Quis dives salvetur?* (Q.D.S.) 29.4, "He poured on our wounded souls wine [Luke 10:34], the blood of the vine of David." Not every reference to "blood" is eucharistic—*Q.D.S.* 34.1.

19. *Str.* 1.10.46.1.

A Response to Robin Darling Young on The Eucharist as Sacrifice

For Clement, as for the later Greek Fathers, the principal eucharistic text was John 6.[20] The first extensive treatment comes in Clement's discussion of new Christians as children, who are to be fed on milk. It is plausible to think that the new converts' initial experiences with the Eucharist suggest Clement's development of the theme. He refers to one interpretation of milk and meat (1 Cor 3:2) according to which the "milk" is the proclamation of the gospel and meat is faith given substance by instruction (*katechesis*). He then explains John 6:53 ("eat my flesh and drink my blood"). Jesus is

> describing allegorically through the symbols of eating and drinking what is the outward manifestation of faith and the promise, by which the church, like a human being composed of many members, is given drink and grows . . . , the body by faith and the soul by hope."[21]

Then Clement follows the medical theory of the day on the blood of the mother becoming milk.[22] He returns to John 6:53–54 and comments that, since the Lord offered his flesh and poured out his blood, nothing more was needed for the growth of his children. "Oh, marvelous mystery!" He presents the following as the "more common" or "more general" understanding:

> He speaks allegorically to us of the Holy Spirit as flesh, because the flesh was created by him, and he hints obscurely to us of the Logos as blood, for the Logos as rich blood has been poured out for life . . . The Lord is Spirit and Logos. The food, that is the Lord Jesus, the Logos of God, is the Spirit who became flesh, the heavenly flesh sanctified. The food is the milk of the Father, by which alone we children are nourished.[23]

Clement here equates the Logos and the Spirit. The Holy Spirit is allegorically the flesh, and the Logos is blood. Clement's concern is not with flesh and blood, but with the invisible realities to which they refer.[24]

---

20. The main texts are well studied by van Eijk, "Gospel of Philip and Clement of Alexandria."
21. *Paed.* 1.6.38.1–3.
22. *Paed.* 1.6.39–40.
23. *Paed.* 1.6.42.3—43.3. Engelbrecht, "God's Milk," esp. 512–16.
24. Van Eijk, "Gospel of Philip and Clement of Alexandria," 111.

Later in the passage Clement affirms, "For us little children who suck as milk the Logos from heaven Christ himself is food."[25] Shortly thereafter Clement may be thought to make a liturgical reference to dipping the bread in the chalice of wine, but the word he chooses makes this doubtful:

> Since [Jesus] said, "The bread that I will give is my flesh" [John 6:51] and flesh is given drink by blood and the blood is spoken of allegorically as wine, therefore one must know that as bread crumbled [*n.b.*] into the mixture of wine and water seizes on the wine and leaves the watery portion, so also the flesh of the Lord, the bread of heaven, absorbs the blood and nourishes what is heavenly in human beings for immortality and leaves only the fleshly lusts for destruction.

Clement continues:

> Thus the Logos is spoken of allegorically in many ways—meat, flesh, food, bread, blood, milk. The Lord is all these for the enjoyment of us who have believed in him. No one should consider it strange that we speak allegorically of the Lord's blood as milk. Is it not spoken of allegorically as wine? Scripture says, "He washes his garment in wine and his cloak in the blood of the grape" [Gen 49:11].[26]

The repeated use of the word "allegorically" makes clear that Clement is not thinking literally. Moreover, he makes the application, "The very blood and milk are a symbol of the Lord's passion and teaching."[27] The incarnation and the necessity of feeding on Christ are clearly present throughout the passage. There seem to be Eucharistic overtones. Given a mind that associates Logos with milk and blood with wine, we should be careful about being too specific about what his thought is. However, all the images—bread, wine, flesh, blood, milk—serve for Clement to describe believing in Christ and growing in spiritual knowledge of him, which will lead to immortality. Whatever is said about bread and wine, however, one must be prepared to say about other food and milk.

Another passage that starts from the contrast of milk and meat (1 Cor 3:1–2), this time between catechesis and contemplation of the highest mysteries, may allude to John 6:53–54. "The flesh and blood of the

---

25. *Paed.* 1.6.46.1.

26. *Paed.* 1.6.47.1–3.

27. *Paed.* 1.6.49.4. Clement's subsequent reference to mixing milk and honey may allude to the practice of giving milk and honey to the newly baptized at their first Eucharist-so argued by van Eijk, "Gospel of Philip and Clement of Alexandria," 113–14.

A Response to Robin Darling Young on The Eucharist as Sacrifice

Logos are the apprehension of the divine power and substance . . . The knowledge of the divine substance is the eating and drinking of the divine Logos."[28] Eating and drinking are for Clement an image of acquiring divine knowledge.[29]

This conclusion is consistent with what Clement says in another reference to the discourse on the Bread of Life in John 6. The context is the discussion of drinking wine, following after a discussion of eating that included instructions about an agape.[30] This discussion of wine includes what is considered the most important eucharistic text in Clement.[31] That it comes shortly after the discussion of the agape would be consistent with Bigg's argument that the agape and the Eucharist were not separated in Clement's Alexandria.[32] Bigg does not persuade me; Clement draws on many associations that he can relate to whatever he is discussing.

The text is introduced by reference to the water from the rock (Exod 17:1–7) and the cluster of grapes brought back from the promised land by Joshua and the other spies (Num 13:23–24). It continues as follows:

> The great cluster was a sign to those being guided from error into rest, the Logos who was oppressed for us, since the Logos desired the blood of the grape to be mixed with water, as also his blood is mixed with salvation. The Lord's blood is twofold: the blood of his flesh by which we have been ransomed from corruption, and the blood of his Spirit by which we have been anointed. To drink this [latter] blood of Jesus is to partake of the Lord's incorruptibility. The Spirit is the strength of the Logos, as blood is of the flesh.

In a comparable way as the wine is mixed with water, the Spirit is with a human being. The former mixture of wine and water nourishes us in faith, and the latter (the Spirit) leads to incorruption. Both mixings, that of the

---

28. *Str.* 5.10.66.1–3, a passage with references to pagan sacrifice, the sacrifice of Christ (our Passover), and Christian spiritual sacrifice as separation from the body's passions, may support the case for an association with the Eucharist, as van Eijk, "Gospel of Philip and Clement of Alexandria," 108–9, argues. Milk and meat are referred to in another passage followed by this statement: "By the 'blazing wine' [Thespis] teaches the perfecting gladness of instruction, the blood of the vine of the Logos"—*Str.* 5.8.48.8.

29. Van Eijk's comment is a propos, "Clement is less interested in the (sacramental) symbols themselves, than in what is communicated by them" (ibid., 109).

30. *Paed.* 2.1.4–8 and 16 on the agape.

31. Mehat, "Clement of Alexandria," 113.

32. Bigg, *Christian Platonists of Alexandria*, 137,n1.

drink and that of the Logos, are called Eucharist, which means grace that is praised and beautiful. Those who participate by faith are sanctified in body and soul, when the Father's will mystically mixes together the divine mixture, a human being with the Spirit and the Logos. For truly the Spirit is akin to the soul it bears and the flesh is akin to the Logos, on account of which "the Word became flesh" [John 1:14].[33]

Once more the Logos and the Spirit are identified. Four different mixtures appear in this passage: wine and water, the Logos's blood and salvation, the Spirit with a human being (the Spirit conveyed in the Eucharist, not the incarnation), and by implication the Logos with flesh in the incarnation.[34] Partaking in faith sanctifies body and soul.

Another commentary on John 6 that appears to represent Clement's own view is found in his *Excerpta ex Theodoto* 13.14:

> [The Son] is "heavenly bread" and "spiritual food" furnishing life by food and knowledge, "the light of human beings," that is, of the church. Therefore those who ate the heavenly bread died [those who ate the manna in the wilderness—John 6:49], but he who eats the true bread of the Spirit shall not die John 6:50]. The Son is the living bread which was given by the Father to those who wish to eat. "And my flesh is the bread which I will give" [John 6:32, 51], he says, that is to him whose flesh is nourished by the Eucharist; or better still, the flesh is his body, "which is the church" [Col 1:24], "heavenly bread," a blessed assembly.[35]

The technical use of Eucharist seems clear. There is once more the double reference to food that nourishes the flesh and to knowledge, the "true bread of the Spirit," that gives life to the church, the real body of the Son of God.[36] Later in the document (82. I), bread and oil are cited as analogies to the water of baptism that has a material effect and by the Spirit an immaterial effect:

---

33. *Paed.* 2.2.19.3–20.1. Cf. the statement that "Scripture names wine the mystical symbol of the holy blood"—*Paed.* 2.2.29.1.

34. Van Eijk, "Gospel of Philip and Clement of Alexandria," 111–12; and Marrou in Mondésert and Marrou, *Clément d'Alexandrie Le Pédagogue* II, 48, give differing lists of the mixtures in the passage, both importing into the passage a mixing of the Logos with the eucharistic elements that is not explicitly there.

35. Casey, *Excerpta ex Theodoto of Clement of Alexandria*, 50–51, whose translation I follow, slightly modified. A fragment ascribed to Clement, but not included in Stählin, from a sermon on Luke 15 is translated in *Ante-Nicene Fathers*, 11, p. 582: "He is both flesh and bread, and has given Himself as both to us to be eaten."

36. Cf. *Str.* 1.1.7.2 on nourishment received through bread and words. The statement may be inspired by the Eucharist, but I question that it is.

A Response to Robin Darling Young on The Eucharist as Sacrifice

> And the bread and the oil are sanctified by the power of the Name, and they are not the same as they appeared to be when they were received, but they have been transformed by power into spiritual power.[37]

The language of John 6 appears to shape the following statement in which Clement presents the Savior as speaking:

> I am the one who nourishes you, giving myself as bread. No one who has tasted of this bread experiences death any more. I daily give the drink of immortality. I am the teacher of supercelestial lessons. I contended with death on your behalf and paid in full for your death.[38]

Here is found the by now familiar combination of feeding on the Savior as on bread and taking his drink, receiving his teachings and the benefits of his death, all resulting in overcoming death.

The intellectualizing and spiritualizing interpretation found in the major works of Clement is found also in his *Hypotyposeis* preserved by Cassiodorus. Thus on 1 John 1:7, "The doctrine of the Lord . . . is called his blood."[39] And on 1 John 4:8, the Spirit is interpreted as life, water as regeneration and faith, and the blood as knowledge.[40]

Professor Young is right to emphasize that for Clement (and for other writers under the influence of Platonism) a symbol mediates and participates in the truth it indicates. But a symbol was still not identical with what was symbolized. I doubt that Clement had a thought-out theology of the Eucharist; it was simply part of his church experience. If I were to characterize his eucharistic thought as exemplified in his treatment of John 6, I would do so by the view that has been called "dynamic symbolism." The Eucharist is symbolism because it participates in the reality symbolized; it is dynamic, for in this instance it conveys the power of the reality that it symbolizes.[41] Clement sees the power or effects of the body and blood of

---

37. Casey, *Excerpta ex Theodoto of Clement of Alexandria*, 88–91.
38. Q.D.S. 23.4.
39. Stählin, III, 211, 7–9.
40. Ibid., 214, 24–25.
41. Völker, *Der wahre Gnostiker nach Clemens Alexandrinus*, in a long note (pp. 598–600) surveys Roman Catholic interpretation of Clement that defends the real presence and transubstantiation and Protestant interpretation that advocates symbolism. He agrees with Tollinton's middle position between spiritualizing and realism. His own exposition (pp. 598, 600–602) emphasizes the close relation for Clement of the Eucharist with the church and with Christ and its function of bringing spiritual life, overthrow of corruption, and immortality. Without using my terminology, his brief

Jesus as conveyed by the taking of the eucharistic elements. They remain bread and wine and so nourish the human body, but there is a heavenly dimension, a spiritual reality that is received by the working of the Logos and the Spirit.[42] In other words, there was a realism of the effects of the Eucharist and a symbolism of the elements, which are associated with the body and blood of Jesus.[43] And, typically for Clement, these effects are described in terms of a heavenly knowledge associated with immortality.

Clement is one of the first to use the language of the Hellenistic mysteries for Christian initiation to any extent.[44] This was part of his general program of borrowing terms familiar to educated Hellenists and using pagan concepts and practices to make Christianity intelligible and acceptable to them. I doubt that we should see in his "mystagogy" more than that. As the terminology became more common, the ideas behind it influenced Christian self-understanding (certainly in the fourth century), but to read Clement in terms of these ideas raises again the question of whether Clement was a Christian who used pagan concepts or a Hellenist not completely immersed. I think Professor Young would join me in voting for the former characterization.

---

statement is consistent with my interpretation.

42. There may be a continuity with David Bentley Hart's characterization of the Byzantine view of the Eucharist as the site or locus where spiritual reality is received.

43. We may compare Origen, *Contra Celsum* 8.33—"We give thanks to the Creator of all, and with thanksgiving and prayer for blessings received we eat the loaves presented to us that become by the prayer a holy body and sanctify those who with sound intentions partake of that body."

44. Marsh, "Use of ΜΥΣΤΗΡΙΟΝ"; Echle, "Sacramental Initiation." Marsh notes Clement's frequent use of mystery terminology but its rarity with reference to the sacraments and concludes that although there was a tendency to surround the sacraments with concepts from the Hellenistic mysteries, the time for that practice had not yet arrived in Clement's Alexandria (p. 80).

6

Psalm-Singing at the Eucharist
A Liturgical Controversy in the Fourth Century

THE REFORMED CHURCHES HAVE been strong advocates of the use of the Psalms in Christian worship and have not been strangers to controversy over this practice. It seems appropriate, therefore, in an article honoring John Jansen, a loyal representative of the Reformed theological tradition, to look at a controversy from early Christian history involving the singing of the Psalms.[1]

Augustine in his *Retractationes* II.11 (37) provides the following information:

> Meanwhile, a certain Hilary, a Catholic layman of tribunician rank, incited to anger, for some reason or other, against the ministers of God, as often happens, in abusive, censorious language, wherever it was possible, was violently attacking the custom which, at the time, had been introduced in Carthage, of singing hymns from the Book of Psalms either before the oblation or when what had been offered was being distributed to the people; he insisted that this should not he done. At the urging of my brethren, I answered him; the book is called *Against Hilary*.
>
> This book begins as follows: "Those who mention the Old Testament."[2]

---

1. See Lamb, *The Psalms in Christian Worship*, for a full historical account of all aspects of the Psalms in Christian worship.

2. Translation by Sister Mary Inez Bogan, *Saint Augustine: The Retractions*, 140.

The work to which Augustine refers was written, according to its position in the *Retractationes*, in the closing years of the fourth century or about 400. Since the *Against Hilary* is lost, we do not know the grounds of Hilary's objection: to the use of the Old Testament, to any singing at the eucharist, or simply to any change from the familiar in the liturgy?[2a] The occasion of the controversy may have been the extension to Carthage of the custom earlier introduced (AD 385-86) at Milan to which Augustine refers in his *Confessions*:

> How freely did I weep in thy hymns and canticles; how deeply was I moved by the voices of thy sweet-speaking Church! . . .
> The church of Milan had only recently begun to employ this mode of consolation and exaltation with all the brethren singing together with great earnestness of voice and heart . . .
> This was the time that the custom began, after the manner of the Eastern church, that hymns and psalms should be sung, so that the people would not be worn out with the tedium of lamentation. This custom, retained from then till now, has been imitated by many, indeed, by almost all thy congregations throughout the rest of the world. (IX.vi.14—vii.15)[3]

This passage, however, has to do with a manner of singing and puts its emphasis on all participating in the singing; this would not fit Hilary's objections, if those were to any singing or to singing of the Psalms. Further, his objections apply to the custom of singing at the eucharist; presumably he had no objections to singing the Psalms at other times or in other parts of the service.

There are a number of indications of liturgical developments in reference to singing in the late fourth century. As was the sixteenth century, the

---

2a. Joseph M. Murphy, "The *Contra Hilarum* of Augustine, Its Liturgical and Musical Implications," *Augustinian Studies* 10 (1979), pp. 133-143 makes the following points: Ambrose made two innovations borrowed from the East—antiphonal singing and non-scriptural hymns; Augustine *Retract*. II,37 refers to the offertory (*oblatio*), not the mass as a whole or the introit; it was written c. 396-400; Hilary was a judicial official, a spokesman for a group of liturgical conservatives; and Augustine is describing the infancy of antiphonal psalmody in the Mass as it was to develop in the West in the Middle Ages. J. Dyer, "Augustine and the 'Hymni ante oblationem': The Earliest Offertory Chants?" *Revue des études augustinennes* 27 (1981) 85-91.

3. Translation by Outler in *Augustine: Confessions and Enchiridion*, 187. Cf. Paulinus, *Vita Amb*. 4.13; Ambrose, *Ep.* 20 *ad Marcellinani* mentions reciting Psalms during the occupation of the basilica. The *Liber Pontificalis* attributes to Celestine (422-32) the introduction of Psalms to the liturgy in Rome.

Psalm-Singing at the Eucharist

fourth century was a time of liturgical change to meet new circumstances in the history of the Church.

It is assumed that the passage in the *Confessions* refers to the introduction into the West of the practice of antiphonal singing, recently having become widespread in the East.[4] Theodoret's church history gives information which would date the introduction of antiphonal singing at Antioch to the time of Bishop Leontius (348–357):

> That excellent pair Flavianus and Diodorus, though not yet admitted to the priesthood and still ranked with the laity, worked night and day to stimulate men's zeal for truth. They were the first to divide choirs into two parts, and to teach them to sing the psalms of David antiphonally. Introduced first at Antioch, the practice spread in all directions, and penetrated to the ends of the earth. Its originators now collected the lovers of the Divine word and work into the Churches of the Martyrs, and with them spent the night in singing psalms to God. (Theodoret, *Ecclesiastical History* 11.19 [24])[5]

The church historian Socrates, in a passage set in the time of Theophilus, bishop of Alexandria 385–412, gives a different account of the origin of the practice:

> We must now however make some allusion to the origin of this custom in the church of antiphonal singing. Ignatius, third bishop of Antioch in Syria from the apostle Peter, who also had held intercourse with the apostles themselves, saw a vision of angels hymning in alternate chants the Holy Trinity. Accordingly he introduced the mode of singing he had observed in the vision into the Antiochian church; whence it was transmitted by tradition to all the other churches. Such is the account [we have received] in relation to these antiphonal hymns. (Socrates, *Ecclesiastical History* VI.8)[6]

The ascription of the practice to Ignatius indicates an awareness that it was not of apostolic origin; but the effort to make it old and base it on a revelation reflects a need to justify this mode of singing. And indeed there was

---

4. See the note by Outler, ad loc. and Duchesne, *Christian Worship*, 115, where the reference in the footnote should read ix.7.

5. Translation by Jackson in *Nicene and Post-Nicene Fathers*, series 2, vol. 3, 85. See Werner, *The Sacred Bridge*, 176, for the Jewish origins of the practice.

6. Translation by Zenos in *Nicene and Post-Nicene Fathers*, series 2, vol. 2, 144.

need to justify antiphonal singing, as may be seen from a letter of Basil, bishop of Caesarea in Cappadocia, dated AD 375:

> Now as to the charge relating to the singing of psalms ... The customs which now obtain are agreeable to those of all the Churches of God. Among us the people go at night to the house of prayer, and, in deep distress, affliction, and continual tears, making confession to God, at last rise from their prayers and begin to sing psalms. And now divided into two parts, they sing antiphonally with one another, thus at once confirming their study of the Gospels [oracles or scriptures], and at the same time producing for themselves a heedful temper and a heart free from distraction. Afterwards they again commit the prelude of the strain to one, and the rest take it up; and so after passing the night in various psalmody, praying at intervals as the day begins to dawn, all together, as with one voice and one heart, raise the psalm of confession to the Lord, each forming for himself his own expressions of penitence. If it is for these reasons that you renounce me, you will renounce the Egyptians; you will renounce both Libyans, Thebans, Palestinians, Arabians, Phoenicians, Syrians, the dwellers by the Euphrates; in a word all those among whom vigils, prayers, and common psalmody have been held in honor.
>
> But, it is alleged, these practices were not observed in the time of the great Gregory [Thaumaturgus] ... We, for our part, are always offering supplication for our sins, but we propitiate our God not as you do, in the words of mere man, but in the oracles of the Spirit ... Beware lest in your disputes about the mode of singing psalms, you are straining at the gnat and setting at nought the greatest of the commandments. (Basil, *Ep.* 207.3, 4.)[7]

Basil here refers to three different modes of rendering the Psalms: antiphonal,[8] responsorial,[9] and unison.[10] Presumably the criticism to which he replies had to do with the antiphonal, for it was the newest of the three modes. There also seems to be some new use of the Psalms them-

---

7. Translation by Jackson in *Nicene and Post-Nicene Fathers* ser. 2, vol. 8, 247–48.

8. Cf. Gregory Nazianzus, *Carm* 18; Sozomen, *H.E.* 3.20.

9. Cf. Methodius, *Symp.* 11.2; *Apos. Const.* 11.57; *Test. Dom.* II.11 and 22; Chrysostom, *Hom.* 36 *in 1 Cor.*; Athanasius, *Apol. de Fuga* 24; Augustine, *Enarr. Ps.* 119.1.

10. Eusebius, *Comm. Ps.* 65:10–15; 91:2f.; Chrysostom, *In Ps.* 145:2; Hilary, *In Ps.* 65; Ambrose, *In Ps.* 1, *Exp.* 9.

Psalm-Singing at the Eucharist

selves, perhaps in vigils, and indeed the monastic movement of the fourth century greatly developed and enlarged their usage.[11]

Basil's affirmation that he approaches God in the very words which the Spirit gives,[12] that is the biblical Psalms and odes, serves as a reminder of another fourth-century controversy: whether non-Biblical songs could be used in the liturgy. The canons of the Council of Laodicea prescribed that "No psalms composed by private individuals nor any uncanonical books may be read in the church, but only the canonical books of the Old and New Testaments" (canon 59). This fourth-century collection of canonical legislation did not originate before c. 345 and probably is twenty years later.[13] The limitation may have been prompted by a concern to exclude heretical ideas from the liturgy. The restriction did not prevail, and it has been argued that the intent was not to restrict singing to the Biblical Psalms but to eliminate unauthorized private compositions.[14] Canon 15, "No others shall sing in the church, save only the canonical singers, who go up into the ambo and sing from a book," is probably to be understood as a similar effort to keep the songs to Biblical or authorized material by restricting private individuals from leading the singing rather than as an exclusion of the laity altogether from participation (something without precedent or subsequent confirmation).[15]

The viewpoint codified in the canons of Laodicea found expression in the *Canons of Basil*, preserved in Arabic:

> Those who sing Psalms at the altar are not to sing with pleasure but with wisdom. They are to sing nothing but the Psalms. If anyone says something that they alone composed or have heard from others that does not stand written by the apostles, they must be excluded . . . The assembly is supposed to respond to all the Psalms with vigor. If anyone is sick in his body so that he responds after them, no guilt rests on him; if however he is well

---

11. Jungmann, *Pastoral Liturgy*, 157–62.

12. Cf. Athanasius, *Ep. ad Marcel*, 10–11, 30–32.

13. Cross and Livingstone, eds., *The Oxford Dictionary of the Christian Church* 2nd ed., 799; 3rd ed. rev., 956.

14. Bingham, *The Antiquities of the Christian Church*, vol. 2, pp. 684ff.; Hefele, *A History of the Councils of the Church*, vol. 2, 322. Cf. the limitation in *Canons of Athanasius* 12 and 59.

15. Hefele, *A History of the Councils of the Church*, vol. 2, 310. Canon 17, "The Psalms are not to be joined together in the congregations, but a lesson shall intervene after every psalm," would confirm this interpretation, for the commentators take the purpose to be to avoid weariness in the congregation by unbroken psalmody—see *Nicene and Post-Nicene Fathers*, series 2, vol. 14, 133.

and remains silent, he is to he placed alone, for he is not worthy of the blessing. (Can. 97)[16]

There were thus at least three points of dispute in regard to liturgical singing in the late fourth century: what could be sung (non-biblical or only biblical psalms), how the singing was performed (antiphonal, responsorial, or congregational singing), and when it was done (at the eucharist or not).

None of the material cited thus far seems to echo exactly Augustine's statement of Hilary's concerns. There is another text, however, with similarities to *Canons of Basil* 97, which does speak directly against Hilary's position and emphasizes the necessity of singing the Psalms of David at the eucharist. I refer to *Visio Pauli* 29-30:

> And I saw in the midst of the city a great and very high altar; and there was standing alongside the altar one whose face shone like the sun and who held in his hands a psaltery and a harp and who sang saying, "Hallelujah!" And his voice filled all the city. And as soon as all who were on the towers and at the gates heard him they replied, Hallelujah, so that the foundations of the city were shaken. And I asked the angel and said: Who, sir, is there here with such great power? And the angel said to me: This is David; this is the city of Jerusalem . . . And I said: Sir, why is it that David alone begins the singing before all the other saints? and the angel answered and said to me: Because (?) Christ, the Son of God, sits at the right hand of his Father, this David will sing psalms before him in the seventh heaven: and just as it is done in the heavens, so it is done below, because it is not permitted to offer to God a sacrifice without David, but it is necessary for David to sing psalms at the time of the offering of the body and blood of Christ: as it is carried out in the heavens, so also on earth
>
> . . . I asked the angel and said: Sir, do all who say Hallelujah bless the Lord? And the angel answered and said to me: That is so: and again, if anyone should sing Hallelujah and there are some present who do not sing (it) at the same time, they commit sin because they do not join in the singing. And I said: Sir, does someone who is doting or very old sin in the same way? And the angel answered and said to me: No, but whoever is able, and does not join in the singing, you know that he is a despiser of the word.[17]

---

16. Riedel, *Die Kirchenrechtsquellen des Patriarchats Alexandrien*, 274, gives a German translation.

17. Hennecke, *New Testament Apocrypha*, vol. 2, 778-79; rev. ed. (1992) 729-30.

Psalm-Singing at the Eucharist

The information in this passage and in the *Canons of Basil* 97 about the manner in which the Psalms were to be recited is instructive and corresponds to other information available. A cantor or singer sang the text and the congregation responded to each phrase with "Hallelujah." This is properly called responsorial singing.[18] The practice is probably reflected already in the book of Psalms, for instance Psalms 136, where each statement is followed by "And the steadfast love of the Lord endures forever." A similar congregational response involving the repeated phrase "I will sing unto the Lord" is attested for Jewish recitation in the synagogue by *b. Sotah* 30b. Several Christian texts mention the united participation of the whole assembly in the singing, at least for the refrains, but there seems to be a special concern in *Visio Pauli* and *Canons of Basil* about non-participation. Were some resisting innovation by their silence? A parallel between the heavenly and earthly worship has been an important idea in the history of liturgy. The thought that at worship the barriers between heaven and earth are lowered and that the church at worship is united with the heavenly praise is reflected in the imagery of the New Testament Apocalypse of John.[19] That the celebration of the eucharist was a participation in the heavenly liturgy was emphasized in the catechetical instruction about the sacraments in the fourth and fifth centuries.[20] Along with such familiar ideas there is in the *Visio Pauli* a new insistence on the use of the Davidic Psalms at the eucharist. The author goes beyond the propriety of the usage to declare that it is not possible to offer the eucharist without the use of the Psalms.[21] The strong language can most plausibly be understood in the context of opposition to this practice such as was voiced by Hilary.

Most studies of the *Visio Pauli* have dealt with its literary relations or with three aspects of its contents: the separation of the soul and body at death, the matching of the punishment of the damned to their sin, and the

---

The translation is based on the Latin version.

18. Jungmann, *The Early Liturgy*, 285–86. See references in n. 9. For the Hallelujah response, note Augustine, *Enarr. in Ps.* 148; *Ep.* 55.

19. And one may think of the Angelic Liturgy from Qumran, for which there is a new edition by Newsom, *Songs of the Sabbath Sacrifice*. And cf. *The History of the Rechabites* 16:1–4, which says that when the angels sing, men respond, and when men sing, the angels respond (edited by Charlesworth, ed., *OTP*, 84–85).

20. Daniélou and du Charlat, *La catéchèse aux premiers siècles*, 201–2. For instance, the psalm singers in church imitate the angels according to Cyril of Jerusalem, *Cat. Lect.* 13.26.

21. [Pseudo?] Hippolytus, *On Ps.* 1:1 (PG 10.712B), perhaps influenced by Jewish thought, suggests the Psalms of David replaced the sacrifices of the Old Testament.

granting of a respite from torment to the damned on Sunday.[22] The work seems to have escaped the notice of liturgists, and students of the work itself have not exploited this liturgically significant passage for evidence relevant to its historical setting.

Some comments about the contents of the *Visio Pauli* will support a connection between it and the controversy agitated by Hilary at Carthage but (as will be seen) not confined to North Africa. According to the work, Paul was conducted, in a fashion typical of many apocalypses,[23] on a journey through heaven, where he encountered many of the Old Testament righteous, and through hell, where he saw various types of sinners suffering excruciating punishments. The passage quoted is the only place in the entire work where a direct application is made to a specific earthly activity by the church. The discussion of David is given the most extensive treatment of all of Paul's encounters in the other world. And this description dwells on David's singing of his Psalms while playing his lyre at the heavenly altar. Furthermore, this is the only part of the work which adopts an argumentative tone; the author insists on the necessity of the same practice at the church's altar as that observed at the heavenly altar. Since the passage occupies a disproportionate place in the work and seems unnecessary to the theme of the work, a polemical purpose unrelated to the context seems evident.

Moreover, R. P. Casey has pointed to a clear sign of interpolation in this section. David's singing in the "seventh heaven" (chapter 29) "appears to be a different source from the main structure which implies a three-fold division of heaven."[24]

Casey's article in which this observation is made has been fundamental to the study of the work. Some of his conclusions pertinent to the history of the work's transmission may be summarized and supplemented here.[25] Knowledge of the work by Origen[26] indicates that it originated in Greek about 240–250 in Egypt.[27] It should be added that this work is dif-

---

22. Silverstein, *Visio Sancti Pauli*, 12, notes these three details as marking the influence of the work in the medieval West.

23. Collins, "Apocalypse."

24. Casey, "The Apocalypse of Paul," 16.

25. Silverstein, *Visio Sancti Pauli*, 1–6, summarizes Casey as the point of departure for his own study of the medieval Latin recensions.

26. That Origen accepted the work as canonical is affirmed by Barhebraeus, *Nomocanon* 7.9, translated by Casey, "The Apocalypse of Paul," 27; and it seems that Origen in *Hom. 5 in Ps.* followed *Visio Pauli* 13ff.

27. Casey, "The Apocalypse of Paul," 26, on the basis that the combination of

ferent from the Coptic *Apocalypse of Paul* found at Nag Hammadi (NHC V, 2),[28] although the latter may have provided one of the sources for the orthodox version.[29] Then in AD 388 the work was revised and expanded, for our existing versions contain an account of its discovery in Tarsus during the consultate of Theodosius and another person whose name is amended to read Cynegius[30] and the subsequent sending of the manuscript to Jerusalem.[31] A Latin version was made, probably in Africa, soon thereafter, for it was used by Prudentius in 402 and referred to by Augustine.[32] Our oldest surviving manuscript is from the eighth century,[33] but it represents a translation no later than the beginning of the sixth century and could be the translation of the late fourth century.[34] The surviving Greek text is

---

Greek and Jewish eschatology is characteristic of Egypt and that the literary sources and associations of *Visio Pauli* are Egyptian.

28. See the observations by Henri-Charles Puech, "Les nouveaux Ecrits gnostiques," 134–37. The Nag Hammadi *Apocalypse of Paul* may be the *Ascension of Paul* referred to by Epiphanius, *Haer.* 38.2.5. English translation by MacRae, et al. in *The Nag Hammadi Library in English*, rev. ed., 257–59.

29. Cf. *Visio Pauli* 15–18 with *Apocalypse of Paul* (NHC V, 2) 19, 29—21, 22.

30. The story of the discovery found in the Latin and Greek versions at the beginning and in the Syriac at the conclusion provides information for the date. Sozomen knew the story of the discovery of the work but rejected it:

> "The Apocalypse of the Apostle Paul," though unrecognized by the ancients, is still esteemed by most of the monks. Some persons affirm that the book was found during this reign [i.e., Theodosius] by divine revelation, in a marble box, buried beneath the soil in the house of Paul at Tarsus in Cilicia. I have been informed that this report is false by Cilix, a presbyter of the church in Tarsus, a man of very advanced age, as is indicated by his gray hairs, who says that no such occurrence is known among them, and wonders if the heretics did not invent the story." (*Ecclesiastical History* VII.19)

The translation is by Hartranft in *Nicene and Post-Nicene Fathers*, series 2, vol. 2, 390.

31. Casey, "The Apocalypse of Paul," 26, on this basis accepts a real connection of the work with Jerusalem.

32. Ibid., 28–29. Prudentius, *Cathemerinon* V.125ff.; Augustine, *In Joh. Tract.* 98.8; cf. *Enchir.* 112–113, for ideas based on it.

33. Paris, Bibliotheque Nationale, *Nouv. acq. Lat.* 1631. Published by James, *Apocrypha Anecdota*, 11–42.

34. Silverstein, *Visio Sancti Pauli*, 5–6.

a later abbreviated recension.[35] Of the many medieval Latin recensions, note may be made of the fragment in Vienna Codex 362 (fourteenth century) which comes from the Greek independent of the other Latin manuscripts.[36] It is generally agreed that the best witnesses to the contents of the "Tarsus" edition of the *Visio Pauli* are the Paris Latin and the Syriac.[37] The Armenian exists in four recensions; in a fashion analogous to the history of the Latin text, the later forms are briefer than the first. It is not simply a translation of the Syriac, and often rearranges and rewrites the material.[38] The Coptic is rambling and has sections displaced, but James thinks that part of its seemingly repetitious long conclusion may be original,[39] and Silverstein suggests that with its assistance one may reconstruct the subject matter of the pre-Tarsus Greek original.[40]

A subsequent study by Theodore Silverstein devoted to "The Date of the 'Apocalypse of Paul'" accepted the main lines of Casey's survey of the history but made an important modification in the date for the "Tarsus" edition.[41] He argued, convincingly it seems, that the name of the consul joined with Theodosius should be read Constantius, so the Theodosius is Theodosius II and the intended date is 420. The Greek version contains an anti-Nestorian reference, so the work was produced between 431 and 450, perhaps soon after AD 431, and pre-dated to 420. Sozomen's reference, therefore, to the discovery of the work "during this reign" (see note 29) refers to the reign in which he was writing, that of Theodosius II. Prudentius does not refer to the *Visio Pauli* but derives the motif of the respite from torment of the Lord's day from another source, and Augustine's reference to the work is to its earlier form known to Origen.

The association to which this article calls attention between the *Visio Pauli* and the controversy in the late fourth century over Psalm singing at the eucharist in Carthage may seem to favor Casey's date, and Silverstein's

---

35. Casey, "The Apocalypse of Paul," 2. It was published by Tischendorf, *Apocalyses Apocryphae*, 34–69.

36. Silverstein, *Visio Sancti Pauli*, 21 and 36.

37. Casey, "The Apocalypse of Paul," 1–5; Silverstein, *Visio Sancti Pauli*, 1ff.; James, *The Apocryphal New Testament*, 525. Kraeling, "The Apocalypse of Paul and the 'Iranische Erlösungsmysterium,'" 209ff., 238, has not been followed in giving preference to the Syriac over the Latin.

38. Leloir, "L'Apocalypse de Paul selon sa teneur armenienne."

39. James, *The Apocryphal New Testament*, 526.

40. Silverstein, *Visio Sancti Pauli*, 20.

41. Silverstein, "The Date of the 'Apocalypse of Paul,'" on which this paragraph is based.

Psalm-Singing at the Eucharist

dismissal of the evidence from Augustine and Prudentius, because hypothetical, is the weakest part of his case. This association is, however, not inconsistent with Silverstein's date. The practice could still have been controverted a few decades later, the controversy could have been slower erupting in the East, or an argument that had been found successful at an earlier time could have been later incorporated into the *Visio Pauli*. Another possibility is to posit an intermediate stage in the growth of the document: a Latin version of the original added the argument from David's practice and this in turn was incorporated into the final redaction of the "Tarsus" edition in Greek about the 430s. Silverstein's statement concerning the medieval Latin redactions that "the history of the Apocalypse of Paul is essentially that of the continuous modification of its contents"[42] applies also to the whole history of the work.

We are now in a position to relate the possible stages in the transmission history of the *Visio Pauli* to chapters 29–30, where Paul in his heavenly journey encounters David singing Psalms at the heavenly altar. With the evidence adduced above for an interpolation in chapters 29–30 we can reconstruct the history of this section of the work and place the various statements about the use of David's Psalms at the altar in the context of controversy over the use of the Psalms in the eucharistic liturgy. An appendix to this article presents in parallel columns an English translation of the principal versional evidence of *Visio Pauli* 29–30 and should be referred to in connection with the following comments.

I submit that the original third-century Greek "Apocalypse of Paul" contained some statement like what I have labelled "Coptic" about Paul on his heavenly journey encountering David in his characteristic function of singing the Psalms. The Vienna Latin conceivably could he a witness to this early form of the work, but more likely it is an abbreviation, omitting reference to the correspondence between the heavenly and earthly liturgy because the controversies which gave rise to this expansion were no longer known. Both the Latin and Armenian texts in their later redactions omit this section. Some references in the original "Apocalypse of Paul" to David's singing in the heavenly temple provided the occasion for a reviser in the late fourth or early fifth century to elaborate on the necessity of employing the Psalms of David in the earthly liturgy of the church. The almost identical statements in the Paris Latin and the Syriac are best accounted for if this revision was done in Greek, but it cannot be ruled out that the expansion was made in Latin and then incorporated

---

42. Silverstein, *Visio Sancti Pauli*, 19.

into the Greek text. The polemic on behalf of the Psalms at the eucharist in this Greek version indicates that Hilary in Carthage was not alone but had his counterparts in the East. Our surviving Greek is an epitome of the "Tarsus" text, keeping the main ideas without the polemical edge.

Any number of places would have been possible locales for the "Tarsus" expansion of the *Visio Pauli*: Alexandria, Jerusalem, Antioch, Tarsus, Constantinople, etc. A social milieu may he suggested more confidently than a geographical provenance. Sozomen attests the popularity of the work among the monks.[43] Favorable notice is given to the monks[44] in a passage which forms a partial exception (the statement is still very general) to what was said above about a lack of concern with a specific earthly activity. The work continued influential in monastic circles.[45] And, as noted above, the monks were especially active in fostering the practice of psalmody.

The use of the Psalms at the eucharist originated in the East, and the practice spread to the West.[46] The introduction of the practice was accompanied by controversy. Augustine mentions it at Carthage, and the *Visio Pauli* implies resistance in the East, comparable to opposition to other fourth-century liturgical changes involving the Psalms. The correspondence posited between the heavenly and earthly liturgy assured the victory of the practice.

---

43. See n. 30. Casey, "The Apocalypse of Paul," 8, suggests the author was a monk; also pp. 20, 31.

44. *Visio Pauli* 9; cf. 24 and 47.

45. Leloir, "L'Apocalypsc de Paul selon sa teneur armenienne," 218–20, 227–30.

46. For Psalms at the eucharist see Cyril, *Cat. Lect* 23.20; *Apos. Const.* VIII.13; Ambrose, *De Elia* 10.34.

Coptic I [A]	Latin (Paris) [B]	Syriac [C]	Coptic II	Greek [D]	Armenian [E]	Latin (Vienna)
And I saw	And I saw in the midst of the city an altar exceeding high And there was one standing by the altar	And I saw in the centre of the city a great altar, which was very high, and I saw standing on the side of the altar an aged man, great and honored,	And I Paul saw in the midst of the city a large altar which was of very great height and there was a man standing before the altar	And I looked and saw in the midst of the city an altar, great and very lofty; and there was one standing near the altar	And there was in the midst of the city a large church and very exalted, and near its pulpit was a man;	Then he saw a tall altar with fire on it. And he saw a very glorious man standing alone beyond it.
a man wearing white apparel,	whose visage shone like the sun,	and his face shone as the sun in the firmament;	and his face was shining like the sun,	whose face shone like the sun,	and he was giving forth, in the manner of the sun, some of the light of the city,	
and there was a harp in his hand and he stood on the right side of the veil; and he sang and played his harp	and he held in his hands a psaltery and an harp	and he held in his hand a harp,	and there was a harp of gold and a psaltery of god in his hands,	and he had in his hands a psaltery and a harp, and he sang the Alleluia	and he was holding in his hands the book of Psalms and he was chanting the antiphon Alleluia.	And he held a psaltery in his hand while he sang with a great voice "Alleluia."
	and sang praises, saying: Alleluia. And his voice filled all the city.	and said: "Hallelujah"; and the whole city was astonished at his voice;	and he was crying out "Hallelujah!"	delightfully, and his voice filled all the city,		
	And when all that were upon the towers and the gates heard him,	and together they shouted— and those who were above the towers,		and all with one consent	And those who were on the walls, the towers, and the gates of the city	And all on the inside
	they answered: Allelulia,	and all said: "Hallelujah."				

Coptic I [A]	Latin (Paris) [B]	Syriac [C]	Coptic II	Greek [D]	Armenian [E]	Latin (Vienna)
		And when I saw those things,		accompanied him,	were responding	responded to him similarly
	so that the foundations of the city were shaken.	the foundations of the city were shaken with their shouting	and the foundations of the city were shaken.	so that the city was shaken by their shouting.	Alleluia.	"Alleluia," so that the foundations of the temple were shaken.
and the angels made answer to his songs. And I answered and said unto the angel,	And I asked the angel and said:	Then I inquired of the angel who was with me:	And I said unto the angel,	And I asked the angel:	I asked the angel and said:	And Paul asked the angel
"Who is this, my lord?"	Who is this, Lord, That is of so great might?	"What is this voice which shakes the city and all its inhabitants?"	"My lord, who is this who is so mighty?"	Who is this that singeth delightfully, whom all accompany?	"Lord, who are those who chant the Psalms before the platform?"	who was the man who appeared more glorious than others.
He said unto me,	And the angel said unto me	And the angel said unto me:	and the angel answered and said unto me,	And he said to me:	The angel said to me:	And the angel said,
"This is David singing praises."	This is David.	"This is David, the king and prophet.	"This is David,	This is the prophet David;	"This is David	"He is David, who was a king and prophet, and he did many wonderful deeds on earth.
	This is the city of Jerusalem;		the father of the Christ according to the flesh.			
		who sings in the Jerusalem of Christ. As he sang on earth,	and this [city] is heavenly Jerusalem,	This is the heavenly Jerusalem,	who chants Psalms before the platform (as he had done in) the Jerusalem which is on the earth.	And this city is called heavenly Jerusalem.

Coptic I [A]	Latin (Paris) [B]	Syriac [C]	Coptic II	Greek [D]	Armenian [E]	Latin (Vienna)
	and when Christ the king of eternity shall come in the fullness (confidence, freedom) of his kingdom,	so sings here David, in spirit, and all the saints are engaged with him, with the voice of shouting;	and when the Christ God showeth Himself	When, therefore, Christ shall come	For, when the king comes and appears	When Christ the holy of holies, will come
	he shall again go before him to sing praises, and all the righteous shall sing praises together answering: Alleluia. And I said: who was with me: Lord, how is it "Why does David	and David the prophet goes forth singing, first, while all the saints after him respond: 'Hallelujah.' And I said to the angel who was with me: "Why does David	in His kingdom, David the king must play music so that the righteous may answer him and cry 'Hallelujah'" and I said unto the angel, "My Lord, why is David the only one	in his second appearing, David himself goes forth with all the saints	in his glory, again before him, David chants psalms and all the righteous respond Alleluia." I asked and said: "Does David alone	with great power, then that one will sing before him, and the rest of the elders will do the same.
	sing before this altar, and these saints respond, each in his own place?" and the angel answered and said unto me: "When (or because) Christ, the Son of God,	sing before this altar, and these saints respond, each in his own place?" and the angel answered and said unto me: "When Christ, the Son of God, ascended on high,	who playeth a harp, and why do not the righteous [play harps]?" And the angel said unto me: "The Christ, our Lord,		chant psalms before God more than all the righteous?" The angel answered and said: "The Son of God	

Coptic I [A]	Latin (Paris) [B]	Syriac [C]	Coptic II	Greek [D]	Armenian [E]	Latin (Vienna)
	sitteth on the right hand of his father,	and sat down on the right had of his father,	sitteth on the right hand of the Father in the heavens		sits in person at the right hand of his Father,"	
	this David shall sing praises before him in the seventh heaven:	this David sang alone, before his ascension and said thus:	and David playeth to him in the Seventh Heaven according to the manner		and David himself chants psalms before him.	
		'Lift up your heads, O ye gates; and be lifted up, ye everlasting doors,	in which	For as it is in the heavens,	According to the example which is done in heaven,	
		that the king of glory may come in.'		so also upon earth:	Thus it must be done also on earth.	
		Many men longed for the singing of that time; but save that man, none reached it.				
	and as it is done in the heavens, so likewise is it below: for without David it is not lawful to offer a sacrifice unto God:	Again, on earth a man hath not permission to offer up sacrifice	he played upon earth. Without David the Prophet it is impossible to offer up a sacrifice	for without David it is not permitted to offer sacrifice.	It is not allowed to offer the sacrifice to God without psalm and alleluia.	
		[celebrate the sacrament] without offering praise in it, with the songs of the blessed David.	in any place.			

Coptic I [A]	Latin (Paris) [B]	Syriac [C]	Coptic II	Greek [D]	Armenian [E]	Latin (Vienna)
		Without the praise of David, A man presumes not to offer:			When indeed the Priests offer the sacrifice,	This is
	But it must needs be that David sing praises at the hour of the offering of the body and blood of Christ: as it is performed in heaven, so also is it upon earth.	It is necessary That he sing his songs, At the time of offering, for it is the body of Christ."	He playeth the harp over the flesh of the Christ and over His Holy Blood, according to the manner of his doing in heaven."	even in the day of the precious body and blood of Christ; but it is necessary for David to sing the Alleluia.	the host of heaven chant psalms also with them."	
	And I said unto the angel: Lord, What is Alleluia? And the angel answered and said unto me:	And I said to him: "O my Lord, what is the meaning of Hallelujah?" and he said unto me:	And I answered and Said unto the angel, "My lord, what is [the meaning of] Hallelujah?" And he said unto me, "Paul, thou master	And I asked the angel: My Lord, what is the meaning of Alleluia?	I asked and said, "Lord, what is this alleluia?" He said to me:	
	Thou dost examine and inquire of all things.	"How much thou examinist, and asketh questions, Paul! Whatever thou desirest to know, know.	of the Church rightly dost thou enquire concerning everything.		"You inquire and search about everything."	
	And he said unto me: Alleluia is spoken in the Hebrew, that is the speech of God and of the angels: now the interpretation of Alleluia is this:	Hallelujah, in the language of the Hebrew means	Now the word 'Hallelujah' is the Hebrew for	It is called in Hebrew	He said: "Alleluia is a Hebrew word, and according to the interpretation of the angels alleluia means	

Coptic I [A]	Latin (Paris) [B]	Syriac [C]	Coptic II	Greek [D]	Armenian [E]	Latin (Vienna)
	tecel. cat. marinth. mach (Gr. thebel marethema). And I said: Lord, what is tecel cat marith macha? And the angel answered and said unto me: This is tecel cat marith macha:			Thebel Marematha	tēklaytʼamaratʼ". He said to me,	
		'Praise the Lord.' Praise God, who was the first of all. Unto him do the angels, without ceasing, raise Hallelujah; and praise him who sent for us salvation, and created for us all things.'	'Give glory unto God,	speech to God	tēklaytʼamaratʼ, according to another interpretation (means) Glory is to God,	the praise of God
			Who created everything, and the interpretation thereof is,	who founded all things;	who has laid the foundations of all things,	and of the holy angels.
	Let us bless him all together. I asked the angel and said: Lord, do all they that say Alleluia bless God?	And I said unto him: "O my Lord, then every one who says 'Hallelujah' praises God';	'Let us bless God together.' And I answered and said unto the angel, "Then any man who saith 'Hallelujah'	let us glorify him in the same.	we bless him together.	

Coptic I [A]	Latin (Paris) [B]	Syriac [C]	Coptic II	Greek [D]	Armenian [E]	Latin (Vienna)
	And the angel answered and said unto me: So it is: and again,	and the angel said unto me:	blesseth God?" And he said "Yea, [and he also] saith, 'Give glory to the Lord.'"			
	if any sing Alleluia, and they that are present sing not with him, they commit sin in that they sing not with him.	"If a man sing in the assembly, and those who are near him do not respond 'Hallelujah', they sin.			Whoever in fact chants Psalms And does not respond Alleluia, sins against God."	
		If those men do not respond, the angels will certainly respond;	And I said unto the angel, "Then he who saith 'Hallelujah' hath no need to translate the word?"			
	And I said: Lord doth A man likewise sin if He be doting or very aged? The angel answered and Said unto me: No so:	and if a man is sick or old, and does not respond, the guardian angel responds in his stead. But I declare that	And the angel said unto me, "If a man be suffering from sickness there is no blame [attached] to him;		The angel said to me:	
	But he that is able	every one who is strong	but if he be strong and vigorous,		"Whoever, when he is able,	

Coptic I [A]	Latin (Paris) [B]	Syriac [C]	Coptic II	Greek [D]	Armenian [E]	Latin (Vienna)
and singeth not with him,		and doth not respond— what do they say of him? "This proud devil turneth aside;	and he answer not,		does not respond Alleluia,	
	know ye that such a one is a despiser of the word,	this man if he despises one response, does he not know that he despises to offer up an offering to God? he does not prize converse with God; for as much as a man offers prayers, he speaks with God; and he who prays not cuts himself off from converse with God.'"	This man			
	for it would be proud		Is arrogant and contemptuous,		is proud;	
	and unworthy that he should not bless the Lord God his creator.		And he is unworthy To bless Him Who created him."		he is not worthy to praise his Creator."	

A. The translation of the Coptic is that of Budge, *Miscellaneous Coptic Texts*, 1081, for what I have labelled Coptic I from the conclusion and pp. 1056–57 for Coptic II from the body of the work.
B. The translation of the Paris Latin is that of James, *The Apocryphal New Testament*, 541. The Latin is the basis of the translation in Hennecke, *New Testament Apocrypha* (see n. 17). It is also translated by Andrew Rutherford in *Ante-Nicene Fathers* vol. 10 (reprinted, Grand Rapids, 1951 reprint), 151ff.
C. The translation of the Syriac is that of Justin Perkins "The Revelation of the Blessed Apostle Paul," 201–2, and reprinted in Tischendorf's edition of the Greek and elsewhere.
D. The translation of the Greek is that of Alexander Walker found in *Ante-Nicene Fathers* (Grand Rapids, 1951 reprint) vol. 8, p. 578.
E. A French translation of the four Armenian recensions is given by Leloir, "L'Apocalypse de Paul selon sa teneur arménienne," 234–85. I have given the fuller first recension, 244.

7

The Art of Praise
Philo and Philodemus on Music

INTRODUCTION: THE SILENCE OF ANCIENT SOUNDS

OF ALL THE CULTURAL expressions of the early Jewish and Christian world, perhaps the least heard by modern scholars has been music. But music was all around in the classical world from the streets to the imperial salon. It was also the subject of extensive technical discussions, especially among philosophers. Two of these, those of Philodemus and Philo, will be the focus of this study. Both give attention to music: Philodemus by a treatise on the subject and Philo by numerous scattered references, but neither author's treatment has attracted extensive analysis. While Abe Malherbe has professed little affinity for Philo, I hope he will accept this study as a melodious tribute, by allowing the tenor of Philo to harmonize with the bass of Philodemus, one of the favorites in his classical chorus.

The neglect of music by scholars may be a result of where one typically encounters it in the extant literary sources. Music, like medicine, grammar, and rhetoric, was considered a τεχνή, a learned "skill" or "art." From the classical Greek tradition it was given stature by its connection to the poetic composition of odes and hymns. Even so, by the Roman period it was not considered an appropriate profession for a person of noble birth. Poetry was now a separate literary art, and music had largely become the province of slaves or women. Unlike rhetoric, elite men were not expected to study music for use in daily life, even though many show substantial awareness of its technical aspects. Jewish and Christian texts give even less attention usually, perhaps because music was often associated with less wholesome activities of the after-dinner entertainment at a symposium. Such carousing with female musicians was to be avoided. Among the moralist philosophers, however, one frequently finds allusions to music and its technical skills as a metaphor or illustration of the precision and practice of pursuing a harmonious moral life. In the arts, skill and training are required to become proficient, as Musonius Rufus said:

> Virtue is not theoretical knowledge (ἐπιστήμη θεωρητική) alone but it is practical application as well, just like medicine and music (ἥ τε ἰατρικὴ καὶ ἡ μουσική). Therefore, just as it is necessary for the doctor or the musician respectively not only to master the theoretical principles of his art (τὰ θεωρήματα τῆς αὐτοῦ τέχνης), it is also necessary for him to exercise (γεγυμνάσθαι) at acting according to the principles; so too, a man who wishes to become good should not only learn the precepts which are conducive to virtue, but should also exercise earnestly and strenuously (γυμνάζεσθαι . . . φιλοτίμως καὶ φιλοπόνως) in accordance with them.[1]

Thus music frequently is found alongside two of the more prominent moral *topoi* that liken philosophy to medical treatment and the virtuous life to an athletic contest.

Philo's frequent statements about music have not drawn much study, perhaps because, as with Musonius, they often occur in discussions of other subjects,[2] but Philo was clearly interested in music and had some knowledge of the technical as well as practical aspects of both instrumental and vocal music. The importance of music for Philo is shown by his abundant use of musical illustrations.[3] Musical ratios and harmonies provide illustrations for his number symbolism, to which he gave much

---

1. *Frag.* 6. Compare also *Frags.* 2, 5. The text is from Lutz, *Musonius Rufus*, 52; the translation is that of the author, adapted from that of Lutz.

2. The major study is the valuable article by Feldman, "Philo's Views on Music." The neglect is illustrated by Grözinger, *Musik und Gesang in der Theologie der frühen jüdischen Literatur*, which includes the Apocrypha, New Testament, and Qumran in its index of passages but omits Philo altogether. The importance of Philo in music history because of his influence on the church fathers is recognized by Schueller, *The Idea of Music*, 130–33.

3. Feldman, "Philo's Views on Music," 511–13.

attention.⁴ Similarly he elucidates peculiarly Jewish rituals with musical metaphors: the thank-offering "is divided into parts in the same manner as are the lyre and other instruments of music."⁵

Philo, it seems, has an illustration for nearly everything, and a large share of his references to music occur in illustrations: "the perfect man like the master of music or of grammar requires no instruction."⁶ In other cases the physical aspects of hearing and sense perception offer a natural opportunity for comment: the pleasures of the "eyes, ears, stomach, and the parts below the stomach" charm us like musical sounds ringing in the ears.⁷ The majority of Philo's illustrations occur in references to philosophy and paraenetic instruction: "let the whole chorus of philosophers chime in, expounding their customary themes";⁸ or "as the things pertaining to music are apprehended through the science of music . . . so that which is wise is perceived through wisdom";⁹ and God gives his blessings to a righteous man "just as he gives to the musician the instru-

---

4. *Op. mun.* 15.48 ("the number four contains the ratios of the musical harmonies"); 31.96 ("most musical is the proportion of these numbers"); 37.107–10 (seven is "most harmonious and in a certain way the source of the most beautiful scale"); *Spec. leg.* 11.32.200 (ten "is the most perfect fullness of musical theories"); *Cong.* 17.89; *Q. Gen.* 4.27. See Feldman, "Philo's Views on Music," 520–22. For the musical ratios in Greek philosophy, cf. Porphyry, *Commentary on the Harmonics of Ptolemy* 107.15–16 on the Pythagoreans (trans. in Barker, *Greek Musical Writings*, vol. 2, 34–35).

5. *Sac.* 20.74. Translations of Philo are for the most part my own but with reference to those in the LCL, whose Greek text I use.

6. *Leg. all.* I.30.94. As often, the musical comparison accompanies an illustration from medicine or grammar; here the vowels of the alphabet like the notes of music are adapted to produce harmony with one another. Compare *Det. pot.* 9.18: the exercise of a virtue in an exaggerated or improper way is like practicing "music unmusically or grammar ungrammatically"; *Det. pot.* 21.75: even as music and grammar remain after the death of a musician or grammarian, virtue survives the death of a virtuous man (cf: Plato, *Phaedo* 86); *Post.* 43.142: not giving to someone according to his needs is as absurd as giving "a lyre to a physician or surgical instruments to a musician."

7. *Post.* 45.155. Compare *Leg. all.* II.3.7: the mind uses a helper, as it does the sense of hearing in recognizing a musician's voice as sweet or out of tune. When Philo thinks about the sense of hearing, he does so in terms of musical sounds (*Leg all.* III.18.57—whether "melodious and rhythmical or out of tune and in discord").

8. *Agr.* 31.139.

9. *Mig.* 8.39. Cf. *Leg all.* II.8.26: when occupied with the tunefulness of a voice it cannot exercise its reasoning power; *Leg. all.* II.7.21: "power" expresses a singer's power in singing; *Leg. all.* III.41.121: a false statement is like naming incorrectly a mode of music or a note on the scale; *Sac.* 5.22 and 29: pleasure takes her stand among various evils "like the leader of a chorus" and her "sound sings in the ears"; *Sac.* 7.37: "that which is pleasing to God and virtue is like a tightly strung and robust harmony" (further on the harmony of the soul, see below).

ments that pertain to music."[10] So, like Musonius, he likens habituation in virtue to practicing at music or the other arts: knowledge without practice is unprofitable, for "What profit is the beautiful voice when it is silent, or of the aulos player if he does not play, or of the kithara player when he does not play?"[11] Even in such metaphorical uses Philo's technical interests show through, as when he employs notions of harmony: the moderation of Moses' laws is like the blending of high and low notes on a musical instrument to produce a life of harmony and concord.[12] Similarly, Moses is called God's special instrument and the Torah his "music": "The sound, moreover, comes when the plectrum, his Logos, melodiously and skillfully strikes a harmony, through which legislation is made known."[13] Elsewhere he compares body and mind to musical instruments: the body is not to be worn out by continuous labor; as musicians loosen the strings of their instruments "lest they snap through unrelieved tension," and as music and voices are adapted to various intensities and relaxations, "so too is it with the mind."[14]

10. *Mig.* 21.120.

11. *Cong.* 9.46. Cf. *Cong.* 25.144: each skill deals with some part of reality—"geometry has its lines, and music its sounds"; *Mut.* 21.122: "habits are superior to the persons practising them, as music is superior to the musician"; *Spec. leg.* II.44.246: we do not punish the servants rather than the actual authors of an act any more than we would praise the instruments instead of the musician who performed on the aulos or lyre; *Spec. leg.* II.47.259: virtue is its own reward as holiness is the most beautiful in the chorus; *Gaium* 11.75: Macro became "like the leader of a chorus" (the same comparison for Helicon in 26.166); *Prob.* 7.49: 'Just as the law of music gives equality with regard to this art to all those practiced in music, so also does the law of human life to those experienced in the matters of living" (for the reverse application see 8.51); *Prob.* 21.157: the declaration that one is a "grammarian, geometrician, or musician" no more makes it so than the declaration that one is free; *Provid.* 2.20: "as it is the height of folly to make the blind judges of color or the deaf of musical sounds, so is it to make evil men the judges of the truly good."

12. *Spec. Leg.* IV.17.102. The illustration of "the harmony which includes a heightening and lowering of the mode, as in a musical instrument for the skillful blending of melody" is applied to individual human beings in *Mut.* 13.87. For other illustrations from "harmony" cf. *Spec. leg.* II.28.157: God "wished to effect a harmony as on a musical instrument"; *Virt.* 27.145: one law "sings together" with others (is in agreement with others), "just as in an all harmonious chorus."

13. *Q. Gen.* IV.196; I use the translation, of Ralph Marcus in LCL (*Philo Supplement* 1.486). Compare *Mut.* 24.139: the prophet Hosea's words were "the voice of the Invisible One whose invisible hand plays on the instrument of the human voice"; *Conf.* 11.41: the words of Gen 42:11 are a "harmonious symphony."

14. *Q. Gen* IV.29 (*Philo Supplement* I:305). Cf. *Q. Gen.* IV.76 (*Philo Supplement* I:354): the one ignorant of the art of a musician has trouble with instruments but to the musician they are "fitting and suitable."

Apart from the seasoning provided by his Jewish heritage and context, Philo's allusions reflect a solid awareness of technical discussions of music in the Greek philosophical thought represented by Pythagoreans, Platonists, Aristotelians, and Stoics,[15] as we would expect from his general use of Platonic and Stoic thought. This kinship is seen especially in regard to the relations between music, the human soul, and cosmic harmony. These relations were especially emphasized by Damon (fifth century BCE) and Diogenes of Babylon (c. 240–152 BCE). But there was another tradition in Greek philosophy in regard to music, represented by some Sophists,[16] the Skeptics,[17] and the Epicureans. For this other tradition, we may take Philodemus as a foil against whom to array Philo.

PHILODEMUS

Philodemus (ca. 110—ca. 40/35 BCE) was originally from Gadara in the Decapolis but moved to Athens, where he became one of the leading Epicurean philosophers of his day. Sometime between 75–55 BCE he moved to Italy where he wrote and taught under the patronage of L. Calpurnius Piso Caesoninus, the father-in-law of Julius Caesar. Philodemus seems to have divided his time between Rome and Piso's luxurious resort villa (now usually called the "Villa of the Papyri") at Herculaneum, where his teaching and literary activities took place.[18] The result was an extensive library of texts on various aspects of philosophy, especially the doctrines of Epicurus and practical ethics, as well as treatises on poetry, rhetoric, and music.[19]

The treatise *On Music* is partially preserved among the charred rolls of papyri (*P. Herc* 1497) found at the villa after it was destroyed in the

---

15. For the views of these philosophical schools on music, Barker, *Greek Musical Writings*. The Pythagoreans posited that "the 'harmony' of the universe (and sometimes those of the microcosms of state and soul) were rooted in mathematical relations of the sort that this musical structure displays" (ibid., 2.28). Platonists, Aristotelians, and Stoics developed this perspective in different ways.

16. The Hibeh Papyrus (c. 280–240 BC), containing an attack on the musical theories of Damon, written c. 390 BC. English translation in Anderson, *Ethos and Education in Greek Music*, 147–49.

17. Sextus Empiricus, *Math.* 6 ("Against the Musicians").

18. In general sec Gigante, *Philodemus in Italy*, 1–28; Asmis, "Philodemus' Epicureanism." See also now Fitzgerald, et al., eds., *Philodemus and the New Testament*, passim.

19. Gigante, *Philodemus in Italy*, 29–37.

eruption of Vesuvius in 79 CE. Most, if not all, of the fragments belong to the Fourth Book,[20] devoted to a refutation of Stoic views on music, especially those of Diogenes of Babylon.[21] Philodemus did not concern himself with the technical and aesthetic features of music but with ethos, the supposed effects of music on its hearers and their theoretical basis. Philodemus' approach of taking up arguments and refuting each one by one results in a less than logically organized counter position.[22] The absence of an English translation for more than selected short passages justifies a fairly full treatment of the contents, even though the fragmentary state of the text leaves many uncertainties.

Philodemus (or his source) summarizes musical activities as "to sing, to play the kithara, and to dance,"[23] or "singing and playing the kithara."[24] He refers to the principal instruments, "auloi and lyres,"[25] and names the percussion instruments—"tympana, rhombi, and cymbals."[26] Philodemus, like Philo, occasionally refers to three elements of music: "harmonies, melodies, and rhythms,"[27] "voice [or sound], pitch, and rhythm,"[28] or in citing Cleanthes, "measures, melodies, and rhythms,"[29] and referring to Archestratus, "the philosophy of music concerns voice, the nature of tone, intervals, and the like."[30] Most often he uses a twofold summary,

---

20. Erler, "Die Schule Epikurs," 1.313. The fullest discussion of the contents in English is Anderson, *Ethos and Education*, 153–76. I use the edition of Neubecker, *Philodemus über die Musik*, and for other fragments Joannes Kemke, ed., *Philodemi De musica librorum quae exstant*. The view put forward by Kemke, that some of the fragments belonged to books 1 and 3, is no longer held. See Fitzgerald, "Philodemus and the Papyri from Herculaneum," which gives a full summary of the contents.

21. Diogenes is named in Book IV, col. 7,1. 24; col. 21, 1. 19; col. 23,1. 28 (Neubecker, *Philodemus über die Musik*, 46, 66, 69).

22. Neubecker, "Beobachtungen," 85. The article develops other features of Philodemus' style in the treatise.

23. Kemke, ed., *Philodemi De musica librorum quae exstant*, 17, VIII 142, 11.4–6 and Book 1V, col. 16, 11.27–28 (Neubecker, *Philodemus über die Musik*, 60). The translations of Philodemus are my own.

24. Kemke, ibid., 7, IX 70, 11.11–12; 55, VIII 7, 11.13–14.

25. Ibid., 28, XI 89, 11.1–2.

26. Ibid., 49, VII 190, 11.3–4. Description of these instruments, in West, *Ancient Greek Music*, 122–26.

27. Kemke, ed., *Philodemi De musica librorum quae exstant*, 23, XI 92, 11.3–5; cf. 1, IX 69, 11.11–13.

28. Ibid., 22, VIII 22, 11.12–13.

29. Book IV, col. 28, 11.10–11 (Neubecker, *Philodemus über die Musik*, 75).

30. Book IV, col. 23, 11.14–19 (Neubecker, *Philodemus über die Musik*, 69).

"melodies and rhythms."[31] He speaks of the "kinds of harmonies,"[32] but when he refers to specific scales he names only the "enharmonic and chromatic."[33] In addition there is a reference to "making the rhythmic and orderly movements of the hands, feet, and other members of the body."[34]

Occasions for Music

A large part of what survives of Book 4 concerns occasions when music was used in Greek life, which were appealed to as part of the arguments for the effects of music on human behavior. The types of activities and songs related to them include encomia, wedding songs, love songs, laments, war songs, athletic songs, dramatic choruses, and women's dances.[35] Philodemus denies that the music accomplishes its alleged usefulness in these areas. The use of music by those launching ships, harvesting grain, trampling grapes, and rowing ships makes the work easier by relaxation and the admixture of pleasure but does not set the work in motion, present the actions to the mind, nor cause them.[36]

---

31. E.g., Book IV, col. 18, 11.15–16; col. 22, 1.14; col. 26, 11.6–7, 16–17; col. 27, 11.18–19; col. 29, 11.42–43 (Neubecker, *Philodemus über die Musik*, 62, 68, 72, 73, 74, 78); Kemke, ed., *Philodemi De musica librorum quae exstant*, 49, VII 190, 11.4–5; cf. "to know rhythm and harmony," Kemke, ibid., 2, IX 69, 11.31ff.; 7, XI 80, 11.9–11; cf. "meters and melodies," Book IV, col. 17, 1.11 (Neubecker, *Philodemus über die Musik*, 60). Sextus Empiricus, *Math.* 6.38, too, considers music the science of melodies and rhythms.

32. Book IV, col. 27, 11.2–3.

33. Book IV, col. 2, 11.15–16 (Neubecker, *Philodemus über die Musik*, 39). Sextus Empiricus, who generally follows Philodemus rather closely, in *Math.* 6.39–51 has a fuller discussion of the technical elements of music.

34. Kemke, ed., *Philodemi De musica librorum quae exstant*, 30, XI 88, 11.4–7. See also below in Philo's description of the Therapeutae.

35. Book IV, col. 5, l.13—col. 7, l.22 (Neubecker, *Philodemus über die Musik*, 43–46); cf. Kemke, 14, XI 74, 11.5–46 for the bridal song, music for war (trumpet, auloi), gymnastics, athletics (for the pentathlon, aulos). Cf. Ps. Plutarch, *Mus.* 26–27 (*Mor.* 1140b–f) for music in education, war, athletic contests, and the theater. Athenaeus, *Deip.* 620a—631c also takes up the occasions when music was employed in Greek life. The similar topics (hymns, private and public celebrations, war, travel, sailing, rowing, and other manual labors, and mourning) in Aristides Quintilianus, *Mus.* 2.6.61 suggest a common topos in reference to music. Cf. Philostratus, *Vita Apol.* 5.21.

36. Book IV, col. 8, 11.4—25, 32 (Neubecker, *Philodemus über die Musik*, 47–48). See below on the acceptance of pleasure as an effect of music. Cf. Sextus Empiricus, *Math.* 6.21–24 on music diverting the mind but not causing the benefits claimed for it.

Occasions from literature and history with which music was associated are given attention because they were already cited by Philodemus' opponent. The erotic drive, with reference to several authors, is declared to be "a great evil" that is stimulated "by the voice and eyes, not melodies." One is corrupted by thoughts, not melody, although music may "distract and make a person heedless just as sexual pleasure and drunkenness do."[37] Music is no more connected to the symposium than it is to erotic vice, for Philodemus does "not consider there to be a so-called banquet virtue [or excellence]." Homer indeed indicates that there is a kinship of music with symposia, but this is because there is "a need to relax and play at symposia."[38] Incidents in history when music was claimed to overcome civil discord are cited below.

The approach taken in dealing with the argument for a likeness of music to friendship is typical to affirm that music produces pleasure, to deny its essential relationship to the topic, to give priority to thoughts and words, and to grant that even if music contributes something to the topic, it does not have the benefits the opponent claims: "Music is useful for pleasure but not for friendship." "Melodies and rhythms do not relax and cheer, but the thoughts combined with them." "Even if [music] should make us relaxed and joyful, ... we would not consider it alone to be the cause of friendship and harmony."[39]

The place of music in education receives only passing mention in the surviving fragments. "[The argument that] music was received by the ancients for the training of children in a model of virtue has produced a discussion . . ." The effect of a musical culture or its absence happens for some persons, but not for others. "They were formed beforehand into the virtue they would have later as men."[40] A detached fragment refers to the main elements of Greek education: "gymnastics for the body and music for the soul."[41] Philodemus' opponent regarded musical speculation

---

37. Book IV, col. 13, 1.4—col. 15, 1.44 (Neubecker, ibid., 55–59).

38. Book IV, col. 16, 1.1—col. 17, l.35 (Neubecker, ibid., 59–61); symposia are discussed also in col. 11, I.4—col. 12, 1.10 (Neubecker, ibid., 51–53); cf. Kemke, ed., *Philodemi De musica librorum quae exstant*, 16, XI 72, 11.1–36 on lovemaking and banquet virtue. Ps. Plutarch, *Mus.* 43 (*Mor.* 1146e-f) argues that Homer did not mean that music is useful only for pleasure.

39. Book IV, col. 17, 1.35—col. 18, 1.33 (Neubecker, ibid., 61–62).

40. Book IV, col. 12, 11.12–35 (Neubecker, ibid., 54); cf. Kemke, ed., *Philodemi De musica librorum quae exstant*, 7, XI 80, 11.9–12, "professing an understanding of harmony and rhythm to be useful for education [or culture]." See references below for Philo on music in education.

41. Kemke, ibid., 3–4, IX 73, 11.8–10; cf. Plato, *Leges* 795d; in *Resp.* 410, 441–42

as "almost equal to the literary critic" and the "writing of music to be almost equal to the art of poetry and grammar." Philodemus disputes this but even allowing a similarity to acting and the art of delivery, since "all these things have an obvious likeness to wit and intellect," more is to be said on behalf of the arts of painting and sculpture.[42] His own viewpoint is expressed in this statement: "To attain theoretical musical knowledge of excellent and bad, or of fitting and unfitting melodies does not itself educate, but philosophy working through musical training does."[43]

Music for the Gods

Philodemus refers to his fuller treatment in book three of the theme "Concerning Music for Divinity" and refers to one [Plato? Aristotle? Diogenes?] who says, "Lawful and excellent music was appointed first for the sake of honor to the divine and then for the education of the freeborn."[44] He gives a fair amount or attention in *On Music* to the argument for the usefulness of music from its presence in religion. Happy to claim a thought shared by others, he affirms right off that "the divine has no need of any honor, but it is natural to us to honor it, especially with holy thoughts." If music profits any group, it is the populace, but the musical practices vary in different places and circumstances, and the music is now performed by hired persons. Many other things besides music are involved in cult, so there is no essential connection of the divine with music.[45] Diogenes had claimed that the hymns sung in Ephesus and by the choruses in Sparta were more impressive because accompaniment was added and so showed the power of music to move us, but Philodemus responds that for one

---

the view is advanced that both are for the benefit of the soul.

42. Book IV, col. 22, 1.10—col. 23, 1.13 (Neubecker, *Philodemus über die Musik*, 68–69).

43. Kemke, ed., *Philodemi De musica librorum quae exstant*, 42–43, VII 187, 11.5–11.

44. Ibid., 12 13, IX 64, 11.3–4, 8–13; Kemke cites as a parallel Ps. Plutarch, *Mus.* 27 (*Mor.* 1140d–f); note also Ptolemy, *Harm.* 3.7.100, "The gods are invoked with music and melody" (Barker, *Greek Musical Writings*, 2.379). Cf. Kemke, ibid., 25–26, XI 90, 11. 1–8 on the gods. Anderson, *Ethos and Education*, 162f. refers to Plato, *Leges* 670 and 803 but considers the main opponent here to be Diogenes, not Plato. Sextus Empiricus, *Math.* 6.18 similarly refers to arguments on behalf of music based on its presence in worship of the gods, its incitement to emulate the good, and its presence in rejoicing and in times of grief.

45. Book IV, col. 4, l1.3–41 (Neubecker, *Philodemus über die Musik*, 41–42); the language is similar to that in the fragment cited in the preceding note.

person the addition of accompaniment added "only the pleasure of hearing" without pious or rational significance and for another person was impressive because of the honor to the gods or men and not on account of the melody."[46]

Diogenes also argued that since the divine is honored by many people through music there is a kinship between music and religion. Philodemus replied that on this premise "magic, the art of making crowns, preparation of unguents, bread making, even agriculture, construction, writing, art, and most occupations" would have to be considered as having a kinship with religion. "Honor occurs rather through the poems, and melody provides a trifling addition."[47] "No god was the inventor of music." Music was not a gift of the gods but was a discovery by human beings, "indeed it was learned gradually," belonging to the last phase of cultural development.[48] "Let it be said that no god is a musician," nor do the gods "stand in need of such things," "for barbarians suppose to honor the gods through these things," which are "out of place among the Greeks" and "have no kinship with religion."[49]

Debates over the Value of Music

The points made by his opponent that are controverted by Philodemus show not only his style of argument but also philosophical concerns. A weighty argument in the Graeco-Roman world was what was honored by the ancients. Philodemus claims that although this is "to be regarded as allowable proof of the useful to the uneducated, to the educated and even more to the philosopher it was a reproach. Divination is esteemed by the Stoics, as are thousands of other things that provide nothing good."[50] Democritus, "most learned of the ancients in natural phenomena," "says music to be comparatively recent, and he gives the cause saying that what is necessary is not put off but it comes into being out of superfluity."

46. Book IV, col. 10, 11.2–28 (Neubecker, ibid., 50).

47. Book IV, col. 20, 1.28—col. 21, l.23 (Neubecker, ibid., 65–66).

48. Book IV, col. 34, 11.23–28 (Neubecker, ibid., 84); Erler, "Die Schule Epikurs," 314 (with reference to *De Poem.* book IV, col, 7, 11.22–25) 315. Cf. Ps. Plutarch, *Mus.* 14 (*Mor.* 1136b) on music as an invention of the gods; specifically Apollo in 1135f.

49. Book IV, col. 35, 11.15–28, 36–39 (Neubecker, *Philodemus über die Musik*, 85, 86).

50. Book IV, col. 10, 11.28–40 (Neubecker, ibid., 50–51).

"Nevertheless, even if it be granted that [music] was most ancient, ... it seems that the foulest things were honored at the beginning."[51]

Another argument by the Stoic Diogenes is that "melody has by nature something stimulating and arousing to action." But, Philodemus replies, music is not like fire, "which has the nature to burn." "To be disposed to action means to set oneself in motion and to choose deliberately, but melody does not urge in the way a word [or reason] does nor is it understood to cause a deliberate choice."[52] Musical instinct does not come by nature.[53]

Because of music's natural affinity with human beings, the claim was made that "Music has power for virtue and vice." Philodemus declares this view "unpersuasive," because "tunes are irrational" and irrational powers influence only irrational things.[54] Those philosophers who learned music did not do so because it was necessary to the attainment of the virtues.[55] On the other hand, Philodemus disputes the possibility that certain melodies are harmful to the composers, performers, and hearers "as if they were not becoming accustomed to shameful words, forms, and thoughts."[56]

Behind Diogenes of Babylon stood Damon, teacher of Pericles, whose ethical theory of music influenced Plato. A fragment from Philodemus has Damon advance the view that "music brings with it both virtues and

51. Book IV, col. 36, 1.29—col. 37, 1.3 (Neubecker, ibid., 87).

52. Book IV, col. 7, 1.22—col. 8, 1.3 (Neubecker, ibid., 46–47); cf the view that "melody by nature is capable of moving and disposing to action"—Kemke, ed., *Philodemi De musica librorum quae exstant*, 15, XI 73, 11.7–9. Kemke, ibid., 48, VIII 9, 11.16–20 refers to "pleasant things that are sought after naturally, not from teaching or custom but as it were automatically." Sextus Empiricus, *Math.* 6.19–20 also denies that melodies are by nature stimulating or repressive, "but they are supposed to be such by us ourselves." Aristides Quintilianus, *Mus.* 2.4.55–56 is a response to those (such as Philodemus and Sextus Empiricus) who doubt whether everyone is moved by melody; in 2.17.86 he overlooks them: "The fact that the soul is naturally stirred by the music of instruments is one that everybody knows" (Barker, *Greek Musical Writings* 2.489).

53. Erler, "Die Schule Epikurs," 314.

54. Kemke, ed., *Philodemi De musica librorum quae exstant*, 38, VII 187, 11.5–11; 55, VIII 7, 11.15–17, associates singing and playing the kithara with courage, prudence, and justice; on the whole subject see Wilkinson, "Philodemus on *Ethos* in Music," 174–81. Ps.Plutarch, *Mus.* frequently affirms the ethos theory of music. Even musical theorists, such as Aristoxenus, accepted the view that music makes persons morally better—*Elementa Harmonica* 2.31.15–30; cf. Ptolemy, *Harm.* 3.5.96—3.7.100 on the elements of music attuned to the different parts and activities of the soul and Aristides Quintilianus, *Mus.* 2.6.61, "The aim set for music is to help us towards virtue" (Barker, *Greek Musical Writings*, 2.465).

55. Book IV, col. 25, 11.12–31 (Neubecker, *Philodemus über die Musik*, 71–72).

56. Book IV, col. 32, 11.4–21 (Neubecker, ibid., 81).

pleasures."⁵⁷ Philodemus' opponent in the *De musica*, furthermore, affirms that music "somehow affects the disposition not only of the body but also of the soul." Philodemus disputes even the effect on the body, for the face of singers causes the ode rather than the ode causing the appearance, and the melody does not move the body, unless the melody is the pretense for this.⁵⁸ Much less was he prepared to accept that "some melodies arouse the understanding and stretch it for instruction and the fitting mode of life."⁵⁹ Rather, "We have the causes of our own proper habits not from without but from within."⁶⁰ Different persons react in different ways to the same melodies:

> It happens that according to certain predispositions there are received varied perceptions, but in regard to what is heard there is not any difference at all; but all perceive alike the same melodies and receive comparable pleasures.

Then citing different opinions of the enharmonic and chromatic scales, Philodemus observes, "Both sides import ideas that belong to neither scale," for "None of the attributed qualities belongs to either scale by its nature."⁶¹ Then comes a strong denial of the ethos theory of music:

> No melody as melody being irrational, arouses that which is sluggish and at rest and leads it to its natural ethical disposition, nor does it calm into a quiet condition the soul carried away with disturbances. It does not turn it from one impulse to another nor bring an increase or diminution in an existing disposition. For music is not imitative, as some imagine, nor, as Diogenes thinks, does it have non-imitative similarities to

---

57. Kemke, ed., *Philodemi De musica librorum quae exstant*, 7, IX 70, 11.4-8; on Damon, see Anderson, *Ethos and Education*, 42, 74-81, 147-53, 161-62, 189-91 and Barker, *Greek Musical Writings*, 1.168-69. Aristides Quintilianus, *Mus.* 2.14.80 attributes to the followers of Damon the demonstration that melodies both instill a character previously absent and draw out a character previously hidden. Plato was concerned with the influence of music—*Leges* 669-70.

58. Book IV, col. 9, 11.1-15 (Neubecker, *Philodemus über die Musik*, 48). Anderson, *Ethos and Education*, 165-66 examines the passage and considers "Less pardonable . . . his claim that music has no effect on the body."

59. Book IV, col. 12. 11.6-11 (Neubecker, ibid., 53).

60. Kemke, ed., *Philodemi De musica librorum quae exstant*, 8, IX 70, 11.3-6; Anderson, *Ethos and Education* 169.

61. Book IV, col. 2, 11.5-36 (Neubecker, *Philodemus über die Musik*, 38-39); the passage is studied favorably by Wilkinson, "Philodemus on *Ethos* in Music," 177. Aristides Quintilianus, *Mus.* 2.4.56 also says music affects people differently, but Philodemus uses this against the ethical influences of music.

> ethical qualities and manifest such qualities as magnificence and humility, manliness and unmanliness, orderliness and rashness, any more than cookery. The different types of music do not contain different ethical qualities ... in so far as the auditory perceptions are concerned.[62]

The last part of the quotation refers to another viewpoint contradicted by Philodemus; the imitative theory of music.[63] No melody has its character by nature, only by convention.[64]

To the claim that music improves the intellect because musicians in creating harmonies set boundaries, Philodemus answers that on the basis of the argument, all things would improve the intellect, for other arts in a similar manner undertake classifications.[65]

Another passage refuting an association of music with virtue leads into a discussion of justice and so the relation of music to community life.

> It has turned out now that the notion of some concerning justice is ridiculous. For it is unthinkable that sounds which stimulate only the hearing of what is irrational contribute something to a disposition of the soul that speculates on the things profitable and unprofitable for the political life shared with one another and of the things that one chooses and another avoids.

Philodemus then corrects the appeal to Plato as saying music is of service to justice. Rather Plato said that justice is analogous to music, not that music is just or the just is music, nor does either contribute to the special knowledge of the other.[66] Since on the Stoic view all the virtues are in-

---

62. Book IV, col. 3, 11.10–41 (Neubecker, ibid., 40–41); Anderson, *Ethos and Education*, 163–65, 167–68. Cf. Kemke, ed., *Philodemi De musica librorum quae exstant*, 33, VIII 17, 11.8–15, "One would consider as exceedingly foolish those who say that we are made mild by music, our souls being softened and their savagery taken away, for only the word that teaches ... does this." On the other side, Athenaeus, *Deip.* 623f—624a cites the view that music "educates characters and calms people of turbulent disposition and those whose thoughts are wayward."

63. Wilkinson, "Philodemus on *Ethos* in Music," 176; Anderson, *Ethos and Education*, 82, 88, 95–103; cf. Kemke, ibid., 45, XI 82, 11.3–10 and Book IV, col. 32, 11.30–33 (Neubecker, *Philodemus über die Musik*, 81).

64. Erler, "Die Schule Epikurs," 314.

65. Book IV, col. 21, 1.24—col. 22, 1.9 (Neubecker, *Philodemus über die Musik*, 67).

66. Book IV, col. 24, 11. 9–35 (Neubecker, ibid., 70–71); see also below on the argument in regard to music bringing an end to civil discord. Plato, *Resp.* 432–33, 441–44. Justice was part of the discussion that music theorists gave to the correlation between the soul and music—Ptolemy, *Harm.* 3.5.97–98.

separable, a refutation of the usefulness of music to one virtue means it contributes nothing to all.

Philodemus thus attacks the prevalent philosophical ideas of a kinship between music and the soul and between music and the political community. He also challenges the theory that there is a correlation between music and celestial powers.

> They talk nonsense who speak concerning the likeness of music to astronomical phenomena. For let it be granted that the movement of the sun and moon and the distance between them are analogous to the distribution of notes and the zodiac is analogous to the distribution of the chords. But this is not a proof of kinship on account of the fact that many things offering such an analogy differ to an even greater extent. To perceive the differentiated arrangement that exists in heaven seems to supply nothing profitable for the possession itself of virtues and the correction of character.[67]

Philodemus proceeds to claim "no one of the musicians themselves recognized these things," which derived from the utterances of "some Pythagoreans."[68]

Philodemus labelled melody "irrational" (ἄλογος).[69] Music, like other things perceived by the senses, brings no cognitive content. Originally "music" to the Greeks was a unity of word, tune, and dance (or gestures),[70] but by Philodemus' time "musician" was commonly used of instrumentalists.

> Not only myself, but also common usage and even Aristoxenos, to name the model of the musician, use the word musicians for those who produce sounds that have no meaning, such as those made by instruments and by humming... Simonides and Pindar were both musicians and poets; as musicians they composed

---

67. Book IV, col. 30, 11.6–24 (Neubecker, ibid., 78); cf. Sextus Empiricus, *Math.* 6.30, 37 for the denial of a correlation between celestial phenomena and ethical theory. The viewpoint opposed here is well preserved in later theorists of music—Ptolemy, *Harm.* 3.8.100–11 (he does not suppose, as some others did, that the celestial bodies emit sounds, but they are arranged in accord with harmonic ratios like those in music); Aristides Quintilianus, *Mus.* 3.9.107—27.133.

68. Book IV, col. 31, 11.13–19 (Neubecker, ibid., 80). See below for Philo on the Pythagorean origins of this common idea.

69. Book IV, col. 3, 1.12; col. 19, 1.15; col. 24, 1.12 (Neubecker, ibid., 40, 63, 71); Wilkinson, "Philodemus on *Ethos* in Music," 178.

70. Neubecker, "Beobachtungen," 86; Wilkinson, "Philodemus on *Ethos* in Music," 175.

> what has no signification but as poets they composed words . . . Therefore, one calls such a person a musician, since everything profitable is made from the thoughts; the bare melodies and rhythms I say to be useful for nothing[71]

This narrowing down of music to the melody and rhythm explains, according to Philodemus, why some in his time attributed to tunes what properly belonged to another element of "music," namely the words. For Philodemus, one must distinguish what someone did as a poet and what as a musician. The things said concerning virtue "are of service to the thoughts, not to the melodies and rhythms. These things are drawn in superfluously even more as a diversion, being blended together so that the audience may pay attention to the thoughts.[72]

Different Types of Music and their Effects

Not everyone agreed with the limitation of the word musician to those who dealt only with instruments.

> I have heard of some who say we are stupid for thinking some philosophers or learned musicians to say melodies and rhythms without verbal significance encourage to virtue. When (actually) men consider the words set to melody and rhythm to contribute to this, while indeed Plato expressly battles with philosophers as uneducated; and they marvel if we should say the composer of instrumental music is a musician, claim musicians to teach things that do not have verbal significance, or do not wish to call Pindar, Simonides, and all the other composers of songs musicians.[73]

Later in the passage Philodemus deals with the appeal to the Stoic philosopher Cleanthes, who was quoted as saying that

> Poetic and musical examples are better than the word of the one who is capable to proclaim the divine and human things of philosophy, since the bare word does not have kindred speeds with

---

71. Book IV, col. 29, 11.14–43 (Neubecker, *Philodemus über die Musik*, 76–78); cf. col. 26, 11.27–35 (Neubecker, ibid., 73). Contrast Ps. Aristotle, *Prob.* 19.27, "Even if there is a melody without words, it has ethical character." Sextus Empiricus, *Math.* 6.1 gives three senses of the word music: "science of melodies, notes, and rhythm-making," instrumental skill, or figuratively correctness in any performance.

72. Book IV, col. 26, 11.1–14 (Neubecker, ibid., 72–73).

73. Book IV, col. 26, 11.14–35 (Neubecker, ibid., 73).

the great gods, but measures, melodies, and rhythms especially touch the truth of speculations about the divine—of which it is not easy to find something more laughable [according to Philodemus]. [Cleanthes says] The thoughts [alone] are not helpful, but when they are set to music, the incitement comes from both, for fitting things come not by thoughts about them but are greater with the melodies.[74]

Philodemus explains what truth there is in this claim is due to the pleasure and distraction afforded by the words exhibited in this way and to other circumstances. "There is no one who would not die laughing upon hearing advice or consolation to those grieving being given with an ode and some instruments."[75]

Philodemus repeatedly asserts that it is not the musical aspects that produce the effects attributed to it, but the texts, the words.[76] For instance, out of the various arguments, he says that it is "the word alone," not the music, that effects "upright conduct" or "bad practices" in love.[77] With regard to religion, one of the fragments raises the question, "Are some of those possessed by the gods who are charmed by the aulos somehow brought to a certain condition, somewhere and in some way indeed, to quit their frightful fancies by the impact of the voice alone, since the melody does not exhibit such power?"[78] Or again, Philodemus' opponent had appealed to occasions when civil strife at Sparta were allayed by the music of Thaletas, Terpander, and others. Philodemus had reservations about the historical details, but

> Even if we allow that the god [Apollo] commanded the Spartans to be of the same mind with those who attended them, it is much easier to find more persuasive that the one who chose to divert them with stirring music and who gave them the commands concerning these affairs was also the one persuading them through the words that were sung.... If indeed each episode happened, they persuaded through words well-arranged

---

74. Book IV, col. 28, 11.1–22 (Neubecker, ibid., 75); cf. col. 11, 11.14–24 for the association of enjoyment with persuasion in poetry and music.

75. Book IV, col. 28, 11.22–41 (Neubecker, ibid., 75–76). Literally, "poured out with laughter."

76. Neubecker, "Beobachtungen" 86.

77. Book IV, col. 15, 11.1–5 (Neubecker, *Philodemus über die Musik*, 58); cf. col. 13, 11.16–21 (Neubecker, ibid., 55).

78. Kemke, ed., *Philodemi De musica librorum quae exstant*, 49–50, VIII 154, 11.7–15.

poetically, not through melodies, and they would have attained their purpose better if they had tried to change minds without use of musical accompaniment[79]

When other considerations are removed, there remains one function for the melodic and rhythmic aspects of music to which allusion is made in the above passages—to give pleasure. This, of course, was a good Epicurean perspective.[80] Epicurus himself was known to have gone to the theatre to hear singers to the kithara and performers on the auloi, but he discouraged the study and discussion of the technical aspects of music, especially at symposia.[81] Philodemus did the same. His slogan was "Everything for rest and enjoyment."[82] With reference to Damon, Philodemus declares that "They speak falsely who say that music alone of the arts is altogether beneficial," for other skills are truly beneficial and helpful to those in need, while music "only brings pleasure physically, not of necessity,"[83] He considered the practice required for musical contests and the effort involved in having something to say about music at symposia as involving too much pain ("For I allow that the pleasure is not necessary, nor is the learning and study that we might enjoy ourselves"). He too considered the speculative aspects of music to be a labor to be avoided. Enjoyment and reputation can be found in other pursuits.[84]

---

79. Book IV, col. 18, 1.33—col. 20, l.27 (Neubecker, *Philodemus über die Musik*, 63–65). The last phrase may be translated "by prose," but "without musical accompaniment" (as suggested here) is another meaning of the phrase. In view of the larger context, I consider the latter to be the more likely meaning. See Sextus Empiricus, *Math.* 6.28—melody only gives pleasure, but poetry, which is concerned with thoughts, is able to benefit and to teach prudence.

80. Sextus Empiricus, *Math.* 6.27 invokes Epicurus as denying Plato's contention that music contributes to happiness. Plato, with everyone else, conceded that music brings pleasure (the art of aulos and lyre playing seeks only pleasure—*Gorgias* 501-2; "pleasure is the characteristic of all music"—*Leges* 802), but wanted it to be the music that delights men of virtue and education—*Leges* 657-59; cf. Aristotle, *Pol.* 1339a. Aristides Quintilianus, *Mus.* 2.6.61 summed up the non-Epicurean philosophical viewpoint: "Not all delight is to he condemned, but neither is delight itself the objective of music" (Barker, *Greek Musical Writings* 2:465).

81. Plutarch, *Non posse vivi* 13 (*Mor.* 1095c—1096c); cf. Diogenes Laertius 10.120, quoting Epicurus' advice to converse about music and poetry but not to engage in the work of writing poems.

82. Kemke, ed., *Philodemi De musica librorum quae exstant*, 37, VIII 148, 11.6–7.

83. Book IV, col. 33, 11.11–22 (Neubecker, *Philodemus über die Musik*, 82–83).

84. Book IV; col. 37, 1.8—col. 38, 1.30 (Neubecker, *Philodemus über die Musik*, 88 83); on music speculation, cf: col. 23, 11.13–27 (Neubecker, ibid., 63); cf. the observation that those who lack natural capacity are not made better by music—col.

PHILO

Philo the Alexandrian Jewish philosopher (ca. 25/20 BCE—ca. 45/50 CE) comes from the next generation after Philodemus and so might have been well-versed in the kinds of technical issues and debates that had gone before.

Occasions for Music and the Types Used

Philo in several passages takes note of the occasions in which music had a place in human life, both pagan and Jewish. Some of those passages not discussed in other connections below will be noted here. Since Philo often uses ὑμνέω to mean "to praise" or "to extoll" with no musical connotation, "song," "ode," or "hymn" are used with it where the musical sense is intended, such as happiness results in "hymning a hymn of joy."[85]

In Roman Alexandria, social entertainment afforded many opportunities for different types of music; often these include forms of instrumental accompaniment. Philo mentions his own presence in a theater, observing the exciting effect on the audience of "a single tune sung by the tragic actors on the stage or played by the kitharodists."[86] The emperor Gaius enjoyed dancers, the singers to the kithara, and choruses.[87] The torture of Jews in Alexandria under the prefect Flaccus was accompanied by "dancers, mimes, aulos players, and other entertainments of theatrical competitions."[88] The description of the incident of the golden calf (Exod 32:6, 17–19) includes reference to the wine song of revelry and in contrast the funeral chant.[89] Instruments also had their place in pagan religious festivals. A long description of activities includes "musical contests, . . . night long celebrations with auloi and kitharas."[90] In reference to the ruler cult, Philo notes "the well trained choruses singing paeans to Gaius" and "honoring him with hymns" when he assumed the appearances of Apollo

---

33,11.27–40 (Neubecker, ibid., 83).

85. *Leg. all.* II.21.82. Cf. *Det. pot.* 43.157: the truly good things of life include the pleasure of hearing "all kinds of melodious sounds"; *Post.* 47.163: the poets "sing."

86. *Ebro* 43.177: cf. *Leg. all.* II.18.75, quoted below.

87. *Gaium* 7.42. See further below on music as bringing pleasure.

88. *Flacc.* 10.85.

89. *Ebr.* 24.95; other references to singing and choruses in this episode in *Mos.* II.31.162; II.49.270; *Spec. leg.* III.22.125.

90. *Gaium* 2.12.

The Art of Praise

and Dionysus.[91] Philo also refers to the mythological basis of this religious use of music among Greeks, the birth of hymnody from Memory.[92] Music occurred in Jewish religious activities, of which more below, but we note now references to the use of trumpets to announce Rosh Hashanah,[93] to music in victory celebrations, particularly a "victory hymn,"[94] and the association of hymns with thanksgiving.[95]

Philo's knowledge of and interest in music came from its place in the educational curriculum.[96] In a first person passage about his own education, Philo mentions that as preliminary to philosophy he studied grammar, geometry, and music.[97] Philo considered philosophy the crown of human intellectual activity by bringing "knowledge" (ἐπιστήμη),[98] but its study was preceded by "the preliminary studies," the *enkyklios paideia* or general education that one received before professional or specialized training. Philo gave a positive value to this general education in spite of his awareness of the dangers Greek culture posed to Jewish faith.[99] He described general education by saying that parents are benefactors of their children, for "they benefitted the body through gymnastic and athletic training . . . and the soul through letters, numbers, geometry, and music, and the whole of philosophy."[100]

91. *Gaium* 13.96.

92. *Plant.* 30.129.

93. *Dec.* 30.159; *Spec. leg.* II.31.188, 192; its use in war is noted in 190. The trumpet "was not used for musical purposes but only for giving signals, especially for battle and in ritual and ceremonial contexts"; so West, *Ancient Greek Music* 118.

94. *Ebr.* 28.110; "victory song" in 30.115; "the victory and thanksgiving hymn" contrasted with the dirge of defeat in 31.121; *Mos.* 1.51.284; *Agr.* 17.79, quoted below.

95. *Ebr.* 27.105—"thanksgiving hymn"; *Somn.* II.5.38—"the thankful person takes in hand praises, encomia, hymns, blessings both in speech and song"; *Somn.* II.41.268—"to give thanks and to hymn"; Plant 33.135. For the theme of thanksgiving in Philo, see J. LaPorte, *Eucharistia in Philo* (New York: Mellen, 1983).

96. Marrou. *A History of Education in Antiquity*, 188-98; Plato, *Leges* 812d-e for his recommendations on musical education; cf. *Resp.* 401d for the potency of musical training because rhythm and harmony penetrate the innermost parts of the soul; Aristotle, *Pol.* 1339b assigns music a place in education for purposes of instruction, amusement, and proper conduct of life; Ps. Plutarch, *Mus.* 26 (Mor. 1140b); Aristides Quintilianus, *Mus.* 2.3.55, "The very young could not be educated through bare words, which contain instruction but no pleasure."

97. *Cong.* 14.74-76; cf. *Agr.* 31.136, 139 for philosophy following grammar, music, and geometry.

98. *Cong.* 25.142.

99. Mendelson, *Secular Education in Philo of Alexandria*, 83.

100. *Spec. leg.* II.40.230 for this division, see above on Philodemus.

Another summary of the educational curriculum gives the benefits of the different branches of study: grammar interprets poetry and history; geometry produces a sense of equality according to proportions; "excellent music by rhythm, meter, and melody heals what is disproportionate, immoderate, and discordant in us"; rhetoric teaches critical thinking and fluency of speech.[101] Moses received this kind of education, and more: "Arithmetic and geometry, rhythmic, harmonic, and metric theory, the whole subject of music through the use of instruments and textbooks, and philosophy"; Greeks taught him the rest of the *enkyklios paideia*, and those from other nations taught him other languages . . . and astrology.[102] Philo sometimes summarized the content of education as "grammar, geometry, and music,[103] but for him "grammar and music [are] the most excellent branches of learning,"[104] and not just grammar, as most would have said. Particularly significant for Philo's evaluation of music is that he ranks it with philosophy as representing those elements of culture that are "like truly divine images of the Godly soul."[105]

His study of music in the educational curriculum gave Philo his knowledge of the technical aspects of music.[106] "She was called music—beautiful in rhythm, harmony, and melody—and from her I begat diatonic, chromatic, and enharmonic scales, conjunct and disjunct melodies, having harmonies of the fourth, fifth, and octave intervals."[107] Rhythm is the one constant in a threefold classification of the components of music; melody, meter, and harmony, in that order of frequency, vie for the remaining two places.[108] The different types of scales or melodies and

101. *Cher.* 30.105; cf. *Cong.* 4.15–18 and *Spec. leg.* I.62.343, from which parts are quoted below.

102. *Mos.* I.5.21–24.

103. *Mut.* 11.80; 26.146, in varying orders; cf. *Agr.* 31.136–38 and "letters, numbers, and music" in *Spec. leg.* I.61.336.

104. *Op. mund.* 42.126; cf. *Cong.* 25.142; Ps. Plutarch, *Mus.* 2 (*Mor.* 1131d) takes music as the second skill after grammar.

105. *Cher.* 27.93.

106. Mendelson, *Secular Education in Philo*, 15; Feldman, "Philo's Views," 517–19.

107. *Cong.* 14.76; almost the same classifications in *Agr.* 31.137, except that the three main parts are "rhythm, meter, and melody" (see note after next); in more summary fashion *Somn.* 1.5.28; 1.35.205; and *Spec. leg.* I.62.342; cf. *Leg. all.* III.41.122; *Post.* 31.104; *Somn.* II.4.27–28. On the three kinds of "scales" or *genera*, cf. Archytas (in Ptolemy, *Harm.* 30–31), Aristoxenus, *El. Harm.* 2.44.20ff. (conjunct and disjunct tetrachords in 3.1); and Ps. Plutarch, *Mus.* 32 (*Mor.* 1142d).

108. Philo has various formulations of the three main elements usually using three out of the following four—rhythm, harmony, meter, and melody. See *Cong.* 4.16;

The Art of Praise

harmonics to which Philo refers are discussed in ancient Greek technical works on music.[109]

Effects of Music

Music was important in shaping culture because of its effects. "Music will lead the discordant into concord, charming the unrhythmic with its rhythms, the inharmonious with its harmony, and the out of tune and unmelodious with its melody."[110] Here Philo espouses the "ethos theory" favored by Stoics and Platonists but repudiated by Philodemus, as we saw above.[111] The positive effects of music resulted in harmony of the soul and of the whole person. Music contributed both to the realization of this harmony and serving as a comparison for its presence or absence.[112] Music can influence how human nature comes to expression.

The almost magical power of music to calm and harmonize a person also made it dangerous. It was a commonplace to recognize that music brings pleasure:

> The aulos, the kithara, and every kind of instrument please the hearing; so do the tuneful sounds of creatures without

---

cf. Plato, *Resp.* 398, "a song or ode has three parts—the words, the melody, and the rhythm"; also *Leges* 669a; "harmony and rhythm" in *Leges* 670b. Cf. Ps. Plutarch, *Mus.* 35 (*Mor.* 1144a) for the note, time, and syllable striking the ear together. Cf. *Cher.* 30.105; *Spec leg.* I.62.342; *Sob.* 8.36; *Vita cont.* 3.29; "melodies, meters, and rhythm" in *Spec. leg.* I.62.342-43 (where "harmonies and consonances" have a different reference); *Spec. leg.* I.5.28; *Mos.* I.5.23.

109. Feldman, "Philo's Views," 518-19 gives references; West, *Ancient Greek Music*, 160-89.

110. *Cong.* 4.16. An almost identical passage says, "Song and speech are healthful and curative medicines, song charming the passions and controlling the unrhythmic in us with its rhythms, the unmelodious with its melodies, and the immoderate with its measures . . . Belief in the musicians and poets becomes habitual in those well educated" (*Spec. leg.* I.62.343).

111. For another statement of the ethos theory of music, cf. *Cher.* 30.105 cited above; cf. Plato, *Prot.* 326a-b; *Resp.* 401d; Aristotle, *Pol.* 1340a-b; Athenaeus, *Deip.* 623f—624a (including a reference to Theophrastus as saying music cures diseases).

112. For the Greek theory of musical ethos, Anderson, *Ethos and Education in Greek Music*. Plato, *Phaedo* 85-86 on the soul as a *harmonia*; Ps. Plutarch, *Mus.* 42 (*Mor.* 1146d) on music as first giving thanks to the gods and second making the soul harmonically well adjusted. Cf. *Plant.* 38.159: At one time poets and others inspired by the Muses "did not sweeten and enfeeble their hearers with rhythmic sounds, but they revived any faculty of the mind that was weakened and broken and they harmonized with the instruments of nature and virtue whatever of the mind that was out of tune."

reason—swallows, nightingales, and other birds that make music—and the euphony of rational beings, singing to the kithara in comedy, tragedy and other theatrical productions.[113]

But music was also associated with unworthy pleasures: myriads every day fill up the theatres where they honor "those who play the kithara and sing to its accompaniment and all the effeminate and unmanly music, approving the dancers and other mimes."[114] In contrast to Jewish festivals, the seductive power of such types of music "through the ears arouse ungovernable lusts"[115] and advance idolatry.[116]

More often than speaking of the effects of music on a person's inner well being, Philo uses music to provide the illustration for harmony or the lack thereof in an individual. Human beings are mixtures of the divine and the mortal, "blended together and harmonized according to the proportions of perfect music.[117] As with Plato this inner harmony is achieved by the reason ruling and guiding the senses.[118] Choral imagery describes the internal harmony that Philo considers the human ideal:

> When the soul enters the intellectual, divine, and truly holy place, the senses aided by virtue and indeed our whole being may join in the hymn just as when a large and melodious chorus sings together one harmonious melody from the different voices blended together, the thoughts of the mind inspiring the preludes—for the leaders of this chorus are the thoughts

---

113. *Leg. all.* II.18.75; for the exciting effects of music, cf. *Leg. all.* III.78.221. See above on Philodemus for music bringing pleasure. Compare *Abr.* 29.148, 150: "We get pleasure from hearing very melodious sounds, and this can be good, being linked with philosophy."

114. *Agr.* 8.35. A tradition of classifying music as male or female was worked out extensively by Aristides Quintilianus, *Mus.* 2.8.66—19.92; Barker, *Greek Musical Writings*, 2.470 n. 71.

115. *Spec. leg.* II.32.193.

116. *Spec. leg.* I.5.28-29. See above on occasions when music was employed in pagan society.

117. *Mut.* 34.184. Cf. *Q. Ex.* 2.38 (trans. by Ralph Marcus in LCL, *Supplement* II: 81): "Disonance from decency [virtue] and disharmony are death to the soul. Therefore ... as in an all-musical chorus with the blended voices of all one should play music in harmonious measures of modulation and with skilled fingers, seeking to show (the harmony) not so much in sound as in mind"; *Fuga* 3.22: Gen 31:27 is applied to the person who does not share in the good things of God: his music is unmusical, and "his kitharas, not instruments but the deeds of life, lack melody and harmony."

118. E.g., *Resp.* 431, 439-41; Aristotle and the Stoics agreed.

of the mind—while the senses sing along together the subsequent parts, which resemble the role of the individual chorus members.[119]

Musical language provides the words to describe the union of the gifts of king, lawgiver, high priest, and prophet in Moses.[120] For ordinary human beings, this harmony pertains to the agreement in good between thoughts, words, and deeds. Observance of the Ten Commandments with "good intentions, wholesome words, and diligent actions" result in the soul being "an instrument that makes music harmoniously in all its parts for a melodious life and blameless concert."[121] Similarly, "If, like tuning all the good sounds of a lyre, one succeeded in bringing speech into harmony with the mind and the mind with the deed, such a person would be considered perfect and in harmony with the truth."[122]

Harmony in Human Nature and the Cosmos

Philo used instrumental analogies for all elements of human nature. "The soul harmonized musically is like a lyre . . . ; [the wise man] keeping it in equal tension strikes and plucks it (ἐπιψάλλειν) melodiously. For the soul is the most perfect instrument fashioned by nature, the archetype (ἀρχέτυπος) of those made by hands."[123] Similarly Philo considered both the mind and the senses as instruments, and the goal was proper harmony

---

119. *Mig.* 18.104; cf. *Ebr* 30.116–17 and *Deus imm.* 6.24–25 below on the harmony of the soul. This passage is relevant to the discussion below of the manner in which songs were sung.

120. *Mos.* II.1.7.

121. *Spec. leg.* IV.25.134; cf. *Deus imm.* 6.25 for this inner harmony expressed in deeds and *Ebr.* 30.117 for it expressed in words; cf. Plato, *Lach.* 188d for harmony of words and deeds better than the harmony of the lyre.

122. *Post.* 24.88. *Q. Ex.* 2.20, For God "wishes him who philosophizes in accordance with Him to be a harmony of all sounds like a musical instrument with no discord or dissonance in any part but with one and the same consonance and harmony of will with word and of word with deed and of deed with both of these" (LCL, *Philo Supplement* II:59–60); *Mos.* 1.6.29.

123. *Deus imm.* 6.24–25; for the comparison of the soul to a lyre cf. *Cher* 31.110; *Ebr.* 30.116. The quotations above show that Philo often compared the soul to a chorus; the analogy of a human being to a lyre found expression in Greek musical theorists like Arisioxertus—Annie Bélis, "La théorie de l'âme chez Aristoxène de Tarente." Note below for heavenly bodies and the human voice as archetypes of music and of instruments.

of the two.¹²⁴ Hence, the confusion of tongues at the tower of Babel offered Philo much opportunity to consider the human condition.¹²⁵

The harmony of the self was extended to the harmony of the community. Indeed, in Genesis 11 the primary reference is to the peoples of the earth. As in persons without the gift of music the vocal organ is tuned to disharmony, so the people of Babel were in harmony and agreement, with no discordant voice, in the doing of iniquity.¹²⁶ But this is not the way things should be. The city is like a soul, and the best constitution is like a hymn to God.¹²⁷ The unity of the whole people is a symphony.¹²⁸

Corresponding to human harmony was cosmic harmony. The Pythagoreans, followed by Plato and then by musical theorists, spoke of the "music of the spheres" and posited the mathematical correspondences of the relations of the heavenly bodies with the ratios of musical intervals.¹²⁹ In some passages Philo combines human harmony with the celestial concert. In a striking statement about the created order as musical combined with a remarkable tribute to the importance he attached to music, Philo says that the creation is the "true music, the original (ἀρχέτυπον) and

---

124. *Agr.* 17.80, quoted below. Cf. *Ebr.* 30.116: The soul is like an instrument in which a single note out of tune can destroy the harmony, but "it is a symphony when all the keys of courage and every virtue are combined and produce one harmonious melody."

125. He took the words of Gen 11:6, "the earth was all one lip and one voice," as referring to the peoples' agreement (*symphonia*) in evil deeds, but he then applied it to the multitude of evils in individuals: "especially when the symphony [or unison of voice] within is disharmonious, dissonant, and discordant"; "the symphony of our self-chosen evils"; or in contrast "the symphony of virtues, all harmonious and musical." See *Conf.* 5.15. (cf. 15.67); 7.21 (cf. 18.83); 11.43.

126. *Conf.* 19.150

127. *Conf.* 23.108, following the reading of the manuscripts, but see the note in LCL, Vol. 4, 68. On the place of music in establishing and sustaining community, see Plato, *Resp.* 424c; *Leges* 701a–b.

128. *Conf.* 13.55, 58: "We like musical instruments with all the notes perfectly in tune echo with our voices all the lessons we have heard, speaking no word and practising no deed that is out of tune or out of harmony"; cf. *Somn.* II.41.270: When wisdom is discovered, "all the people will sing not with one part of music but with all its harmonies and melodies."

129. Plato, *Resp.* 530d–531b); cf. *Tim.* 34b—36d on the musical structure of the soul of the universe; Ps. Plutarch, *Mus.* 44 (*Mor.* 1147a) says Pythagoras and Plato claimed that the movement of the stars came about through the influence of music; Ptolemy, *Harm.* 3.4.95 found harmony in all things that are perfect in their nature but most fully revealed through human souls and through the movements in the heavens; Aristides Quintilianus, *Mus.* 2.8.66–68, 14.79–82, 16.84–89; and 3.7.105, 9.107–27.133 developed an elaborate system of the soul as corresponding to the elements of music and of the cosmic harmony to which earthly music is an imperfect imitation.

model (παραδειγματικήν)" of everything from which human beings derived "this most necessary and beneficial art."[130] He moves from human concord to harmony of the cosmos.[131] The same Logos that ordered the cosmos and created the nine intervals of music is also the leader of the human chorus.[132] Following Aristotle Philo makes a parallel between heavenly music and human music.[133]

Praise of God and the Music of the Cosmos

In keeping with this theme of the continuity between the harmony of the cosmos and that of the soul, Philo makes numerous brief references to the

---

130. *Op. mund.* 25.78. Nicomachus, *Enchiridion* 3.241-42 expressed the view that music among human beings is an imitation of the music of the planets.

131. *Conf.* 13.56: "the whole world, which is the instrument of him who is the All, may make melody musically with its harmonies." Also on the world as God's instrument cf. *Virt.* 11.74 quoted below.

132. *Q. Gen.* 4.110 (*Philo Supplement* I, 393-94): the Logos is "the leader and ruler of harmony" so that "melodies and songs sound as one"; the number ten trumpets "the theme of forgiveness in concordant and antiphonal chants leading to one and the same mixture of harmony." For the place of the "divine Logos" in achieving the universal harmony, cf. *Plant.* 2.10, and the human being in tune with nature, cf: *Plant.* 38.159 quoted above. The Armenian fragment of *De Deo* contains the statement, "The Being has ordered the universe by his Word, and [the universe] has been made vocal and rational by his providence" (section 5); see Siegert, "The Philonian Fragment *De Deo*," 5. For the seven planets and two spheres corresponding to the number nine in music, Aristides Quintilianus, *Mus.* 3.6.102 (Philo, however, may have counted the sun and moon with the planets—see quotation at n. 137 below) and 12.112; for the number ten, ibid. 3.6.103 and 23.124-25.

133. *Q. Gen.* 3.3 (*Philo Supplement* I, 181): "Birds are singers," and Moses alludes "to the music which is perfected in heaven and is produced by the harmony of the movement of the stars. For it is an indication of human skill that all harmonic melody is formed by the voices of animals and living organs through the mechanism of the intelligence. But the heavenly singing does not extend" to the earth, because "that most harmonious and truly heavenly music, when it strikes the organ of hearing" would drive human beings to madness. For Aristotle, see *De caelo* 290b, which explained that humans cannot hear the music of the spheres because the sound is there from our birth and so has no contrasting silence by which it may be discerned; the Pythagorean Archytas offered several possibilities why our nature could not discern the heavenly music—the weakness of its impact, its distance from us, or the very loudness too great to be received (Porphry, *Comm.* 56 57; for the last explanation cf. Cicero, *Rep.* 6.18-19); Aristides Quintilianus, *Mus.* 3.20.120 said we could not hear it because of the distance and the debilitating influence of the body, but men of virtue can hear it (as Philo said Moses did, see below).

theme of cosmic music.¹³⁴ Second only to seeing God is seeing "the visible heaven and the harmonious and all musical order of the stars truly like a chorus."¹³⁵

Philo considered a principal function of music to be for praising God. *On Dreams* 1.6.35–37 is an important passage that brings together several themes under the heading of praise to God:

> Both heaven and the mind have the capacity to declaim praises, hymns, and blessings to the Father who is the One who brought them into being. For the human being was assigned the excellent reward above all other living things to worship the One who is, while the heaven is always melodious, producing all-musical harmony by the movements of its parts. If its sound ever reached our hearing, there would be mad, ceaseless frenzies . . . [Such] inspired songs of perfect music Moses heard [when he fasted forty days and nights] . . . The heaven, then, the archetypical instrument of music, appears to have been tuned perfectly for no other purpose than that the hymns being sung to the honor of the Father of all might be accompanied (ἐπιψάλλωνται) musically.¹³⁶

---

134. *Cher.* 31.110: The reciprocity of the whole created order, earthly as well as heavenly is like "a lyre, harmonized out of unlike notes, and comes into fellowship and concord." Cf. *Det. pot.* 33.125: In God's creation there are "no meters, rhythms, and melodies of sound attracting the ears through music but the most perfect works of nature itself allotted its own beautiful harmony"; *Op. mund.* 17.54: The human faculty of vision observed the harmonious movement of the stars and "their rhythmic dances, ordered by the harmonious laws of perfect music"; *Spec. leg.* I.18.61: "Evil has been excluded from the divine choir" (for the phrase "divine choir" see Plato, *Phaedrus* 247a); *Cher.* 7.23: "The fixed stars dance as in a truly divine choral order"; Cf. *Mos.* I.38.212: "the choral dance of the planets and fixed stars"; II.4.9.271, "the chorus of the stars"; *Spec. leg.* I.6.34, "the choral movements of the planets, fixed stars, and the whole heaven"; *Aet.* 2.4, "the cosmos [is] the choric movements and revolutions of the stars." See also *Mig.* 32.178: That "the most harmonious symphony of the universe" is "like the laws of music" was the basis of Chaldean astronomy; cf. *Abr.* 17.77.

135. *Cong.*10.51.

136. *Somn.* 1.6.35—7.37. For the heavenly music producing madness in human beings, see *Q. Gen.* 3.3 cited above; for the heavenly bodies as the archetypical music, see *Op. mund.* 25.78 cited above. Ἐπιψάλλω meant "to play on a lyre," then in 2 Macc 1:30 "to sing," and in patristic literature "to sing responses" (e.g., Clement of Alexandria, *Str.* 5.8). All three meanings are possible here. Philo reflects classical Greek musical terminology; therefore, he avoids ψάλμοί as the title of the Psalms and calls them ὕμνοι (e.g. *Cont.* 3.25; *Plant.* 7.29; *Mig.* 28.157; *Somn.* II.37.245), ὑμνῳδία (as in *Plant.* 9.39), or ᾄσμα (as in *Somn.* II.37.246; *Mut.* 20.115). Rather than the "Psalmist" David is the ὑμνῳδός, in *Deus imm.* 16.74 and "the one who hymns" in *Conf.* 28.149. Consequently, here I have opted for a translation alluding to instrumental accompaniment.

The Art of Praise

Similarly, a long passage on the end of Moses's life brings together a number of these themes regarding heavenly music and the praise of God:

> He began to praise God in song [Deut 32:1–43], rendering thanksgiving . . . Gathering together a divine assembly, the elements of the universe and the most essential parts of the cosmos, the earth and heaven, one the home of mortals and the other the house of the immortals, in their midst he sang his hymn of praise with all harmony and every kind of symphony so that both men and ministering angels might hear . . . , the angels themselves skilful in music observing lest there be any discordant note in the song and doubting that someone bound in a corruptible body [Moses] was able like the sun, moon, and the all holy chorus of the other stars to harmonize his soul so as to make music in accompaniment with God's instrument, the heaven and all the cosmos. Having taken his position in the presence of the ethereal chorus, the hierophant blended with his thanksgiving hymns his genuine feelings for the well being of the nation.[137]

The one duty of human beings is to honor God with thanksgiving, voiced with or without melody.[138] In response to the magnificent blessings of God, Philo asks rhetorically, "What is more fitting for one to do than to return to the Benefactor words, and songs, and hymns?"[139] or more fully, "to return to him in a pure manner hymns, blessings, prayers, and other thanksgivings, in a word, praise."[140] Thus it is natural that Philo includes song as typical of Jewish worship[141] and especially in the religious festivals. Moses "called the people to the sanctuary to share in hymns, prayers, and sacrifices";[142] at Passover those gathered for the banquet "fulfill the custom

---

137. *Virt.* 11.72–75; cf. *Spec. leg.* I.V24.177 for Moses as the "hierophant who hymned the excellencies of Him who is."

138. *Plant.* 31.131; for "to speak" and "to sing" praise to God, cf. *Somn.* 1.43.256; 2.5.38; and the correction adopted in LCL (V, 562) at 2.41.268.

139. *Sob.* 11.58.

140. *Spec. leg.* I.41.224; cf. II.32.199, "to reverence, worship, and honor the Giver with harmonious hymns and blessings: and II.33.209, "they honor God for the good things of the present with songs and words." Cf. Plato, *Leges* 800–802, "hymns, prayers, and encomia."

141. *Somn.* II.5.34: the allegorical interpretation of Judah as "songs and hymns to God." Also in an expository vein, compare *Mos.* I.46.255: "The people loved by God [Israel] in their gladness and joy set up choruses in a circle around the well and sang a new song to God"; cf. Balaam "singing the most exalted hymns to God" in *Mig.* 20.113 and Jacob "singing and hymning" in *Ios.* 42.253.

142. *Spec. leg.* I.35.193.

handed down from the fathers with prayers and hymns";[143] at Tabernacles the worshipper brings baskets from the fruit-harvest to the priest, reciting "a beautiful and marvellous song."[144] While Philo has various combinations of words to formulate the response of praise to God,[145] he affirms that "the best and most perfect product of all right actions brought to birth is the hymn to the Father of the universe.[146] Yet from an ultimate standpoint, Philo considered it impossible to render adequate praise to God.[147]

The Therapeutae and Choral Music

Although Philo does not describe music at the temple in Jerusalem nor specifically speak of any musical practices in synagogues,[148] he tells us a great deal more about how the vocal music he preferred was performed among the Jews than is usually acknowledged. Bare references to actual singing, however, are not always informative on the manner of performance.[149] He frequently uses several words for vocal music without any apparent sharp distinction in meaning; e.g., "praise, hymns, and songs fitting for God."[150] Like other ancient writers, Philo recognized the differences in human voices. The parts of the human self and the different members of the people correspond to these different kinds of voices. So too with the celestial music, the combination of different sounds makes a more complete melody: "For if there had not been produced in the world the harmonious blending into a symphony of antiphonal voices as if of a

---

143. *Spec. leg.* II.27.148.

144. *Spec. leg.* II.35.216 and 220; cf. *Virt.*18.95 for "hymns composed to God," which are preserved in the sacred books, accompanying the offerings.

145. *Heres* 22.110, 111: As the "mind should think of nothing else than God and his excellencies, speech should honor the Father of all with unbridled mouth, with encomia, hymns, and blessings," "hymning with the voice's instrument the world and its Creator"; cf. "sing with sweet melody the excellencies of Him who is" (*Somn.* 1.43.256); for hymning God's excellencies (virtues) see *Spec. leg.* IV.34.17.

146. *Plant.* 33.135.

147. *Mos.* II.43.239: "O Master, how can one hymn you? With what mouth, what tongue, what organ of speech, what leading part of the soul? If the stars become one chorus, what melody will they sing that is worthy?"

148. Feldman, "Philo's Views," 527.

149. E.g., *Cong.* 21.115, "sing a refrain."

150. *Leg. all.* III.8.26. Given Philo's avoidance of the word "psalms," the statement is a close parallel to Eph 5:19, "psalms, hymns and spiritual songs."

choir sounding as one, it would not have received its full perfection."[151] Philo refers to "precentors" (ἔξαρχοι) or "leaders (ἡγεμόνες) of the chorus who led the singing."[152]

More significant with regard to the practice of choral music within the Alexandrian synagogue communities is the account of their response to the news, which arrived during the Feast of Tabernacles, of the arrest of the prefect Flaccus, who had allowed the pogrom against the Jews in 37 CE. "Extending their hands to heaven, they sang hymns and songs of victory to God," and "all through the night they continued in hymns and odes." At dawn they went to the beach, since their synagogues had been taken from them, and offered prayer to God.[153] Doubts have been raised about the presence of psalmody or any kind of singing in synagogues during New Testament times.[154] Such a conclusion requires a discounting of the account by Philo, who had immediate knowledge of the events. Even if a sharp distinction were maintained between what was done "in synagogue" and other religious activities, based on the wording of the passage,[155] it testifies nonetheless to a rich experience of vocal religious music among Alexandrian Jews.

This testimony is extended by Philo's fullest and most informative account of the musical activities of some Jews, namely that found in his description of a sectarian community known as the Therapeutae, who

---

151. *Q. Ex.* II.120 (*Philo Supplement* II, 172); cf. II.38, with reference to inner harmony, quoted above, "In an all-musical chorus" there are "the blended voices of all."

152. *Ebr.* 31.121; cf. 29.112. We should not think of the "leader" as a modern director of a chorus but perhaps more like a lead singer whom the chorus joined as the song began or to whom it responded. Cf. *Mig.* 18.104 quoted above. West (*Ancient Greek Music*, 339) notes that the pattern of a leader (*exarchos*) and an answering chorus was well established in Greek cultic practice; the practice of a solo singer who leads off and a chorus that answers was widespread throughout the Near East (388).

153. *Flacc.* 14.121-22.

154. Smith, "The Ancient Synagogue, the Early Church and Singing"; McKinnon, "On the Question of Psalmody in the Ancient Synagogue."

155. It might be argued, for example, that the setting of the singing is a public, "outdoor" festival (Succoth), to be distinguished from the act of praying, which is said to have taken place at the beach because their "prayerhalls" (προσευχαί) had been confiscated. On the other hand, prayer for the Jews was not as distinct from song as in modern usage, and the festival cycle was closely tied to scripture readings and prayers usually associated with synagogue activity. We should see the first-century synagogues as integral to the total community life of the Jewish residents of Alexandria. The concerted group participation described by Philo with formal acts of song and prayer suggest joint religious activity with which the whole community was familiar.

lived together not far from Alexandria.[156] An introductory summary of their musical interests states, "They not only engage in contemplation, but they also compose songs and hymns to God in all kinds of meters and melodies, which they mark with rhythms necessarily more solemn."[157] The description of their actual singing occurs in the account of their celebration on the fiftieth day, presumably Pentecost, a description which because of its fullness of musical information deserves to be quoted extensively.

> [Following a discourse by the president,] The president having stood up sings a hymn addressed to God, either a new one composed by himself or an old one by poets of an earlier time [one of the Psalms?], for they have left behind in many meters and melodies verses in trimeters, hymns for processions, at libations, and at the altars, and careful metrical arrangements for the stops and varied movements of choruses.[158] After him the others [sing] in proper order according to their rank, while all the rest listen in great silence except when they must sing the closing phrases or refrains, for then all, both men and women, lift up their voices. [When each has finished his hymn, the meal is served.]
>
> [Then came an all-night vigil of the community that was spent in song.] They all rise together in the midst of the dining room and first form two choruses, one of men and one of women. For each chorus the most honored and most musical is chosen as precentor and leader. Then they sing hymns to God composed in many meters and melodies, sometimes singing together and at other times with antiphonal harmonies, motioning with their hands, and dancing, inspiring in turn processional odes and then performing the stops, turnings, and movements of a choric dance. Then when each of the choruses has taken its own part in the feast, . . . they combine and out of the two become one chorus, a copy of what was constituted at the Red Sea on account of the marvelous things done there . . . At that time filled with divine enthusiasm, the men together with the women, becoming one chorus, sang thanksgiving hymns to God their Savior, the prophet Moses leading the men and the prophetess Miriam the women. On this model the male and female members with

---

156. Conybeare, *Philo about the Contemplative Life*; Riaud, "Les Thérapeutus d'Alexandrie"; Taylor and Davies, "The So-Called Therapeutae of *De Vita Contemplativa*."

157. *Cont.* 3.29.

158. Alternatively, instead of referring to the dances, "the stationary choral songs well arranged with versatile strophes."

> responsive and antiphonal strains, blending the bass sound of the men with the treble of the women, perform a harmonious and truly musical symphony. Truly beautiful are the thoughts, truly beautiful the words, reverent are the chorus members. The goal of the thoughts, the words, and the choruses is godliness.[159]

By employing technical vocabulary Philo intends for the reader to be reminded of the choral music and dances of the Greek theater and religious festivals. Philo describes solo, responsorial (when the leader's text is followed by the others singing a refrain), and unison singing by the Therapeutae. Whether the "antiphonal harmonies" (84) and "antiphonal strains" (88) are to be thought of as yet another style of singing with the choruses of men and women responding to each other antiphonally (suggested by the context of the former statement) or as indicating the contrasting pitches of male and female voices (indicated by the latter statement) is not clear. Philo closes the description with a statement recalling his concern for the harmony of thoughts, words, and actions, and he brings it all under the umbrella of religious piety.

There might be a suspicion that Philo invented the whole account of the Therapeutae, including their musical activities, in order to advance his philosophical ideas or to claim a Jewish version of a Pythagorean-like community; but on the matter of musical practices, there is too much concurrence with other passages in Philo to think that these are made up, even if this specific community did not exist.[160] Perhaps the most surprising feature of this account is its emphasis on antiphonal choruses of men and women. Male and female choruses were common in the Greek world, but not among Jews (see below), another indication that most of what Philo writes about music reflects his Greek education and social world. A specifically Jewish setting is provided by the parallel with the account in Exod 15:1–21 of the celebration by the Israelites of their escape from Egyptian bondage.

---

159. *Cont.* 10.80; 11.83–85, 87–88.

160. For a defense of the historicity of the group, see Hay, "Things Philo Said and Did Not Say about the Therapeutae." For Philo's account as a fabricated story, see Engberg-Pedersen, "Philo's *De vita contemplativa* as a Philosopher's Dream." My own opinion is that there was such a group, however much idealized Philo's account might be. On the other hand, if it were fabricated, it becomes all the more significant as evidence for what Philo thought religious music ought to be. The agreements especially concern his treatment of Exodus 15, a particularly important passage for him, judging by the frequency of his references to it, although oddly enough not in his *Questions and Answers on Exodus*.

In addition to the book of Psalms, which he calls "Hymns,"¹⁶¹ Philo refers to a number of other songs in the Bible, for example the "song sung by Hannah."¹⁶² There are frequent references to Deuteronomy 32, "the Greater Song" (μείζων ᾠδή) by reason of its length.¹⁶³ But the most important Biblical song in its influence on Philo in regard to musical performance was the Song of Victory sung after the crossing of the Red Sea in Exodus 15.¹⁶⁴ It is "the Song (τὸ ᾆσμα) in which Moses hymns God."¹⁶⁵ Although the passage was important for Jews generally,¹⁶⁶ it made a significant impression on Philo, who made a distinctive use of it. It is not clear whether this passage occasioned the practice of the Therapeutae or their practice influenced Philo's interpretation of what happened in Exodus 15.¹⁶⁷ The separate statements of Exod 15:1 and 21 gave the possibility of presenting separate choruses of men and women as doing the singing.¹⁶⁸ Philo seems to emphasize particularly that the women participated. This sets him at odds with later rabbinic literature, which disapproved of mixed choirs.¹⁶⁹

---

161. See n. 136 above.

162. *Mut.* 25.143 (1 Samuel 2).

163. *Post.* 35.121; 48.167; *Plant.* 14.59; *Sob.* 3.10; *Mut.* 34.182; *Somn.* II.29.191; "Great Song" in *Leg. all.* III.34.105; *Det. pot.* 30.114; simply "a Song" in *Virt.* 11.72.

164. Goldin, *The Song at the Sea*, 248 gives a commentary on this passage, *Shirta*, in the *Mekilta de-Rabbi Ismael*. He makes frequent reference to Philo in his notes and offers other evidence for this song sung antiphonally.

165. *Leg all.* II.25.102–26.103; *Sob.* 3.13 reverses the verb and noun, "sings the hymn to God"; other references to the song in Exodus 15—*Plant.* 12.48; *Ebr.* 19.79; 29.111; *Conf.* 10.35–36; *Somn.* II.41.269 ("We sing the most sacred ode").

166. Exod 15 provided the wording for the benediction following the recitation of the Shema—Dembitz, "Ge'ullah,") 5.648; text translated in McNamara, *Targum and Testament*, 39. See *m. Sota* 5.4 for Exod 15 in temple worship.

167. Perhaps both considerations were present, the Biblical account taken by the Therapeutae as authorizing their activity and that activity in turn filling in details in Philo's understanding of the text.

168. *Mos.* 1.32.180: "Seeing the total destruction of their enemies in a moment, they set up on the shore two choruses, one of men and one of women, and sang thanksgiving hymns to God, Moses being the precentor for the men and his sister for the women, for these became the leaders of the choruses." Earlier Greek choruses were either male or female, but sources contemporary with Philo mention men and women singing in unison (Ps. Aristotle, *Mund.* 399a; Seneca, *Ep.* 84.9); see West, *Ancient Greek Music*, 40.

169. *b. Sotah* 48a: "Rabbi Joseph [third-century Babylonian Amora] said: 'When men sing and women join in it is licentiousness; when women sing and men join in it is like fire in town.' For what practical purpose is this mentioned? To abolish the latter before the former." The footnote to the translation in the Soncino edition, ed. I. Epstein

The Art of Praise

Whatever the actual practice, Philo's allegorical expositions on Exod 15 develop the musical aspects of the episode rather fully and bring in themes already identified. In the first[170] we find the union of song by heavenly powers with human beings, the harmony of the self (mind and senses), which is an instrument to be played in praise to God, song associated with thanksgiving, vocal praise proceeding from the mind, both women and men singing, each with their own leader to start the hymn and responding to each other in harmony.

Similar motifs occur in the exposition from the *Life of Moses*;[171] however, here Philo emphasizes the harmony of the people instead of the harmony of the individual. In this connection, the different qualities of male and female voices are highlighted. Otherwise, the same manner of singing is described: a leader beginning, the chorus joining in, and the separate choruses of men and women either alternating antiphonally, responding with the refrain together, or perhaps doing both at different times.

Evaluating Different Types of Music

Philo followed philosophical thought in the evaluations he gave to different kinds of music. A further preference derives from the goal of praise to God and the continuity of the human soul with the cosmos. The different types of music, therefore, are graded accordingly: stringed instruments over wind and percussion instruments, the voice over instrumental music, and "silent singing" (the thoughts of the mind) over vocal music.

(London: Soncino, 1936) explains that the men joining in is more serious because it is a willful act by the men to listen to female voices. Feldman, "Philo's Views on Music," 525 cites the opinion of the third-century rabbi Samuel that "A woman's voice is a sexual incitement" (*b. Ber.* 24a) to support the conclusion that a man was not permitted to hear her sing and so women did not sing in the synagogue.

170. *Agr.* 17.79—18.82; Ps. Aristotle, *Prob.* 19.39 says the correspondence of different voices is pleasanter than unison singing and gives the example of the blending of children's with men's voices.

171. *Mos.* II.46.256–57. "Moses appropriately honors the Benefactor with thanksgiving hymns. He divided the nation into two choruses, one or men and one of women, and he himself leads the men and he appoints his sister precentor of the women in order that responding together they might sing hymns to the Father and Creator with answering [or concordant] harmonies, a blending of temperaments and melodies, ... a symphony of the combination of bass and treble. For the voices of men are deep and the women's high, and when their blending occurs in proper proportion there is produced the sweetest and most harmonious melody. He persuaded these myriads of people to be of one mind and to sing together the same hymn ... He led off the song, and his hearers assembled in two choruses and sang together the words spoken above."

Philo often refers in summary fashion to the different ways of making music, "to play on the aulos, to play on the kithara, to sing, or any similar kind of performance,"[172] and to the principal instruments: "aulos, kithara, and every kind of instrument,"[173] "aulos, lyre, and other instruments of music,"[174] or "psalterion and kithara" as standing for "all music."[175] Of these instruments, Philo considered the lyre the best and the standard for other instruments: "In music the seven-stringed lyre is generally regarded as the best of instruments, because the enharmonic mode, which is the most dignified of all the classes of melodies, is considered somehow best when rendered by it."[176] Again, "The seven-stringed lyre, which corresponds to the choir of the [seven] planets, produces notable harmonies, and is (one might say) the chief of all the instruments for making music."[177] Philo was particularly negative about percussion instruments, since they did not make music but "noises inarticulate and meaningless."[178]

Vocal music is related to the harmony of a person in which reason rules the senses, and, moreover, instruments are hand-made, but the voice is nature's instrument: "The musician accommodates meters, rhythms, and all kinds of melody to the auloi, kitharas, and other instruments, and he is able apart from the handmade instruments to use the instrument of nature through the voice attuned to all the notes."[179] Interpreting Jubal allegorically as "sounding speech," Philo finds it fitting that he is called the "father of music and all musical instruments" (Gen 4:21). And he proceeds to declare the organ of sound the most perfect of all instruments and the pattern for artificially fashioned instruments:

---

172. *Sob.* 8.36; cf. *Leg. all.* 3.78.221.

173. *Leq. all.* II.18.75.

174. *Sac.* 4.18; cf. *Post.* 32.105.

175. *Post.* 32.111.

176. *Leg. all.* I.5.14.; the preference of the lyre over the aulos was Pythagorean according to Aristides Quintilianus, *Mus.* 2.19.91f. (but Sextus Empiricus, *Adv. Math.* 6.7–9, 23 relates a story about Pythagoras that gives a positive evaluation to the aulos); Cf. Plato, *Resp.* 397a, 399c–e; there was an association of the lyre with the rational and the aulos with emotional frenzy—*Leges* 790e—791b); so also Aristotle, *Pol.* 1339a, 1341a-b, hence he rejected the aulos from his educational curriculum; he reports Socrates' disapproval of the instrument in 1342a-b.

177. *Op. mund.* 42.126.

178. *Fuga* 3.22.

179. *Sob.* 8.36. Plato, *Resp.* 398d, 400a,d and *Leges* 669 subordinated melody and rhythm to the words. "Music is the sound of the voice that reaches and educates the soul"—*Leges* 673a.

> Nature, fashioning for living creatures the vocal organ as the chief and most perfect instrument, granted to it immediately all the harmonies and kinds of melodies so that it might become, the pattern made beforehand for those instruments going to be fashioned by (human) skill . . . Nature made for living creatures the rough windpipe, stretching it like a musical scale [or chord], harmonizing the enharmonic, chromatic, and diatonic classes according to the various kinds of conjunct and disjunct melodies, and established it the pattern of every musical instrument.[180]

The passage continues with a praise of natural music over instrumental, of the voice over all other kinds, including a contrast of what is pleasing to the ear (instrumental music) with what is pleasing to both the ear and the mind (vocal music):

> Whatever melodious sounds auloi, lyres, and other such instruments produce, they fall as much short of the music of nightingales and swans as a copy and imitation does of an original pattern . . . None of the other kinds of music is worthy to be compared to that of the human voice, since it has the incomparable privilege, for which it is honored, of articulate expression. By using the modulation of sound and successive changes of tones the other types please only the hearing, but the human being, having been given articulation by nature for speaking and singing, wins over both the hearing and the mind, charming the one by the melody. and leading the other by the thoughts. For just as an instrument given to an unmusical person is tuneless but becomes tuneful according to the skill of the musical person, in the same way speech set in motion by a worthless mind is without harmony but by a diligent mind is found altogether melodious. A lyre or any similar instrument, unless it is struck by someone, is quiet, and speech also unless struck by the ruling faculty of necessity remains silent . . .[181]

180. *Post.* 31.103–4; cf. *Deus imm.* 6.25 below for the soul as the archetype of man-made instruments. The same view was expressed by Nicomachus (beginning of second century AD): sounds of stringed. blown, and percussion instruments are imitations of the sounds we ourselves make—*Enchiridion* 2.240.20ff. Ptolemy, *Harm.* 1.20.9 has the reverse comparison that the windpipe is something of a natural aulos.

181. *Post.* 32.105–8. In classical Greece instruments accompanied song but by Philo's time they were used independently; Ps. Aristotle, *Prob.* 19.39 still subordinates the accompaniment to the song. Ps. Plutarch, *Mus.* 2 (*Mor.* 1131d) offers a comparable statement to Philo: "For it is an act of piety and a principal concern to human beings to hymn the gods, who have given articulate speech to them alone." Ibid., 34 (*Mor.* 1143f) for the ear and the mind working together (so also Aristoxenus, *El. Harm.*

Since speech can proceed from a "worthless mind" and can be itself soulless,[182] Philo ascribed to the proper thoughts of the mind the highest level of praise, the philosophical concept of "silent singing."[183]

> The loudest cry is not with mouth and tongue . . . but with the all musical and loudest sounding organ of the soul, which is not heard by anyone mortal but only by the uncreated and imperishable One. For only the mind's Musician, not anyone entangled in sense perception, is capable of apprehending the beautiful and symphonic melody of the mind's harmony.[184]

In one of his noblest passages, Philo expressed the basis for this concept of spiritual sacrifice. "God is in need of nothing, but he rejoices in God-loving thoughts and in the human exercise of holiness," and from such worshipers he accepts simple grain offerings, "holding the things of least cost as most precious more than those things of highest price." He continues:

2.33.2–10—vocal and instrumental music involve hearing and reason) and 37 (*Mor.* 1144f) for Pythagoras saying the excellence of music is to be apprehended by the mind and not judged by sense perception. For the voice having the twofold capacity "for speaking and singing" cf. *Spec. leg.* I.62.342; for articulation as making sound "truly rational" cf. *Q. Gen.* II.3 and III.3 (the melody of voices comes by means of the intelligence). "Swallows, nightingales, and other birds"—*Leg. all.* II.18.75; even grasshoppers have a song—*Cont.* 4.35. Cf. Aristotle, *An.* 420b-421a on "voice" in some animals (but not all sounds they produce are from a "voice") and *Gen. animal.* 788a on rough and smooth voices. *Det. pot.* 34.126: The Creator "has made speech like a compound instrument, the articulate utterance of our whole being," and it has its excellence because it is a "brother of the mind," whose thoughts it brings to expression. Cf. Theophrastus (in Porphyry, *Comm.* 61) on the soul turning the voice (itself wordless or non-rational) as it wishes. *Dec.* 9.33: God's voice at Sinai was declared to be "more marvelous than all instruments." It might be nothing remarkable for this to be said of God, but the explanation seems to reflect Philo's general estimate of voices in relation to instruments: "it was fitted with perfect harmonies, not soulless. . . . but a rational soul full of clarity and distinctness." Aristotle had said, "Nothing that is without soul utters voice"—*An.* 420b; for the description of instruments as "soulless" cf. 1 Cor 14:7.

182. *Det. pot.* 34.130.

183. On this concept see Apollonius of Tyana, *De sacrif.* quoted in Eusebius, *Praep. Evang.* 4.13; *Corp. Herm.* 1.31; 13.18–19; from Nag Hammadi *Disc.* 8–9 (NHC VI, 58,20–60,5); and Porphyry (building on Theophrastus), *De abst.* 2.34.

184. *Heres* 4.14–15; cf. without the musical analogy *Leg. all.* III.14.44. Compare also *Plant.* 30.126: "It is not possible genuinely to give thanks to God through those things most people consider—buildings, offerings, and sacrifices—for the whole world would not be an adequate temple for his honor; but through praises and hymns, not which the spoken voice sings but which the formless and purest mind resounds in uplifted strains"; *Ebr.* 23.94, "those who sing the thanksgiving hymn not with the spoken voice but rather with the understanding" and *Somn.* 1.6.35 quoted above for hymns coming from the mind. Cf. *Leg. all.* II.15.56 for sacrificing the whole mind.

Although the worshipers bring nothing else, in offering themselves they bring the best sacrifice—the full and most truly perfect sacrifice of noble living—as they honor their Benefactor and Savior, God, with hymns and thanksgivings, sometimes with the organs of speech, sometimes without tongue or lips when within the soul alone their minds recite or cry out. These expressions one ear alone receives, the divine ear.[185]

CONCLUSION

Philo and Philodemus provide the philosophical thought in regard to music that sets the context in which to see the references to music in the NT[186] and the development of Christian music in the church.[187] Philo's preference for vocal music and his description of the musical practices of the Therapeutae provide close parallels to early Christian practice. His philosophical observations are also significantly similar to the comments found in patristic literature, but that is another subject.[188] Rabbinic literature agrees with Philo on the centrality of words and on music as "performative."[189] Philodemus too agrees with Philo on the centrality of words. It appears that there was a common cultural assumption, at least among the educated, on the priority of words and so a special regard for vocal music.

---

185. *Spec. leg.* I.50.271–72. For parallels in Greek and Roman poets and philosophers, see the passages collected in my article "Spiritual Sacrifice in Early Christianity and Its Environment," 1152–56 [pp. 1-44 in this volume].

186. W. S. Smith, *Musical Aspects of the New Testament.*

187. McKinnon. ed., *Music in Early Christian Literature*; Foley, *Foundations of Christian Music.*

188. Ferguson, "Towards a Patristic Theology of Music"; in this vol., pp. 162-182.

189. Grözinger, *Musik and Gesang,* 335, "At the center of the [rabbinic] evaluation of music stands the human voice, which is esteemed as the living medium and organ of the call and encounter between God and men," and this voice is "performative music."

8

Toward a Patristic Theology of Music

References in Patristic literature to music have been examined from various standpoints.[1] Seldom, however, have these passages been studied from a theological perspective.[2] Most explicitly theological is Robert A. Skeris, *Chroma Theou*.[3] He finds four significant theological ideas in the literature of the first three Christian centuries referring to music: (1) the hierarchical order of the Christian community, (2) the pneumatic nature of Christian song, (3) the interior aspect of worship signaled by the concept of "rational worship," and (4)

---

1. In comparison to music in pagan antiquity: Quasten, *Musik und Gesang* (ET = *Music and Worship*); see also Haldanae, "Musical Instruments in Greek Worship." In comparison to Jewish forms and styles: Werner, *The Sacred Bridge*. In the context of Roman culture: Wille, *Musica Romana*; see also Mountford, "Music and the Romans." On the use of the Psalms: Lamb, *The Psalms in Christian Worship*; and Gélineau, "Antiphona." For aspects of musical performance: Wellesz, *A History of Byzantine Music and Hymnography* (his "Early Christian Music" is dropped in the new 1990 edition). Collected sources for music history: McKinnon, *Music in Early Christian Literature*. Musical aesthetics: Schueller, *The Idea of Music*, marred by numerous errors. Musical terminology: Schlötter, "Die kirchenmusikalische Terminologie der griechischen Kirchenväter," which I have not seen and know through Skeris (*Chroma Theou*).

2. Gerold, *Les Pères de l'église et la musique*, includes theology as part of broader interests. Söhngen, *Theologie der Musik*, 12–25, is a helpful treatment of the New Testament, but the main interest is the Reformation, spending only two and one-half pages (126–28) on patristics, principally Augustine.

3. Skeris, *Chroma Theou*, a valuable collection of original texts and translations, accompanied by commentary and extensive bibliographical references.

the logocentric character of early Christian music (pp. 158–59). His collection of passages using music imagery to illustrate theological points overlaps significantly this contribution toward a theology of music, but the literature surveyed and perspective are different. I broaden the scope to the fourth and fifth centuries and focus on certain recurring ideas of doctrinal import: theological, cosmological, ethical, and ecclesiological. H.-I. Marrou's observation about Gregory of Nyssa, *In inscriptiones Psalmorum* 1.3, that he was content, without transforming it substantially,[4] to integrate a classical theory into a Christian perspective applies to much of the patristic comment on music. Our concern here will be with the Christian theological perspective, with only occasional allusion to the philosophical antecedents of the thoughts. (Similarly, I leave aside the theoretical treatises on music—such as those written by Augustine, Martianus Capella, and Boethius—and deal with the remarks, often incidental, about Christian practice.) Nevertheless, those familiar with Greek philosophy and its use of musical imagery will recognize in what follows the Pythagorean/Platonic application of harmony to the cosmos, to human nature, and to society.[5]

Augustine stated that musicians say that there are three kinds of music:

> By voice, by breath, and by striking: by voice, that is by the throat and wind pipe of a singing man without any sort of instrument; by breath, as with the tibia or anything of that kind; by striking, as with the cithara or anything of that sort.[6]

Although patristic literature comments on both vocal and instrumental music, liturgical music was vocal. Many of the fathers, in fact, feared instrumental music even in private life,[7] and the positive or neutral references to instruments occur for the most part only in illustrations. Modern scholars often explain this preference for vocal music as a negative result of the associations of instruments with idolatry and immorality.[8] The fa-

---

4. "Une théologie de la musique chez Grégoire de Nysse?"

5. Schueller, *The Idea of Music*, 36f.

6. *In Ps.* 150:8. Trans. McKinnon, 160. Cf. *De doct. chris.* 2.17.27. For the Psalms I follow the numbering of the Hebrew/English Bibles rather than the Greek/Latin.

7. McKinnon, "The Meaning of the Patristic Polemic against Musical Instruments," based on his unpublished dissertation, "The Church Fathers and Musical Instruments"; Ferguson, *A Cappella Music in the Public Worship of the Church*, 3rd. ed., esp. 47–81. The pagan historian Ammianus Marcellinus included music (vocal as well as instrumental) in his description of the decadence of his times (14.6.18).

8. Although church leaders often warned against music in idolatrous or immoral

thers do make these associations, but it is not often noted that vocal music as well was subject to the same abuses and that the fathers warned also against vocal music used for improper purposes.[9] Hence, consideration must be given to the positive theological reasons given by the fathers for the preference for vocal music, and some of these will emerge in the course of the exposition to follow.

Musical instruments occur frequently in the Psalms, and there were two principal ways of dealing with these references. One approach was historical, to treat musical instruments in the Old Testament as belonging to the childhood of the human race's spiritual development and as abolished from Christian assemblies along with other types and shadows in Old Testament worship.[10] Another approach was to give an allegorical interpretation of the instruments, on which more below.[11] Neither approach gave any indication of the presence of instrumental music in the Christian liturgy.

I

As to the theology of music, the church fathers present Christian music as directed to the praise of God and Christ. Niceta's statement is typical: "The songs which the Church of God sings . . . are pleasing to God, since everything about them is directed solely to the glory of the Creator."[12] Leo the

---

settings, this negative side of the patristic views on music will not be the concern of this paper. (See the literature already cited.) The tortuous reasoning applied by some modern scholars to get around the strictures against instruments in the church fathers is illustrated by Schueller, *The Idea of Music*, 206. There was philosophical support for the view that the human voice produces more pleasure than do instruments—Ps. Aristotle, *Problems* 918a. An argument of more validity, therefore, would be that Greek philosophers too preferred vocal music yet allowed a place as well for instrumental; but if this explanation should be thought to have allowed a place in the thinking of the church fathers for instruments in liturgical music, the conclusion would be fallacious.

9. E.g., Clement of Alexandria, *Paed.* 3.11.80.4; Gregory of Nazianzus, *Or.* 5 (PG 35.709B); John Chrysostom, *Ps.* 42 (PG 55.157).

10. Eusebius of Caesarea, *Ps.* 92:2–3; Niceta, *Util. hymn.* 9; John Chrysostom, *Exp. in Ps.* 149:3; Theodoret [?], *Quaes. et resp. ad Orth.* 107; Theodoret, *Graec. affec. cur.* 7.16; Theodoret, *Comm. Isa.* 1.11 (PG 81.226); Theodoret, *Ps.* 150:4 (PG 80.1996); Cassiodorus, *Ps.*, praef. 6; *Ps.* 97:4.

11. An example is Gregory of Nyssa, *In inscrip. Ps.* 2.3, the basis of my study of "Words from the Ψαλ- Root in Gregory of Nyssa," chapter 12 below.

12. *Util. hymn.* 7. Trans. Gerald G. Walsh, 70.

Great says succinctly, "We have sung with one voice the Psalm of David to give praise to Christ the Lord" (*Serm.* 3.1).

Such statements are obvious, considering how often the Psalms speak of praising God. Not so obvious is the common interpretation that the human body is the true instrument to be used in praising God. Clement of Alexandria set the tone of many later comments: "A beautiful breathing instrument of music the Lord made a human being, after his own image" (*Prot.* 1.5).[13] Chrysostom takes up the refrain: "The soul is an excellent musician, an artist; the body is an instrument, holding the place of the kithara, aulos, and lyre. . . . Since it is necessary to pray unceasingly, the instrument is always with the artist unceasingly" (*Ps.* 146.3). Theodoret elaborates the theme in a typical way:

> We [the churches] play the divine melody with the spiritual kithara. We make our bodies rational kitharas, and we use instead of chords the teeth, instead of brass the lips; higher pitched than any plectrum the tongue when moved performs the harmonious sound of the notes. The mind moves the tongue like a musician skillfully changing the sound. This kithara is more pleasing to God than a lifeless one. (*Ps.* 98.5)[14]

Common was the interpretation that referred the kithara and psalterion of the Psalms respectively to the body and the spirit or soul.[15]

---

13. A few lines before Clement referred to instruments, in contrast, as "soulless" or "lifeless"—note Quasten, *Musik und Gesang*, 142 (ET = *Music and Worship*, 92). Cf. *Strom.* 6.11 and esp. *Paed.* 2.4.41, where individual instruments are allegorized as parts of the body, including the statement, "For a human being is truly an instrument of peace." In *Prot.* 10.107 "the immortal person" is "a beautiful hymn to God." The varied use of the imagery is shown by *Strom.* 6.11.88, where Clement says the primary signification of the kithara by the Psalmist is the Lord, but the secondary is "those who continually strike the chords of their souls under the direction of the Choirmaster, the Lord." The body as an instrument used by the mind—Gregory of Nyssa, *Making of Man* 9. Different is Tertullian, *An.* 14, which compares the body to a water organ for solely anthropological purposes without reference to praise. Later Iamblichus, from the pagan side, described enthusiasm as God using human beings as instruments (*Mys.* 3.7).

14. A virtually identical statement in Ps. Eusebius, *Ps.* 98:4-6. Other references in Gérold, *Les Pères de l'église et la musique*, 123-34. Add among others "Athanasius" [Hesychius?], *Tit. Ps.* 150 and Augustine, *Serm.* 243.4 (the constitution of the human body compared to the strings of an instrument that produces different sounds). Bardesanes denied that human beings were instruments played on by God if this entailed a denial of free will (trans. B. P. Pratten in *Ante-Nicene Fathers*, vol. 8 [1886], 724).

15. Origen, *Ps.* 33.2-3. Other references and discussion in Ferguson, "The Active and Contemplative Lives" (chapter 9 in this collection). Add Athanasius, *Ps.* 43. The application of these instruments to the "active soul moved by the commandments of

Vocal music was justified by the fathers because it has a direct connection with the thoughts of the mind and so comes from the highest part of human nature.[16] Praise is to be offered by the whole self—by voice, thoughts, and good works. Chrysostom expresses it this way: "As the Jews are commanded to praise God with all musical instruments, so we are commanded to praise him with all our members—the eye, the tongue, the ear, the hand" (*Ps.* 150). Athanasius offers as one of the justifications for the use of melody in rendering the words that "In this way it will be ensured that people love God with their whole strength and power" (*Ep. ad Marcell.* 27).[17] And so, music was a way of involving the whole self in praise to God.[18]

Moreover, music moves the mind to God. Not only is song the expression of the reason, but it is also true that the words lift our thoughts to God. Augustine and Cassiodorus in their comments on the Psalms agree on this spiritual purpose and have some similarities in their metaphorical treatment of the instruments mentioned, but they had different emphases.[19] Augustine was mainly interested in the intent of the heart, whereas Cassiodorus was interested in what makes musical instruments suitable comparisons to invisible realities. Augustine treats music more theoretically as a single entity, both instrumental and vocal, and draws attention away from specifically instrumental sounds to the spiritual purpose of praise. Cassiodorus, on the other hand, emphasizes the distinct qualities of different instruments each viewed as a body. Music for him lends itself to metaphorical comparisons and so is particularly well suited to making invisible realities understandable.

The praise offered in song was understood as a spiritual sacrifice. Following his interpretation of the instruments in Psalm 150 as members of the body, Chrysostom says, "Let us praise God continually . . . For this is our sacrifice and offering" (*Ps.* 150). Hymn singing is "a spiritual sacrifice

---

God" and "the pure mind moved by spiritual knowledge" comes from Evagrius—Ferguson, "The Active and Contemplative Lives," 17 (p. 187 in this collection).

16. "The rational pertains to the human voice, the irrational to musical instruments" (Cassiodorus, *Ps.* praef. 2; cf. praef. 1). See other references in Ferguson, "The Active and Contemplative Lives," which studies the different ways the imagery of higher and lower was worked out in various musical contexts.

17. Quotations from this work are from my translation in "Athanasius, *Epistola ad Marcellinum*." On the work's authenticity see Rondeau, "L'Épitre à Marcellinus sur les Psaumes," and on its differences from the inauthentic commentary on the Psalms attributed to Athanasius see Stead, "St. Athanasius on the Psalms."

18. Cf. Theodoret, *Ps.* 33:2 cited in section III below.

19. For this paragraph I follow Van Deusen, "Medieval Organologies."

Toward a Patristic Theology of Music

that is greater than all sacrifices of victims," according to Niceta, who explains that instead of shedding the blood of irrational animals, "from the soul and a good conscience rational praise is offered up" (*Util. hymn.* 7).[20]

The praise of God in song, furthermore, unites one with the angels in their ceaseless activity.[21] When "the reasoning soul employs the body . . . as an instrument for sounding forth a fitting tribute of praise" to God's name, "the voice of mortal man is blended with the harmony of the angelic choirs in heaven" (Eusebius, *Laud. Const.* 10).[22] "As the angels of heaven and the hosts and all (His) ministers praise God, so too on earth all men should praise God" (*Didas.* 11 [2.56.]).[23] That in songs of praise human beings join the heavenly chorus is a common motif.[24] A striking musical image is that of human praise as an antiphon to the angelic voices led by Christ.[25] Or, it can be stated that singing is an imitation of the angels[26]: "The chanters of the church imitate the angelic hosts and continually sing praises to God" (Cyril of Jerusalem, *Cat.* 13.26).[27]

Christian music was an expression of the activity of the Holy Spirit, instead of the product of inspiration by the Muses as in pagan thought. Although Dohmes exaggerates the pneumatic, inspired character of song,[28] there was a connection established by the fathers between the indwelling Spirit and Christian song. The Holy Spirit makes possible acceptable song: "[Our mind] is not able to sing and hymn the Father in Christ with proper

---

20. The same contrast of the blood sacrifices of animals with the sacrifice of song occurs in Eusebius of Caesarea, *Ps.* 33:2f., and Cyril of Alexandria, *Ps.* 33.2. Cf. Eusebius, *Ps.* prol. (PG 23.76A) that after Moses gave the law of sacrifices, David introduced the new manner of worshipping God through hymns and jubilations. Cf. Hesychius, *Ps.* 69:31, "Rational praise pleases God more than worship according to the law." For further references to singing as a sacrifice and other items of spiritual sacrifice see Ferguson, "Spiritual Sacrifice in Early Christianity and Its Environment," (in this collection, chapter 1). Add Paulinus of Nola, *Carm.* 27.556, "sacrifice of sung praise."

21. Gregory of Nazianzus, *Or.* 4.71, "angelic psalmody"; Ambrose, *Ps.* 1 praef 2, "angels praise the Lord"; "hear the divine psalmody . . . and imagine one is high above in paradise," Palladius, *Hist. Laus.* 7.5.

22. Trans. by E. C. Richardson in *Nicene and Post-Nicene Fathers*, 2nd ser., vol. 1, 595.

23. Connolly, trans., *Didascalia Apostolorum*, 118. The Greek text of the *Apostolic Constitutions* elaborates, "all with one mouth and one purpose should praise."

24. Gregory of Nyssa, *In inscrip. Ps.* 1:9; Niceta, *Util. hymn.* 10.

25. Methodius, *Symp.* 3.6.

26. Werner, *The Sacred Bridge*, vol. 1, 141 notes the reverse in rabbinic sources, where the songs of the Jewish community stimulate the angels in their praise to God.

27. Cf. *Cat.* 23.6; Basil of Caesarea, *Ep.* 2.2.

28. Dohmes, "Der pneumatische Charakter des Kultgesanges."

rhythm, melody, meter, and harmony, unless the Spirit ... has first praised and hymned him" (Origen, *Or.* 2.4). According to Ambrose, "[Our flesh] is a cithara when it receives the sevenfold Spirit in the sacrament of baptism ... so that we may sing even when we are not singing and proclaim the Lord in a symphony of good works" (*Interpell. Iob et Dav.* 4.16).[29] Athanasius found it fitting for one to praise God with the words God himself by the Spirit had given in the Psalms (*Ep. ad Marcell.* 10-12, 21, 24).

II

Praise of the Creator is something the church has in common with the heavenly bodies:

> We sing praise to God and his only Son, as do also the sun, moon, and stars, and all the heavenly host. For all these form a divine choir and with just human beings sing praise to the God over all and his only Son. (Origen, *C. Cels.* 8.67)[30]

The Pythagorean parallel between musical harmony and the harmony of the universe lies behind many patristic statements referring to music.[31] Athenagoras takes the lead among the church fathers in giving a monotheistic turn to the idea, declaring: "Thus if the world is a harmonious instrument, rhythmically moved, I worship not the instrument but the one who tuned it and strikes the strings and sings to its accompaniment the melodious strain" (*Leg.* 16.3).[32] Clement of Alexandria picks up the theme but gives a specifically Christian coloring to the idea by asserting that it is the Logos who makes music on the universe:

29. Trans. M. McHugh in Fathers of the Church 65 (Washington, 1972) 363. Cf. Ambrose, *Ps.* 49:7, "the plectrum of the Holy Spirit striking the interior and exterior chord."

30. Note Ignatius' imagery of the "stars together with the sun and moon" forming a chorus at the birth of Jesus (*Eph.* 19.2). Skeris notes that the imagery of the stars as a chorus was often used by Stoics but was older (*Chroma Theou*, 177–78 n. 122). For the church joining with the heavenly bodies, cf. Hesychius, *Ps.* 69:30: "He calls praise and doxology that which is offered to him by the whole creation, praising him in its physical movements. The church is commanded now to offer not only the praise with the creation, but to praise with ode, that is to offer spiritual and intellectual hymnody. This is properly to sing to God."

31. Gérold, *Les Pères de l'église et la musique*, 72–80, and Marrou, "Une théologie de la musique chez Grégoire de Nysse?" on Gregory of Nyssa, who are followed in this section of the paper. Pythagoras' view that the world sings is referred to by Hippolytus, *Ref.* 1.2.2–3.

32. Schoedel, ed. and trans., *Athenagoras*, 33. Cf. Tertullian, *Nat.* 2.5.

> [The Logos (the new song)] composed the universe into melodious order, and tuned the discord of the elements to harmonious arrangement so that the whole world might become harmony ... [A]nd having tuned by the Holy Spirit the universe, and especially humankind, who composed of body and soul is a universe in miniature, [the Logos] makes melody to God on this instrument of many tones. (*Prot.* 1.5)[33]

Eusebius combines the ideas of creation and Christology with an elaborate imagery of God framing the world as a great instrument on which the Word of God then produces melody (*Tric. Or.* 12.11).

Gregory of Nyssa puts his "philosophy of melody" in the cosmic perspective of the symphony of the universe.

> I heard a wise man explain our nature as a little cosmos having within itself the things of the big cosmos. The orderly arrangement of the whole is a kind of musical harmony, intricate and complex, harmonized to itself according to a certain order and rhythm and singing with itself and never separated from this symphony, even if the difference of things is considered great in themselves individually. For it is like what happens to the plectrum striking the tones skillfully and bringing forth the melody in the variety of sounds, when if indeed the sound in all was singular, the melody would assuredly not be exhibited ... The mind ... hears the melody of the heavens ... The concord of all creation with itself is truly a hymn, brought forward by such rhythm, of the glory of the unattainable and inexpressible God ... All the other powers in heaven, the astral light, the sun, the moon, the heavens of the heavens, and the water above the heavens praise God. The breathing together and sympathy of all things to one another administered in rank, order, and sequence, is the first, archetype, and true music. (*In inscrip. Ps.* 1.3)[34]

According to Marrou's summary of Gregory, human beings as microcosms of the universe are homogeneous with the whole, so there is a correlation between cosmic music and our nature. The harmony of the spheres is an

---

33. Cf. Athanasius, *Gent.* 42, "Just as a musician, tuning his lyre and skillfully combining [the notes], produces a single melody, so the Wisdom of God, holding the universe like a lyre, combines the whole with the parts, ... producing in beauty and harmony a single world and a single order" (Thomson, trans., *Athanasius*, 117–19).

34. This is the passage studied by Marrou ("Une théologie de la musique chez Grégoire de Nysse?"), on whom the following comments are based. The passage is substantially repeated in the *Catena on the Psalms* (PG 106.1072).

intellectual or spiritual hymn to the glory of God. Music, based on the harmony of the spheres, corresponds to our nature, and this gives it a mystical power over us. Therefore, David mixed melody with words of philosophy, pouring out exalted dogmas as if honey.

Gregory's brother Basil, although describing the elements as forming a harmonious choir, was negative about the spheres producing actual music (*Hex.* 3.3). Ambrose, *Hexaemeron* 2.2.6f., following Basil, was also sceptical, in spite of what modern writers say, perhaps because they did not read to the end of the passage.

III

The harmony of the celestial bodies provided a model for the ethical harmony of the self. The comparison of the body to an instrument also contributed to this theme of internal harmony. Theodoret explained that under the law the people played various musical instruments, but these things apply to Christians spiritually: "We are able to express a pleasant sound and to be ourselves a harmonious instrument and to praise God through all our sensible and intellectual faculties" (*Ps.* 33:2). For this to occur there must be harmony in the soul. Athanasius justified pleasing the people in church with melodious sounds, not for their own sake, but because melody accomplishes as well as represents the harmony of the soul.[35] One of the reasons he gives for "sweet and beguiling melody" (see above, section I for another reason) is its benefit for the soul. He first states the point negatively: "Even as harmony puts together the pipes and accomplishes one symphony, so the Word desires the human being not to be inharmonious and divided, although there appear in the soul different movements" (*Ep. ad Marcel.* 27).[36] He then states the benefits positively in a more extensive manner.

> The purpose is that, like a plectron in making harmony, man himself (becoming a psalterion) should devote himself entirely to the spirit and obey and serve the will of God with all his members and emotions. The harmonious oral reading of the Psalms

35. Sieben, "Athanasius über den Psalter," about which I learned after preparing my own study, Ferguson, "Athanasius, *Epistola ad Marcellinum*." chapter 10 in this collection.

36. Cf. Clement, *Strom.* 5.4.19, "The one who is discordant, disordered, and material must still stand outside the divine choir." For the philosophical background of the idea that sounds and rhythms are able not only to reflect but also to produce the movements of the soul, see Skeris, *Chroma Theou*, 134–35 and 200 n240.

Toward a Patristic Theology of Music

> is an image and type of such a tranquil and calm constitution of the mind. For as we make known and signify the thoughts of the soul through the words which we utter, so the Lord wishing the melody of the words to be a symbol of the spiritual harmony in the soul has decreed the odes to be sung harmoniously and the psalms to be recited as an ode. (*Ep. ad Marcel.* 28)

The fathers several times comment on the way in which the message of the words was enhanced by the emotional impact of the melody. Often cited is Augustine's testimony, "What tears I shed in your hymns and canticles! How deeply was I moved by the voices of your sweet singing church! Those voices flowed into my ears and the truth was distilled into my heart, which overflowed with my passionate devotion" (*Conf.* 9.6.14).[37] As Athanasius stated above, the emotional effect was precisely one of the values of melody: It served to calm the soul and control the emotions for good.

> The blessed David, therefore, as he made music to Saul pleased God and drove away the disturbed and depressed condition of Saul and secured calmness for his soul. Even so when the priests sang, they summoned the souls of the people to tranquility and to the harmony of the chorus in heaven. The saying of the Psalms with melody is not, therefore, a zeal for euphony but a sign of the harmony of the reasonings in the soul. The harmonious recitation is a symbol of the ordered and calm constitution of the mind. [There follows the comparison of the body to instruments.] . . . So also singing well trains the soul and leads it out of disturbance to equanimity, so that the soul by being naturally constituted may not be disturbed by anything but rather may be imagining good things and even more may receive a desire for the good things to come. For the soul sympathetically affected by the chanting of the words forgets the passions, and joyfully looks to the mind of Christ, thinking on the best things. (*Ep. ad Marcel.* 29)

This is accomplished when "all these things move and live by the sound and command of the Spirit" (ibid.). Basil, closely following Athanasius, says psalmody "soothes the passions of the soul" (*Ps.* pref.). Niceta put it, "[The songs of the church] put out, rather than excite, the passions" (*Util. hymn.* 7).[38]

---

37. Trans. R. Warner for New American Library (New York, 1963) 194.

38. Unaccompanied singing "awakens the soul to a fervent desire for that which is described in the songs, it quiets the passions that arise from the flesh, it removes

Since some monks were resistant to the use of melody,[39] there was some need to justify its use.[40] And this was done in terms that the melody makes "pleasant" (*hedus*) the spiritual influence of the words. This wording[41] is often employed, as by Athanasius (*Ep. ad Marcel.* 27), Gregory of Nyssa (*In inscrip. Ps.* 1.3), Basil of Caesarea (*Ps.* pref.), and Chrysostom. The last, noting the difficulty with which the majority of people are persuaded to take an interest in spiritual things, says of God:

> [He] mixed melody with prophecy in order that all, being attracted by the rhythm of the melody, might send up to him holy hymns with much eagerness. For nothing, nothing at all, so stirs up and excites the soul, sets free from the earth and releases from the bonds of the body, and produces philosophy and a deriding of everything pertaining to this life as harmonious melody and divine song mixed with rhythm. For our nature responds naturally and with pleasure to songs and melodies. (*Ps.* 42:1)

Thus, he continues, there is both pleasure and profit in the Psalms. Niceta elaborates as follows:

> Through David, his servant, the Lord prepared a medicine powerful enough to cure the wounds of sin, yet sweet to the taste by reason of the melody. For, when a psalm is sung, it is sweet to the ear. It enters the soul because it is pleasant. It is easily retained if it is often enough repeated.[42] Confessions that no severity of law could extort from the heart are willingly made under the sweet influence of song. (*Util. hymn.* 5)

To accomplish these spiritual purposes the melody must be "suitably religious" and not "melodramatic," for it is "carried out in the presence of God, not with a view to pleasing men" (Niceta, *Util. hymn.* 13).

---

the evil thoughts that are implanted in us by invisible foes, it waters the soul to make it fruitful in the good things of God, it makes the soldiers of piety strong to endure hardships, it becomes for the pious a medicine to cure all the pains of life" (*Quaes. et resp. ad orth.* 107). Such praises of the Psalms and of psalm singing often occur in the introductions to the commentaries on the Psalms.

39. Mitsakis, "The Hymnography of the Greek Church," 40–41, 43.

40. See the justification for melody in terms of cosmic harmony in Gregory of Nyssa, *In Inscrip. Ps.* 1.3, cited above.

41. Cf. Cyprian, *Don.* 16, "if the sweetness of religion delights our ears," in reference to singing Psalms at meals, and Basil of Caesarea, *Ps.*, pref., "gentle and smooth."

42. Basil of Caesarea, *Ps.*, pref. (PG 29.213 C) noted that the Psalms, since they were sung, were more easily retained in the memory than the injunctions of an apostle or a prophet.

Toward a Patristic Theology of Music

Aesthetics posed a problem. Augustine wrestled with the conflict he felt between the spiritual benefits that he knew from experience could come from singing in church and the fear he had of gratifying the senses.

> So I fluctuate between the danger of pleasure and my experience of the good that can be done. I am inclined on the whole (though I do not regard this opinion as irrevocable) to be in favor of the practice of singing in church, so that by means of the delight in hearing the weaker minds may be roused to a feeling of devotion. Nevertheless, whenever it happens to me that I am more moved by the singing than by what is sung, I confess that I am sinning grievously, and then I would prefer not to hear the music.[43]

Lactantius, recognizing the seductive power of pleasure, warned:

> Let nothing be agreeable to the hearing but that which nourishes the soul and makes you a better person. And especially this sense ought not to be distorted to vice, since it is given to us for this purpose, that we might gain the knowledge of God. Therefore, if it be a pleasure to hear melodies and songs, let it be pleasant to sing and hear the praises of God. This is true pleasure, which is the attendant and companion of virtue. (*Inst.* 6.21).[44]

The fathers did not extend the same concession to instrumental melody as they did to vocal melody, presumably because words gave opportunity for praise and instruction that instrumental sounds did not.

For all the fathers, music was not primarily a matter of aesthetics but of ethics, a view that they shared with their philosophical predecessors.[45] As a result, the fathers, while recognizing the benefit of melody, gave priority over the melodiousness of the song and the voice of the singers to the words of the song and the meaning of what was sung.[46] A commentary on

---

43. *Conf.* 10.33; trans. Warner, 242–43. See Brennan, "Augustine's *De Musica*." Chrysostom stated that God allowed rhythm with song because of human weakness—Ps. 41.

44. W. Fletcher, trans., in *Ante Nicene Fathers*, vol. 7 (1888) 188.

45. See Werner, *The Sacred Bridge*, vol. 1, sec. 10; cf. the comment of Holleman, "The Oxyrhynchus Papyrus 1786," 15: "Platonic or rather Neo-Platonic conceptions about music not as an aesthetic but as an ethical value presented the only link between [ancient Greek and early Christian music]." For the Greek view that music molded character see the references in J. Mountford, "Music and the Romans."

46. Wille, *Musica Romana*, 384–88. Contrast the judgment of Dionysius of Halicarnassus, *On Literary Composition* 11, that music subordinates the words to melody instead of melody to the words.

the Psalms preserved under the name of John Chrysostom sets forth the following explanation:

> David sings, intending not to delight and bring pleasure to the ears but wanting to rejoice and benefit the understanding. He sets up the things sung not for the hearing alone, but he sends along the things spoken also for the soul. For he delivers [them] to the hearing for the instruction and knowledge of the truth, and he puts [them] in the soul for the security and confirmation of salvation. He sings the song, sending forth the things said not with bare words but with benefits correcting the life of those who sing. For this song does not pertain to this world and the things of this life but is divine and spiritual and filled with all adornment. (*Ps.* 101.1; PG 55.629-30)

The passage continues by contrasting worldly songs and melodies that draw away the soul to pleasures with heavenly songs that lead the understanding to good order. Such is the power and influence of song and melody.

Music not only brought tranquility to the soul, but it also nourished the soul.[47] Singing served to teach both virtue and doctrine.[48] It served to control the thoughts. John Cassian quoted Abba Moses: "This is the purpose of singing psalms often, so that feelings of repentance may be continually elicited" (*Conf.* 1.17.2).[49] Clement of Alexandria includes music among the educational disciplines to be appropriated by Christians: "Music is then to be employed for the sake of the ordering and adornment of character" (*Strom.* 6.11.89).[50]

Harmony with God required not only harmony within the soul but also harmony between body and soul.[51] This requires, again according to

---

47. "Nourish the soul"—Niceta, *Util. hymn.* 12; "train the soul"—Athanasius, *Ep. ad Marcel.* 29, quoted above; "educate the soul"—Basil of Caesarea, *Ps.* pref. (PG 29.213 C); Cassiodorus, *Ps.*, praef., "delights ears and instructs souls."

48. Modern studies often comment on the moral purpose of the music—Gérold, *Les Pères de l'église et la musique*, 81–87—and the use of the Psalms in religious education—Wille, *Musica Romana*, 384–86; Quasten, *Musik und Gesang*, 190–94 (ET = *Music and Worship*, 137–39).

49. Trans. O. Chadwick in Library of Christian Classics, vol. 12 (Philadelphia, 1958) 207.

50. Clement proceeds to contrast this useful music to the extravagant music to be avoided "which enfeebles souls and leads to changefulness—now mournful, and then licentious and luxurious, and then frenzied and mantic."

51. The harmony between soul and body is quite different from Lactantius, *Op. Dei* 16.13–18, which rejects the comparison, drawn from Terpander or Aristoxenus, of the

good Greek philosophical precedents, that the rational soul control the senses of the body.[52] Athanasius compares the senses to the strings of the lyre, each having its own sound, and the mind to the skillful musician who brings these sounds into harmony (*Gent.* 31). The Christian emphasis on words carried this thought further.

The need to please God, not others, and the connection between virtue and song required that there be agreement between the words sung and the thoughts in the heart. Athanasius again sets the theme:

> Those who do not sing with the understanding but give pleasure to themselves are blameworthy... Those who do sing... so that the melody of the words is offered from the rhythm of the soul and from harmony with the spirit sing with the tongue and with the mind, and profit greatly not only themselves but also those who want to hear them. (*Ep. ad Marcel.* 29)

And once more Niceta is in agreement:

> Only, brothers, let us please God by singing with attention and a mind wide awake... We must sing with our intelligences; not only with the spirit (in the sense of the sound of the voice), but also with our mind. We must think about what we are singing. (*Util. hymn.* 13)[53]

John Chrysostom explained the phrase "in your hearts to the Lord" (Eph 5:19) as follows: "It means giving attention with the understanding. For those who do not pay attention merely sing, sounding the words while their hearts roam elsewhere" (*Hom. 19 in Eph.*).[54] There must be an understanding of the words spoken, as Theodoret affirms in commenting on the same passage: "He sings in heart who not only moves the tongue but also arouses the mind to the understanding of the words spoken" (Eph 5:19). Similarly Jerome says we ought to sing "more with spirit than the voice,"

---

soul in the body to the harmony in the lyre.

52. Skeris, *Chroma Theou*, 131, 135 for the Neopythagorean fondness for the imagery of the body as the instrument of the soul. Cf. Augustine, *Ps.* 146.2 that the soul rules, the body obeys.

53. Cf. chap. 2, where 1 Cor 14:15, "spirit and understanding," is interpreted as "with both voice and thought." A different turn, in the direction of "silent singing," is given by Paulinus of Nola, "hymn ... not only aloud but with silent heart" (*Ep.* 15.4). On silent singing see Philo, *Ebr.* 94; *Plant.* 126; *Spec. Leg.* I.272; and Porphyry, *Abst.* 2.34. Niceta, *Util. hymn.* 1–2 opposes the arguments of Christians who advocated "silent singing" exclusively.

54. Cf. John Chrysostom, *Ps.* 42.1; *Hom. 9 in Col.* 3.2; *Hom. 35 in 1 Cor.* 14.15.

"not with the voice but with the heart," "so that not the voice of the singer but the words that are read give pleasure" (*Comm. Eph.* 5.19).⁵⁵

Harmony of the self required, moreover, an agreement between words and life. Augustine is representative here:

> Will you then sing a Psalm? Let not your voice alone sound the praises of God; but let your works also be in harmony with your voice . . . To please then the ear, sing with your voice; but with your heart be not silent, with your life be not still. (Ps 147:2)

Chrysostom provides the Greek counterpart: "It is not sufficient simply to make melody to please God with praise, but the life, prayer, and attention of the one singing must please God" (Ps 147:1).⁵⁶

IV

The harmony of the spheres corresponded not only to the harmony of the individual but also to the harmony of the church. Congregational participation in the singing exemplified the unity of the church and the harmony of human beings with God, which is the goal of God's plan for humanity. The motif of spiritual unity is sounded already in one of the earliest patristic references to music:

> By your concord and harmonious love Jesus Christ is being sung. Now all of you together become a choir so that being harmoniously in concord and receiving the key note from God in unison you may sing with one voice through Jesus Christ to the Father. (Ignatius, *Eph.* 4.2)⁵⁷

Origen concluded a long discussion of the uses of the word "symphony" in scripture, based on Matt 18:19, with this statement: "We ought to practice the symphony [agreement] derived from the divine music, so that when we are gathered together in the name of Christ, Christ may be in our midst" (*Mt.* 14.1 on Matt 18:19).⁵⁸ Jerome applies the musical imagery

---

55. Trans. by McKinnon, *Music in Early Christian Literature*, 145.

56. Musical imagery (instrumental) is used for a "life which harmonizes with the sacred law in all things" by Paulinus of Nola, *Carm.* 21.327ff. Cf. Cassiodorus, *Ps.* 26, "singing means uttering praises with the voice alone, whereas reciting a psalm means proclaiming the Lord's glory by good works" (trans. P. G. Walsh in Ancient Christian Writers, vol. 51 [New York, 1991]) 266; *Ps.* 25 (ibid., 256); *Ps.* 56.8 (ibid., vol. 52, 43).

57. Clement, *Strom.* 6.14.87 calls the church "the spiritual and holy choir." See the discussion of "one voice" below.

58. Cf. Origen, *Ps.* 149.3, "If the many praise the name and characteristics of the

pointedly: "Where there is dissension, where there is jealousy, there is no choir" (*Hom.* 59 on Ps 149:3).[59] Eusebius of Caesarea is representative in bringing into concert unison singing and the unity of the church. In a context contrasting Jewish and Christian worship and likening the human body to an instrument, he trumpets forth:

> The unison voices of Christians would be more acceptable to God than any musical instrument. Accordingly in all the churches of God, united in soul and attitude, with one mind and in agreement of faith and piety, we send up a unison melody in the words of the Psalms. (*Ps.* 91.2–3).[60]

Niceta gave the practical application that for the harmony to be evident in the singing "No one should sing unbecomingly louder or slower than the rest" (*Util. hymn.* 13).[61]

Clement of Alexandria counseled individuals that their attention be first "toward God in thanksgiving and psalmody, and second toward neighbors in decorous fellowship" (*Paed.* 2.4.43). Once again, it should be noted that the words were to be accompanied by deeds: "Similarly, let one follow after unity by doing good works, seeking the Good Monad. The union of many into one, bringing a divine harmony out of the many scattered sounds, becomes one symphony, following one Choirleader and Teacher" (*Prot.* 9.88). Right faith, as well as good works, was necessary for the unity of the church: Augustine applied the language of congregational harmony to warn against heresy, which "throws into confusion the harmony of them who praise" (*Ps* 149:3). Fellowship was expressed in the church's singing, which not only taught virtue to the self but also instructed others. As Niceta said, a well-tuned voice "will be a joy to ourselves and source of edification to those who hear us" (*Util. hymn.* 13)[62]

King with the same mind and same consent with one accord in the same spirit and heart, then they indeed praise his name with harmonious union."

59. Trans. Marie Liguori Ewald in *Fathers of the Church*, vol. 48 (Washington, DC, 1964) 424.

60. Cf. his comments on *Ps.* 70.22–24, which contain the same motifs. Ps. Eusebius, *Ps.* 97.4–6 likens the kithara of the text not to the individual, as is usual, but to "the whole people of Christ harmonized from their diverse souls as from a multitude of strings."

61. Augustine, noting that a voice out of harmony offends the ear, says "If we sing, let us sing in concord" (*Ps.* 149.3).

62. Athanasius once more is in tune with Niceta, declaring that those who sing from the soul "profit greatly not only themselves but also those who want to hear them" (*Ep. ad Marcel.* 29, context quoted above). See Gérold, preface, for the importance of

A chorus of passages proclaims the participation of the whole church in the singing.[63] Variety of sounds, not sameness, was necessary to create harmony. Gregory of Nyssa noted that if the sound in all was singular, the melody would not be exhibited" (*In inscrip. Ps.* 1.3). Augustine similarly describes the sounding together in "most harmonious diversity":

> The saints of God will have their differences, accordant, not discordant, that is agreeing, not disagreeing, just as sweetest harmony arises from sounds differing indeed, but not opposed to one another. (*Ps.* 150.4)

This diversity in a congregation included the blending of voices of different quality. Chrysostom, declaring that the Lord "gathers all into his own chorus," says:

> Our tongues are the strings of our kithara, putting forth a different sound yet a Godly harmony. For indeed women and men, old and young, have different voices but they do not differ in the word of hymnody, for the Spirit blends the voice of each and effects one melody in all. (*Ps.* 146.2).[64]

Ambrose makes the same point, in a passage which deserves to be quoted extensively, for it emphasizes the participation of the whole congregation and the effect of singing together in effecting reconciliation of the members.

> When the psalm is recited . . . all are speaking and there is no disturbance . . . Each person does the utmost in singing what will be a blessing. The apostle commands women to be silent in church, but they may sing the psalms; this is fitting for every age and for both sexes. [There follows reference to old men, middle-aged men, younger men, youth, tender maidens, and young widows.] Psalmody unites those who disagree, makes friends of those at odds, brings together those who are out of charity with

---

edification, and hence of the words, for the patristic view of music.

63. Some of the principal passages are cited below; add Eusebius, *Ps.* 66.10–15; John Chrysostom, *Hom. Mt.* 11.9 on Matt 3:7; Paulinus of Nola, *Ep.* 29.13 and *Carm.* 23.111 at vigils and night offices.

64. See Paulinus of Nola, *Carm.* 21.272–275, where an instrument of discordant notes brought into harmony serves as an illustration of vocal harmony ("the holy lyre of our combined voices"); cf. 327ff. (a family assembled from different strings to sing the same song, "harmonious hearts like a single lyre" "united in body, mind, and faith"). Athanasius, *Gent.* 43 uses the different quality of voices—"men, children, women, old people, and youths"—blended together into a chorus under one leader as an illustration of the harmony of the universe.

one another. Who could retain a grievance against the person with whom one sings to God in one voice? Singing of praise is the very bond of unity, when the whole people come together in one chorus. The strings of the cithara are of varying lengths, but they all sound in harmony. The musician's finger too, may often make mistakes on the small strings, but in the congregation that great Musician, the Spirit, cannot err. (*Ps.* 1, *Exp.* 9).[65]

Basil of Caesarea chimes in with a consequence for personal relations from the congregational singing of the Psalms: "Who can still regard as an enemy one with whom he has sent forth one voice [or] to God? . . . Psalmody harmonizes the people into a symphony of one chorus" (*Ps.* 1.2). Basil also provides the most comprehensive statement of the different ways in which the congregation participated in the singing. In describing the all night vigils of his church (*Ep.* 207.3)[66] he describes antiphonal,[67] responsorial,[68] and congregational or unison[69] singing.

The praise of God united not only the local church but also all the churches: Even as a kithara produces one sound from many separate chords, so "the church [is] gathered together from many nations so that from separate places and from diverse regions and customs, one choir may sound forth the praise of God" (Jerome, *Hom.* 65 on Ps 88:1).[70] This harmony encompassed Christians temporally as well as geographically, for it united the saints of all the ages (Niceta, *Util. hymn.* 11).

---

65. I follow but modify the translation of Erik Routley, *The Church and Music*, 229; also translated by McKinnon, *Music in Early Christian Literature*, 126–27. Cf. his *Hex.* 3.5.23, "Song of men, women, virgins, children." Cf. Basil of Caesarea, *Hex.* 4.7 (PG 29.93C), "mingled voice of men, women, and children." Also, Jerome: "Wherever there is a choir many voices blend into one song. In the same way that separate chords produce a single effect, so, too, do separate voices harmonize as one. In other words, when the faithful gather together, they form the Lord's choir. Let them praise his name in choir" (*Hom.* 59 *in Ps.* 149; cf. *Hom.* 65, *in Ps.* 87). Jerome, however, opposed women singing in church (*C. Pel.* 1.25).

66. Cf. Paulinus of Nola, *Carm.* 23.111–46, after a meal "we began to sing hymns of joy to the Lord and so prolong the night with Psalms."

67. Theodoret, *HE* 2.19; Augustine, *Conf.* 9.7. Socrates, *HE* 6.8 is incorrect; see Ferguson, "Psalm-Singing at the Eucharist," reprinted in this collection (pp. 107–127).

68. Tertullian, *Or.* 27; *Const. App.* 2.57.6; 8.12.4; Eusebius, *Ps.*, prol. (PG 23.73B, 76B); John Chrysostom, *Hom.* 36 *in 1 Cor.* 14.33. Cf. the distinction between *antiphona* and *responsorios* in Isidore, *Etymol.* VI.19.7–8.

69. *Mart. Matt.* 8; Eusebius, *Ps.* 92.4; Hilary, *Ps.* 66.1; and passages cited above and below and in n. 63.

70. Trans. Marie Liguori Ewald in *Fathers of the Church*, vol. 57 (Washington, DC, 1966) 56.

The "one soul and one heart" of the church was expressed in singing with "one voice" and from "one mouth."[71] "For it is necessary that there be one voice in the church, since it is one body . . . Even when all respond [to the solo singing of the Psalms], the sound is carried as by one mouth" (Chrysostom, *Hom.* 36 *in* 1 *Cor.* 14.33). There were biblical precedents for these phrases, but they were used in pagan literature as well.

"With one mouth" occurs metaphorically in 2 Chr 18:12 for the prophets speaking the same message. Of more importance for this study is The Song of the Three (Dan 3:51 in both LXX and Theodotion), "The three sang a hymn to God as from one mouth." Romans 15:6 does not include the qualification "as" in exhorting to unity, "so that together with one mouth you may glorify the God and Father of our Lord Jesus Christ."

The metaphorical use of "one mouth" continued in Christian literature, as when Irenaeus describes the church scattered throughout the world teaching the same faith "as if possessing one mouth" (*Adv. haer.* 1.10.2), and another writer speaks of the doctrinal agreement of the authors of scripture, who taught us "as if with one mouth and one tongue" (Ps. Justin, *Cohort.* 8). For Clement of Rome the cry of the heavenly hosts, "Holy, Holy, Holy" is a pattern for Christians: "Let us therefore, having gathered together in one place in harmony with conscience, cry earnestly to God as from one mouth" (1 *Clem.* 34.7).[72] "One mouth" was used explicitly for unison singing, sometimes with allusion to the Song of the Three (as in the words of Paulinus of Nola, "so let the holy lyre of our combined voices resound as though three tongues were singing with one mouth"),[73] sometimes with allusion to Romans 15:6 (as in Gregory of Nazianzus, "so that together with one mouth you may glorify the Father, and the Son, and the Holy Spirit"[74]). Basil speaks of the unison singing of the congregation (in contrast to antiphonal and responsorial singing) by saying, "All in common as from one mouth and one heart, offer up to the Lord the psalm of confession" (*Ep.* 207.3). John Chrysostom uses "one mouth" to describe the unison singing of monks: Having arisen and "having made one choir,

---

71. Quasten, *Musik und Gesang*, 91–102 (ET = *Music and Worship*, 66–72); cf. Skeris, *Chroma Theou*, 122 and notes on 176–77 and 202 n256; Dohmes, "Die Einstimmigkeit des Kultgesanges." See now my more comprehensive study, Ferguson, "Praising God with 'One Mouth'/'One Voice.'" [Pp. 45–61 in this collection.].

72. See n. 23 above.

73. *Carm.* 21.275, trans. P. G. Walsh in *Ancient Christian Writers* 40 (New York, 1975) 181. See n64 for instruments in this passage as an illustration of vocal harmony as well as of agreement in mind.

74. *Or.* 23.4 (PG 35.1153), a passage alluding also to the "one voice" of Gen 11:1.

with their conscience bright, all harmoniously as if from one mouth, they sing hymns to the God of all."[75]

Mia phone had several possible meanings in Greek literature and consequently occurs more frequently than "one mouth." The Greek Bible reflects some of these meanings: "one language" (Gen 11:1) and "a single voice" (Rev 9:13). The interest here is the usage to describe agreement, especially as expressed verbally. Thus, Exodus 24:3 says that all the people of Israel "with one voice" declared their acceptance of the words of the Lord. Second Chronicles 5:13 uses the phrase for the sounds of instruments and singers in unison, as does 4 Macc 8:29 for the united response of the seven brothers to the inducements to apostatize. Similarly Acts 19:34 speaks of the mob in Ephesus "with one voice" shouting, "Great is Artemis!"[76]

"One voice" continued to occur frequently in Christian literature. In the metaphorical sense of agreement[77] the phrase was used for the writing of the scriptures[78] and the unity of the faith.[79] The references to vocal activities include prayer (Origen, *C. Cels.* 8.37, in a qualified sense),[80] acclamation ("Amen"—Irenaeus, *Haer.* 1.14.1; "O Christ, help"—Athanasius, *Apol. Const.* 10), and confession of faith by the martyrs (Gregory of Nyssa, *Enc. in xl mart.* (PG 46.764). One use was in reference to song. Clement of Alexandria in describing Greek banquets notes as alternatives singing by all together "with one voice after the manner of the Hebrew Psalms" or taking turns in the singing (*Paed.* 2.4.44).[81] Epiphanius insists that the angels say "Holy" to the Trinity "in one voice, one word, and one perfection" (*Ancor.*

---

75. *Hom. Mt.* 68.3 (PG 58.644). In the same context, he contrasts the songs of the monks with the music of the theater: "Here the grace of the Spirit sounds forth, employing instead of aulos, kithara, or syrinx the mouths of the saint" (68.4).

76. The phrase "one voice" was common in Greek literature for acclamations and shouting in unison. Note Diodore of Sicily, *Bib. hist.* 11.9 and 16; 17.33 and 106; 19.81; 40.5a; Dionysius of Halicarnassus, *Ant. Rom.* 7.22; Josephus, *Ant.* 11.332; Lucian of Samosata, *Nigrinus* 14; secular acclamations in John Chrysostom, *De inani gloria* (twice). The thought was sometimes qualified, "as if with one voice"—Diodore of Sicily, *Bib. hist.* 11.92; 16.10 and 79.

77. Cf. Eusebius, *Praep. evang.* 14.3 (PG 21.719D); Gregory of Nyssa, *C. usur.* (GNO 9, 204, 11).

78. Origen, *Mt.* 14.1 on Matt 18:19.

79. [Ps.] Basil, *In Isa.* (PG 30.573B).

80. Cf. Clement of Alexandria, *Strom.* 7.6.31, "congregation of those who devote themselves to prayers, having as it were one common voice and one mind." Without the qualification "as it were" but more stressing the common mind than indicating joint vocal participation are John Chrysostom, *Ad pop. Ant.* 15.3 (PG 49.155) and *De proph. obsc.* 1 (PG 56.182).

81. Cf. Plutarch, *Mor.* 615B.

26).[82] Passages reflecting church practice, in addition to Ignatius, *Ephesians* 4 quoted above,[83] include Niceta's advice on suitable performance:

> [After quoting Daniel 3:51–52, he says,] Therefore, let us sing all together, as with one voice, and let all of us modulate our voices in the same way. If one cannot sing in tune with the others, it is better to sing in a low voice rather than drown the others.[84]

Gregory of Nazianzus incorporates several themes when he says, "Taking up one voice, harmonized by the one Spirit, let us sing that victory ode which Israel then sang over the Egyptians" (*Or.* 4.12 [PG 35.541]).

The Pythagorean/Platonic application of the theme of harmony to the celestial spheres, the human body and soul, and the state[85] was continued by the church fathers, with the significant substitution of the church for the state. And this was set in a distinctively Christian theological context. The participation of the assembled Christians in singing exemplified their spiritual unity with one another in the church and their ethical harmony within themselves and united them with the cosmological and angelic symphony which was a sacrifice of praise to God in Christ by the Holy Spirit.

---

82. For angels praising with "one voice," cf. *Asc. Isa.* 7.15; 8.18; 9.28; *Pass. Perp.* 12 (*vocem unitam*). According to *Apoc. Pet.* 19 (Akhmim Frg., not in the Ethiopic) all those in glory, angels and the redeemed, praise God "with one voice" (E. Preuschen, *Antilegomena* [Giessen, 1901] 49).

83. At n. 57. Ignatius uses "one voice" in reference to singing but with an emphasis more on unity than on unison performance.

84. *Util. hymn.* 13, trans. Walsh, 75. From Latin writers note also Pope Celestine, "*una voce Deo canere*" (PL 50.457), quoted from a fragment of a sermon in Arnobius Younger, *Confl. Serap.* 2.13 (PL 53.289).

85. Cf. Boethius' classification of cosmic music, human music (the harmony of body and soul), and instrumental music (i.e., music proper, for vocal music is included along with that produced by striking and blowing)—summarized in Schueller, *The Idea of Music*, 265–66.

9

The Active and Contemplative Lives
The Patristic Interpretation of Some Musical Terms

THE RECENTLY PUBLISHED PAPYRUS manuscripts of the "Commentary on the Psalms" written by Didymus the Blind[1] contain the following interpretations of certain central musical terms. First, concerning Ps 26:6, "I will sing and make melody to the Lord":

> We were saying in the earlier psalms that "to sing" [ᾆσαι] signifies contemplation [θεωρίαν], to offer praises and songs without an instrument. "To make melody" [ψάλλειν] signifies to sound forth the victory song in activity [πρακτικῶς].[2]
>
> "Both, therefore," he says, "pertain to me, and I will make melody and I will sing. I will sing, contemplating the truth." He who apprehends the dogmas of godliness and contemplates them learnedly and wisely is the one who sings. He who takes the body as an instrument, a kithara and a psalterion, and plays all its emotions and feelings like strings (being able to produce melodiously a psalm) is the one who makes melody.
>
> This holy person then promises to do two things—to sing and to make melody. He who mortifies his body, brings it into

---

1. Gronewald, trans. *Didymos der Blinde, Psalmenkommentar*. The following three quotations are from vol. 2, pp. 214–16 (105,21–106,3), vol. 3, pp. 4–8 (129.21—130,6), and vol. 5, p. 96 (307,3–5).

2. I have adopted "make melody" as the uniform translation of ψάλλω. The names of musical instruments will be transliterated.

subjection, and practises the ethical virtues (such as giving alms, showing gentleness, making progress in manliness) is the one who "makes melody." He who contemplates each mystery of the truth and is able to relate with skill every dogma of godliness "sings."

Then Didymus says concerning the title of Psalm 29, "Psalm of an Ode":

> We were saying when we began the twentieth psalm that there are psalms, there are odes, and there are psalms of odes and odes of psalms. And I was saying that the psalm signifies activity. He who makes melody plays the instrument called the psalterion.
>
> But it is possible to sing without the psalterion. He who uses contemplation alone—to conceptualize God, to know the truth and participate in it . . .—he then who contemplates and apprehends scientifically what is knowledge and what is the mystery of the kingdom, this one sings. Again, whoever perform deeds and take their stand on activity alone make melody.
>
> He who makes melody and is active and who sings and contemplates, if he begins from activity that is the psalm of an ode, but if he begins from contemplation that is an ode of a psalm. Let us see these things happening. Many times some who wish to contemplate come to understand the virtues and their deeds and from this knowledge receive power to live correctly and come to activity. It has become an ode of a psalm. The ode led, that is contemplation came first . . . He kept the commandments, he was making melody. And having made melody, he has wisdom well-supplied. It signifies therefore to begin sometimes with the ode and the psalm to follow, or again the psalm to show the way and lead the soul to an ode. If therefore the beginning and the understanding of the beginning occurs from an activity, it is a psalm of an ode. But whenever one begins with contemplation and receives a love for the life of virtue, it is an ode of a psalm.

On Psalm 42:4, "I will confess to you, O God, on the kithara," Didymus comments:

> I have said many times that the kithara signifies active virtue or the body being played by the soul which has the characteristics of music.

The parts of Didymus' Psalm commentary which were previously known contain similar interpretations. The statement about the kithara is made clearer in the comments on Ps 32:2. After noting that the kithara may be considered the body (in which case "the extended strings would

The Active and Contemplative Lives

be none other than the senses which we employ in praising the Lord") or the soul (in which case its faculties "such as memory, assent, refusal, and others in accordance with reason shall confess the Lord mystically and be played by the mind like strings") Didymus gives this information:

> Musicians say that the psalterion differs from the kithara in this way. The kithara makes its sound from its lower parts, but the psalterion from its upper parts, being straight up and down. When the soul is explained to be the kithara, the spirit of man in him (perhaps nothing other at times than the mind) is the psalterion, making melody to none other than God.[3]

The psalterion is considered the superior instrument because according to its construction the sound comes from its upper part, therefore it corresponds to the higher part of human nature.

The noun for the sound made by plucking the psalterion, ψαλμός, however, is treated as inferior to the song made by the voice:

> An ode is a triumphal or thanksgiving praise offered with the voice alone. A psalm is a hymn played on the instrument called a psalterion or a kithara. It may be by analogy that an ode is the contemplation of the truth with the mind alone given the power of song, but the psalm is a deed performed according to right reason.

Didymus continues in the same vein concerning the verbs:

> So "to make melody" is the active life, and "to sing" the contemplative. Since David contemplates God and his truth with a pure heart, he presents an ode which it says is in the psalms, because he also accomplished many things practically.[4]

Didymus is part of a tradition in these interpretations. One of the fullest statements describing the stringed instruments is in [Pseudo] Hippolytus:

> David alone of the prophets prophesied with an instrument, called by the Greeks the "psalterion," and by the Hebrews the "nabla," which is the only musical instrument that is quite straight, and has no curve. And the sound does not come from

---

3. *Exp. in Psalmos* 32:2 (PG 39.1321D-1324A). Cf. 150:3 (PG 39.1616A).

4. *Exp. in Psalmos* 4 (PG 39. 1164D-1165B). For psalm and ode see also on Psalm 64 (PG 39.1433C), "Psalm is the deed; ode is the contemplation." For the verbs see 12:6 (PG 39.1217B), "To sing is contemplation; to make melody is practical activity." Cf. 67:25 (PG 39.1448A-B); 97:5 (PG 39.1509D).

the lower parts, as is the case with the kithara and certain other instruments, but from the upper. For in the kithara and the lyre the brass when struck gives back the sound from beneath. But the psalterion has the source of its musical numbers above, in order that we, too, may practice seeking things above, and not suffer ourselves to be borne down by the pleasure of melody to the passions of the flesh.[5]

Augustine's musical interest is shown in his descriptions:

These two instruments of the musicians have each a distinct meaning of their own, worthy of our consideration and notice. They are both borne in our hands, and played by the touch; and they stand for certain bodily works of ours. Both are good, if one knows how to play the psalterion [*psallere*] or the kithara [*citharizare*]. But since the psalterion is that instrument which has the shell (i.e., that drum, that hollow piece of wood, by straining on which the chords resound) on the upper part of it, whereas the kithara has that same concave sounding-board on the lower part, there is to be a distinction made between our works, when they are "upon the kithara," when "on the psalterion."[6]

The distinction between sounding from the upper or lower part of the instrument was used to support a distinction between the contemplative and active lives. The interpretation of the kithara as the lower part of a human being and the psalterion as the higher appears to derive from Origen. His comment on Ps 32:2 is, "The kithara, speaking figuratively, is the body; the psalterion is the spirit."[7] Origen associates the kithara with the body[8] and the psalterion with the spirit.[9] The ten-stringed psalterion is the body (in the sense of person) having five senses and five powers of the soul.[10] The extension of this body-spirit interpretation to the active

    5. PG 10. 716 D–717A. The translation is that of the *Ante-Nicene Fathers*, vol. 5, p. 199, with slight changes.

    6. *Expositions on the Psalms* XLIII, 5. The Augustine quotations are taken from the *Nicene and Post-Nicene Fathers*, Series 1, Vol. 8, with modernization and adaptation to the terminology of the Greek fathers. Cf. on Ps. CL, 4–6.

    7. PG 12.1304C.

    8. PG 12.1421C.

    9. PG 12.1680D.

    10. PG 12.1304C. This is continued in later authors: Eusebius, *Comm. on Ps.* 143:9 (PG 24.56A) and "Athanasius," *Exp. in Ps.* 91:4 and 143:9 (PG 27.404D and 544A). Others made the association with the ten commandments, e.g., Pseudo Chrysostom [Hesychius?], *In Ps.* 91 (PG 55.762) and Augustine, *Exp. on Ps.* XXXIII, 2 and CXLIV, 7.

The Active and Contemplative Lives

and contemplative lives in the *Selecta in Psalmos* belongs to those passages now attributed to Evagrius and reflect his debt to Didymus.[11] "The kithara is the active soul moved by the commandments of God; the psalterion is the pure mind being moved by spiritual knowledge."[12]

Basil of Caesarea connects the information about the instruments with the distinction between the active and contemplative lives in the same way as Didymus. The following comments are also on Ps 32:2.

> It is necessary to praise the Lord first with the kithara, that is to perform harmoniously the deeds done through the body. Then after this confession you are worthy to make melody to God on the ten-stringed psalterion. For it is necessary first to perform right actions with the body so as to act harmoniously with the divine word, and in this way to ascend to the contemplation of spiritual things. For the mind which seeks the things above is called the psalterion, because in the construction of this instrument the power of sound comes from the upper parts.[13]

Not all interpreters of the Psalms took this Origenist approach. Chrysostom alludes to this interpretation but prefers the historical interpretation which puts the instruments under the old covenant in contrast to the vocal music of Christians.[14] Hesychius fits the covenantal interpretation into the allegorical interpretation of the instruments.

> "Psalterion with kithara," that is the New with the Old . . . Why are these compared to psalterion and kithara? Since the instruments have an affinity to one another, but the nexus of the chords is different. One is bound at the top, and the other at the bottom. So the Old and New have an affinity; they look to the one purpose of godliness. But the commandments of one are below on account of the lowliness of the legislation, and those of the other are above on account of the exceeding height of the disciples of Christ.[15]

---

11. Von Balthasar, "Die Hiera des Evagrius," esp. 93–100; and Rondeau, "Le commentaire sur les Psaumes d'Evagre le Pontique."

12. PG 12.1304 B–C. The same statement in reversed order occurs in 1552D. Cf. 1472C. Note 1684D, "The organ is the church of God composed of contemplative and active souls."

13. PG 29.325C–328B. Cf. *Hom. on Ps.* 1:2 (PG 29. 213B–C). When related to the voice, the psalterion becomes "deeds performed in accord with reason" (*Hom. in Ps.* 48:5 [PG 29.436C]). For the description of the psalterion cf. PG 27.548A quoting Basil.

14. *Exp. in Ps.* 149:3 (PG 55.494).

15. PG 55.728–29.

Eusebius of Caesarea, too, makes a covenantal distinction. But he so strongly emphasizes the contrast between the Jewish use of instruments in worship and the purely vocal praise of the churches that he refers both kithara and psalterion to the body which now spiritually offers praise to God.[16]

Augustine follows his description of the instruments, quoted above, by referring the psalterion to the active life of obeying God's commands (as the angels do) and the kithara to the passive experience of suffering (since we suffer from the lower parts of our nature).[17] Yet another variation on the interpretation of higher and lower is Augustine's comparison of the psalterion and kithara to two kinds of deed worked by the Lord—miracles from above, and sufferings from below.[18] Or, again, "The psalterion praises God from things above, the kithara praises God from things below; I mean from things in heaven and things in earth."[19] Augustine appears acquainted with the line of Greek interpretation which has been noted, for he says, "There seems to be signified by the psalterion the spirit, by the kithara the flesh."[20] Or again, praise to the Lord on the psalterion and kithara is to sing and work, "He who sings and works makes melody with psalterion and kithara."[21]

The patristic disparagement of instrumental music in contrast to vocal music comes out in the higher evaluation given to an ode than to a psalm. The long history of Christian admiration and use of the psalms may leave the modern reader unprepared for this. But a look at etymology will make clear the basis for the quotations which follow. Ψάλλω properly means "twitching or twanging with the fingers" and so "the sound of the kithara or harp."[22] The Greek translation of the Old Testament used the

---

16. *Comm. in Ps. 146:7* (PG 24.68B). But he observes the body-soul distinction on the instruments at 56:8 (PG 23.513B) and 107:2 (PG 23.1329B). Another author strongly against instruments, Theodoret, also makes both instruments stand for a person—*In Ps. 56:9* and *107:2* (PG 80.1293B and 1749C). The pseudo-Athanasius, *De titulis Psalmorum*, now attributed to Hesychius, similarly makes the two instruments together stand for the person—PG 27.996D, 1069C, 1341C. For the rejection of instruments in favor of singing see n. 40.

17. See n. 6.

18. *Exp. on Ps. LVIII*, 14.

19. *Exp. on Ps. CL*, 4–6.

20. *Exp. on Ps. LXXII*, 28.

21. *Exp. on Ps. XCVIII*, 5; cf. *CXLVII*, 11 and more fully *CXLIV*, 1–2.

22. Liddell and Scott, *A Greek-English Lexicon*, s.v.

word in the titles of the psalms[23] and by this means apparently the word came to be used among Jews and Christians for the poems and songs themselves. Josephus maintained the classical meaning of ψάλλω, using it of the tune plucked on a stringed instrument.[24] Therefore, he referred to the Old Testament Psalms not as ψαλμοί but as ὕμνοι.[25] Philo, too, regularly used hymns or songs instead of psalms in his quotations.[26] The Greek translations of the Old Testament, most other Jewish writers, and early Christian writers used "psalms," "hymns," and "odes" interchangeably.[27] The fathers in their comments on the Psalms often found ψαλμός and ᾠδή together, and they were well aware of their proper meanings in Greek and explained the Old Testament musical practices accordingly. They would then make use of the etymological meanings in the service of their spiritual and edifying interpretations.

[Pseudo] Hippolytus, once more, gives a full explanation.

> As there are "psalms," and "songs," and "psalms of song," and "songs of psalmody" [in the titles of the Psalms], it remains that we discuss the difference between these. We think, then, that the "psalms" are those which are simply played to an instrument, without the accompaniment of the voice, and (which are composed) for the musical melody of the instrument; and that those are called "songs" which are rendered by the voice in concert with the music; and that they are called "psalms of song" when the voice takes the lead, while the appropriate sound is also made to accompany it, rendered harmoniously by the instruments; and "songs of psalmody" when the instrument takes the lead, while the voice has the second place, and accompanies the music of the strings. And thus much as to the letter of what is signified by these terms. But as to the mystical interpretation, it would be a "psalm" when, by smiting the instrument, viz., the body, with good deeds we succeed in good action, though not wholly proficient in speculation; and a "song" when, by revolving the mysteries of the truth, apart from the practical, and assenting fully to them, we have the noblest thoughts of God and his oracles, while knowledge enlightens us, and wisdom shines

23. Delling, Ψαλμός, in *TDNT* 8:497.
24. *Ant.* VI.xi.214; XII.vii.323; VII.iv.80.
25. *Against Apion* I.40.
26. See also his *Migration of Abraham* 147 and *Contemplative Life* 25. Philo does on occasion use psalm.
27. Delling, op. cit., p. 502; Smith, *Musical Aspects of the New Testament*, 61ff. See further n30.

brightly in our souls; and a "song of psalmody" when, while good action takes the lead, . . . we understand wisdom at the same time, and are deemed worthy by God to know the truth of things, till now hid from us; and a "psalm of song" when, by revolving with the light of wisdom some of the more abstruse questions pertaining to morals, we first become prudent in action and then also able to tell what, and when, and how action is to be taken.[28]

It may be noticed that the information corresponds to Didymus but exactly reverses the understanding where psalm and ode occur together.

Origen was not limited to a knowledge of the Septuagint text, and he knew that it was precarious to draw these precise distinctions. He notes that where the Septuagint has ψαλμός, Aquila regularly has μελῴδημα and Symmachus ᾠδή or ἆσμα. On the other hand, where the Septuagint has "hymns," Aquila has "psalms" and Symmachus "psalterion." Hence, not all of those entitled ψαλμός are said with musical accompaniment.[29] In their own practice and terminology Christians made no distinctions in these nouns,[30] and separate definitions are employed only in 'historical' notices about Old Testament usage or as a basis for a spiritual lesson to Christians.

Eusebius gives the same interpretation as [Pseudo] Hippolytus above concerning the historical practice, but he does not continue with an allegorical application.[31] Elsewhere Eusebius makes the spiritual application but in connection with different words:

> He says literally, "Combine hymns and psalmic instruments." Anagogically, kithara is the practical, "voice of a psalm" [Ps 97:4, 5] is contemplation. Praise therefore, he says, the Lord with deeds and contemplation . . . And this law it is possible to see fulfilled continuously in the churches, for by the spiritual kithara we play the divine melody. We make therefore our tongues

---

28. PG 10.717 B–C, Ante-Nicene Fathers, V, pp. 200–201.

29. PG 12.1072 B–1073A.

30. Athanasius, Exp. in Ps. 70:22 (PG 27.321C), interprets ψαλμός as ὑμνολογί as Theodore of Mopsuestia defines psalm as ode—Devreesse, *Le commentaire de Théodor de Mopsueste sur les Psaumes*, 556. Pseudo-Justin, *Epistle to Zeno and Serenus* 9, gives as the kinds of words which may be spoken "hymns, psalms, odes, and verbal praise" (Otto, IV, 82). Other passages where the original etymological meaning of psalm is recognized include Eusebius, *Comm. in Ps. 47* (PG 23.417C); Asterius, *Frg.* 17, in Ps. 17:1 (Richard, ed. *Asterii Sophistae*, 263–64). Augustine reflects the intermediate stage in the history of the word psalm when he defines it as "a song to a psalterion" (*Exp. in Ps. CXLVII, 2*).

31. *Comm. in Ps.*, proem. (PG 23.72D–73B and cf. 76B).

rational kitharas, and we employ instead of strings odes, instead of brass the lips. The tongue moves to a greater interval than any plectrum.³²

This higher evaluation of vocal music accounts for placing the ode on a higher level than the psalm.

Basil of Caesarea once more offers a close parallel to Didymus. Commenting on the title of Psalm 29 he says this:

> The deeds of the body which are performed for the glory of God are a psalm, whenever by harmonious reason we accomplish nothing unmelodious in our actions. An ode is whatever is present of a higher and divine contemplation . . . Here, then, since it is entitled "Psalm of an Ode," we consider the words to intimate that action follows on contemplation.³³

Although not explicitly stated, the basis for interpreting the word psalm as the active life would seem to be the physical activity employed in plucking the strings of an instrument; the ode could stand for contemplation because singing was related to the rational activity of the mind.³⁴ This background of interpretation accounts for Chrysostom regarding hymnody as superior to psalmody as "a thing of more perfection," as "a diviner thing" chanted by the angels above.³⁵

Gregory of Nyssa often exhibits a considerable independence and originality in his interpretations, even while working within the same principles of interpretation as the other fathers. His treatment of ψαλμός and ᾠδή shows this independence. Gregory avoided the apparent contradiction of taking the psalterion as the intellectual part of man and psalm (the sound made on the psalterion) as the working part of man by reversing the usual interpretation of psalm and ode. He exalts the psalms as representing mental activity and odes as outward deeds:

> There is a distinction between psalm, ode, praise, hymn, and prayer. A psalm is the melody of a musical instrument. An ode is the expression with words of a melody made by the mouth . . . The interpretation which by these designations leads us to virtue is as follows. The psalterion is a musical instrument making its

---

32. *Comm. in Ps.* 97:5 (PG 23.1233B-C). Cf. Theodoret, *In Ps.* 97:5 (PG 80.1661).

33. PG 29.305 B-C. Notice the interpretation of "psalm of an ode," which follows Hippolytus and not Didymus.

34. Athanasius, *Ep. ad Marcellinum* 29 (PG 27.40D-41A); Theodoret, *Interp. Eph.* 5:19 (PG 82.545C); Hesychius, *Frg. in Ps.* 98:30, 31 (PG 93.1232 C). See further n. 40.

35. *Hom. IX on Col. 3:13* (PG 62.363).

sound from the upper parts of its construction, and the music from this instrument is called "psalm." Therefore the word which exhorts to virtue has a significance from the very shape of its construction, for it informs us that the life which is not characterised by earthly sounds is a psalm. I say "sounds" meaning "thoughts"... When we read "ode" we understand through a figure the respectable life with reference to outward things... Whenever the good is accomplished, when practical philosophy accompanies contemplative philosophy, there is the ode of a psalm or the psalm of an ode. Whenever one of these terms is placed by itself before the praises, either the good according to the mind alone is signified by the word "psalm" or the activity and respectability in outward things is the interpretation of the word "ode."[36]

Augustine too takes "psalm" of the words, but in a different context. On Psalm 81:4, 5, "Take the psalm, and give the tabret," he says, "Take your voice, return your hands... To the preaching of God's word we make answer by bodily works."

The same distinctions and applications are sometimes made in connection with the corresponding verbs, ᾄδω and ψάλλω. The classical meaning of ψάλλω was first "to pluck" and then "to play a stringed instrument."[37] The Septuagint represents the transition in Jewish usage, sometimes referring to singing to an instrument and sometimes referring to purely vocal music.[38] Christian singing was unaccompanied.[39] When the fathers met instruments in the Old Testament, either they put them in the category of material sacrifices which had now been replaced by spiritual worship[40] or else they allegorized the instruments as parts of the body or as spiritual principles.[41] Ψάλλω in Christian usage ordinarily means "to sing

36. *On the Titles of the Psalms* II. iii (Jaeger, V, 74-79).

37. Liddell and Scott, op. cit., s.v.

38. The Septuagint usage is conveniently tabulated by Roberson et al., "The Meaning and Use of *Psallo*: Part II."

39. Quasten, *Musik und Gesang* (ET = *Music and Worship*); Gérold, *Les pères de l'église et la musique*; McKinnon, "The Church Fathers and Musical Instruments"; and my booklet, Ferguson, *A Cappella Music in the Public Worship of the Church*.

40. Theodoret, *Quaes. et Resp. ad Orth.* 107 (PG 6.1354); Niceta of Remesiana, *De Util. Hymn.* 9; Eusebius, *Comm. in Ps. 32:2,3 and 91:2,3* (PG 23.281A and 1172D-1173A); Chrysostom, *Exp. in Ps. 149:2 and 150* (PG 55.494 and 498); Cyril of Alexandria, *In Ps.* 32.2 (PG 69.869D-872B); Theodoret, *In Ps.* 32:2 (PG 80.1093C) and 150:4 (PG 80.1996).

41. Origen, *Sel. in Ps. 150:3-5* (PG 12.1684B-D); Hesychius, *De tit. Ps. 150* (PG 27.1341 B-D); Gregory of Nyssa, *Inscrip. Ps. I.ix* (Jaeger, V, 66); Chrysostom, *Exp. in*

The Active and Contemplative Lives

the psalms," "to praise," or "to chant."⁴² There are places, however, in the interpretation of the Psalms where the etymological meaning is recalled and a contrast is made with ᾄδω along the same lines as the contrast between psalm and ode.

Eusebius in commenting on Ps 67:5, "Sing to the Lord and make melody to his name," is a good point of reference.

> And if of these two, I mean "to sing" and "to make melody," it was better "to sing" and inferior to play on an instrument, the better is referred "to God" and to play the instrument is referred "to his name"... For he sings to God who educates his soul with healthful doctrines and sends up a fitting theology to him from a purified mind. He makes melody to his name who practises these things by his bodily movements and activities of his senses so that the name of God is glorified by the things seen through him.⁴³

Augustine makes a similar conjunction of word and deed: "you speak words alone, you have, as it were, the song only, and not the kithara; if you work and speak not, you have the kithara only. On this account both speak well and do well, if you would have the song together with the kithara."⁴⁴ Jerome spoke of *cantare* (to sing) as superior to *psallere* (to make melody). *Cantare* is to

> sing meditatively, that is, to think about the mystery and the sense of divine Scripture. '*Psallere*,' on the other hand, implies the chanting of praise to God through a good work, for example, that the sense of hearing offer its service, and likewise the mouth, and the eyes, and the hands, all the members of the body harmonize, as it were, and thereby pluck the chords of the psalterion in noble acts.⁴⁵

Ps. 150 (PG 55.497); and see n. 32.

42. E. A. Sophocles, *Greek Lexicon of the Roman and Byzantine Periods*, s.v., and Lampe, *A Patristic Greek Lexicon*, s.v. Notice the usage in Asterius, *In Ps. 20:2–5*; *In. Ps. IV, Hom. I*; *In Ps. VIII, Hom. I*; *In Ps. XI, Hom. II*; *In Ps. XII, Hom. I*; *In Ps. IX* (Richard, *Asterii Sophistae*, 270, 23, 105–6, 167, 176, and 136); in Theodore of Mopsuestia, *In Ps. 46:9* (Devreesse, *Le commentaire de Théodore de Mopsueste sur les Psaumes*, 309); and in Theodoret, *In Ps. 17:50; 20:14; and 46:9* (PG 80.988D, 1008C, and 1209B).

43. PG 23.685A–B.

44. *Exp. in Ps. XCII*, 5. Cf. references in n. 21.

45. *Homily 7 on Ps. 67*. The translation follows Ewald, *The Homilies of Saint Jerome*, 51.

One perhaps should not look for complete consistency where allegory is concerned, but there does seem to be some underlying harmony in these interpretations. The unifying idea is the contrast and conjunction of the higher and lower. Where there are two kinds of stringed instruments concerned, the instrument which sounds from its top is the contemplative side of a human being, whereas the instrument which sounds from the bottom is the active side. Where there are two kinds of music, that made with the hand and that made with the voice, the latter as coming from the "higher" part of human nature is superior. Vocal praise is considered superior to instrumental sounds, since contemplation is a higher activity than physical exertion. The fathers shared with Hellenistic philosophy a high evaluation of the contemplative life. Nevertheless, the frequent conjunction in the Psalms of kithara and psalterion, psalm and ode, to make melody and to sing led the fathers to consider the combination of the active and the contemplative as the ideal.

10

Athanasius' *Epistola ad Marcellinum in Interpretationem Psalmorum*, Part I

ATHANASIUS' *EPISTOLA AD MARCELLINUM* (PG 27.12–45) has received little published study.[1] Its authenticity seems well established.[2] The work holds a favored place in the textual transmission of Athanasius' writings. It is preserved in the biblical codex *Alexandrinus*, a prized possession of the British Museum. This fifth-century manuscript gives us a text considerably older than what is preserved in the manuscripts of the main body of Athanasius' writings, which "depart rather considerably from the text of Alexandrinus."[3] It is the Alexandrinus text as edited by Grabbe and reprinted by Migne which I have used in this study, and citations are to the chapter divisions given in Migne.

Opitz declared that this is the only work where one can arrive definitely at the Alexandrian text of an Athanasian writing.[4] Not surpris-

---

1. Quasten, *Patrology*, vol. 3, 37. But note Sieben, "Athanasius über den Psalter"; and Stead, "St. Athanasius on the Psalms" (where he shows that the *Exp. in Psalmos* is not by Athanasius when compared with the *Ep. Marcell.*). There is a German translation by Jos. Fisch in *Bibliothek der Kirchenväter* (1875), a French translation by F. Cavallera, *Saint Athanase* (Paris, 1908), and an English translation by a religious of C.S.M.V. Sister Penelope, *Saint Athanasius on the Psalms* (Oxford, 1949).

2. Rondeau, "L'Épître à Marcellinus sur les Psaumes."

3. Opitz, *Untersuchungen zur Überlieferung der Schriften des Athanasius*, 206.

4. Ibid.

ingly, then, the Psalms quotations in the *Epistola ad Marcellinum* follow consistently the readings of *Alexandrinus*, where these depart from the readings of other Septuagint witnesses.⁵ So faithful is this agreement that one can feel confident in taking the readings of *ad Marcellinum* as evidence for the text of *Alexandrinus* in that section missing from the biblical codex (Ps. 49:20—79:11). Unless the text of Athanasius has been altered to conform with that of the biblical codex in which the work appears, then the *ad Marcellinum* carries the text preserved in *Alexandrinus* back to the life-time of Athanasius.

The patrologies have not ventured a date for the letter.⁶ If some of the descriptions of the Psalms reflect an existential situation and are to that extent autobiographical, as I am inclined to think, then we must date the work during or after Athanasius' escapades while hiding with the monks in the deserts of Egypt. There is much emphasis on persecution: the nobles turned against him (chap. 20); he was discredited before an evil king (chap. 20), and an enemy tyrant arose against the people (chap. 25); the enemies were like a company of soldiers (chap. 17)⁷ and they guarded the house from which he fled, going into the desert (chap. 20); the enemies "defiled the house of God, killed the saints, and threw their bodies to the birds" (chap. 21)⁸; finally wrath ceased and captivity ended (chap. 22). I would suggest a date, therefore, between the closing years of his third exile (c. 360) and shortly after the death of Julian (which occurred in 363), depending on whether Constantius or Julian is the ruler in mind.

In spite of the paucity of modern studies on the *ad Marcellinum*, the work had influence in the patristic period, as its position in *Alexandrinus* as an introduction to the Psalms attests. Basil the Great repeats in summary form the main ideas of the *Epistola* in his prolegomenon to Psalm 1.⁹ The work has some contemporary interest, especially for understanding the patristic interpretation of the Psalms. My concern in this paper will not be exegesis strictly speaking, but the use of Scripture, particularly the

---

5. I have noted these exceptions: ὡσεὶ for ὡς in Ps. 125:1; πορευσώμεθα for πορευσόμεθα in Ps 121:1 (chap. 4); ἐνδυναμώθησαν for ἐδυναμώθησαν in Heb 11:34; and see n19. For the text of the Psalms I have used *Septuaginta X, Psalmi cum odis*, ed. Rahlfs (Göttingen, 1967). References to the Psalms are to the Septuagint numbering.

6. See Rondeau, op. cit., pp. 192–94 for considerations which support the date suggested below.

7. Cf. *Apol. pro fuga*; *Ar. Hist.* 81.

8. Cf. *Ap. ad Const.* 27. See further under the devotional use of the Psalms below.

9. PG 29.213C. English-speaking students know this passage better than they do Athanasius through its translation in NPNF, 2nd ser., vol. 8, pp. xlv–xlvi.

Athanasius' Epistola ad Marcellinum in interpretationem Psalmorum

Psalms, as reflected in the Athanasian treatise. There follows an outline of the contents of the *Epistola ad Marcellinum.* Then will be presented a topical discussion of the contents arranged according to the devotional, liturgical, Christological, doctrinal, and catechetical uses of the Psalms.

OUTLINE

I. Occasion of the letter—chap. 1. Marcellinus, recovering from an illness, has leisure to read the scriptures. The author will relate what a studious old man taught him about the Psalter.

II. The Psalms encompass the entire Old Testament—chap. 2-9.

    A. An outline of the Old Testament: each part has its own function—chap. 2.

    B. The Psalms contain everything—chap. 3-9.

        1. Law—chap. 3.

        2. History—chap. 4.

        3. Prophecy (especially of Christ)—chap. 5-8.

        4. There are Psalms in the other books, so different kinds of literature are found in each part—chap. 9.

III. Special qualities of the Psalms—chap. 10-14.

    A. The Book of Psalms not only contains what the other books do, but it also describes each person's conditions and emotions. Moreover, it gives the words by which to express these feelings and to carry out the commands given in the other books—chap. 10.

    B. Unlike the other biblical books, the words of the Psalms (except those about Christ or other nations) become one's own words and can be spoken as one's own—chap. 11.

    C. The words of the Psalms help men to understand their own emotions: they are a mirror of the soul, a reminder of duty, and a corrective of conduct—chap. 12.

    D. The purpose of the incarnation was to give a perfect example in human life of virtue. The Psalms beforehand expressed Christ's perfect humanity and divinity, and they too bring healing and correction to humanity—chap. 13.

E. Summary of chapters 10–13—chap. 14a.

F. Classification of the contents of the Psalms—chap. 14b.

IV. In what circumstances of life which psalms are to be said—chap. 15–26. This is the main part of the letter. In substance it is a running summary of the contents of the Psalms, *seriatim*, except that when later psalms in the collection deal with the same thing, they are listed with the first one which fits the description. These references to the contents are primarily based on the Septuagint headings or on the opening verses. Twenty-nine receive no specific mention in this listing.[10] A few are mentioned twice; Psalms 104 and 106 are favorites, each being included four times.

V. Why the Psalms are sung with melody—chap. 27–29.

A. Not for the sake of euphony but for two reasons—chap. 27–28:

1. To praise God with all of one's strength.

2. To symbolize and to effect the harmony which the Logos desires in man.

B. The proper singing of the Psalms is with a harmonious soul and from the heart. The saying of the Psalms with melody is symbolic of inner calm and trains the soul in good things—chap. 29.

VI. The value of the Psalms—chap. 30–33.

A. All of the life of a human being is encompassed in the Psalms: select from them according to one's needs—chap. 30.

B. No addition is to be made to the words of the Psalms—chap. 31.

C. God answers prayers spoken in the words of the Psalms, whatever the circumstances: biblical examples of the value of reading the Scriptures—chap. 32.

D. The value of the Psalms is for those of a holy life—chap. 33.

---

10. Twenty-six of these are included in the classification in chapter 14; Psalms 119 and 133 are covered in the group reference to the fifteen Psalms of Ascent (119–33); and Psalm 71 is prominent in chapter 8; hence all are covered in the treatise.

Athanasius' Epistola ad Marcellinum in interpretationem Psalmorum

USES OF THE PSALMS

Devotional

A distinctive principle of Athanasius' interpretation of the Psalms is that each person is able to use the words of the Psalms as his own. "Each psalm has been spoken and arranged by the Spirit so that the movements of our soul may be understood in them according to what was written before time and so that all of them may have been written as about us and be the very words proper to us" (chap. 12). Athanasius demonstrates this point by reading his own life situation in the Psalms, especially in those about the persecution of the righteous. Athanasius' typical form of expression is this: "If you [find yourself in a given situation], say the words in [a given psalm]." Thus in chapter 17 he says: "When you need prayer because of those opposing you and encompassing your soul, sing the 16th, 85th, 87th, and 140th."[11] And later, "Your enemies are around you, but lift up your soul to God and say the 24th . . . Your enemies remain and their hands are full of blood, and they seek to drag you away and destroy you . . ." Some might seem to be contrived, as when he speaks of the pursuer entering "the cave where you are hiding" (chap. 20) in reference to Psalms 56 and 141; but even this may not be, for Athanasius had to hide in caves during his exile.[12] Athanasius knew all too well "those who seem to be friends" who "discredit you" (chap. 20). There is even a personal touch, as when Athanasius speaks of "being little" (chap. 25), a feature of his stature at which Julian sneered.[13]

Athanasius saw not only his own experiences but also all needs and moods reflected in the Psalms. "For I consider that in the words of this book is included and encompassed all the life of men, both the dispositions of the soul and the movements of the reason" (chap. 30).[14] Chapter ten is programmatic of the use of the Psalms to express emotions in all circumstances. The Psalter "has this marvel proper to itself that it describes and represents both the movements of each soul and their changes and corrections." "The one singing these things is confident that he says things written properly concerning himself" (chap. 11). From the Psalms one can gain an understanding of what is going on within himself. "Also from the Psalter he is able to have the form of words for what he experiences

---

11. Cf. the opening two sentences of chapter 19.
12. *Apol. pro fuga* 25.
13. Julian, *Ep.* 47 (435C).
14. Cf. similar statements in chapters 11 and 32.

and in what he is distressed" (chap. 10). Athanasius proceeds to cite some examples:

> In the Psalms it has been written and described how one is to bear affliction and what to say while afflicted, and what to say afterward ... Again, there is the command "in everything" to give thanks, but the Psalms teach what one is to say in giving thanks ... We are commanded to bless God and acknowledge him, but in the Psalms we find expressed how one must praise the Lord.[15]

In this regard notice the classification of the Psalms given in chapter 14. Many of the categories have to do with types of address to God: prayer, petition, thanksgiving, confession, praise, invocation, proclaiming vows, announcing words of glory in the Lord, and various combinations of these. "When you need prayer," Athanasius says (chap. 17), there is an appropriate psalm to provide the words for the occasion.

Athanasius twice gives the same list of psalms to be used "when you have need of *exomologesis*" (chap. 14 and 21). Each of these psalms has a form, of *exomologeō* in its opening verses in the Greek.[16] The type of confession indicated is that of praise and thanksgiving to God. This is a further indication of the basic meaning "acknowledgement" in Christian usage.[17] "Confession" (again *exomologesis*) in the sense of confession of sins occurs in chapter 20: "You sinned, and having turned you repent and ask to receive mercy, you have the words of confession and repentance in the fiftieth" [the great penitential psalm].

Athanasius' suggestions for blessing and praising God are as follows:

> Since it is fitting for us to give thanks to God always and in all things, when you want to bless him, you have as a means of urging on your soul the words of the 102nd and 103rd. Do you want to praise God and to know how one ought to praise for something and for what things it is fitting to speak praise? You have the 104th, 106th, 134th, 145th, 146th, 147th, 148th, and 150th.

The Psalms give expression to the individual's longing for God.

> Then, if you have a very great desire for God and hear enemies casting reproaches, do not be troubled. Rather understand the eternal fruit of such desire, comfort your own soul in the hope

---

15. Cf. also chapter 14.
16. Psalms 9; 74; 91; 104; 105; 106; 107; 110; 117; 135; 137.
17. Ledogar, *Acknowledgement*.

of God, and by this lightening and alleviating of the soul's sorrows, say the 41st psalm.[18]

"As the hart longs for flowing streams, so longs my soul for thee, O God" (Ps 41:2). For the words of Scripture to be effective, they must be supported by a holy life. "For there is need of faith and a genuine disposition for the law to cooperate in the things prayed for" (chap. 32). The demons make sport of those who use the right words but are unrighteous, "but they fear the words of the saints or are not even able to endure them" (chap. 33). Hence, one must dedicate himself to the Lord:

> Consecrating your house and your soul in which the Lord is welcomed, even your bodily house in which you dwell bodily, give thanks and say the 29th ["for the dedication of the temple"] and the 126th ["Unless the Lord build the house"].

This last statement illustrates the tropological interpretation of the Psalms by which statements are applied to the individual and his moral life. Athanasius does this not only with Psalms about the temple but also those about the nation. Thus Psalm 136 about Israel in Babylon is applied to the soul "taken captive by alien thoughts" (chap. 25).

The devotional use of the Psalms seems to be what predominates in this letter. There is an explicit reference to singing privately in chapter 26. Much of the contents of the letter probably has reference to this individual use of the Psalms, but it is often difficult to say what reflects a private and what a liturgical use of the Psalms. Some statements do give some information relating to the liturgical use of the Psalms.

Liturgical

A fair amount of the *Epistola ad Marcellinum* may in fact be based on liturgical use, but I shall confine the remarks here to what explicitly bears on it. Some of the information included under doctrine (e.g., about the meaning of baptism) also reflects liturgical use. The teaching noted above that the Psalms give acceptable words with which to address God laid the theological foundation for their liturgical use.

The use of the Psalms in the daily office is reflected at several points, although no distinction is made in the comments between a private and a church use. The assigning of certain psalms to certain days of the week follows the headings in the Septuagint. "Do you want to sing on the Sabbath?

---

18. Chapter 19.

You have the 91st. Do you want to give thanks on the Lord's day? You have the 23rd" (chap. 22, 23). This follows the normal early Christian terminology, continued in the modern languages of southern Europe, of designating Saturday as the Sabbath and Sunday as the Lord's day (the heading of the Psalm, following Jewish terminology, says "first day of the week"). The use of Psalm 23 ("Be lifted up, O ancient doors! that the King of glory may come in") on the first day of the week may be connected with the belief that the ascension (see chap. 8) occurred on Sunday.[19] The passage continues, "Do you wish to sing on Monday? Say the words in the 47th. Does one want to praise on Friday? You have the praise in the 92nd." The crucifixion occurred on Friday,[20] and Athanasius explains that it is fitting to sing a victory song on that day because the Lord rules in spite of the attempts of enemies to interfere.

> Do you want to sing on Wednesday? You have the 93rd. For then the Lord was betrayed . . . When therefore you read the Gospel and see on Wednesday the Jews taking counsel against the Lord and you see him speaking boldly in vindication against the Devil on your behalf, sing the words in the 93rd itself.

This tradition, which places the betrayal on Wednesday rather than Thursday night, has become important in the efforts to correlate the Gospel accounts of the Passion with the calendar information supplied by the book of Jubilees and the Dead Sea Scrolls.[21] Some annual commemoration is indicated, but what is not specified, in the instructions. "At the festival [Ps. 80:4] when you want to sing to the Lord, call together the servants of God and sing the words in the 80th and 94th" (chap. 22). Such corporate singing of the Psalms is referred to in chapter 18, When you wish to sing with many, coming together with men righteous and upright in life, say the 32nd (but that need not be understood as a stated assembly of the church).

The public oral reading of the Scriptures, including the Psalms, seems to be indicated by the references to "the hearer" in chapter 10. This is made more explicit in the following chapters' references to "he who hears" and "he who speaks" (chap. 11) and "he who hears the reader" (chap. 12). There is even allusion to the action of handing the book to the reader (chap. 11).

Chapter 12 uses cantor (ὁ ψάλλων) and reader (ὁ ἀναγινώσκων) synonymously for the same person. This interchange of singer and reader may

---

19. Rordorf, *Sunday*, 235–36.

20. The heading of Psalm 92 has προσαββατου but *Alexandrinus* has σαββατου.

21. Jaubert, *La Date de la Cène*. She does not include this passage in her list of patristic testimonies (79–102). For the betrayal on Wednesday, see *Didas.* V.14.

Athanasius' Epistola ad Marcellinum in interpretationem Psalmorum

serve to introduce what is surely the most interesting liturgical information supplied by this treatise, namely the manner of rendering the Psalms. Athanasius' own statements may serve to balance the statement better known in the history of music made by Augustine about Athanasius' practice. "I remember that it has been often told me that Athanasius bishop of Alexandria caused the reader of the psalm to sound it forth with so little modulation of the voice that it was nearer to speaking than to singing."[22]

Athanasius himself explains as follows:

> Some of the unlearned among us, although believing the words to be inspired by God, nevertheless think that the Psalms are sung [chanted] on account of the euphony and for pleasure to the ear. But it is not so, for the Scripture does not seek what is sweet and beguiling, but even these qualities were appointed for the benefit of the soul. (Chap. 27)

He offers two purposes for the presence of melody [or chant].

> First, it was fitting that the divine Scripture hymn God in voice not only in its length [συνεχείᾳ] but also in its breadth [πλάτος]. Therefore it has spoken according to the length such as are the words of the law and the prophets, and all the things told as history, along with the New Testament; but according to the breadth it has said such words as those of the psalms, odes, and songs.[23]

The second purpose is obviously the more important to Athanasius and more fully developed.

> As we make known and signify the thoughts of the soul through the words which we bring forth, so the Lord wishing the melody of the words to be a symbol of the spiritual harmony in the soul has decreed the odes to be sung harmoniously and the psalms to be recited as a song ... The saying of the psalms with melody [chant] is not therefore a zeal for euphony but a sign of the harmony of the reasonings in the soul. (Chap. 27, 28, 29)[24]

22. *Confessions* X.33. Cf. Athanasius' frequent use of λέγω for reciting the Psalms.

23. Archibald Robertson understands the "breadth" to mean that chanting gave a longer time to dwell on the meaning of the words—*Nicene and Post-Nicene Fathers*, 2nd ser., vol. 4, p. lxv. However, the word "breadth" or "broadly" occurs in chapter 9 for the melody aspect of the Psalms.

24. Athanasius understands the kithara and psalterion as the harmony of the body to the soul in his *Exp. in Ps.* 80:3 and 97:5 (PG 27.361 D and 420C). This varies the interpretation of these instruments which is studied in my communication, "The Active and Contemplative Lives," chapter 9 in this volume.

Without listing a separate purpose, Athanasius actually elaborates this one in such a way as to make it into two purposes. Not only does the harmony of the chanting symbolize the harmony of one's being, but the melody also elevates the soul away from disturbances toward higher things.

> Singing well trains the soul and leads it out of disturbance to equanimity, so that the soul constituted by nature may not be disturbed by anything but rather may be imagining good things and even more may receive a desire for the good things to come. For the soul sympathetically affected by the chanting of the words forgets the passions, and rejoicing, looks to the mind of Christ and thinks on the best things. (Chap. 29)

I conclude that Athanasius had a positive assessment of the melodic element in psalmody. But it was not for its own sake. Melody might even seem to be minimized, but it is not disparaged, nor does it seem to be feared. Melody was to serve spiritual purposes. To that end he opposed additions to the words of the Psalms.

> Let no one surround these words with appealing words from outside [scripture?] nor attempt to alter or wholly change the phrases. Let him say and sing simply the things written, as they were said, so that the men who ministered these words might recognize them as their own and join in prayer with us. Or rather, so that the Spirit who spoke in holy men, perceiving the words which he inspired to resound in them, might come to our assistance. For in so far as the life of holy men is better than others, so far also their words are better and stronger than those devised by us, even if spoken rightly. (Chap. 31)

Athanasius is perhaps protesting against the embellishments on the biblical texts which became a feature of Byzantine hymnody or is reflecting the spirit which attempted to limit the singing in church to the biblical hymns.[25] On the other hand, this restriction could be considered the reverse side of Athanasius' insistence that the Psalms provide a perfect expression for all spiritual needs.

The Psalms were rendered without instrumental accompaniment.[26] We might infer that instrumental music would provide for Athanasius an

---

25. Council of Laodicea, canon 59.

26. See my booklet, Ferguson, *A Cappella Music in the Public Worship of the Church*, for documentation. So also McKinnon, "The Church Fathers and Musical Instruments," with his conclusions summarized in "The Meaning of the Patristic Polemic against Musical Instruments."

Athanasius' Epistola ad Marcellinum in interpretationem Psalmorum

instance of euphony without the spiritual and edifying purposes which he found acceptable in making melody with the words, but there is no indication that Athanasius even considered the possibility of instruments in the church's assemblies. How the Psalms were to be performed is expressed in this way:

> Those who do not recite the divine odes [from an ordered soul] do not sing with the understanding but delight themselves and are blameworthy ... Those who do sing according to this manner so that the melody of the words is offered from the rhythm of the soul and from harmony with the spirit, the ones singing in this way sing with the tongue and with the mind and profit greatly not only themselves but also those who want to hear them. (Chap. 29)

The word translated singing in this passage is ψάλλω. Although this word meant "to play" or "to sing to accompaniment" in classical Greek, it was commonly used in Christian literature to mean "to sing the Psalms" or "to sing praise" with no instrumental connotations.[27] It does seem to be used by Athanasius in places especially for the melodious aspect of the singing.[28] Even this aspect is apparently lost in much of the treatise. Throughout ψάλλω is interchangeable with ᾄδω or even λέγω. The Lord "taught by word of mouth in the ones pronouncing the psalms [ψάλλουσι]" (chap. 13). Even where Athanasius found ψάλλω in the Septuagint referring to instruments (as 4 Kingdoms 3:15), he understood it vocally (chap. 33). The musical instruments in the Psalms he allegorized as parts of the human body (chap. 28, 29).[29]

Christological

The Psalms contain, according to Athanasius, all of Scripture, but they especially point to Christ. "When you want to sing privately the things concerning the Saviour, you find in almost every psalm such things" (chap. 26). Athanasius shares the conviction of early Christianity that in

---

27. Ibid.

28. It is in parallel with μελωδεῖ in chapter 2 and μελῳδία in chapter 28. Cf. chapter 29, "singing well."

29. Athanasius, following the Alexandrian exegetical tradition, regularly does this in his Psalms commentary—e.g., on Pss 32:1; 91:4; 97:5; 143:9 (PG 27.164B; 404D; 420C; 544A).

the Psalms the Saviour was either speaking or spoken about.[30] The Psalms, more so than any other Old Testament book, were read Christologically in the early church. The principle that the Psalms are to be interpreted Christologically was the common standpoint of early Christian exegesis.

Athanasius gives at two points a kerygmatic summary of prophecies about Christ in the Psalms: an extensive list in chapters 5–8 and a briefer list in chapter 26. These Christological summaries proceed from his eternal generation to the present session and coming destruction of the devil. The basic outline follows other early Christian summaries of the Gospel in emphasizing the facts of the incarnate life of Christ.[31] But Athanasius adds an emphasis on the deity of the Word, true Son of the Father, and upon his function as judge.

Psalm 117:26, 27 says in the Septuagint, "Blessed is he who comes in the name of the Lord . . . God the Lord has appeared to us." The designation of "Lord" as "God" in the Old Testament (Ps 49:2, 3 is also cited) is seen as an affirmation that the Christian's Lord is God. "This very God who comes is also the Word who is sent" (chap. 5, citing Ps 106:20). Psalms 44:2 and 109:3 are cited for the generation of the Word by the Father, making him "Son of God." Since this is the one to whom the Father spoke in the creation (Genesis 1), Ps 32:6 says, "By the word of the Lord the heavens were established."

The coming of this one was no illusion (chap. 6). Psalm 86:5 marks his true humanity by saying, "Mother Zion will say, 'Man, even a man was born in her.'" The birth from a virgin was known, for David in Ps 44:11, 12 addresses her as "Daughter." The same Psalm declares the coming One as Christ, the Anointed (vv. 7, 8).

Athanasius gives much attention to the passion (chap. 7). The plot of the Jews against Jesus is seen in Ps 2:1, 2: "The peoples considered vain things . . . and the rulers were gathered together against the Lord and his Christ." The betrayal by Judas was read in Psalm 108:6–8.[32] "In the 21st it tells what kind of death he had, the Saviour himself speaking" followed by a quotation of vv. 16–19 (chap. 7), a Psalm which was already prominent in the passion narratives of the Gospels. Athanasius seized upon the word ὤρυξαν ("gouged, pierced") for the hands and feet as especially referring to death on a cross. Athanasius emphasizes that "not for himself, but for

---

30. See Linton, "Interpretation of the Psalms in the Early Church," for the concern with "Who is the speaker?" in the Christian interpretation of the Psalms.

31. See Ferguson, *Early Christians Speak*, 3rd ed., 19–22 for a collection of such summaries of Christian belief.

32. Already in Acts 1:20.

us, the Lord suffered these things" (chap. 7). He appeals to Pss 87:8; 68:5; 137:8; and 71:4, 12 for the redemptive power of Christ's death. Chapter 26 gives a general reference to Psalms 92, 95, 97, and 98 for "the Saviour's benefits accomplished for us by his sufferings."

"The 15th Psalm shows his resurrection from the dead" (chap. 26), a psalm already used for this purpose in the New Testament (Acts 2:25ff.; 13:35). "The 23rd and 46th announce his ascension to heaven." Athanasius cites particularly 23:7 and 46:6 (chap. 8). The Psalms announce the session in 109:1, one of the most frequently cited Psalms in early Christian literature.[33] Athanasius includes the calling of the nations in his list of the Saviour's deeds, as is done in some early Christian kerygmatic summaries.[34] He says it is found "in many places, but especially" in Pss 46:2 and 71:9–11. Athanasius makes much of Christ's "kingdom and judicial power" (chap. 26). He cites particularly Ps 71:1–2, "O God, give your justice to the king and your righteousness to the son of the king, to judge your people with righteousness and your people with justice," and Pss 49:4, 6, and 81:1 (chap. 8). Jesus will come again and the Devil will be destroyed: "You have sat upon the throne, O righteous judge; you have rebuked the nations, and the wicked one is destroyed" (Ps 9:5, 6).

"These things then are sung in the Psalms, while in each of the other books [of the prophets] they are announced beforehand" (chap. 8). The most prominent Christological Psalms according to the usage of this treatise are 2; 21; 23; 44; 46; 49; 68; 71; and 109. But Athanasius was prepared to affirm that the Psalter "signifies the things of the prophets more or less in each psalm" (chap. 5).

Doctrinal

The appropriation of the Psalter as a Christian book implicit in its Christological use meant that Christian doctrine could be learned from it. Some of the following points pertain to doctrine that is found in the treatise, not to specifically the doctrinal use of the Psalms, but there is enough of the doctrinal use to indicate that one value of the Psalms in Athanasius' estimation was that Christian doctrine could be found there.

We may make the transition from the Christological reading of the Psalms to the doctrinal use of the Psalms by looking first at the incarnation. Athanasius gives a twofold purpose to the incarnation in chapter 13.

---

33. Hay, *Glory at the Right Hand*.
34. Justin, *Apology* I, 31.7.

There was first the redemptive purpose: "This again is the grace of the Saviour. Becoming man for us, he offered his own body for death on our behalf in order that he might deliver all from death." There was further an instructional and exemplary purpose. The Lord did not want us easily deceived by the Devil and gave a pledge of the victory over the Devil. Therefore, "he not only taught but did the things which he taught in order that each one might hear him speaking, and seeing as in a picture, might receive from him the example of doing . . . No one would find a more perfect teaching in virtue than what the Lord expressed in himself." Unlike other lawgivers, Jesus "not only gives the law but also has given himself as a type" for those who want to see it in action.

Very striking is that Athanasius seems to say that Scripture shares in this task. The statements about the purpose of the incarnation lead into statements about the Lord teaching in the Psalms and about their role in improving mankind.

> On account of this, therefore, before his visit to us he taught by word of mouth also in the Psalmists in order that he might express and show in himself the earthly and heavenly man. Even so, also, he who wants is able to learn from the Psalms the emotions and dispositions of souls, finding in them also the healing and correction of each emotion.

Is there a suggestion here that the Psalms partake of Christ's redemptive work? The Psalms may share in this divine work because "the Lord is in the words of the scriptures" (chap. 33). The words of the Psalms, like all of Scripture, are "inspired by God" (chap. 2, quoting 2 Tim 3:16, and chap. 27 and 30). This doctrine of Scripture is in a way the foundation for all of the values of the Psalms which Athanasius finds and the uses to which they were put in the church. Each part of Scripture—law, history, prophecy—has its own ministry, but it is "one and the same Spirit" which administers these distinctions and gives unity to Scripture (chap. 9).

When Athanasius wants to make a shorthand reference to the Christological content of the Psalms, it is in terms of the incarnation: they have "repeated prophecies concerning the appearance in the body of our Lord and Saviour Jesus Christ" (chap. 27). The purpose of the incarnation, as noted above, was "to deliver all from death" (chap. 13). Although only once is a psalm recalled in support of Christ's resurrection (Psalm 15 in chap. 26), Athanasius twice refers to the Christian's resurrection by appeal to Psalm 65 "concerning joy and the resurrection" (chap. 14 and 21). Some witnesses have "Of the resurrection" as part of the title of the psalm. That

Athanasius' Epistola ad Marcellinum in interpretationem Psalmorum

which led to this association, unless there was already a Jewish use of it on the first day of the week, might have been verse 9, "Who placed my soul in life and did not give my feet to be moved." However the association came about, Athanasius could say, "If you wish to instruct some concerning the resurrection, sing the words in the 65th" (chap. 21).

The human condition which requires that one be delivered from death is a result of sin. Athanasius finds in Psalm 35 evidence that humans are the cause of their own sin (note verse 2, "to sin in oneself"). "Do not consider," he declares, "the evil in transgressors to be according to nature, as the heretics [Gnostics, Manichaeans] say, but speak the 35th and see that they themselves are the cause of their sinning" (chap. 18).

Athanasius occasionally speaks of the human part in appropriating salvation. He offers rather incidentally a definition of repentance: "To repent is to cease from sin" (chap. 10). He proceeds to explain that the Psalms express how one is to repent and what one is to say in repentance. Furthermore, hearing the words of the Psalms can prick the conscience and produce repentance, or hearing about God's grace can bring joy (chap. 12). The doctrine of baptism common in the ancient church is reflected in the following statement: "When you see some being baptized and redeemed from the corruptible birth and marvel at God's love for humans, sing for them the 31st" (chap. 18). In view of Athanasius' avowal (cited above) that sin is not by nature, I take it that he is not referring to birth sin or original sin, but to the fact that at our fleshly birth we are mortal or perishable; there would be an unexpressed contrast with the new birth of baptism as conferring eternal life. The exclamation of Psalm 31:1, "Blessed are those whose transgressions are forgiven and whose sins are covered," made it an important baptismal psalm in the ancient church. Its use in the baptismal liturgy is well-attested.[35]

Baptism, because it brings one within the circle of salvation, makes one a member of the church. This connection between salvation and church membership is seen in Athanasius' comment on Psalm 92 for Friday, "When the cross [i.e., crucifixion] occurred, the house of God was built, although the enemies made an attempt to hinder it" (chap. 23). The house of God or temple is the church. The atoning death of Christ is the foundation of the church. Athanasius' doctrine of the church is further amplified in his interpretation of the Old Testament language of the temple, city, and nation as the church. The references to the temple and

---

35. Cyril of Jerusalem, *Procat.*; Gregory Nazianzus, *Or.* XL, *De bapt*. See further Lamb, *The Psalms in Christian Worship*.

the nation of Israel were sometimes applied to the individual believer, as noticed in connection with the devotional use of the Psalms. As instances of the ecclesiological use of such terminology, notice chapter 22: "If you want to know the difference between the catholic church and schisms and to overturn the latter, you are able to say the words written in the 86th," which speaks of God's love for the city of Zion. Similarly he says, "When you wish to confound the opinions of pagans and heretics to the effect that the knowledge of God is not found among them but only in the catholic church, you can sing with understanding and say the words in the 75th" (chap. 21). That Psalm declares that God is known in Israel and makes his dwelling in Zion. Since the church is the saved, it has eschatological significance, and Athanasius can blend the ideas of the church and heaven: "And if seeing the house of God and its eternal habitations, you have a longing for these things say the 83rd" (chap. 22), a psalm which speaks of the soul's longing for the courts of the Lord. The Christian appropriation of the Psalms meant an ecclesiological as well as a Christological reading of the Psalms.

Catechetical

"All the divine Scripture is a teacher of virtue" as well as of "true faith" (chap. 14). I adopt the word catechetical not as a technical term but to embrace some of the general instructional material which Athanasius finds in the Psalms.

Although I am not limiting this section to baptismal catechesis, there is a considerable evangelistic thrust in Athanasius' comments. "When you see the providence of the Lord for all things and his lordship and wish to instruct [κατηχῆσαι] some in his faith and obedience, persuading them first to confess, sing the 99th" (chap. 23) with its exultant invitation to "Know the Lord" and "Enter his courts." Again, "When the Enemy is conquered and a creature is saved, do not boast in yourself but knowing that the Son of God accomplished this, say that which is spoken to him in the 9th psalm" (chap. 16), which has several appropriate thoughts—the wicked one destroyed, trusting in the Lord, and telling of his characteristics. This concern with conversion recalls again the confounding of the heretics (chap. 21, 22) and the inclusion of the calling of the nations in the summary of the faith (chap. 8). "If you see the grace of the Saviour extended everywhere and the race of men saved," salute the Lord with the 8th psalm (chap. 16).

Athanasius' Epistola ad Marcellinum in interpretationem Psalmorum

As to other kinds of teaching notices in his letter, Athanasius picks up the frequent attention to the poor in the Psalms, and uses the Psalms as an encouragement to benevolence. "When you see many in need and poor and you want to show mercy to them, you are able to approve those who have already shown mercy and to persuade others to do it by saying the 40th" (chap. 16), which opens, "Blessed is he who considers the poor and needy."

I am continually impressed with the concern among the fathers that everything contribute to virtue. Moral instruction was very important to Athanasius. He pointed to the incarnate life of Jesus, as noted above, for a perfect example of virtue. "Whether forbearance, love of mankind, goodness, manliness, mercy, righteousness—one will find all these things in him so that nothing pertaining to virtue is lacking to the one who understands his human life" (chap. 13). Then he points to the Psalms as providing "healing and correction" for human dispositions.[36] The Psalms are a "corrective of our conduct" (chap. 12).[37] Athanasius commends Psalm 14 ("Who shall dwell on your holy hill?") for learning "what sort of person is the citizen of the kingdom of heaven" (chap. 16). Indeed it may be thought that the goal of the whole letter is the spiritual improvement of the reader. The last word may appropriately be Athanasius' conclusion:

> And you, meditating on these words, such as are in the Psalms, and reading them with understanding, "being led by the Spirit," you will be able to understand the reason in each. Emulate such a life as the holy men inspired by God had who spoke these things. (Chap. 33)

---

36. Cf. chapter 33 for the imagery of therapy again.
37. Cf. chapter 15.

11

Athanasius, *Epistola ad Marcellinum in Interpretationem Psalmorum*, Part II

INTRODUCTION

Text

A THANASIUS' *EPISTOLA AD MARCELLINUM* holds a privileged position in the textual history of the father's writings. It is preserved as an introduction to the Psalms in the biblical codex *Alexandrinus*, once in the possession of the patriarchate of Alexandria and now in the British Museum, London. This manuscript is dated in the first half of the fifth century and so is considerably older than other manuscripts of Athanasisus' works. The text of this letter in *Alexandrinus* was the basis of the printed edition by J. E. Grabe,[1] reprinted in Migne, *Patrologiae Graeca*, vol. 27, cols. 12–45, from which the following translation was made. With few exceptions the text of the Psalms quotations in *Ad Marcellinum* is that of *Alexandrinus*, confirming that *Alexandrinus* preserves the text of the Psalms used by Athanasius. Conversely, the early date of *Alexandrinus* and its Alexandrian provenance argue that it most nearly preserves the original wording of Athanasius' treatise.

1. *Septuaginta interpretum*, vol. 4.

Athanasius, Epistola Ad Marcellinum In Interpretationem Psalmorum

Genuineness

The Athanasian authorship of the *Epistola ad Marcellinum* is well established. The manuscript tradition is unanimously favorable. Cassiodorus[2] and the Second Council of Nicaea[3] cite it as by Athanasius. If an objection to the genuineness of the work is made because Jerome[4] lists as an Athanasian work *De titulis Psalmorum*[5] but not the *Ad Marcellinum,* it may be replied that Jerome also notes "other works too numerous to mention." Moreover, in view of the contents it seems possible that the *Ad Marcellinum* could be described as a work "On the Topics of the Psalms."

M. J. Rondeau has confirmed the external evidence for Athanasian authorship by a study of the Christology and terminology of the treatise.[6] There seems to be no basis for serious doubt about the authorship.

Athanasius presents the teaching which he records as coming from an old man. His identity is unknown. The ascription may simply be a literary device. Of known personages one thinks of bishop Alexander or the monk Antony.

Date

Rondeau dates the treatise in Athanasius' maturity and notes its deep roots in a monastic milieu.[7] There are perhaps indications of a more precise date. Some of the statements are so closely parallel to other statements in Athanasius' writings as to appear autobiographical. The references to a company of soldiers in chapter 17 and to the house where he stayed being guarded and from which he fled to hide in a cave in the desert in chapter 20 remind one of *Apologia pro fuga* 24 and 25 and *Arianorum historia* 81. The statement that the enemies "rush in, defile the house of God, kill the saints, and throw their bodies to the birds of heaven" in chapter 21 is closely parallel to *Apologia ad Constantium* 27. The references to an evil king (chapter 20) and an enemy tyrant (chapter 25) could have had either

   2. *Institutiones* IV.3; *In Psal.* pref. 16.
   3. Sixth session—Mansi 13, 721 C.
   4. *De viris illustribus* 87.
   5. The work by this title in the Athanasian corpus (Migne, PG 27, 649–1344) has been ascribed to Hesychius of Jerusalem by G. Mercati, "'Sull' autore del De titulis psalmorum stampato fra le opere di S. Atanasio," *Orientalia Christiana Periodica* 10 (1944) 7–22.
   6. Rondeau, "L'Epître à Marcellinus sur les Psaumes."
   7. Ibid.

Constantius or Julian in mind. When Athanasius wrote, wrath had finally ceased and captivity had ended (chapter 22). These statements point to a date either after the third exile (361) or after the death of Julian (363).

Importance

The *Epistola ad Marcellinum* is informative on the uses or functions of scripture in the early church.[8] Its greatest importance is its enormous influence in the history of Christian spirituality. The central thesis of the work is that the Psalms cover all the moods and emotions of the human soul and, unlike other parts of Scripture, provides words that each person can use as his own. The reader of the Psalms "comprehends and is taught the emotions of his own soul" and receives "the form of words for what he experiences and for what distresses him" (chapter 10). "The one singing [the Psalms] is bold to speak these words as especially written concerning himself and as his own words" (chapter 11). Athanasius thus encouraged the personal devotional reading of the Psalms in addition to their liturgical use in churches and monasteries. He further offered important reflections toward a theology of music (chapters 27–29).

Basil the Great appears to be indebted to the *Ad Marcellinum*, for his prolegomenon to Psalm 1 gives in summary form the main ideas of this letter:

> The prophets, the historians, the law, give each a special kind of teaching, and the exhortation of the proverbs furnishes yet another. But the use and profit of all are included in the book of Psalms. There is prediction of things to come. There our memories are reminded of the past. There laws are laid down for the guidance of life. There are directions as to conduct. The book, in a word, is a treasury of sound teaching, and provides for every individual need. It heals the old hurts of souls, and brings about recovery where the wound is fresh. It wins the part that is sick and preserves that which is sound. As far as lies within its power, it destroys the passions which lord it in this life in the souls of men. And all this it effects with a musical persuasiveness and with a gratification that induces wise and wholesome reflection. The Holy Spirit saw that mankind was hard to draw to goodness, that our life's scale inclined to pleasure, and that so we were

---

8. This was the subject of my major theme paper at the Seventh International Conference on Patristic Studies at Oxford, September, 1975; published in *Studia Patristica* 16.2 (1985) 295–308 and now chapter 10 above.

Athanasius, Epistola Ad Marcellinum In Interpretationem Psalmorum

neglectful of the right. What plan did he adopt? He combined the delight of melody with his teaching, to the end that by the sweetness and softness of what we heard we might, all unawares, imbibe the blessing of the words ... So the melodious music of the Psalms has been designed for us, that those who are boys in years, or at least but lads in ways of life, while they seem to be singing, may in reality be carrying on the education of the soul.[9]

The *Epistola ad Marcellinu*m was fairly widely circulated in the Middle Ages as an introduction to the Psalms. This is especially true of excerpts from the letter, known as *Opusculum in Psalmos*. The *Opusculum* comprises chapters 14a and 15 through 26, modified, of the longer work. This section of the treatise applying the Psalms to personal circumstances of life may be the most original as well as most influential contribution made by the letter. The *Opusculum* was printed in Latin translation in the sixteenth century before the other works of Athanasius were printed.[10] An English translation under the title "A Treatise made by Athanasius the Great concerning the use and vertue of the Psalmes" [*sic*] was published in 1580(?).[11]

The longer work has not fared so well in modern times. It has been translated into German by J. Fisch for the series Bibliothek der Kirchentväter,[12] into French by F. Cavallera,[13] and into English by a religious of C.S.M.V. [Sister Penelope].[14] This earlier English version does not stay with the best Greek text and is often loose. It had limited circulation and is difficult to obtain now.

Contents

The contents of the *Epistola ad Marcellinum* may be outlined as follows:

I. Occasion of the letter—chapter l.

---

9. Migne, PG 29.212A–B.

10. See for editions the *British Museum Catalogue of Printed Books* under Athanasius, *Opusculum in Psalmos*.

11. It was reprinted in Prideaux, *The Doctrine of Prayer*, 261–82.

12. *Ausgewählte Schriften des heiligen Athanasius*, vol. 2.

13. *Saint Athanase* (Paris, 1908).

14. *St. Athanasius on the Psalms* (Oxford, 1949). Since the publication of my translation, English translations have appeared by Gregg, trans., *The Life of Antony and the Letter to Marcellinus*; and Bright, trans. *Early Christian Spirituality*.

II The Psalms in relation to the other parts of the Old Testament—Chapters 2-9.

III. Distinctive features of the Psalms—chapters 10-13.

    A. They give the words by which to express human feelings and to carry out the commands found in the other books. Chapter 10.

    B. The words of the Psalms can he spoken as one's own words. Chapter 11.

    C. The Psalms help men to understand their own emotions and conditions. Chapter 12.

    D. They spoke beforehand of Christ's perfect humanity and divinity and so share in his work of healing and improving mankind. Chapter 13.

IV. Classification of the contents of the Psalms—chapter 14.

V. A Running summary of the contents of the Psalms—chapters 15-26.

VI. The Purpose of melody in singing the Psalms—chapters 27-29.

    A. Melody is not for the sake of euphony, but in order to praise God with all of one's strength and to express the harmony which the Logos desires in human beings. Chapters 27-28.

    B. The proper singing of the Psalms is from the heart. Chapter 29.

VII. The Value of the Psalms in prayer and exorcism—chapters 30-33.

TRANSLATION

MG. 27. 12A 1. Dear Marcellinus, I admire you for your devotion in Christ. Although you are suffering much in the present testing, you are bearing it well and are not neglecting spiritual exercises. Since learning from the bearer of your letter how you pass your time after your illness, I know that you have time to study all the divine scriptures, but that with special frequency you read the book of Psalms and are eager to acquire an understanding of each Psalm. I approve of this, since I too have a great desire for this book, as indeed for all the scrpitures. Once while filled with this desire, I met with a studious old man, and I want to write to you the things which he mastered from the Psalter and led me to understand concerning

Athanasius, Epistola Ad Marcellinum In Interpretationem Psalmorum

it. For he has a certain grace and persuasiveness B as well as an eloquent way of expressing himself. He spoke as follows.

2. My son, all our Scripture, both old and new, is inspired of God and profitable for instruction, as the text says.[15] The book of Psalms has a persuasive and exact manner of expression to those who give attention to it. Each book in the Bible ministers and reports its own particular message. For instance, the Pentateuch reports the beginning of the world and the deeds of the patriarchs, the exodus of Israel from Egypt, and the arrangements of the law; the Triteuch[16] the distribution of the land and the deeds of the judges and the genealogy of David; Kingdoms and Chronicles the deeds of the kings; and Esdras the release from captivity, return of the people, and building of the C temple and the city; the Prophets prophecies concerning the life of the Savior, reminders of the commandments, censures of transgressors, and prophecies to the nations. The book of Psalms contains and sings all these things within itself, like a paradise; and it exhibits and sings its own particular contents in addition.

3. The Psalter sings[17] the contents of Genesis in the 18th Psalm: "The heavens declare the glory of God, and the firmament announces his handiwork."[18] Also in the 23rd "The earth and its fullness is the Lord's, the world and all those who dwell in it. He founded it upon the seas."[19] The contents of Exodus, Numbers, and Deuteronomy it sings well in the 77th Psalm. 13A Also in the 13th Psalm, when it says, "At the Exodus of Israel from Egypt, the house of Jacob from a people of strange language, Judah became his sanctuary and Israel his dominion."[20] It sings about these things also in the 104th: "He sent Moses his servant and Aaron whom he had chosen. He performed by them the words of his signs and his wonders in the land of Ham. He sent darkness, and it became dark; they rebelled at his words. He turned their waters into blood, and he killed their fish. Their land swarmed with frogs, even in the chambers of their kings. He spoke, and there came flies and gnats in all their borders."[21] Indeed all this Psalm

---

15. 2 Tim 3:16.

16. Joshua, Judges, Ruth.

17. Athanasius uses ψαλλω (here) and αδω (introducing the next quotation) interchangeably; hence the translation makes no effort to distinguish them. The nouns psalm and ode are similarly interchangeable.

18. Ps 18:2 (19:1). References will be given to the Septuagint numbering first and the English numbering in parentheses.

19. Ps 23:1, 2 (24:1, 2).

20. Ps 113:1, 2 (114:1, 2).

21. Ps 104:26–31 (105:26–31).

and the 105th are found to be written concerning these things. The details concerning the priesthood and tabernacle are proclaimed at the procession of the tabernacle in the 28th Psalm: "Bring to the Lord, sons of God; bring to the Lord, sons of strength; bring to the Lord glory and honor."[22]

B 4. The stories of [Joshua] the son of Nave and of the Judges it exhibits somewhat in the 106th when it says, "And they establish cities to live in, they sow fields, and they plant vineyards."[23] For under the son of Nave the land of promise was distributed to Israel. Continuing from the same Psalm, "They cried to the Lord in their trouble, and he saved them from their distress."[24] This signifies the book of Judges, for when they cried out, he raised up judges at that time who saved the people from their oppressors. And it sings of the kings somewhat in the 19th, saying: "Some boast of chariots, some of horses, but we boast of the name of the Lord our God. They were overthrown and fell, but we arose and stood upright. 13C Lord, save the king, and answer us in the day we call upon you."[25] The Psalms sing the things of Esdras in the 125th of the Psalms of Ascents: "When the Lord overturned the captivity of Zion, we became like those who are comforted."[26] And again in the 121st Psalm: "I was glad when they said to me, 'Let us go to the house of the Lord!' Our feet have been standing in your courts, O Jerusalem. Jerusalem is built as a city which is bound firmly together. The tribes, the tribes of the Lord, go up there, a testimony to Israel."[27]

5. The things of the Prophets are signified more or less in each Psalm. Concerning the coming of the Savior and that although God he should dwell among us, it speaks thus in the 49th Psalm: "The Lord will come openly, our God, and he will not keep silence."[28] D In the 117th: "Blessed is he who comes in the name of the Lord. We blessed you from the house of the Lord. The Lord is God, and he appeared to us."[29] That this one is the Word of the Father it sings in the 106th: "He sent his word, and he healed them. He delivered them from destruction."[30] For the very God who comes

22. Ps 28:1 (29:1).
23. Ps 106:36, 37 (107:36, 37).
24. Ps 106:19 (107:19).
25. Ps 19:8–10 (20:8, 9).
26. Ps 125:1 (126:1).
27. Ps 121:1–4 (122:1–4).
28. Ps 49:2, 3 (50:2, 3).
29. Ps 117:26, 27 (118:26, 27).
30. Ps 106:20 (107:20).

is also the Word who is sent. Knowing this Word to be the Son of God, the Psalter sings by the voice of the Father in the 44th Psalm: "My heart has given forth a good word."[31] 16A And again in the 109th: "Out of the womb, before the morning star, I begat you."[32] For who else would one say is the offspring of the Father than his Word and Wisdom? Knowing this one to be the one to whom the Father said, "Let there be light, firmament, and all things,"[33] this book contains this statement: "By the word of the Lord the heavens were established, and by the spirit of his mouth all their power."[34]

6. The Psalms were not ignorant that the one coming was the Christ [Anointed One] but speak especially concerning this one in the 44th Psalm: "Your throne, O God, is forever and ever. Your royal staff is a staff of equity. You loved righteousness and hated iniquity. Because of this, God, your God, anointed you with the oil of gladness above your fellows."[35] 16B And lest one think his coming was in appearance only, it marks him as a man who will come and as the very one through whom all things were made, saying in the 86th Psalm: "Mother Zion will say, 'Man, a man, was born in her, and the Most High himself established her.'"[36] And this is the equivalent of saying, "And the Word was God. All things were made by him. And the Word became flesh."[37] Because of this, and knowing the birth from a virgin, the book was not silent, but indeed gives a certain emphasis to it, saying in the 44th Psalm: "Hear, O daughter, and see, and incline your ear. Forget your people and the house of your father, because the king has desired your beauty."[38] This again is like what is said by Gabriel, "Hail, full of grace, the Lord is with you."[39] C For having called him Christ,[40] it immediately revealed the human generation from the virgin, saying, "Hear, daughter." Notice, Gabriel calls Mary by a title, being a stranger to her by race; but David, knowing that she will be of his own seed, addresses her as "daughter."

31. Ps 44:2 (45:1).
32. Ps 109:3 (110:3).
33. Gen 1:3ff.
34. Ps 32:6 (33:6).
35. Ps 44:7, 8 (45:6, 7).
36. Ps 86:5 (87:5).
37. John 1:2, 3, 14.
38. Ps 44:11, 12 (45:10, 11).
39. Luke 1:28.
40. From the verb anointed in 44:8 (45:7) above.

7. Knowing that he will become a man, the book consequently signifies also that he will suffer in the flesh. Seeing the treachery of the Jews, it sings in the 2nd Psalm: "Why did the nations rage, and the people imagine vain things? The kings of the earth were present, and the rulers were gathered together against the Lord and against his Christ."[41] In the 21st it tells of the kind of death, the Savior himself speaking: "You led me into the dust of death, because many dogs encircled me and a synagogue of evildoers surrounded me. They pierced my hands and my feet. They counted all my bones. They stared, and they despised me. D. They parted my garments among themselves, and for my clothing they cast lots."[42] By saying his hands and feet are pierced, what else is meant than a cross? It teaches all this, and it adds that the Lord suffered these things not for himself, but for us. And he speaks for himself again in the 87th: "Your wrath was confirmed against me."[43] In the 68th: "The things which I did not steal, I was repaying."[44] 17A For he died, not being under liability to do so. He suffered for us, and he took upon himself the wrath against us because of transgression, as is said by Isaiah: "He took our infirmities."[45] And when we say in the 137th Psalm, "The Lord will make recompense on my behalf,"[46] the Spirit also says in the 71st: "He will save the sons of the poor, and he will humble the accuser, because he delivered the poor man out of the hand of the powerful and the poor who had no helper."[47]

8. Because of this the Psalter predicts also his bodily ascension to heaven and says in the 23rd: "Lift up the gates, O rulers of yours, and be lifted up you eternal gates, and the king of glory will come in."[48] B And in the 46th:[49] "God went up with joy, the Lord with the voice of a trumpet."[50] It announces the session and says in the 109th: "The Lord said to my Lord, 'Sit on my right hand until I make your enemies the footstool of your feet.'"[51] In the 9th it calls out the coming destruction of the devil: "You who

---

41. Ps 2:1, 2.
42. Ps 21:16-19 (22:16-18).
43. Ps 87:8 (88:7).
44. Ps 68:5 (69:4).
45. Isa 53:4.
46. Ps 137:8 (138:7).
47. Ps 71:4, 12 (72:4, 12).
48. Ps 23:7 (24:7).
49. The Greek text has 40th, the word for sixth obviously having dropped out.
50. Ps 46:6 (47:5).
51. Ps 109:1 (110:1).

judge in righteousness sat upon the throne: you rebuked the nations, and the wicked one is destroyed"[52] And that he received all judgment from the Father it does not hide but predicts that he will come as the judge of all in the 71st: "O God, give to the king your judgment, and your righteousness to the son of the king, to judge your people in righteousness and your poor in justice."[53] 17C. And in the 49th it says: "He calls upon the heaven above and the earth that he judges his people. And the heavens shall declare his righteousness, because God is the judge."[54] And in the 81st: "God stood in the assembly of the gods; in the midst of the gods he holds judgment."[55] It is possible to learn even the calling of the nations from it in many places but especially from the 46th: "All you nations, clap your hands; rejoice in God with a voice of gladness."[56] In the 71st: "The Ethiopians will fall down before him, and his enemies will lick the dust. The kings of Tarshish and the islands will offer gifts. The kings of Arabia and Seba will bring gifts. All the kings of the earth will worship before him, and all the nations will serve him."[57] These things then are sung in the Psalms, while in each of the other books [of the Prophets] they are announced beforehand.

17D 9. The old man, not lacking in understanding, says again that in each book of scripture these things concerning the Savior are said in a special way. This announcement is in them all, and the agreement is from the Spirit. And even as one can find the contents of other books in the Psalms, so also the contents of this book are found many times in the others. For Moses writes an ode,[58] and Isaiah sings,[59] and Habakkuk prays with an ode.[60] And again in each book it is possible to see prophecy, legislation, and history. For the same Spirit is in every book. 20A Each book ministers and fulfils the grace given to it according to what is distinctive in each, whether it is prophecy, law, historical reminder, or the grace of the Psalms. Since it is one and the same Spirit from whom are all the distinctives, the scripture is indivisible in nature. Therefore, the whole is in each part, and the manifestations and distinctions of the Spirit occur according

52. Ps 9:5, 6 (9:4, 5).
53. Ps 71:1, 2 (72:1, 2).
54. Ps 49:4, 6 (50:4, 6).
55. Ps 81:1 (82:1).
56. Ps 46:2 (47:1).
57. Ps 71:9–11 (72:9–11).
58. Deut 31:30.
59. Isa 5:1.
60. Hab 3:1.

to his ministry in each part. As the Spirit wills, each part ministers the word according to the use which is reserved for each. The result is, as I said before, that the legislator Moses sometimes prophesies and sings. And the prophets who prophesy sometimes lay down laws: "Wash yourselves; be made clean. Cleanse your heart from evil, Jerusalem."[61] Sometimes the prophets write history, as Daniel about Susannah[62] and Isaiah about Rabshakeh and Sennacherib.[63] B The same is true of the book of Psalms, whose special quality is to sing odes. The things which are said in detailed narrative in the other books, this book sings with melody in a musical voice,[64] as I said above. Therefore, it sometimes legislates. "Refrain from anger and forsake wrath,"[65] and "Depart from evil and do good; seek peace and pursue it."[66] And it sometimes narrates history concerning the journey of Israel and prophesies concerning the Savior (as was said before).

10. Such grace of the Spirit, therefore, is common to all the books, and the grace which is present in each is found also in all, as need requires and the Spirit wills. For "more and less" makes no difference in this use, as each discharges and perfects its own ministry unceasingly. 20C Even so the book of Psalms has a grace of its own and a special manner of expression. In addition to those things in which it bears an affinity to other books, it has also this marvel proper to itself that within it are represented and portrayed in all their variations and corrections the emotions of the human soul. The result is that anyone who wishes, even though inexperienced, may learn from it so to express himself as is written therein. In the other books one hears only the law being laid down (the things he must do and must not do), or he hears only prophecy so that he knows only the coming Savior, or he gives attention to history from which he can know about the deeds of the kings and holy men. D In the book of Psalms the one who listens in order to learn these things also comprehends and is taught the emotions of his own soul. Finally, he is able also from this book to have the form of words for what he experiences and for what distresses him. The result is that it teaches the hearer not only to escape but how also by speaking and doing to heal the passion. For there are in the other books

---

61. Isa 1:16; Jer 4:14.

62. Daniel 12 (Greek).

63. Isaiah 36–37.

64. The terminology here offers the most difficult point in interpretation in the translation. See the note to the parallel statement in chapter 27.

65. Ps 36:8 (37:8).

66. Ps 33:15 (34:14).

Athanasius, Epistola Ad Marcellinum In Interpretationem Psalmorum

preventive words to dissuade from evil, but in this book it has also been expressed how one should abstain. 21 A Take for example the command to repent. To repent is to cease from sin. Here it has been expressed also how to repent and what one must say in repentance. Again, Paul has said, "Affliction produces endurance, and endurance produces character, and character produces hope, and hope does not disappoint."[67] In the Psalms it has been written and described how one is to hear afflictions, what to say while afflicted, what afterward, how each one is tested, and some words of those who trusted in the Lord. Again, there is the command "in everything" to give thanks,[68] but the Psalms teach what one is to say in giving thanks. Then, hearing from others, "Whoever would live godly will be persecuted,"[69] B we are taught by the Psalms how those who flee are to call upon God and how those who are persecuted and after the persecution are delivered are to offer up words to God. We are commanded to bless God and acknowledge him, but in the Psalms we find expressed how one should praise the Lord and how by saying certain words we should acknowledge him properly. And thus for each circumstance would one find the divine odes deposited for us and for our emotions and conditions.

11. Furthermore, there is another marvel in the Psalms. The readers[70] of those things which holy men say in the other books and of those things about which they might speak, are reporting the things written by another. And the hearers of these other books which the Word speaks consider 21C the proclaimed deeds until they marvel and desire them and come to imitate them. But he who receives the book of Psalms not only goes through in detail the usual prophecies concerning the Savior found in the other scriptures (marveling and worshipping), but he also reads the other Psalms as if his own words. And the hearer too, when the reader finishes, is also affected by the words of the odes as if they were his own. For the sake of clarity one must not hesitate, according to the blessed Apostle, to repeat the same thing.[71] Most of the words spoken by the patriarchs belong to them alone. Moses was speaking, and God answered. Elijah and Elisha seated on Mount Carmel called upon the Lord and were saying repeatedly, "As the Lord lives, in whose presence I stand today."[72] D The words of the

67. Rom 5:3–5.
68. 1 Thess 5:18.
69. 2 Tim 3:12.
70. Athanasius refers to oral reading.
71. Phil 3:1.
72. 1 Kgs 17:1; 2 Kgs 3:14.

other holy prophets primarily concern the Savior. In the next place most of their words concern the nations and Israel. Accordingly, no one would speak the words of the patriarchs as his own, nor would one dare to imitate and speak the words belonging to Moses, nor those of Abraham concerning his family, Ishmael, or the great Isaac. Even if the same need and necessity should seize someone, he would not dare to speak their words as his own. Even if one should suffer with those who suffer and take a desire for something better, he would never say as Moses, 24A. "Show me yourself,"[73] or again, "If you forgive them their sin, forgive; but if you do not forgive, wipe me out of your book which you wrote."[74] Neither would one take the words of the prophets as his own words to censure or praise the persons who do the same things which they censured or praised. Neither would one repeat, "As the Lord lives, in whose presence I stand today" as his own word. For indeed the reader from books is clearly not speaking the words as his own but as words of the holy men and those indicated by them. But the marvel with reference to the Psalms is this: beyond the prophecies concerning the Savior and the nations, the one saying the other things is speaking as his 24B own words, and each person sings them as if written concerning himself and he receives and relates them not as if another were speaking and not as if they signified another. He recites them as himself speaking. Whatever is spoken, he offers these things to God as he himself acting and speaking. For not as the words of the patriarchs, Moses, and the other prophets will these words be honored; but the one singing is bold to speak these words as especially written concerning himself and as his own. The Psalms include the deeds of both the one who keeps the commandment and the one who transgresses it. It is necessary for every one to be included in the Psalms, and either as keeping or as transgressing the commandment to speak the words written concerning the one or the other.

12. I think that these words become like a mirror to the singer for him to be able to understand in them the emotions of his own soul and thus perceiving them to explain them. C Moreover, he who hears the reader also receives the ode which is spoken as about himself. Either pricked and convicted by the conscience he will repent, or hearing about the hope toward God and the support which comes to believers he rejoices when this grace comes to him and he begins to give thanks to God. When, therefore, someone sees his own afflictions and sings the third Psalm, he thinks the

---

73. Exod 33:13.
74. Exod 32:32.
74a 1 Kgs 17:1. [AQ: placement?]

Athanasius, Epistola Ad Marcellinum In Interpretationem Psalmorum

words in the Psalm are his own. And then he recites the 11th and the 16th as his own confidence and prayer and the 50th Psalm as speaking his own repentance. When someone sings the 53rd, 55th, 56th, and the 141st, he is affected not as if another person D were being persecuted but as if he himself were suffering, and he sings to the Lord these words as properly his own. And thus all the psalms have been spoken and arranged by the Spirit so that the emotions of our soul may be understood in them according to what was written before time and so that all of them may have been written as about us and become our very own words, for a reminder of our emotions and a corrective of our conduct. What things the psalmists have said are able to be types and characteristics of ourselves.

13. This now is another grace of the Savior. Not only did he become man for us and offer his own body for death on our behalf in order that he might deliver all from death. 25A He also wished to show us his own heavenly and acceptable manner of conduct and expressed it in himself in order to prevent some from being easily deceived by the Enemy. This is possible because they now have a pledge of safety—the victory against the devil accomplished by him for us. For this reason he not only taught but also did the things which he taught in order that each person might hear him speaking, and seeing as in a picture, might receive from him the example of doing. "Learn from me that I am gentle and humble in heart."[75] No one would find a more perfect teaching in virtue than what the Lord expressed in himself. Whether forbearance, love of mankind, goodness, manliness, mercy, righteousness—one will find all these things in him so that nothing pertaining to virtue is lacking to the one who comprehends the Savior's human life. 25B Paul knew this and said, "Be imitators of me as I am of Christ."[76] For the lawgivers among the Greeks have attractiveness as long as they speak, but the Lord (as being truly Lord of all[77] and concerned about the things he made) not only gives the law but also has given himself as a type in order that those who desire the power to do may see it done. On account of this, therefore, before his visit to us he taught by word of mouth also in the psalmists in order that he might express and show in himself the earthly and the heavenly man. Even so also he who wants to do so is able to learn from the Psalms the emotions and dispositions of souls, finding in the Psalms also the healing and correction of each emotion.

---

75. Matt 11:29.
76. 1 Cor 11:1.
77. Acts 10:36; Rom 10:12.

C 14. If it is necessary to speak more persuasively, all the divine scripture is a teacher of virtue and true faith, but the book of Psalms has also the image somehow of the very course of the life of souls. Just as he who approaches a king is prescribed a certain form and certain words, lest saying the wrong things he be ejected as rude, even so the divine book through its reading first makes a reminder of the emotions of the soul to the one pursuing virtue, and wanting to understand the Savior's manner of life in the flesh and then finally typifies and teaches the readers by its words. In order that one may observe this carefully from the book, there are words spoken in narrative, D some in exhortation, some in prophecy, some in prayer, and others in confession.

Those in the form of narrative are 18, 43, 48, 49, 72, 76, 77, 88, 106, 113, 126, 136.

Those as a prayer: 16, 67, 89, 101, 131, 141.

Those as in petition, prayer, and request: 5, 6, 7, 11, 12, 15, 24, 27, 30, 34, 37, 42, 53, 54, 55, 56, 58, 59, 60, 63, 82, 85, 87, 137, 139, 142.

As in petition and thanksgiving: 138.

As petition only: 3, 25, 68, 69, 70, 73, 78, 79, 108, 122, 129, 130.

28A Those in confession: 9, 74, 91, 104, 105, 106, 107, 110, 117, 135, 137.

Those having a combination of confession and narrative: 9, 74, 105, 106, 117, 137.

One having a combination of confession and narrative with praise is 110.

One in exhortation is 36.

Those in prophecy: 20, 21, 44, 46, 75.

Announcement with prophecy: 109.

Exhortation and advice are: 28, 32, 80, 94, 95, 96, 97, 102, 103, 113.

An exhortation is spoken with a song in 149.

Those describing the virtuous life are 104, 111, 118, 124, 132.

28B Those declaring praise are these: 90, 112, 116, 134, 144, 145, 146, 148, 150.

The thanksgiving Psalms are 8, 9, 17, 33, 45, 62, 76, 84, 114, 115, 120, 121, 123, 125, 128, 143.

Athanasius, Epistola Ad Marcellinum In Interpretationem Psalmorum

Those preaching blessedness are 1, 31, 40, 118, 127.

Another exhibiting ready kindness with an ode is 107.

One exhorting to manliness is 80.

Those condemning the impious and lawless are 2, 13, 35, 51, 52.

An invocation is 4.

Those proclaiming vows, as 19 and 63.

Those announcing words of glory in the Lord are 22 and 26, 38, 39, 41, 61, 75, 83, 96, 98, 151.

28C Those of reproach are 57, 81.

Those speaking words of hymn are 47, 64.

One of joy and concerning the resurrection is 65.

And another speaks words of joy only: 99.

15. Such being the arrangement of the Psalms, it is possible for those who read them to find in each, as I said, the emotions and constitution of his own soul and so the type and teaching for each. And saying such words one is able to please the Lord and through these words he is able to correct himself and to give thanks to the Lord, because the one who says these words does not fall into impiety. D We must give account to the Judge not only for our works but also for an idle word.[78] If you wish to bless someone, you have how, why, and what you must say: the 1st, 31st, 40th, 111th, 118th, and 127th.[79] If you want to censure the treachery of the Jews against the Savior, you have the 2nd ode. If you are persecuted by your own or if you have many rising up against you, say the 3rd Psalm. If afflicted, call upon the Lord; and if when you are heard you want to give thanks, sing the 4th, 74th, and 114th. And if you see the wicked still trying to ensnare you and you want your prayer to be heard, arise early in the morning and sing the 5th. 29A If you feel the threat of the Lord, and because of this you see yourself fearful, you can say the 6th and 37th. And if some plot against you, as Ahithophel against David,[80] and someone tell this to you, sing the 7th and take courage in the God who delivers you.

16. If you see the grace of the Savior extended everywhere and the race of men saved and you want to salute the Lord, sing the 8th. Again, if you want to sing the vintage song and give thanks to the Lord, you have

---

78. Matt 12:36.
79. Each begins with *Makarioi.*
80. 2 Samuel 17.

again the 8th and 83rd. When the Enemy is conquered and a creature is saved, do not boast in yourself but knowing that the Son of God accomplished this, say that which is spoken to him in the 9th Psalm. B. If someone should wish to frighten you exceedingly, have confidence in the Lord and sing the 10th. Whenever you see the arrogance of many and evil multiplying so that there is nothing sacred to men, flee to the Lord and say the 11th. When the treachery of enemies continues for a long time, do not be discouraged as if you were forgotten by God, but implore the Lord singing the 12th. When you hear some blaspheming against Providence, do not share in their impiety, but supplicating God, say the 13th and 52nd. And finally, if you wish to learn what sort of person is the citizen of the kingdom of heaven, sing the 14th.

17. When you need prayer because of those opposing you and encompassing your soul, sing the 16th, 85th, 87th, and 140th. C. You want to learn how Moses prayed? You have the 89th. You were saved from your enemies, and you were delivered from those persecuting you, sing the 17th Psalm. You marvel at the order of the creation and the favor of Providence upon it and at the holy precepts of the law, sing the 18th and 23rd. When you see the afflicted, encourage them and pray for them with the words in the 19th Psalm. You see yourself shepherded and guided by the Lord, rejoice in this and sing the 22nd. Your enemies are around you; lift up your soul to God, say the 24th, and see them doing wrong in vain. Your enemies remain, their hands are full of blood, and they seek to drag you away and destroy you: do not give the D judgment to man (for all things human are suspect), but esteeming God to be the judge (for he alone is just) say the words in the 25th, 34th, and 42nd. If your enemies press yet harder after you and become a multitude like a company of soldiers, despising you as if you were not yet anointed and so wanting to fight you, do not be alarmed but sing the 26th Psalm. Since human nature is weak, if again the plotters treat you shamelessly so that you have no ease from them, cry to God using the words in the 27th. And if you wish to give thanks and to learn how to make an offering to the Lord, sing the 28th with spiritual understanding. And finally consecrating your house and your soul in which the Lord is welcomed, even your bodily house in which you dwell bodily, give thanks and say the 29th and the 126th of the Psalms of Ascents.

32A 18. Whenever you see yourself being hated and persecuted because of the truth by all your friends and relatives, do not be discouraged when you consider them and yourself. Nor, if you see the notables turning away from you, be alarmed, but stand aside from them, look to the

Athanasius, Epistola Ad Marcellinum In Interpretationem Psalmorum

things to come, and sing the 30th. When you see some being baptized and redeemed from the corruptible birth and marvel at God's love for man, sing for them the 31st. When you wish to sing with many, coming together with men righteous and upright in life, say the 32nd. Having fallen among enemies and wisely having fled from them and escaped from their snare, if you wish to give thanks, summon meek men and sing to them the 33rd. And if you see the zeal for evil B by transgressors, do not consider the evil in them to be according to nature, as the heretics say; but speak the 35th, and see that they themselves are the authors of their sinning. If you see evil men doing many lawless things and rising up against little people, and if you wish to advise some not to approach them lest they imitate them (on account of their influence not being extinguished quickly), say to yourself and others the 36th.

19. Then you also, proposing to give attention to yourself, if you see the enemy attacking (for then especially one is aroused against such persons) and you wish to encourage yourself against him, sing the 38th Psalm. And if, when the enemies are attacking, you endure afflictions and you want to learn the value of endurance, sing the 39th Psalm. C When you see many in need and poor and you want to show mercy to them, you are able to approve those who have already shown mercy and to persuade others to do the same by saying the 40th. Then if, having a very great desire for God, you hear enemies casting reproaches, do not be troubled. Rather understand the eternal fruit of such desire, comfort your own soul in the hope of God, and in this way lightening and easing the soul's sorrows in life, say the 41st Psalm. Wishing to remember continuously the benefactions of God to the fathers, both in the Exodus from Egypt and the journey in the wilderness, how God is good and men are ungrateful, you have the 43rd, 77th, 88th, 104th, 105th, 106th, and 113th. D Having fled to God and having been delivered from the afflictions about you, if you want to thank God and relate his philanthropy extended to you, you have the 45th.

20. You sinned, but you turned, repented, and ask to receive mercy, you have the words of confession and repentance in the 50th, If you were slandered before an evil king, and if you see the Devil boasting, retire and say the things in the 51st Psalm. When you are persecuted and some slander you, wishing to betray you as the Ziphites and foreigners did to David,[81] do not be discouraged but take heart in the Lord. Praise him and say the 53rd and 55th. 33A. If the pursuer come upon you and without

---

81. 1 Sam 23:19; 26:1; cf. Ps 53:2 (Ps 54 heading).

knowing it enters the cave where you are hiding,[82] do not crouch in fear, for you have words useful for comfort and memorial in such necessity in Psalms 56 and 141. If the persecutor command your house to be guarded and you flee, render thanks to the Lord and write it on your soul as on a pillar as a memorial of your not being destroyed and say the 58th Psalm. If the enemies who oppress you cast reproaches, and if those who seem to be friends prate against you and slander you, and you are grieved in your conversation for a short time, yet you can be comforted and hymn God by saying the words in the 54th. Against hypocrites and those boasting in appearance say to their reproach the 57th Psalm. B. Against those raging savagely against you and wanting to take your life, set up your obedience to God and take courage. As much as they rage, so much the more submit to the Lord and say the 61st. And if you are persecuted and go into the wilderness, do not fear as if you were alone there, but having God there rise up early and sing before him the 62nd. If enemies terrify and do not cease from lying in wait but seek out everything against you, and if they are a multitude, do not give way even a little. For their blows will be the toy weapons of children as you sing the 63rd, 64th, 69th, and 70th.

21. Whenever one wishes to hymn the Lord, sing the words in the 64th. C If you wish to instruct any concerning the resurrection, sing the words in the 65th. When asking mercies from God, hymn him and sing the 66th. When you see the ungodly thriving in peace while living according to their own whims and the righteous in afflictions, and that you will not be made to stumble nor to be unsettled, say the words in the 72nd Psalm. Whenever God is showing wrath toward the people, you have for consolation the wise words in the 73rd. When you have need of confession, sing the 9th, 74th, 91st, 104th, 105th, 106th, 107th, 110th, 117th, 135th, and 137th.[83] When you wish to convince the pagans and heretics that the knowledge of God is not found among them but only in the catholic church, you can sing with understanding and say the words in the 75th. D When enemies overpower those who flee and you are persecuted everywhere, even if you are terrified, do not lose hope but pray. And if, when you cry out, you are heard, give thanks to God and say the words in the 76th. But if the enemies persist and rush in, defile the house of God, kill the saints, and throw their bodies to the birds of heaven, to the end that you be not drawn down and cower at their cruelties, you are to suffer with those that suffer and entreat God with the 78th Psalm.

82. 1 Sam 24:3.
83. The same Psalms are listed in the classification in chapter 14.

Athanasius, Epistola Ad Marcellinum In Interpretationem Psalmorum

22. At the festival, when you want to sing to the Lord, call together the servants of God and sing the words in the 80th and 94th. When all the enemies are gathered together again from every side and threaten the house of God 36A and make pacts against the godly, so that you may not be disheartened on account of their multitude and power you have as an anchor of hope the words in the 82nd. And if seeing the house of God and its eternal habitations, you have a longing for these things, as the apostle had,[84] say also the 83rd Psalm. When wrath ceases and captivity is ended, if you want to give thanks, you may say the words in the 84th and 125th. If you want to know the difference between the catholic church and schisms and to overturn the latter, you are able to say the words written in the 86th. When you wish to encourage yourself and others to godliness and to show how hope in God does not disappoint but makes the soul fearless, praise God saying the words in the 90th. Do you want to sing on the Sabbath? You have the 91st.

B 23. Do you want to give thanks on the Lord's day? You have the 23rd.[85] Do you wish to sing on Monday? Say the words in the 47th. Does one want to praise on Friday? You have praise in the 92nd. For, when the crucifixion occurred, the house of God was built although the enemies made an attempt to hinder it. Therefore, it is fitting to sing as a song of victory the words spoken in the 92nd. If captivity comes and God's house is destroyed and then rebuilt, sing the words in the 95th. When the earth receives stability after wars and finally is at peace and the Lord rules, if you want to sing about this, you have the 96th. Do you want to sing on Wednesday? You have the 93rd. For then the Lord was betrayed and began to take vengeance against death and to triumph over it boldly. C When, therefore, you read the Gospel and see on Wednesday the Jews taking counsel against the Lord and you see him speaking boldly in vindication on your behalf against the Devil, sing the words in the 93rd itself. Again, seeing the providence of the Lord for all things and his lordship, and wishing to instruct some in faith and obedience toward him, persuading them first to confess, sing the 99th. And if learning his judicial power and that the Lord mixes judgment with mercy, you should want to approach him, you have for this the words in the 100th.

---

84. Cf. 2 Cor 4:18—5:2; Phil 1:23.

85. The "gates" of the Psalm could be understood as the gates of Hades and so make this a reference to the resurrection (cf. *Gospel of Nicodemus* 21), but chapter 8 applies Psalm 23 to the ascension, so Athanasius must be putting the ascension on a Sunday. See *Fathers according to R. Nathan* (pp. 11-12) for these psalms sung in the temple on these days.

24. Since our nature is weak, if on account of the distresses of life you become weary as one who is poor and if you want to be comforted, you have the 101st Psalm. 6--36 D Since it is fitting for us to give thanks to God always and in all things, when you want to bless him, you have as a means of urging on your own soul and for words to say the 102nd and 103rd. Do you want to praise God and to know how and for what one should praise and with what words it is fitting to speak praise? You have the 104th, 106th, 134th, 145th, 146th, 147th, 148th, 150th. Do you have faith, as the Lord said,[86] and do you believe in the prayers you say?[87] Say the 115th. But when you perceive yourself ascending in your deeds so as to say, "I forget the things which are behind, and I stretch forward to the things which are before me,"[88] you have at each attainment the fifteen Songs of Ascents[89] to say.

37A 25. You were taken captive by alien thoughts and felt yourself carried away, and you change your mind, cease from following through, and check yourself in your sinning while living among such things; sit and weep (as the people of Israel did then) and say the words in the 136th. Considering temptations to be your proving, after the temptations if you want to give thanks, you have the 138th Psalm. Are you encompassed again by enemies and you want to be delivered? Say the words in the 139th. Do you want to make supplication and pray? Sing the 5th and 142nd. An enemy tyrant rises up against the people and you, as Goliath against David,[90] do not be alarmed. Rather believe, as David did, and say the words in the 143rd. Then marveling at all the good works of God and remembering his goodness to you and to all, if you want to B bless God for these things, say the words of David which he said in the 144th Psalm. Do you want to sing to the Lord? You may say the 92nd and 97th. If in spite of being small you were preferred for some rulership before your brothers, do not exalt yourself against them, but give glory to the Lord who chose you and sing the 151st, which especially belongs to David. You want to sing Psalms resounding with hallelujah? You have 104, 105, 106, 111, 112, 113, 114, 115, 116, 117, 118, 134, 135, 145, 146, 147, 148, 149, and 150.

26. When you want to sing privately the things concerning the Savior, you find such things in more or less every Psalm. You have especially

---

86. Mark 4:43, changed from the plural to the singular.
87. 2 Cor 4:13 (Ps 116:10, Eng.).
88. Phil 3:13.
89. Psalms 119–33.
90. 1 Sam 17.

Athanasius, Epistola Ad Marcellinum In Interpretationem Psalmorum

the 44th and 109th to make clear his true generation from the Father and his incarnate appearance.[91] 37C The 21st and 68th predict his divine cross and that he submitted to such a plot on our behalf and how much he suffered. The 2nd and 108th signify the evil plot of the Jews and the betrayal of Judas Iscariot. The 20th, 49th, and 71st declare his kingship and judicial power and on the other hand his coming in the flesh for us and the calling of the Gentiles. The 15th shows his resurrection from the dead. The 23rd and 46th announce his ascension to heaven. Reading the 92nd, 95th, 97th, and 98th you are able to contemplate the Savior's benefits accomplished for us by his sufferings.

27. Such therefore is the character of the book of Psalms, and its profit D for men, that it has Psalms proper and also repeated prophecies (as I said before) concerning the appearance in the body of our Lord and Savior Jesus Christ. It is necessary now to include the reason why such words are sung with melody and song. For some of the unlearned among us, although believing the words to be inspired by God, nevertheless think that the Psalms are sung on account of the euphony and for pleasure to the ear. But it is not so, for the Scripture does not seek the sweet and beguiling, but even these qualities were appointed for the benefit of the soul in all things. Melody has these two purposes. First, it was fitting that the divine Scripture hymn God vocally not only in prose but also in poetry.[92] 40A Therefore it has spoken in prose such words as those of the law, the prophets, the things told as history, and the New Testament; but in poetry it has said such words as those of the psalms, odes, and songs. In this way it will be ensured that men love God with their whole strength and power. Second, even as harmony puts together the pipes and accomplishes one symphony, so the Word desires man in himself not to be inharmonious and divided in himself, although there appear in the soul different movements and it is possible by it to reason, to desire, and to be spirited[93] and the activity of the members of the body comes from these movements. Disharmony happens when a person thinks the best things but practices

---

91. For this paragraph compare chapters 5–8.

92. The phrase is literally "according to length . . . according to breadth." See the parallel in chapter 9, where the contrast may be between the details of a continuous narrative and the more general expression of song or just a contrast between melody and its absence. Breadth may refer to the drawing out of the sound in a chant. In some way ordinary prose is seen as providing "length," whereas poetry or song provides "depth."

93. This threefold division of the soul derives from Plato, *Republic* 439d; 588h; *Phaedrus* 246b but became commonplace.

evil things by his inclinations, as Pilate said, "I find nothing worthy of death in him,"[94] but 40B concurred in the judgment of the Jews; or one desires evil but is not able to practice it, as the elders against Susannah; or again not to commit adultery but to steal, or not to steal but to kill, or not to kill but to blaspheme.

28. In order, therefore, that no one among us may be troubled in such a way, the Word wishes the soul to have "the mind of Christ"[95] (as the apostle says) and to use this guide and by it to control the passions and to rule the members of the body so as to obey the Word. The purpose is that, like a plectron in making harmony, man himself (becoming a psalterion) should devote himself C entirely to the spirit and obey and serve the will of God with all his members and emotions. The harmonious oral reading of the Psalms is an image and type of such a tranquil and calm constitution of the mind. For as we make known and signify the thoughts of the soul through the words which we utter, so the Lord wishing the melody of the words to be a symbol of the spiritual harmony in the soul has decreed the odes to be sung harmoniously and the psalms to be recited as an ode. And this is the soul's desire, to dispose itself well, as it is written, "Is any among you happy? Let him sing."[96] Even so, what is confused, rough, and disordered in the soul is smoothed out; what causes pain is healed, when we sing "Why are you cast down, O my soul, and why are you disquieted within me?"[97] D What is in error will be discovered, saying, "My feet almost stumbled."[98] What is fearful will flow into hope when we say, "The Lord is my help; I will not fear what man will do to me."[99]

29. Those who do not recite the divine odes in this manner, that is those who do not sing with the understanding but give pleasure to themselves, are blameworthy, because "Praise is not fitting in the mouth of the sinner."[100] Those who do sing according to the aforementioned manner so that the melody of the words is offered from the rhythm of the soul and from harmony 41A with the spirit sing with the tongue and with the mind, and profit greatly not only themselves but also those who want to hear them. The blessed David, therefore, as he made music to Saul pleased God

---

94. John 18:38; Luke 23:22.
95. Phil 2:5.
96. James 5:13.
97. Ps 41:6, 12; 42:5 (42:5, 11; 43:5).
98. Ps 72:2 (73:2).
99. Ps 117:6 (118:6).
100. Sirach 15:9.

Athanasius, Epistola Ad Marcellinum In Interpretationem Psalmorum

and drove away the disturbed and depressed condition of Saul and secured calmness for his soul.[101] Even so when the priests sang, they summoned the souls of the people to tranquility and to the harmony of the chorus in heaven. The saying of the Psalms with melody is not, therefore, a zeal for euphony but a sign of the harmony of the reasonings in the soul. The harmonious recitation is a symbol of the ordered and calm constitution of the mind. 41B For to praise God with euphonious cymbals, kithara, and ten-stringed psalterion[102] was again a symbol signifying the members of the body to be compounded in an orderly manner like chords and the reasonings of the soul to be like cymbals. Finally, by the sound and command of the spirit all these things move and live. The result is that, according to what is written, "Man lives by the spirit, and puts to death the deeds of the body."[103] So also singing well trains the soul and leads it out of disturbance to equanimity, so that the soul by being naturally constituted may not be disturbed by anything but rather may be imagining good things and even more may receive a desire for the good things to come. For the soul sympathetically affected by the chanting of the words forgets the passions, and joyfully looks C to the mind of Christ, thinking on the best things.

30. It is necessary, therefore, my son, for each of those who read this book to read all of the things in it as truly inspired of God and to take from them as from the fruit of paradise some profit in that for which he sees himself in need, For I consider that in the words of this book is included and encompassed all the life of men, both the dispositions of the soul and the movements of the reasonings, and nothing more of these things is to be found among men. For whether there is need of repentance and confession, or affliction and temptation overtake one, or he is persecuted, or being plotted against he is delivered, or if one becomes deeply grieved and is troubled and suffers such as was said above, or sees himself making progress and the enemy defeated and wants to praise, thank, and bless the Lord—he has instruction for all these things in the divine Psalms. Let the words spoken in the Psalms concerning each of these things be selected, and thus saying what is written as though it concerned himself and being affected by the things written, he offers them to the Lord.

31. Let no one embellish these things with appealing words from outside Scripture nor attempt to alter or wholly change the phrases. Let him say and sing artlessly the things written just as they were said, so that

101. 1 Sam 16:23.
102. Ps 150:3–5.
103. Rom 8:13 paraphrased.

the men who 44A ministered these words might recognize them as their own and join with us in prayer. Or rather, let him use these words in order that the Spirit who spoke in the holy men, perceiving the words which he inspired to resound in them, might come to our assistance. For in so far as the life of holy men is better than others, so far also their words are better and stronger than those composed by us, even if spoken rightly. For in these words they were pleasing to God, and by saying these things, as the apostle said: "They conquered kingdoms, enforced justice, received promises, stopped the mouths of lions, quenched raging fire, escaped the edge of the sword, won strength from weakness, became mighty in war, put foreign armies to flight, women received their dead by resurrection."[104]

B 32. Therefore, now, let each one say these words and be of good courage, because through them God will quickly answer those who pray. For if one says these words while distressed, he will see a great consolation in them. If while tested and persecuted he sings thus, he will appear more acceptable and will be sheltered by the Lord who protected the one who first spoke these words. By them he will overturn the Devil and drive away his demons. If he sins and he speaks these words, he will turn himself around and cease. If he did not sin, he will see himself rejoicing, because he will stretch forward to the things ahead[105] and by his struggling he will become strong and so will sing. C He will not be moved from the truth forever, but he will reprove the deceivers and those attempting to mislead. The guarantor of this is not man, but divine Scripture itself. For God commanded Moses to write the great Ode and to teach the people.[106] He orders the person who is appointed a ruler to copy Deuteronomy and to have this book in hand and always to meditate on its words,[107] since these words are a sufficient reminder of virtue and convey help to those meditating sincerely on them. The son of Nave at the time of the entrance into Canaan was without a care when he saw the formations of the enemies and the kings of the Amorites gathering for war. He read Deuteronomy in the hearing of all, reminded the people of the words of the law, and equipped them with these words instead of armor and swords.[108] And he prevailed over the adversaries. D King Josiah, when the book was found

---

104. Heb 11:33–35.
105. Phil 3:13.
106. Deut 31:19.
107. Deut 17:18.
108. Josh 8:34, 35.

Athanasius, Epistola Ad Marcellinum In Interpretationem Psalmorum

and was read in the hearing of all, no more feared his enemies.[109] And if there was war for the people of Israel, the ark containing the tablets of law went before all[110] and was sufficient to help them more than any battle line, provided no sin or hypocrisy had previously seized its bearers or someone among the people.[111] For there is need of faith and sincere motives in order for the law to cooperate in the things prayed for.

45A 33. "I, therefore," the old man used to say, "heard also from wise men how in ancient times in Israel the readers of the Scriptures by themselves put to flight demons and by their reading confused the schemes plotted by them against men." Whence he also said that they are worthy of all censure who omit these words and frame for themselves persuasive words from the outside and call themselves exorcists. Rather they are playing and allow themselves to be scorned by the demons, as the Jews (sons of Sceva) experienced when they undertook to exorcize in this manner.[112] For the demons, when they hear from such men these words, play with them. But they fear the words of the saints, or they are not even able to endure them. For the Lord is in the words of the Scriptures. The demons were not able to endure him and cried, "I beseech you, do not torment me before the time."[113] For they were burning when they only B saw the Lord's presence. Even so Paul also commanded the unclean spirits,[114] and so also the demons were subject to the disciples.[115] And the hand of the Lord came upon the prophet Elisha, and he prophesied at the place of the waters to the three kings, when the one singing[116] sang at his command. So also now if anyone is distressed for those in suffering let him speak these words. He will profit the sufferer and he will exhibit his own true and firm faith. When God sees this, he prepares for those who pray the perfect therapy. Knowing this, the holy one said in the 118th Psalm, "I will meditate on your judgments, I will not forget your words."[117] And again,

---

109. 2 Kgs 22:8–11.
110. Josh 3:3, 14.
111. Joshua 7; 1 Sam 4:1–11.
112. Acts 19:14–16.
113. Luke 8:28 and Matt 8:29.
114. Acts 16:18.
115. Luke 10:17.
116. 2 Kgs 3:15. The more ambiguous "make melody" might be a better translation here: the Old Testament context is clearly "play," but Athansaius understands the music as vocal.
117. Ps 118:16 (119:16).

"Your judgments were songs to me in the place of my sojourning."[118] 45C For in these they gain salvation, saying, "Unless your law is my meditation, I would perish in my humiliation."[119] Whence also Paul fortifies his disciple, saying, "Meditate on these things, stand in them, in order that your progress may he manifest."[120]

And you, meditating on these words and reading the Psalms thus with understanding, "being led by the Spirit,"[121] will be able to understand the meaning in each. Emulate such a life as the holy men inspired of God had who spoke these words.

---

118. Ps 118:54 (119:54).
119. Ps 118:92 (119:92).
120. 1 Tim 4:15.
121. Rom 8:14 or Gal 5:18, neither quoted exactly.

12

Words from the Ψαλ- Root in Gregory of Nyssa

GREGORY OF NYSSA GIVES the following definition and discussion of ψαλμός:

> There is a distinction between psalm, ode, praise, hymn and prayer. A psalm is the melody made by a musical instrument. An ode is a melodious expression made by the mouth with words. A prayer is a supplication brought to God with reference to something of concern. A hymn is the honor rendered to God for the good things which are ours. Praise includes a panegyric for the divine accomplishments, for a panegyric is nothing but an increase of praise. Many tines these terms are joined with one another in some combination in the titles [of the Psalms] so that one becomes two through the combination: either psalm of an ode or ode of a psalm or psalm with hymns or (as we have learned in Habakkuk) a prayer with an ode. The deeper meaning which by these titles leads us to virtue is as follows. The psaltery is a musical instrument which makes its sound from the upper parts of its construction, and the music from this instrument is called "psalm." Therefore, the Word that exhorts to virtue provides a significance from the very shape of the instrument's construction, for it admonishes you that your life be a psalm, not characterized by earthly sounds. (I say "sounds" meaning "thoughts.") Rather it has the pure and audible sound produced from the upper and heavenly parts. When we read "ode," we understand through a figure the respectable life with reference

to outward things. Even as from musical instruments the sound alone of the melody falls on the ears and no words that belong to the melody are articulated by voices, but in an ode both together occur—both the rhythm of the melody and the meaning of the words which comes through with the melody, a meaning which cannot be understood when the melody occurs by the musical instruments alone; so it happens to those who give up virtue. For those devoting their mind to the contemplative and mystical philosophy of being accomplish virtue in many things invisibly and shut up virtue in their own conscience. But those who at the same time diligently perform the ethical life display publicly the gracefulness of their life in the respectability of outward action exactly like some word. Whenever the good is accomplished by both, when practical philosophy accompanies contemplative philosophy, there is the ode of a psalm or the psalm of an ode. Whenever one of these terms stands alone before the panegyrics, either the good according to the mind alone is signified by the word "psalm" or the activity and respectability in outward things is the interpretation of the word "ode."

. . .

The psalm with hymns leads us to a higher condition, which the divine apostle also knew, as he says to the Corinthians that he makes melody (ψάλλω) now with the spirit and now with the mind. Therefore, the psalmody mixed with the mind interprets the previously explained word. It is necessary for the outward appearance to be worthy of what is hidden, in order that the ode might agree with the thought. The psalmody which is accomplished by the spirit alone indicates the superlative condition of the saints, since that which leads to God is better than the indications of outward appearances. For he does not say the psalm with certain odes, which distinguish through words the meaning of the thoughts, but he says the psalm with hymns. This is, according to my judgment, a teaching of what it is necessary to know by a hymn. For we learn that the higher life and the thinking on things above and having our instrument from the heavenly and superior thoughts is the hymn of God, not in the power of words but accomplished in the superlative life. Whenever the Word writes the voice of understanding with the hymns, it seems to me to speak symbolically that we should not employ words of praise to God senselessly.[1]

---

1. *In Inscriptiones Psalmorum* 2,3 (GNO V 74,23—76,13; 77,6-26 (PG 44,493B-497B). I published a preliminary study of the same material, based on a less nearly

Gregory in this passage presents the definition of ψαλμός in classical Greek: "the sound of the cithara or harp."[2] The passage continues to be cited for the meaning, even the Christian meaning, of the word.[3] Actually, however, this is an isolated usage by Gregory, not representative of his usual meaning. As with other patristic authors, Gregory employs the classical meaning as the basis of an allegorical interpretation.[4] Otherwise, Christians, as Jews before them, used ψαλμός to refer to the biblical book of Psalms.

Outside the quoted passage, a form of ψαλμός occurs in the same treatise, *In inscriptiones Psalmorum*, sixty-five times, all with the Judaeo-Christian meaning.[5] Classification of meanings is often somewhat arbitrary, but (1) I count twelve references to the book of Psalms. The phrase "book of Psalms" occurs three times.[6] Gregory refers also to the division of the Psalms into five books.[7] (2) I have assigned fourteen occurrences to the category of individual Psalms as part of the collection but without specific identification. This includes such phrases as "order of the Psalms,"[8] "a few of the untitled Psalms,"[9] "such Psalms"[10] and "each Psalm."[11] (3) Most frequently, as the nature of the work required, the reference is to a specific Psalm: eighteen times. The reference could be indefinite, "David spoke

---

complete listing of Gregory's references, under the title "Gregory of Nyssa and Psalmos." The whole treatise is now translated by Heine, *Gregory of Nyssa's Treatise on the Inscriptions of the Psalms*.

2. Liddel, Scott, Jones, *Greek-Engish Lexicon*, 2018. Other patristic texts giving a similar definition include (Ps.) Hippolytus, *In Pss*. 5 (PG 10,717B–C); Eusebius, *Ps*. pr (PG 23.72D); Basil of Caesarea, *Hom. in Ps*. 29.1 (PG 29,305B–C).

3. Trench, *Synonyms of the New Testament*, 296; Lampe, *Patristic Greek Lexicon*, 1539.

4. See my "Active and Contemplative Lives: The Patristic Interpretation of Some Musical Terms," chapter 9 above. Gregory's philosophy of music is discussed by H. I. Marrou, "Un théolegie de la musique chez Grégoire de Nysse?"

5. I gratefully acknowledge the assistance of Daniel Ridings at the Institute of Classical Studies, Göteborg University, Sweden, and Dr. Friedhelm Mann and Klaus Wachtel of the Forschungsstelle Gregor von Nyssa an der Westfälischen Wilhelms-Universität, Münster, for providing indexes of the ψαλ- words in Gregory of Nyssa. See now Fabricius and Ridings, *A Concordance to Gregory of Nyssa*.

6. *Inscr Ps* 1 pr (GNO V 24,7); 2,7 (91.1); 2,10 (114,5).

7. Ibid., 1 pr (25,5f.); 1,9 (65,5).

8. Ibid., 1 pr (25,3); 2,8 (93,24) 2,11 (117,2); 2,14 (151,15); etc.

9. Ibid., 2,8 (94,1).

10. Ibid., 93,15.

11. Ibid., 2,10 (110,6).

in one of the Psalms"[12] or "in another Psalm,"[13] but often the reference is definite: "the fourth Psalm,"[14] the ninth Psalm,"[15] "the one hundred third Psalm,"[16] and elsewhere. Other definite expressions are "the last Psalm,"[17] "the following Psalm,"[18] "the Psalm before us,"[19] and the like. Sometimes the Psalm is characterized, as "Psalm of ecstasy"[20] or "the Psalm 'for confession.'"[21] (4) Nine additional times Gregory refers to the word Psalm in a title[22] or to the title of a given Psalm: "the titles of the Psalms,"[23] "the title in some of the Psalms,"[24] "title of this Psalm."[25] (5) Overlapping some of the other categories, but in order to underscore the normal usage by Gregory, I have noted three instances where Gregory speaks of the Psalms as written: "written in these Psalms,"[26] "David wrote this Psalm."[27] (6) In keeping with the interpretive purpose of the treatise, Gregory five times refers to the "deeper meaning" (διάνοια) of the Psalm[28] or "the mystery in this Psalm"[29] or "this great philosophy in the Psalms."[30] (7) Finally, returning to the passage at the beginning, there are other places where Gregory, uses ψαλμός in connection with ode or hymn but seemingly with the text of the Psalms in mind.[31]

---

12. Ibid., 1,3 (32,7) = *Ps* 148,1ff. I follow Gregory's numbering of the Psalms, which is that of the Septuagint.
13. Ibid., 1,8 (62,18) = *Ps* 17,5.
14. Ibid., 1,4 (35,2).
15. Ibid., 2,10 (114,6).
16. Ibid., 2,9 (107,19).
17. Ibid., 1,9 (65,23).
18. Ibid., 2,16 (174,6); cf. "the next Psalm": 2,9 (104,6).
19. Ibid., 2,13 (136,15).
20. Ibid., 2,6 (88,16) = *Ps* 30.
21. Ibid., 2,7 (89,9).
22. Ibid., 2,6 (88,18).
23. Ibid., 1 pr (24,3); 2,1 (69,15).
24. Ibid., 2,1 (71,3); cf. 2,7 (90,1) "in many of the Psalms."
25. Ibid., 2,9 (103,6); cf. 2,13 (138,12).
26. Ibid., 2,11 (117,15).
27. Ibid., 2,9 (107,23); cf. 2,6 (88,1) quoted from the title, "Psalm by David."
28. Ibid., 1,9 (68,8); 2,8 (93,6); 2,9 (107,27).
29. Ibid., 2,8 (95,14).
30. Ibid., 1,9 (67,11).
31. Ibid., 2,1 (69,20; 70,4f.); 2,6 (88,2).

The same usage of ψαλμός for the biblical Psalms characterizes Gregory's other writings. Thus, he refers to the "book of Psalms"[32] or "books of the Psalms";[33] cites a particular Psalm;[34] declares that David wrote that Psalm";[35] and refers to "the word resounding in our hearing all night long with Psalms, hymns, and spiritual songs."[36] This is not an exhaustive cataloging of the references, but there are no exceptions outside the passage quoted at the beginning to the usage for the biblical Psalms.

To summarize, except where Gregory makes an allegorical point from the etymology of ψαλμός he always follows the biblical meaning of the word. It is, therefore, very precarious to cite *In Inscriptiones Psalmorum* 2,3 for lexical purposes; indeed it can be misleading to do so, for the definition given there does not correspond to Gregory's normal vocabulary, and the same applies for all of early Christian usage.

If we expand the examination to other words from the ψαλ- root, we find the same pattern. In fact, the most common word in the family in Gregory's usage is ψαλμῳδία—136 times in the works attributed to Gregory. Ψαλμῳδία in classical Greek meant "singing to the harp";[37] in Christian usage "singing" or "composing Psalms."[38] Gregory, however, used ψαλμῳδία for the Psalms themselves. The equivalence of ψαλμός and ψαλμῳδία for Gregory is shown by a passage where they are interchangeable in the same context: "The mysteries of the ψαλμῳδία . . . Understanding these in the titles of the ψαλμοί read aloud to us."[39] The same meanings of ψαλμός noted above are found for ψαλμῳδία and in the same phrases. (1) About one-third of the occurrences of ψαλμῳδία refer to the book of Psalms: e.g., "the Psalmody cries from beginning to end,"[40] "the book of Psalmody,"[41] "the third part of the Psalmody,"[42] "the words of the Psalmody."[43] Especially noteworthy is the summary of the books

---

32. *Ascens* (GNO IX 323,20).
33. *Melet* (GNO IX 453,2).
34. *Ps 6* (GNO V 187,11; 190,4; 192,26).
35. *S pas* (GNO IX 265,16).
36. *Sal* (GNO IX 309,12).
37. Liddel, Scott, Jones, *Greek-Engish Lexicon*, 2018.
38. Lampe, *Patristic Greek Lexicon*, 1540.
39. *Mart* 1 (PG 46,749B-C).
40. *Inscr Ps* 1,4 (GNO V 37,23).
41. Ibid., 2,10 (110,1).
42. Ibid., 2,14 (148,16); 2,15 (161,12); *CE* III,V 14 (GNO II 165,3).
43. *Inscr Ps* 1,6 (40,24).

of the Bible: "In every church Moses and the Law are read, the Prophets, the Psalmody, all the History, and if there is anything of the Old or New Covenant, all things are proclaimed to the churches."[44] (3)[45] About another one-third of the occurrences of ψαλμῳδία refer to a specific Psalm: "He says at the end of the ψαλμῳδία (Psalm)" followed by a quotation of *Psalms* 83,13;[46] "In this Psalmody," *Psalms* 94,1;[47] "In the forty-fourth Psalmody";[48] "That which was spoken in the word of Psalmody";[49] "The Psalmody preaches the mystery of the new covenant in the introduction, saying" (Ps 95), then "After the evangelical voices which have been composed in the introduction of the Psalmody."[50] In fact there are numerous references to "this Psalmody,"[51] "the following Psalmody,"[52] or to the "beginning,"[53] "middle," or "end"[54] of a Psalmody. (2) Indefinite references to individual Psalms are few, but there are comparable phrases to those used with ψαλμός: "the order of the Psalmody"[55] and "according to the sequence of the Psalmody."[56] (4) Use of ψαλμῳδία is rare in reference to the titles of the Psalms, but does occur: "The title of the Psalmody includes such mysteries";[57] "The title ascribes the Psalmody to David"[58] (5) As in the last reference, several statements ascribe the Psalmody to David: "Uttering the . . . hymn, which often we hear from the Psalmody of David, who says";[59] "I heard often from David in the holy Psalmody."[60] A favorite characterization is "Great David."[61] This characterization, at least, is au-

---

44. *Eccl* 1 (GNO V 279,6).
45. I deliberately follow the numbering of the classification used for ψαλμός.
46. *Hom opif* 22 (PG 44,208 D).
47. *Spir* (PG 47,700 A).
48. *CE* III,IX 15 (GNO II 269,4).
49. *Ps* 33,8: *Cant* (GNO VI 237,5).
50. *Inscr Ps* 2,9 (GNO V 103,4 and 7; cf. 104,18).
51. Ibid., 2,13 (136,13).
52. Ibid., 2,11 (120,10).
53. Ibid., 116,27.
54. Ibid., 2,13 (125,21).
55. Ibid., 2,11 (115,12).
56. Ibid., 2,10 (108,10); 2,14 (150,15) and 2,15 (163,6).
57. Ibid., 2,14 (148,10; cf. 20).
58. Ibid., 2,9 (104,9).
59. *Ps* 123,6: *v Gr. Thaum.* (PG 46,949 B).
60. *Pulch.* (GNO IX 467,13).
61. *CE* I 338 (GNO I127,13–14); *Eccl* 5 (GNO V 354,3); *or dom* 2 (PG 44,1140B).

thentic in *Oratio in diem natalem Christi*: "Let as also ourselves say the word of the Psalmody, joining the chorus with the great voiced David."[62] Similarly, several statements speak of the ψαλμῳδία as written: "Divine scripture of Psalmody";[63] "Written word of Psalmody";[64] "Let him read the inspired words of the Psalmody."[65] (6) Even as he did with the word ψαλμός, Gregory speaks of the "deeper meaning" (διάνοια) of ψαλμῳδία, also of the "philosophy witnessed to by Psalmody"[66] and "the θεωρία of the thoughts" of Psalmody.[67] (7) The compound ψαλμῳδία left no need for contrast with ode or hymn. Gregory had no reservations about using the word ψαλμός, but perhaps his preference for ψαλμῳδία reflects his awareness of the classical meaning of ψαλμός and its different meaning in the Bible. One may compare Philo[68] and Josephus,[69] who preferred the term "hymns" in speaking of the biblical Psalms. Gregory himself likewise once identified the Psalms as hymnody.[70] Gregory too preferred a word which, although keeping the same ψαλ- root, brought out the vocal element in the Psalms.

In non-exegetical works where reference is made to actual Psalm-singing, Gregory reflects the more common Christian use of ψαλμῳδία to refer to the singing of the Psalms. In view of the classical meaning of ψαλμός and ψαλμῳδία, it is to be noted that there is no indication of instrumental accompaniment of this Psalm-singing. Although Gregory uses ψαλμῳδία in his usual sense of the Psalter in his *Vita Macrina*,[71] this work provides a cluster of statements where the meaning is "sing Psalms":[72] "Changing the wailing of our lamentation into a common

---

62. *Ps* 117,25: *nat.* (PG 46,1128B).
63. *Inscr. Ps.* 1,1 (GNO V 26,14f.).
64. Ibid., 2,7 (GNO V 90,27).
65. Ibid., 2,14 (GNO V 144,10).
66. *Inscr. Ps.* 1,9 (GNO V 67,22).
67. Ibid., 1,4 (35,1).
68. Philo, *mig. Abr.* 157 (II 299,12 Wendland); *v. cont.* 25 (VI 52,25 Cohn).
69. Josephus, *Ap.* 1.40 (CSEL 37,11,16).
70. *Steph.* 2 (PG 46,729 A).
71. GNO VIII/I 373,23; 374,4.
72. McKinnon, *Music in Early Christian Literature*, in his generally excellent collection of sources includes from Gregory of Nyssa only two passages from the *Life of Macrina* (pp. 73-74). As this paper shows, Gregory of Nyssa offers considerably more information about early Christian musical terminology.

singing of Psalms";[73] "the Psalm-singing of the virgins";[74] "broke in on the Psalm-singing with cries of grief";[75] "I arranged for the Psalm-singing to come rhythmically and harmoniously from the group, blended well as in choral singing with the common responses of all";[76] "The Psalm-singing continuing from beginning to end harmoniously";[77] "When there was a lull in the Psalm-singing";[78] "Confusion drowned out the orderly and sacred Psalm-singing."[79] This meaning appears elsewhere: "His dwelling resounded night and day with Psalm-singing."[80] This occasional usage makes possible the meaning "sing the Psalms" in the passage quoted at the beginning and later in the treatise[81] and probable in the doubtful work *De occursu Domini*, "so that we heard the sound (or voices) of Psalmody."[82]

Even as ψαλμῳδία was commonly the "Psalter," in whole or any of its parts, so ψαλμῳδός was the "Psalmist," the writer or singer of the Psalms, and ψαλμῳδέω was "to sing the Psalms." Ψαλμῳδός was a common way—twenty-one times—for Gregory to refer to the author of the Psalms: "The Psalmist exhorts";[83] "The Psalmist says . . .";[84] "According to what was set down by the Psalmist";[85] "The Psalmist also calls by name."[86] Ψαλμῳδέω is rare: "She [Macrina] was not ignorant of the writing of the one who sang the Psalms."[87]

Ψαλμικός (five times) and ψαλμικῶς (once) follow the pattern evident in other words in the family: "Psalm-like," "in the manner of the Psalms," or even "the Psalmic passage." Gregory shows great flexibility in the use of the adjective: "According to Psalmic voice" (the voice of the

---

73. *V. Macr* (GNO VIII/I 401,17).
74. Ibid., 406,22.
75. Ibid., 407,4.
76. Ibid., 407,12.
77. Ibid., 408,10.
78. Ibid., 408,20.
79. Ibid., 409,4.
80. *Ep.* 19 (GNO VIII/II 65,2).
81. *Inscr Ps* 2,7 (GNO V 90,8).
82. PG 46,1156 B.
83. Ps 56: *Inscr Ps* 2,14 (GNO V 154,26).
84. Ps 106,17: *Eccl* 2 (GNO V 300,17); cf. *hex* (PG 44,73 C; and frequently).
85. *V. Mos* II 191 (GNO VII/I 373,22).
86. *Mart* 2 (PG 46,781 B).
87. *V Macr* (GNO VIII/I 373,22).

Psalm—Ps 1,3);[88] "The Word shows the way through all the Psalmic guidance" (guidance of the Psalms);[89] "In the fourth step of the Psalmic ascent" (ascent of the Psalms);[90] "Paraphrasing the Psalmic reading [the words of the Psalm], I set down words."[91] Notable is the use of the adjective as a noun: "The book of Psalms [τὸ ψαλμικόν, the Psalmic word] spoke of his habits."[92] The adverb is used in the statement "The word [of the Synod] is as far from the word [of Apollinaris], to speak Psalmically [in the manner or in the language of the Psalms], as the east is from the west."[93]

Largely irrelevant for this inquiry is Gregory's effort to find a meaning for the word διάψαλμα, which the Septuagint had used to render the Hebrew *selah* in the Psalms. The discussion of this word occurs in *In inscriptiones Psalmorum* 2,10. Since "the interval [between the parts of the Psalm] was named by the interpreters διάψαλμα,"[94] Gregory suggests "one might define the διάψαλμα as the teaching from the Spirit in the soul which occurs without being expressed."[95] The interpretation proposed by Gregory follows from his understanding of ψαλμός as the words of the Psalms.

Gregory mentions the stringed instrument named ψαλτήριον mainly in Old Testament quotations or allusions without significance given to it.[96] The kind of allegorical interpretation of the ψαλτήριον reflected in the opening quotation and characteristic of patristic exegesis,[97] whereby musical instruments are understood figuratively as the human body, is found again in Gregory's comments on Psalms 150:

> He says, "Praise the Lord" with the sound of the trumpet when human nature represents complete harmony in the variety and diversity of virtues and becomes an instrument in melodious rhythm to God. The Word in a figurative way of speaking names this instrument a psaltery and cithara. After this the human nature puts away all that is earthly, dumb, and inarticulate by

88. *Diem lum* (GNO IX 237,10).
89. *Inscr Ps* 1,2 (GNO V 27,3).
90. Ibid., 1,7 (51,21).
91. Ibid., 2,15 (161,24).
92. *V Ephr* (PG 46,828 A).
93. Ps 102,12: *Apol* 9 (GNO III/I 143,18).
94. *Inscr Ps* 2,10 (GNO V 109,26).
95. GNO V, 109, 8.
96. Ibid., 2,12 (130,16); 2,14 (157,19 and 25); 2,16 (167,21); *s pas* (GNO IX 246,6).
97. See my article "The Active and Contemplative Lives," chapter 9 above.

the loud sound of the tympanies and joins the sound of its own strings to the heavenly choruses. The strings attached to the instrument would be that in each virtue which is taut and unyielding toward evil.[98]

Not stated here, but implicit in the interpretation, is the explanation given in the opening quotation that the ψαλτήριον has its sounding board at the top, so Gregory understands its music in reference to thoughts in contrast to what is "earthly and inarticulate." The use made of the ψαλτήριον underscores the thrust of the passage with which we began as making distinctions in the service of a non-literal interpretation that brings a contemporary spiritual lesson.

The usage of other words in the ψαλ- family by Gregory corresponds with Christian liturgical usage. Thus ὑπόψαλμα refers to the unison response sung by the congregation to the recitation of the Psalm by a cantor or precentor (responsorial singing): "I heard the refrain [ὑποψάλματος] which we all in common add in confession" [Ps 146, 5].[99]

The verb ψάλλω in classical Greek meant "to pluck," "to play a stringed instrument,"[100] but in ecclesiastical Greek "to sing Psalms," "to praise." Ψάλλω occurs ten times in the Gregorian corpus and keeps the ecclesiastical meaning. Even in the passage quoted at the beginning, where the classical meaning of ψαλμός is cited, ψάλλω is used in the sense of "sing," as in 1 Cor 14:15, to which allusion is made. There is another allusion in the phrase "sing with the understanding."[101] Two other passages take ψάλλω from the text of a Psalm: once without comment;[102] the other commenting, "to sing . . . through harmonious and suitable contemplation."[103] The use of ψάλλω for unaccompanied vocal music is clear in certain texts: "Let him bless, and not revile; sing [ψαλλέτω] and not blaspheme; speak favorably and not slander";[104] "The voice of the singers [τῶν ψαλλόντων] called out the thanksgiving at lamp lighting."[105] The participle used for a choir also occurs in another text where the simple verb occurs synonymously with ἐπᾴδω:

98. *Inscr. Ps.* 1,9 (GNO V 66,2–29).
99. Ps 146:5; *deit* (GNO IX 339,16).
100. Liddel, Scott, Jones, *Greek-Engish Lexicon*, 2018.
101. *Inscr. Ps.* 2,12 (GNO V 126,28).
102. *Cant.* 2 (GNO VI 57,14).
103. *Inscr. Ps.* 2,11 (GNO V 123,16).
104. *Benef.* (GNO IX 96,5).
105. *V. Macr.* (GNO VIII/I 395,3).

"[The martyr Theodore] recited [ἐπῇδεν] to his tormentors this line from the Psalms [ψαλμῳδίας] [Ps 33,1]. He sang a Psalm [ἔψαλλεν] in the same way as another who submitted to vengeance. He received the punishment, imprisonment, and again there in prison occurred a marvel concerning this holy man. At night he heard the voice of a multitude of singers [ψαλλόντων], and torches were shining so that light as at a night festival was seen by those outside."[106]

The doubtful work *De occursu Domini* twice uses the singular participle ὁ ψάλλων to mean "the Psalmist," for which Gregory normally used ψαλμῳδός.[107]

The occurrence of the compound συμψάλλω in Gregory's description of a pilgrimage well summarizes his information on the liturgical use of the ψαλ- root: "The chariot was a church and monastery for us, all singing together and fasting together to the Lord all the way."[108] The normal usage of the words in Gregory of Nyssa, therefore, referred to the church's practice of singing (the Psalms) unaccompanied.

Even experienced lexicographers are sometimes led astray by dependence on etymology or on such definitions as Gregory gives in the passage quoted at the beginning. Thus Lampe's *Patristic Greek Lexicon*[109] includes in its definition of ψαλμός a reference to Basil, *Homilia in Psalmum* I,[110] as giving a "reason for musical accompaniment." Basil, however, is referring to melody, use of the Psalms with melody, not to musical instruments. The statements before and after the words cited by Lampe make clear that the discussion pertains to the "book of Psalms" and "words of the Psalms." Μελῳδία is the chanting or singing, i.e. the musical aspect of the Psalms and not any instrumental accompaniment. Because worshipers were beguiled to listen to the melody instead of the words, the use of melody had to be defended.[111]

To summarize the results of this examination, Gregory always follows the biblical usage of ψαλμός except in the one place where he makes

106. *Thdr.* (PG 46,745 B).
107. *Occurs.* (PG 46,1153 D and 1157 D).
108. *Ep.* 2,13 (GNO VIII/II 17,15).
109. Lampe, *Patristic Greek Lexicon*, 1539.
110. PG 29,212 B.
111. Athanasius, *ep Marcell* 27–29 (PG 27,37 D–41 C). See my English translation: "Athanasius, *Epistola ad Marcellinum in interpretationem Psalmorum*," (chapter 11 above), and my study "Athanasius' *Epistola ad Msarcellinum in interpretationem Psalmorum*." (chapter 10 above).

an allegorical point from the etymology of the word. It is, therefore, inappropriate to cite *In Inscriptiones Psalmorum* 2,3 for the meaning of the word in Christian usage: indeed, it is misleading, if not erroneous, for the meaning of the word in Gregory's vocabulary. Gregory's usage does not differ from the usage of other early Christian authors.

This narrow philological inquiry has implications of broader significance for cultural history. It provides a specific example of how Gregory took the classical heritage, which he knew quite well, and reshaped it and used it according to Christian doctrine and practice. His normal use of words followed their Christian meaning, except in self-conscious reflections on the classical meaning. One can rightly claim that in philosophy and world view. Gregory did the same as he did in philology, a sample of which usage is demonstrated by this word study.

13

Progress in Perfection
Gregory of Nyssa's Vita Moysis

GREGORY OF NYSSA'S THEOLOGY of the spiritual life has come in for special study in recent years.[1] Cardinal Daniélou has called attention to the importance in Gregory's thought of the theme of perpetual progress.[2] Ekkehard Mühlenberg has emphasized the grounding of this idea in Gregory's doctrine of the divine infinity.[3] This progress was especially in the sphere of the moral life.[4] Others have contributed to the elucidation of special themes related to Gregory's spiritual theology.[5]

Gregory's treatment of the "Life of Moses" occupies a central place in this recent study. The treatise touches on some of the main points of his spiritual doctrine and its theological underpinnings. Our purpose here will be to consider some features of the contents which are important for Gregory's understanding of Christian spirituality.

---

1. Daniélou, *Platonisme et théologie mystique*; von Balthasar, *Présence et Pensée*; von Ivánka, *Hellenisches und Christliches im frühbyzantinischen Geistesleben*; Völker, *Gregor von Nyssa als Mystiker*; Leys, "La théologie spirituelle de Grégoire de Nysse."

2. Daniélou, *Platonisme*, 291–307; Daniélou, "La colombe et la ténèbre dans la mystique Byzantine ancienne"; Daniélou, *From Glory to Glory*, 46ff.

3. Mühlenberg, *Die Unendlichkeit Gottes bei Gregor von Nyssa*.

4. Cf. Völker, *Gregor von Nyssa als Mystiker*, 225ff. Konstantinou, *Die Tugendlehre Gregors von Nyssa*, makes only passing reference to the theme of eternal progress, e.g., 96, 174.

5. For example, Merki, ὉΜΟΙΩΣΙΣ ΘΕΩ; Balás, ΜΕΤΟΥΣΙΑ ΘΕΟΥ; Gaïth, *La conception de la liberté chez Grégoire de Nysse*.

The alternate title of the *Vita Moysis* is "Concerning Perfection in Virtue." Gregory takes the experiences of Moses recorded in the Biblical text of Exodus and Numbers as an example or pattern to be imitated by those who "pursue the life of virtue."[6] He goes through Moses' life in outline form in the first part of the treatise according to the literal events (*historia*). Then he gives in the second part a spiritual interpretation (*theoria*) in order to gain lessons for the virtuous life. Moses' life is presented as an example not only in specific qualities but especially in its feature of constant growth in virtue, or to use a favorite figure of Gregory's, of never stopping in the race of virtue.[7]

The prologue of the *Vita Moysis* offers a definition of perfection in virtue which underlines the thesis of the work. Perfection in regard to objects of the senses can be defined, for objects perceived by the senses have definite limitations. The only definition of virtue, in contrast, is that it has no limitation.[8] Gregory's scriptural proof is found in Paul's statement, "I have not attained . . . but stretching forth to the things that are before" (Phil 3:13). This is the text verse of the treatise, appealed to again in the central passage in the body of the work.[9] Gregory's philosophical proof comes from the consideration that Good is limited "by the presence of its opposite, as life by death and light by darkness." But the Supreme Good (God) has no opposite to bound it, so "the divine nature is unlimited and infinite,"[10] The same language which is used about the infinity of God later in the treatise is used here of virtue, namely that they have no boundary.[11] Since God is the Good, or "absolute virtue," the Good must be unlimited. Hence, grasping or possessing perfection is impossible. On the other hand, there is the Biblical command, "Be perfect" (Matt 5:48). Gregory answers the dilemma, "Perhaps the perfection of human nature consists in its very growth in goodness."[12] Perfection is a continual progress. And this is the theme illustrated from the events of Moses' life.

---

6. PG 44.301A, 304C; I, 6 and 15. We shall give both the Migne divisions of the text, which can also be located in Musurillo's edition, and Daniélou's paragraph numbers in Sources Chrétiennes. The Old Testament heroes take a prominent place as examples of virtues for Gregory—cf. Daniélou in *Moïse, L'homme de l'alliance*, 269ff.

7. E.g., PG 300 A, 301 A, 408 C; I, 1, 6; II, 249.

8. PG 300 C-D); I, 5.

9. PG 401 A; II, 225.

10. PG 301 A; I, 7. See Mühlenberg, *Die Unendlichkeit Gottes bei Gregor von Nyssa*.

11. PG 404 B; II, 236 and 300 C–301 C; I, 5–10.

12. PG 301 C; I, 10.

The two parts of virtue for Gregory are the knowledge of God and right conduct.[13] The three theophanies received by Moses—at the burning bush, at the giving of the Law at Sinai, and when Moses saw the glory of God while he stood in the cleft of the rock—are important in relating these two.[14] The life of virtue is a quest for God, hence a right knowledge about God is necessary to right action. In each case the knowledge gained about God is related to the incarnation, results in service, and is made possible by Moses' own preparation.

At the vision of the burning bush (Exodus 3) Moses gained an understanding of the nature of God. Truth is "not to have a mistaken apprehension of being."[15] Moses came to know, on the basis of the Septuagint of Exod 3:14, that God alone is self-existent. Neither things perceived by the senses nor those contemplated in the mind truly subsist; the Creator alone has made possible their existence.[16] The knowledge attained by Moses on that occasion is available to everyone who, like him, will turn away from earthly things and look at the divine Radiance.

The second theophany received by Moses occurred in connection with the giving of the Law. There according to the text "Moses entered the darkness where God was" (Exod 20:21). The first vision was of light, but the second was of darkness. This was not a contradiction. The more the mind progresses in the contemplation of reality, the more it sees what is uncontemplated of the divine nature.[17] The mind leaves behind sense experience and what the intelligence thinks it sees. It comes to understand that God is invisible and incomprehensible. This is the true knowledge of God, "the seeing that consists in not seeing."[18] At the burning bush Moses had learned that God is the only true existence. Now he learns that knowledge of the divine essence is unattainable. The "seeing of God," therefore, was coming to know that what is divine is "beyond all knowledge and comprehension."[19] So Gregory speaks of the "luminous darkness."[20]

---

13. PG 377C; II, 166.

14. Marechal, Études sur la psychologie des mystiques, II, 108–9, writes on Moses' three theophanies.

15. PG 333A; II, 23.

16. PG 333A-B; II, 23, 24.

17. τὸ τῆς θείας φύσεως ἀθεώρητον. PG 376 D; II 162.

18. PG 377A; II, 163.

19. PG 377B; II, 164.

20. PG 377A; II, 163.

The Law which was given to Moses confirmed by word his experience in the darkness, for it forbade the making of any image of the divine, whether material or intellectual. The knowledge of God is recognizing that "none of the things known by human comprehension is to be ascribed to him."[21] Although the essence of God is inaccessible, Gregory goes on to explain that its existence is manifested by his actions in the world. The theme of progress is more explicitly introduced in connection with this theophany—along with the idea of following Moses' example:

> What person will follow him who makes his way through such places and elevates his mind to such heights, who, as though he were passing from one peak to another ever comes higher than he was through his ascent to the heights? First, he leaves behind the foot of the mountain, and is separated from all those too weak for the ascent. Then he hears the sounds of the trumpets as he rises higher in his ascent. Thereupon, he slips into the inner sanctuary of divine knowledge. And he does not remain here, but he passes on to the tabernacle not made with hands.[22]

The third theophany is the most extensively treated of the three, and its discussion clearly constitutes the climax of Gregory's presentation about the knowledge of God and eternal progress.[23] We refer to the story in Exod 33:17ff. where Moses asked to see God's glory and was told he could not see God's face. Instead he was placed in the cleft, of a rock and permitted to see the "back parts" of God as he passed by. Here we get one of Gregory's most original interpretations of the Biblical text as he applies it to the theoretical basis for and content of the spiritual life.

The Moses who has talked with God "face to face" (Exod 33:11) yet asks that God appear to him. Why? The soul is ever attracted to the Good and desires further experience of the divine.[24] Gregory quotes Phil 3:13 as he comes now to the central passage of his book. The soul, made more desirous by the things already attained, renews its intensity for the upward flight. "Activity directed toward virtue causes the soul's capacity to grow

---

21. PG 377C; II, 166.

22. PG 377C-D; II, 167.

23. Thus I judge Leys, *L'image de Dieu chez Saint Grégoire de Nysse*, 33–34, to err when he says the third theophany did not differ essentially from the second, and is treated separately only because the plan of the work obligated Gregory to take up this other experience of Moses. But he does note the importance of "following God" at the conclusion of the theophany, pp. 42ff.

24. PG 401A; II, 225.

through exertion."²⁵ This experience is unlike the recurrence of desires for physical things. Elsewhere Gregory compares the desire for material pleasures to a brick-maker throwing yet more clay into his mold while it is constantly being emptied.²⁶ Yearning after material pleasures always leaves the soul empty. The desire for the Good brings the paradox of satisfaction and an enlarged capacity for greater attainment. Other types of activity do not produce the same kind of progress that virtuous activity does. For instance, the doubting and uncertain man is like those who climb a sand hill. They toil endlessly but slip downward. There is much motion but no progress.²⁷

There is attainment without satiety in the spiritual life because the soul enlarges with its desire for heavenly things.²⁸ "Once having set foot on the ladder which God set up, Moses continually climbed to the step above and never ceased to rise higher, because he always found a step higher than the one he had attained."²⁹ From each summit attained, new vistas continually unfold before one on the journey to God. Gregory rehearses the attainments of Moses narrated thus far.³⁰ Nevertheless, Moses "is still unsatisfied in his desire for more."³¹ The ever increasing participation in the Good is always the point of departure for new progress.³²

Gregory explains that Moses' request to see God is both granted and denied, indeed it was granted in what was denied. God fulfilled Moses' desire, but did not promise any cessation or satiety of the desire. God would not have granted the request if it would have ended Moses' desire.³³ Because of the infinite nature of God, one is able to grow greater in proportion to his growth in grace.³⁴ Thus the spirit, unlike the flesh, never knows satiety. The true sight of God is that the "one who looks to God never ceases" in the desire to see him.³⁵

---

25. PG 401B; II, 226.
26. PG 344A; II, 60.
27. PG 405C; II, 244.
28. PG 401A; II, 225.
29. PG 401B; II, 227.
30. PG 401B-D; II, 228–30.
31. PG 401C; II, 230.
32. See Daniélou, *Platonisme*, 291–307.
33. PG 404A; II, 232–33.
34. Cf. *In Cant.* PG 44.1033D–1036 A; 940D–941 B; 1084C–D.
35. PG 404A-B; II, 233–35.

The desire can be infinite because its object is infinite. The statement "man shall not see me and live" (Exod 33:20) is interpreted to mean that, since the divine transcends all characteristics, the one who thinks he sees God has turned from true being to what does not have life.[36] There follows a demonstration of the divine infinity which repeats and applies the idea of the Prologue. The application to the theme of the treatise is this: "This truly is the vision of God—never to be satisfied in the desire to see Him."[37] Gregory summarizes in a statement which corresponds to his initial definition of perfection: "Thus, no limit would cut off growth in the ascent to God, since no limit to the good is to be found nor is the increase of desire for the good brought to an end because it is satisfied."[38] Again, "Moses, your desire for *what is before* has expanded and you have not reached satisfaction in your progress and since you do not see any limit to the good, but your yearning always looks for more, the place with me is so great that the one running in it is never able to cease from his progress."[39] Thus is achieved the demonstration of the thesis stated in the introduction—that perfection is to be found in progress.

One should note the advance of the formula, "the vision of God is never to be satisfied in the desire to see him," over the one which characterized the earlier vision at Sinai, "the seeing that consists in not seeing."[40] This would seem to be a more fundamental concept, at least for this treatise. And this concept connects with the thought of "following God" with which Gregory concludes this section of the treatise. Here he develops a further aspect of the spiritual life: not only to seek God but to follow God. The reader should not neglect Gregory's application of the meaning of this third theophany. The one who sees "face to face" is going in the opposite direction, but the one who sees the "back parts" is following behind. Thus is provided another explanation of God's words "man shall not see my face and live." The one who looks at the face of God is going in the opposite direction from God. The nature of discipleship is to follow behind God. The journey of virtue can be safely completed only by following after the divine guide.[41] This is the essence of the life of virtue, always to follow after

---

36. Ibid.
37. PG 404D; II, 239.
38. PG 405A; II, 239.
39. PG 405B; II, 242.
40. PG 377A; II, 163.
41. PG 408C–409B; II, 249–55.

Progress in Perfection

God. "To follow God wherever he might lead is to behold God."[42] Living in obedience to God is the highest knowledge of God granted to man on earth. Thus Moses learned that his desire for God would be ever expanding and that the true knowledge of God was to follow him.

Each of these three theophanies is brought into relation with Christology. The *Vita Moysis* is notable for the large number of types of the incarnation that it finds in the Old Testament narrative.[43] Thus the burning bush represents the two natures—the light of divinity which shone in the flesh. Moses saw the divine Radiance through the thorny bush.[44] At the next theophany at Sinai Moses was given the tables of stone written with the finger of God. This too is interpreted of the two natures in the incarnation. The tables are the human nature, the "God-receiving flesh." The finger is the Holy Spirit by which the true Lawgiver carved his divine nature on our human nature.[45] Finally, the rock where Moses stood when he saw the "back parts" of God is Christ.[46] All the treasures of good are in him,[47] and the hope of all good things is found in standing steadfast in him. Thus in every crucial passage on the knowledge of God, Christ stands at the forefront. Here is the specifically Christian emphasis in Gregory's spirituality. By the incarnation of Christ is made possible the knowledge of God and so also progress in the spiritual life.

The three theophany texts serve further to demonstrate that for Gregory "practical philosophy should be joined to the contemplative philosophy."[48] Each of the experiences of Moses in "seeing" the divine is followed by an act of service. Such a person as has seen the divine light in the thorny bush "becomes able to assist others to salvation, to destroy tyranny . . . and to deliver to freedom."[49] It is only the one so equipped who is prepared to go and speak among the people.[50] Again, the Moses who has seen God in the darkness receives the commandments to deliver

---

42. PG 408D; II, 252.

43. In addition to those discussed in the text, other types are Moses' rod changed into a serpent (PG 333D and 336B; II, 26–27 and 31–33), Moses' hand becoming leprous (PG 333D–336A; II, 26–30), the manna (PG 368C; II, 139), and the tabernacle (PG 381A-B; II, 174).

44. PG 332D and 333C; II, 20 and 26.
45. PG 397B-C; II, 216.
46. PG 405D and 408B; II, 244, 248.
47. PG 408B; II, 248.
48. PG 392D; II, 200; cf. PG 377C; II, 166.
49. PG 333C; II, 26.
50. PG 341B; II, 55.

to the people. "He went down to the people to share with them the marvels which had been shown him."[51] Finally, after seeing God from behind, Moses followed as a disciple according to the command of Christ.[52] The meaning of this climax episode in the life of Moses is that one runs in the racecourse of virtue.[53] To obey God is to know God.

Thus we are led to the practical side of this treatise, which comes out in its emphasis on "right conduct." This includes meditation, ascetic denial, and virtuous acts. Before the light of truth shone on Moses at the burning bush, he had to have spent a quiet and peaceful time in solitary meditation.[54] Moreover, he had to remove the sandals from his feet, meaning that the dead and earthly covering of skins, which was placed around our nature" at the first transgression, must be removed from the soul.[55] Before one ascends the mountain of God he must be "pure in soul and body, washed stainless of every spot."[56] Asceticism is commended as the "greater philosophy,"[57] and there is repeated emphasis on control of the passions.[58] Finally, standing on the rock at the third theophany is understood as being firmly stationed on the good. It is only by standing firm in virtue that one can follow God. Ascent takes place by means of standing firm in the good.[59] And so we have the paradox of stable movement.

These activities are a matter of human effort. When it comes to the life of virtue, "we are in some manner our own parents."[60] We have within ourselves the power of choice, and so are the cause of light or darkness in ourselves.[61] We may become "capable of receiving God."[62] The help of the Holy Spirit is for those who are worthy.[63] This human mutability, or capacity to change, is the counterpart of the divine infinity in providing a

---

51. PG 321A; I, 56.

52. PG 408D; II, 251.

53. PG 405B and 405D–408A; II, 242, 245–46.

54. PG 332C; II, 18–19.

55. PG 333 A; II, 22. This idea is prominent in discussions of Gregory's anthropology—e.g., Daniélou, *Platonisme*, 56–60; Ladner, "The Philosophical Anthropology of Saint Gregory of Nyssa," 88ff.

56. PG 373B; II, 154.

57. PG 305B; I, 19; cf. PG 385D; II, 187.

58. PG 352C–356B; II, 90–101.

59. PG 405C; II, 243.

60. PG 328B; II, 3.

61. PG 349A; II, 80.

62. PG 368A; II, 136.

63. PG 361B; II, 121.

basis for eternal progress. "Everything placed in a world of change never remains the same but is always passing from one state to another, the alternation always bringing about something better or worse."[64]

But to reduce his teaching to the moral and ascetic and to human effort would be to reduce the range of discipleship. As Gregory draws his writing to a close he states the goal of life. We should have "but one purpose in life: to be called servants of God by virtue of the lives we have lived."[65] The servant of God is the one who follows God.

> For he who truly has come to be in the image of God and who has in no way turned away from the divine character bears in himself its distinguishing marks and shows in all things his assimilation to the archetype, beautifying his own soul with what is incorruptible, unchangeable, and has no part in any evil.[66]

Gregory refers again to his definition in the prologue: "continual development of life to what is better is the soul's way to perfection."[67] That Moses ever rose higher in his ascent demonstrates the definition of perfection.[68] One thing follows another in his life, but the concern is not with logical connection but with progress, not with chronology but with sequence.[69] The stages of Moses' life are a pattern, not in their order, but in their demonstration that the life of virtue is a constant advance to new things. Perfection in virtue is to be always making progress in virtue.

64. PG 428B; II, 315.
65. PG 328A-B; II, 2-3.
66. PG 429 A; II, 318.
67. PG 425 A; II, 306.
68. There are frequent summaries throughout the work of Moses' attainments; the most extensive one coming as a summary at the end—PG 425 B-D; II, 308-13. These summaries serve the purpose of emphasizing the theme of constantly going on to new attainments.
69. Daniélou, "*Akolouthia* chez Grégoire de Nysse," 236ff., has called attention to the importance of the idea of sequence in Gregory. Sometimes the order of the texts in Scripture is important, but frequently in the *Vita Moysis* it seems that the events are taken simply as they come in the Bible without making something of the order. The meaningfulness of the sequence is not in some inner connection or logical order but in the theme of continual progression which is illustrated. The point of going on to something new as opposed to stopping, which is the leading idea (σκόπος) of the whole work. Even on the larger question of stages of the spiritual life Gregory has different patterns. Thus Moses' three visions of God listed *In Cant.* 11, PG 44, 1000 C do not correspond exactly to the theophanies in *Vita Moysis*. The three Solomonic books form a different three-fold scheme (*Eccl. I*, PG 44, 617 A-B; *In Cant.* 1, PG 44, 765D-772A); Abraham shows four steps (*C. Eun.* ii, 89); and the five books of Psalms provide five steps of ascent (*In Ps.* I, 7, PG 44, 465 B).

14

God's Infinity and Man's Mutability
Perpetual Progress according to Gregory of Nyssa

GEORGE BEBIS WROTE AN excellent article for the Fall, 1967, issue of the *Greek Orthodox Theological Review* on "Gregory of Nyssa's 'De Vita Moysis': A Philosophical and Theological Analysis." That analysis may serve as a point of departure for this paper.

The subtitle of the *Vita Moysis* is "Concerning Perfection in Virtue." The theme of the work is perpetual progress in virtue.[1] "Continual development to what is better is the soul's way to perfection."[2] "Perfection is growth in goodness."[3] This is no less the theme of Gregory's *Commentary on Canticles*.

> Created being is ever changing for the better in its growth in perfection; along these lines no limit can be envisaged, nor can its progressive growth in perfection be limited by any term. In this way, its present state of perfection, no matter how great and

---

1. See my "Progress in Perfection," chapter 13 above.

2. *Vita Moysis* II, 306; PG 44, 425A. (I shall give the section numbers from the edition prepared by Daniélou for *Sources Chrétiennes*, Paris, 1955, and the reference in Migne, which is also given in the margins of Musurillo's edition, Leiden, 1964. For other works I shall be content with the Migne references, which again can be found in the Leiden edition.)

3. Ibid., I, 10; PG 44, 301C. Cf. *On Perfection* (PG 46, 285C), "For this is truly perfection: never to stop growing towards what is better and never placing any limit on perfection." English translation by Virginia Woods Callahan in Fathers of the Church 58 (Washington, DC, 1967) 122.

perfect it might be, is merely the beginning of a greater and superior stage. Thus the words of the Apostle are verified: the stretching forth to the things that are before involves the forgetting of what has already been attained (Phil. 3:13). For at each stage the greater and superior good holds the attention of those who enjoy it and does not allow them to look at the past; their enjoyment of the superior perfection erases all memory of that which was inferior.[4]

Or again,

> Thus though the new grace we may obtain is greater than what we had before, it does not put a limit on our final goal; rather, for those who are rising in perfection, the limit of the good that is attained becomes the beginning of the discovery of higher goods. Thus they never stop rising, moving from one new beginning to the next, and the beginning of ever greater graces is never limited of itself.[5]

Cardinal Daniélou and others have noted that a central doctrine for Gregory is the understanding of perfection as perpetual progress.[6] This is an original contribution of Gregory to the theology of the spiritual life.

The present study will look briefly at the background to the idea of perpetual progress, then note the imagery under which Gregory of Nyssa presents the idea, consider in some detail the theological grounding of the idea in the divine infinity and human mutability, and conclude with some observations relative to the nature of the spiritual life.

BACKGROUND OF THE IDEA

Some hints and components of the idea of perpetual progress in virtue may be found scattered in Gregory's predecessors and contemporaries.

Philo's *The Posterity of Cain* 14–15 takes up a favorite text of Gregory's, Exodus 20:21. He declares that the quest for the essence of God is an unattainable quest, because God is incomprehensible. Still the undertaking

---

4. *Comm. on Cant.* PG 44, 885D–888A. English translations of this work will be taken from Daniélou and Musurillo, *From Glory to Glory*. This quotation is from 197.

5. Ibid., 941C; *From Glory to Glory*, 213.

6. Daniélou, *Platonisme et théologie mystique*, esp. 291ff.; Daniélou, "La colombe et la ténèbre," esp. pp. 409ff.; Daniélou, "Mystique de la ténèbre chez Gregoire de Nysse"; and the Introduction to *From Glory to Glory*, 46–71. Völker, *Gregor von Nyssa als Mystiker*, 186ff., does not emphasize the idea of progress so much.

produces "a great good, namely to comprehend that God is incomprehensible and to see that he is invisible." Philo concludes that the quest itself is a foretaste of happiness (21).[7]

Irenaeos, *Against Heresies* IV. xi. 2, affords a good parallel to Gregory in his contrast between the Creator and the created and the assertion, "For as God is always the same, so also man, when found in God, shall always go on toward God." Later Irenaeos says man "should always possess something toward which he might advance" (IV. xx. 7).

Clement of Alexandria is one of the more important forerunners of Gregory's thought. He speaks of "the soul which is ever improving in the knowledge of virtue and growth of righteousness ... progressively stretching forth to the possession of impassibility until it attains to a perfect man" (*Stromata* VII. ii. 10). Clement, like Philo, anticipates features of Gregory's use of Moses entering the dark cloud where God was (Exod 20:21): God is invisible, and he is "infinite" in the sense of being without dimensions and having no limit and so without any form (*Stromata* V. xii).

Although the general structure of Origen's system was antithetical to the theme of perpetual progress, he has a passage based on personal experience which corresponds to Gregory's emphasis.[8] In the *Homilies on Numbers* XVII.4 Origen likens the search for wisdom to a journey. "Where is the limit of the wisdom of God?" Anyone who has made any progress in knowledge knows well that discoveries in spiritual things lead to other advances. Philippians 3:13 says to reach out to what is beyond the first attainments. Rather than dwelling in a permanent house, the soul which seeks wisdom "appears to advance like nomads with their tents." Another anticipation of the language of Gregory of Nyssa comes in the treatise *On Prayer* 25:2, which explains how the kingdom of God can be both present and prayed for as if it were not present. There is an advancement toward perfection. We journey toward perfection if "stretching forward to the things that are before" we "forget the things which are behind." As we advance unceasingly, the kingdom of God will be fully established in us, and then 1 Cor 15:24–28 will be fulfilled.

A parallel to Gregory of Nyssa is found in the *Commentary on Isaiah* 1:17 ascribed to Basil of Caesarea: "For as he who is being perfected stretches forward to the things before, so the sinner returns to the things

---

7. Cf. *On the Change of Names* 7; 9.

8. See the distinctions made by Otis, "Nicene Orthodoxy and Fourth Century Mysticism."

behind" (PG 30, 144D). The majority opinion, however, according to Quasten, is against the authenticity of this work.[9]

Gregory of Nazianzos approaches Nyssa's view of the divine infinity in *Oration* XXXVIII. 7, 8. God is "like some great sea of Being, limitless and unbounded," and he is without beginning and end. As such he is incomprehensible, but this very fact becomes an enticement: as an object of wonder he becomes more an object of desire.[10] The conclusion of the oration presents the life of Christ as something to be imitated as a continuous journey.

Unlike these incidental references, the theme of perpetual progress becomes characteristic of Gregory of Nyssa.[11] Völker, who emphasizes Gregory's indebtedness to the Alexandrian tradition and tends to play down his originality, yet says Gregory puts this idea in the middle point, repeats it almost endlessly, expresses it in paradoxical formulas, and finds it a true expression of his piety.[12]

IMAGERY AND EXAMPLES

Gregory of Nyssa employs a wide range of imagery to suggest the theme of perpetual progress in the soul's advancement in virtue. A favorite illustration, influenced by Phil 3:13, is that of running a race.[13] "For him who runs to the Lord the open field of the divine course is never exhausted."[14] "Just as the end of life is the beginning of death, so also the stopping of the race of virtue becomes the beginning of the race of evil."[15] "The place with Me is so great that the one running in it is never able to cease from his progress."[16]

Equally popular with Gregory is the imagery of climbing higher.[17] This may be by steps: "We see the Word, then, leading the bride up a rising

---

9. Quasten, *Patrology*, vol. 3, 218–19.

10. The same language is found in *Oration* XLV. 3. *Oration* XXVIII. 2–4 makes the familiar point that man may know that God is but not what he is.

11. Cf. Otis, "Nicene Orthodoxy and Fourth Century Mysticism," on the essential difference in Gregory from his predecessors. Cf. also Otis, "Cappadocian Thought as a Coherent System."

12. Völker, *Gregor von Nyssa als Mystiker*, 283–84.

13. Daniélou, *Platonisme*, 294, 297ff.

14. *Comm. on Cant.* PG 44, 876C; *From Glory to Glory*, 191.

15. *Vita Moysis* I, 6; PG 44, 301A.

16. Ibid., II, 242; PG 44, 405B. Cf. the "wide and roomy stadium" of II, 246; PG 44, 408A.

17. Daniélou, *Platonisme*, 293–94.

staircase, as it were, up to the heights by the ascent of perfection."[18] Or the figure may be of a ladder: "Once having set foot on the ladder which God set up (as Jacob says), Moses continually climbed to the step above and never ceased to rise higher, because he always found a step higher than the one he had attained."[19]

The general language of ascent leads in one passage to the specific imagery of flight: "For he who elevates his life beyond all things through such ascents does not fail to become ever higher than he was so that, as I think, in all things like an eagle his life might be seen above and beyond the cloud whirling around the ether of spiritual ascent."[20] "Once it is released from its earthly attachment, the soul becomes light and swift for its movement upward, soaring from below up to the heights... The soul ever rises higher and will always make its flight yet higher."[21]

A frequently recurring image of another kind is that of growth. "The soul grows by participation in what transcends it."[22]

Removing garments is used as an illustration of progressive purification:

> For after removing her old tunic and divesting herself of all further clothing, the bride became much purer than she was. And yet, in comparison with this newly acquired purity, she does not seem to have removed her head-covering. Even after that complete stripping of herself she still finds something further to remove.
>
> So it is with our ascent towards God: each stage that we reach always reveals something heavy weighing on the soul. Thus in comparison with her new found purity, that very stripping of her tunic now becomes a kind of garment which those who find her must once again remove.[23]

The progress in perfection is like a continual creation: "Thus, in a certain sense, it is constantly being created, ever changing for the better in its growth in perfection."[24] There is always a new beginning: "Because of

18. *Comm. on Cant.* PG 44, 876B; *From Glory to Glory*, 190.
19. *Vita Moysis* II, 227; PG 44, 401B.
20. Ibid., II, 307; PG 44, 425B.
21. Ibid., II, 224-25; PG 44, 401A. Cf. Daniélou, "La colombe et la ténèbre," 396ff. on the wings of the dove.
22. *Comm. on Cant.* PG 44, 876A; *From Glory to Glory*, 190. Cf. *On the Soul and the Resurrection* PG 46, 105B-C.
23. *Comm. on Cant.* PG 44, 1029B-C; *From Glory to Glory*, 264.
24. Ibid., PG 44, 885D; *From Glory to Glory*, 197.

God's Infinity and Man's Mutability

the transcendence of the graces which the bride finds ever beyond her, she always seems to be beginning anew."[25]

Gregory connects the theme of progress with some of his favorite conceptions, for example that of the vision of God. The man living the life of virtue is always desirous to see God. "This truly is the vision of God: never to be satisfied in the desire to see him. One must always, by looking at what he can see, rekindle his desire to see more."[26] "The pure in heart will see God, according to the Lord's infallible word, according to his capacity, receiving as much as his mind can sustain; yet the infinite and incomprehensible nature of the Godhead remains beyond all understanding."[27]

One of Gregory's profoundest insights is that the vision of God consists in following God. Here he unites the images of motion and sight. "So Moses, who eagerly seeks to behold God, is now taught how he can behold him: to follow God wherever he might lead is to behold God."[28] The *Commentary on Canticles* makes the same application of the episode in Exod 33:21–23: "By this I think we are taught that he who wishes to see God, will see his Beloved only by constantly following after Him, and the contemplation of His face is really the unending journey towards Him, accomplished by following directly behind the Word."[29]

Gregory's favorite theme of participation is also related to the perpetual progress, for one's advancement in virtue increases with his participation in God.[30]

> Since then no limit to virtue except evil has been shown, and the Divine does not admit of an opposite, the divine nature is found to be unlimited and infinite. Certainly he who follows after true virtue participates in nothing other than God, because he himself is absolutely virtue. Since then those who know what is good by nature desire participation in it and since this good has no limit, the participant's desire itself necessarily has no stopping place but stretches out with the limitless.[31]

---

25. Ibid., 876B; p. 190.

26. *Vita Moysis* II, 239; PG 44, 404D.

27. *Comm. on Cant.* PG 44, 941A; *From Glory to Glory*, 212. Cf. *On the Beatitudes*, Sermon 6, on Matt 5:8.

28. *Vita Moysis* II, 252; PG 44, 408D.

29. *Comm. on Cant.* PG 44, 1028A; *From Glory to Glory*, 263.

30. Balás, Μετουσια Θεου, esp. 152–57.

31. *Vita Moysis* I, 7; PG 44, 301A–B.

Gregory not only gives comparisons of the perpetual progress, but he also points to Biblical personages who exemplified it. Moses is a prime example, for the theme of the *Vita Moysis* is continual progress in virtue. Representative of several statements in the work is the following: "The great Moses, as he was ever becoming greater, at no time stopped in his ascent, nor did he set a limit for himself in his upward course."[32] The appeal to Moses is not limited to the work based on his life. "Everyone is familiar with those elevations which Moses enjoyed, for no matter how great he had become, he never stopped in his growth towards perfection,"[33] and there follows a summary of the course of his life. The bride of Canticles is described in the same terms of progress as Moses. Just as the soul that looks to God constantly experiences an ever new yearning for him, "so the bride that ever runs towards her Spouse will never find any rest in her progress towards perfection."[34] Then follows a recapitulation of her experiences identical in form to the summaries of Moses' experience which punctuate the narrative of the *Vita*.

Abraham, too, serves as an exemplar of the life that journeys to the knowledge of God. His mind,

> unimpeded by any object of sense, was never hindered from its journeying in quest of what lies beyond all that is known . . . All the other things which in the course of his reasoning he was able to apprehend as he advanced. . . . using them all as supplies and appliances for his onward journey, ever making one discovery a stepping-stone to another, ever reaching forth unto those things which are before.[35]

Moreover, David is seen as one who knew the exaltation of unending progress. "The great David enjoyed in his heart those glorious elevations as he progressed from strength to strength."[36]

Paul is another representative of continual advancement.

> Paul does not let the graces he has obtained become the limit of his desire, but he continues to go on and on, never ceasing his ascent. Thus he teaches us, I think, that in our constant participation in the blessed nature of the Good, the graces that

---

32. Ibid., II, 227; PG 44, 401B.
33. *Comm. on Cant.* PG 44, 1025B; *From Glory to Glory*, 261.
34. Ibid., 1036A; p. 268; cf. 888C.
35. *Against Eunomios* 12 (PG 45, 940D–941A; Jaeger I, 252–53). English translation from NPNF, series 2, vol. 5, p. 259.
36. *Comm. on Cant.* PG 44, 941A; *From Glory to Glory*, 212.

we receive at every point are indeed great, but the path that lies beyond our immediate grasp is infinite.[37]

DIVINE INFINITY

Gregory's doctrine of perpetual progress is grounded in his doctrines of God and man. God's infinity is fundamental to Gregory's distinction between Creator and creation and so to his whole philosophy and theology.[38] He gives an expanded explanation of what the divine infinity means in *Against Eunomios* II, 70 (*NPNF*, V, p. 257), but we need not explore the passage, since our concerns are the application Gregory makes of this to the spiritual life. Suffice it to say that "the Divine Nature, being limited in no respect, but passing all limitations on every side in its infinity, is far removed from those marks which we find in creation."[39]

Writing against Eunomios, he lays down a principle which connects his theology and his mysticism:

> For to the Godhead it properly belongs to lack no conceivable thing which is regarded as good, while the creation attains excellence by partaking in something better than itself; and further, not only had a beginning of its being, but also is found to be constantly in a state of beginning to be in excellence, by its continual advance in improvement, since it never halts at what it has reached, but all that it has acquired becomes by participation a beginning of its ascent to something still greater, and it never ceases, in Paul's phrase, "reaching forth to the things that are before."[40]

Continual improvement distinguishes creation from the Creator, who lacks no good thing.

> For as long as a nature is in defect as regards the good, the superior existence exerts upon this inferior one a ceaseless attraction towards itself: and this craving for more will never stop: it will

---

37. Ibid., 940D–941A, p. 211.

38. See Mühlenberg, *Die Unendlichkeit Gottes bei Gregor von Nyssa*, 100ff. for his doctrine of infinity, and 147ff. for this doctrine as a grounding for the theme of progress. James E. Hennessy, "The Background, Sources, and Meaning of Divine Infinity in St. Gregory of Nyssa," should be better known.

39. *Against Eunomios* 8 (PG 45, 796A; Jaeger, II, 210. 9–11; NPNF V, 209); cf. also PG 45, 772A (Jaeger, II, 188. 11–26; NPNF V, 201).

40. Ibid. (PG 45, 797A; Jaeger, II, 212. 5–14; NPNF V, 210).

> be stretching out to something not yet grasped: the subject of this deficiency will be always demanding a supply, always altering into the grander nature, and yet will never touch perfection, because it cannot find a goal to grasp, and cease its impulse upward. The First Good is in its nature infinite, and so it follows of necessity that the participation in the enjoyment of it will be infinite also, for more will be always being grasped, and yet something beyond that which has been grasped will always be discovered, and this search will never overtake its Object, because its fund is as inexhaustible as the growth of that which participates in it is ceaseless.[41]

The soul of man stretches out after the infinity of God.[42]

One of the arguments advanced for the infinity of God is the following:

> The divine by its very nature is infinite, enclosed by no boundary. If the divine be perceived as though bounded by something, one must by all means along with that boundary consider what is beyond it. For certainly that which is bounded leaves off at some point, as air provides the boundary for all that flies. . . . In the same way, God, if he be conceived as bounded, would necessarily be surrounded by something different in nature.[43]

The same argument is used to establish that perfection in virtue is infinite:

> Perfection in regard to all other things which are measured by sense perception is marked off by certain definite bounds . . . But in the case of virtue we have learned from the Apostle that the one limit of perfection is that it has no limit . . . No Good has a limit in its own nature but is limited by the presence of its opposite, as life by death and light by darkness.[44]

The passage continues with the quotation marked by note 31. Gregory concludes the passage with the definition of virtue quoted at the beginning, "For perhaps the perfection of human nature consists in its very growth in goodness."[45]

---

41. *Against Eunomios* I, 290-91 (PG 45, 340D; Jaeger, I, 112. 7-20; NPNF V, 62).

42. Cf. *Comm. on Cant.* PG 44, 873D-876A; *From Glory to Glory*, 190.

43. *Vita Moysis* II, 236; PG 44, 404B.

44. Ibid., I, 5; PG 44, 300C-D. Cf. *Comm. on Cant.* PG 44, 885C-D; *From Glory to Glory*, 196.

45. See note 3.

God's Infinity and Man's Mutability

Since the nature of God is the nature of Good (Perfection), if God is infinite, so also is perfection. The infinity of God is the basis for the infinity of virtue. Several passages touch on this point. God is unlimited in the good, for the eternal substance of God "contains all perfection within itself and cannot be limited... But every perfection that He is conceived to have is present to an infinite and unlimited degree."[46] The good, unchecked by its opposite, goes on to infinity.[47] In a remarkable, but for Gregory not unusual, juxtaposition of metaphors Gregory says that the path of those who ascend to God is unlimited because God is like a never failing Fountain of which one could never say he had seen all.[48] There is no limit to the advance that can be made toward the good, because the good has no limit.[49] Therefore, Gregory provides a grounding for the idea of perpetual progress in the infinity of virtue, which in turn is a corollary of the infinity of God.

An early expression of the idea of progress is based on the inexhaustible nature of virtue. "For the possession of virtue is such that all men should partake of it according to their capacity, yet it will be always in abundance for those who thirst after it."[50] Since virtue is unlimited, it follows that participation in virtue brings no diminution or division of it. In later writings the divine infinity becomes explicitly the basis for human progress.

> We are thus taught never to set any bounds to the immensity of the Godhead; nor can any measure of human knowledge ever become a limit to our comprehension of our goal, so as to force us to stop in our ever forward progress towards heaven.[51]

Vita Moysis II, 219–48 develops the theme of eternal progress in relation to the divine infinity. A key statement is the following:

> No consideration will be given to anything as enclosing the infinite nature. It is not in the nature of what is unenclosed to be grasped. But every desire for the good which is attracted to that ascent constantly expands as one progresses in pressing on to

---

46. *Comm. on Cant.* PG 44, 873C; *From Glory to Glory*, 189.
47. *On the Soul and the Resurrection* PG 46, 96C–97A; NPNF V, 450.
48. *Comm. on Cant.* PG 44, 997D and 1000B; *From Glory to Glory*, 245f.
49. *Catechetical Oration* 21 (PG 45, 57D–60A).
50. *On Virginity* 4 (PG 46, 337B).
51. *Comm. on Cant.* PG 44, 892A–B; *Glory*, 200. Cf. 885C–888A; *From Glory to Glory*, 196–97.

> the good.... Thus no limit would cut off growth in the ascent to God, since no limit to the good is to be found.[52]

Because of the infinite nature of virtue, participation in virtue can never be expressed as an attainment; it can only be expressed as movement. "In reference to virtue the grasping of perfection is impossible."[53] "The beloved face of the Lord once passed Moses by, and thus the soul of the Lawgiver kept going out of the state in which it had arrived, constantly following after the Word Who walked before."[54]

Although limitless progress in the good is possible, evil, in contrast, is limited and finite. Progress in evil cannot go on indefinitely; a reversal to the good must follow. The limitation of evil in contrast to the good is expressed in the following selection:

> Now that which is always in motion, if its progress be to good, will never cease moving onwards to what lies before it, by reason of the infinity of the course to be traversed:—for it will not find any limit of its object such that when it has apprehended it, it will at last cease its motion: but if its bias be in the opposite direction, when it has finished the course of wickedness and reached the extreme limit of evil, then that which is ever moving, finding no halting point for its impulse natural to itself, when it has run through the lengths that can be run in wickedness, of necessity turns its motion towards good: for as evil does not extend to infinity, but is comprehended by necessary limits, it would appear that good once more follows in succession upon the limit of evil.[55]

Gregory's presupposition here is the mutability of human nature, which will be considered below. It may be noted that this reasoning is consistent with the idea of universal salvation.[56]

The progress in the good is not limited to the present life. Another significant passage connecting infinite progress with the nature of God shows that since God is infinite, there is a greater and greater participation

---

52. *Vita Moysis* II, 238–39; PG 44, 404C–D. Cf. *On the Soul and the Resurrection* PG 46, 96C–97A; NPNF V, 450. Mühlenberg, *op. cit.*, 160.

53. *Vita Moysis* I, 6; PG 44, 301A; cf. II, 252–55; PG 44, 409A–B.

54. *Comm. on Cant.* PG 44, 1025A; *From Glory to Glory*, 261. Cf. 1032C; p. 266.

55. *On the Making of Man* 21:2 (PG 44, 201B–04A; NPNF V, 410f.). Cf. Balás, Μετουσια Θεου, 137; Gaïth, *La conception de la liberté chez Grégoire de Nysse*, 137–42; Daniélou, *L'être et le temps chez Grégoire de Nysse*, 186ff. discusses the "acme of evil."

56. Daniélou, "L'apocatastase chez Saint Grégoire de Nysse."

in grace throughout eternity. Gregory's theme of participation thus is a movement.

> In our constant participation in the blessed nature of the Good, the graces that we receive at every point are indeed great, but the path that lies beyond our immediate grasp is infinite. This will constantly happen to those who thus share in the divine Goodness, and they will always enjoy a greater and greater participation in grace throughout all eternity . . .
> In all the infinite eternity of centuries, the man who runs towards Thee constantly becomes greater as he rises higher, ever growing in proportion to his increase in grace.[57]

God always remains beyond and incomprehensible, but man receives a knowledge of God and participates in his goodness "according to his capacity." Man's knowledge of God is limited by his capacity, not by the transcendent object.[58]

> This, then, is the doctrine that I think the Apostle is teaching about the ineffable nature of the Good, when he says that the eye does not know it even though it may see it. For the eye does not see it completely as it is, but only insofar as it can receive it.[59]

The note of "according to capacity" brings this study to the second theological grounding of perpetual progress, the nature of man.

HUMAN MUTABILITY

Gregory of Nyssa sees the contrast between God and man to consist especially in the fact that God is unchangeable but man is mutable.[60] Human mutability is due to the created condition of man and so rests on the fundamental distinction between Creator and created. Man's very existence involved a change, a coming into being out of non-being. God, in contrast, always is. This distinction between Creator and created is one of Gregory's

---

57. *Comm. on Cant.* PG 44, 940D–41A; *From Glory to Glory*, 211–12. Gaïth, *La conception de la liberté chez Grégoire de Nysse*, 200ff.
58. Daniélou, *L'être et le temps*, 108.
59. *Comm. on Cant.* PG 44, 941B; *From Glory to Glory*, 212.
60. Daniélou, *L'être et le temps*, 95ff.

basic theological propositions,⁶¹ and stress on the changeableness of man is a key feature of his anthropology.⁶²

> What difference then do we discern between the Divine and that which has been made like to the Divine? We find it in the fact that the former is uncreate, while the latter has its being from creation: and this distinction of property brings with it a train of other properties; for it is very certainly acknowledged that the uncreated nature is immutable, and always remains the same, while the created nature cannot exist without change; for its very passage from non-existence to existence is a certain motion and change.⁶³

This difference between God and man is brought into the discussion of the spiritual life.

> In our changeable natures good and evil exist by turns, because of the power we have to choose equally either side of a contradiction. The consequent evil becomes the limit of our good . . . But the divine nature is simple, pure, unique, immutable, unalterable, ever abiding in the same way, and never goes outside of itself. It is utterly immune to any participation in evil and thus possesses the good without limit, because it can see no boundary to its own perfection, nor see anything that is contrary to itself.⁶⁴

That human beings are always changing is a frequently reiterated theme. "Everyone knows that everything placed in a world of change never remains the same but is always passing from one state to another, the alteration always bringing about something better or worse."⁶⁵ The soul partakes of this nature and is always unstable.⁶⁶ Once more there is an early

---

61. Balás, Μετουσια Θεου, 43–49.

62. For studies of Gregory's anthropology to Gaïth add Ladner, "The Philosophical Anthropology of Saint Gregory of Nyssa"; Cavarnos, "Gregory of Nyssa on the Nature of the Soul"; McClear, "The Fall of Man and Original Sin in the Theology of Gregory of Nyssa"; J. Pelikan, "The Mortality of God and the Immortality of Man in Gregory of Nyssa."

63. *On the Making of Man* 16:12 (PG 44, 184C; NPNF V, 405).

64. *Comm. on Cant.* PG 44, 873C–76C; *From Glory to Glory*, 190. The whole passage contains many ideas encountered in this study. Cf. ibid., 885D–888A (*From Glory to Glory*, 196–97) for Gregory's classification of being into spiritual and material, and the spiritual into Creator and created.

65. *Vita Moysis* II, 2; PG 44, 328A.

66. *On the Soul and the Resurrection* PG 46, 113B–C; NPNF V, 455f.

statement of a cardinal principle for Gregory in the treatise *On Virginity*: "For it is impossible for our human nature ever to stop moving; it has been made by its Creator ever to keep changing."[67]

There are different types of change and movement. Daniélou has taught us to see Gregory's distinction between cyclic change and progressive change.[68]

> There are two forms of movement; the one being ever towards what is good, and in this the advance has no check, because no goal of the course to be traversed can be reached, while the other is in the direction of the contrary, and of it this is the essence, that it has no subsistence.[69]

There is such a thing as motion without progress, like attempting to climb a sand dune.[70] There is the cycle of bodily appetites in which there is a filling up and becoming empty again. "And we never stop this until we depart from this material life."[71] Gregory's *Funeral Oration on Flacilla* describes life as a repetitious cycle.[72] In contrast to the filling and emptying which is characteristic of this life, there is a good which is not limited.[73] More on this will come in the analysis of the nature of the spiritual life.

Gregory sees a virtue in human mutability. Unlike the cyclical change in which there is no progress there is the possibility of change to the better. The very fact that created beings change opens up the possibility of improvement. Creation itself was such a change. The passage from nonbeing to being means that the first and natural movement of created being is progress. Man's constant changeableness gives the possibility of change to the better.

The mutability of our nature becomes a pinion in our flight to higher things.

> For man does not merely have an inclination to evil, were this so, it would be impossible for him to grow in good, if his nature possessed only an inclination towards the contrary. But in truth

---

67. *On Virginity* 7 (PG 46, 352C). Michel Aubineau in his edition of the treatise in Sources Chrétiennes 119 (Paris, 1966) 347 (cf. p. 176) notes parallels from earlier authors and considers this idea a root of Gregory's doctrine of progress.

68. "La Colombe," 400ff.

69. *Catechetical Oration* 21 (NPNF V, 492).

70. *Vita Moysis* II, 244; PG 44, 405C.

71. Ibid., II, 61; PG 44, 344A–B.

72. Jaeger, IX, 485. 10–13.

73. *De Mortuis* PG 46, 500D–501D.

the finest aspect of our mutability is the possibility of growth in good; and this capacity for improvement transforms the soul, as it changes, more and more into the divine. And so . . . what appears so terrifying (I mean the mutability of our nature) can really be a pinion in our flight towards higher things, and indeed it would be a hardship if we were not susceptible of the sort of change which is towards the better.[74]

Again,

> Though we are changeable by nature, the Word wants us never to change for the worse; but by constant progress in perfection, we are to make our mutability an aid in our rise towards higher things, and so by the very changeability of our nature to establish it immovably in good.[75]

The "change from the worse to the better" is a characteristic idea.[76] But Gregory knows that the change can go either way.

> The divine nature alone is beyond all change and variation, for it has nothing to which it needs to turn, being wholly incapable of evil and unable to turn to something better . . . But we men who exist in change and variation become through the activity of change either better or worse—worse whenever we depart from participation in the good, better again when we happen to change to the better. Since we are associated with evil through change, we need to change to the good.[77]

Man's ability to change is a part of Gregory's characteristic emphasis on the freedom of the will. Man has the power of choice between good and bad.[78]

> Since being changeable you departed from the good, use your changeableness again for the good. And whence you are fallen turn again to that, since men have power of free will to choose which things they want, whether good or evil.[79]

Man's mutability means his freedom of choice.

    74. *On Perfection* PG 46, 285B–C; *From Glory to Glory*, 83–84.
    75. *Comm. on Cant.* PG 44, 945C; *From Glory to Glory*, 216.
    76. *Comm. on Cant.* PG 44, 885D–888A; 980B–992B.
    77. *On the Inscriptions of the Psalms* II. iv (PG 44, 500B).
    78. Jaeger, *Two Rediscovered Works of Ancient Christian Literature*, 85–107; Gaïth, *La conception de la liberté chez Grégoire de Nysse*.
    79. *On the Inscriptions of the Psalms* I. vii (PG 44, 460B–C).

God's Infinity and Man's Mutability

> In mutable nature nothing can be observed which is always the same . . . We are in some manner our own parents, giving birth to ourselves by our own free choice according to whatever we wish to be.[80]

It was noted above that man's advancement in relation to the divine infinity was limited by his capacity. "According to capacity," however, is not a fixed limitation. Human mutability means that there is a growth in capacity to apprehend virtue.

> The All-creating Wisdom fashioned these souls, these receptacles with free wills, as vessels as it were, for this very purpose, that there should be some capacities able to receive his blessings and become continually larger with the inpouring of the stream. Such are the wonders that the participation in the Divine blessings works: it makes him into whom they come larger and more capacious.[81]

With each blessing God dilates the capacity to receive other blessings. "Activity directed toward virtue causes its capacity to grow through exertion."[82] The recipient remains filled with what he has attained, and in contrast to the cycle of filling and emptying the capacity is enlarged. This observation is already an infringement on the final phase of this study.

NATURE OF THE SPIRITUAL LIFE

Gregory's doctrine is not solely grounded in theology. He seems also to speak out of his own experience. Certainly his writings contain much profound insight into the nature of spirituality and express truths which have been verified in the experience of other practitioners of the spiritual life. The theme of perpetual progress is particularly true to the nature of religious experience.

One area where this is the case pertains to the unlimited enjoyment of spiritual things. The spirit, unlike the flesh, does not know satiety in its enjoyment of spiritual things. The filling up and emptying of bodily appetites considered above is contrasted by Gregory with the satisfaction and growth of spiritual desires.

---

80. *Vita Moysis* II, 3; PG 44, 328B. Cf. *On Ecclesiastes* 6 (PG 44, 704A); *Catechetical Oration* 39.
81. *On the Soul and the Resurrection* PG 46, 105A–C (NPNF V, 453).
82. *Vita Moysis* II, 226; PG 44, 401B.

> Satiety stops the greed of the glutton, and the drinker's pleasure is quenched at the same time as his thirst. And so it is with the other things. They all require a certain interval of time to rekindle the desire for the delights which enjoyment carried to satiety has caused to flag. The possession of virtue, on the other hand, where it is once firmly established, is neither circumscribed by time nor limited by satiety. On the contrary, it always offers its disciples the ever-fresh experience of the fullness of its own delights. . . . The desire of virtue is followed by the possession of what is desired; and the interior goodness brings at the same time unceasing joy to the soul. For such is the nature of this wonderful thing that it not only delights at the moment while one is enjoying it, but brings actual happiness at every instant of time.[83]

This idea of continual enjoyment offers a different explanation from the one treated above where Gregory spoke of the capacity for enjoyment being enlarged, but the two ideas seem to be merged in a related passage:

> The pleasure of drinking ceases with satiety, and likewise with eating an abundance extinguishes the appetite. If there is any other desire, it withers in the same manner at the participation in what is desired, and if it should come again, it is quenched again . . . But I sought that good which to every age and time of life is equally good, whose satiety is not desired and whose surfeit is not found. Rather the appetite is extended with the participation, and the desire flourishes with the enjoyment and is not circumscribed by the attainment of what is desired. By as much as desire revels in the good, by as much more is it kindled for the pleasure. And the pleasure is stretched out with the desire and becomes always good according to the extension of time to those who participate in it.[84]

Thus Gregory can declare that there is no satiety in love for the Beautiful.[85] And he extols "the enjoyment which does not cut off the desire by satiety, but rather nourishes the longing through the participation in the things desired."[86]

---

83. *The Beatitudes* 4 (PG 44, 1244D–1245A). English translation by Hilda C. Graef in Ancient Christian Writers 18 (Westminster, MD, 1954) 127.

84. *On Ecclesiastes* 2 (PG 44, 648D–649A).

85. *On the Soul and the Resurrection* PG 46, 96C–97A.

86. *Comm. on Cant.* PG 44, 1084C-D.

God's Infinity and Man's Mutability

Closely related to the above point is the experience of an ever increasing desire for God.

> The soul that looks up towards God, and conceives that good desire for His eternal beauty, constantly experiences an ever new yearning for that which lies ahead, and here desire is never given its full satisfaction.[87]

"For any enjoyment of Him only increases our desire for a greater share in His goodness."[88] The bride's "desire grows as she goes on to each new stage of development."[89] Participation renders the desire more intense, and the growth of the desire is in proportion to the participation.[90] The desire is never satisfied, because the object is infinite. Nor is it good for the spiritual nature of man for the desire to be satisfied. Moses desired to see God, not "according to his capacity" (see above), but according to God's true being, but God would not grant any request that brought to an end man's longing for Him.[91]

This never satisfied desire might seem to introduce a problem of despair into the spiritual life. Is it not a disappointment never to attain the goal, to be always "on the way"? Here is the paradox, but one faithful to spiritual experience. Every attainment is a real attainment, and one has the sense of accomplishment or fulfillment; yet there is no stopping. There is both satisfaction and expanding desire. When Moses asked to see God "face to face," Gregory first explains that his petition was (in a sense) granted and yet Moses was led to despair by being told that what he requested was impossible to human life.[92] More boldly, Gregory later resolves the paradox of satisfaction and desire in another paradox: "The divine voice granted what was requested in what was denied."[93] Moses was permitted to see (the "back parts" of) God but was not promised any cessation of his desire for God. So there is an attainment. In another way of looking at the problem, the satisfaction consists in going on with the quest.

> In this way the bride is, in a certain sense, wounded and beaten because of the frustration of what she desires, now that she

---

87. Ibid., 1033D–1036A; *From Glory to Glory*, 268. Cf. 1025C–D and 1037B.
88. Ibid., 777B; p. 155.
89. Ibid., 876B; p. 190.
90. Daniélou, *Platonisme*, 295.
91. *Vita Moysis* II, 232–33; PG 44, 404A.
92. Ibid., II, 220; PG 44, 400A.
93. Ibid., II, 232; PG 44, 404A.

thinks that her yearning for the Other cannot be fulfilled or satisfied. But the veil of her grief is removed when she learns that the true satisfaction of her desire consists in constantly going on with her quest and never ceasing in her ascent, seeing that every fulfillment of her desire continually generates a further desire for the Transcendent.[94]

The soul desirous of God always discovers more and more of the Object. Here again it is true to the nature of the spiritual life that there are always new vistas which open up with each new height gained in the advance toward God. What is attained is the beginning point for new discoveries.[95] Every taste of the Lord is an incitement to further enjoyment.

> The fountain of grace constantly draws to itself all those who thirst . . . Here He puts no limit on our thirst, nor on our movement towards Him nor, on the satisfaction of our thirst; but He has created our tendency to thirst, to drink, and to move towards Him by a command that is constant and perpetual. To those who have tasted and seen by experience *that the Lord is sweet* (Ps. 33.9), this taste becomes a kind of invitation to further enjoyment. And thus the one who is rising towards God constantly experiences this continual incitement towards further progress.[96]

Every perfection is the beginning of a greater good.

> And yet the final stage of all a soul's previous attainments becomes the beginning of her introduction to all that still lies beyond . . .
>
> And yet this climax [seeing God] of all she has now attained becomes the beginning of her hope for the things that lie ahead . . .
>
> Rather, the soul that is rising towards transcendent truth in the ways of higher understanding should be so disposed that every stage of perfection that is possible for human nature should be merely the beginning of a yearning for things more sublime.[97]

---

94. *Comm. on Cant.* PG 44, 1037 B–C; *From Glory to Glory*, 270. Cf. 885D–888A.

95. See passages cited at footnotes 4, 5, and 40. *Vita Moysis* II, 226f1; PG 44, 401B–D. Mary Emily Keenan, "*De Professione Christiana* and *De Perfectione*: A Study of the Ascetical Doctrine of Saint Gregory of Nyssa," *Dumbarton Oaks Papers* 5 (1950) 174.

96. *Comm. on Cant.* PG 44, 941D; *From Glory to Glory*, 213. Cf. 1033D–36A. The idea is amply documented in earlier references.

97. Ibid., 889B, D and 892B; *From Glory to Glory*, 199–200.

Gregory sees the greatest obstacle to grace to be a relaxation of effort to make progress.

> To one who stretches himself up to the higher life what has been said provides amply for true wisdom. To him who shows weakness in toiling for virtue there would be no gain even if many more things should be written ... The continual development of life to what is better is the soul's way to perfection.[98]

The need for human effort is constantly stressed.[99] At the same time, God gives us the power.

> We must therefore constantly arouse ourselves and never stop drawing closer and closer in our course. For as often as He says *Arise*, and *Come*, He gives us the power to rise and make progress.[100]

Here we meet Gregory's synergism. To the human effort God opens the path of progress.[101]

CONCLUSION

Virtue is "both the work and the reward of those who have accomplished it."[102] The desire for God is joy, and the seeking is the vision of God. Here is perhaps the ultimate answer to the problem of despair in an ever-expanding system. The final word should be Gregory's. "The finding is the continuous search itself, for the seeking is not one thing and the finding another. But the reward of the search is the seeking itself."[103]

---

98. *Vita Moysis* II, 305f; PG 44, 425A.

99. See *On the Christian Mode of Life* (Jaeger, VIII, 1, pp. 44–45; Callahan, *op. cit.*, 129–30).

100. *Comm. on Cant.* PG 44, 876C; *From Glory to Glory*, 191.

101. On the necessity of free will for perfection cf. ibid. 876D–77A and n. 78.

102. *Beatitudes* 4 (PG 44, 1245C; Graef, *op. cit.*, 128). For virtue as its own reward cf. *Comm. on Cant.* PG 44, 765 B–C.

103. *On Ecclesiastes* 7 (PG 44, 720C).

15

Some Aspects of Gregory of Nyssa's Moral Theology in the Homilies on Ecclesiastes

INTRODUCTION

THE "LIFE OF VIRTUE" (280,1) or "training in the virtues" (333,16) is the theme of Gregory of Nyssa's *Homilies on Ecclesiastes*.[1] The subject of the Being of God and certain aspects of his creation requires a moment of silence (Eccl 3:7), but there is "a moment to speak of the things through which our life increases in virtue" (415,17—416,9; cf. 414,17–19).[2] Thus, of the two parts of religious virtue, the knowledge of God and right conduct,[3] the *Homilies on Ecclesiastes* concentrate on the latter.

Virtue is prominent in a large number of Gregory's writings, including *Vita Moysis*, *In psalmorum inscriptiones*, *De virginitate*, *De professione Christiana*, *De perfectione*, *De instituto Christiana*, and *Vita Macrinae*.[4]

---

1. For the importance of virtue in the *Homilies* see also 288,14; 292,22; 318,1; 333,19; 354,1; 361,10; 362,14; 365,12; 368,22; 373,12; 374,21; 379,21; 380,12; 385,4; 404,7; 407,1; 416,8; 428,3; 436,14–17.

2. Cf. *V. Moys.* II,110 for a similar listing of questions into which human curiosity is not to inquire.

3. *V. Moys.* II,166. See the discussion in Heine, *Perfection*, 115ff.

4. See Konstantinou, *Die Tugendlehre Gregors von Nyssa*, 27–36. I have not seen

The researcher can very nearly reconstruct Gregory's moral theology from the *Homilies on Ecclesiastes*, for they touch on many of Gregory's characteristic emphases; the full significance of these ideas in Gregory's thought, however, must be learned from his other writings. This paper will impose a systematic presentation on Gregory's comments, which emerge from the sequence of the biblical text.

THEOLOGICAL TENETS

Looking to God

As a result of the Eunomian controversy, Gregory continued, even in his moral and spiritual treatises, to emphasize the ultimate unknowability of God. "The divine is beyond knowledge" (411,13). No thoughts or ideas about God, "compared with what is truly worthy of the subject," can be spoken by human beings (293,16—294,5).[5] Nevertheless, there is a "grasp of the transcendent which is gained by analogy" (308,18). This permits an understanding of God as the Good, the source and the goal of virtue.

God as Creator "is the source both of the soul and of the body." Therefore, "anyone trained in the divine mysteries is surely aware that the life conformed to the divine nature is proper and natural to mankind" (284,12–20).

The life of virtue is a life directed toward God. Gregory's last words in the *Homilies on Ecclesiastes* are these:

> What food and drink are to the body, the means by which natural life is preserved, that, for the soul, is to look towards the Good; and that truly is a gift of God, to gaze upon God ... For as the fleshly man, he says, gets strength by eating and drinking, so the one who looks at the good (the true good is he who alone is Good) has the gift of God in all his toil—just this, to look upon the good forever, in Jesus Christ our Lord ... (441,12—442,2)

As in this passage, Gregory elsewhere defines God as the Good.[6] The vision of God (or at least the longing to look upon God) has entered prominently

---

Vollert, *Die Lehre Gregors von Nyssa vom Guten und Bösen*.

5. See the continuation of the passage through 416,10 (referred to above), with which compare *V. Moys.* II,110. For the influence of the Eunomian controversy on Gregory's spiritual theology, see Heine, *Perfection*, chapter 3.

6. *V. Moys.* I,7; II,237; *De an. et res.* (PG 46.93B).

into studies of Gregory's spirituality.[7] The inability to experience a direct vision of God in this life and the limitations on the knowledge of God available to human beings led Gregory to reformulate what it means to see God: "the seeing that consists in not seeing"; "this truly is the vision of God: never to be satisfied in the desire to see him"; "to follow God wherever he might lead is to behold God."[8] With such an understanding, looking toward God provides direction for the virtuous life.

Grounded in Christ

The looking to God occurs "in Christ Jesus our Lord." "Every name and thought of virtue leads back to the Lord of virtues" (436,17), who is himself "perfect virtue" (358,9). "The way back for the wanderer, and the way of escape from evil, and towards good" is the Christ, "who took our weaknesses upon" himself. He "speaks to us from our own condition," and "through these very weaknesses of our nature shows us the way out of the reach of evil" (305,14-19). The Lord's coming in the flesh to dwell among human beings ("the great mystery of salvation") was in order to investigate the condition of life on the earth (299,20—300,3; cf. 301,4-6 quoted below) and bring salvation to mankind (299,18-19). The incarnation was central to Gregory's spiritual theology. It is related to each of the theophany texts in *Vita Moysis*,[9] and that work provides the imagery of Christ as the ground or foundation ("rock") of virtue (II,244). Christ leads his people in the way to God and as Commander of the forces of good gives victory over the Adversary and brings peace with God (435,14—436,14).

---

7. Völker, *Gregor von Nyssa als Mystiker*, 196-218; Lieske, "Die Theologie der Christusmystik Gregors von Nyssa," 60-75; Daniélou, *Platonisme*, 190-99; Daniélou, *L'être et le temps chez Grégoire de Nysse*, 1-17. Cf. the related idea in Merki, ὉΜΟΙΩΣΙΣ ΘΕΩ, esp. 124-64. For an analysis of the three theophany texts in the *V. Moys.* see my "Progress in Perfection," chapter 13 above; cf. Bebis, "Gregory of Nyssa's 'De Vita Moysis,'" esp. 382-92.

8. *V. Moys.* II,163, 239, 252.

9. See my "Progress in Perfection," 312; and Malherbe and Ferguson, *Gregory of Nyssa: The Life of Moses*, 15. Cf. Völker, *Gregor von Nyssa als Mystiker*, 48-57; Lieske, "Die Theologie der Christusmystik Gregors von Nyssa"; Gaïth, *La conception de la liberté*, 148-57.

Free Will

The principal anthropological affirmation of Gregory's moral teaching has to do with free will. As is well known. Gregory was a champion of human freedom, and this was an important foundation of his understanding of virtue.[10] The *Homilies on Ecclesiastes* have a great deal to say about freedom of the will. "What is not within our control [ἐφ' ἡμῖν] cannot be described as either virtue or vice" (379,21). "Free choice [προαίρεσις]," Gregory says, "is wealth" (326,17).

Birth, the very thing over which we might seem to have no control, becomes for Gregory an analogy for the effects of free choice. "For we become in a way our own parents when through good choice we shape ourselves and bear ourselves and bring ourselves forth to the light . . . Again, we miscarry and produce premature births or mere wind, when the shape of Christ . . . has not been formed in us . . . [S]omeone makes himself a child of God through virtue" (380,3-13).[11] The same positive imagery of becoming our own parents through free choice and the negative imagery of a miscarriage or being full of wind occur in connection with free will in *Vita Moysis* (II,1-11).

In protecting the nature of God from the charge of causing evil, Gregory in Homily 2 explains that evil results from the abuse of God's gift of freedom: "The good gift of God, that is free will [αὐτεξούσιον], became a means to sin through the sinful use mankind made of it. For unfettered freedom of the will is good by nature . . . but . . . man through folly used God's good gifts in the service of evil" (301,20-302,8; cf. 302,18-303,2; 438, 14-439,10).[12] The impulses of the soul were created for good, but they can be used for evil. "Though our power of free will is a good, when it is active for evil it becomes the worst of evils" (428,1-2).

Being and Non-Being

Free will is important for Gregory's whole understanding of the structure of reality.

---

10. The most extensive study is Gaïth, *La conception de la liberté*, but see also Heine, *Perfection*, 27-61, 228-40; Konstantinou, *Tugendlehre Gregors von Nyssa*, 81-95. For the modern theological discussion of the relevance of Gregory's thought, see Mühlenberg, "Synergism in Gregory of Nyssa."

11. Cf. another use of the birth analogy in 344,21—345,7.

12. The same strategy is employed in *V. Moys.* II,73ff.; see Malherbe and Ferguson, *Gregory of Nyssa: The Life of Moses*, 167 n. 93.

> So, since evil is regarded as the opposite of good, and absolute virtue is God, evil must be outside God, because its nature is not apprehended in its being something, but in its not being good . . . Thus evil is regarded as the opposite of good, in the same way as non-being is distinguished from being. So, when in the freedom of our impulse we fell away from the good . . . then the unreal nature of evil took substance in those who had fallen away from the good (406,17—407,10).[13]
>
> An evil resting by itself apart from our free choice does not exist (407,14).

These same ideas, including the illustration of those who close their eyes to the light being responsible for their darkness, are found in Gregory's major discussion of free will in connection with the hardening of Pharaoh's heart in *V. Moys.* II,73-8.

For Gregory, "evil has no substance" (300,22), "does not exist" (356,9-10), and "is the deprivation of being" (356,15). Consequently, "the life of the senses" when "compared with the true life is unreal and insubstantial" (284,10-11; cf. 289,21—290,1). One purpose of the incarnation was to investigate "how being became the slave of non-being, how the unreal dominates being" (301,4-6). This view of the substantial unreality of evil and its Neoplatonic background have been often studied.[14] There are numerous parallels in Gregory's other writings.[15] Whereas sin is turning to unreality and non-existence, the life of virtue, on the other hand, not only does the good but also participates in that which really is (see the whole passage 406,1-407,17). "Whatever the thing that is shared in naturally is, what shares in it must conform" (422,14-15).

God as true Being is a "stable reality" (285,10). Always the same, he is unchanging good (313,17-18). This nature of God as absolute Being and absolute Good left the human misuse of free will as the only explanation for evil in the world, but it also provided the basis and the goal for human endeavors in virtue.[16] "Those who cling to what is unstable do not reach out for what stands for ever" (422,8-9).

---

13. Cf. *V. Moys.* 1,5-7.

14. E.g., Cherniss, *The Platonism of Gregory of Nyssa*, 49–53; Balás, ΜΕΤΟΥΣΙΑ ΘΕΟΥ, 108-20; Völker, *Gregor von Nyssa als Mystiker*, 80-91; Heine, *Perfection*, 32-39; Mosshammer, "Non-Being and Evil in Gregory of Nyssa."

15. E.g., *V. Moys.* II,22-25; *In Inscr. Psal.* I,8; *De virg.* 12; *De beat.* 5.

16. Daniélou, *L'être et le temps*, 95-115; cf. Heine, *Perfection*, 57, 60, 78-79, with reference to *V. Moys.* II,243-244.

Continual Progress

One of the most distinctive emphases in Gregory's moral theology is that perfection in virtue is always to be making progress in virtue.[17] Gregory gave his classic exposition of this theme of perpetual progress in *V. Moys.*,[18] but he alludes to it elsewhere, including the *Homilies on Ecclesiastes*. Seeking the Lord is a pursuit of one's entire life: "For it is not at a fixed moment and an appointed time that it is good to seek the Lord, but never to cease from continual search" (401,2–13).

The two metaphysical bases of continual progress are human mutability and divine infinity.[19] The "truly good things" belong to the "one divine and everlasting nature," but sensual things are "naturally subject to flux and transient," "unstable" in contrast to "what stands forever" (422,3–9). These truly good things can be summed up as "one good thing, the perpetual joy in good things, and that is the child of good deeds" (441,5–6).

Because of the infinite extension of the uncreated Good and the nature of created beings always to be changing, there is no satiety in the enjoyment of spiritual goods.[20] Using Epicurean observations about the kinetic pleasures of food and drink, Gregory describes the cycle of satisfaction and return of appetite in sensual things. In contrast, there is no satiety expected nor fullness found in the search for the true Good (313,8–11). "Appetite for it and partaking of it are exactly matched, and longing flourishes together with enjoyment, and is not limited by the attainment of what is desired; the more it delights in the Good, the more it flames up with delight; the delight matches the desire" (313,11–15). The work of faith lasts "in full strength continuously throughout life" (314,8).

---

17. See my "Progress in Perfection," chapter 13 above; Heine, *Perfection*, 58–59, 63–71, 97–107; and literature cited in these works, esp. Daniélou, *Platonisme*, 291–307.

18. Especially I,5–10 and II,225–55. For other references see the notes in Malherbe and Ferguson, *Gregory of Nyssa: The Life of Moses*.

19. See Ferguson, God's Infinity and Man's Mutability," chapter 14 above. On the divine infinity see Hennessy, The Background, Sources, and Meaning of Divine Infinity in St. Gregory of Nyssa," 273–84; Mühlenberg, *Die Unendlichkeit Gottes bei Gregor von Nyssa*, 147–65. For Gregory's philosophy of change, see Daniélou, *L'être et le temps*, 95–115.

20. Cf. *V. Moys.* II,232, 235, 239 and Heine, *Perfection*, 42, 76–78; also Daniélou, "La colombe et la ténèbre," 400–418.

PSYCHOLOGICAL PERSPECTIVES

Gregory's rejection of satiety already involves a consideration of the psychological perspectives from which he views the life of virtue. These in turn involve some related practical points for attaining that life.

Soul and Body

Although Ecclesiastes does not offer Gregory opportunity to develop his anthropology,[21] he does define human nature as twofold. The more familiar way of expressing this dichotomy is to pair soul and body (cf. 403,5–6 for higher and lower). The soul is impassible and immortal, but the body is mortal and temporal (284,1–11). The Creator is the source of both, but the person "trained in the divine mysteries" has "escaped from the flesh" and "glimpsed the higher life" (284,13–19). There is a twofold manner of life corresponding to the twofold nature of human beings as soul and body (389,8–10).

Rational and Sensory

In the Homilies on Ecclesiastes the dichotomy of human nature is also commonly described in terms of its rational and sensory aspects. "Our nature is a double one, a combination of mind [νοητῷ] and sense [αἰσθητῷ]" (419,9), and Gregory makes much of the need for the latter (the flesh) to be submissive to the former (the intellectual) (311,20—312,1). The purpose of Ecclesiastes was "to raise the mind above sensation" (280,2–3). Gregory expresses the goal that "intelligible things [νοητῶν] might overcome the inclinations of the flesh, so that our nature might not be at war with itself, with the mind choosing some things and the body pulling it towards others, but instead might make the pride of our flesh submissive and obedient to the rational [νοητῷ] part of the soul" (311,17—312,1). Even in the first passage noted in the preceding paragraph Gregory shifts to speaking of "the life of sense-perception" that should be guided by "knowledge" (284,21—285,1). This manner of speaking does not mean that there is a

---

21. For Gregory's anthropology, in addition to Gaïth and Merki, see A. H. Armstrong, "Platonic Elements in St. Gregory of Nyssa's Doctrine of Man," *DomSt* 1 (1948) 113–26; Ladner, "The Philosophical Anthropology of Saint Gregory of Nyssa," 59–64; and Cavarnos, *St. Gregory of Nyssa on the Origin and Destiny of the Soul*.

simple equation of mind with soul and senses with body, but the senses are the point of contact between the rational part of the soul and the body.[22]

Gregory emphasizes the need for the rational faculties to control the non-rational part of human nature. He does not regard the impulses or desires as evil in themselves, but inasmuch as they are the means through which temptation and sin enter human life, they frequently have a negative connotation for him (as in "the evil array of the passions [παθημάτων]," 383,20–21).[23] He states:

> Every impulse [κίνησις] of the soul was framed for good by the One who created our nature, but the mistaken use of such impulses produces the drives [ἀφορμάς] towards evil . . . Conversely, the power to reject unpleasant things, whose name is hate, is an instrument of virtue when it is deployed against the enemy, but becomes a weapon of sin when it is opposed to the good. (427,15—428,6; cf. 303,7–11)

Control of Pleasures

Gregory gives many warnings against the pursuit of pleasure. Although there is a disposition toward the good in the soul (371,20–21), "the things pursued by humans for the sake of bodily pleasure are pursuit of error and distraction of a soul dragged down from the things above to the things below." Such things are a damage to rational thought (λογισμοῖς) (372,3–6).[24] Gregory interprets Eccles. 2:2 as meaning "I set my face against pleasure, being suspicious of its approach" (311,2–4). He proceeds to compare pleasure to a wild animal (311,7), a common comparison with him.[25] In particular, because of the biblical connotations, the passion of pleasure is identified with a serpent (348,15). Hence, he gives the advice to kill the head first,[26] that is to prevent evil from entering in the first place, because

---

22. The components of the soul are described in more Platonic, and more colorful, terms in *V. Moys.* 11,96–97.122–23, on which see Heine, *Perfection*, 221–27.

23. For the πάθη in Gregory, see Völker, *Gregor von Nyssa als Mystiker*, 87–90, 117–22; Merki, ὈΜΟΙΩΣΙΣ ΘΕΩ, 93–100; Daniélou, "La colombe et la ténèbre," 390–95.

24. Such warnings are, of course, common in Gregory's moral writings. Cf. *V. Moys.* II,60–61, 122, 271, 297–304.

25. Cf. *V. Moys.* 276–277, and Malherbe and Ferguson, *Gregory of Nyssa: The Life of Moses*, 191 n. 390; *De prof. chr.* (GNO VIII, 1, 137,17ff.). See Daniélou, *Platonisme*, 74–80.

26. The same imagery and advice in *V. Moys.* II,90, 94; cf. *In natalem Christi* (PG

"the one who has let in the beginning of passion has admitted the whole beast into himself" (349,11—350,10).

Gregory advocates limiting physical needs. "If any one, yearning for greater possessions, and letting his desire become as boundless as a sea, has an insatiable greed for the streams of gain flowing in from every side, let him treat his disease by looking at the real sea," which "does not exceed its boundary but remains at the same volume" (289,3-10). "Enjoyment cannot exceed the amount fixed by nature" (289,16). Whereas spiritual matters bring continuous enjoyment without satiety, "there is no bodily activity which can give lasting pleasure" (312,22).[27] Therefore, Gregory's advice is for moderation: "As long as he lives in the flesh he will care for the physical nature of his own body just enough to prevent its being deprived of anything" (326,18-20).[28]

Inducements to Correction

There is implanted in our nature by God "a great and powerful weapon for avoiding sin" (315,13-14), the sense of modesty [αἰδώς] and of shame [αἰσχύνη]. These two emotions, Gregory says, are closely related, but "shame is modesty intensified, and modesty . . . is shame moderated" (316,3-4). Modesty is often better than fear in turning a person away from sin; and shame, the stronger emotion, "which follows criticisms of a fault is enough by itself to correct the sinner" (315,22-316,1).

Confession of sin (ἐξομολόγησις),[29] defined as "public acknowledgment" (ἐξαγόρευσις), produces the emotion of shame (315,11-12). The public acknowledgment of wrongdoing, then is a means of correction (317, 1-4), because of the sense of shame inherent in our nature. "The person who has branded himself by confessing his secret sins will be given lessons by the memory of his feeling of shame for the rest of his life" (317,10-12). The text of Ecclesiastes contains Solomon's confession of his sins (328,23—329,1).

46.1133A).

27. See discussion of satiety above. Cf. *De beat.* 4 (ACW 18, 126).

28. Cf. Gaïth, *La conception de la liberté*, 157-68, for "Liberation by Ascesis" in Gregory.

29. For penance and exomologesis in Gregory, see Völker, *Gregor von Nyssa als Mystiker*, 106-9, who gives other references but not *In Ecclesiasten*.

Some Aspects of Gregory of Nyssa's Moral Theology

MEANS OF MORAL PROGRESS

Having surveyed Gregory's remarks relevant to the theological and psychological bases for the life of virtue, we may proceed to note some of his observations about some of the means for carrying out the continuous progress toward virtue.

Necessity for Effort

As an ascetic himself and a spiritual guide for other ascetics. Gregory placed considerable emphasis on human effort in the moral life.[30] "Effort and diligence" are necessary in order to learn wisdom and knowledge (308,9–16; cf. 307,24—308,1), so pain is involved in the pursuit of learning (309,16) (as students of Gregory can attest). Gregory was keenly conscious of the labor involved in giving a morally edifying interpretation of Ecclesiastes (277,3; 278,5–17; 373,2–3). Similarly "all words are laborious" (Eccl 1:8), because "those who instruct in virtue first achieve within themselves the things which they teach" (292,222–223). One must make an effort to live virtuously (362,15).

Help from Angels

To those who make the effort in the life of virtue, divine assistance is provided. "The array of angels of the host of heaven" make up an army under Christ, the heavenly Commander. Gregory exhorts the human warrior to join forces with the angels in the fight against the Adversary. With the angels as allies true peace is achieved (435,1—436,10). The *Vita Moysis* II,45–53 offers a fuller exposition of the angels as helpers in the fight against the forces of evil.

Scripture Heals

Scripture is part of the divine assistance offered as a means for moral improvement.[31] The very exposition of Ecclesiastes, as is true for all of Gregory's exegetically based works, indicates a belief that instruction in attaining

---

30. E.g., *V. Moys.* II,226, 305; *De oratione dominica* 2; and the whole of *De instituto Christiano*.

31. Cf. Völker, *Gregor von Nyssa als Mystiker*, 111, 156–62, on Scripture in Gregory's spirituality.

virtue is to be found in the Scriptures. Gregory was concerned about the meaning of the titles of the biblical books, the aim of each book, and the book's service to the church (279,4–20). Moreover, there are express statements of the healing power conveyed through the Scripture writer. The Ecclesiast "heals our life through his account of his own" (319,11–12).[32] More explicit is the statement that one may learn how to "live virtuously by obtaining from the text [λόγου] some art and method, so to speak, of successful living" (373,12–13). The Word directs our life to "what is right" (374,13–14). Not expressly referring to Scriptures but probably including them is the reference to "the heavenly spring, from which the virtues of the soul germinate and are watered, so that the grove of good desires may flourish in our souls" (333,19—334,2).

Gregory often comments on the sequence or order of the words and events in the Scriptures.[33] He could even find a lesson in the order of the books in the canon, finding in Genesis and Exodus a connection between birth and death (378,18–23). Although Gregory finds significance in the order in which the account proceeds (307,4–8), his references to sequence in the *Homilies* do not always attribute a spiritual meaning to it (307,17–18).

Examples

Gregory found the examples provided by biblical persons to be demonstrations of his spiritual theology and to be an instruction and encouragement to contemporary aspirants of the virtuous life.[34] In other writings he takes as examples Abraham,[35] Paul,[36] and especially Moses.[37] The *Homilies on Ecclesiastes* offer Solomon as an example. Gregory's method of interpretation permits him to take the "Ecclesiast" sometimes as Christ (as in 280,8–13; 298,5–13)[38] and sometimes as Solomon, the putative author of

---

32. Admittedly "account" is supplied by the translator, but it is a legitimate inference.

33. Cf. *V. Moys.* II,136, 148; Daniélou, "*Akolouthia* chez Grégoire de Nysse."

34. The use of personal examples was a common device in the Hellenistic moral literature. Malherbe, *Moral Exhortation*, 135–38, and see the index.

35. *Contra Eunomium* 2.85–92 (GNO 1,251,15–254,20); *V. Moys.* I,11–14.

36. *De perfectione* (174,24—175,13).

37. *V. Moys.* I,15; II,319.

38. The section continues to list other names or titles of Christ in addition to "the Ecclesiast." This was a favorite exercise by Gregory: the treatise *De perfectione* is built around the names of Christ; cf. *V. Moys.* II,177; Malherbe and Ferguson, *Gregory of*

Ecclesiastes (305,20). Since "we do not learn everything from our own experience" (306,3–4), we learn from the experience of others. Solomon's experiences with the different forms of pleasure provide the basis for the lessons presented subsequently, especially *Homilies* 2–4.

It is not only persons who provide examples in Gregory's teachings. The earth itself furnishes a lesson in steadfastness. "As for those to whom a life directed towards virtue seems burdensome, let their soul be trained by the example of the earth so as to persevere under hardship" (288,13–15). The occasion for this surprising conclusion is the text of Ecclesiastes 1:4, "The earth stands to eternity," an unchanging state which Gregory understands as tedious.

VICES AND VIRTUES

The Goal of Life

The Hellenistic philosophical schools were differentiated not so much by the specific moral advice they gave as by how they defined the goal or purpose of life. Gregory gives a characteristically Christian statement of the goal.[39] The goal (σκοπός) of the church is "godliness" (εὐσέβεια) (279,19). On this basis, virtue is "to turn one's soul to nothing here on earth, but to have one's effort directed toward what through faith lies in our hopes before us" (379,11–13; cf. 354,21–22). The goal or purpose of life excludes the vices and gives unity to the individual virtues.

Virtue as the Mean

Gregory sometimes defined virtue in Aristotelian terms as the mean between extremes. His wording in the *Homilies on Ecclesiastes* is "the middle point between contrasting things" (375,4–5). The same description employed in this passage, in terms of deficiency or excess, and the same illustration of cowardice and rashness as the extremes in relation to courage, taken from Aristotle, occur in *V. Moys.* II,288.[40]

Nyssa: *The Life of Moses*, 180 n. 223.

39. Merki, ΌΜΟΙΩΣΙΣ ΘΕΩ, 108–10, and Konstantinou, *Tugendlehre Gregors von Nyssa*, 182, define the goal for Gregory as to become like God in the state of blessedness. Gregory had various ways of formulating the goal: in *V. Moys.* II,317 the goal (τέλος) is to be "called a servant of God."

40. See Malherbe and Ferguson, *Gregory of Nyssa: The Life of Moses*, 92 n. 403;

Use of Lists and Opposites

A favorite device of Hellenistic moralists was to compile lists of vices and virtues.[41] Gregory continued this tradition. A long list of vices occurs in describing the evil results of an immoderate use of wine: "licentiousness, self-indulgence, injury to youth, deformity to age, dishonour for women, . . . death to the understanding, estrangement from virtue" (328, 19—329,2).[42] There continues a list of other effects of wine. A list of virtues occurs in describing the qualities that a person who gathers riches will not acquire (340,10-12).

The *Homilies on Ecclesiates* show a fondness for arranging lists of opposites.[43] For instance, the list of miseries in the natural world: "pitiable childhood, dementia in age, unsettled youth, the constant toil of adult life, burdensome marriage, lonely celibacy, the troublesome multitude of children, sterile childlessness, miserliness over wealth, the anguish of poverty" (387,8-13). A contrast of virtues and vices occurs at 427,6-8: "Restraint and pleasure, self-control and indulgence, humility and pride, goodwill and perversity, and all the things which are regarded as the opposite of one another" (cf. 402,19-21). Opposites are also used by Gregory in his definitions of words (as 371,3-4) and concepts (355,3-5).

Illustrations

As with any preacher who seeks to communicate with his hearers, Gregory made rich use of illustrations in order to make his points about the moral life. Even in the *Homilies on Ecclesiastes* the illustrations would be a study in themselves.[44] Gregory draws lessons from athletics (278,5),[45] carpentry (303,14—304,6), pearl divers (318,10-14), irrigation (319,21—320,4), agriculture (331,1-10; 375,19—376,5; 382,3-9), and shyster lawyers (358,20—359,1).

Konstantinou, *Tugendlehre Gregors von Nyssa*, 48–52, 112–18.

41. Malherbe, *Moral Exhortation*, 32, 37, 39, 42, 45–46, 73, 130, 136, 138–41, 159.
42. Cf. the list of vices in *V. Moys.* II,25.
43. Cf. *V. Moys.* II,14.
44. Coggin, *The Times of Saint Gregory of Nyssa*, draws on the illustrations used in the named works.
45. Cf. *V. Moys.* II,36. For athletic imagery in the Hellenistic moralists, see Malherbe, index.

In view of the language of warfare about the struggle between good and evil, the military imagery is fully developed (428,19—433,7). The text of Eccl 2:4 gives occasion for the most elaborately developed illustration in the *Homilies*, the adornment of a house (324,3—326,18).[46] Each part of the house is identified with a virtue, providing one of the longer listings of virtues in the *Homilies*. By far, the most popular discipline drawn on as a source for illustration in the *Homilies* is medicine,[47] a favorite with the Hellenistic moralists and a subject with which Gregory had considerable familiarity.[48]

Particular Sins

Out of the many sins referred to in the Homilies on Ecclesiastes certain ones come in for special treatment. In different works Gregory concentrates on different sins, as he singled out envy for special treatment in *V. Moys.* II,256-263. In the *Homilies* at least three subjects get this distinction. Special interest attaches to the subject of slavery (334,4—338,22).[49] Drunkenness comes in for full treatment (327,21—330,11; cf. 347,16ff.). Note may be made too of Gregory's condemnation of usury (343,10—346,14). Furthermore, Gregory designates the love of money, citing 1 Tim 6:10, as the greatest of [Solomon's] sins" (338,23—339,2; cf. 433,1-3).[50]

Faith and Works

The importance of the incarnation as the divine means of bringing salvation to humanity was noted above. This "Gospel must be proclaimed *in the whole world* (Matt 26:13), *every tongue* must confess that *Jesus Christ is Lord, to the glory of God the Father* (Phil 2:11)" (382,12-15). The church is established through the gospel message (280,19-20). The gospel must be received in faith: "There is the same moment for both receiving the saving

---

46. The adornment of a house is not one of the more common illustrations in the resources of rhetoricians, but see the briefer use in *V. Moys.* II,71.

47. 317,5-9; 319,6-10; 346,17-347,1; 354,13-16; 376,7-9; 384,3-15.

48. See the index in Malherbe, *Moral Exhortation*; and Malherbe, "Medical Imagery in the Pastoral Epistles"; Coggin, *The Times of Saint Gregory of Nyssa*, 22-25, 137-44. In the *V. Moys.* medical illustrations occur at I,87, 272, 278.

49. See Bergadà, "La Condemnation de l'Esclavage dans l'Homilie IV," 193-204.

50. Money was treated by the Hellenistic moralists too as the root of all evil; see Malherbe, *Moral Exhortation*, 109.

plant of faith and pulling up the weeds of unbelief" (382,21—383,2). "The one who comes forward in faith finds purification by baptism" (404,21–22).[51]

"The escape from evil is the beginning of the virtuous life" (354,1). The divine initiative did not free human beings from responsibility. "If you shape your soul in every respect with good characteristics, if you free yourself from the defilements of evil, if you wash away from your nature all stain of the filth of matter, what will you become as you beautify yourself in such ways? What loveliness will you put on?" (295,9–13). For every sin there is a corresponding virtue that must be put in its place. Faith replaces unbelief; justice, what is unjust; humility, pride; and love, hatred (cf. 383,2–12; 399,9–20).

Gregory links faith and works (or righteous deeds) inseparably together: "Faith without the works of justice is not enough to save one from death, nor again is the justice of one's life a guarantee of salvation if it is on its own, divorced from faith" (434,3–8; cf. "work of faith," 314,6).[52]

Love

The one virtue receiving the fullest treatment in the *Homilies on Ecclesiastes* is love, the subject of the first half of the eighth homily. Gregory sets the discussion of love in the context of the contrast between loving and hating. Love and hate are related to an "inner disposition" (ἐνδιάθετος σχέσις) of the soul, which must be trained to discriminate between good and evil (417,13; 418,6–8). "The mistaken disposition of the soul towards bad things," however, is not really love (421,5–6). Love has a transforming effect: "The one who loves the good will also be good himself, as the goodness which comes to be in him changes the one who receives it into itself" (423,2–4). Hence, love is truly the sum of virtue, being directed toward that which is truly Good, namely God. "What truly exists is the one and only intrinsically Lovable," whom scripture commands to love "with all your heart"; "and again the only thing to be hated in truth is the Inventor of evil, the Enemy of your life" (425,4–10).

---

51. See Gregory's sermon *In baptismum Christi*; *V. Moys.* II, 124–129, 185, 277.
52. On justice, or righteousness, cf. *De beatitudinibus* 4 (ACW 18, 118–20).

CONCLUSION

At the beginning and end of his *Vita Moysis* Gregory defined perfection as always going on towards perfection (I,10; II,306). His closing words spoke of the goal of the virtuous life and motives for it:

> This is true perfection: not to avoid a wicked life because like slaves we servilely fear punishment, nor to do good because we hope for rewards ... On the contrary, ... we regard falling from God's friendship as the only thing dreadful and we consider becoming God's friend the only thing worthy of honor and desire. This, as I have said, is the perfection of life. (II,320)

In a similar vein, his *Homilies on Ecclesiastes* declared, "It is not one thing to seek, and another to find, but the reward of seeking is the actual seeking" (400,21—401,2).[53]

---

53. Cf. *V. Moys.* II,239; *De beatitudinibus* 4 (ACW 18, 128); *In Canticum* 12 (GNO VI,369,24–370,3).

16

Some Aspects of Gregory of Nyssa's Interpretation of Scripture
Exemplified in his *Homilies on Ecclesiastes*

GREGORY OF NYSSA'S PROLOGUE to his *Commentary on the Song of Songs* offers a theoretical justification for allegorical interpretation.¹ His actual practice in the *Homilies on Ecclesiastes* reflects some of these basic principles but also shows the more practical methods he employed in interpretation.²

One of Gregory's fundamental principles is that the interpretation of Scripture must be consistent with Christian doctrine. Hence, the words of Ecclesiastes 1.2, "All things are vanity," must not be taken as an indictment of creation (283,18–21).³ Gregory is especially concerned to protect the

---

1. Alexandre, "La théorie de l'exégèse dans le de Hominis Opificio et l'In Hexaemeron," 103–4, lists the pointers to an allegorical meaning as (1) theological impropriety, (2) physical or logical impossibility, (3) uselessness, and (4) immorality of the letter. Heine, "Gregory of Nyssa's Apology for Allegory," shows Gregory's indebtedness to Origen for the Pauline texts used in justification for allegory.

2. The Seventh International Colloquium on Gregory of Nyssa, devoted to his Homilies on Ecclesiastes, held at St. Andrews, 5–10 September 1990, under the direction of Stuart G. Hall provided the incentive for this study. My quotations from the *Homilies* are based on the translation prepared for that conference by Stuart G. Hall and Rachel Moriarty, now published in Hall, ed., *Gregory of Nyssa Homilies on Ecclesiastes*.

3. References are to the page and lines of the edition by P. Alexander in *Gregorii Nysseni Opera*, vol. 5 (Leiden, 1962).

nature of God. Evils cannot be the responsibility of God but must, therefore, be due to the wrongful exercise of free will (301,3—303,11).[4] Every interpretation must be worthy of God (395,16-17).[5]

As an extension of the regulative role of doctrine, Gregory gives a specifically Christian interpretation to the text. Revelation comes through Christ, and it is Christ who speaks in the book of Ecclesiastes. For example, the "true Ecclesiast . . . who assembles into one congregation those who have been led astray" is Christ (280,8-13; cf. 298,5-13).[6] This meaning is "not unreasonable," he says (280,15-16), but, of course, only from the Christian perspective. Furthermore, specifically Christological interpretations are to be found: "For Christ is perfect virtue" (358,9, as summing up the interpretation in the context).

This Christian reading of the text has as its corollary that the text speaks directly to Gregory's listeners. "The Ecclesiast speaks to us," Christians (299,5).[7] Gregory moves smoothly back and forth from Christ speaking (298,5-13) to Solomon speaking (306,11-13). The church is instructed through the reading of what is written in Ecclesiastes by Solomon (317,13-19). Gregory was not the last to expand the text of Scripture according to the practices of his own day, as when he describes Solomon's building of houses (Eccl 2:4) according to the expensive buildings of his own day (320,13—324,2).

Another important regulative principle for Gregory was that the interpretation serve "the goal of Godliness" (279,19). "Now the teaching of this book looks exclusively to the conduct of the church and gives instruction in those things by which one would achieve the life of virtue" (279,20—280,2). This statement may be taken as the theme of the *Homilies on Ecclesiastes*, and much of Gregory's work is concerned with excellence in the moral life.[8] The words of the text of Ecclesiastes are the occasion for

---

4. For Gregory's teaching on free will see Gaïth, *La conception de la liberté*; Heine, *Perfection*, 27-61, 228-40; and the collection of references in Malherbe and Ferguson, *Gregory of Nyssa: The Life of Moses*, 16-17. The same concern to protect the nature of God is evident in the treatment of the same passage in Gregory's predecessor and namesake, Gregory Thaumaturgus, *Metaph. Eccl.* 1.13.

5. A literal meaning unworthy of God is one of the important indicators of an allegorical meaning for Gregory; see n. 1 and cf. Malherbe and Ferguson, *Gregory of Nyssa: The Life of Moses*, 8.

6. Contrast Gregory Thaumaturgus, *Metaph. Eccl.*, where it is always Solomon and never Christ who speaks in the book; see Jarwick, *Gregory Thaumaturgos' Paraphrase of Ecclesiastes*, 314-16.

7. Ibid., 8 and 314 for the same being true in Gregory Thaumaturgus' *Metaph. Eccl.*

8. My paper for the St. Andrews Colloquium dealt with "Some Aspects of Gregory

moral lessons: on slavery (Eccl 2:7—334,4—338,22), on the use of money (Eccl 2:8—338,23—343,9), against usury (Eccl 2:8—343,10—346,14), and against drunkenness (Eccl 2:8—346,15—348,14). Gregory expands on the literal meaning of Eccl 1:8, "All words are laborious," in order to get a spiritual point: speaking words is easy, but words spoken for spiritual benefit require effort (291,15—293,1). Even the illustrations that Gregory takes from nature are applied to the life of virtue (288,13-17).

Gregory repeatedly interprets the text according to spiritual matters, not the earthly things of which it speaks, as on Eccl 3:5-7 (390,1—400,9), in the discussion of which he expressly says that a text in the Psalms speaks "figuratively" or "symbolically" (398,16).[9] The purpose of moral instruction encounters difficulties in the text of Ecclesiastes, for, as Gregory acknowledges, the author speaks "of things which nobody who was aiming at virtue would willingly be associated with" (317,22—318,1). In explanation Gregory suggests that what is written about in Ecclesiastes need not have happened literally.

> Whether it is by benevolent design that he discusses things which had not happened as if they had, and condemns them as though he had experienced them, in order that we might turn away from desire for what is condemned before the experience, or whether he deliberately lowered himself to the enjoyment of such things, so as to train his senses rigorously by using alien things, is for anyone who wishes to decide freely, according to the speculation he wants to make. (318,1-8)[10]

To sum up thus far, consistency with Christian doctrine (especially what is worthy of God), revelation through Christ, applicability to the people of his day, and the goal of Godliness provide the guiding principles of Gregory's interpretation. These principles of doctrine (theology, Christology, and ecclesiology) and virtue (moral and spiritual benefit) were applied by specific methods of exegesis, to which we now turn.

Gregory proceeds in his interpretation by logical analysis. A prime example is his treatment of Eccl 3:1 ("there is a time for every activity under the heaven"), which connects the theme of the virtuous life with

---

of Nyssa's Moral Theology in the Homilies on Ecclesiastes," chapter 15 above. For Gregory's teachings on virtue, see Konstantinou, *Die Tugendlehre Gregors von Nyssa*.

9. *Di' ainigmatos*. Hall and Moriarty translate "allegorically."

10. Gregory Thaumaturgus' treatment of the passage (Eccl 2.3-6) avoids the suggestion that Solomon actually engaged in drunkenness—Jarick, *Gregory Thaumaturgos' Paraphrase of Ecclesiastes*, 28-29.

the principal programmatic statement on interpretation to be found in these *Homilies*. According to his definition elsewhere that the life of virtue has two parts, "that which pertains to the Divine and that which pertains to right conduct,"[11] so here Gregory proposes that interpretation must be twofold, both theoretical and practical. There is "much philosophy in the words [of the text], both theoretical and providing practical advice about duty" (373,17–19). In his analysis of "the things that are, one part is material and sensory, and one part intellectual and immaterial." Since the material things obscure the heavenly things, Ecclesiastes deals with "things on earth and under heaven, so that we may go through life on earth without stumbling" (373,21—374,8). Hence, the main theme in these *Homilies*, as indicated above, is not the theoretical but the practical side of virtue, right conduct: "It is made clear to us by the Word how our life is directed to what is right" (374,13–14).

The use of logic occurs in many places in less studied ways. Gregory seeks a logical explanation for why the text speaks as it does. Thus on Eccl 2:2 he describes the characteristics of laughter that could properly be called madness (310,6—311,2). He also appeals to what "everybody knows" (393,20) to support an interpretation. He undertakes a "word-by-word interpretation systematically, following the sequence of the words" (307,17–18), but, unlike some of his other works, he gives no special significance to the sequence in the *Homilies*.[12]

Gregory frequently interprets Ecclesiastes by other Scriptures. Interpreting Scripture by the Scriptures is, of course, a long-standing technique. Gregory at one place can declare, "these ideas cannot possibly become clear to us unless the passage has first been interpreted through the Scripture" (397,19–20 on Eccl 3:5). He explains Eccl 1:13, "God gave evil distress to men," by appealing to other similar statements in scripture where God is said to cause what he gives the capacity or free will to do (301,3—303,2). Gregory often introduces parallel phrases or expressions from elsewhere in the Bible to interpret a passage.[13] In interpreting the common phrase in Ecclesiastes "vanity of vanities," he refers to analogous expressions, such as "holy of holies," which were the scriptural way of showing intensification or speaking of extremes (282,10—283,17 on Eccl 1:2).

---

11. *Vita Moysis* II, 166; see Heine, *Perfection*, 115–27 for Gregory's "stress on virtue involving both right thinking about God and right living."

12. Daniélou, "*Akolouthia* chez Grégoire de Nysse."

13. E.g., 381,19—382,11 on Eccl 3:2; 388,17—389,4 on Eccl 3:4.

Overlapping this use of other passages to explain ideas and phrases is the definition of a word by its occurrences elsewhere in Scripture. The word "want" (ὑστέρημα, lack or deficiency) in Eccl 1:15 is defined by its occurrence in several New Testament passages (304,6-23). Similarly, what it means to seek (Eccl 3:6) is explained by the usage of the word in other Old Testament texts (400,10-21).

Gregory gives considerable attention to the meaning of words. The crucial word "vanity" (ματαιότης)[14] is examined in its various meanings in ordinary speech: what is insubstantial, what is done to no purpose, or what turns out to be useless (281,3—282,9). He, furthermore, explores the meaning of words by considering their opposites, invoking the principle that "The definition of things pursued becomes more exact when they are compared with their opposites" (355,1-3). In exemplification of this approach, he says, "What is understood by goodness is clear from its opposite" (371,4-5). The longest exploration of the meaning of a text based on definitions examines loving and hating in Eccl 3:8 (417,10—428,21).

As a preacher, Gregory makes rich use of illustrations. "As the chorus looks to its conductor, the rowers to the helmsman, and an army in line to its general, so we who belong to the church look to the leader of the church" (299,6-9). He appeals to the example of Jesus, who taught his "message about the kingdom with visual images, speaking about a pearl, or treasure, or a wedding, or a seed, or yeast" (309,2-5). Gregory draws illustrations from the sun, the sea, and the earth to describe human life (286,1—289,18). More often he draws his illustrations from contemporary activities. These may be introduced as direct analogies to the Biblical text: As the carpenter works to make his materials straight, so the Ecclesiast (in Eccl 1:15) speaks about what is crooked (303,12—304,6). Gregory has a large rhetorical warehouse of contemporary illustrations. Besides carpentry, he illustrates the teaching he finds in the text from the practice of medicine (his favorite—317,5-12; 319,6-10; 346,17-21; 354,13-16; 384,3-15), athletics (278,5-8), pearl diving (318,10-19), irrigation (319,21—320,4), farming (331,1-11; 382,1—383,8), lawyers (358,19-359,1), and military operations (429,1—433,7).

Gregory was willing to consider alternative interpretations, as in the case of those who understood "a time for throwing stones and a time for collecting stones" (Eccl 3:5) in terms of the law that required stoning for breaking the Sabbath (391,5-10). He rejected this interpretation on the basis that it gave no adequate explanation for the gathering up again of the

---

14. "Futility" in the Hall-Moriarty translation.

stones, and proceeded to develop an allegorical interpretation in terms of "spiritual stones," thoughts and words (395,18—397,15).

Gregory's use of logic, comparative Scriptures, definitions of words, illustrations, and alternative interpretations serve theological and especially moral purposes. Despite these considerations, the application of his methods of interpretation demonstrate definite shortcomings. Subtle distinctions in different details of the text carry more weight than they can bear. Thus the phrases "what has come to be" and "what has been made" (Eccl 1:9) are referred to the soul and the body, respectively (296,3-8). Gregory, of course, was not alone in not understanding Hebrew fondness for parallelism.

Gregory's interpretation is quite atomistic. Phrases and sentences yield a spiritual teaching in isolation from their context and even from Gregory's own exegesis. This is true throughout, but an example is the digression on words and their inability to express heavenly things (291,15—294,17, on Eccl 1:8). As another instance, after defining the meaning of the word "want" or "lack," he goes immediately to a theological point about humanity falling into sin (304,23—305.19).

For all Gregory says about sequence (see above and 312,11), in the *Homilies on Ecclesiastes* sequence is more what comes one after another in the text rather than conveying any sense of a unified whole derived from the text itself. What holds the interpretation together is what is brought to the text from the outside, namely Christian doctrine and specifically Gregory's own moral theology.

17

Images of the Incarnation in Gregory of Nyssa's *Vita Moysis*

IN ATTEMPTING TO EXPLAIN and to make understandable the mystery of the incarnation,[1] Gregory of Nyssa employed both analogies from nature and typologies from scripture.

ANALOGIES FROM NATURE

Gregory drew on philosophical discussions of physical union to describe the "mixture" of the divine and human as a union of "predominance." In this type of union the result of the mixture is the more powerful of the constituents, but the weaker component is not destroyed but remains identifiable.[2] Accordingly, Gregory says:

> We say that even the body in which the Son of God accepted his passion, by being mixed with the divine nature, was made by that mixture to be what the assuming nature is. We avoid holding any low idea concerning the only begotten God, so that if he assumed anything belonging to our lowly nature on account of

---

1. On Gregory's Christology see Lenz, *Jesus Christus nach der Lehre des hl. Gregor von Nyssa*; and on the incarnation, Moutsoulas, Η σαρκωσις του Λογου και η θεωσις του ανθρωπου κατα την διδασκαλιαν Γρηγοριου του Νυσσης.

2. Wolfson, *The Philosophy of the Church Fathers*, 385, 397–99.

his dispensation of love for humanity, we believe that even this was transformed into what is divine and incorruptible.[3]

Later he adds:

> For it is the nature of even physical mixtures, when one part is greater than the other by a significant measure, the lesser is assuredly changed to what is more powerful.[4]

After defending the humanity as well as the divinity of Christ, he affirms that "On account of the union and coalescence of natures, the proper attributes of each belong to both."[5]

Gregory uses another analogy from nature for the union of the divine and human in Christ, one popular with the church fathers and alluded to in the context of the passages quoted above,[6] that of the flame and the material that burns. After using the relation of soul and body in a human

---

3. *C. Eun.* 3.3.34 (GNO 11, 1 19, 21–27) = Migne 5.3 (PG 45.693A).

4. *C. Eun.* 3.3.45 (GNO 11, 123, 24–27) =Migne 5.3 (PG 45.697C).

5. *C. Eun.* 3.3.66 (GNO 11, 131, 10–11) =Migne 5.5 (PG45.705D). Gregory then adduces another type of union (in which the weaker element loses its identity) to explain the absorption of the human into the divine after the exaltation of Christ: "Whatever is piously perceived to be in God the Word we make also to be in what is assumed by the Word. Accordingly, these attributes no longer seem to be in either nature by way of division, but that the perishable nature, by its mixture with the divine, is made anew in conformity with the nature that is more powerful and participates in the power of the Godhead, as if one were to say that the mixing makes a drop of vinegar that was mixed in the deep to become sea, because the natural quality of this liquid does not continue in the boundlessness of that which overwhelms it." *C. Eun.* 3.3.68 (GNO 11. 132, 24—133, 4) = Migne 5.5 (PG 45.708C). The same illustration occurs in *Ad Theoph. adv. Apol.*: "The first fruit of human nature having been taken up by the all powerful Deity, like a drop of vinegar mixed with the boundless sea (to use a picture to express the idea), exists in the Deity but not with the specific properties of its own nature" (GNO 111.1, 126, 14-127, 10 = PG 45.1276C-D for the whole context); also *Ant. ad Apol.* 42 (GNO 111.1, 201, 1–16 = PG 45.1221C–1224A); cf. *C. Eun.* 3.4.43 (GNO 11, 150,21-27) = Migne 6.4 (PG 45.728D). Bouchet, "A propos d'une image christologique de Gregoire de Nysse," notes that vinegar in water had a medicinal use, so this may fit Gregory's fondness for medical analogies as well as expressing his therapeutic view of the incarnation.

6. *C. Eun.* 3.3.68 (GNO 11, 132, 7–24 = Migne 5.5 [PG 45.708A-C]): "As fire in wood is often hidden within what can be seen and escapes the notice of those watching or even of those touching the material but becomes visible when it blazes up, so . . . the Lord of glory despised what is shameful among human beings, as if covering the embers of his life in the bodily nature by the dispensation of death, again kindled and enflamed his life by the power of his own divinity and warmed up again what had been put to death."

being as comparable to the relation of divinity and humanity in Christ (another common analogy)[7] Gregory offers this illustration:

> If the soul of a human being commingled with the body according to the necessity of its nature is by its power present everywhere, what necessity is there for saying that the Deity is limited by the fleshly nature, and why may we not by examples current among us obtain some fitting approximation of the divine economy? As an example, the flame in a lamp is seen grasping the underlying matter. Reason distinguishes between the flame upon the material and the material that kindles the flame, although in fact it is not possible to cut off the one from the other so as to exhibit the flame separate from the material, but united they both form one single thing.[8]

The flame and the olive oil co-exist in the lamp. The flame is attached to the olive oil, but is distinct from it and not encompassed by it. And this approximates to the union of the divine nature with humanity. At the same time, Gregory warns against taking the analogy beyond this point of comparison, for a flame may be extinguished but the divine nature is not.

THE STONE CUT WITHOUT HUMAN HANDS

Gregory found a biblical type or foreshadowing of the incarnation in Daniel 2:34 and 45 about a stone cut from the mountain but not by human hands that destroyed the statue symbolizing four kingdoms. In discussing Old Testament types of baptism, Gregory comes to the story of the stone covering the well that Jacob rolled away for Rachel (Gen 29:1–12). He understands the well as representing ("the living water") given to the church. The stone represents Christ:

> For what is the stone that is laid but Christ himself'? For of him Isaiah says, "And I will lay in the foundations of Zion a costly stone, precious, elect" [Isa 28:16]. And Daniel likewise, "A stone was cut out without a hand" [Dan 2:45], that is, Christ was born without a man. For as it is a new and marvelous thing for a stone to be cut from rock without a stone-cutter and stone-cutting

---

7. Wolfson, *Philosophy of the Church Fathers*, 364–72.

8. *Or.catech.* 10 (GNO 111.4, 38, 18—39, 1=PG 45.41C-D); note the fire hidden in wood: The Lord of glory "concealed the flame of his life in his bodily nature by the dispensation of his death and kindled and inflamed it once more by the power of his own Godhead" (C. Eun. 3.3.68 [GNO 11, 132,7—133,l] =Migne 5.5 (PG 45.708A-B); there follows the illustration of the vinegar in the ocean (n. 5 above).

tools, so it is beyond all wonder that a child should appear from an unwedded virgin.[9]

The interpretation of Christ as the "stone cut out without hands" was traditional by Gregory's time.[10] It is found in Irenaeus with specific reference to the virgin birth, "Joseph having no part in it, but Mary alone cooperating in the divine plan."[11]

THE BURNING BUSH

Particularly notable is the concentration of biblical types of the incarnation in Gregory of Nyssa's *Vita Moysis*. Gregory finds six types of the incarnation of the Word of God in events recorded in the Old Testament story of Moses. These types enabled him to emphasize the virginity of Mary even after giving birth, the two natures of Christ as both preexistent deity and a fully human person, and salvation effected by Christ's assuming our sinful nature and transforming it. These interpretations occur in the second part of the *Vita Moysis*, the *theoria*, which gives the spiritual interpretation of the events that he surveyed in a literal manner in the first part, the *historia*. Gregory's discovery of frequent images for the incarnation in the life of Moses shows the importance of this theme for him and probably reflects the growing Christological controversy of the late fourth century.

We will take these Old Testament types in the order in which they are discussed by Gregory, which, with one exception, is the order in which the events appear in the book of Exodus. The first object interpreted as representing the incarnation is the burning bush, in which God appeared to Moses according to Exod 3:1–6. The analogy from nature discussed

---

9. *In diem lum.* (GNO IX, 23 1, 23—232,9 = PG 46.589A-B).

10. Justin, *Dial.* 76.1. "When Daniel speaks of 'the stone cut without human hands,' he has proclaimed in a mystery the same thing [that Christ became a human being but not from human seed], for to say that he was 'cut without human hands' makes clear that it is not a human work but a matter of the will of God the Father of all who brought him forth." Hippolytus, *Comm. Dan.* 2.13, "No other king than Christ, who came from heaven as the stone detached from the mountain in order to overthrow the kingdoms of this world and inaugurate the heavenly kingdom of the saints)). Cf. Cyprian, *Test.* 2.17, and for Origen see n. 57. The *Physiologus* 19 on the Vulture refers to the stone cut without hands as meaning Christ born of the virgin without insemination; cf. Basil, *Hom. Hex.* 8.6, also on the vulture, "a virgin gave birth while preserving inviolate the signs of her virginity."

11. *Adv. haer.* 3.21.7; 4.20.11; 5.26.1–2.

above of fire and the material that burns perhaps suggested this biblical story as a type of the incarnation.

Gregory offers this explanation of the phenomenon of the burning bush:

> And if the flame by which the soul of the prophet was illuminated was kindled from a thorny bush, even this fact will not be useless for our inquiry. For if truth is God and truth is light—the Gospel testifies by these sublime and divine names to the God who made himself visible to us in the flesh—such guidance of virtue leads us to know that light which has reached down even to human nature. Let one think that the radiance did not come from a material substance, this light did not shine from some luminary among the stars but came from an earthly bush and surpassed the heavenly luminaries in brilliance.
>
> From this we learn also the mystery of the Virgin: The light of divinity which through birth shone from her into human life did not consume the burning bush, even as the flower of her virginity was not withered by giving birth. (*Vit. Moys.* 2.20–21)[12]

According to Gregory's interpretation, even as God appeared to Moses in the burning bush, so "God made himself visible to us in the flesh." The divine light was manifest in "a material substance," that is it reached down even to "human nature." This earthly bush was more brilliant than the heavenly bodies, for the "light of divinity" came forth from Mary into human life. God was truly present, but that appearance was in a truly human nature.

Prior to Gregory both Jews and Christians interpreted the burning bush in reference to God's people. Philo saw the thorny bush as a symbol of the suffering of God's people and the appearance of the heavenly being as a symbol of God's presence among them.

> For the burning bramble was a symbol of those who suffered wrong, as the flaming fire [was] of those who did it. Yet that which burned was not burnt up, and this was a sign that the sufferers would not be destroyed by their aggressors, who would find that the aggression was vain and profitless which the victims of malice escaped unharmed. The angel was a symbol of

---

12. I use the translation of Malherbe and Ferguson, *Gregory of Nyssa: Life of Moses*), 59. The notes in this work and in Daniélou, *Gregoire de Nysse*, provide the basis for this paper.

God's providence, which all silently brings relief to the greatest dangers, exceeding every hope.[13]

Rabbinic interpretation was similar: The burning bush that was not consumed meant the Egyptians would not be able to destroy Israel.[14] Christian writers continued the interpretation in terms of the people of God, only now as the church. Hippolytus says that "God speaks with the saints in a church as in a bush."[15] And Hilary of Poitiers understood the bush as the church experiencing the flames of persecution and temptations but not consumed.[16]

Many Christian interpreters followed Philo in emphasizing that the person who spoke with Moses was an angel distinct from the supreme God.[17] Clement of Alexandria made the comparison of the burning bush with Christ by way of the crown of thorns and so connected the theophany of the Word in Exodus with the end of Jesus' earthly life rather than with its beginning.[18] Justin Martyr, on the other hand, anticipated Gregory's interpretation by paralleling the appearance at the bush with the incarnation. He declared:

> [No one] saw in the strict sense the Father and indescribable Lord of all and of Christ himself, but they saw that one who according to God's will as his Son is God and who as serving the purpose of God is an angel, who also willed to be born as a human being by the virgin and who also at that time became fire when he talked with Moses from the bush.[19]

---

13. Philo, *Vita Mosis* 1.12.67 (1.12.66 interprets the light as referring to an angel rather than God himself, and 1.12.68 elaborates on the sufferings). Translation by Colson in *Philo*, vol. 6, 311.

14. *Midrash Rabbah, Exodus* 2:5. See Bloch, "Quelques aspects de la figure de Moïse dans la tradition rabbinique," 103–4.

15. *Ben. Mos.* (PO 27, pp. 172–73).

16. *Tract. Mys.* 1.30.

17. Justin, *Dial.* 59; Ps. Clement, *Hom.* 16.14.1 and *Recog.* 1.34: Eusebius, *Dem.* 5.1.1.5; 5.13.3.6. Cf. Irenaeus, *Adv. Haer.* 4.10.1 for the Son of God as the one who spoke with Moses, and Origen, *Comm. Joh.* 1.218 for the Savior becoming a human being to human beings and an angel to angels with Exod 3:2, 6 quoted as proof of the latter. Although most Christian interpreters understood the "angel" to be Christ, Cyprian applied Exod 3:2 to the Holy Spirit—*Test.* 3.101; cf. *Rebapt.* 17.

18. Clement's wording makes a parallel between the thorn bush at the beginning of God's legislation through Moses with the crown of thorns at the end of the Lord's giving of the law and his stay among humanity—*Paed.* 2.8.73–75.

19. *Dial.* 127.4; cf. 59–60 and *1 Apol.* 63 on the angel as distinct from God. Tertullian, *Adv. Marc.* 3.10 understands the person talking in the bush to be the Creator

This interpretation of the divine person as a manifestation of the supreme God but somehow distinct from him prepared for Gregory's interpretation of the burning bush as a revelation of Christ, but Gregory goes further in not simply laying the two events alongside each other but making a specific application of the burning bush to the incarnation.

Gregory appears to be the first to connect the burning bush with the virginity of Mary postpartum. The bush burned, but it was not burned up. In a similar way, the divine light did not wither Mary's virginity. Giving birth to Jesus did not destroy her virginity, for Mary was still a virgin after giving birth. The burning bush is interpreted in reference to the mystery of the virgin birth also in the sermon *In diem natalem Salvatoris* attributed to Gregory.

> Oh how wonderful! The virgin became a mother and remained a virgin ... This seems to me to have been contemplated beforehand in the theophany that occurred to the great Moses through the light, when the fire was kindled from the bush and the bush was not consumed ... For what was typified beforehand in the flame and the bush ... was revealed in the mystery concerning the virgin. For as there the shrub kindles the fire and is not burned, so also here the virgin both gives birth to the light and is not corrupted. If the bush typified beforehand the God-bearing body of the virgin, you should not be ashamed at the figure of speech. For all flesh on account of receiving sin is this thorn bush; because it is only flesh, it is sin. And sin is given by scripture the derived name of thorn.[20]

The imagery of the burning bush for the virgin birth was picked up by later Greek fathers and included in the Byzantine liturgy.[21]

---

himself.

20. *In diem nat. Salv.* (GNO X. 2, 246, 15–248, 4 = PG 46.1 136B–C). Elsewhere Gregory develops the thorns as the human sinful nature and in the same way as Clement of Alexandria makes an association of the thorn bush with Christ's crown of thorns: "He made those who were formerly changed through sin into a thorny nature into a crown for himself through the dispensation by his death, transforming the thorn through his passion into honor and glory"—*De perf.* (GNO 8.1, 206, 18–19). Cf. Clement of Alexandria above, n. 18.

21. Cyril of Alexandria, *Adv. anthropom.* 26 (PG 76.1129A): "That which was symbolized in the flame and the bush ... was revealed clearly in the mystery of the virgin. For as there the bush is on fire but the light did not consume, so also the virgin here both gives birth to the light and is not corrupted. If the bush prefigured the God-bearing body of the virgin, do not be ashamed at the figure. For all flesh through the reception of sin, in itself, because it is only flesh, is sin. And sin by scripture is named by the designation 'thorn.'" Blanc, "La Fête de Moïse dans le rite byzantine," 345–53

Images of the Incarnation in Gregory of Nyssa's Vita Moysis

THE LEPROUS HAND OF MOSES

Gregory next discusses two types of the incarnation together: Moses' rod that became a serpent and returned to being a rod (Exod 4:1–5) and Moses' hand that became leprous and was then cleansed (Exod 4:6–9). In his interpretation Gregory elaborates these signs of the incarnation in the reverse order of their appearance in the biblical text, taking up the leprous hand first.[22]

> The transformation of the right hand and the rod's changing into a snake became the first of the miracles.
>
> These seem to me to signify in a figure the mystery of the Lord's incarnation, a manifestation of deity to men which effects the death of the tyrant and sets free those under his power (*Vit. Moys.* 2.26–27).

The incarnation had as its purpose salvation, described here as a deliverance from the tyranny of the Evil One.[23]

Gregory supports the incarnational interpretation by appeal to the Prophets (Psalms) and the Gospel. He quotes Psalms 76:11 (LXX, Eng. 77:10), "This is the change of the right hand of the Most High," and John 1:18 according to some manuscripts of the Alexandrian family, "The only begotten God who is in the bosom of the Father." The "only begotten God" of the Gospel is interpreted as "the right hand of the Father" of the Psalms. Gregory's interpretation of Moses' hand becoming leprous and being restored to its normal condition is as follows:

> Although the divine nature is contemplated in its immutability, by condescension to the weakness of human nature it was changed to our shape and form.
>
> When the hand of the lawgiver was extended from his bosom it was changed to an unnatural complexion, and when placed again in his bosom, it returned to its own natural beauty . . .
>
> When he was manifested to us from the bosom of the Father, he was changed to be like us. After he wiped away our infirmities, he again returned to his own bosom the hand which had been among us and had received our complexion. (The Father is the bosom of the right hand.) What is impossible by nature

---

translates into French, "Textes tires de la fête de Moïse du 4 Septembre," in which the connection of the burning bush with the virgin birth is twice made (349, 352).

22. He mentions them in their biblical order in his historical survey, 1.21.

23. The connection of incarnation and salvation is elaborated in *Or. catech.* 8–32, where the predominant image of salvation is medicinal, but the passage includes the ransom theory of the atonement that involves release from the captivity of the devil.

311

did not change into what is passible, but what is mutable and subject to passions was transformed into impassibility through its participation in the immutable. (*Vit. Moys.* 2.28–30)[24]

Gregory's refutation of Eunomius also uses "the change of the right hand of the Father" from the Psalms text to indicate Christ was the same nature as the Father but contemplated as an individual existence and was God himself manifested in the flesh.[25] The change to our condition is also developed in the *Refutatio confessionis Eunomii*, where Gregory affirms that the Word in taking flesh took the whole of human nature, including hunger, thirst, fear, dread, desire, sleep, tears, and trouble of spirit.[26]

Two themes from Irenaeus provide a background for Gregory's interpretation. Irenaeus had spoken of the "hands of God" in reference to his Word (the Son) and Wisdom (the Holy Spirit).[27] He also had expressed the thought, better known from Athanasius, of Christ becoming what we are so that we could become what he is.[28] Origen at one time interpreted the leprous hand as pure deeds and on another occasion its insertion into Moses's bosom as representing the works of the law that produce no perfect work and so are hidden from sight.[29] Cyril of Jerusalem used the two miracles of Moses' hand becoming leprous and restored again and Moses's rod becoming a serpent (in the same reversal of the Biblical order as Gregory) as arguments against Jews in support of Christ being born of a virgin.[30]

Latin authors gave other interpretations of the transformation of Moses' hand. Tertullian described Moses' hand as becoming "dead" when he first put in into his bosom and drew it out and then becoming "alive" when he did it again; he used this, as well as the subduing of the serpent in the double transformation of the rod, in support of the resurrection

---

24. Malherbe and Ferguson, *Gregory of Nyssa: Life of Moses*, 61.

25. *C. Eun.* 3.4.24 (GNO 11, 143, 5–19) = Migne 6.3 (PG 45.720C-D).

26. *Ref. conf. Eun.* 181 (GNO 11, 388, 24–389, 4) = Migne 2.13 (PG 45.549A).

27. Irenaeus, *Adv. haer.* 4.pref.4; 4.20.1; 5.1.3; 5.28.4, all with reference to the creation of humanity. Discussed in Lawson, *The Biblical Theology of St. Irenaeus*, chap. 10.

28. Irenaeus, *Adv. haer.* 3.10.2 ("He was made son of man for this purpose that man might be made son of God"); 3.19.1; 5.pref. ("The Word of God, Jesus Christ our Lord, who because of his great love was made what we are so that we might become what he himself is"); 5.1 .1; Athanasius, *De incarn. Verbi* 54.3 ("He was made man that we might be made God").

29. Origen, *Comm. Joh.* 32.267–268; *Hom. Ex.* 12.3.

30. *Catech. illum.* 12.28, using also Sarah's giving birth in her old age (Gen 18:10–11; 21:1–2) and Aaron's rod that budded (Num 17:1–10).

of the flesh.[31] Hilary of Poitiers saw in the episode a teaching of the two senses of scripture, literal and spiritual.[32] Ambrose, however, here as elsewhere follows the Greek fathers, in this case it seems Gregory of Nyssa, in interpreting both events, but following the biblical order, in reference to the incarnation.

> Moses cast down his rod and it became a serpent that devoured the serpents of Egypt; this signifies that the Word should become flesh to destroy the poison of the dread serpent by the forgiveness and pardon of sins . . .
> Another sign that Moses gave points to our Lord Jesus Christ. He put his hand into his bosom and drew it out again, and his hand became as snow. A second time he put it in and drew it out, and it was again like the appearance of human flesh. This signified first the original glory of the Godhead of the Lord Jesus and then the assumption of our flesh, in which truth all nations and peoples must believe. So he put in his hand, for Christ is the right hand of God, and whoever does not believe in his Godhead and incarnation is punished as a sinner.[33]

Among the Greek fathers, Cyril of Alexandria follows Gregory in interpreting the leprous hand as teaching the incarnation of Christ.[34]

THE ROD AND THE SERPENT

Gregory's interpretation of Moses' rod that became a snake and then returned to be a rod follows immediately on his interpretation of Moses' leprous hand. He anticipates that his readers will find his application of this episode to the incarnation problematic, for the snake would be an unworthy image of Christ.

The change from a rod into a snake should not trouble the lovers of Christ—as if we were adapting the doctrine of the incarnation to an

---

31. Tertullian, *De res. mort.* 28.1; cf. 55.8.

32. Hilary of Poitiers, *Tract. myst.* 16.

33. Ambrose, *De off. minis.* 3.15.94–95. Translation by H. de Romestin, modified, in NPNF, 2nd ser., Vol. X, 82–83. Ambrose's description of the rod in terms of the later incident when Aaron's staff that became a snake swallowed the Egyptians' snakes (Exod 7:8–12) may explain why Gregory treated the rod after the hand of Moses.

34. *Glaph. in Ex.* 2.299, "It is the custom for the divinely inspired scripture to call the Son a Hand" . . . "Understand the mystery and the manner of the incarnation" of the Son, who was in the bosom of the Father (PG 69,2. 473D), but "Human nature is unclean before God" (476A).

unsuitable animal (*Vit. Moys.* 2.31). He justifies the comparison by quoting John 3:14, where the lifting up of the Son of Man is likened to the Moses' lifting up the image of a serpent in the wilderness (Num 21:8–9). Gregory continues:

> The teaching is clear. For if the father of sin is called a serpent by Holy Scripture and what is born of the serpent is certainly a serpent, it follows that sin is synonymous with the one who begot it. (*Vit. Moys.* 2.32)

He then quotes 2 Cor 5:21 for the Lord being made sin for our sake when he took on our sinful nature.

> This figure therefore is rightly applied to the Lord. For if sin is a serpent and the Lord became sin, the logical conclusion should be evident to all: By becoming sin he became also a serpent, which is nothing other than sin. For our sake he became a serpent that he might devour and consume the Egyptian serpents produced by the sorcerers.[35]
>
> This done, the serpent was changed back into a rod by which sinners are brought to their senses, and those slackening on the upward and toilsome course of virtue are given rest. (*Vit. Moys.* 2.33–34)[36]

Gregory thus once more gives a soteriological emphasis to the incarnation. Christ assumed sinful human nature and so became a "serpent." This was done on our behalf, for the purpose was to devour the serpents of sorcery and remove us from the power of sin. His return to a rod is applied by Gregory to a twofold function: A rod disciplines sinners but also protects and supports those striving for virtue and so gives them rest.

Gregory had a nearly exact predecessor for interpreting the turning of the rod into a snake as a figure of the incarnation, once more in Irenaeus. As part of a series of arguments for the virgin birth, preceded by reference to the stone cut out not by human hands (Dan 2:34), Irenaeus appeals to the episode under consideration:

> Moses also, showing forth a type, threw his rod on the ground, so that by becoming flesh it might prove false and devour every sinful device of the Egyptians that was raised up against the plan of God. And so the Egyptians themselves testify that it is the

---

35. The allusion is to Exod 7:8–13.

36. The quotations from *Vit. Moys.* 3.31–34 are from Malherbe and Ferguson, *Gregory of Nyssa: The Life of Moses*, 61–62.

finger of God that effects salvation for the people and not the son of Joseph.[37]

In his *Proof of the Apostolic Preaching* 59, Irenaeus in commenting on Isa 11:1-10 seems to identify the rod with the virgin, but the text is ambiguous and continues by referring to Christ.[38] Justin Martyr has a passage that includes all the elements brought together in the later typology—the Son of God who became a man by the virgin, a "Rod" included among the titles of the Son, disobedience introduced by the serpent to the virgin Eve, and God's destruction of the serpent—but he does not mention the rod turning into a snake, the event that tied the elements of the typology together for Gregory.[39] Hilary of Poitiers interpreted the rod (=royal power) of Moses as Christ and the serpent as the devil, but he relates the rod to the resurrection as demonstrating what Christ really is, "the God of the ages," in response to the Jews' charge that he was associated with Beelzebub (Matt 10:25), the serpent.[40]

Cyril of Alexandria once more follows Gregory in referring the change of the rod into a snake to the incarnation.[41]

---

37. Irenaeus, *Adv. haer.* 3.21.8. Ps. Clement, *Hom.* 20.6.7 uses the turning of the rod into a serpent as an illustration of God's power to take whatever bodily form he likes but without reference to the incarnation.

38. J. P. Smith, *St. Irenaeus Proof of the Apostolic Preaching*, 195 n266, discusses the Armenian text.

39. *Dial.* 100.3-6. Justin elsewhere included the rod of Moses in his list of types of the wood of the cross, but he refers to those events where the rod was associated with water—parting the Red Sea, water from the rock, and the tree that sweetened the bitter waters of Marah—and does not mention the change into a serpent—*Dial.* 86.1. *Dial.* 126.1 also includes "Rod" among the names for Christ.

40. *Tract. mys.* 1.31. Hilary does not give a Christological interpretation to the hand in the bosom. His order of the rod and then the hand follows the biblical order, reinforced by the fact that the turning of the rod into a serpent was the first of the wonders performed by Moses and Aaron in the presence of Pharaoh (Exodus 7). Clement of Alexandria too understood a rod (=Christ) as representing correction, government, and sovereignty, but without specific reference to Ex. 4:2-4 (*Paed.*1.7.61). Cyril of Jerusalem used the rod of Moses becoming a serpent as proof of the possibility that the bodies of the righteous shall live and rise again—*Catech. illum.* 18.12.

41. *Glaph. in Ex.* 2.299: "The divinely inspired scripture compares the Word born of God to a rod" (PG 69,2.469D); the Word became a "snake" on account of being in the likeness and same form as we are (472A); the only begotten became a human being (472B); if we believe on him we find him a rod (symbol of kingship) (472C).

MANNA FROM HEAVEN

The fourth image of the incarnation that Gregory found in the story of Moses is the manna that fed Israel during her wilderness wanderings (Exodus 16). The Gospel of John had already identified Jesus as the bread from heaven with the manna (John 6:30–51). Gregory's exposition is as follows:

> Coming down from above, the bread is found upon the earth already prepared without the wheat's having been sown or ripened.
>
> You no doubt perceive the true food in the figure of the history: The bread which came from heaven is not some incorporeal thing. For how could something incorporeal be nourishment to a body? Neither ploughing nor sowing produced the body of this bread, but the earth which remained unchanged was found full of this divine food, of which the hungry partake. This miracle teaches in anticipation the mystery of the Virgin.
>
> This bread, then, that does not come from the earth is the Word. He changes his power in diverse ways to suit those who eat. (*Vit. Moys.* 2.138–140)[42]

The subsequent sentences show that Gregory's main interest here is the way the divine Word accommodates himself to the needs of those who receive him: milk for little children, greens for the young and weak, and meat for the more mature.[43] This theme had been developed by Origen.[44]

---

42. Malherbe and Ferguson, *Gregory of Nyssa: The Life of Moses*, 88.

43. The tradition of diverse taste of the manna according to the needs of the one eating was suggested by Wis 16:20–21. Rabbinic interpretation said the manna was suited to the capactiy of each individual (*Midrash Rabbah, Exodus* 5.9), contained the taste of every kind of food (*b. Yoma* 75a; *Mekilta de Rabbi Ishmael, Tractate Amalek* 3), and tasted to each Israelite what he particularly liked (*Midrash Rabbah, Exodus* 25.3; *Mekilta de Rabbi Ishmael, Tractate Vayassa'* 5). The interpretation that the manna was adapted to each individual is found in Philo, according to Basil, *Ep.* 190.3. Gregory, *In Eccl.* 8 (GNO V, 423, 4–18 = PG 44.740A-B) notes that the "flesh of the Word" that we eat has "not one particular grace, but is sweet to those who taste it, and desirable to those who long for it, and to those who love it, adorable" (trans. by Stuart George Hall and Rachel Moriarty, in Hall, ed., *Gregory of Nyssa Homilies on Ecclesiastes*, 132).

44. With reference to Rom 14:2, Origen says of the manna that God is flesh, bread, milk, and vegetable "for the capacity of those believing or the ability of those appropriating it" (*Hom. Ex.* 7.8; cf. also 7.5 for the different qualities of manna). Origen also notes (with reference to Wis 16:20–21) that the heavenly manna has a different taste to each one (*Comm. Mt.* ser. 100).

Gregory elsewhere elaborates on the language of God's revelation accommodated to our capacity to understand.[45]

The interpretation of the manna as representing the divine Word was well established by Gregory's time. It is found in Philo[46] and in Origen.[47] The distinctively Christian theme of this Word becoming incarnate through the virgin Mary is prepared for by Irenaeus's view (without reference to the manna) of the birth of Adam from the virgin earth (untilled and unrained on) as a figure of the Word's virgin birth[48] and was approximated in Origen.[49] For Gregory, as the manna was of heavenly origin and not produced by ploughing the earth and sowing seed, so the incarnation was effected through a virgin in whom no human seed was sowed. He alludes to the point made in connection with the burning bush that Mary remained a virgin after the birth by speaking of the earth remaining "unchanged," although it was full of the divine food. The soteriological implications of Christ as the heavenly manna are not drawn here but may be inferred from his designation of Christ, "clothed in our human nature," as the "firstfruits of the dough"[50] and his declaration with reference to John 6:55 that by eating Christ we become what he is.[51]

THE TABERNACLE

A fifth image of Christ is the tabernacle erected in the wilderness. Although the incarnational aspect is not so pointedly made, it provides the framework for Gregory's interpretation. God showed Moses a pattern for the tabernacle and its furniture that Israel was to make as a sanctuary

45. *C. Eun.* 2.242 (GNO I, 297,2–15) = *Ans. to Eun. 2nd Bk.* (PG 45.992C–D).

46. *Quod det.* 31.1 18, "Manna is the divine Word, the oldest of the things that exist"; *Quis rer. div.* 15.79, "The manna, the divine Word, the heavenly, incorruptible nourishment of the soul that is fond of contemplation."

47. *Hom. Ex.* 7.5.

48. *Adv. haer.* 3.21.10; *Dem.* 32; cf. *Frg.* 19 for manna as a type of the body of Christ. Eusebius seems to be more typical of earlier interpreters in simply paralleling Moses's giving the manna with Jesus feeding the multitude as part of a series of parallels between what Moses did and what Jesus did—*Dem.* 3.2.14.

49. In interpreting the manna Origen says, "We for whom at the end of the age and in the evening of the world 'the Word was made flesh' [John 1:14] say the Lord is known in that flesh which he received from the virgin" (*Hom. Ex.* 7.8). One may contrast Hilary of Poitiers, who, while repeating the theme that the manna was efficacious for all ages and sexes, suggested that it alludes to the resurrection (*Tract. mys.* 1.30).

50. *In Cant.* 14 (GNO VI, 427, 20—428,7 = PG 44.1085B–C).

51. *In Eccl.* 8 (GNO 5,423,4–6 = PG 44.740A).

(Exod 25:9, 40). Gregory understood this heavenly pattern as a tabernacle not made with hands that was to serve as an archetype for the handmade structure on earth (*Vit. Moys.* 2.169–170). He offers the following Christological interpretation:

> Taking a hint from what has been said by Paul, who partially uncovered the mystery of these things, we say that Moses was earlier instructed by a type in the mystery of the tabernacle which encompasses the universe. This tabernacle would be Christ who is the power and wisdom of God [1 Cor 1:24], who in his own nature was not made with hands, yet capable of being made when it became necessary for this tabernacle to be erected among us. Thus, the same tabernacle is in a way both unfashioned and fashioned, uncreated in preexistence but created in having received this material composition.
>
> What we say is of course not obscure to those who have accurately received the mystery of our faith. For there is one thing out of all others which both existed before the ages and came into being at the end of the ages. It did not need a temporal beginning (for how could what was before all times and ages be in need of a temporal origin?), but for our sakes, who had lost our existence through our thoughtlessness, it consented to be born like us so that it might bring that which had left reality back again to reality. This one is the Only Begotten God [John 1:18], who encompasses [John 1:14] everything in himself but who also pitched his own tabernacle among us (*Vit. Moys.* 2.174–175).[52]

Gregory then proceeds to justify calling Christ "tabernacle" on the basis that he is also called by many other names of material objects (*Vit. Moys.* 2.176–177). To take a specific example of this incarnational interpretation, Gregory (on the basis of Hebrews 10:20) identifies the curtain of the tabernacle with the flesh of Christ (*Vit. Moys.* 2.178). After giving this Christological interpretation of the heavenly tabernacle, Gregory gives an ecclesiological interpretation of the earthly tabernacle (*Vit. Moys.* 2.184–188).

For Philo the celestial tabernacle is the intelligible world of archetypal ideas, and the earthly tabernacle is the universe.[53] Accordingly, Philo interpreted the tabernacle mainly in terms of cosmology but with

---

52. Malherbe and Ferguson, *Gregory of Nyssa: The Life of Moses*, 98–99.
53. Philo, *Quaest. Ex.* 1.52, 59, 83; *Spec. leg.* 1.12.66.

some reference to psychology and philosophy.[54] In this he was followed by Christian interpreters.[55]

Origen, taking his cue from Hebrews 9, interpreted the tabernacle as heaven, then as collectively the church, and also individually of the person making himself a tabernacle for God.[56] Origen also gave an incarnational interpretation that exactly corresponds to Gregory's later interpretation. He combined the imagery of the tabernacle and of the stone cut from a mountain. After quoting Exod 15:17, "A habitation that you, Lord, prepared," and Prov 9:1, "Wisdom built a house for herself," Origen explains:

> I think that this is understood more correctly of the Lord's incarnation. For "it was not made by the hand of men," that is the temple of flesh is not built in the virgin by human work, but as Daniel had prophesied, "a stone cut without hands separated and became a great mountain" (Dan 2:34–35). That is, the "sanctuary" of the flesh which was taken up and "cut" from the mountain of human nature and the substance of flesh "without hands," that is, apart from the work of men.[57]

Irenaeus and Methodius anticipated the ecclesiological interpretation of Gregory by comparing the tabernacle to the church.[58] In another place Methodius gave an eschatological interpretation to the feast of Tabernacles: Our bodies are tabernacles that will be raised to incorruption at the resurrection.[59]

Gregory elsewhere compares the incarnation to a building[60] and specifically to the construction of a tabernacle without human corruption.[61]

54. *Vita Moysis* 2.15.71–2.22.108; *Quaest. Ex.* 2.51–106.

55. Clement of Alexandria, *Strom.* 5.6.32–40; Ps. Justin, *Coh. ad Graecos* 29–30 (PG 6.296B-C—Plato got his theory of ideas from reading Exod 25:9, 40); Gregory of Nazianzus, *Or.* 28.31 (PG 36.72A).

56. *Hom. Ex.* 9.

57. Origen, *Hom. Ex.* 6.12.

58. Irenaeus, *Dem.* 26; Methodius, *Symp.* 5.8.

59. *De res.* 1.14.

60. Commenting on Prov 9:1, he says, "True Wisdom did not dwell in another's building but built for herself a dwelling place from the body of the virgin . . . I speak of both the house and of Wisdom that dwells in the house, that is of the humanity and of the deity mixed with the human person"—*C. Eun.* 3.1.44–45 (GNO 11, 19, 6–12) = Migne, 3.2 (PG 45.580D).

61. Wisdom built her house in Mary, with allusion again to Prov 9:1 and also Luke 1:35—*Ep.* 3.19–20 (GNO VIII.2,25, 1–16, esp. 12–13) = Migne 17 (PG 46.102 1C). "God was manifest in the flesh . . . and tabernacled among us . . . After he once for all absorbed to himself through its firstfruits the perishable nature of flesh that he received

The sermon *In diem natalem Salvatoris* alludes to several manifestations of the tabernacle: the tabernacle of the Jews, the incarnation, the world, and the resurrection.[62]

The soteriological purpose of the incarnation finds expression in the passage quoted above: "Christ came into being at the end of the ages . . . for our sakes" so that we "who had lost our existence" might be brought back to "reality." The whole section on the heavenly tabernacle closes with a reference to the "saving passion" contemplated in the skins dyed red and the woven hairs of the covering for the tabernacle. The redness pointed to blood, and the hair (since it has no feeling) was a symbol of death (*Vit. Moys.* 2.183). Human salvation was never far from Gregory's doctrine of the incarnation.

STONE TABLETS WRITTEN BY THE FINGER OF GOD

The last image of the incarnation that Gregory discovered in the life of Moses was the stone tablets written by the finger of God (Exod 31:18; 32:15–16). He once again found significance in the combination of a material element and the divine activity: "Both the material and the writing on [the tablets] were equally the work of God" (*Vit. Moys.* 1.57). They represent respectively human nature and the work of the Holy Spirit, according to Gregory's Christological interpretation:

> The true Lawgiver, of whom Moses was a type, cut the tables of human nature for himself from our earth. It was not marriage which produced for him his "God-receiving" flesh, but he became the stonecutter of his own flesh, which was carved by the

---

through the uncorrupted virgin he continues to sanctify by the firstfruit the common dough of our nature . . . nourishing his own body, the church [and so Gregory passes from the incarnation to the church] . . . The one who looks at the church looks directly at Christ, who builds and increases it by the addition of those being saved"—*Comm. Cant.* 13 (GNO VI, 38 1, 1—383,6 = PG 44.1045C—1048C).

62. "The present purpose of the feast is the mystery of the true feast of Tabernacles. On this occasion the human tent was pitched in the one who was clothed with a human being for our sakes. On this occasion our bodily tents that have been struck down by death have been set up again by the One who took up residence from the beginning in our habitation . . . He crossed over to human life through virginal incorruption . . . [The trumpets of the prophets and apostles sound the word of truth] through the covering of the tabernacle of the lower creation . . . In the fellowship of this feast the human nature is completely covered in the renewal of our bodies and is joined to the [heavenly powers] through the setting up of the tabernacle at the resurrection." *In diem nat. Salv.* (GNO X.2, 236, 6—12, 15—16; 237, 12—17; 238, 2—5 = PG 46.1 128A—1129B).

divine finger, for the Holy Spirit came upon the virgin and the power of the Most High overshadowed her [Luke 1:35 adapted]. When this took place, our nature regained its unbroken character, becoming immortal through the letters written by his finger. The Holy Spirit is called "finger" in many places by Scripture.[63]

... For when the restorer of our broken nature (you no doubt perceive in him the one who healed our brokenness) had restored the broken table of our nature to its original beauty— doing this by the finger of God ... (*Vit. Moys.* 2.216-217)[64]

Gregory once more emphasizes the virgin birth, for Christ's flesh was not the result of marriage. He attributes the creation of his flesh to both Christ himself and to the Holy Spirit. Gregory appears to be the first author to use the term θεοδόχος ("God receiving"), certainly the first to make extensive use of it in reference to Christology.[65] In addition to Jesus' flesh, as in this quotation,[66] he uses the word of Jesus' body[67] and of his humanity.[68]

Previous authors generally did not make the Christological application of the passage. Clement of Alexandria contrasted the laws of reason written on human hearts to what was written on stone.[69] Irenaeus connected the finger of God in this episode with the Holy Spirit but only with reference to the commandments delivered to Israel.[70] Novatian saw the "finger of God" as an instance of scripture turning the divine appearance

---

63. Luke 11:20 and Matt 12:28 (cf. Exod 8:19 and Deut 9:10).

64. Malherbe and Ferguson, *Gregory of Nyssa: The Life of Moses*, 110-11.

65. Lampe, *A Patristic Greek Lexicon*, 625, cites no writing earlier.

66. "That God-receiving flesh"—*Or. catech.* 37 (GNO 111.4, 97, 20-21 = PG 45.97B).

67. "That God-receiving body alone received this grace [of immortality]"—*Or. catech.* 37 (GNO 111.4, 94, 8-10 = PG 45.93C); "As the virgin did not know how the God-receiving body would exist in her body, neither did she feel the birth that the prophecy testified to her concerning the painless birth pangs [Isa 66:7]"—*Comm. Cant.* 13 (GNO VI, 388,21—389, 1 = PG 44.1053B).

68. "We refer this name Christ not to his eternal deity but to the God-receiving humanity"—*Comm. Cant.* 13 (GNO VI, 390, 22—391, 2 = PG 44.1056A); "The God-receiving human being was nothing other than part of our own human dough" [Rom 11:16]—*Or. catech.* 32 (GNO 111.4, 78, 9-10 = PG 45.80B).

69. *Paed.* 3.12.94.

70. Irenaeus, *Dem.* 26. Origen interpreted the writing of the commandments a second time after Moses broke the first tablets as a preparing of the soul after transgression to receive again the commandments of God—*C. Cels.* 1.4. Ambrose, following the usual identification of the "finger of God" with the Holy Spirit (note 63), interpreted the tablets as written by the Holy Spirit rather than by Christ—*De Sp. Sanct.* 3.3.13-14.

into a human form, but does not relate this to the incarnation.[71] Hippolytus did interpret the handwriting on the wall in Dan 5:1-9 as, "The Word himself in the last times became incarnate and took the form of a human being," and then identified the writing on the wall with the writing on the tablets of stone in Exodus.[72]

Gregory underscores the soteriological results of his interpretation. As the stone tablets broken by Moses were replaced (Exod 32:19; 34:1-4), so human nature regains "its unbroken character" and becomes immortal through the incarnation. This restoration of our broken nature is described in the medical imagery Gregory so much preferred as a "healing."

CONCLUSION

Gregory of Nyssa showed great interest in the incarnation. We could say that it was a central element in his theological system. In working with the prior exegetical tradition, both Hellenistic Jewish and Christian, he showed both a measure of dependence and also considerable originality. Three special emphases emerge from his interpretations of the history of Moses. One is that the birth of Jesus did not affect the virginity of Mary. The virginity of Mary supported Gregory's ascetic moral theology. The second emphasis is that Christ had two natures; he was fully divine and fully human. The divine predominated in the union, but Christ was fully identified with human nature and assumed for himself human sinfulness without his divine impassibility being affected. The third emphasis is that the incarnation had as its purpose and goal human salvation. By assuming human nature, Christ transformed it into divine incorruptibility.

---

71. *De Trin.* 6.1.

72. Hippolytus, *Comm. Dan.* 3.14.

Bibliography

Anderson, Warren D. *Ethos and Education in Greek Music.* Cambridge: Harvard University Press, 1966.
Asmis, Elizabeth. "Philodemus' Epicureanism." In *ANRW* II.36.4 (1990) 2370–73.
Atchley, E. G. Cuthbert F. *On the Epiclesis of the Eucharistic Liturgy and in the Consecration of the Font.* Oxford: Alcuin Club Collections 31. Oxford University Press, 1935.
Audet, Jean-Paul. *La Didache: Instructions des apôtres.* EB. Paris: Lecoffre, 1958.
Augier, B. "La transsubstantiation d'après S. Thomas d'Aquin." *Revue des sciences philosophiques et théologiques* 17 (1928) 427–59.
Augustine. *Augustine: Confessions and Enchiridion.* Translated by Albert C. Outler. Library of Christian Classics 7. 1955. Reprinted, Hendrickson Christian Classics. Peabody, MA: Hendrickson, 2004.
———. *Saint Augustine: The Retractions.* Translated by Mary Inez Bogan. FC 60. Washington, DC: Catholic University of America Press, 1968.
Balas, David L. "Gregory of Nyssa." In *Encyclopedia of Early Christianity*, edited by Everett Ferguson, 400–402. Garland Reference Library of the Humanities 846. New York: Garland, 1990.
———. ΜΕΤΟΥΣΙΑ ΘΕΟΥ: *Man's Participation in God's Perfections according to Saint Gregory of Nyssa.* Studia Anselmiana philosophica theologica 55. Rome: Herder, 1966.
Balthasar, Hans Urs von. "Die Hiera des Evagrius." *Zeitschrift für katholische Theologie* 63 (1939) 86–106.
———. *Présence et Pensée: Essai sur la philosophie religieuse de Grégoire de Nysse.* Paris: Beauchesne, 1942.
Barnard, Leslie W. *Athenagoras: A Study in Second Century Christian Apologetic.* Théologie historique 18. Paris: Beauchesne, 1972.
———. *Justin Martyr: His Life and Thought.* London: Cambridge University Press, 1967.
Barker, Andrew, ed. *Greek Musical Writings.* Vol. 2, *Harmonic and Acoustic Theory.* Cambridge Readings in the Literature of Music. Cambridge: Cambridge University Press, 1989.
Barnes, Timothy David. *Tertullian: A Historical and Literary Study.* Oxford: Oxford University Press, 1971.
Basil of Caesarea. *Epistles.* Translated by Blomfield Jackson. NPNF ser. 2, vol. 8. Reprinted, Grand Rapids: Eerdmans, 1955.

Bibliography

Battenhouse, Roy, ed. *A Companion to the Study of St. Augustine*. Oxford: Oxford University Press, 1955.

Batiffol, Pierre. *L'Eucharistie: La présence réelle et la transubstantiation*. 9th ed. Paris: Gabalda, 1930.

Baumgarten, Joseph M. "Sacrifice and Worship among the Jewish Sectarians of the Dead Sea (Qumran) Scrolls." *HTR* 46 (1953) 141–59.

Behm, Johannes. "θύω, θυσία, θυσιαστήριον." In *Theologisches Wörterbuch zum Neuen Testament*, edited by Gerhard Kittel, 3:180–91. Stuttgart: Kohlhammer, 1938.

Beckwith, Roger T. "Qumran Calendar and the Sacrifices of the Essenes." *Revue de Qumran* 7 (1971) 587–91.

Bellis, Annie. "La théorie de l'âme chez Aristoxène de Tarente." *Revue de philologie, de littérature et d'histoire ancienne* 59 (1985) 239–46.

Bernays, Jacob. *Theophrastos' Schrift über Frömmigkeit: Ein Beitrag zur Religionsgeschichte*. Berlin: Hertz, 1866.

Best, Ernst. "I Peter 2:4–10." *Novum Testamentum* 11 (1969) 270–93.

———. "Spiritual Sacrifice: General Priesthood in the New Testament." *Interpretation* 14 (1960) 273–99.

Bigg, Charles. *The Christian Platonists of Alexandria*. 1913. Reprinted, Hildesheim: Olms, 1981.

Bingham, Joseph. *The Antiquities of the Christian Church*. London: Rivingtons, 1845.

Blanc, Jean. "La Fête de Moïse dans le rite byzantine." In *Moïse: L'homme de l'alliance*, edited by H. Cazelles et al., 345–53. Paris: Desclee, 1955.

Bloch, Renée. "Quelques aspects de la figure de Moïse dans la tradition rabbinique." In *Moïse: L'homme de l'alliance*, edited by H. Cazelles et al., 93–167. Paris: Desclee, 1955.

Botte, Bernard. *La tradition apostolique de Saint Hippolyte*. Liturgiewissenschaftliche Quellen und Forschungen 39. Münster: Aschendorff, 1963.

Bouchet, Jean-René. "A propos d'une image christologique de Gregoire de Nysse." *Revue Thomiste* 67 (1967) 584–88.

Bradshaw, Paul, Maxwell E. Johnson, and L. Edward Phillips. *The Apostolic Tradition: A Commentary*. Hermeneia. Minneapolis: Fortress, 2002.

Brennan, Brian. "Augustine's *De Musica*." *VigChr* 42 (1988) 267–81.

Bright, Pamela, trans. *Early Christian Spirituality*. Edited by Charles Kannengiesser. Sources of Early Christian Thought. Philadelphia: Fortress, 1986.

Brightman, F. E. *Liturgies Eastern and Western*. Oxford: Clarendon, 1896 [1965].

Brinktrine, Johannes. *Der Messopferbegriff in den ersten 2 Jahrhunderten: Eine biblisch-patristische Untersuchung*. Freiburger theologische Studien 21. Freiburg: Herder, 1918.

Briolioth, Yngve. *Eucharistic Faith and Practice: Evangelical and Catholic*. Translated by A. G. Hebert. London: SPCK, 1930.

Brown, James Russell. *Temple and Sacrifice in Rabbinic Judaism*. Winslow Lectures 1953. Evanston, IL: Seabury-Western Theological Seminary, 1963.

Budge, E. A. Wallis. *Miscellaneous Coptic Texts in the Dialect of Upper Egypt*. London: Longmans, 1915.

Campenhausen, Hans von. *Die Idee des Martyriums in der alten Kirche*. 2nd ed. Göttingen: Vandenhoeck & Ruprecht, 1964.

Casel, Odo. *Die Liturgie als Mysterienfeier*. Ecclesia orans 9. Freiburg: Herder, 1923.

———. "Die Λογική Θυσία der antiken Mystik in christlichliturgischer Umdeutung." *Jahrbuch fur Liturgiewissenschaft* 4 (1924) 41–44.
Casey, R. P. "The Apocalypse of Paul." *JTS* 34 (1933) 16.
———. *The Excerpta ex Theodoto of Clement of Alexandria*. Studies and Documents 1. London: Christophers, 1934.
Chadwick, Henry. "Eucharist and Christology in the Nestorian Controversy." *JTS* n.s. 2 (1951) 145–64.
Charles, R. H. *Apocrypha and Pseudepigrapha of the Old Testament*. 2 vols. Oxford: Clarendon, 1913.
Charlesworth, James A. *The History of the Rechabites*. Texts and Translations 17. Pseudepigrapha Series 10. Chico, CA: Scholars, 1982.
Childs, Brevard S. *Memory and Tradition in Israel*. Studies in Biblical Theology 1/37. Naperville, IL: Allenson, 1962.
Clark, M. T. "Irenaeus." In *Encyclopedia of Early Christianity*, edited by Everett Ferguson, 471–73. Garland Reference Library of the Humanities 846. New York: Garland, 1990.
Clements, R. E. et al. *Eucharistic Theology Then and Now*. Theological Collections 9. London: SPCK, 1968.
Collins, John J. "Apocalypse: Toward the Morphology of a Genre." *Semeia* 14 (1979) 1–20.
Colson, F. H., trans. *Philo*. Vol. 6. Loeb Classical Library. Cambridge: Harvard University Press, 1935.
Conybeare, E. C. *Philo about the Contemplative Life*. Oxford: Clarendon, 1895.
Congar, Yves M.-J. *Jalons pour une théologie du lacat*. 2nd ed. Unam Sanctam 23. Paris: Cerf, 1954.
Connolly, R. Hugh. *Didascalia Apostolorum: The Syriac Version Translated and Accompanied by the Verona Latin Fragments*. 1929. Reprinted, Ancient Texts and Translations. Eugene, OR: Wipf & Stock, 2010.
Corwin, Virginia. *St. Ignatius and Christianity in Antioch*. Yale Publications in Religion 1. New Haven: Yale University Press, 1960.
Crockett, William R. *Eucharist: Symbol of Transformation*. New York: Pueblo, 1989.
Cross, F. L., and E. A. Livingstone, eds. *The Oxford Dictionary of the Christian Church*. 2nd ed. London, 1974. 3rd ed. rev., 2005.
Cuming, Geoffrey J. *Liturgy of St. Mark*. Orientalia Christiana Analecta 234. Rome: Pontificium Institutum Stordiorum Orientalium, 1990.
Cuming, G. J. "ΔΙ' ΕΥΧΗΣ ΛΟΓΟΥ (Justin, *1 Apol.* 66.2)." *JTS* n.s. 31 (1980) 80–82.
Dahl, Nils Alstrup. "*Anamnēsis*: Mémoire et Commémoration dans le christianisme primitif." *Studia Theologica* 1 (1947) 69–95.
———. "*Anamnēsis*: Memory and Commemoration in Early Christianity." In *Jesus in the Memory of the Early Church*, 11–29. Minneapolis: Augsburg, 1976.
Daly, Robert J. *Christian Sacrifice: The Judaeo-Christian Background before Origen*. Catholic University of America Studies in Christian Antiquity 18. Washington, DC: Catholic University of America, 1978.
———. *The Origins of the Christian Doctrine of Sacrifice*. Philadelphia: Fortress, 1978.
———. "Sacrifice in Origen." *StPatr* 11 (1972) 125–29.
Daniélou, Jean. "La colombe et la ténèbre dans la mystique Byzantine ancienne." *Eranos Jahrbuch* 23 (1954) 403ff.

Bibliography

———, ed. *From Glory to Glory: Texts from Gregory of Nyssa's Mystical Writings*. Translated and edited by Herbert Musurillo. New York: Scribner, 1961.

———. *Origen*. Translated by Walter Mitchell. New York: Sheed & Ward, 1955.

———. *Origène. Le Génie du christianisme*. Paris: La Table Ronde, 1948.

———. *Platonisme et théologie mystique: essai sur la doctrine spirituelle de saint Grégoire de Nysse*. Thélogie 2. Paris: Aubier, 1944.

Daniélou, Jean, and R. du Charlat. *La catéchèse aux premiers siècles*. Fayard-Mame, 1968.

Dembitz, Lewis N. "Ge'ullah." In *Jewish Encyclopedia*, edited by Isadore Singer, 5:648. New York: Funk & Wagnalls, 1910.

Devreesse, Robert. *Le commentaire de Théodore de Mopsueste sur les Psaumes I–LXXX*. Studi e Testi 93. Vatican City: Biblioteca apostolica vaticana, 1939.

Dix, Gregory. *The Shape of the Liturgy*. Westminster: Dacre, 1945.

———. *The Treatise on the Apostolic Tradition of St. Hippolytus of Rome*. Reissued with corrections by Henry Chadwick. London: SPCK, 1968.

Dodd, C. H. *The Bible and the Greeks*. London: Hodder & Stoughton, 1954.

Dohmes, Ambrosius. "Die Einstimmigkeit des Kultgesanges als Symbol der Einheit." *Liturgie und Mönchtum* 1 (1948) 67–72.

———. "Der pneumatische Charakter des Kultgesanges nach frühchristlichen Zeugnissen." In *Vom Christlichen Mysterium: Gesammelte Arbeiten zum Gedächtnis von Odo Casel*, edited by Anton Mayer et al., 35–53. Düsseldorf: Patmos, 1951.

Dölger, Franz Joseph. *Sol Salutis: Gebet und Gesang im christlichen Altertum: mit besonderer Rücksicht auf die Ostung in Gebet und Liturgie*. Liturgiegeschichtliche Forschungen 4/5. Münster: Aschendorff, 1920.

Duchesne, L. *Christian Worship: Its Origin and Evolution. A Study of the Latin Liturgy up to the Time of Charlemagne*. Translated by M. L. McClure. 5th ed. London: SPCK, 1949.

Dugmore, C. W. "Sacrament and Sacrifice in the Early Fathers." *JEH* 2 (1951) 24–37. Reprinted in Everett Ferguson, *Studies in Early Christianity*, vol. 15, *Worship in Early Christianity*, 178–91. New York: Garland, 1993.

Echle, Harry A. "Sacramental Initiation as Christian Mystery-Initiation according to Clement of Alexandria." In *Vom Christlichen Mysterium*, edited by A. Mayer et al., 54–65. Düsseldorf: Patmos, 1951.

Eijk, A. H. C. van. "The Gospel of Philip and Clement of Alexandria: Gnostic and Ecclesiastical Theology on the Resurrection and the Eucharist." *VigChr* 25 (1971) 94–120.

Engberg-Pedersen, Troels. "Philo's *De vita contemplativa* as a Philosopher's Dream." *Journal for the Study of Judaism* 30 (1999) 40–64.

Engelbrecht, Edward. "God's Milk: An Orthodox Confession of the Eucharist." *Journal of Early Christian Studies* 7 (1999) 509–26.

Erler, Michael. "Die Schule Epikurs." In *Die Hellenische Philosophie*. Die Philosophie der Antike 4.1. Basel: Schwabe, 1994.

Ewald, Marie Liguori, trans. *The Homilies of Saint Jerome*. FC 48. Washington, DC: Fathers of the Church, 1964.

Fabricius, Cajus, and Daniel Ridings. *A Concordance to Gregory of Nyssa*. Studia Graeca et Latina Gothoburgensia 50. Göteborg: Acta universitatis Gothoburgensis, 1989.

Fahey, J. F. *The Eucharistic Teaching of Ratramn of Corbie*. Pontificia Facultas Theologica Seminarii Sanctae Mariae ad Lacum, Dissertationes ad lauream 2. Mundelein, IL: St. Mary of the Lake Seminary, 1951.

Feldman, Louis H. "Philo's Views on Music." *Journal of Jewish Music and Liturgy* 9 (1985-86) 36–54. Reprinted in Feldman, *Studies in Hellenistic Judaism*, 504–28. Arbeiten zur Geschichte des antiken Judentums und des Urchristentums 30. Leiden: Brill, 1996.

Ferguson, Everett. *A Cappella Music in the Public Worship of the Church*. 3rd. ed. Fort Worth, TX: Star Bible, 1988. 4th ed., 2013.

———. "The Active and Contemplative Lives: The Patristic Interpretation of Some Musical Terms." *StPatr* 16 (1985) 15–23. [Included in this volume as chapter 9.]

———. "The Art of Praise: Philo and Philodemus on Music." In *Early Christianity and Classical Culture: Comparative Studies in Honor of Abraham J. Malherbe*, edited by John T. Fitzgerald et al., 391–426. NovTSup 110. Leiden: Brill, 2003. [Included in this volume as chapter 7.]

———. "Athanasius, *Epistola ad Marcellinum in Interpretationem Psalmorum*." *Ekklesiastikos Pharos* 16 (1978) 378–403. [Included in this volume as chapter 10.]

———. "Athanasius, *Epistola ad Marcellinum in Interpretationem Psalmorum*." *StPatr* 16 (1985) 295–308. [Included in this volume as chapter 11.]

———. *Early Christians Speak*. Rev. ed. Abilene, TX: ACU Press, 1987.

———. *Early Christians Speak*. 3rd ed. Abilene, TX: ACU Press, 1999.

———, ed. *Encyclopedia of Early Christianity*. Garland Reference Library of the Humanities 846. New York: Garland, 1990.

———. "God's Infinity and Man's Mutability: Perpetual Progress according to Gregory of Nyssa." *Greek Orthodox Theological Review* 18 (1973) 59–78. [Included in this volume as chapter 14.]

———. "Gregory of Nyssa and Psalmos." *Restoration Quarterly* 22 (1979) 77–83.

———. "Images of the Virgin Birth in Gregory of Nyssa's *Vita Moysis*." In *Jesus Christ in St. Gregory of Nyssa's Theology: Minutes of the Ninth International Conference on St Gregory of Nyssa, Athens 7–12 September 2000*, edited by Elias D. Moutsoulas, 285–305. Athens: Eptalophos, 2005. [Included in this volume as chapter 17.]

———. "The Liturgical Function of the *Sursum Corda*." *StPatr* 13 (1975) 360–63. [Included in this volume as chapter 3.]

———. "The Lord's Supper in Church History: The Early Church through the Medieval Period." In *The Lord's Supper: Believers' Church Perspectives*, edited by Dale R. Stoffer, 21–45. Scottdale, PA: Herald, 1997. [Included in this volume as chapter 4.]

———. "Praising God with 'One Mouth'/'One Voice.'" In *Renewing Tradition: Studies in Texts and Contexts in Honor of James W. Thompson*, edited by Mark Hamilton et al., 3–23. Princeton Theological Monograph Series; Eugene, OR, 2006. [Included in this volume as chapter 2.]

———. "Progress in Perfection: Gregory of Nyssa's *Vita Moysis*." *StPatr* 14 (1976) 307–14. [Included in this volume as chapter 13.]

———. "Psalm-Singing at the Eucharist: A Liturgical Controversy in the Fourth Century." *Austin Seminary Bulletin* 98 (1983) 52–77. [Included in this volume as chapter 6.]

———. "A Response to Robin Darling Young on the Eucharist as Sacrifice according to Clement of Alexandria." In *Rediscovering the Eucharist: Ecumenical Conversations*,

Bibliography

edited by Roch A. Kereszty, OCist., 104–15. New York: Paulist, 2003. [Included in this volume as chapter 5.]

———. "Some Aspects of Gregory of Nyssa's Moral Theology in the Homilies on Ecclesiastes." In *Gregory of Nyssa: Homilies on Ecclesiastes*, edited by Stuart George Hall, 319–36. Berlin: de Gruyter, 1993. [Included in this volume as chapter 15.]

———. "Some Aspects of Gregory of Nyssa's Interpretation of Scripture Exemplified in His *Homilies on Ecclesiastes*." *StPatr* 27 (1993) 29–33. [Included in this volume as chapter 16.]

———. "Spiritual Sacrifice in Early Christianity and Its Environment." In *ANRW* II.23.2 (1980) 1151–89. [Included in this volume as chapter 1.]

———. "Towards a Patristic Theology of Music." *StPatr* 24 (1993) 266–83. [Included in this volume as chapter 8.]

———. "Wine as a Table Drink in the Ancient World." *Restoration Quarterly* 13 (1970) 141–53.

———. "Words from the Ψαλ- Root in Gregory of Nyssa." In *Studien zu Gregor von Nyssa and der christlichen Spätantike*, edited by H. R. Drobner and C. Klock, 57–68. Vigiliae Christianae Supplements 12. Leiden: Brill, 1990. [Included in this volume as chapter 12.]

Fini, Mario. "'Sacrificium spiritale' in Tertullian: Ricerca sul significato del culto Cristiano." PhD diss., Pontificio Ateneo Anselmiano, Rome, 1976.

Fisch, Jos., trans. *Ausgewählte Schriften des heiligen Athanasius*. Kempten: Kösel, 1875.

Fitzgerald, John T. "Introduction: Philodemus and the Papyri from Herculaneum." In *Philodemus and the New Testament*, edited by John T. Fitzgerald et al., 1–14. Novum Testamentum Supplements 111. Leiden: Brill, 2003.

Fitzgerald, John T. et al., eds. *Philodemus and the New Testament*. NovTSup 111. Leiden: Brill, 2003.

Foley, Edward. *Foundations of Christian Music: The Music of Pre-Constantinian Christianity*. Collegeville, MN: Liturgical, 1996.

Fontaine, Jacques, and Charles Kannengiesser, eds. *Epektasis: Mélanges patristiques offerts au Cardinal Jean Daniélou*. Paris: Beauchesne, 1972.

Gaïth, Jérôme. *La conception de la liberté chez Grégoire de Nysse*. Etudes de philosophie médiévale 43. Paris: Vrin, 1953.

Garrett, James Leo, Jr. "The Pre-Cyprianic Doctrine of the Priesthood of All Christians." In *Continuity and Discontinuity in Church History: Essays Presented to George Huntston Williams on the Occasion of His Sixty-fifth Birthday*, edited by Frank Forrester Church and Timothy Francis George, 45–61. Studies in the History of Christian Thought 19. Leiden: Brill, 1979.

Gaster, T. H. "Sacrifices and Offerings, OT." In *Interpreter's Dictionary of the Bible*, edited by George Arthur Buttrick, 4:147–59. New York: Abingdon, 1962.

Gélineau, Joseph. "Antiphona: Recherches sur les formes liturgiques de la psalmodie aux premiers siècles." In *Chant et musique dans le culte chrétien: principes, lois et applications*. Collection "Kinnor," séries études 1. Paris: Fleurus 1962.

———. *Voices and Instruments in Christian Worship: Principles, Laws, Applications*. Translated by Clifford Howell. Collegeville, MN: Liturgical, 1964.

Gelston, Anthony. "ΔΙ' ΕΥΧΗΣ ΛΟΓΟΥ (Justin, *1 Apol.* 66.2)." *JTS* n.s. 33 (1982) 172–75.

Gérold, Théodore. *Les Pères de l'église et la musique*. Études d'histoire et de philosophie religieuses, publiées par la Faculté de théologie protestante de l'Université de Strasbourg 25. Paris: Alcan, 1931.

Gibson, Margaret. *Lanfranc of Bec*. Oxford: Clarendon, 1978.

Gigante, Marcello. *Philodemus in Italy: The Books from Herculaneum*. Translated by Dirk Obbink. The Body, in theory : Histories of materialism in the human sciences. Ann Arbor: University of Michigan Press, 1995.

Goldin, Judah. *The Song at the Sea: Being a Commentary on a Commentary in Two Parts*. New Haven: Yale University Press, 1971.

Grabar, André. *The Beginnings of Christian Art, 200–395*. London: Thames & Hudson, 1967.

———. *Christian Iconography: A Study of Its Origins*. Translated by Terry Grabar. Princeton: Princeton University Press, 1968.

Grabe, Johannes Ernst. *Septuaginta interpretum*. Vol. 4. Oxford: Sheldonian Theatre, 1709.

Gregg, Robert C., trans. *The Life of Antony and the Letter to Marcellinus*, by Athanasius. Classics of Western Spirituality. New York: Paulist, 1980.

Gregory of Nyssa. *Gregorii Nysseni Opera*. Edited by W. Jaeger et al. Leiden: Brill, 1952–.

Gronewald, Michael, trans. *Didymos der Blinde, Psalmenkommentar*. Papyrologische Texte und Abhandlungen. Bonn: Habelt, 1967.

Grözinger, Karl Erich. *Musik und Gesang in der Theologie der frühen jüdischen Literatur: Talmud, Midrasch, Mystik*. Texte und Studien zum Antiken Judentum 3. Tübingen: Mohr/Siebeck, 1982.

Gy, Pierre-Marie. "Les paroles de la consécration et l'unité de la priere eucharistique selon les théologiens de Pierre Lombard à S. Thomas d'Aquin." In *Lex Orandi Lex Credendi: Miscellanea in onore di P. Cipriano Vagaggini*, edited by G. J. Békés and G. Farnedi, 221–33. Studia Anselmiana 79. Rome: Anselmiana, 1980.

Haldane, J. A. "Musical Instruments in Greek Worship." *Greece & Rome* 13 (1966) 98–107.

Hall, Stuart George, ed. *Gregory of Nyssa Homilies on Ecclesiastes*. Berlin: de Gruyter, 1993.

Hamman, Andre. "Irenaeus of Lyons." In *The Eucharist of the Early Christians*, by Willy Rordorf et al., 86–98. Translated by Matthew J. O'Connell. New York: Pueblo, 1978.

———. *The Mass: Ancient Liturgies and Patristic Texts*. Staten Island, NY: Alba House, 1967.

———. *Vie liturgique et vie sociale: Repas des pauvres, diaconie et diaconat, agape et repas de charité, offrande dans l'antiquité chrétienne*. Bibliothèque de théologie. Paris: Desclée, 1968.

Harnack, Adolf. *History of Dogma*. Translated by Neil Buchanan. 1900. Reprinted, New York: Dover, 1961.

Harris, Rendel, and Alphonse Mingana. *The Odes and Psalms of Solomon*. 2 vols. Manchester: University of Manchester Press, 1916–20.

Hay, David M. *Glory at the Right Hand: Psalm 110 in Early Christianity*. Society of Biblical Literature Monograph Series 18. Nashville: Abingdon, 1973.

———. "Things Philo Said and Did not Say about the Therapeutae." In *SBL Seminar Papers*, 673–83. Atlanta: Scholars, 1992.

Hefele, Charles Joseph. *A History of the Councils of the Church: From the Original Documents*. Translated by William R. Clark. Vol. 2. Edinburgh: T. & T. Clark, 1896.

Bibliography

Heine, Ronald E. *Gregory of Nyssa's Treatise on the Inscriptions of the Psalms*. Oxford Early Christian Studies. Oxford: Clarendon, 1995.

Heinemann, Isaak. *Philons griechische und jüdische Bildung: Kulturvergleichende Untersuchungen zu Philons Darstellung der jüdischen Gesetze*. Breslau: Marcus, 1932.

Hennecke, Edgar. *New Testament Apocrypha*. 2 vols. Edited by R. McL. Wilson. Philadelphia: Westminster, 1965. Rev. ed. Louisville: Westminster John Knox, 1992.

Hermans, Theo. *Origène: Théologie sacrificielle du sacerdoce des chrétiens*. Théologie historique 102. Paris: Beauchesne, 1996.

Hitchcock, F. R. M. "Tertullian's Views on the Sacrament of the Lord's Supper." *Church Quarterly Review* 134 (1942) 21–36.

Höfling, J. W. F. *Die Lehre der ältesten Kirche vom Opfer im Leben und Cultus der Christen*. Erlangen: Palm'schen Verlagsbuchhandlung, 1851.

Holleman, A. W. J. "The Oxyrhynchus Papyrus 1786 and the Relationship between Ancient Greek and Early Christian Music." *VigChr* 26 (1972) 1–17.

Ivánka, Endre von. *Hellenisches und Christliches im frühbyzantinischen Geistesleben*. Vienna: Herder, 1948.

James, M. R. *Apocrypha Anecdota*. Texts and Studies 2.3. 1893. Reprinted, Eugene, OR: Wipf & Stock, 2004.

———. *The Apocryphal New Testament*. Corrected ed. Oxford: Clarendon, 1953.

Jaubert, Annie. *La Date de la Cène: Calendrier biblique et liturgie chrétienne*. EB. Paris: Gabalda, 1957.

Jorissen, Hans. *Die Entfaltung der Transubstantiationslehre bis zum Beginn der Hochscholastik*. Münsterische Beiträge zur Theologie 28. Münster: Aschendorff, 1965.

Jourjon, M. "Justin." In *The Eucharist of the Early Christians*, by Willy Rordorf et al., 71–85. Translated by Matthew J. O'Connell. New York: Pueblo, 1978.

———. "Remarques sur le vocabulaire sacerdotal dans la *Ia Clementis*." In *Epektasis: Mélanges patristiques offerts au Cardinal Jean Daniélou*, edited by Jacques Fontaine and Charles Kannengiesser, 107–10. Paris: Beauchesne, 1972.

Jungmann, Josef A. *The Early Liturgy*. Translated by Francis A. Brunner. Liturgical Studies 6. Notre Dame: University of Notre Dame, 1959.

———. *The Mass of the Roman Rite: Its Origins and Development (Missarum sollemnia)*. 2 vols. Translated by Francis A. Brunner. New York: Benziger, 1951–55.

———. *Pastoral Liturgy*. New York: Herder & Herder, 1962.

Kemke, Joannes, ed. *Philodemi De musica librorum quae exstant*. Bibliotheca scriptorum Graecorum et Romanorum Teubneriana. Leipzig: Teubner, 1884.

Kereszty, Roch A., OCist., ed. *Rediscovering the Eucharist: Ecumenical Conversations*. New York: Paulist, 2003.

Kilmartin, Edward J. "*Sacrificium laudis*: Content and Function of Early Eucharistic Prayers." *TS* 35 (1974) 268–87.

Kraeling, Carl H. "The Apocalypse of Paul and the 'Iranische Erlösungsmysterium.'" *HTR* 24 (1931) 209–44.

Lamb, John Alexander. *The Psalms in Christian Worship*. London: Faith Press, 1962.

Lampe, G. W. H. "Eucharist in the Thought of the Early Church." In *Eucharistic Theology Then and Now*, by R. E. Clements et al., 34–46. Theological Collections 9. London: SPCK, 1968.

———. *A Patristic Greek Lexicon*. Oxford: Clarendon, 1968.

Lawson, John. *The Biblical Theology of Saint Irenaeus*. London: Epworth, 1948.

Lecuyer, J. "Sacerdote des fideles et sacerdoce ministeriel chez Origene." *Vetera Christianorum* 7 (1970) 253–64.

Le Déaut, Roger. "Le titre de Summus Sacerdos donne a Melchisedech est-il d'origine juive?" *Recherches de science religieuse* 50 (1962) 222–29.

Ledogar, Robert J. *Acknowledgment: Praise-Verbs in the Early Greek Anaphora.* Rome: Herder, 1968.

Leloir, Louis. "L'Apocalypse de Paul selon sa teneur armenienne." *Revue des Études Arméniennes* 14 (1980) 217–85.

Lenz, Johann. *Jesus Christus nach der Lehre des hl. Gregor von Nyssa: Eine dogmengeschichtliche studie..* Trier: Paulinus, 1925.

Léon-Dufour, Xavier. *Sharing the Eucharistic Bread: The Witness of the New Testament.* Translated by Matthew J. O'Connell. New York: Paulist, 1987.

Leys, R. "La théologie spirituelle de Grégoire de Nysse." *StPatr* 2 (1957) 495–511.

Linton, O. "Interpretation of the Psalms in the Early Church." *StPatr* 4 (1961) 143–56.

Lutz, Cora E. *Musonius Rufus, "The Roman Socrates."* Yale Classical Studies 10. New Haven: Yale University Press, 1947.

MacDonald, A. J. *Berengar and the Reform of Sacramental Doctrine.* London: Longmans, Green, 1930.

———, ed. *The Evangelical Doctrine of Holy Communion.* Cambridge: Heffer, 1930.

———. *Lanfranc: A Study of His Life, Work, and Writing.* 2nd ed. Oxford: Oxford University Press, 1944.

MacRae, George W., William R. Murdock, and Douglas M. Parrott, trans. "The Ascension of Paul." In *The Nag Hammadi Library in English*, edited by James M. Robinson, 257–59. Rev. ed. San Francisco: HarperSanFrancisco, 1988.

Macy, Gary. *The Banquet's Wisdom: A Short History of the Theologies of the Lord's Supper.* New York: Paulist, 1992.

———. *The Theologies of the Eucharist in the Early Scholastic Period: A Study of the Salvific Function of the Sacrament according to the Theologians c. 1080–1220.* Oxford: Clarendon, 1984.

Magne, Jean. *Sacrifice et sacerdoce.* Origines chrétiennes 2. Paris: Magne, 1975.

Malherbe, Abraham J. "The Structure of Athenagoras' *Supplicatio pro Christianis*." *VigChr* 23 (1969) 1–20.

Marrou, H. I. *A History of Education in Antiquity.* Translated by George Lamb. New York: Sheed & Ward, 1956.

———. "Une théologie de la musique chez Grégoire de Nysse?" In *Epektasis: Mélanges patristiques offerts au Cardinal Jean Daniélou*, edited by Jacques Fontaine and Charles Kannengiesser, 501–8. Paris: Beauchesne, 1972.

Marsh, H. G. "The Use of ΜΥΣΤΗΡΙΟΝ in the Writings of Clement of Alexandria with Special Reference to His Sacramental Doctrine." *JTS* 37 (1936) 64–80.

Mazza, Enrico. *The Celebration of the Eucharist: The Origin of the Rite and the Development of Its Interpretation.* Collegeville, MN: Liturgical, 1999.

McCormick, Scott. *The Lord's Supper: A Biblical Interpretation.* Philadelphia: Westminster, 1966.

McCracken, George E., trans. *Early Medieval Theology.* Library of Christian Classics 9. Philadelphia: Westminster, 1957.

McCue, James F. "The Doctrine of Transubstantiation from Berengar through Trent: The Point at Issue." *Harvard Theological Review* 61 (1968) 385–430.

Bibliography

McInerny, Ralph. "Aquinas, St. Thomas." In *Dictionary of the Middle Ages*, edited by Joseph R. Strayer, 1:353–66. New York: Scribner, 1982.

McKinnon, James W. "The Church Fathers and Musical Instruments." PhD diss., Columbia University, 1965.

———. "The Meaning of the Patristic Polemic against Musical Instruments." *Current Musicology* 1 (1965) 69–82.

———, ed. *Music in Early Christian Literature*. Cambridge Readings in the Literature of Music. Cambridge: Cambridge University Press, 1987.

———. "On the Question of Psalmody in the Ancient Synagogue." *Early Music History* 6 (1986) 159–91.

McNamara, Martin. *Targum and Testament*. Rev. ed. Grand Rapids: Eerdmans, 2010.

Meer, F. van der, and Christine Mohrmann. *Atlas of the Early Christian World*. Translated and edited by Mary F. Hedlund and H. H. Rowley. London: Nelson, 1958.

Megivern, James J. *Concomitance and Communion: A Study in Eucharistic Doctrine and Practice*. Studia Friburgensia n.s. 33. New York: Herder, 1963.

Mehat, André. "Clement of Alexandria." In *The Eucharist of the Early Christians*, by Willy Rordorf et al., 99–131. Translated by Matthew J. O'Connell. New York: Pueblo, 1978.

Mendelson, Alan. *Secular Education in Philo of Alexandria*. Monographs of the Hebrew Union College 7. Cincinnati: Hebrew Union College Press, 1982.

Merki, Hubert. ΟΜΟΙΩΣΙΣ ΘΕΩ: *Von der platonischen Angleichung an Gott zur Gottähn-lichkeit bei Gregor von Nyssa*. Paradosis 7. Freiburg: Paulusverlag, 1952.

Miles, Margaret R. "Augustine." In *Encyclopedia of Early Christianity*, edited by Everett Ferguson, 121–26. Garland Reference Library of the Humanities 846. New York: Garland, 1990.

Mitsakis, K. "The Hymnography of the Greek Church in the Early Christian Centuries." *Jahrbuch der Oesterreichischen Byzantinistik* 20 (1971) 31–49.

Mondésert, Claude, and Henri-Irénée Marrou. *Clément d'Alexandrie Le Pédagogue* 11. Sources Chrétiennes 108. Paris: Cerf, 1965.

Montefiore, C. G., and H. Loewe, eds. *A Rabbinic Anthology*. Philadelphia: Jewish Publication Society of America, 1960.

Moore, George Foot. *Judaism in the First Centuries of the Christian Era: The Age of the Tannaim*. 3 vols. Cambridge: Harvard University Press, 1927.

Mountford, James. "Music and the Romans." *Bulletin of the John Rylands Library* 47 (1964) 198–211.

Moutsoulas, Elias D. Η σαρκωσις του Λογου και η θεωσις του ανθρωπου κατα την διδασκαλιαν Γρηγοριου του Νυσσης. Athens, 1965.

Muñoz, Antonio. *Il Codice Purpureo di Rossano e il Frammento Sinopense*. Rome: Danesi, 1907.

Neubecker, Annemarie Jeanette. "Beobachtungen zu Argumentationsweise und Stil Philodems in der Schrift 'Über die Musik', Buch IV." *Cronache ercolanesi* 13 (1983) 85.

———. *Philodemus über die Musik IV. Buch: Text, Übersetzung, und Kommentar*. La Scuola di Epicuro 4. Naples: Bibliopolis, 1986.

Newsom, Carol. *Songs of the Sabbath Sacrifice: A Critical Edition*. Harvard Semitic Studies 27. Atlanta: Scholars, 1985.

Nikiprowetzky, Valentin. "La spiritualisation des sacrifices et le culte sacrificiel au temple de Jerusalem chez Philon d'Alexandrie." *Semitica* 17 (1967) 97–116.

Bibliography

Nilson, Jon. "To Whom Is Justin's Dialogue with Trypho Addressed?" *TS* 38 (1977) 538–46.
Noll, R. R. "The Search for a Christian Ministerial Priesthood in I Clement." *StPatr* 13 (1975) 250–54.
Norden, Eduard. *Agnostos Theos: Untersuchungen zur Formengeschichte religiöser Rede.* 1913. Reprinted, Darmstadt: Wissenschaftliche Buchgesellschaft, 1974.
Norris, Fred W. "Cyril of Jerusalem." In *Encyclopedia of Early Christianity*, edited by Everett Ferguson, 250–51. Garland Reference Library of the Humanities 846. New York: Garland, 1990.
Opitz, Hans-Georg. *Untersuchungen zur Überlieferung der Schriften des Athanasius.* Arbeiten zur Kirchengeschichte 23. Berlin: de Gruyter, 1935.
Osborne, Eric Francis. *Justin Martyr.* Beiträge zur historischen Theologie 47. Tübingen: Mohr/Siebeck, 1973.
———. *The Philosophy of Clement of Alexandria.* Texts and Studies 3. Cambridge: Cambridge University Press, 1957.
Palmer, Paul F., ed. *Sacraments and Worship: Liturgy and Doctrinal Development of Baptism, Confirmation, and the Eucharist.* Sources of Christian Theology 1. Westminster, MD: Newman, 1963.
Pelikan, Jaroslav. *The Christian Tradition.* Vol. 3, *The Growth of Medieval Theology (600–1300).* Chicago: University of Chicago Press, 1978.
Perkins, Justin. "The Revelation of the Blessed Apostle Paul." *Journal of the American Oriental Society* 8 (1866) 183–212. https://archive.org/details/jstor-592239.
Prideaux, John. *The Doctrine of Prayer.* New ed. Oxford: Parker, 1841.
Prigent, Pierre. *L'Épître de Barnabe I, XVI et ses sources.* EB. Paris: Gabalda, 1961.
———. *Justin et l'Ancien Testament.* EB. Paris: Lecoffre, 1964.
Prigent, Pierre, and Robert A. Kraft. *Épître de Barnabé.* Sources Chrétiennes 172. Paris: Cerf, 1971.
Puech, Henri-Charles. "Les nouveaux Ecrits gnostiques decouverts en Haute-Egypte (Premier inventaire et essai d'identification)." In *Coptic Studies in Honor of Walter Ewing Crum*, 134–37. Second Bulletin of the Byzantine Institute. Boston: Byzantine Institute, 1950.
Quacquarelli, A. "L'epiteto sacerdote (ἱερεύς) ai cristiani in Giustino Martire (*Dial.* 116.3)." *Vetera Christianorum* 7 (1970) 5–19.
Quasten, Johannes. *Music and Worship in Pagan and Christian Antiquity.* Translated by Boniface Ramsay. NPM Studies in Church Music and Liturgy. Washington, DC: National Association of Pastoral Musicians, 1983.
———. *Musik und Gesang in den Kulten der Heidnischen Antike und Christlichen Frühzeit.* Liturgiegeschichtliche Quellen und Forschungen 25. Münster: Aschendorff, 1930.
———. *Patrology.* Vol. 3, *The Golden Age of Greek Patristic Literature from the Council of Nicaea to the Council of Chalcedon.* Utrecht: Spectrum, 1960.
Quasten, Johannes, and A. Di Berardino. *Patrology.* Vol. 4, *The Golden Age of Latin Patristic Literature from the Council of Nicaea to the Council of Chalcedon.* Westminster, MD: Christian Classics, 1986.
Ratcliff, E. C. "The Eucharistic Institution Narrative of Justin Martyr's First Apology." *JEH* 22 (1971) 97–102.
Reitzenstein, Richard. *Die hellenistischen Mysterienreligionen: Nach ihren Grundgedanken und Wirkungen.* 3rd ed. Leipzig: Teubner, 1927.

Bibliography

———. *Hellenistic Mystery Religion: Their Basic Ideas and Significance*. Translated by John E. Steely. Pittsburgh Theological Monograph Series 15. Pittsburgh: Pickwick, 1978.

Riaud, Jean. "Les Thérapeutus d'Alexandrie dans la tradition et dans la recherche critique jusqu'aux découvertes de Qumran." In *ANRW* II.20.2 (1987) 1189–295.

Richard, Marcel, ed. *Asterii Sophistae Commentariorum in Psalmos quea supersunt: Accedunt aliquot homiliae anonymae*. Symbolae Osloense 16. Oslo: Brøgger, 1956.

Riedel, Wilhelm. *Die Kirchenrechtsquellen des Patriarchats Alexandrien*. Leipzig: Deichert, 1900.

Robertson, Charles H. et al. "The Meaning and Use of *Psallo*: Part II." *Restoration Quarterly* 6.2 (1962) 57–66.

Rondeau, Marie-Joseph. "Le commentaire sur les Psaumes d'Evagre le Pontique." *Orientalia Christiana Periodica* 26 (1960) 307–48.

———. "L'Épitre à Marcellinus sur les Psaumes." *VigChr* 22 (1968) 176–97.

Rordorf, Willy. *Sunday: The History of the Day of Rest and Worship in the Earliest Centuries of the Christian Church*. Translated by A. A. K. Graham. Philadelphia: Westminster, 1968.

Rordorf, Willy, et al. *The Eucharist of the Early Christians*. Translated by Matthew J. O'Connell. New York: Pueblo, 1978.

———. "Le sacrifice eucharistique." *Theologische Zeitschrift* 25 (1969) 335–53. Reprinted in Everett Ferguson, ed., *Worship in Early Christianity*, 193–211. Studies in Early Christianity 15. New York: Garland, 1993.

Routley, Erik. *The Church and Music: An Enquiry into the History, the Nature, and the Scope of Christian Judgement on Music*. London: Duckworth, 1950.

Saxer, Victor. "Tertullian." In *The Eucharist of the Early Christians*, by Willy Rordorf et al., 132–55. Translated by Matthew J. O'Connell. New York: Pueblo, 1978.

Schlötter, Reinhold. "Die kirchenmusikalische Terminologie der griechischen Kirchenväter." PhD diss., University of Munich, 1953.

Schmitz, Otto. *Die Opferanschauung des späteren Judentums und die Opferaussagen des Neuen Testaments*. Tübingen: Mohr/Siebeck, 1910.

Schoedel, William R., ed. and trans. *Athenagoras, Legatio and De Resurrectione*. Oxford Early Christian Texts. Oxford: Clarendon, 1972.

Schroeder, H. J., OP. *Disciplinary Decrees of the General Councils*. St. Louis: Herder, 1937.

Schueller, Herbert M. *The Idea of Music: An Introduction to Musical Aesthetics in Antiquity and the Middle Ages*. Early Drama, Art, and Music Monograph Series 9. Kalamazoo, MI: Medieval Institute Publications, 1988.

Sheedy, Charles Edmund. *The Eucharistic Controversy of the Eleventh Century against the Background of Pre-Scholastic Theology*. Studies in Sacred Theology 2/4. Washington, DC: Catholic University of America, 1947.

Sheerin, Daniel J. *The Eucharist*. Message of the Fathers of the Church 7. Wilmington, DE: Glazier, 1986.

Sider, Robert D. *Ancient Rhetoric and the Art of Tertullian*. Oxford Theological Monographs. Oxford: Oxford University Press, 1971.

———. "Tertullian." In *Encyclopedia of Early Christianity*, edited by Everett Ferguson, 883–85. Garland Reference Library of the Humanities 846. New York: Garland, 1990.

Sieben, H.-J. "Athanasius über den Psalter: Analyse seines *Briefes an Marcellinus*." *Theologie and Philosophie* 48 (1973) 157–73.

Siegert, Folker. "The Philonian Fragment *De Deo*: First English Translation." *Studia Philonica Annual* 10 (1998) 1–33.

Silverstein, Theodore. "The Date of the 'Apocalypse of Paul.'" *Medieval Studies* 24 (1962) 335–48.

———. *Visio Sancti Pauli: The History of the Apocalypse in Latin, Together with Nine Texts*. Studies and Documents 4. London: Christophers, 1935.

Skeris, Robert A. *Chroma Theou: On the Origins and Theological Interpretation of the Musical Imagery Used by the Ecclesiastical Writers of the First Three Centuries, With Special Reference to the Image of Orpheus*. Musicae sacrae melethmata 1. Altötting: Coppenrath, 1976.

Smith, J. A. "The Ancient Synagogue, the Early Church and Singing." *Music and Letters* 65 (1984) 1–16.

Smith, Joseph P. *St. Irenaeus Proof of the Apostolic Preaching*. Ancient Christian Writers 16. New York: Newman, 1952.

Smith, William Sheppard. *Musical Aspects of the New Testament*. Amsterdam: Ten Have, 1962.

Snaith, J. G. "Ben Sira's Supposed Love of Liturgy." *Vetus Testamentum* 25 (1975) 167–74.

Snyder, Graydon F. "The Text and Syntax of Ignatius ΠΡΟΣ ΕΦΕΣΙΟΥΣ 20:2c." *VigChr* 22 (1968) 8–13.

Socrates. *Ecclesiastical History*. Translated by A. C. Zenos. NPNF ser. 2, vol. 2. Reprinted, Grand Rapids: Eerdmans, 1952.

Söhngen, Oskar. *Theologie der Musik*. Kassel: Stauda, 1967.

Solaro, Jesus. *Textos eucaristicos primitivos*. 2 vols. Madrid: La Editorial Catolica, 1952–54.

Southern, R. W. "Lanfranc of Bec and Berengar of Tours." In *Studies in Medieval History Presented to Frederick Maurice Powicke*, edited by R. W. Hunt et al., 27–48. Oxford: Clarendon, 1948. Reprinted, Westport, CT: Greenwood, 1979.

Sozomen. *Ecclesiastical History*. Translated by Chester D. Hartranft. NPNF series 2, vol. 2. Reprinted, Grand Rapids: Eerdmans, 1952.

Spengel, Leonhard von, and C. Hammer, eds. *Rhetores Graeci*. Vol. 1. Bibliotheca scriptorum Graecorum et Romanorum Teubneriana. Leipzig: Teubner, 1853.

Stählin, Otto. *Clemens von Alexandrien*. Die griechischen christlichen Schriftsteller. Berlin: Akademie, 1905–1972.

Stead, G. Christopher. "St. Athanasius on the Psalms." *VigChr* 39 (1985) 65–78.

Stott, Wilfrid. "The Conception of 'Offering' in the Epistle to the Hebrews." *New Testament Studies* 9 (1962) 62–67.

Srawley, J. H. "Eucharist (to end of Middle Ages)." In *Encyclopedia of Religion and Ethics*, edited by James Hastings, 5:540–63. New York: Scribner, 1922.

Stylianopoulos, T. "Justin Martyr." In *Encyclopedia of Early Christianity*, edited by Everett Ferguson, 514–16. Garland Reference Library of the Humanities 846. New York: Garland, 1990.

Swete, H. B. "Eucharistic Belief in the Second and Third Centuries." *JTS* 3 (1902) 161–77. Reprinted in Everett Ferguson, *Studies in Early Christianity*, vol. 15, *Worship in Early Christianity*, 109–25. New York: Garland, 1993.

Bibliography

Swetman, J. "Malachi 1,11: An Interpretation." *Catholic Biblical Quarterly* 31 (1969) 200–209.

Swift, Louis J. "Ambrose." In *Encyclopedia of Early Christianity*, edited by Everett Ferguson, 30–32. Garland Reference Library of the Humanities 846. New York: Garland, 1990.

Taylor, Joan E., and Philip R. Davies. "The So-Called Therapeutae of *De Vita Contemplativa*." *HTR* 91 (1998) 3–24.

Theodoret. *Ecclesiastical History*. Translated by Blomfield Jackson. NPNF ser. 2, vol. 3. 1892. Reprinted, Grand Rapids: Eerdmans, 1953.

Thomas Aquinas. *St. Thomas Aquinas Summa Theologiae*. Vol. 58. Edited by Thomas Gilby. New York: McGraw-Hill, 1965.

Thomson, Robert W., trans. *Athanasius*. Oxford Early Christian Texts. Oxford: Clarendon, 1971.

Tischendorf, Constantin. *Apocalyses Apocryphae Mosis, Esdrae, Pauli, Johannis, item Mariae dormito*. Leipzig: Mendelssohn, 1866.

Tollinton, R. B. *Clement of Alexandria: A Study in Christian Liberalism*. Vol. 2. London: Williams & Norgate, 1914.

Trench, R. C. *Synonyms of the New Testament*. London: Parker, 1880.

Trudinger, L. Paul. "Sens de la Sécularité selon l'Evangile: Un Mot au sujet de l'Épître aux Hébreux 13:10–13." *Foi et Vie* 74 (1975) 52–54.

Van Deusen, Nancy E. "Medieval Organologies: Augustine vs. Cassiodor on the Subject of Musical Instruments." In *Augustine on Music: An Interdisciplinary Collection of Essays*, edited by Richard R. LaCroix, 53–96. Studies in the History and Interpretation of Music 6. Lewiston, NY: Mellen, 1988.

Völker, Walther. *Gregor von Nyssa als Mystiker*. Wiesbaden: Steiner, 1955.

Wagner, Walter. "Clement of Alexandria." In *Encyclopedia of Early Christianity*, edited by Everett Ferguson, 214–16. Garland Reference Library of the Humanities 846. New York: Garland, 1990.

Wallace, David H. "The Essenes and Temple Sacrifice." *Theologische Zeitschrift* 13 (1957) 335–38.

Walsh, Gerald G., trans. *Writings, Niceta of Remesiana*. FC 7. New York: Fathers of the Church, 1949.

Watteville, J. de. *Le sacrifice dans les textes eucharistiques des premiers siècles*. Bibliothèque théologique. Neuchâtel: Delachaux & Niestlé, 1966.

Wellesz, Egon. "Early Christian Music." In *New Oxford History of Music*. Vol. 2, *Early Medieval Music up to 1300*, edited by Don Anselm Hughes, 1–13. London: Oxford University Press, 1954.

———. *A History of Byzantine Music and Hymnography*. 2nd ed. Oxford: Clarendon, 1961.

Wenschkewitz, Hans. *Die Spiritualisierung der Kultusbegriffe: Tempel, Priester, und Opfer in Neuen Testament*. Angelos 4. Leipzig: Pfeiffer, 1932.

Werner, Eric. *The Sacred Bridge: The Interdependence of Liturgy and Music in Synagogue and Church during the First Millennium*. Vol. 1. New York: Columbia University Press, 1959. Vol. 2, New York: Ktav, 1984.

West, M. L. *Ancient Greek Music*. Oxford: Clarendon, 1992.

Wetter, Gillis Petersson. *Altchristliche Liturgien II: Das christliche Opfer: Neue Studien zur Geschichte des Abendmahls*. Forschungen zur Religion und Literatur des Alten und Neuen Testaments 17. Göttingen: Vandenhoeck & Ruprecht, 1922.

Whalen, Teresa. T*he Authentic Doctrine of the Eucharist*. Kansas City: Sheed & Ward, 1993.
Wieland, Franz. *Der vorirenäische Opferbegriff*. 1909. Reprinted, Aalen, 1970.
Wiles, Maurice F. "The Theological Legacy of St. Cyprian." *JEH* 14 (1963) 139–49.
Wilkinson, L. P. "Philodemus on *Ethos* in Music." *Classical Quarterly* 32 (1938) 174–81.
Wille, Günther. *Musica Romana: Die Bedeutung der Musik im Leben der Römer*. Amsterdam: Schippers, 1967.
Wolfson, Harry A. *Philo: Foundations of Religious Philosophy in Judaism, Christianity, and Islam*. 2 vols. Cambridge: Harvard University Press, 1948.
———. *The Philosophy of the Church Fathers: Faith, Trinity, Incarnation*. Structure and Growth of Philosophic Systems from Plato to Spinoza 3. Cambridge: Harvard University Press, 1956.
Woodhall, J. A. "The Eucharistic Theology of Ignatius of Antioch." *Communio* 5 (1972) 5–21.
Young, Frances M. "The Idea of Sacrifice in Neoplatonic and Patristic Texts." *StPatr* 11 (1972) 278–81.
———. "New Wine in Old Wineskins: XIV. Sacrifice." *Expository Times* 86 (1975) 305–9.
———. "Temple Cult and Law in Early Christianity." *New Testament Studies* 19 (1973) 325–38.
———. "The Use of Sacrificial Ideas in Greek Christian Writers from the New Testament to John Chrysostom." PhD diss., University of Cambridge, 1967.
———. *The Use of Sacrificial Ideas in Greek Christian Writers from the New Testament to John Chrysostom*. Patristic Monograph Series 5. Philadelphia: Philadelphia Patristic Foundation, 1979.
Zandee, J. *"The Teachings of Silvanus" and Clement of Alexandria, a New Document of Alexandrian Theology*. Mededelingen en verhandelingen van het Vooraziatisch-Egyptisch Genootschap "Ex Oriente Lux" 19. Leiden: Brill, 1977.

Subject Index

Abraham, as perpetual progress example, 268
acclamation (Amen), as expression of "one voice," 54, 56, 58, 183
active vs. contemplative life, musical terms as symbolic of, 185–96
"Acts of Apollonius," 24
Acts of Paul, "one voice" metaphor, 54
Acts of Thomas, on spiritual sacrifice, 41
Against Eunomius (Gregory of Nyssa), divine infinity, 269–70
Against Hilary (Augustine, lost work), psalm-singing in Eucharist, 107–8
agape meal, 65, 103
agreement, "one mouth"/"one voice" as expression of, 48, 52, 56, 57, 59, 183
Alexandrians
  Cyril on incarnation types in Exodus, 310n21, 313, 315
  on spiritual sacrifice, 33–38
  See also Clement of Alexandria; Philo
altar, Ignatius's metaphorical use of for community unity, 20–21
alternative interpretations of Scripture, Gregory of Nyssa's use of, 302–3
Ambrose, bishop of Milan
  on Eucharist, 78–80
  on Moses' leprous hand, 313
  "one voice" metaphor, 59–60

singing as agent of reconciliation in congregation, 180–81
skepticism on cosmos/music connection, 172
"Amen" (acclamation), as expression of "one voice," 54, 56, 58, 183
angels as allies in life of virtue, 291
animal sacrifice, Greek and Christian repudiation of, 3–4, 6
antiphonal singing, 108n2a, 109–10, 154–55, 157, 181
Apocalypse of Paul (Visio Pauli), analysis of, 112–26
Apocalypse of Peter, "one voice" in praising God, 53
apocryphal, pseudepigraphal, and sectarian literature, on spiritual sacrifice, 7–9
Apollodorus, "one voice" metaphor, 51
Apollonius of Tyana, on spiritual sacrifice, 4, 24, 29
apologists, on spiritual sacrifice, 23–30
Apostolic Constitutions, "one mouth"/"one voice" metaphors, 47
apostolic fathers, on spiritual sacrifice, 17–23
Aquinas, Thomas, on Eucharist, 92, 93–95
Aristophanes, "one mouth"/"one voice" metaphors, 46

339

Subject Index

Aristotle
  and Aquinas on transubstantiation, 94
  and Gregory of Nyssa on virtue as the mean, 293
  "one voice" metaphor, 50
  view of reality applied to real presence in Eucharist, 88–91, 93–94, 95
ascension of Christ, as reflected in Psalms, 209, 222–23
Ascension of Isaiah, on "one voice" metaphor, 53
asceticism
  as Christian sacrifice, 37–38, 40
  Gregory of Nyssa on, 260, 290
"as if" qualification for metaphorical use of "one voice," 50
Athanasius
  ethical take on use of music, 177
  on melody as context for words of praise, 168
  on music as beneficial to soul, 172–73
  "one voice" metaphor, 56
  See also *Epistola ad Marcellinum in Interpretationem Psalmorum*
Athenaeus, on "one voice" metaphor, 51
Athenagoras
  on music as sign of divine harmony, 170
  on rational sacrifice, 24
atoning sacrifice, 12, 14, 100
Augustine of Hippo
  on Eucharist, 80–82
  harmony of self as agreement between words and life, 178
  melody as enhancement of message in words, 173
  on music, 165, 168, 194
  on musical instruments, 188, 190
  on psalm-singing in Eucharist, 107–8
  sense gratification vs. spiritual use of music, 175
  on superiority of vocal music, 195

baptism, 42, 70, 104–5, 211
Basil the Great of Caesarea
  appreciation of *Epistola ad Marcellinum,* 216–17
  vs. Gregory of Nyssa on use of ψαλμός, 251
  on musical instruments, 189
  "one mouth"/"one voice" metaphors, 47, 56–57, 182
  on perpetual progress, 264–65
  on psalm-singing in Eucharist, 110–11
  singing as agent of reconciliation in congregation, 181
  skepticism on cosmos/music connection, 172
being and non-being, Gregory of Nyssa on, 285–86
beneficium, 2
benevolence, as Christian sacrifice, 15, 22, 37, 40–41
Berengar of Anger, and transubstantiation debate, 87–90
biblical consecration in Eucharist, 77
biblical-Jewish religious reality and eucharistic real presence, 67–68, 75
biblical persons as moral examples, 292–93. See also *Vita Moysis*
biblical songs, influence on Philo, 158
birth and free will, 285
body and soul
  Gregory of Nyssa's twofold anthropology, 288
  harmony between, 176–77
  and kithara vs. psalterion instruments, 186–91
  soul's intent as most important part of sacrifice, 3, 10
body as musical instrument, 172
body of Christ. *See* real presence in Eucharist
"The Book of Similitudes," 52
bread and wine
  catechesis and contemplation of highest mysteries, Clement of Alexandria, 102–3

Subject Index

and Jesus' words as inspiration to speak well and act well, 100
as only legitimate eucharistic substances, 99
as spiritual nourishment, 104
bride of Canticles, 268
burning bush, images of incarnation in *Vita Moysis*, 255, 307–10

Canons of Basil, on psalm-singing at Eucharist, 111–12, 113–15
cantor and reader in *Epistola ad Marcellinum*, 204–5
capacity for virtue, enlargement of human, 277
Cassiodorus, on music, 168
Catacomb of Callistus, 64
catechesis and contemplation of highest mysteries, 102–3
catechetical psalms, Athanasius on uses of, 209–12
Cathars, 93
Catholics, focus on connection between symbol and reality in Eucharist, 75
changeability of humans. *See* mutability of human nature
chastity and celibacy, as Christian sacrifice, 42
choruses/choral singing, Philo on, 157, 158n168
Christian doctrine
 and cosmological ideas in early church music, 165
 doctrinal use of Psalms, 209–12
 and ethical ideas in early church music, 165, 172–78
 "one mouth" metaphor as agreement on, 182
 as only appropriate lens for scriptural interpretation, 298–300
Christological perspectives in Scripture
 analogies from nature, 304–6
 burning bush, 307–10
 as ensurance of virtuous interpretation, 299–300
 images of incarnation in *Vita Moysis*, 259, 304–22
 Jacob and Rachel and the well stone, 306–7
 leprous hand of Moses, 311–13
 manna from heaven, 316–17
 reading of Psalms, 207–11, 220–23, 235–36
 rod and serpent, 313–15
 stone tablets written by finger of God, 320–22
 tabernacle, 317–20
Chrysostum, Dio, "one voice" metaphor, 50
Chrysostum, John
 diversity in congregational singing as model for organizational harmony, 180
 ethical take on use of music, 177, 178
 on human as finest musical instrument, 167, 168
 on hymnody over psalmody, 193
 on musical instruments, 189
 "one mouth"/"one voice" metaphors, 48, 58–59, 182–83
 praise offered in song as spiritual sacrifice, 168
 words as primary in spiritual purpose of song, 176
church
 death (crucifixion) of Christ as foundation of, 211
 hierarchical order of Christian community, as found in music, 164
 musical harmony as symbolism of agreement in, 178–79
 salvation through baptism as connection to, 211–12
 unity of, 81, 179, 182
 See also congregation
classical Greek and Roman poets and philosophers
 on "one voice," 49–51, 55
 spiritual sacrifice, 1–6
 See also Aristotle; Plato

Subject Index

Clement of Alexandria
  on allegorical symbolism of Eucharist, 73–74, 98–106
  on burning bush symbolism, 309
  catechesis and contemplation of highest mysteries, 102–3
  on human as finest musical instrument, 167
  importance of God and fellowship as focus of singing, 179
  music as element of Christian education, 176
  on music as originating in Logos, 170–71
  "one voice" metaphor, 55, 183
  on perpetual progress, 264
  on spiritual sacrifice, 33, 34, 35–36, 37
  on stone tablets of the Law, 321
Clement of Rome
  "one mouth"/"one voice" metaphors, 46, 182
  on spiritual sacrifice, 17–18
climbing imagery for Gregory of Nyssa's perpetual progress, 265–66
comfort, Athanasius on psalms of, 231–32, 234
Commentary on Canticles (Gregory of Nyssa), 262–63, 267
communion in one kind, eucharistic, 94
community. *See* church; congregation
confession
  as Christian sacrifice, 40
  psalms of, 202, 228, 231
Confessions of Cyprian (of Antioch), "one voice" metaphor, 58
congregation
  equality of congregants in unity of song, 58–59
  fellowship as expressed in singing, 179
  as focus for spiritual sacrifice, 20
  participation in singing, 108, 113, 158, 180
  singing as agent of reconciliation in, 180–81
  singing as force for unity in, 58–60

Constantine, 56
consubstantiation, 95
contemplative vs. active life, musical terms as symbolic of, 185–96
conversion of elements in Eucharist
  Ambrose on, 78–80
  Aquinas on, 93–95
  Augustine's spiritual/symbolic perspective, 80–82
  Berengar on, 88–90
  Cyril of Jerusalem on, 76–77
  Gregory of Nyssa on, 77
  Guitmund on, 91–92
  Radbertus' use of reality and figure, 82–85
  Ratramnus on, 85–86
  See also real presence in Eucharist
"Corpus Hermiticum," 4
cosmic harmony and harmony of soul, 49, 148–51, 170–72, 178
cosmological ideas of doctrinal import in early church music, 165
Council of Laodicea, 111
Council of Trent, 95
Creator and created, and human mutability, 273–74
cyclic vs. progressive change, 275
Cyprian of Carthage
  on eucharistic prayer, 64, 65–66
  on spiritual sacrifice, 39–41
Cyril of Alexandria, incarnation types in Exodus, 310n21, 313, 315
Cyril of Jerusalem
  on Eucharist, 76–77
  on Moses' leprous hand, 312

daily psalm recommendations from Athanasius, 203–4, 233
David, as perpetual progress example, 268–69
death (crucifixion) of Christ
  Christians as participating in, 15
  as foundation of church, 211
  and spiritual sacrifice, 14
  See also Eucharist
desire for God, 256–58, 277–81, 287
devotional use of Psalms, Athanasius on, 201–3, 216

Subject Index

Didache, on Eucharist, 18–20
Didascalia Apostolorum, on sacrifices, 41–42
Didymus the Blind, musical term interpretations, 185–87
Diodore of Sicily, "one voice" metaphor, 50
Dionysius of Halicarnassus, "one voice" metaphor, 50
diversity in congregational singing as model for organizational harmony, 180
divine infinity, 258, 260–61, 265, 269–73, 287
divinity
  in harmony with humanity, 148, 170
  Philodemus' on music's relationship to, 135–36, 140
  Philo's musical metaphors for praising God, 151–54
  Scripture as source of, 238–39, 291–92
  in two-part nature of Christ, 305–10
  See also God
Docetism, Tertullian's opposition to, 74
doctrinal use of Psalms, 209–12. *See also* Christian doctrine
dualist heresy, 93
Duns Scotus, 95
dynamic symbolism in Eucharist, 86–87, 105–6

Eastern Orthodox Church, psalm-singing at the Eucharist, 118
ecclesiological ideas of doctrinal import in early church music, 165
ecclesiological reading of Psalms, 212
education
  Philodemus on music in, 134–35, 138
  Philo on music in, 145–46
Eleazar, Rabbi, on spiritual sacrifice, 13
emotional benefits of music to Christian soul, 172–74

emotional/personal impact of Psalms, 201–2, 225–27
Epiphanius, on "one voice" among angels, 183–84
Epistola ad Marcellinum in Interpretationem Psalmorum (Athanasius), 197–240
  catechetical use of Psalms, 209–12
  Christological perspective on Psalms, 207–9
  date of, 215–16
  devotional use of Psalms, 201–3
  doctrinal use of Psalms, 209–12
  importance for functions of Scripture in early church, 216–17
  liturgical use of Psalms, 203–7
  outline of, 199–200, 217–18
  text of, 214–15, 218–40
erotic drive, music's contribution immorality, 134
Essenes, 9
ethical perspective
  classical authors on requirements for spiritual sacrifice, 1–3
  doctrinal import in early church music, 165, 177–78
  harmony of celestial bodies as model for ethical harmony of self, 172
  Hebrew focus on vs. sacrificial cultus, 7
  melody's purpose in, 173–74, 175
  singing as teacher of virtue and doctrine, 176
  See also right conduct; virtue
ethos theory of music, 132–41, 147–49
Eucharist
  as Christian sacrifice, 19, 20–21, 26–27, 31–32, 36–37, 39–40, 42, 43, 100
  Clement of Alexandria on, 73–74, 98–106
  figurative/symbolic view of, 74–75, 80–81
  in history of church, 67–96
  Irenaeus' on, 72–73, 74, 77–78
  Justin Martyr on, 70–72, 77

Subject Index

Eucharist *(continued)*
  literalism in, 82–86
  as memorial, 68–69, 70, 74
  Old Testament anticipations, 98, 103
  philosophical explanation, 87–90
  prayer in, 20–21, 100n17
  presence of Jesus as real but not literal, 67–75
  psalm-singing at, 107–26
  as sacrament, 78–79, 81, 85–87, 89, 90, 95
  substance vs. accidents, and Aristotelian view of Eucharist, 88
  as symbolic of intermediary sacrifice of Christ, 6
  taking while standing, 64
  Tertullian's *figura* perspective, 73, 74–75, 79
  in transformation between sacred and secular, 76–78
  transubstantiation theory, 90–95
  See also real presence in Eucharist
eucharistic prayer, 62–66
Eunomian controversy, 283
Eusebius of Caesarea
  on distinguishing musical terms, 192–93
  God's creation as musical instrument, 171
  "one voice" metaphor, 56
  on spiritual sacrifice, 43–44
  on superiority of vocal music, 195
  unison singing as emblematic of unity of church, 179
evil
  as finite (in opposition to the good), 272
  God's lack of responsibility for, 298–99
  as insubstantial, 286
  as sourced in free will, 285, 286
exhortation, psalms of, 228, 229

faith
  as central to Radbertus on Eucharist, 84
  as central to real presence in Eucharist, 91
  congregational harmony as ensurer of, 179
  in moral theology of Gregory of Nyssa, 295–96
fasting, 13, 22
Felix, Minucius, 29–30
fellowship as expressed in singing, 179
figura, Radbertus vs. Ratramnus on, 86–87
financial support of preaching, as Christian sacrifice, 16–17
Flaccus, 155
flame and material that burns, as metaphor for divine and human in Christ, 305–6, 307–10
flight imagery for Gregory of Nyssa's perpetual progress, 266
following God as path to seeing God, 258–59, 267
Fourth Lateran Council, 92, 93
free will, Gregory of Nyssa on, 276–77, 285–86

Gnostics
  Alexandrians' interpretation of "true Gnostic," 33–34
  Apologists' use of spiritual sacrifice to oppose, 30–32
  dualist heresy, 93
  Irenaeus' use of eucharistic perspective to oppose, 72
  "one voice" viewpoint, 54–55
goal of life, in moral theology of Gregory of Nyssa, 293
God
  desire for, 277–81, 287
  distinction between Creator and created, 273–74
  divine infinity, 258, 260–61, 265, 269–73, 287
  as focus of singing, 179
  following God as path to seeing God, 258–59, 267
  as the Good, 271, 283, 286, 298–99
  Gregory of Nyssa on absolute virtue of, 254

Subject Index

knowledge of, 24, 255–60, 267–68, 283
as luminous darkness, 255–56
music as inspiration of mind to turn to, 168
as in need of nothing, 5, 23, 30–31, 162
participation in, 267–69, 272–73
role in Moses' growth toward perfection, 255
See also divinity; praising God
Godliness goal for scriptural interpretation, 299–300
"God receiving" (Θεοδόχος), virgin birth as, 321
the Good, God as, 257, 271, 283, 286, 298–99
good works. *See* works
Gospel, imperative of proclaiming for salvation, 295–96
Gospel of the Egyptians (Coptic), 54–55
grammatical argument for real presence, 88–89
Gregory of Nazianzus
  "one mouth"/"one voice" metaphors, 47, 57, 184
  on perpetual progress, 265
Gregory of Nyssa
  on Eucharist, 77
  integration of classical music theory into Christian perspective, 165
  interpretation of Scripture, 298–303
  moral theology, 282–97
  on music as allegory of cosmic harmony, 171–72
  "one voice" metaphor, 57
  on perpetual progress toward virtue, 262–81
  philosophy of melody, 171, 242
  on psalm vs. ode, 193–94
  word study from the Ψαλ-root in Psalms, 241–52
  See also Vita Moysis
growth imagery for Gregory of Nyssa's perpetual progress, 266

Guitmund of Bec, on Eucharist, 91–92

habituation and virtue, Philo on, 130n11
harmony
  of church, 178–84
  cosmic harmony and harmony of soul, 49, 148–51, 170–72, 178
  ethical harmony of self, 172–78
  and music's power to bring social peace, 147
  "one voice" metaphor, 48–60, 182, 183–84
  Philodemus on, 132
  Philo on, 130–31, 146–47, 148–51, 159
  Psalms in service of harmony of soul, 167, 225–27, 236–37
healing through Scripture, 291–92
"Hearts above" or "Up with our hearts" in eucharistic prayer, 63, 65
Hellenistic philosophy, impact on real presence in Eucharist, 69–70
heresy
  dualist, 93
  as likened to musical discord in community, 179
  need for leadership unity in opposition to, 20
  restrictions on non-Biblical songs to exclude, 108n2a, 111
  See also Gnostics
Hesychius, on musical instruments, 189
hierarchical order of Christian community, as found in music, 164
Hilary of Poitiers, on Christological interpretation of Exodus, 309, 313, 315
Hippolytus
  on Christological interpretation of Exodus, 309, 322
  eucharistic prayer, 62, 64, 65
  on spiritual sacrifice and Eucharist, 42
  See also Pseudo-Hippolytus

345

Subject Index

holiness, as Christian requirement, 6, 203
The Holy Book of the Great Invisible Spirit, 54–55
Holy Spirit
  as agent of conversion of elements in Eucharist, 76–77, 83, 84
  Clement of Alexandria on, 101, 103–4
  as moving in the soul through the Psalms, 201
  music as consecrated by, 169–70
Homilies on Ecclesiastes, 282–97
  means of moral progress, 291–93
  psychological perspectives, 288–90
  theological tenets, 283–87
  vices and virtues, 293–96
human as most appropriate musical instrument for worship, 167, 185–86, 190. *See also* vocal music
human effort
  in making progress toward God, 260, 281
  in moral life, 291
human mutability, 260–61, 272, 273–77, 287
human nature, Gregory of Nyssa on, 288
Humbert, Cardinal-Bishop, and condemnation of Berengar, 91
hymns/hymnody
  as Christian sacrifice, 27–28, 42
  definition compared to psalms and odes, 191
  embellishments on Biblical texts in Byzantine, 205
  as expressions of purified mind to God, 11
  Gregory of Nyssa on definition of, 241
  non-scriptural hymns, 108n2a
  as superior to psalmody, 193

Ignatius
  antiphonal singing introduction as ascribed to, 109–10
  on martyrdom as spiritual sacrifice, 21

"one voice" metaphor, 53
illustrations, Gregory of Nyssa's use of, 302
imitative theory of music, 139
incarnation of Christ
  connection to salvation, 311–12
  life of virtue as grounded in, 284
  as reflected in Exodus, 259, 304–22
  as reflected in Psalms, 208, 209–10, 221
In diem natalem Salvatoris (Gregory of Nyssa), 310
Innocent III, Pope, 92
instrumental music
  inferiority compared to vocal music, 140–41, 175–76, 187, 193–94, 195
  patristic disapproval of, 165–66, 175, 189–90, 192–95
  Philo on, 149–50, 159–60
interval between parts of psalm (διάψαλμα), 249
invocation in Eucharist, 76–77
Irenaeus
  on Eucharist, 72–73, 74, 77–78
  "hands of God" metaphor for Son and Holy Spirit, 312
  "one mouth"/"one voice" metaphors, 46–47, 54, 182
  on perpetual progress, 264
  on rod-to-serpent episode, 314–15
  on spiritual sacrifices, 30–32
  on stone tablets of the Law, 321
  on tabernacle as symbol of church, 319
  on virgin birth, 307
irrationality of music, Philodemus on, 137, 138–39
Isocrates, on spiritual sacrifice, 3

Jerome
  church agreement as akin to symphony, 178–79
  ethical take on use of music, 177–78
  on superiority of vocal music, 195
Jesus Christ
  as altar, 20

Subject Index

ascension of, 209, 222–23
as bread and wine of Eucharist, 78, 79, 80, 84, 105
eucharistic commentary on real humanity of, 72
fleshly vs. docetic, 32
as foundation of church, 211
as observant Jew, 14
as present in Psalms, 207–11, 220–23, 227, 229, 235–36
resurrection of, 210–11, 229, 312–13
two-part nature of, 304–10
See also incarnation of Christ
Jewish perspective
vs. Christians on music, 153–54, 157–58, 179, 191, 194
meal as form of sacrifice, 19–20
music's role in ritual, 128–29, 145, 153–56
rabbinic authors on "one voice," 52
and real presence in Eucharist, 67–68, 75
role of music in morality, 148–49
on spiritual sacrifice, 7–13, 25–26, 77
See also Philo
Johanan ben Zakkai, on spiritual sacrifice, 13
joy, as defined in desire for God, 281
Jubal, Philo on, 160
judgement, Christ/God's in Psalms, 222–23
justice
identification of Christ with in Psalms, 209
Philodemus on relationship with music, 139
Justin Martyr
on burning bush symbolism, 309–10
on Eucharist, 70–72, 77
eucharistic prayer, 64–65
"one mouth"/"one voice" metaphors, 47
on spiritual sacrifice, 25–27, 29

kithara, 167, 186–89, 190

kneeling vs. standing in prayer, 63n8
knowledge of God
as Christian sacrifice, 24
as focus of perpetual progress, 267–68
as found in life of virtue, 255–60, 283

Lactantius, on seductive power of music as pleasure, 175
Lanfranc, vs. Berengar, 90–91
leitourgia, 18–19
Leontius, Bishop, and introduction of antiphonal singing, 109
Leo the Great, on directing music to praise of God, 166–67
leprous hand of Moses, image of incarnation in *Vita Moysis*, 311–13
"Lift up your hearts" in eucharistic prayer, 64–66
literalism in Eucharist, 82–83, 90–91
literal sacrifices, Philo's moral allegory of, 10
literal use of "one voice," 52, 57
liturgical practices
Athanasius on uses of Psalms, 203–7
Clement of Alexandria on, 98–99
fasting for benevolence as, 22–23
sursum corda, 62–66
vocal music as primary music for liturgy, 165, 194
See also Eucharist
living sacrifice, Christian adoption of, 6, 17, 19–20
logical analysis in Gregory of Nyssa's scriptural interpretation, 300–301
logocentric character of early Christian music, 164–65
Logos
as blood (Clement of Alexandria), 101
in Clement of Alexandria's view of Eucharist, 103–4
Jesus as last sacrifice, 100n13
longing for God, psalms for expression of, 202–3

Subject Index

looking to God, theological tenets in morality, 283–84
Lord's Supper. *See* Eucharist
love, in Gregory of Nyssa's moral theology, 296
Lucian of Samosata, "one voice" metaphor, 51
luminous darkness, God as, 255–56
lyre, Philo's preference for, 160

manna from heaven, as image of incarnation in *Vita Moysis,* 316–17
martyrdom, as Christian sacrifice, 21–22, 34, 40
meal as form of sacrifice, Christian vs. pagan or Jewish forms, 19–20
medieval period, eucharistic developments, 82–95
melody
   Athanasius on elevation of soul by, 206, 207
   construction of divine unity from congregational voices, 180
   Didymus on sacrificial definition, 185–86, 187
   as enhancement of message in words, 168, 173–74
   ethical perspective on, 173–74, 175
   Gregory of Nyssa on, 171, 242
   Philodemus on, 132, 140, 141–42
   Philo on, 146
   superiority of words over, 195, 205
memorial, Eucharist as, 68–69, 70, 74
metabolic realism, 82, 91–92
meter, Philo on musical, 146
Methodius
   on good works as sacrifice, 42
   on tabernacle as symbol of church, 319
Midrash Rabbah on Song of Solomon, 52
milk and meat, Clement of Alexandria's evangelistic use of, 101
mind
   condition of as Christian sacrifice, 34
   as instrument according to Philo, 149–50
   as source of vocal music, 168
   See also rational faculty
ministry of word as sacrifice, 19
modesty, as inducement to moral correction, 290
monetary donations to preaching, as Christian sacrifice, 16–17, 31
monody, 49–50, 53
monophonic singing, 45
moral theology (Gregory of Nyssa), 282–97
   means of moral progress, 291–93
   psychological perspectives, 288–90
   theological tenets, 283–87
   vices and virtues, 293–96
   See also ethical perspective; right conduct; virtue
Moses, 153, 158, 159n171. *See also Vita Moysis*
music
   ancient music, 127–31
   and church harmony, 178–84
   debates on value of, 136–41
   effects of, 141–43, 147–49
   evaluating different types, 159–63
   and harmony in human nature and cosmos, 149–51, 170–78
   as inspiration of mind to turn to God, 168
   instrumental music, 149–50, 159–60, 165–66, 175, 189–90, 192–95
   monody, 49–50, 53
   musical instruments, 149–51, 160, 249–50
   occasions for, 133–35, 144–47
   patristic theology of, 164–84
   Philodemus on, 131–43
   Philo on, 128–30, 144–63
   praise of God and music of cosmos, 151–54
   spiritual purpose of, 135–36, 168
   terminology interpretation, 185–96, 241–52
   Therapeutae and choral music, 154–59
   See also melody; singing
musical instruments

Subject Index

Gregory of Nyssa on, 249–50
Philo on, 149–50, 160
musicians, and music's relationship to virtue, 140–41
mutability of human nature, 260–61, 272, 273–77, 287

"name," "one voice" as, 51
narrative psalms, 228
nature metaphors in *Vita Moysis* images of incarnation, 304–6
Nehemian, Rabbi, on spiritual sacrifice, 13
Neo-Platonism, 6
New Testament
"one mouth"/"one voice" metaphors, 45–46, 49
as perpetual progress example, 268–69
on spiritual sacrifice, 14–17
See also Jesus Christ
Niceta of Remesiana
on community singing as reflecting harmony within group, 179
ethical take on use of music, 174, 177
"one voice" metaphor, 60, 184
praise offered in song as spiritual sacrifice, 168
non-Biblical songs, early church controversy over using, 108n2a, 111–12
North Africans, on spiritual sacrifice, 38–41
Novation, on stone tablets of the Law, 321–22

obedience
as center of Jewish sacrifice to God, 77
as gateway to knowledge of God, 260
odes distinguished from psalms, 186, 190–92, 193, 241–42
"Odes of Solomon," on spiritual sacrifice, 23
offertory *(oblatio)*, 108n2a
Old Testament

on "one voice," 49
on spiritual sacrifice, 7
See also *Vita Moysis*
"one altar" as unified community in worship of God, 20
one language, "one voice" as expression of, 49, 52
"one mouth" (unified expression), 45–48, 54–55, 182–83
oneness of universe in "one voice," 54
"one saying" as "one voice" for Gregory of Nyssa, 57
"one voice" (harmony, unified expression), 48–60, 182, 183–84
opposites, list of, *Homilies on Ecclesiastes*, 294, 302
Opusculum in Psalmos, 217
orans gesture, 64
Origen
on church agreement as akin to symphony, 178
on distinguishing musical terms, 192
on manna from heaven, 316n44, 317n49
on Moses' leprous hand, 312
"one mouth"/"one voice" metaphors, 45–46, 55–56
on search for wisdom as journey, 264
on spiritual sacrifice, 34–35, 36–38
on tabernacle symbolism, 319

participation in God, and infinite progress, 267–69, 272–73
participation in singing
all congregants, 108, 113
construction of unity from congregational voices, 180
women as participants, 158
particular sins, in Gregory of Nyssa's moral theology, 295
passion of Christ, as reflected in Psalms, 208–9, 222, 235–36
patristic perspective
ethical harmony of self/individual, 172–78
harmony of church, 178–84

349

Subject Index

patristic perspective *(continued)*
   harmony of music and harmony of the spheres, 170–72
   on musical terms, 185–96
   purpose of music to praise God, 166–70
   on spiritual sacrifice, 17–20
Paulinus of Nola, "one mouth"/"one voice" metaphors, 48
Paul the Apostle
   "one mouth"/"one voice" metaphors, 45–46
   as perpetual progress example, 268–69
   on spiritual sacrifice, 16–17
perfection in virtue, Gregory of Nyssa on, 254, 262, 270–72
perpetual progress toward virtue
   Basil on, 264–65
   Clement of Alexandria on, 264
   divine infinity, 269–73
   human effort in, 260–61
   human mutability, 273–77
   imagery and examples, 265–69
   Irenaeus on, 264
   nature of spiritual life, 277–81
   perfection as continual progress, 253, 254–58
   Philo on, 263–64
   and soul's progress toward God, 256–58
   theological tenets in morality, 287
Persius, on spiritual sacrifice, 2
petition, psalms of, 58, 228
Philo
   on burning bush from Jewish perspective, 308–9
   effects of music, 147–49
   evaluating different types of music, 159–63
   on harmony, 130–31, 146–47, 148–51, 159
   interest in music, 128–30
   occasions for music and types used, 144–47
   "one voice" metaphor, 52
   on perpetual progress, 263–64
   praise of God and music of cosmos, 151–54
   on spiritual sacrifice, 9–10
   on tabernacle symbolism, 318–19
   Therapeutae and choral music, 154–59
Philodemus
   debates on value of music, 136–41
   different types of music and their effects, 141–43
   music for divinity, 135–36
   occasions for music, 133–35
philosophical perspective
   explanation of Eucharist, 69–70, 87–90
   Gregory of Nyssa's philosophy of melody, 171, 242
   and paraenetic instruction, 129–30
   Philodemus on relationship to music, 135, 136–41
   spiritual conception of worship, 6
piety of person over content of sacrifice to gods, 2–3
Plato
   "one mouth"/"one voice" metaphors, 46, 49–50
   on spiritual sacrifice, 1–2
Platonic relationship between symbol and reality, 75, 80, 88n59
pleasure
   Athanasius' exhortation not to use psalms for, 236–37
   cyclical filling and emptying of self in, 257, 275, 287
   music as a part of, 129, 134, 143, 144, 147–48
   Plato on music as, 143n80
   seductive power of music as, 175, 176
   as source of sin for Gregory of Nyssa, 289–90
Plotinus, "one voice" metaphor, 51–52
Plutarch, "one voice" metaphor, 50–51
pneumatic nature of Christian song, 164
poetry vs. music, Philodemus on, 141–42

Subject Index

Polycarp of Smyrna, and martyrdom as spiritual sacrifice, 21–22
the poor, Psalms' call to care for, 213
Porphyry, theory of sacrifice, 5, 6
possessions, as Christian sacrifice, 31
praising God
    as Christian sacrifice, 15, 24, 41
    as expressions of purified mind to God, 11
    Gregory of Nyssa on definition of, 241
    Gregory of Nyssa's use of ψάλλω, 250
    music's role in, 144–45
    in "one voice," 53–55
    Philo's musical metaphors for, 151–54
    psalms of, 202, 228, 229
    as purpose of Christian music, 166
    as unifier of Christian community, 169, 181
    vocal music as most appropriate instrument for, 168
prayer
    as benevolence, 29
    as Christian sacrifice, 22, 25–27, 31, 35–36, 38–39, 41–42, 43, 100
    of consecration, 98
    in Eucharist, 100n17
    Gregory of Nyssa on definition of, 241
    as Jewish sacrifice, 25–26
    "one mouth" and unity of faithful, 45–46
    and "one voice," 55, 58, 183
    Philo's coupling with sacrifice, 9–10
    psalms of, 228
    vs. public singing, 155n155
    as replacement for animal sacrifice, 12–13
    sacrifice as medium of, 6, 10
preaching, as Christian sacrifice, 16, 18–19, 37
priestly status of Christians, 15, 16, 25
progressive purification, Gregory of Nyssa, 266
prophecy, psalms of, 228. *See also* Christological perspectives in Scripture
prophets, and ministry of word as sacrifice, 19
Protestantism, focus on symbolic/figurative interpretation of Eucharist, 75
psalm, Gregory of Nyssa on definition of, 241
psalmist (ψαλμῳδός), Gregory of Nyssa on, 248, 251
psalm-like/psalmic passage/psalmic voice (Ψαλμικός and ψαλμικῶς), Gregory of Nyssa's use of, 248–49
psalmody
    Chrysostum on hymnody over, 193
    early Christian focus on, 166–67
    Gregory of Nyssa's use of ψαλμῳδία, 245–48
    as higher calling for soul, 242
    melody as carrier of divine moral message, 174
    as sung in unison, 183
    as unifier of congregation, 181
    as unity of word and belief in singing, 59–60
Psalms
    Athanasius on uses of, 170, 201–13
    Christ's presence in, 207–11, 220–23, 227, 229, 235–36, 311
    Philo's description of for religious singing, 155–58
    See also *Epistola ad Marcellinum*
psalm-singing
    antiphonal singing development, 108–11
    Athanasius' choices, 232
    Augustine on, 107–8
    Didymus' definition, 185–86
    at the Eucharist, 107–26
    liturgical method with "Hallelujah," 111–13
    non-Biblical songs controversy, 111–12
    Visio Pauli on, 112–26
    See also psalmody

Subject Index

Psalms (ψαλμός can mean Book of Psalms but basic Greek is sound of cithara or harp)
  Athanasius' classifications for devotional purposes, 202–3
  Athanasius on reading vs. singing of, 204–5
  as encompassing all human emotions, 201–2
  as personal spiritual guidance, 201, 224–25
  as source for understanding Christ's teaching, 210, 227
psalterion, 167, 187–89, 190
Pseudo-Hippolytus
  on distinguishing musical terms, 191–92
  on stringed instruments, 187–88
psychological perspectives in Gregory of Nyssa's moral theology, 288–90
Ptolemy the Gnostic, on spiritual sacrifice, 23
public oral readings of Scriptures, according to Athanasius, 204
purification, in Clement of Alexandria's eucharistic symbolism, 102
purity of heart
  as Christian sacrifice, 23, 34
  Hebrew philosophers and poets on, 7
  Philo's moral allegories of literal sacrifice in Pentateuch, 10
  as sacrificial gift to God, 6, 8
Pythagoras, 4
Pythagoreans
  lyre as preferred instrument, 160n176
  mathematics of music, 131n15, 140
  on music and harmony of the cosmos, 165, 170

rabbinic literature, spiritual sacrifice, 10–13
Radbertus, Paschasius, on Eucharist, 82–85, 91
rational faculty
  as Christian sacrifice, 34–35

  musical harmony as allegory for rational control over senses, 177
  as requirement for worthiness before God, 10–11
  and sensory aspects of human nature, 288–89
  in worship and spiritual sacrifice, 3–6, 164
rational sacrifice, 3–5
Ratramnus, on Eucharist, 85–87
reading and study of the Law, as substitute for literal sacrifice, 12
realist vs. symbolic understanding of Eucharist, 75n25
real presence in Eucharist
  Berengar on, 88–89
  as both reality and figure, 82–86
  as conversion of elements, 76
  Lanfranc's overthrow of Berengar, 90–91
  as real but not literal, 67–75
  transubstantiation theory, 90–95
  See also conversion of elements in Eucharist
redemption
  Christ's sacrifice as key to, 14
  Psalms as tool for, 210–11, 229–30
"remembrance" in Eucharist, 67
removing garments imagery for Gregory of Nyssa's progressive purification, 266
repentance
  as Christian sacrifice, 40
  as equivalent to literal sacrifice for rabbis, 12
  and human role in salvation, 211
responsorial singing, 110, 113, 157, 181, 250
resurrection of Christ
  as reflected in Psalms, 209, 210–11, 229
  as reflected in transformation of Moses' leprous hand, 312–13
resurrection of the body, 72
rhythm
  Philodemus on, 132, 141–42
  Philo on, 146
right conduct

faith as inextricably linked to, 296
music's influence on, 137
as one part of virtue for Gregory of Nyssa, 255, 258–61
rectitude as necessary to success of prayers on Psalms, 203
as sacrificial gift to God, 8
Solomon as teacher of in Ecclesiastes, 299–300
See also moral theology; virtue
righteousness
kindness and almsgiving as appropriate sacrifices, 7
"one voice" and joining the angels, 53
rod and serpent, as image of incarnation in *Vita Moysis,* 313–15
Roman Stoics on sacrifice, 2

sacrament, Eucharist as
Augustine on, 81
Berengar's influence on, 89, 90
consecration's role in moving from physical to spiritual, 78–79
Franciscans vs. Aquinas on, 95
Radbertus on, 85
Ratramnus on, 86–87
sacred and secular
Eucharist as point of transformation between, 71–74, 76–78
and "one mouth"/"one voice," 48, 58
sacrifice. *See* spiritual sacrifice
Sallustius, as Christian sacrifice, 6
salvation
and connection to church through baptism, 211–12
Exodus from Egypt interpreted in light of, 311, 320, 322
incarnation of Christ as connection to, 311–12
and proclaiming of Gospel, 295–96
and real presence in Eucharist, 84–85
sanctification of food for Eucharist, 68–69
satisfaction and desire in spiritual life, paradox of, 279–80
Scripture

Athanasius on divine power of, 238–39
as divine assistance in life of virtue, 291–92
Gregory of Nyssa's interpretation, 298–303
public oral readings of, 204
as source of divinity, 238–39, 291–92
unity of and "one voice" metaphor, 55
See also Christological perspectives in Scripture; *specific Scriptures by name*
seeing God, 258–59, 267, 283–84. *See also* knowledge of God
self as sacrifice to God, 33–34, 38, 43
Seneca, on spiritual sacrifice, 2
senses
dilemma of music's use for pleasurable vs. spiritual purposes, 175
as instrument according to Philo, 149–50
musical harmony as allegory for rational control over senses, 177
rational and sensory aspects of human nature, 288–89
See also pleasure
sequence issue in Gregory of Nyssa's work, 303
sexuality, music as corruptive influence, 148
shame, as inducement to moral correction, 290
"Shepherd of Hermas," on spiritual sacrifice, 22–23
Sibylline Oracles, on spiritual sacrifice, 27–28
sin
evidence in Psalms for human responsibility, 211, 224–25
Moses' rod and serpent and Christ's adoption of human nature, 314
as sourced in senses of the body, 289
singing
antiphonal, 108n2a, 109–10, 154–55, 157, 181

353

Subject Index

singing *(continued)*
  Basil on unifying quality in, 56–57
  choruses/choral singing, 157, 158n168
  Didymus on definition, 185–86, 187
  effect on congregation, 58–60, 108, 113, 158, 179, 180–81
  Gregory of Nyssa's use of ψαλμῳδία, 245–48
  monophonic, 45
  and "one voice," 53–55
  Philo's use of as metaphor, 129n9
  prayer vs. public singing, 155n155
  responsorial, 110, 113, 157, 181, 250
  superiority over instrumental music, 140–41, 175–76, 187, 193–94, 195
  unison, 53, 110, 157, 181, 182–83
  See also psalm-singing; vocal music
skolion, 55
social use of music
  Philodemus on, 133–35
  Philo on, 144–63
Socrates (church historian), on antiphonal singing, 109
Solomon
  as example of virtue, 292–93
  as instructor in Ecclesiastes, 299–300
"The Song of the Three Youths," 46
songs
  Biblical songs' influence on Philo, 158
  as Christian sacrifice, 27–28, 37, 168
  musical term definition in relation to Psalms, 191–92
  and "one mouth"/"one voice" metaphors, 48
  pneumatic nature of Christian, 164
  restrictions on non-Biblical, 108n2a, 111
  as spiritual sacrifice, 168–69
  See also singing
soul
  as archetype of manmade instruments, 161–62, 161n180
  as ever-changing and mutable, 274–75
  importance of words vs. melody for, 205
  influence of music according to Philo, 147–48
  music as beneficial to, 172–73
  perpetual progress toward God, 256–58
  psalmody as higher calling for, 242
  Psalms in service of harmony within, 167, 225–27, 236–37
  See also body and soul
spiritual desires, Gregory of Nyssa on continuity of, 277–81, 287
spiritual doctrine, Gregory of Nyssa's. *See Vita Moysis*
spiritualizing interpretation of Eucharist, Clement of Alexandria, 105
spiritual life, Gregory of Nyssa on nature of, 277–81
spiritual sacrifice
  Alexandrians on, 33–38
  apologists on, 23–30
  apostolic fathers on, 17–23
  Eucharist as, 19, 20–21, 26–27, 31–32, 36–37, 39–40, 42, 43, 100
  in eucharistic prayer of lifting up hearts, hands, 65
  Eusebius on, 43–44
  Greek and Roman poets and philosophers on, 1–6
  Irenaeus on, 30–32
  Judaism on, 7–13
  New Testament on, 14–17
  North Africans on, 38–41
  and "one voice" in writing, 55
  other third-century sources on, 41–42
  Philo on, 162–63
  praise offered in song as, 168–69
  See also prayer
standing in prayer with eyes to heaven and palms up, 63–64
Stoicism

Subject Index

Philodemus' argument against music as virtue, 135–43
on sacrifice, 2
stone cut without human hands, as image of incarnation in *Vita Moysis*, 306–7
stone tablets written by finger of God in *Vita Moysis*, 255–56, 320–22
structure of reality, free will as integral to Gregory of Nyssa's, 285–86
substance vs. accidents, and Aristotelian view of Eucharist, 88, 93, 94
suffering, as equivalent to literal sacrifice for rabbis, 13
sursum corda, 62–66, 98–99
symbolic realism, in Augustine's Eucharist perspective, 82
symbolic vs. realist understanding of Eucharist, 75n25
symphony, church agreement as akin to, 178–79
symposium, as center of immoral activity, 134

tabernacle, as image of incarnation in *Vita Moysis*, 317–20
Tertullian of Carthage
on Eucharist, 74–75
on Moses' leprous hand, 312–13
on spiritual sacrifice, 38–39, 40, 41
thank offering, Eucharist as, 100
thanksgiving
as Christian sacrifice, 25–27, 43–44
in Eucharist, 100n17
as Jewish sacrifice, 25–26
psalms of, 228
sacrifice as medium of, 10
Thaumaturgus, Gregory, "one mouth"/"one voice" metaphors, 47
Theodoret
on antiphonal singing, 109
ethical take on use of music, 177
on human as finest musical instrument, 167
on purpose of human music to praise God, 172

Theophrastus, on rational sacrifice, 3–4
Therapeutae, 155–57, 158n167
thusia, 20
transubstantiation theory, 87–95
tropological interpretation of Psalms, 203
"true Gnostic," Alexandrians' interpretation of, 33–34
two-part nature of Christ (divine/human), 304–10

unaccompanied singing, Gregory of Nyssa's use of ψαλ- root words for, 251
unified expression
"one mouth" metaphor, 45–48, 54–55, 182–83
"one voice" metaphor, 48–60, 182, 183–84
unison acclamations, and community agreement, 150n125
unison singing
Basil's report of, 181
as emblematic of church unity, 179
as expression of congregation as "one mouth," 182–83
Philo on, 157
for Psalms, 110
theme of in early church, 53
unity of church
altar as metaphor for, 20–21
Augustine on bread and wine symbolism and, 81
effect of praising God on, 169, 181
good works coupled with right faith, 179
"one mouth"/"one voice" as expression of, 182
singing as force for, 58–60
unison singing as emblematic of, 179
universal salvation, 272
unknowability of God, Gregory of Nyssa on, 283

"vanity" (ματαιότης), in *Homilies on Ecclesiastes*, 302

355

Subject Index

vices and virtues
- Gregory of Nyssa's list of, 294
- Philodemus on music's relationship to, 137–43
- See also sin; virtue

virgin birth, 307, 308, 310, 314–15, 321

virtue
- Athanasius' appeal to Psalms for moral instruction, 213, 225, 228, 229, 234, 236
- disharmony as metaphor for lack of, 148n117
- Gregory of Nyssa on role of music in inspiring, 241–42
- Gregory of Nyssa's definition, 293
- Jesus as best example, 213
- loss of as disharmony to the soul, 148n117
- as the measure of worthiness for God, 10
- Moses' journey toward moral perfection as model of, 254
- music practice as, 130
- Philodemus on music's relationship to, 137–43
- Philo on habituation and virtue, 130n11
- See also perpetual progress toward virtue

virtuous life
- as Christian sacrifice, 28–30, 31, 35–36
- goals of, 297
- positive influence of music according to Philo, 147
- as proper sacrifice for God, 3–5

virtus sacramenti, 84

vision of God, 258–59, 267, 283–84. See also knowledge of God

Visio Pauli, analysis of, 112–26

Vita Moysis (Life of Moses) (Gregory of Nyssa)
- analogies from nature, 304–6
- burning bush, 255, 307–10
- divine infinity, 258, 260–61, 271–72
- knowledge of God, 255–60
- leprous hand of Moses, 311–13
- manna from heaven, 316–17
- progress in perfection, 253–61, 271–72
- right conduct, 255, 258–61
- rod and serpent, 313–15
- sequence issue, 261n69
- stone cut without human hands, 306–7
- stone tablets written by finger of God, 255–56, 320–22
- tabernacle, 317–20

vocal music
- Athanasius' assumption of in worship, 206–7
- choruses/choral singing, Philo on, 157, 158n168
- Gregory of Nyssa's use of ψάλλω, 250
- as most appropriate instrument for praising God, 168
- "one mouth" (unified expression), 45–48
- "one voice" (harmony, unified expression), 48–60
- Philo on Jewish preference for, 154–55
- as primary liturgical music, 165, 194
- superiority of for worship music, 160–61, 190–91, 194–95
- as superior to instrumental, 140–41, 175–76, 187, 193–94, 195
- Therapeutae, 155–56
- See also singing

women, as religious singing participants, 59–60, 158

"word of God" in Irenaeus on Eucharist, 72–73

words
- emphasis on as source of human virtue, 163
- explaining ideas through different Scripture definitions of, 302
- Gregory of Nyssa on ψαλμός and Psalms, 243–45
- moral primacy over music, 140–41, 175–76, 193–94

need for agreement with thoughts in the mind, 177–78
word study from the Ψαλ-root, Gregory of Nyssa, 241–52
works
  as Christian sacrifice, 15–16, 22, 28–30, 37, 40–41, 42
  coupled with right faith equaling communal harmony, 179
  as equivalent to literal sacrifice for rabbis, 13
  in moral theology of Gregory of Nyssa, 295–96

Ancient Sources Index

OLD TESTAMENT

Genesis

1:3ff.	221n33
4:21	160
11	47
11:1	49, 52, 182n74, 183
11:6	150n125
14:18	98
18:10–11	312n30
21:1–2	312n30
29:1–12	306
31:27	148n117
42:11	130n13
49:11	98

Exodus

3:2, 6	309n17
3:14	255
4:1–5	311
4:6–9	311
7:8–12	313n33
7:8–13	314n35
8:19	321n63
12:11	68
12:14	68
15	158nn165–166
15:1, 21	158
15:1–21	157
15:17	319
16	316
17:1–7	103
20:21	255, 263, 264
24:3	49, 183
25:9, 40	318
31:18	320
32:15–16	320
32:19	322
32:32	226n74
33:11	256
33:13	226n73
33:17ff.	256
33:20	258
33:21–23	267
34:1–4	322

Leviticus

7:12	7n30

Numbers

13:23–24	103
17:1–10	312n30
21:8–9	314

Deuteronomy

9:10	321n63
17:18	238n107
31:19	238n106
31:30	223n58
32:1–43	153, 158

Joshua

3:3, 14	239n110
7	239n111
8:34, 35	238n108

Ancient Sources Index

1 Samuel

2	158n162
4:1–11	239n111
15:22	7
16:23	237n101
17	234n90
24:3	232n82

2 Samuel

17	229n80

1 Kings

17:1	225n72, 226n74a

2 Kings

3:14	225n72
3:15	239n116
22:8–11	239n109

2 Chronicles

5:13	49, 183
18:12	46

Psalms

	197–240
1	216–17, 229, 246, 249, 251
2	209, 235
2:1, 2	208, 222n41
3	249
4	229
5	229, 234, 250n99
6	229, 246n59
7	229
8	212, 229–30, 246n49
9	212, 230, 232
9:5, 6 (9:4, 5)	209, 223n52
10	230
11	227, 230
12	230, 249n93
13	219, 230, 246
14	230
15	209, 210, 235
16	227, 230
17	230, 248n84
17,5	244n13
18	230
18:2 (19:1)	219n18
19	230
19:8–10 (20:8, 9)	220n25
20	235
21	209, 222, 235
21:16–19 (22:16–18)	222n42
22	7n30, 230
23	204, 209, 219, 222, 230, 233, 235
23:1, 2 (24:1, 2)	219n19
23:7 (24:7)	209, 222n48
24	230
25	230, 247n62
26	230
26 [27]:6	7n30, 185
27	230
28	220, 230
28:1 (29:1)	220n22
29	185, 230
30	244n20
31	229, 231
31:1	211
32	231
32:2	186–187
32:6 (33:6)	208, 221n34
33	231, 246n49, 251
33:15 (34:14)	224n66
34	230
35	211, 231
36	231
36:8 (37:8)	224n65
37	229
39	231
39:7–9 [40:6–8]	7
40	213, 229, 231
41	231
41:2	203
41:6, 12 (42:5, 11)	236n97
42	230
42:4	186
42:5 (43:5)	236n97
43	231
44	221, 234–235, 246
44:2	208
44:2 (45:1)	209, 221n31
44:7, 8 (45:6, 7)	221n35
44:11, 12 (45:10, 11)	208, 221n38
45	231

Ancient Sources Index

46	209, 222, 223, 235	85	230
46:2 (47:1)	209, 223n56	86	221, 233
46:6 (47:5)	209, 222n50	86:5 (87:5)	208, 221n36
47	204, 233	87	222, 230
49	209, 220, 235	87:8 (88:7)	209, 222n43
49:2, 3 (50:2, 3)	220n28	88	231
49:4, 6 (50:4, 6)	209, 223n54	91	204, 232, 233
49:7–15 [50:8–15]	7	92	204, 209, 211, 233–35
50	231	93	233
50:18, 19 [51:16, 17]	7, 231	94	204, 233, 246
50:19	7	95	209, 233, 235
51	231	96	233
52	230	97	209, 234, 235
53	227, 231	98	209, 235
54	232	99	212, 233
55	227, 231	100	233
56	227, 232, 248n83	101	234
57	232	102	234, 249n93
58	232	103	234
61	232	104	219, 231, 232, 234
62	232	104:26–31 (105:26–31)	219n21
63	232	105	219–220, 231, 232
64	232	106	220, 231, 232, 234, 248n84
65	210–211, 232	106 [107]	7n30
66	232	106:19 (107:19)	220n24
68	209, 235	106:20 (107:20)	208, 220n30
68:5 (69:4)	209, 222n44	106:36, 37 (107:36, 37)	220n23
68:31, 32 [69:30, 21]	7	107	232
69	232	108	235
70	232	108:6–8	208
71	209, 222, 223, 235	109	209, 222, 234–35
71:1, 2 (72:1, 2)	209, 223n53	109:1 (110:1)	209, 222n51
71:4, 12 (72:4, 12)	209, 222n47	109:3 (110:3)	208, 221n32
71:9–11 (72:9–11)	209, 223n57	110	232
72	232	111	229
72:2 (73:2)	236n98	113	231
73	232	113:1, 2 (114:1, 2)	219n20
74	229, 232	114	229
75	212, 232	115	234
76:11 (77:10)	311	115:8 [116:17]	7n30
77	219, 231	117	220, 232, 247n62
78	232	117:6 (118:6)	236n99
80	204, 233	117:26, 27 (118:26, 27)	208, 220n29
81	223	118	229, 239
81:1 (82:1)	209, 223n55	118:16 (119:16)	239n117
82	233	118:54 (119:54)	240n118
83	212, 229–230, 246	118:92 (119:92)	240n119
84	233	119–133	234n89

Psalms *(continued)*

121	220
121:1–4 (122:1–4)	220n27
123	246n59
125	220, 233
125:1 (126:1)	220n26
126	230
127	229
134	234
135	232
136	203
137	222, 232
137:8 (138:7)	209, 222n46
139	234
140	230
140:2 [141:2]	7
141	227, 232
142	234
143	234
144	234
145	234
146	234, 250n99
147	234
148	234
148:1	244n12
150	234, 249–250
150:3–5	237n102
151	234

Proverbs

9:1	319, 319nn60–61
15:28	7
21:3	7, 13
21:27	7

Ecclesiastes

1:2	298, 301
1:4	293
1:8	291, 300, 303
1:9	303
1:13	301
1:15	302
2:2	289, 301
2:3–6	300n10
2:4	295, 299
2:7	300
2:8	300
3:1	300
3:5	301, 302
3:5–7	300
3:6	302
3:8	302

Song of Solomon (Canticle of Canticles)

8:13, 14	52

Isaiah

1:10–17	7
1:11, 13	13
1:16	224n61
5:1	223n59
11:1–10	315
28:16	306
36–37	224n63
53:4	222n45
61:6	16n86
66:7	321n67

Jeremiah

4:14	224n61
6:20	7
7:21–23	7

Ezekiel

20:40, 41	16n89

Daniel

2:34	306, 314
2:34–35	319
2:45	306
3:38–40	8n37
3:51	182
5:1–9	322
7:10	18n94
12 (Greek)	224n62

Hosea

6:6	7
6.6	7, 13
14:2	12, 15n81

Amos

5:20–25	7

Jonah

2:10	7n30

Habakkuk

3:1	223n60

Malachi

1:10–12	27, 98
1:10–14	7, 26
1:11	12, 19n103

NEW TESTAMENT

Matthew

5:48	254
8:29	239n113
9:13	16n84
10:25	315
11:29	227n75
12:28	321n63
12:36	229n78
18:19	178
20:22	100
26:13	295
26:27–29	100
26:28	14

Mark

4:43	234n86
6:4	19n104
10:45	14
12:33	12n58
14:12ff	14
14:22	19n104, 68

Luke

1:28	221n37
1:35	319n61
2:41–49	14
8:28	239n113
10:17	239n115
11:20	321n63
23:22	236n94

John

1:14	104
2:1–11	76
2:19–22	14
3:14	314
4:24	14
6	73n21, 101, 103, 104, 105
6:30–51	316
6:32, 51	104
6:50	81
6:51	102
6:53	81n42, 83, 101
6:53–54	101, 102–103
6:53–56	73
6:54	79
6:55	317
18:38	236n94

Acts

2:25ff.	209
2:46	14
3:1	14
10:36	227n77
13:2	19n101
13:35	209
16:18	239n114
19:14–16	239n112
19:34	49, 183
21:20ff.	14
27:35	19n104

Romans

5:3–5	225n67
8:13	237n103
8:14	240n121
10:12	227n77
12:1	17, 24
14:2	316n43
15:5–6	45
15:6	47, 182
15:15–21	16

1 Corinthians

1:24	318
3:1–2	102
3:2	101
3:16	14
11:1	227n76
11:24–25	68
14:7	162n181
14:15	177n53, 250
14:33	48
15:24–28	264

2 Corinthians

4:13	234n87
4:18—5:2	233n84
5:21	314
6:16	14
18:12	182
29:31	15n81

Galatians

5:18	240n121
6:16; Phil 3:3	15

Ephesians

1:7	14
2:18–22	14
5:19	177–178
5.19	154n150

Philippians

1:23	233n84
2:11	295
2:17	16
3:1	225n71
3:13	238n105, 254, 256, 263, 264, 265
4:18	16–17

Colossians

1:24	104

1 Thessalonians

1:9	17
5:18	225n68

1 Timothy

2:8	24, 63n5
4:5	69, 71, 77
4:15	240n120
5:5	22
6:10	295

2 Timothy

3:12	225n69
3:16	210, 219
4:6	21

Hebrews

3:6	14
6:20	14
7:15–28	14
8:1, 2	14
8:3	14
9:1–14, 24	15
9:9, 14	14
9:11, 12	14
9:11–14	14
9:12–14, 25–28	14
9:14	14
10:1–14	14
10:19	15
10:19–22	14
10:21	14
10:23–25	14
11:33–35	238n104
12:28	15–16
13:10	15
13:11, 12	15
13:15	15
13:16	15

James

5:13	236n95

1 Peter

2:5	15n79, 16, 17
2:9	15n78, 37, 100n14

1 John

1:7	105

4:8	105

Revelation

1:6	15n77
5:8	21, 31
6:9	21
8:3, 4	21
9:13	49, 183

APOCRYPHA AND PSEUDEPIGRAPHA

Tobit

4:10, 11	8n38

Judith

16:16	8n34

2 Maccabees

1:30	152n136

4 Maccabees

6:29	9n39
8:29	183
17:22	9n39
68:29	183

Wisdom

16:20–21	316n43, 316n44

Sirach

15:9	236n100
34:18—35:11	7

Ascension of Isaiah

7.15	53, 184n82
8.18	53, 184n82
9.28	53, 184n82

Book of the Secrets of Enoch

45:3	8n35

Enoch

61.6, 9, 11	52

Epistle of Aristeas

234	8n33

Gospel of the Egyptians (Coptic)

IV, 2, 66, 14–23	54–55

Jubilees

2:22	8

Testament of Levi

3.5.6	8

DEAD SEA SCROLLS AND RELATED TEXTS

1QS

9:4, 5	9

PHILO

De aeternitate mundi

2.4	152n134

De agricultura

8.35	148n114
17.79—18.82	159n170
17.80	150n124
31.136	145n97
31.136–38	146n103
31.137	146n107
31.139	129n8

De cherubim

7.23	152n134
27.93	146n105
30.105	146n101, 147n108, 147n111
31.110	149n123, 152n134

De confusione linguarum

1.1	52
5.15	52, 150n125
7.21	150n125
10.35–36	158n165
11.41	130n13
11.43	150n125
13.55, 58	150n128
13.56	151n131
15.67	150n125
18.83	150n125
19.150	150n126
23.108	150n127
28.149	152n136

De congressu eruditionis gratia

4.15–18	146n101
4.16	146–147n108, 147n110
9.46	130n11
10.51	152n135
14.74–76	145n97
14.76	146n107
17.89	129n4
21.115	154n149
25.142	145n98, 146n104
25.144	130n11

De decalogo

9.33	162n181
30.159	145n93
158	10n44

De ebrietate

19.79	158n165
23.94	162n184
24.95	144n89
27.105	145n95
28.110	145n94
29.111	158n165
29.112	155n152
30.116	149n123, 150n124
30.116–17	149n119
30.117	149n120
31.121	155n152
43.177	144n86

66	10n44
79	10n44
94	177n53

In Flaccum

10.85	144n88
14.121–22	155n153
17.144	10n51

De fuga et inventione

3.22	148n117, 160n178

De Iosepho

42.253	153n141

Legatio ad Gaium

2.12	144n90
7.42	144n87
11.75	130n11
13.96	145n91
26.166	130n11

Legum allegoriae

3.78.221	160n172
I.5.14	160n176
I.30.94	129n6
II.3.7	129n7
II.7.21	129n9
II.8.26	129n9
II.15.56	162n184
II.18.75	144n86, 148n113, 160n173, 162n181
II.21.82	144n85
II.25.102–26.103	158n165
III.8.26	154n150
III.14.44	162n184
III.18.57	129n7
III.34.105	158n163
III.41.121	129n9
III.41.122	146n107
III.78.221	148n113

De migratione Abrahami

8.39	129n9
17.77	152n134

18.104	149n119, 155n152
20.113	153n141
21.120	130n10
28.157	152n136
29.148, 150	148n113
32.178	152n134
89–93	10n46
147	191n26
157 (II 299,12 Wendland)	247n68

De mutatione nominum

11.80	146n103
13.87	130n12
20.115	152n136
21.122	130n11
24.139	130n13
25.143	158n162
26.146	146n103
34.182	158n163
34.184	148n117

De opificio mundi

15.48	129n4
17.54	152n134
25.78	151n130, 152n136
31.96	129n4
37.107–10	129n4
42.126	146n104, 160n177

De plantatione

1.107	10n51
1.108	10n51
2.10	151n132
2.126	11n56
7.29	152n136
9.39	152n136
12.48	158n165
14.59	158n163
30.126	162n184
30.129	145n92
31.131	153n138
33.135	145n95, 154n146
38.159	147n112, 151n132
126	177n53
162	10n44

De posteritate Caini

14–15	263–264
21.75	129n6
24.88	149n122
31.103–4	161n180
31.104	146n107
32.105	160n174
32.105–8	161n181
32.111	160n175
35.121	158n163
43.142	129n6
45.155	129n7
48.167	158n163

De providentia

2.20	130n11

Quaestionis et solutiones in Exodum

1.52, 59, 83	318n53
2.20	149n122
2.38	148n117
2.51–106	319n54
2.98	10n49
2.120	155n151

Quaestionis et solutiones in Genesin

3.3	151n133, 152n136
4.27	129n4
4.110	151n132
II.3	162n181
III.3	162n181
IV.29	130n14
IV.76	130n14
IV.196	130n13

Quis rerum divinarum heres sit

4.14–15	162n184
22.110, 111	154n145

Quis rerum divinarum heres sit

15.79	317n46

Quod Deus sit immutabilis

6.24–25	149n119, 149n123
6.25	149n120, 161n180
16.74	152n136

Quod deterius potiori insidari soleat

9.18	129n6
21	11n54
21.75	129n6
30.114	158n163
31.1 18	317n46
33.125	152n134
34.126	162n181
34.130	162n182

Quod omnis probus liber sit

7.49	130n11
8.51	130n11
21.157	130n11

De sacrificiis Abelis et Caini

4.18	160n174
5.22, 29	129n9
7.37	129n9
20.74	129n5

De sobrietate

3.10	158n163
3.13	158n165
8.36	147n108, 160n172, 160n179
11.58	153n139

De somniis

1.5.28	146n107
1.6.35	162n184
1.6.35–7.37	152n136
1.6.35–37	152
1.32.256	153n138
1.35.205	146n107
1.43.256	154n145
1.215	10, 10n44
2.5.38	153n138
2.41.268	153n138
2.72	10n44
2.299	10n44
II.4.27–28	146n107
II.5.34	153n141
II.5.38	145n95
II.29.191	158n163
II.37.245	152n136
II.37.246	152n136
II.41.269	158n165

De specialibus legibus

1.12.66	318n53
1.97	10n44
1.113	10n44
1.193	10n44
1.195	10n45
1.201	11n53
1.224	10n44
1.229	10n44
1.253	10n52
1.272	11n55
1.277	10n50
1.287	10n47
1.290	10n48
1.297	10
I.5.28	147n108
I.5.28–29	148n116
I.6.34	152n134
I.18.61	152n134
I.35.193	153n142
I.41.224	153n140
I.50.271–72	163n185
I.61.336	146n103
I.62.342	146n107, 147n108, 162n181
I.62.342–43	147n108
I.62.343	146n101, 147n110
I.272	177n53
II.17	10n44
II.27.148	154n143
II.28.157	130n12
II.31.188, 192	145n93
II.32.193	148n115
II.32.199	153n140
II.32.200	129n4

II.33.209	153n140
II.35.216, 220	154n144
II.40.230	145n100
II.44.246	130n11
II.47.259	130n11
III.22.125	144n89
IV.17.102	130n12
IV.24.177	153n137
IV.25.134	149n120
IV.34.17	154n145

Virtutibus

11.72–75	153n137
11.72	158n163
11.74	151n131
18.95	154n144
27.145	130n12

De vita contemplativa

3.25	152n136
3.29	147n108, 156n157
4.35	162n181
10.80	157n159
11.83–85, 87–88	157n159
25	191n26
25 (VI 52,25 Cohn)	247n68

De vita Moysis

I.5.21–24	146n102
I.5.23	147n108
1.6.29	149n122
1.12.66	309n13
1.12.67	309n13
1.12.68	309n13
1.32.180	158n168
I.38.212	152n134
I.46.255	153n141
II.1.7	149n120
II.4.9.271	152n134
2.15.71—2.22.108	319n54
II.31.162	144n89
II.43.239	154n147
II.46.256–57	159n171
II.49.270	144n89
2.147	10n44
2.174	10n44

JOSEPHUS

Antiquities

11.8.5, 332	52
11.332	183n76
18.19	9n41
VII.iv.80	191n24
VI.xi.214	191n24
XII.vii.323	191n24

Against Apion

1.40 (CSEL 37,11,16)	247n69
I.40	191n25

RABBINIC LITERATURE

Aboth de Rabbi Nathan

4	12
4, 11 a	13

Baba Bathra

9a	13

Berakoth

5a,b	12n60
10b	13
17a	13
24a	159n169
26a,b	13n67
32b	13n70

Deuteronomy Rabbah

5.1–3	13n73

Exodus Rabbah

38.4	12n64

Leviticus Rabbah on Zaw

7.2	12n63

Megillah

31b [= *Ta'anith* 27b]	12n60

Mekilta, Bahodesh, Yitro

10	13n71

Mekilta de Rabbi Ishmael

Tractate Amalek 3	316n43
Tractate Vayassa' 5	316n43

Menahot

110a	12n59

Midrash Psalms

5.4	12
118.18	13

Midrash Rabbah

Exodus

2.5	309n14
5.9	316n43
25.3	316n43

Song of Solomon

8.13.2	52

Moed Katan

28a	13

Pesachim

10.5	68

Rosh Hashanah

18a	13

Shabbath

30 a end	12

Shebuoth

13a [= *Kerioth* 7a]	12n62

Sifre Deuteronomy

30b	12n60

Siphre Num.

143	12n57

Sotah

5b [= *Sanhedrin* 43b]	13n72
30b	113
48a	158–159n169

Sukkah

49b	13

Tanhuma

1, 31b	13n68

Tanhuma B., Aharè Mot

14 (34b–35a)	12n66
16–17 (35a)	12n60

Tanhuma B., Zaw

8, 9a	12n65

Tosefta Yoma

5.9	12n61

Yoma

8:8	12n62
75a	316n43

APOSTOLIC FATHERS

Clement of Rome

1 Clement	17–18
2	63n5
4:1–2	17n92
8:1	18n99
9:2, 4	18n94
10:7	17n92
18:16, 17	17n92
20:10	18n94
29	63n5
31:3	17n92
32:4	18n94
34.5	18n94
34.6	18n94
34.7	46, 182
35:12	17n92
36:1	18

36:40–44	18
36.3	18n94
40:2, 3, 5	18n96
41:1	18n97
41:2	18n94
41:3	17n92
43:4	18n94
44:2–4, 6	18
52:3, 4	17n92
62:1	18

2 Clement

6:3	19n105

Didache

1–4	20
4:1	19
6:3	19
7:1	20
9:3	20
10:2	20
11	19
14:1	19n102
15:1	19n100

Epistle of Barnabas

2.4	23
2.4–10; 7.3	14n76

Ignatius

Ephesians

4.1–2	53
4.2	178
5.2	20n109
19.2	170n30

Magnesians

7.2	20n106

Philadelphians

4	20n110

Romans

2.2	21n111
4.2	21n112

Smyrnaeans

9.1	20n108

Trallians

7.2	20n107

NEW TESTAMENT APOCRYPHA AND PSEUDOEPIGRAPHA

Acts of John

43	66n18
109	27n136

Acts of Paul

Papyrus Hamburg 5, 4	54

Acts of Paul and Thecla

34	63n5

Acts of Thomas

76	41

Apocalypse of Peter

19	53, 184n82

Visio Pauli

9	118n44
13ff.	114n26
24	118n44
29–30	112
47	118n44
NHC V, 2	115

GREEK, LATIN, AND SYRIAC CHRISTIAN AUTHORS

Acta Apollonius

44	29n145

Aesclepius

41.2	5n20

Ambrose

De elia

10.34	118n46

Ambrose (continued)

De fide
- 4.10.125 — 79

De mysteriis
- 8.49 — 79
- 9.50–58 — 79n38

De officiis ministrorum
- 3.15.94–95 — 313n33

De sacramentis
- 4.4.13 — 79n36
- 4.5.23 — 79
- 6.1.3, 4 — 78

De Spiritu Sancto
- 3.3.13–14 — 321n70

Enarrationes in Isaac
- 1 — 110n10
- 38.25 — 79n37

Enarrationes in Psalmos
- 1 — 180–181
- 1 praef 2 — 169n21
- 1.9 — 59–60
- 49:7 — 170n29
- 118 — 79n39

Epistola 20 ad Marcellinani
- 20 — 108n3

Expositio evangelii
- 9 — 110n10, 180–81

Hexaemeron
- 2.2.6f — 172

Interpellatione Iob et David
- 4.16 — 170

Sermones
- 18.26 — 79n39

Apostolic Constitutions

- 2.57.6 — 181n68
- 7.56.1 — 47
- 8.12.4 — 181n68
- 8.13 — 118n46
- 11.57 — 110n9

Aristides of Athens

Apology
- 1.5 — 24n124
- 16.1 — 24n126

Arnobius

Adversus nationes
- 6.1 and 3 and book 7 — 33n163

Asterius

Fragmenta
- 17 — 192n30

In Ps.
- 20:2–5 — 195n42
- IV, Hom. I — 195n42
- IX — 195n42
- VIII, Hom. I — 195n42
- XI, Hom. II — 195n42
- XII, Hom. I — 195n42

Athanasius

Apologia de Fuga
- 24 — 110n9, 215
- 25 — 201n12, 215

Apology to Constantius
- 10 — 56, 183
- 16 — 56
- 27 — 215

Arianorum historia
- 81 — 215

De incarnatione Verbi
- 54.3 — 312n28

Epistola ad Marcellinum
- 10–11, 30–32 — 111n12
- 10–12, 21, 24 — 170
- 27 — 168, 172, 174
- 27–29 (PG 27,37 D–41 C) — 251n111
- 28 — 173
- 29 (PG 27.40D–41A) — 173, 176n47, 177, 179–180n62, 193n34
- PG 27.12–45 — 197–240

Exp. in Psalmorum
- 43 — 167–168n15
- 70:22 (PG 27.321C) — 192n30
- 80:3 (PG 27.361D) — 205n24
- 97:5 (PG 420C) — 205n24

Contra Gentes
- 31 — 177
- 42 — 171n33
- 43 — 180n64

Ancient Sources Index

Athenagoras

Legatio pro Christianis
13	24n125, 63n9
16.3	170

Augustine

Civitate Dei
19.23	5–6n26

Confessionis
1.17.2	176
9.6.14	173
9.7	181n67
10.33	175n43
IX.vi.14—vii.15	108
X.33	205n22

Doctrina Christiana
3.16.24	81n42

Enarrationes in Psalmos
3.1	81
33, 2	188n10
33:1, 3, 11 [Engl 34]	80n41
43.5	188n6
98.8 [Engl 99.8]	80n41
119.1	110n9
144	188n10
146.2	177n52
147:1	178
147:2	178
148	113n18
149:3	179
149.3	179n61
150.4	180
CL, 4–6	190n19
CXLIV, 1–2	190n21
CXLVII, 2	192n30
CXLVII, 11	190n21
LVIII, 14	190n18
LXXII, 28	190n20
XCII, 5	195n44
XCVIII, 5	190n21

Epistolae
55	113n18
98.9	81

In Iohannis evangelium tractatus
25.2	81
26.11, 12	81
26.13	81n45
26.18	81
98.8	115n32

Retractationes
II.11 (37)	107

Sermoni
57.7 [7.7]	81n45
131.1	82
227	80
234.2	80n40
243.4	167n14
272	81n43, 81n45

Sermo Denys
3	81n45
6	80n40

Sermo Mai
129	81n42

Sermo Morin
7	80, 81n45

De Trinitate
3.4.10	80n40

Barhebraeus

Nomocanon
7.9	114n26

Basil of Caesarea

Comm. Ps.
pref.	173, 174
pref. (PG 29.213 C)	176n47
1.2	57, 181, 189n13
29 (PG 29.305 B–C)	193n33, 243n2
48:5	189n13
I (PG 29,212 B)	251n110
PG 29.212	57

Epistolae
2.2	169n27
96.1	56
190.3	316n43
207.3	47, 110, 181, 182
207.3, 4	110
243.2	56

Hom. Hexaemeron
3.3	172
4.7 (PG 29.93C)	181n65
8.6	307n10

373

Ancient Sources Index

Basil of Caesarea (continued)

Hom. Hexaemeron (continued)
9.4.32	56

Hom. Pent.
3	56
PG 52.811	56

In Isa.
1:17 (PG 30, 144D)	264–265
(PG 30.573B)	183n79

Canons of Basil

97	111–112

Cassiodorus

In Psalmorum
praef.	176n47
praef. 1	168n16
praef. 2	168n16
praef. 6	166n10
praef. 16	215n2
26	178n56
97:4	166n10

Institutiones Divinarum et Saecularium Litterarum
IV.3	215n2

Clement of Alexandria

Excerpta ex Theodoto
13.14	104
82	74n22

Fragmenta
61 Sacr. Par. 300 (Stählin III, 227, 28)	100n14
Hyp. 1 Pet 2:9	100n14

Paedagogus
1.5.153-4	98n3
1.6.38, 43, 47	73
1.6.38.1-3	101n21
1.6.39-40	101n22
1.6.42.3—43.3	101n23
1.6.46.1	100n15
1.7.61	315n40
1.12	33n165
2.1.4-8, 16	103n30
2.2.19-20	74
2.2.19.3	99n8
2.2.19.3-20.1	104n33
2.2.29.1	104n33
2.2.32	73
2.2.32.2	100n18
2.4.41	167n13
2.4.43	179
2.4.43.3	100n17
2.4.44	183
2.4.44.3	55
2.8.67	100n13
3.11.80.4	99n10, 166n9
3.12.90	33n164
3.12.94	321n69

Protepticus.
1.5	167, 171
9.88	179
10.107	167n13

Quis dives salvetur? (Q.D.S.)
23.4	105n38
29.4	100n18
34.1	100n18

Stromata
1.1.5	99n9
1.1.7.2	104n36
1.1.14.4	55
1.10.46.1	100n19
1.19.96	99n8
1.19.96.1	36n184
4.9.75.1	100n15
4.25.161	98n2
4.25.162.3	98n2
5.1 1.70.4	100n13
5.4.19	172n36
5.6.32–40	319n55
5.8	152n136
5.8.48.8	103n28
5.11.67.1	34n171
5.11.70.4	33n163
5.11.74.5	33n164, 100n13
5.14.136.2	98n4
6.11	167n13
6.11.88	167n13
6.11.89	176
6.14.87	178n57
6.14.113.3	99n11
7.3	33n166
7.3–7	35
7.3.13.2	33n165

Ancient Sources Index

7.3.14.1	35n176
7.6.31	183n80
7.6.31.7	35–36n178, 100n14
7.6.31.8	55, 100n14
7.6.32	3n11
7.6.32.6	100n14
7.6.32.7	33n164
7.6.34.2	100n14
7.7.3 6.4	100n17
7.7.35.4, 6	100n17
7.7.40.1	98n5
7.7.41.67	100n17
7.7.49.4	37n186, 100n14
7.7.49.5	37n189
7.12	33n165
13.23–24	103n28
V. xii	264
VII. ii. 10	264
VII. vii. 40. 1	63n5

Confessions of Cyprian [of Antioch]

17	58

Cyprian

De dominica oratione

23	38
31	66n18
33	41n212

Ad donatum

16	174n41

Epistulae

15.1	39n200
57.3	40n209
63	39
63.9	39n202
63.14	39n203
63.17	40n204
69.6	39n201
73.2	39n199
76.3	40n208

De Lapsis

16	40n210

De opere et eleeomosynis

1, 2	40n211
15	40n205

Ad Quirinum testimonia adversus Judaeos

1.16	33n164
2.17	307n10
3.101	309n17

Rebaptism

17	309n17

Cyril of Alexandria

Adversus anthropom.

26 (PG 76.1129A)	310n21

Glaphyra in Exodus

2.299 (PG 69,2 473D and 476A)	313n34, 315n41

In Psalmos

32.2 (PG 69.869D-872B)	194n40
33.2	169n20

Cyril of Jerusalem

Catecheses mystagogicae

12.28	312n30
18.12	315n40

Catechical Lectures

1.7	76
4.1, 2, 3, 6	76
5.7	76–77
13.26	113n20, 169
23.6	169n27
23.20	118n46

Procatechesis 211n35

Didascalia Apostolorum

9	41n217
11 [2.56]	169
XI (Connolly, 117)	63n6
XII (Connolly, 119)	63n6

Didymus the Blind

Expositiones in Psalmos 185–188

4 (PG 39. 1164D–1165B)	187n4
12:6 (PG 39.1217B)	187n4
32:2 (PG 39.1321D-1324A)	187n3, 188
64 (PG 39.1433C)	187n4

Didymus the Blind (continued)

Exp. in Psalmos (continued)
67:25 (PG 39.1448A-B)	187n4
97:5 (PG 39.1509D)	187n4
150:3 (PG 39.1616A)	187n3

Epistola ad Diognetus

2.8	25n127
3.2,5	25n127
3.4	23

Epistle Philip

4.3	22n116

Epiphanius

Ancoratus
26	183–184

Advsus haereses
33.5.10	23n122
38.2.5	115n28

Eusebius of Caesarea

Commentarius in Psalmos
32:2,3 (PG 23.281A)	194n40
33:2f	169n20
47 (PG 23.417C)	192n30
56:8 (PG 23.513B)	190n16
65:10–15	110n10
66.10–15	180n63
67:5 (PG 23.685A-B)	195n43
70.22–24	179n60
91:2–3 (PG 1172D– 1173A)	194n40
91:2f.	110n10
91.2–3	179
92:2–3	166n10
92.4	181n69
97:5 (PG 23.1233B-C)	193n32
97.4–6	179n60
98:4–6	167n14
107:2 (PG 23.1329B)	190n16
146:7 (PG 24.68B)	190n16
pr (PG 23.72D)	243n2
proem. (PG 23.72D–73B and cf. 76B)	192n31
prol. (PG 23.73B, 76B)	181n68
prol. (PG 23.76A)	169n20

Demonstratio evangelica
1.10	43n225
3.2.14	317n48
3.6	56
5 int. 25	56
5.1	309n17
132a	56
208d	56

Historia ecclesiastica
4.69	43n228
5.1.14–17	73n17
5.18.2	22n118
6.11.2	56
10.2.1	43n228
10.4.1	43n228
10.4.20	43n229
10.4.22	43n229
10.4.68	43n227
VII.ix	64n12

De laudibus Constantini
2.5–3.1	43n224
10	169
16.9,10	43n226

Or. ad sanctos
12	43n230

Praeparatio evangelica
4.13	162n183
14.3	56
14.3 (PG 21.719D)	56
719d	56

Questions of the Gospel to Stephen
PG 22.912	56

Tricennial Orations
12.11	171

Vita Constantini
1.41.2	56
3.7	44n231
3.15	44n231
3.40	43n228

Gregory of Nazianzus

Carmina
18	110n8

Ancient Sources Index

Letters
46.4	57
Oration	211n35
4.12	57, 184
4.15	57
4.71	169n21
5 (PG 35.709B)	166n9
23	47
23.4 (PG 35.1153)	182n74
28.2-4	265n10
28.31 (PG 36.72A)	319n55
38.7, 8	265
41.15	57
43.68	47
45.3	265n10

Gregory of Nyssa

Ad Theophilum.
GNO 111.1, 126, 14-127, 10 = PG 45.1276C-D	305n5

Antirrheticus
42 (GNO 111.1, 201, 1-16 = PG 45.1221C-1224A)	305n5

Apollinaris
9 (GNO III/I 143,18)	249n93

Ascension
GNO IX 323,20	245n32

On the Baptism of Christ
9, 225	77

The Beatitudes
4 (ACW 18, 118-20)	296n52
4 (ACW 18, 126)	290n27
4 (PG 44, 1244D-1245A)	278n83
4 (PG 44, 1245C)	281n102
5	286n15

Beneficiis
GNO IX 96,5	250n104

Catena on the Psalms
1.3 (PG 106.1072)	171n34

Commentary on Usury
9	57
GNO 9, 204, 11	57, 183n77

Contra Eunomium
1.203 [16]	57
2.85-92 (GNO 1,251,15-254,20)	292n35
2.242 (GNO I, 297,2-15) = Ans. to Eun. 2nd Bk. (PG 45.992C-D)	317n45
3.1.44-45 (GNO 11, 19, 6-12) = Migne, 3.2 (PG 45.580D)	319n60
3.3.34 (GNO 11, 1 19, 21-27) = Migne 5.3 (PG 45.693A)	305n3
3.3.45 (GNO 11, 123, 24-27) =Migne 5.3 (PG 45.697C)	305n4
3.3.66 (GNO 11, 131, 10-11) =Migne 5.5 (PG45.705D)	305n5
3.3.68 (GNO 11, 132, 7-24) = Migne 5.5 (PG 45.708A-C)	305n6
3.3.68 (GNO 11. 132, 24—133, 4) = Migne 5.5 (PG 45.708C)	305n5
3.3.68 (GNO 11, 132,7—133,l) =Migne 5.5 (PG 45.708A-B)	306n8
3.4.24 (GNO 11, 143, 5-19) = Migne 6.3 (PG 45.720C-D)	312n25
3.4.43 (GNO 11, 150,21-27) = Migne 6.4 (PG 45.728D)	305n5
8 (PG 45, 796A; Jaeger, II, 210. 9-11; NPNF V, 209)	269n39
12 (PG 45, 940D-941A; Jaeger I, 252-53)	268n35
GNO 1,86,3	57
I, 290-91 (PG 45, 340D; Jaeger, I, 112. 7-20; NPNF V, 62)	270n41
I 338 (GNO I127,13-14)	246n61
II, 70 (NPNF, V, 257)	269
ii, 89	261n69
III,IX 15 (GNO II 269,4)	246n48
III,V 14 (GNO II 165,3)	245n42
PG 45	57
PG 45, 772A (Jaeger, II, 188. 11-26; NPNF V, 201)	269n39
PG 45, 797A (Jaeger, II, 212. 5-14; NPNF V, 210)	269n40

De mortuis
PG 46, 500D-501D	275n73

De occursu Domini
PG 46,1153 D and 1157 D	251n107
PG 46,1156 B	248n82

377

Ancient Sources Index

Gregory of Nyssa (continued)

De oratione dominica
2	291n30
2 (PG 44,1140B)	246n61

De perfectione
174,24—175,13	292n36
GNO 8.1, 206, 18–19	310n20
PG 46, 285B–C	276n74
PG 46, 285C	262n3

De professione Christianum
GNO VIII, 1, 137,17ff.	289n25

Deit
GNO IX 339,16	250n99

Encomium on the Forty Martyrs
1 (PG 46,749B–C)	245n39
1b [GNO 10.1, 149, 25; PG 46.764]	57
2 (PG 46,781 B)	248n86
PG 46.764	183

Epistolae
2.13 (GNO VIII/II 17,15)	251n108
3.19–20 (GNO VIII.2,25, 1–16, esp. 12–13) = Migne 17 (PG 46.102 1C)	319n61
19 (GNO VIII/II 65,2)	248n80

Funeral Oration on Flacilla
Jaeger, IX, 485. 10–13	275n72

Hexaemeron
PG 44,73 C	248n84

Homilies on Ecclesiastes 282–303
1 (GNO V 279,6)	246n44
2 (GNO V 300,17)	248n84
2 (PG 44, 648D–649A)	278n84
5 (GNO V 354,3)	246n61
6 (PG 44, 704A)	277n80
7 (PG 44, 720C)	281n103
8 (GNO 5,423,4–6 = PG 44.740A)	317n51
8 (GNO V, 423, 4–18 = PG 44.740A–B)	316n43
277,3	291
278,5	294
278,5–8	302
278,5–17	291
279,4–20	292
279,19	293, 299
279,20—280,2	299
280,1	282
280,2–3	288
280,8–13	292, 299
280,15–16	299
280,19–20	295
281,3—282,9	302
282,10—283,17	301
283,18–21	298
284,1–11	288
284,10–11	286
284,12–20	283
284,13–19	288
284,21—285,1	288
285,10	286
286,1—289,18	302
288,13–15	293
288,13–17	300
288,14	282n1
289,3–10	290
289,16	290
289,21—290,1	286
291,15— 294,17	303
291,15—293,1	300
292,22	282n1
292,222-223	291
293,16—294,5	283
295,9–13	296
296,3–8	303
298,5–13	292, 299
299,5	299
299,6–9	302
299,18–19	284
299,20—300,3	284
300,22	286
301,3—303,2	301
301,3—303,11	299
301,4–6	284, 286
301,20–302	285
302,18–303,2	285
303,7–11	289
303,12—304,6	302
303,14—304,6	294
304,6–23	302
305,14–19	284
305,20	293
306,3–4	293
306,11–13	299
307,4–8	292

Ancient Sources Index

307,17–18	292, 301	338,23—339,2	295
307,24—308,1	291	338,23—343,9	300
308,9–16	291	340,10–12	294
308,18	283	343,10— 346,14	295
309,2–5	302	343,10–346,14	300
309,16	291	344,21—345,7	285n11
310,6—311,2	301	346,15—348,14	300
311,2–4	289	346,17–21	302
311,7	289	346,17–347,1	295n47
311,17—312,1	288	347,16ff.	295
311,20—312,1	288	348,15	289
312,11	303	349,11—350,10	290
312,22	290	354,1	282n1, 296
313,8–11	287	354,13–16	295n47, 302
313,11–15	287	354,21–22	293
313,17–18	286	355,1–3	302
314,6	296	355,3–5	294
314,8	287	356,9–10	286
315,11–12	290	356,15	286
315,13–14	290	358,9	284, 299
315,22–316,1	290	358,19–359,1	302
316,3–4	290	358,20—359,1	294
317, 1–4	290	361,10	282n1
317,5–9	295n47	362,14	282n1
317,5–12	302	362,15	291
317,10–12	290	365,12	282n1
317,13–19	299	368,22	282n1
317,22—318,1	300	371,3–4	294
318,1	282n1	371,4–5	302
318,1–8	300	371,20–21	289
318,10–14	294	372,3–6	289
318,10–19	302	373,2–3	291
319,6–10	302	373,12	282n1
319,11–12	292	373,12–13	292
319,21—320,4	294, 302	373,17–19	301
320,13—324,2	299	373,21—374,8	301
324,3—326,18	295	374,13–14	292, 301
326,17	285	374,21	282n1
326,18–20	290	375,4–5	293
327,21—330,11	295	375,19—376,5	294
328, 19—329,2	294	376,7–9	295n47
328,23—329,1	290	378,18–23	292
331,1–10	294	379,11–13	293
331,1–11	302	379,21	282n1, 285
333,16	282	380,3–13	285
333,19	282n1	380,12	282n1
333,19—334,2	292	382,1—383,8	302
334,4—338,22	295, 300	382,3–9	294

379

Ancient Sources Index

Gregory of Nyssa *(continued)*

Homilies on Ecclesiastes (continued)

382,12–15	295
382,21—383,2	296
383,2–12	296
383,20–21	289
384,3–15	295n47, 302
385,4	282n1
387,8–13	294
389,8–10	288
390,1—400,9	300
391,5–10	302
393,20	301
395,16–17	299
395,18—397,15	303
397,19–20	301
398,16	300
399,9–20	296
400,10–21	302
400,21—401,2	297
401,2–13	287
402,19–21	294
403,5–6	288
404,7	282n1
404,21–22	296
406,1–407,17	286
406,17—407,10	286
407,1	282n1
407,14	286
411,13	283
414,17–19	282
415,17—416,9	282
416,8	282n1
417,10—428,21	302
417,13	296
418,6–8	296
419,9	288
421,5–6	296
422,3–9	287
422,8–9	286
422,14–15	286
423,2–4	296
425,4–10	296
427,6–8	294
427,15—428,6	289
428,1–2	285
428,3	282n1
428,19—433,7	295
429,1—433,7	302
433,1–3	295
434,3–8	296
435,1—436,10	291
435,14—436,14	284
436,14–17	282n1
436,17	284
438, 14–439,10	285
441,5–6	287
441,12—442,2	283
I, PG 44, 617 A–B	261n69

Homilia de opficio

22 (PG 44,208 D)	246n46

In Canticum Canticorum

1 (PG 44, 765D–772A)	261n69
7	57
11, PG 44, 1000 C	261n69
13 (GNO VI, 38 1, 1—383,6 = PG 44.1045C—1048C)	320n61
13 (GNO VI, 388,21—389, 1 = PG 44.1053B)	321n67
13 (GNO VI, 390, 22—391, 2 = PG 44.1056A)	321n68
14 (GNO VI, 427, 20—428,7 = PG 44.1085B-C)	317n50
GNO 6, 228, 14	57
GNO VI 237,5	246n49
PG 44, 765 B–C	281n102
PG 44, 777B	279n88
PG 44, 873C	271n46
PG 44, 873C–76C	274n64
PG 44, 873D–876A	270n42
PG 44, 876A	266n22
PG 44, 876B	266n18, 267n25, 279n88
PG 44, 876C	265n14, 281n100
PG 44, 876D–77A and n. 78	281n101
PG 44, 885C–888A	271n51
PG 44, 885C–D	270n44
PG 44, 885D	266n24
PG 44, 885D–888A	262–263, 274n64, 276n76, 280n94
PG 44, 889B, D and 892B	280n97
PG 44, 892A–B	271n51
PG 44, 940D–41A	273n57
PG 44, 940D–941 B	257n34
PG 44, 940D–941A	269n37

PG 44, 941A	267n27, 268n36	1,9	169n24
PG 44, 941B	273n59	1,9 (65,5)	243n7
PG 44, 941C	263n5	1,9 (65,23)	244n17
PG 44, 941D	280n96	1,9 (67,11)	244n30
PG 44, 945C	276n75	1,9 (68,8)	244n28
PG 44, 980B-992B	276n76	1,9 (GNO V 66,2-29)	250n98
PG 44, 997D and 1000B	271n48	1,9 (GNO V 67,22)	247n66
PG 44, 1025A	272n54	1.3	165, 171, 174, 180
PG 44, 1025B	268n33	2,1 (69,15)	244n23
PG 44, 1025C-D and 1037B		2,1 (69,20)	244n31
	279n87	2,1 (70,4f.)	244n31
PG 44, 1028A	267n29	2,1 (71,3)	244n24
PG 44, 1029B-C	266n23	2,3 (GNO V 74,23—76,13;	
PG 44, 1033D-36A	280n96	77,6-26) (PG 44,493B- 497B)	
PG 44, 1033D-1036A	279n87		242n1, 252
PG 44, 1036A	268n34	2,6 (88,1)	244n27
PG 44, 1037 B-C	280n94	2,6 (88,2)	244n31
PG 44, 1084C-D	257n34, 278n86	2,6 (88,16)	244n20
PG 44.1033D-1036 A	257n34	2,6 (88,18)	244n22

In diem lum.
  GNO IX, 23 1, 23—232,9 = PG
  46.589A-B   307n9
  GNO IX 237,10   249n88

In diem natalem Christi
  PG 46,1128B   247n62
  PG 46.1133A   289-290n26

In diem natalem Salvatoris
  GNO X. 2, 246, 15-248, 4 = PG
  46.1 136B-C   310n20
  GNO X.2, 236, 6-12, 15-16
                               320n62
  GNO X.2, 237, 12-17   320n62
    GNO X.2, 238, 2-5 = PG 46.1
  128A-1129B   320n62

In Inscriptiones Psalmorum

1 pr (24,3)	244n23	2,7 (89,9)	244n21
1 pr (25,3)	243n8	2,7 (90,1)	244n24
1 pr (25,5f.)	243n7	2,7 (91.1)	243n6
1 pr (GNO V 24,7)	243n6	2,7 (GNO V 90,8)	248n81
1,1 (GNO V 26,14f.)	247n63	2,7 (GNO V 90,27)	247n64
1,2 (GNO V 27,3)	249n89	2,8 (93,6)	244n28
1,3 (32,7)	244n12	2,8 (93,24)	243n8
1,4 (35,1)	247n67	2,8 (94,1)	243n9
1,4 (35,2)	244n14	2,8 (95,14)	244n29
1,4 (GNO V 37,23)	245n40	2,9 (103,6)	244n25
1,6 (40,24)	245n43	2,9 (104,6)	244n18
1,7 (51,21)	249n90	2,9 (104,9)	246n58
1,8 (62,18)	244n13	2,9 (107,19)	244n16
		2,9 (107,23)	244n27
		2,9 (107,27)	244n28
		2,9 (GNO V 103,4 and 7; cf.	
		104,18)	246n50
		2,10 (108,10)	246n56
		2,10 (110,1)	245n41
		2,10 (110,6)	243n11
		2,10 (114,5)	243n6
		2,10 (114,6)	244n15
		2,10 (GNO V, 109, 8)	249n95
		2,10 (GNO V 109,26)	249n94
		2,11 (115,12)	246n55
		2,11 (117,2)	243n8
		2,11 (117,15)	244n26
		2,11 (120,10)	246n52
		2,11 (GNO V 123,16)	250n103

Gregory of Nyssa *(continued)*

In Inscriptiones Psalmorum (continued)

2,12 (130,16)	249n96
2,12 (GNO V 126,28)	250n101
2,13 (125,21)	246n54
2,13 (136,13)	246n51
2,13 (136,15)	244n19
2,13 (138,12)	244n25
2,14 (148,10, 20)	246n57
2,14 (148,16)	245n42
2,14 (150,15)	246n56
2,14 (151,15)	243n8
2,14 (157,19 and 25)	249n96
2,14 (GNO V 144,10)	247n65
2,14 (GNO V 154,26)	248n83
2,15 (161,12)	245n42
2,15 (161,24)	249n91
2,15 (163,6)	246n56
2,16 (167,21)	249n96
2,16 (174,6)	244n18
2.3	166n11
6 (GNO V 187,11; 190,4; 192,26)	245n34
93,15	243n10
116,27	246n53
150:8	165n6
I, 7, PG 44, 465 B	261n69
I. vii (PG 44, 460B-C)	276n79
I,8	286n15
II. iv (PG 44, 500B)	276n77
II.iii	194n36
I.ix	194n41

Meletius

GNO IX 453,2	245n33

On the Making of Man

9	167n13
16:12 (PG 44, 184C; NPNF V, 405)	274n63
21:2 (PG 44, 201B-04A; NPNF V, 410f.)	272n55

On the Soul and the Resurrection

PG 46, 96C-97A	278n85
PG 46, 96C-97A; NPNF V	272n52
PG 46, 96C-97A; NPNF V, 450	271n47
PG 46, 105A-C (NPNF V, 453)	277n81
PG 46, 105B-C	266n22
PG 46, 113B-C; NPNF V, 455f	274n66
PG 46.93B	283n6

Or. Catech.

8-32	311n23
10 (GNO 111.4, 38, 18—39, 1=PG 45.41C-D)	306n8
21 (NPNF V, 492)	275n69
21 (PG 45, 57D-60A)	271n49
32 (GNO 111.4, 78, 9-10 = PG 45.80B)	321n68
37	77
37 (GNO 111.4, 94, 8-10 = PG 45.93C)	321n67
37 (GNO 111.4, 97, 20-21 = PG 45.97B)	321n66
39	277n80

On Prayer

25:2	264

Pulcheria

(GNO IX 467,13)	246n60

Refutatio confessionis Eunomii

181 (GNO 11, 388, 24-389, 4) = Migne 2.13 (PG 45.549A)	312n26

Spas Selecta

GNO IX 246,6	249n96
GNO IX 265,16	245n35

Sal

GNO IX 309,12	245n36

Spiritu

PG 47,700 A	246n47

Stephen

2 (PG 46,729 A)	247n70

In Praise of Thodore the Martyr.

PG 46,745 B	251n106

Vita Ephraim

PG 46,828 A	249n92

Vita Gregorius Thaumaturgus

PG 46,949 B	246n59

On Virginity

4 (PG 46, 337B)	271n50
7 (PG 46, 352C)	275n67
12	286n15

Vita Macrina

GNO VIII/I 373,22	248n87

Ancient Sources Index

GNO VIII/I 373,23	247n71	II, 232–33; PG 44, 404A	279n91
GNO VIII/I 374,4	247n71	II, 236; PG 44, 404B	270n43
GNO VIII/I 395,3	250n105	II, 238–39; PG 44, 404C–D	
GNO VIII/I 401,17	248n73		272n52
GNO VIII/I 406,22	248n74	II, 244; PG 44, 405C	275n70
GNO VIII/I 407,4	248n75	II, 252; PG 44, 408D	267n28
GNO VIII/I 407,12	248n76	II, 252–55; PG 44, 409A–B	
GNO VIII/I 408,10	248n77		272n53
GNO VIII/I 408,20	248n78	II, 305f; PG 44, 425A	281n98
GNO VIII/I 409,4	248n79	II, 306; PG 44, 425A	262n2
Vita Moysis 253–281, 304–322		II, 307; PG 44, 425B	266n20
1,5–7	286n13	II,1–11	285
1.57	320	II,14	294n43
2.20–21	308	II,22–25	286n15
2.26–27	311	II,25	294n42
2.28–30	311–312	II,36	294n45
2.31–34	314n36	II,45–53	291
2.138–140	316	II,60–61, 122, 271, 297–304	
2.169–170	318		289n24
2.174–178	318	II,71	295n46
2.183	320	II,73–8	286
2.184–188	318	II,73ff.	285n12
2.216–217	321	II,90, 94	289n26
11,96–97.122–23	289n22	II,110	282n2, 283n6
191 (GNO VII/I 373,22)	248n85	II,136, 148	292n33
276–277	289n25	II,163, 239, 252	284n8
I, 5; PG 44, 300C–D	270n44	II,166	282n3
I, 6; PG 44, 301A	272n53	II,177	292n38
I, 7; PG 44, 301A–B	267n31	II,225–55	287n18
I, 10; PG 44, 301C	262n3	II,226, 305	291n30
I,5–10	287n18	II,232, 235, 239	287n20
I,7; II,237	283n6	II,243–244	286n16
I,10	297	II,244	284
I,11–14	292n35	II,256–263	295
I,15	292n37	II,288	293
I,87, 272, 278	295n48	II,306	297
II, 2; PG 44, 328A	274n65	II,317	293n39
II, 3; PG 44, 328B	277n80	II,319	292n37
II, 61; PG 44, 344A–B	275n71	II,320	297
II, 124–129, 185, 277	296n51	PG 44.301A, 304C; I, 6 and 15	
II, 219–48	271–272		254n6
II, 220; PG 44, 400A	279n92	PG 300 A, 301 A, 408 C; I, 1, 6;	
II, 224–25; PG 44, 401A	266n21	II, 249	254n7
II, 226; PG 44, 401B	277n82	PG 300 C–D; I, 5	254n8
II, 226f1; PG 44, 401B–D	280n95	PG 301 A; I, 7	254n10
II, 227; PG 44, 401B	266n19, 268n32	PG 301 C; I, 10	254n12
		PG 305B; I, 19	260n57
II, 232; PG 44, 404A	279n93	PG 321A; I, 56	260n51

383

Gregory of Nyssa *(continued)*

Vita Moysis (continued)

PG 328A-B; II, 2–3	261n65
PG 328B; II, 3	260n60
PG 332C; II, 18–19	260n54
PG 332D and 333C; II, 20 and 26	259n44
PG 333 A; II, 22	260n55
PG 333A; II, 23	255n15
PG 333A-B; II, 23, 24	255n16
PG 333C; II, 26	259n49
PG 333D and 336B; II, 26–27 and 31–33	259n43
PG 333D–336A; II, 26–30	259n43
PG 341B; II, 55	259n55
PG 344A; II, 60	257n26
PG 349A; II, 80	260n61
PG 352C–356B; II, 90–101	260n58
PG 361B; II, 121	260n63
PG 368A; II, 136	260n62
PG 368C; II, 139	259n43
PG 373B; II, 154	260n56
PG 376 D; II 162	255n17
PG 377A; II, 163	255n18, 255n20, 258n40
PG 377B; II, 164	255n19
PG 377C; II, 166	255n13, 256n21, 259n48
PG 377C-D; II, 167	256n22
PG 381A–B; II, 174	259n43
PG 385D; II, 187	260n57
PG 392D; II, 200	259n48
PG 397B-C; II, 216	259n45
PG 401 A; II, 225	254n9
PG 401A; II, 225	256n24, 257n28
PG 401B; II, 226	257n25
PG 401B; II, 227	257n29
PG 401B-D; II, 228–30	257n30
PG 401C; II, 230	257n31
PG 404 B; II, 236 and 300 C–301 C; I, 5–10	254n11
PG 404A; II, 232–33	257n33
PG 404A-B; II, 233–35	257n35, 258n36
PG 404D; II, 239	258n37
PG 405A; II, 239	258n38
PG 405B; II, 242	258n39
PG 405B and 405D–408A; II, 242, 245–46	260n53
PG 405C; II, 243	260n59
PG 405C; II, 244	257n27
PG 405D and 408B; II, 244, 248	259n46
PG 408B; II, 248	259n47
PG 408C–409B; II, 249–55	258n41
PG 408D; II, 252	259n42
PG 408D; II, 251	260n52
PG 425 A; II, 306	261n67
PG 425 B-D; II, 308–13	261n68
PG 428B; II, 315	261n64
PG 429 A; II, 318	261n66

Gregory Thaumaturgus

Epistolae canonicae

XI	63n8

Metaphrases on Ecclesiastes

1.13	299n4
12:11	47

Hesychius

De titulis Psalmorum

150	167n14
150 (PG 27.1341 B-D)	194n41
PG 27.996D, 1069C, 1341C	190n16

Fragments in Ps.

98:30, 31 (PG 93.1232 C)	193n34

Psalms

69:30	170n30
69:31	169n20
PG 55.728–29	189n15

Hilary of Poitiers

In Psalmos

65	110n10
66.1	181n69

Tractatus de mysteriis

1.30	309n16, 317n49
1.31	315n40
16	313n32

Hippolytus

Apostolic Tradition

4	42n218
26.1, 6, 29–30	42n219
Dix: 6–7; Botte, 10, 12; Bradshaw, 38.	62n1
III.xxvi.19–23	65n17
I.iv.12, 13	65n16

Benediction of Moses

PO 27, pp. 172–73	309n15

Commentary on Daniel

2.13	307n10
3.14	322n72
II.24	63n9

On Psalms

1:1 [PG 10.712B]	113n21
5 (PG 10,717B–C)	243n2
PG 10, 712B	42n220

Refutation of all Heresies

1.2.2–3	170n31

Hortatory Address to the Greeks

8	47

Irenaeus

Adversus haereses

1.10.2	47, 182
1.13.2	73n18
1.14.1	54, 183
1.18.3	31
3.10.2	312n28
3.19.1	312n28
3.21.7	307n11
3.21.8	315n37
3.21.10	317n48
4.10	309n17
4.14.3	30n148
4.16.5	30n148
4.17.1	30n151
4.17.1–5	30n148
4.17.5	30n148, 32n160, 72n15, 100n17
4.17.6	30n149, 31n153
4.18.1	30n150, 32
4.18.2	30n148, 31n155
4.18.3	31n152, 31n156
4.18.4	31n157, 31n158, 32
4.18.4–5	72n15
4.18.5	32, 32n161, 72, 72n16
4.18.6	31n154, 73
4.20.1	312n27
4.20.11	307n11
4.33.2	72n15
4.pref.4	312n27
5.1.1	312n28
5.1.3	312n27
5.2.2–3	72n15
5.2.3	72n16
5.26.1–2	307n11
5.28.4	312n27
5.pref.	312n28
IV. xi. 2	264
IV. xx. 7	264

Demonstration of the Apostolic Preaching

26	319n58, 321n70
32	317n48
59	315

Frg.

19	317n48

Isidore of Seville

Etymologies

VI.19.7–8	181n68

Jerome

Contra Pelagius

1.25	181n65

Commentary on Ephesians

5.19	178

Homilies on Psalms

7 on Ps. 67	195n45
59	179, 181n65
65	181, 181n65

John Chrysostom

Ad populum Anttiochenum de statuis

15.3	58
15.3 (PG 49.155)	183n80

On the Ascension

4 [PG 52.799]	58

John Chrysostom (continued)

De inani gloria	183n76
De prophetarum obscuritate	
1 (PG 56.182)	183n80
PG 56.182	58
De studio praesentium	
5.1 [PG 63.487]	58–59
Expositiones in Psalmos	
41	175n43
42 (PG 55.157)	166n9
42:1	174
42.1	177n54
101.1 (PG 55.629–30)	176
145 [English 146].2 [PG 55.521]	59
145:2	110n10
146.2	180
146.3	167
149:2 (PG 55.494)	194n40
149:3	166n10
150	168
150 (PG 55.497)	194–195n41
150 (PG 498)	194n40
Homilies on 1 Corinthians	
35	177n54
36	110n9, 181n68, 182
Homilies on Acts	
38 [PG 60.270]	58
Homilies on Colossians	
3.2	177n54
IX on Col. 3:13 (PG 62.363)	193n35
Homilies on Ephesians	
19	177–178
Homilies on Matthew	
11.9	180n63
68.3 (PG 58.644)	183n75
68.4	183n75
68[69].3	48
68[69].4	48
Homilies on Romans	
7	58
On Vainglory and Education of the Young	
4	58

John of Damascus

On the Orthodox Faith	
4.13	77n29

Julian

Ep.	
47 (435C)	201n13

Justin Martyr

1 Apology	
9.1	25n127
10.1	29n146
13	25n128
13.1	71n11
24.2	25n127
31.7	209n34
62	25n127
63	309n19
65	63n7
65.3	27n139–140
66.1	27, 27n138
66.2	71
67	64n11
Dialogue with Trypho	
13	25n127
19,6	25n127
22	25n127
22.1	25n127
28	25n127
29	25n127
40	25n127
41.1–3	27n134
43.1	25n127
46.7	25n127
59	309n17
59–60	309n19
67.8	25n127
70.4	70
72	25n127
73	25n127
86.1	315n39
92,5	25n127
100.3–6	315n39
111	25n127
111.3	307n10
116.3	25n130, 26
117.1	26n132

117.2	26n131	1–2	177n53
117.3	70	7	166n12, 169, 173
117.3,5	26n133	9	166n10, 194n40
118.2	25n129	10	169n24
126.1	315n39	11	181
127.4	309n19	12	176n47
		13	60, 174, 177, 179, 184n84

Lactantius

Novatian

Divine Institutes

6.21	175
6.24	38n194
6.25	41nn214–215

De Trinitate

6.1	322n71

De Opificio Dei

Odes of Solomon

16.13–18	176–177n51
20	23n121

Leo the Great

Origen

Sermons

Contra Celsum

3.1	167
1.4	321n70
8.37	183
8.67	170

Martyrdom of Matthew

Commentarius in evangelium Johannis

8	181n69	1.35, 37, 39, 40	14n76
		1.218	309n17

Martyrdom of Polycarp

		6.52.33	34–35n174
8.2	21	6.54.36	34n169
12.2	21	32.267–268	312n29
14.1	22n113	XXVIII. 4	63n8
14.2	22n114		

Commentarius in evangelium Matthaei

Methodius

14.1	178
ser. 100	183n78, 316n44

De resurrectione

Contra Celsus

1.14	319n59	6.70	33n163
Symposium		8.17	36n180
3.6	169n25	8.21	36n181
5.4	42n221	8.33	106n43
5.6	42n222	8.37	55
5.8	319n58	8.57	37n185
8	42n222		
11.2	110n9		

De oratione

2.4	170
28.9,10	36n183

Minucius Felix

Exhortation to Martyrdom

Octavius

32	30n147	30	34n170

Homilae in Exodum

Niceta of Remesiana

6.12	319n57
7.5	316n44, 317n47

Utility of Hymn Singing

Origen (continued)

Homilae in Exodum (continued)
7.8	316n44, 317n49
9	319n56
12.3	312n29
13.2	35n175

Homilae in Jesu Nave
9.5	33–34n168

Homilae Lam.
2.7	34n173

Homilae in Leviticum
5.8	37n188

Homilae in Numeros
11.9	36n182, 37n190
12.3	35n177
23.3	35, 38n191
24.1	36n183
24.2	38n192
XVII.4	264

Homilae in Psalmos
5	114n26
33.2–3	167n15
49.5, 6	33n164
65:13, 15	33n167
149.3	178–179n58
150:3–5 (PG 12.1684B–D)	194n41
PG 12.1072 B–1073A	192n29

Sacra Parallela
300	36n179

Palladius

Hist. Laus.
7.5	169n21

Passion of Perpetua

12	184n82

Paulinus

Vita Ambrosii
4.13	108n3

Paulinus of Nola

Carmina.
21.272–275	180n64
21.275	48, 182n73
21.327ff.	178n56
23.111	180n63
23.111–46	181n66
27.556	169n20
327ff.	180n64

Ep.
15.4	177n53
29.13	180n63

Prudentius

Cathemerinon
V.125ff.	115n32

Pseudo-Clement

Homilies
16.14.1	309n17
20.6.7	315n37

Recognitions
1.34	309n17
1.39	42n223

Pseudo-Hippolytus

PG 10. 716 D–717A	188n5
PG 10.717 B–C	192n28

Pseudo-Justin

Cohartatio ad Graecos
8	182
29–30 (PG 6.296B–C)	319n55

Epistle to Zeno and Sernus
9	192n30

Ptolemy (the Gnostic)

Ad Floram
3	23n122

Quaestiones et responsiones ad orthodoxos

107	166n10, 173–174n38
107 (PG 6.1354)	194n40
115	63n8

Sentences of Sextus

47	37n190a

Ancient Sources Index

Shepherd of Hermas

Mandates
5.1.2,3	23n120
10.1.6	63n4
10.3.2	22n117

Similitudes
5.3.7,8	22n118
7.6	23n120
9.27.2,3	22–23n119

Vision
3.10.9	63n4

Sibylline Oracles

8.332–336	28n142
8.380–90	28
8.401–408	28n144
8.487–92	27–28
8.496–500	28n143

Socrates of Constantinople

Historia ecclesiastes
6.8	109, 181n67

Sozomen

Historia ecclesiastica
3.20	110n8

Tertullian

Ad uxorum
2.8	39

Adversus Judaeos
5	33n164

Adversus Marcion
1.14.3	75
2.22	33n164
3.10	309n19
3.19.3–4	75
3.22	41n213
4.1	39
4.40.3–6	74
5.8	74

Apology
30.4	63n7
30.5	38n195

De anima
14	167n13
17.3	74

De corona
3	63n8, 74

De cultu feminarum
II.9	40n207

De idolatria
7.1	63n7

De ieiunis
7	40
16	40

De oratione
14	63n7
17	63n7
19.3	64n13
23	63n8
27	181n68
28	38–39n196
31.2	63n8

De pudicitia
9.16	74

De resurrectioni carnis
8	40n206
8.3	74
28.1	313n31
55.8	313n31

De spectaculis
25	63n7

De virginibus velandis
13	38n193

De Exhortatione castitates
7	39

Ad nationes
2.5	170n32

Testamentum Domini

II.11 and 22	110n9

Theodore of Mopsuestia

In Psalmos
46:9	195n42

Theodoret of Cyprus

Commentary on Isaiah
1.11 (PG 81.226)	166n10

Graecorum affectionum curatio
7.16	166n10

Ancient Sources Index

Theodoret of Cyprus (continued)

HE
2.19	181n67
11.19 [24]	109
VI.8	109

Interpretatio in Psalmos
17:50 (PG 80.988D)	195n42
20:14 (PG 1008C)	195n42
32:2 (PG 80.1093C)	194n40
33:2	168n18
46:9 (PG 1209B)	195n42
56:9	190n16
97:5 (PG 80.1661)	193n32
98.5	167
107:2 (PG 80.1293B and 1749C)	190n16
150:4 (PG 80.1996)	166n10, 194n40

Interp. Ephesians
5:19 (PG 82.545C)	193n34

CLASSICAL AUTHORS

Anaximenes

Ars Rhetorica
2	3n9

Apollodorus

Library
3.5.8	51

Apollonius of Tyana

De sacrif.	4n16, 162n183
Ep. 26	4n15

Aristides Quintilianus

De Musica
2.3.55	145n96
2.4.55–56	137n52
2.4.56	138n61
2.6.6.1	137n54
2.6.61	133n35, 143n80
2.8.66–68	150n129
2.8.66—19.92	148n114
2.14.80	138n57
2.17.86	137n52
2.19.91f	160n176
3.6.102	151n132
3.6.103	151n132
3.7.105	150n129
3.9.107—27.133	140n67
3.20.120	151n133
9.107— 27.133	150n129
12.112	151n132
14.79–82	150n129
16.84–89	150n129
23.124–25	151n132

Aristophanes

Knights
	670

Aristotle

Analytics
420b	162n181
420b-421a	162n181

De caelo
290b	151n133

De generatione animalium
788a	162n181

Interpretation
11, 20b	50

Politics
1339a	143n80, 160n176
1339b	145n96
1340a-b	147n111
1341a-b	160n176
1342a-b	160n176

Aristoxenus

Elementa Harmonica
2.31.15–30	137n54
2.33.2–10	161–162n181
2.44.20ff	146n107

Athenaeus

Chaerea Callirhoe
8.1	51

Deipnosophistae
1.6.87	51
2.1	51

Ancient Sources Index

620a–631c	133n35
623f–624a	147n111
623f—624a	139n62

Cassius Dio

Roman History

44.36.2	51

Cicero

De republica

6.18–19	151n133

Corpus Hermeticum

1 [Poimandres].31	4n17
1.31; 13.18–19	162n183
12.23	5n19
13.18,19	4n18

Dio Chrysostom

Oration

39.3	50

Diodore of Sicily

Library

11.9	183n76
11.19.3	50
11.26.6	50
11.92	183n76
16	183n76
16.10	183n76
16.10.3	50
17.33	183n76
19.81	183n76
19.81.2	50
40.5a	183n76
79	183n76
106	183n76

Diogenes Laertius

10.120	143n81

Dionysius of Halicarnassus

Antiquitates Romanae

4.67.2	50
6.87.1	50

7.22	183n76

Epictetus

Enchiridion

31.5	3n7
112–113	115n32

Euripides

Hercules furens

1345	1n1

Iamblichus

De mysteriis

3.7	167n13
5.14	5n24

Isocrates

Orations

11 (To Nicocles).20	3n8

Libanius

Letters

1350.3	52

Lucian of Samosata

On Dance

76	51

Nigrinus

14	51, 183n76

Musonius Rufus

Fragments

2, 5	128n1
6	128n1

Nicomachus

Enchiridion

2.240.20ff	161n180
3.241–42	151n130

Persius

Satirae

11.69–75	2n6

Ancient Sources Index

Philodemus

De Musica	131–143
1V, col. 16, ll.27-28	132n23
IV, col. 2, ll.5-36	138n61
IV, col. 2, ll.15-16	133n33
IV, col. 3, l.12	140n69
IV, col. 3, ll.10-41	139n62
IV, col. 4, ll.3-41	135n45
IV, col. 5, l.13—col. 7, l.22	133n35
IV, col. 7, l.22—col. 8, l.3	137n52
IV, col. 7, l. 24	132n21
IV, col. 8, ll.4-25, 32	133n36
IV, col. 9, ll.1-15	138n58
IV, col. 10, ll.2-28	136n46
IV, col. 10, ll.28-40	136n50
IV, col. 11, ll.14-24	142n74
IV, col. 12. ll.6-11	138n59
IV, col. 12, ll.12-35	134n40
IV, col. 13, l.4—col. 15, l.44	134n37
IV, col. 15, ll.1-5	142n77
IV, col. 16, l.1—col. 17, l.35	134n38
IV, col. 17, l.11	133n31
IV, col. 17, l.35—col. 18, l.33	134n39
IV, col. 18, l.33—col. 20, l.27	143n79
IV, col. 18, ll.15-16	133n31
IV, col. 19, l.15	140n69
IV, col. 20, l.28—col. 21, l.23	136n47
IV, col. 21, l. 19	132n21
IV, col. 21, l.24—col. 22, l.9	139n65
IV, col. 22, l.10—col. 23, l.13	135n42
IV, col. 22, l.14	133n31
IV; col. 23, ll.13-27	143n84
IV, col. 23, ll.14-19	132n30
IV, col. 23, l. 28	132n21
IV, col. 24, l.12	140n69
IV, col. 24, ll. 9-35	139n66
IV, col. 25, ll.12-31	137n55
IV, col. 26, ll.1-14	141n72
IV, col. 26, ll.6-7, 16-17	133n31
IV, col. 26, ll.14-35	141n73
IV, col. 27, ll.2-3	133n32
IV, col. 27, ll.18-19	133n31
IV, col. 28, ll.1-22	142n74
IV, col. 28, ll.10-11	132n29
IV, col. 28, ll.22-41	142n75
IV, col. 29, ll.14-43	141n71
IV, col. 29, ll.42-43	133n31
IV, col. 30, ll.6-24	140n67
IV, col. 31, ll.13-19	140n68
IV, col. 32, ll.4-21	137n56
IV, col. 32, ll.30-33	139n63
IV, col. 33, ll.11-22	143n83
IV; col. 33, ll.27-40	143-144n84
IV, col. 34, ll.23-28	136n48
IV, col. 35, ll.15-28, 36-39	136n49
IV, col. 36, l.29—col. 37, l.3	137n51
IV; col. 37, l.8—col. 38, l.30	143n84
IX 64, ll.3-4, 8-13	135n44
IX 69, ll.11-13	132n27
IX 69, ll.31ff.	133n31
IX 70, ll.3-6	138n60
IX 70, ll.4-8	138n57
IX 70, ll.11-12, 55	132n24
IX 73, ll.8-10	134n41
VII 187, ll.5-11	135n43
VII 187, ll.5-11, 55	137n54
VII 190, ll.3-4	132n26
VII 190, ll.4-5	133n31
VIII 7, ll.13-14	132n24
VIII 7, ll.15-17	137n54
VIII 9, ll.16-20	137n52
VIII 17, ll.8-15	139n62
VIII 22, ll.12-13	132n28
VIII 142, ll.4-6	132n23
VIII 148, ll.6-7	143n82
VIII 154, ll.7-15	142n78
XI 73, ll.7-9	137n52
XI 74, ll.5-46	133n35
XI 80, ll.9-11	133n31
XI 82, ll.3-10	139n63
XI 88, ll.4-7	133n34
XI 89, ll.1-2	132n25
XI 92, ll.3-5; cf. 1	132n27

Philostratus

Vita Apollonii

Ancient Sources Index

1.1	4n13	588h	235n93
4.11	4n13	*Timaeus*	
5.21	133n35	34b—36d	150n129

Plato

Gorgias
501–2	143n80

Leges
1, 634e	46
4, 716D-E	2, 2n3
6, 777c	49
657–59	143n80
669	160n179
669–70	138n57
669a	147n108
670	135n44
670b	147n108
673a	160n179
701a–b	150n127
790e—791b	160n176
795d	134n41
800–802	153n140
802	143n80
803	135n44
812d–e	145n96

Phaedo
85–86	147n112
86	129n6

Phaedrus
246b	235n93
247a	152n134

Philebus
17b	49

Protagoras
326a–b	147n111

Republic
2, 364a	46
10, 617b	49–50
397a, 399c–e	160n176
398	147n108
398d, 400a,d	160n179
401d	147n111
410, 441–442	134n41
424c	150n127
431, 439–41	148n118
432–33, 441–44	139n66
439d	235n93
530d–531b	150n129

Plotinus

Enneads
6.4.14	51–52

Plutarch

Aratus
10.2	51

Cato the Younger
71.1	51

De musica
2 (Mor. 1131d)	146n104, 161n181
14 (Mor. 1136b)	136n48
26 (Mor. 1140b)	145n96
26–27 (*Mor.* 1140b–f)	133n35
27 (Mor. 1140d–f)	135n44
32 (Mor. 1142d)	146n107
34 (Mor. 1143f)	161n181
35 (Mor. 1144a)	147n108
37 (Mor. 1144f)	162n181
42 (Mor. 1146d)	147n112
44 (Mor. 1147a)	150n129

Demetrius
18.7	50

Galba
14.5	51
26.3	50

Moralia
414c	50
502d	50
615b	51, 183n81
1135f	136n48

Non posse vivi
13 (Mor. 1095c—1096c)	143n81

The Obsolescence of Oracles
8	50

Pompey
72.2	50

Table-Talk
1.1	51

Talkativeness
1	50

Timoleon
38.3	51

Porphyry

Commentaries
56, 57	151n133
61	162n181

De abstinentia
2.32	3n12
2.34	5nn22–23, 162n183, 177n53
2.61	5n25

De philosophia ex oraculis   5n26

Pseudo-Aristotle

De mundo
399a	158n168

Problems
10.38, 895a	50
19.16, 918b	50
19.27	141n71
19.39	159n170, 161n181

Pseudo-Plato

Alcibiades
II, 149E	2n4

Ptolemy

Harmonics
1.20.9	161n180
3.4.95	150n129
3.5.96–3.7.100	137n54
3.5.97–98	139n66
3.7.100	135n44
3.8.100–11	140n67
30–31	146n107

Sallustius

Concerning the Gods and the Universe
15	6nn27–28
16	6nn27–28

Seneca

De beneficiis
1.6.3	2n5

Epistulae morales
84.9	158n168

Sextus Empiricus

Adversus mathematicos
6	131n17
6.1	141n71
6.7–9	160n176
6.18	135n44
6.19–20	137n52
6.21–24	133n36
6.23	160n176
6.27	143n80
6.28	143n79
6.30, 37	140n67
6.38	133n31
6.39–51	133n33

Xenophon

Anabasis
5.7.32	1n2

Memorabilia
1.3.3	1n2

MEDIEVAL CHRISTIAN WRITERS

Radbertus

De corpore et sanguine Domini
1.2	84
1.5	84–85
3.1	85
3.4	84
4.1, 2	83
4.2	83
4.3	84
5	85n52
6.2	84

Ratramnus

De corpore et sanguine Domini
7–10	86n54
11	87n57
16	87n56
37–38	87n55
43	86
47	86
48	87
49	86

62	87n56	**Thomas Aquinas**
69	86n53	*Summa theologiae*
97	85–86	3:Q. 73–83 94
		3:Q. 76, art. 1–3 94

www.ingramcontent.com/pod-product-compliance
Lightning Source LLC
Chambersburg PA
CBHW051204300426
44116CB00006B/433